TUNISGRAD

Also by Saul David

TUNISGRAD

Victory in Africa

SAUL DAVID

**WILLIAM
COLLINS**

William Collins
An imprint of HarperCollins*Publishers*
1 London Bridge Street
London SE1 9GF

WilliamCollinsBooks.com

HarperCollins*Publishers*
Macken House
39/40 Mayor Street Upper
Dublin 1, DO1 C9W8

First published in Great Britain in 2025 by William Collins

1

HB ISBN 978-0-00-865381-1
TPB ISBN 978-0-00-865382-8

Typeset in Bembo MT Pro by Jouve (UK), Milton Keynes

Printed and bound in Great Britain by CPI Group (UK) Ltd, Croydon

To Richard

Contents

Maps

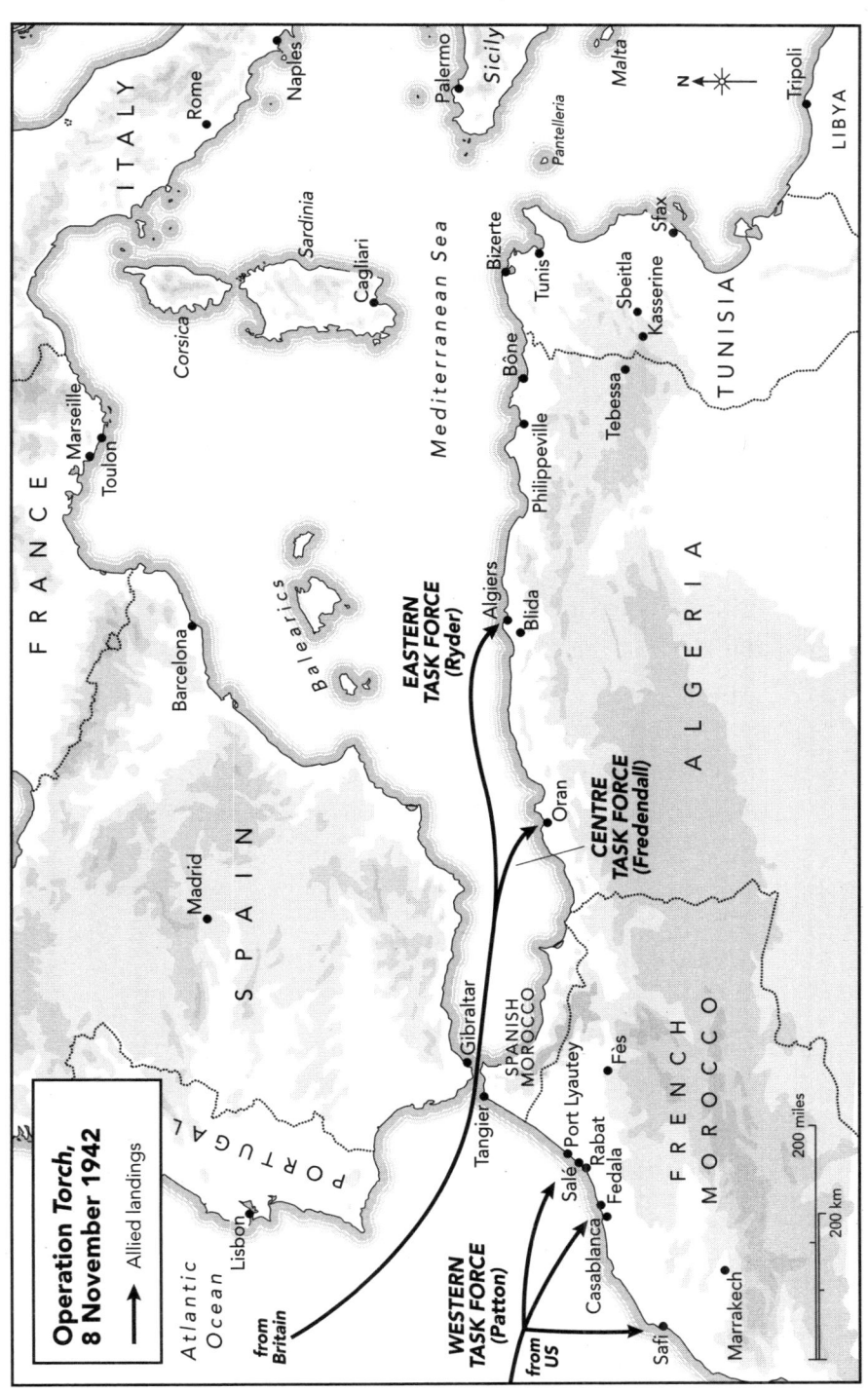

Operation Torch,
8 November 1942

→ Allied landings

**EASTERN
TASK FORCE
(Ryder)**

**CENTRE
TASK FORCE
(Fredendall)**

**WESTERN
TASK FORCE
(Patton)**

*from
Britain*

*from
US*

*Atlantic
Ocean*

PORTUGAL

Lisbon

SPAIN

Madrid

Barcelona

FRANCE

Marseille

Toulon

ITALY

Rome

Naples

Corsica

Sardinia

Cagliari

Balearics

Mediterranean Sea

Palermo

Sicily

Pantelleria

Malta

Tripoli

LIBYA

Sfax

Bizerte

Tunis

Sbeitla

Kasserine

TUNISIA

Bône

Philippeville

Tebessa

Algiers

Blida

Oran

ALGERIA

Gibraltar

Tangier

SPANISH
MOROCCO

Port Lyautey

Salé

Rabat

Fedala

Casablanca

Fès

FRENCH
MOROCCO

Marrakech

Safi

200 miles

200 km

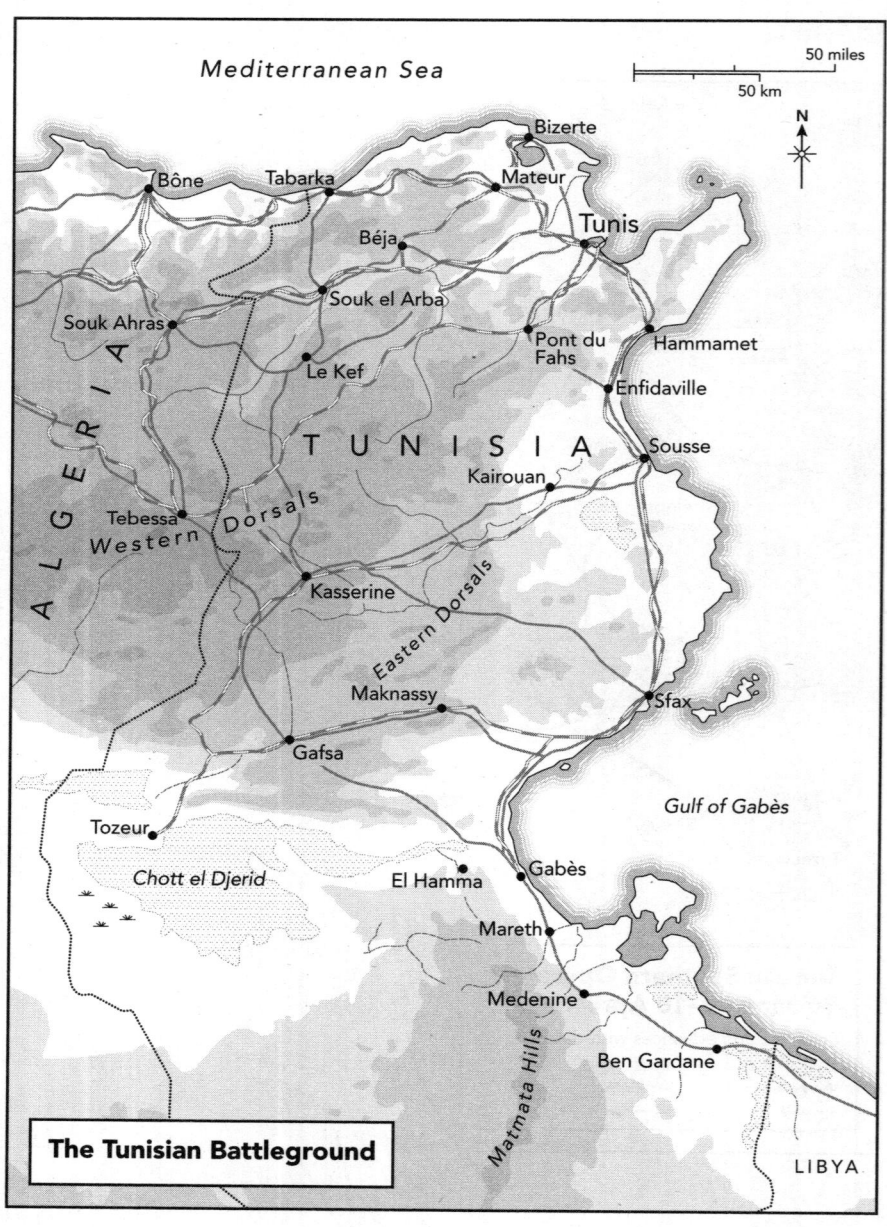

The Tunisian Battleground

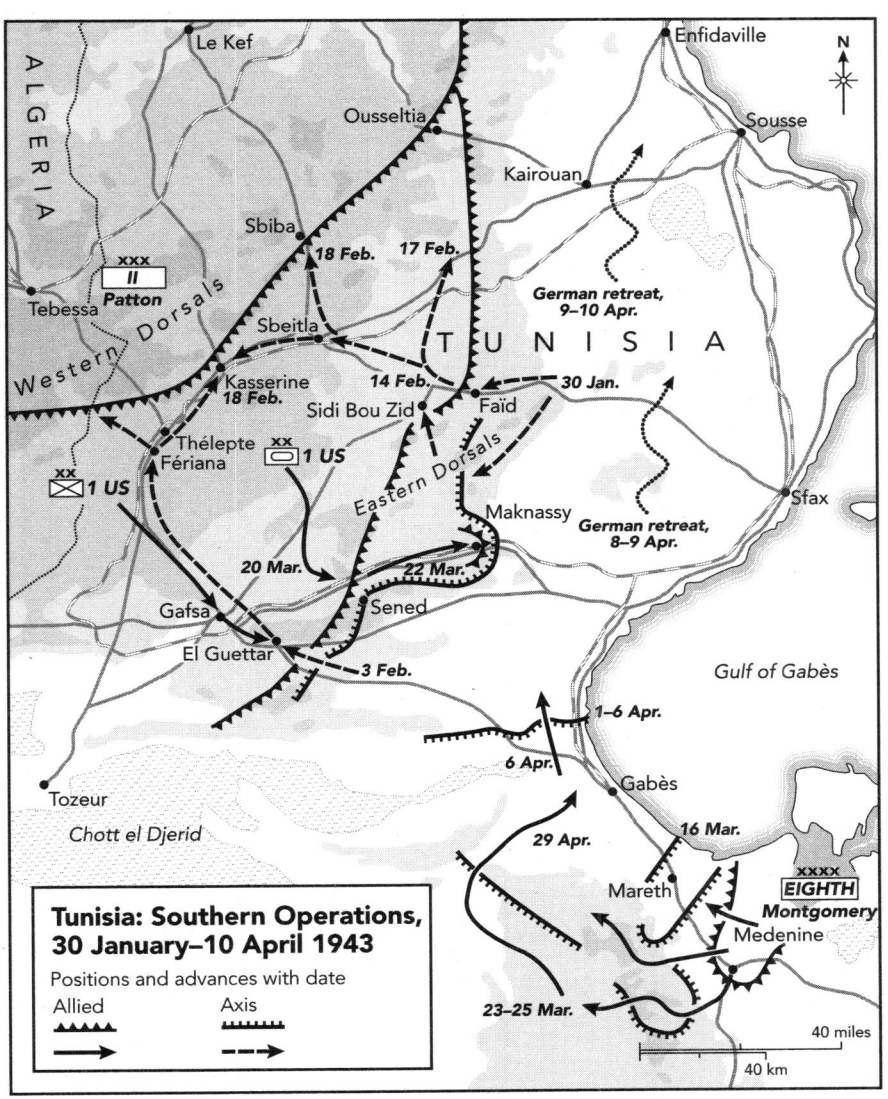

Tunisia: Southern Operations, 30 January–10 April 1943

Positions and advances with date

Allied

Axis

ALGERIA

Le Kef

Ousseltia

Enfidaville

Sousse

Kairouan

N

XXX
II
Patton

Tebessa

Sbiba

18 Feb.

17 Feb.

German retreat, 9–10 Apr.

T U N I S I A

Western Dorsals

Sbeitla

Kasserine
18 Feb.

14 Feb.

30 Jan.

Sidi Bou Zid

Faïd

Thélepte
Fériana

XX
1 US

Eastern Dorsals

Maknassy

German retreat, 8–9 Apr.

Sfax

XX
1 US

20 Mar.

22 Mar.

Gafsa

Sened

El Guettar

3 Feb.

Gulf of Gabès

Tozeur

Chott el Djerid

1–6 Apr.

6 Apr.

Gabès

16 Mar.

29 Apr.

Mareth

XXXX
EIGHTH
Montgomery

Medenine

23–25 Mar.

40 miles

40 km

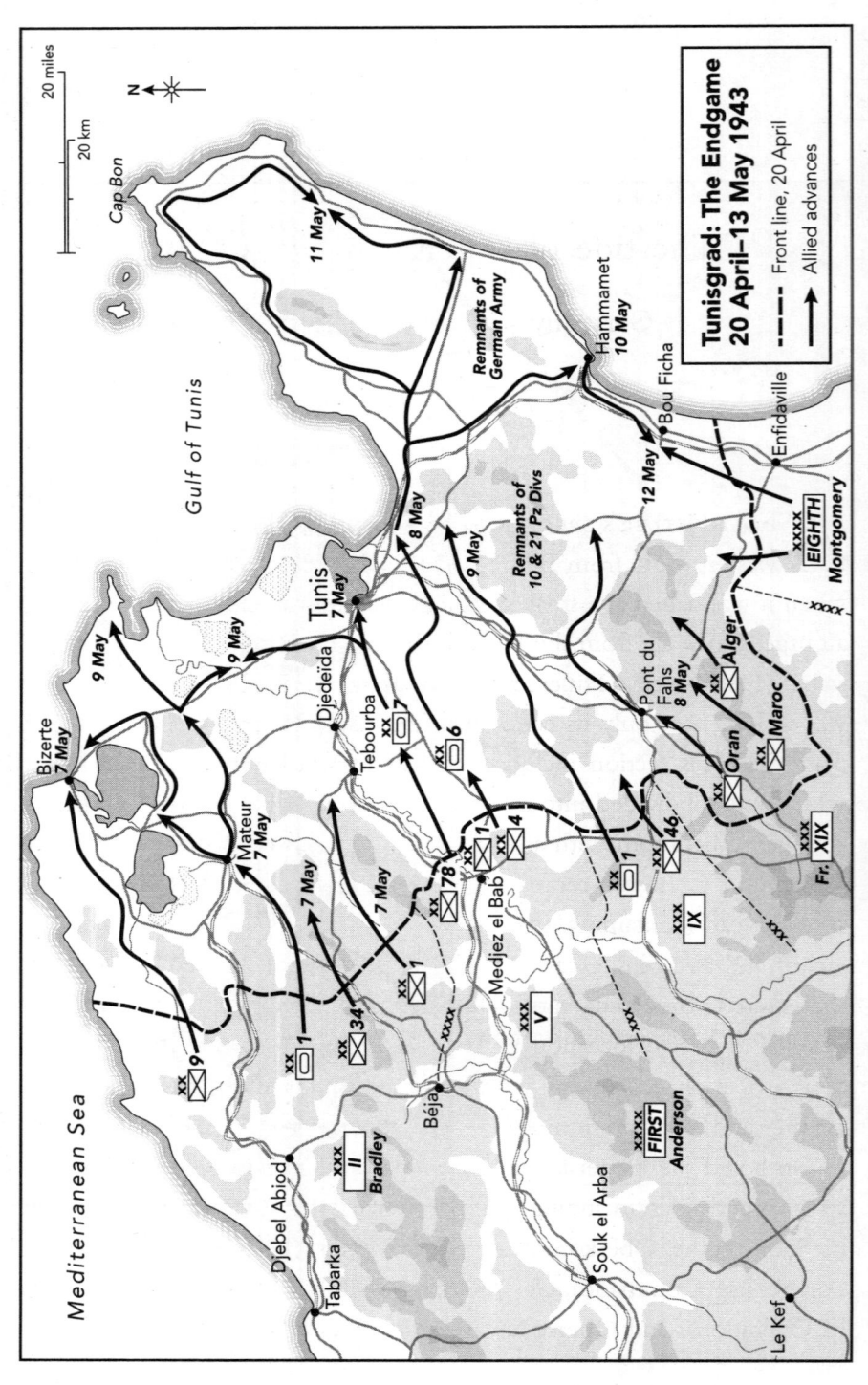

Tunisgrad: The Endgame
20 April–13 May 1943

Front line, 20 April
Allied advances

Mediterranean Sea

Cap Bon

Gulf of Tunis

Bizerte
7 May

9 May

9 May

Tunis
7 May

11 May

Hammamet
10 May

Remnants of
German Army

Bou Ficha

12 May

Enfidaville

Mateur
7 May

Djedeïda

Tebourba

8 May

9 May

Remnants of
10 & 21 Pz Divs

XXXX
EIGHTH
Montgomery

xxxx

7 May

7 May

xx 7

xx 6

Pont du
Fahs
8 May

xx
Alger

xx
Oran

xx
Maroc

XXX
Fr, XIX

Djebel Abiod

xx 9

7 May

34

xx 1

xx 1

78

xx 1

xx 4

Medjez el Bab

xx 1

46

xx 1

XXX
IX

Tabarka

xxx
II
Bradley

Béja

xxx
V

Souk el Arba

xxxx
FIRST
Anderson

Le Kef

20 miles

20 km

N

Prologue

'The tide of war had really turned'

Germany, 8–30 November 1942

ADOLF HITLER'S SPECIAL TRAIN – the *Führersonderzug* 'Amerika' – was en route from Berlin to Munich early on 8 November 1942 when it was halted at a small station in the Thuringian Forest to receive an urgent message from the Foreign Office. The huge 1,200-ton luxury train, which served as Hitler's mobile headquarters (or *Führerhauptquartier*), was so long that only its central portion could be accessed via the tiny platform. This section included Hitler's personal car, the *Führerwagen*, which was subdivided into a lounge with a big table and veined maple couches, a bedroom with a single bed, a marble bathroom, three guest rooms and a shower room; a command and communications car; a security car (containing twenty-two SS men from Hitler's personal guard) and two dining cars. Making up the rest of the 500-metre-long train were two sleeping cars, a press car, two *Flakwagens* for anti-aircraft defence, and two locomotives, in case of engine failure. The interior design of each coach was art deco, and, for comfort, there was both heating and air conditioning.[1]

On board the 'Amerika' that day were Hitler and his senior military advisors and aides, including Generalfeldmarschall Wilhelm Keitel, Chief of Staff of the Oberkommando der Wehrmacht (OKW, or Armed Forces High Command), Generalleutnant Alfred Jodl, the OKW's Chief of Operations, and Oberst Nicolaus von Below, Hitler's Luftwaffe (air

I

force) adjutant. A day earlier, Below recalled, they had received a 'very disturbing signal' from German agents in Gibraltar at the entrance to the Mediterranean reporting the departure of a large Allied troop convoy in an easterly direction. Most on the train assumed the convoy was bound for Libya, a colony of Germany's fascist ally Italy since 1912. But its true destination was confirmed by the Foreign Office communiqué on the 8th: 'a US expeditionary corps was disembarking in Algiers and Oran', two ports in French Algeria.[2]

The news left Hitler aghast, but it should not have done. A week earlier, he had asked Jodl's staff to prepare 'a survey of the overall situation in Autumn 1942'. The task was given to Jodl's deputy, Generalleutnant Walter Warlimont, who came to the following conclusions: on the Eastern Front – where General der Panzertruppe Friedrich Paulus's 320,000-strong Sixth Army had tried and narrowly failed to capture Stalingrad on the River Volga, as part of a broader German drive to secure the oilfields of the Caucasus (Operation 'Blue') – the 'utmost limits of the Wehrmacht and its allies had now been reached' and a strategic withdrawal to a shorter defensive line might be necessary;* as for the 'most likely area for the attack by the Western powers', which was clearly imminent, Warlimont suggested French North Africa as offering 'the best jumping-off point for further attacks against "Fortress Europe"'.

For Germany, the biggest new threat to its continental hegemony was the United States which, eleven months after Hitler had unwisely declared war on it in the wake of the Japanese sneak attack at Pearl Harbor, was about to bring its economic and military might to bear in

---

* Warlimont was correct. The gamble to capture Stalingrad, as flank cover for the advance south into the Caucasus, had not paid off. The Sixth Army's chief problem, now, was resupply. In the September battles alone, it had used 25 million bullets, 500,000 anti-tank shells, 750,000 artillery shells and 178,000 hand grenades. Every day, the army required 20 tonnes of food, 50 tonnes of horse fodder, and up to 40 tonnes of fuel. Yet the nearest railhead was 50 miles away. It would become almost impossible to replenish supplies and, just as important, manpower. (MacGregor, *The Lighthouse of Stalingrad*, p. 164)

Europe. Hitler knew a storm was brewing in the Atlantic that threatened to burst over Germany. The question was: where first? Even President Roosevelt and his advisors were unable to agree on the best strategy: to invade France immediately or enter Europe via the backdoor route of North Africa. The Foreign Office communiqué, however, was confirmation that – in the short term at least – the Allies had chosen the less risky Mediterranean strategy.

Fearing this might be the case, Warlimont had urgently recommended a resumption of military discussions with the pro-German Vichy government of unoccupied France to beef up the defences of its North African colonies. But nothing was done, Warlimont recalled, because the survey 'never got further than Jodl and Keitel', and neither they nor the Comando Supremo (the Italian High Command) 'had any conception that the landing was so imminent'.[3]

When Hitler was informed on his train on 8 November that 'a large American army had now appeared on the confines of the European theatre of war', and in an area of the 'greatest political and strategic importance', he asked Keitel and Jodl what forces or resources were immediately available to meet the threat. The answer was none. Oran, moreover, was beyond the range of German bombers based in Sicily, a detail that caused Hitler to rail against the Luftwaffe's incompetent lack of planning.

In truth, he had only himself to blame. Long before penning his autumn 1942 'survey', Warlimont had consistently argued that the Vichy regime should be allowed to reinforce its forces in North Africa from metropolitan France. At one point, Jodl had agreed. But Hitler had 'invariably brought' all these efforts 'to naught'.[4]

Further down the track, at Bamberg, Foreign Minister (and former champagne salesman) Joachim von Ribbentrop boarded the train and, with the Allied landings in mind, pleaded with Hitler to let him put out peace feelers to Stalin, via the Soviet embassy in Stockholm, offering 'far-reaching concessions in the East'. Hitler dismissed the idea: a 'moment of weakness was not the proper time to negotiate with an enemy'. Instead he ordered Jodl to 'organise the Wehrmacht for the defence of Tunis', the capital of French Tunisia, which was a short flight and sea journey from Sicily.[5] By securing Tunisia, Hitler hoped to stymie Allied plans to trap Generalfeldmarschall Erwin Rommel's Italo-German Panzer Army in Libya between General Sir Bernard Montgomery's Eighth Army advancing from Egypt in the east, and the forces just landed in Algeria to the west. The Allies had the same idea, and the subsequent 'Race for Tunis' would set the scene for one of the decisive campaigns of the war.

Looking back, Warlimont acknowledged that the 'moment at which the strategic initiative passed out of Hitler's hands' was November 1942, 'the month of doom in modern German history, when the enemy struck both in East and West'. It began during the evening of 2 November with the receipt at Wolfsschanze (the 'Wolf's Lair'), Hitler's Eastern Front HQ in the Masurian woods near Rastenburg, East Prussia, of a 'thunderclap' message from Rommel that, after an eight-day battle against the British Eighth Army at El Alamein in Egypt, he 'could see no alternative to the total annihilation of his army other than to begin a withdrawal on his own initiative and contrary to all orders from Rome and Rastenburg'.[6]

Lacking fuel and supplies, and facing a numerically superior foe, Rommel knew his only hope of survival was to fall back into Libya. Hitler disagreed. 'In the situation in which you find yourself,' he messaged Rommel on 3 November, 'there can be no other thought than to stick it out, not to yield a step, and to throw every weapon and available fighter into the battle.' Reinforcements would be sent, said Hitler, but it was now a contest of wills. 'You can,' he concluded, 'show your troops no other way than victory or death.'[7]

Unwilling to disobey the Führer, Rommel countermanded the withdrawal which had already begun. But by the afternoon of the following day, with his 'front broken' and enemy tanks 'streaming' towards his rear, Rommel reissued orders for an immediate retreat. 'We had lost the decisive battle of the African campaign,' he admitted. 'It was decisive because our defeat had resulted in the loss of a large part of our infantry and motorised forces.'[8]

Infuriated by Rommel's insubordination, Hitler chose to blame a relatively junior operations staff officer who had failed to pass on the original message in time. He even, for a while, seemed to accept the logic of Rommel's withdrawal, issuing a post-facto authorisation that, in the event, would have been too late. But the more he thought about it, the more convinced Hitler became that Rommel should have 'stayed put up front', that that was 'the only hope of saving the whole thing', and that only 'an unfortunate chain of events' had prevented him from intervening.[9]

As far as Hitler was concerned, wrote Nicolaus von Below, 'Rommel had lost much of the glamour he had attracted in the outward [desert] campaign. From now on he was the commander of an army driven ever westwards across the desert towards Tunisia.'[10]

The second major blow – news of the American landings in North Africa – came a couple of days after Rommel's defeat at El Alamein. It prompted Hitler to demand a robust reaction – preferably a declaration of war on the Allies – from Vichy France. When that failed to materialise, and instead word reached Hitler on 10 November that French resistance in North Africa was crumbling, he ordered his troops to occupy the remainder of France and Corsica the following day, the anniversary of the 1918 Armistice. It was necessary, said Hitler, to defend the coast of southern France against Allied invasion from North Africa. At the same time he demanded permission from Vichy to land troops in Tunisia. This was given by Marshal Pétain, but only under 'official protest'.[11]

Hitler then retired for a few days' rest at the Berghof, his palatial Alpine retreat near Berchtesgaden in Bavaria which he had developed from a much smaller chalet bought with the royalties from his political manifesto *Mein Kampf* in 1933. A spell at the Berghof – his favourite residence with its wood-beamed great hall, heavy German antique furniture and spectacular views of snow-capped mountains – rarely failed to raise Hitler's spirits. But the news that the Western Powers – the USA and Britain – had joined forces in North Africa was, for him, a 'very serious development' that left him feeling depressed. He was well aware of the difficulty of shipping supplies across the Mediterranean and, moreover, had 'no confidence' in his Italian allies. His one hope, noted Nicolaus von Below, who spoke to him privately, was that there were 'no new surprises in store on the Eastern Front'.[12]

There were. On 19 November, while still at the Berghof, Hitler was informed by General der Infanterie Kurt Zeitzler, the Chief of the Army General Staff (OKH), that a huge Russian offensive (Operation Uranus) had broken through a weak section of the line held by Romanian troops to the west and northwest of Stalingrad. Hitler ordered a counter-attack, but it failed. On 20 November, a separate Russian force pierced Romanian defences to the south of the city, and two days later the pincers closed behind Stalingrad, encircling the Sixth Army's remaining 220,000 men.

Zeitzler requested permission for the Sixth Army to fight its way out of Stalingrad. Hitler refused. That evening, as he began a twenty-hour train journey back to Rastenburg, he ordered Paulus to hold on. 'The Sixth Army must know,' he promised, 'that I am doing everything to help it and relieve it.'[13]

By the end of November, the smooth occupation of Vichy France, the successful landing of Axis troops in Tunisia, and plans for the relief of Stalingrad, had produced a 'deceptive atmosphere of confidence' at Führer HQ in Rastenburg. But it masked the reality that, in Warlimont's words, 'the tide of war had really turned and we went back to the dance of tactical expedients with Hitler as master of ceremonies'.[14]

Within six months, three Axis defeats had changed the course of the war: at Guadalcanal in the Pacific, Stalingrad in Russia and Tunisia in North Africa. Historians have long recognised the significance of the first two campaigns, but not that of Tunisia which they have either ignored or characterised (as the Americans did at the time) as a sideshow.

Yet it ended Axis sea power in the Mediterranean, destroyed more than 2,400 Axis aircraft (40 per cent of the Luftwaffe's strength), and resulted in the surrender of over 250,000 German and Italian troops, more than were lost at Stalingrad. Comparing the scale of the defeat to the destruction of General Paulus's Sixth Army in Russia, many Germans called it a 'second Stalingrad' or 'Tunisgrad'.[*][15]

It was the first campaign fought by the Anglo-American alliance, and it would determine how and where the Allies would fight for the rest of the war. It was where America first brought to bear the full weight of its industrial strength, and where the Allies learned, after early setbacks, how to defeat the Germans with a combination of air, land and sea power. It was where many of the great commanders of the Second World War emerged: 'Ike' Eisenhower, George S. Patton Jr, Omar Bradley, Harold Alexander, Bernard Montgomery, Arthur Coningham, Andrew Cunningham, Alphonse Pierre Juin, Albert Kesselring, Erwin Rommel, Hans-Jürgen von Arnim and Giovanni Messe. And it was where the Allies agreed on unconditional surrender as the only way the war could end, thus ruling out any hope of a negotiated peace and forcing the Nazis to fight to the finish. But the campaign's chief significance is that it extinguished any lingering hopes in Italy that the war could be won and led, inexorably, to the dissolution of the Axis in Europe when Italy surrendered unilaterally in September 1943. By destroying the Axis it marked, for Hitler, the beginning of the end.

The Tunisian campaign was fought in a particularly harsh climate: through the wet and chill of winter and spring, and across an unforgiving terrain that encompassed parched and featureless deserts in the south, semi-arid highlands in Central Tunisia, and the mountainous,

---

[*] Britain's Public Warfare Executive, tasked with black propaganda, also used the term 'Tunisgrad' in leaflets dropped over Germany in 1943, informing readers in the Ruhr that the twin defeats at Stalingrad and in Tunisia were unprecedented, and the only way to avoid total defeat was to get rid of Hitler (Stiastny, *Believable Lies*, p. 290).

if relatively fertile, territory of the north which, 2,000 years earlier, had served as the Roman Empire's breadbasket.

The outcome was never a foregone conclusion. At first, the Axis troops took advantage of air superiority and greater combat experience to defeat the Allies in a number of key engagements on land. When they took the offensive, in January and February 1943, they won a string of startling victories over the French and the Americans that came within an ace of cutting the Allies' supply lines and inflicting a major strategic defeat. To remedy the situation, Alexander was appointed theatre commander, incompetent generals like Fredendall were sacked (allowing Patton, for example, to come to the fore), and the First Army regrouped, helped, it must be said, by the measured advance of Montgomery's veteran Eighth Army from the south.

Other key players in the story include Oberstleutnant Claus Graf von Stauffenberg, Operations Officer of the 10th Panzer Division, who, a year after losing his left eye and right hand in a strafing attack by a P-40 Kittyhawk fighter-bomber in Tunisia, would come so close to assassinating Hitler in the 'Bomb Plot' of July 1944; Major Vladimir 'Popski' Peniakoff, the extraordinary Belgian-born leader of the irregular force known as Popski's Private Army, who discovered the route that enabled Montgomery to outflank the Mareth Line, and who later conducted a series of sabotage missions behind the lines in Tunisia; Lieutenant Colonel David Stirling, the founder of the SAS, who was captured by the Italians on a hare-brained mission to link up with the First Army in Tunisia; Ernie Pyle, the celebrated American war correspondent, who wrote a series of memorable dispatches from the perspective of ordinary soldiers on the front line in Tunisia that were syndicated across America; and 23-year-old Second Lieutenant Te Moanunui-a-Kiwa Ngarimu of New Zealand's 28th (Maori) Battalion, who became the first Maori recipient of the Victoria Cross for leading an attack on Point 209, at the Tebaga Gap, on 26 March 1943, destroying German machine-gun posts and repelling a counter-attack before he was killed the following day.

Scores of books have been written about Guadalcanal and Stalingrad. But outside the world of academia, only two histories have covered the 'Tunisgrad' timeline in recent years: Rick Atkinson's Pulitzer prize-winning *An Army at Dawn: The War in North Africa, 1942–1943* (2001), and James Holland's *Together We Stand: North Africa 1942–1943 – Turning the Tide in the West* (2005). Atkinson's book concentrates on the American contribution; Holland's devotes most of its space to the earlier campaign by Montgomery's Eighth Army in Egypt and Libya.

Tunisgrad, on the other hand, is the first comprehensive 360-degree history, drawing on memoirs, unpublished diaries, letters and interviews with participants, from politicians and senior commanders to ordinary servicemen, war correspondents and nurses. For the first time, the Tunisian campaign takes its rightful place as the third great hinge moment of the war, in an epic tale, told in the words of those who were there.

I

'The most dismal setting'

Europe, USA and North Africa, September 1939–November 1942

A T THE SOUTHERN TIP of the Iberian peninsula, guarding the narrow entrance to the Mediterranean, lies the tiny two-square-mile enclave and port of Gibraltar, a British possession since 1704 when it was captured by Anglo-Dutch forces during the War of the Spanish Succession. It is dominated by the 'Rock', a sheer-sided limestone feature 1,400 feet high, home to Barbary monkeys and riddled with tunnels. In late 1942, these deep subterranean passages were used to house the head-quarters of Lieutenant General Dwight D. 'Ike' Eisenhower, the American Commander-in-Chief of the Allied Expeditionary Force for Operation Torch, the invasion of French North Africa.

It was, Eisenhower remembered, 'the most dismal setting we occupied during the war'. The darkness was only 'partially pierced by feeble electric bulbs', and the 'damp, cold air' seemed impervious to the 'clattering efforts of electric fans'. From the arched ceilings, meanwhile, 'came a constant drip, drip, drip of surface water that faithfully but drearily ticked off the seconds of the interminable, almost unendurable, wait which occurs between completion of a military plan and the moment action begins'.

The tunnels were being used as the nerve centre for what, at the time, was the greatest amphibious operation in history because, noted Eisenhower, beggars could not be choosers. In November 1942, the fortress of Gibraltar was the only Allied possession in western Europe, and the only safe haven west of the Mediterranean island of Malta, a sea journey of 1,100 nautical miles. Without Gibraltar's port and airfield, the invasion of northwest Africa would not have been possible.

As Eisenhower and his staff paced Gibraltar's caverns in the early hours of 8 November 1942, waiting anxiously for news from the three Allied naval expeditions that were nudging ever closer to the Moroccan and Algerian shores, they realised the stakes were impossibly high. As Eisenhower wrote:

> Within a matter of hours, the Allies would know the initial fate of their first combined offensive gesture of the war. Aside from the see-saw campaigns of advance and retreat that had been going on in the Western Desert for two full years and the island battle of Guadalcanal, nowhere in the world had the Allies been capable of undertaking on the ground anything more than mere defense. Even our defensive record was tragically draped in defeats of which Dunkirk, Bataan, Hong Kong, Singapore, Sourabaya, and Tobruk were black reminders.[1]

Since Germany's invasion of Poland on 1 September 1939, the start of a war that would last 2,174 days and claim a life every three seconds, the Western Allies had known mostly defeat.[2] Poland capitulated to German aggression in October 1939 (and was cynically partitioned between Germany and the Soviet Union), followed by Denmark in April 1940, Norway, Holland, Belgium and Luxembourg in May, and France in June, leaving Britain to fight on alone. In late May, with the writing on the wall, some senior members of the British government – notably the Foreign Secretary Lord Halifax – thought it best to sue for peace, using the Italians as intermediaries. Even Winston S. Churchill, who had replaced Neville Chamberlain as prime minister on 10 May, considered the possibility. Short, balding and stout, a superb orator whose rejection of 'appeasement' had angered the Conservative Party leadership and caused him to spend much of the 1930s in the political wilderness,

Churchill quickly concluded that there was more to lose by throwing in the towel than by fighting on. He was backed by his three Chiefs of Staff – who insisted that it was possible to continue the war alone against Germany, and probably Italy, as long as the Royal Air Force (RAF) maintained air superiority to prevent an invasion.[3]

On 4 June 1940, buoyed by the news that 224,000 British and 111,000 Allied (mostly French) soldiers had been rescued from Dunkirk,★ Churchill gave a speech of defiant brilliance to the House of Commons: 'We shall fight on the beaches, we shall fight on the landing grounds, we shall fight in the fields and in the streets, we shall fight in the hills, we shall never surrender.'[4]

But more disasters were in store. On 10 June, with the conflict seemingly won, Italian dictator Benito Mussolini cynically declared war on France in the hope of sharing Germany's spoils. It was not unexpected, and prompted Churchill to tell his private secretary Jock Colville: 'People who go to Italy to look at ruins won't have to go as far as Naples and Pompeii again.'[5]

Churchill's chief hope was that the industrial might of America would come to its fellow liberal democracies' rescue. On 15 May, as German panzers were overrunning western Europe, he had asked US President Franklin Delano Roosevelt (or FDR, as he was known), mostly confined to a wheelchair since contracting polio in 1921, to send military support. 'The small countries,' wrote Churchill, 'are simply smashed up, one by one, like matchwood . . . If necessary, we shall continue the war alone, and we are not afraid of that. But I trust you realise, Mr President, that the voice and force of the United States may count for nothing if they are withheld too long.'

While sympathetic, Roosevelt was bound by the Neutrality Acts of

---

★ Despite the relative success of the ad hoc evacuation, the British Expeditionary Force (BEF) left behind 68,111 personnel (killed, wounded and missing), and the vast majority of its weapons and supplies: 2,400 artillery pieces, 63,000 vehicles, 76,000 tons of ammunition, and almost 200,000 tons of stores and fuel.

the 1930s that were designed to keep America out of other people's wars, and to limit the trade and production of arms. He also knew, in a presidential election year, that the powerful 'isolationist' lobby, backed by famous aviator Charles A. Lindbergh, made overt support for the Allies a potential vote loser. He would provide planes, anti-aircraft weapons, ammunition and steel – invoking the 1939 Neutrality Act's 'cash-and-carry' clause that allowed belligerent nations to pay for such items and carry them on non-American ships – though not the forty or fifty 'older destroyers' that the prime minister had also asked for because that would require Congress's permission and the time was 'not opportune'.[6]

But the news of Italy's perfidy caused FDR to drop all pretence of neutrality. That evening, giving the commencement address at the University of Virginia in Charlottesville (where his son, FDR Jr, was graduating from law school), he declared that 'the hand that held the dagger has struck it into the back of its neighbor'. It was 'an obvious delusion' to believe that America could exist as 'a lone island in a world dominated by the philosophy of force', said Roosevelt, and its duty now was to 'extend to the opponents of force the material resources of this nation', while at the same time equipping and training American forces. The 'stab-in-the-back' speech was, wrote Roosevelt's biographer, a 'decisive turning point in American policy'. At a time when only 30 per cent of the nation believed an Allied victory possible, Roosevelt had aligned himself shoulder to shoulder with Britain and France.[7]

Churchill was delighted, telling the US president that the statement had given the Allies 'a strong encouragement in a dark but not unhopeful hour'. But it was not enough to convince France's leaders to continue the fight from their northwest African colonies. Churchill even offered a political union between the United Kingdom and the French Republic, in a desperate last-ditch attempt to prevent the powerful French navy from falling into German hands. The French prime minister Paul Reynaud and Under-Secretary of State for War Brigadier General Charles de Gaulle (an aggressive tank commander who had performed well in recent battles) were supportive. But the other senior ministers and military commanders had already made up their minds to throw in the towel.

The chief defeatists were Marshal Philippe Pétain, the legendary hero of the Battle of Verdun in 1916, who ironically had been brought out of retirement by Reynaud in late May to stiffen resolve as Vice President of the Council; and General Maxime Weygand, Commander-in-Chief of the French army. A political union was pointless, Weygand told Pétain, because in 'three weeks England will have her neck wrung like a chicken'. Pétain agreed. To make a union with Britain, he said, was 'fusion with a corpse'.[8]

Reynaud resigned on 16 June and was replaced by Pétain who began peace negotiations with Germany. The armistice – a betrayal of France's agreement with Britain not to conclude a separate peace – was duly signed, in Hitler's presence, on 22 June in the same railway carriage in the Forest of Compiègne, near Paris, in which the German generals had capitulated in 1918.[*] 'The disgrace is now extinguished,' reported Josef Goebbels, Hitler's propaganda chief. 'It's a feeling of being born again.'[9]

The surrender terms, as in 1918, were harsh. France was to be divided: the north and western seaboard, including Paris, under German occupation; the centre and south (about two-fifths of the total) to be left as a vassal state, under Pétain, with its seat of government at the spa town of Vichy in central France. Germany, in addition, reannexed the provinces of Alsace and Lorraine. Pétain retained control of France's huge overseas empire, including the colonies of Morocco, Algeria and Tunisia. To defend it, he was allowed a reduced army of 120,000 men. This, the Germans hoped, would be large enough to keep out the British; but not so big as to threaten the Axis powers if Vichy ever chose to switch sides. To ensure the French kept their side of the bargain, the Germans retained one and a half million French prisoners of war as insurance.

---

[*] A separate Italian-French armistice was signed on 24 June, bringing hostilities in southern France to a close.

De Gaulle was horrified. On 18 June, a day after his escape to Britain, he had appealed on BBC radio for all French soldiers to join him in London to continue the fight. 'Whatever happens,' he said, 'the flame of French resistance must not and shall not die.' But of the more than 100,000 French soldiers then in Britain – recently evacuated from Norway and Dunkirk – only 7,000 answered his call. The rest were repatriated and quickly made prisoners of war. When de Gaulle made a second broadcast from London on 22 June, denouncing the armistice, he was dismissed from the French army. The response of the British government was to recognise de Gaulle as leader of the Free French.[10]

Churchill's main concern was still the French fleet. He had tried and failed to get Amiral de la flotte François Darlan, the Commander-in-Chief of the French navy (and Minister of Marine under Vichy) to order the fleet to British, American or French colonial harbours on 17 June. Darlan had repeatedly assured Churchill that, whatever happened, French ships would not fall into German hands. Yet Churchill put little store by French promises, and was determined to force the issue.

On 1 July, he authorised Operation Catapult, the 'simultaneous seizure, control or effective disablement or destruction of all the accessible French fleet'. Two days later, French ships were taken with minimal resistance at Portsmouth and Plymouth, and at Alexandria after their gun mechanisms had been removed and the fuel oil discharged. Only at Dakar in French West Africa and Mers-el-Kébir, near Oran in French Algeria, did the French refuse to surrender or scuttle their ships. At the former the battleship *Richelieu* was attacked by British torpedo-bombers and badly damaged; at the latter, a superior British fleet sank the battleship *Bretagne* and damaged five other ships, an attack that killed 1,297 French sailors.

It was a ruthless, unprovoked assault on a neutral nation the French would find hard to forgive. But Churchill – fearful that French warships would be used to protect a German invasion fleet – had no regrets. 'Here was this Britain which so many had counted down and out,' he wrote, 'which strangers had supposed to be quivering on the brink of surrender to the mighty power arrayed against her, striking ruth-lessly at her dearest friends of yesterday and securing for a while to herself the undisputed command of the sea. It was made plain that the British Cabinet feared nothing and would stop at nothing.'[11]

On a personal level, however, the Francophile Churchill was not unaffected. 'It was a terrible decision,' he admitted later, 'like taking the life of one's own child to save the State.'[12]

De Gaulle agreed. In a broadcast of 8 July, he said the attack was a 'hateful tragedy not a glorious battle', yet necessary to prevent the enemy from using the ships against Britain or the French Empire. He added: 'Our two ancient nations . . . remain bound to one another. They will either go down both together or both together they will win.'[13]

Hitler, meanwhile, was perplexed by Churchill's decision to fight on. On 19 July, in a speech to the Reichstag, he made a final attempt to bring the British to the negotiating table by emphasising the hope-lessness of their position and the likelihood that continued resistance would result in the destruction of Britain and its Empire. It was, he insisted, an 'appeal to reason'. The 'offer' was rejected within an hour. 'England's position is hopeless,' said Hitler. 'The war is won by us.'

He had already authorised 'Directive No. 16 for Preparations of a Landing Operation against England'. But for that to succeed, the Luftwaffe first needed to gain air superiority over southern England. By mid-September, the Luftwaffe's failure to defeat the RAF and win the so-called 'Battle of Britain' meant the plan to invade – Operation Sealion – was first postponed and then abandoned.

Hitler consoled himself with the belief that a victorious campaign against Josef Stalin's Soviet Union, planned for the following spring, would extinguish Britain's last hope and leave Germany master of Europe and the Balkans.[14] To bolster his position, he authorised the signing of the defensive Tripartite Pact with Italy and Japan, which was fighting its own war of aggression in China. 'All his efforts in these autumn months of 1940,' noted his Luftwaffe adjutant Nicolaus von Below, 'were directed towards welding a powerful and effective alliance against Britain.'[15]

Not all were successful. In November 1940, following their first face-to-face meeting at Hendaye in France, the Spanish dictator Francisco Franco refused Hitler's offer to join the Axis or permit a German attack on Gibraltar. Mussolini, meanwhile – keen to carve out a new 'Roman Empire' in North Africa and the Balkans, and ignoring his military experts who insisted Italy would not be ready for war until 1943 – had ordered Marshal Rodolfo Graziani's Italian Tenth Army in Libya to invade Egypt, a former British protectorate that was still garrisoned by British and Commonwealth troops. Despite being heavily outnumbered, Lieutenant General Richard O'Connor's Western Desert Force counter-attacked in December 1940 (Operation Compass) and, within two months, had destroyed the bulk of Graziani's army – capturing 130,000 prisoners, and taking or destroying 400 tanks and 800 guns – and conquered the whole of Cyrenaica, Libya's eastern province.[16]

Just as O'Connor was preparing to deliver the *coup de grâce* by advancing to Tripoli, the last Italian foothold in North Africa, Churchill intervened. The Greek leader, General Ioannis Metaxas, had died on 29 January and his successor, Alexandros Koryzis, told the British ambassador that he welcomed military assistance. The Greeks had already defeated an Italian invasion from Albania with the help of British planes. But enemy signals decrypted at Bletchley Park – a source known as Ultra – indicated a threat to Greece from German troops massing in Romania, prompting Churchill to act. On 12 February, he ordered General Sir Archibald Wavell, the Commander-in-Chief in the Middle East, to halt the advance into Tripolitania, transfer to Greece 'the fighting portion of the Army which has hitherto defended Egypt and make every plan for sending and reinforcing it to the limit'.

The first contingent of a force that would eventually number 50,000 arrived at Salonika on 7 March. The Germans invaded Greece and Yugoslavia a month later, and within weeks had overrun both countries, forcing the British to evacuate the bulk of their force to the island of Crete. They left behind 12,000 men, all their tanks and most of their equipment.[17]

On 20 May, the Germans launched Operation Mercury, a huge airborne assault on Crete using 8,000 paratroopers and 14,000 men of the airlanding 5. *Gebirgs-Division*, under Generalleutnant Kurt Student. Despite very heavy casualties – 4,000 killed and 2,500 wounded – the Germans eventually overwhelmed the numerically superior British garrison of 42,000 men (including 9,000 Greeks). British and Dominion losses included 3,500 killed and wounded, and 12,000 captured. A further 1,800 Royal Navy sailors were killed when three cruisers and six destroyers were sunk, and thirteen ships badly damaged, including the only aircraft carrier in the Mediterranean.[18]

In North Africa, meanwhile, Hitler had again come to Mussolini's assistance by sending an Afrika Korps of two divisions – the 5th Light and 15th Panzer – to Tripoli in mid-February. It was led by the dashing and fearless Erwin Rommel who had commanded Hitler's personal bodyguard in Poland, and later displayed his mastery of armoured warfare with the 7th Panzer Division in France in 1940. Rommel attacked in late March and within a fortnight had driven the bulk of the British and Dominion troops back into Egypt, capturing O'Connor and another senior commander in the process. Only a small force holding the port of Tobruk remained in Cyrenaica. For the next eighteen months the contest would ebb and flow, as first the Germans and then the British took the initiative.[19]

But for Churchill's intervention, O'Connor would probably have ejected the Italians from Libya before Rommel's troops could intervene. Even the Germans were convinced of this. 'We could not understand at the time,' wrote Generalleutnant Walter Warlimont, the OKW's Deputy Chief of the Operations Staff, 'why the British did not exploit the difficulties in Cyrenaica by pushing on to Tripoli. There was nothing to check them. The few Italian troops who remained there were panic-stricken, and expected the British tanks to appear at any moment.'[20]

2

'We had won after all!'

Soviet Union, USA, UK and Iran,
June 1941–August 1942

B Y THE SUMMER OF 1941, a desperate Britain was hoping for a
miracle. It came on 22 June with Hitler's invasion of the Soviet
Union, in flagrant violation of the German–Soviet Non-aggression
Pact of August 1939. Operation Barbarossa was the largest ground
offensive in history, and involved over 3 million soldiers, 3,600 tanks,
7,000 artillery pieces and 2,500 aircraft. It was, Hitler had told 200 of
his senior officers in late March, a 'clash of two ideologies' and a 'war
of annihilation' in which functionaries of the Bolshevik state were to
be killed out of hand.[1] As his men poured across the border, Hitler
commented: 'It will be the most difficult battle which our soldiers
will have to undergo in this war.'[2]

He was right. When General Sir Alan Brooke, commanding Britain's
Home Forces, heard the news he felt a mixture of relief and dread.
Like most people, he believed Russia would 'not last long, possibly 3
or 4 months, possibly longer'. But that might be enough to postpone
an invasion of Britain until 1942. That evening, Churchill put aside
his long-held aversion to communism in general, and the Soviet Union
in particular, by offering Stalin all the economic and technical assistance that Britain could provide.[3]

In the event, 40 per cent of Russia's air force – 3,100 planes – were
destroyed in the first three days. By early September, more than 4 million

Russian troops had been killed, wounded or captured. Smolensk and Kiev were in German hands, Leningrad was under siege and Hitler's troops were closing in on Moscow. The battle for the capital began in early October and involved seventy German divisions, totalling a million men, 1,700 tanks, 14,000 artillery pieces and almost 1,000 aircraft. They came within forty miles of Moscow before a desperate Russian defence and worsening weather brought them to a grinding halt. 'The troops are finished,' noted Generaloberst Franz Halder, the German Army Chief of Staff, on 22 November. In his old division, the 7th, one regiment was commanded by a first lieutenant, the battalions by second lieutenants.[4]

A Russian counter-attack in early December by wide-tracked T-34 tanks and ski troops pushed the Germans back fifty miles and saved Moscow. By the turn of the year, Hitler had lost 200,000 killed, 726,000 wounded, 400,000 captured and 113,000 hospitalised with frostbite.[5]

Even as Operation Barbarossa was faltering, Germany's Axis ally Japan launched a sneak attack by 366 carrier-borne planes on the US naval base at Pearl Harbor in Hawaii on 7 December 1941, sinking four American battleships, seriously damaging one and inflicting minor damage on another three. Churchill wrote later that, on hearing the momentous news, he knew 'the United States was in the war, up to the neck and in to the death', and that 'we had won after all!'.[6] But at the time he did not regard America's entry into the war with Germany 'as a foregone conclusion', nor was he alone. President Roosevelt was acutely aware that the powerful isolationist lobby in Congress would have preferred a war exclusively against Japan. What changed everything was Hitler's declaration of war on the United States on 11 December, thus letting Roosevelt and the American interventionists off the hook.

Why did he do it? Because, according to a recent study by Brendan Simms and Charlie Laderman, Hitler was convinced that the US president, international 'plutocratic' capitalism and 'world Jewry' were together bent on his destruction. 'Declaring war on the United States,' they write, 'was the culmination of Hitler's career, both ideologically and strategically.'[7]

With America now a belligerent, Churchill and his Chiefs of Staff rushed across the Atlantic to coordinate Allied plans. It helped greatly that, thanks to Roosevelt, the two countries were already closely aligned. Following his re-election in November 1940, Roosevelt had offered Churchill more goods and weapons under a scheme known as Lend-Lease. 'This is tantamount to a declaration of war by the United States,' the prime minister told his private secretary.[8]

If that was a little premature, Churchill worked hard to transform American economic aid into active belligerency. The US Navy extended its patrols deeper into the Atlantic to protect the sea-lanes from German submarine attack, and American servicemen were stationed in Greenland and Iceland. Roosevelt also felt confident enough of popular support to ramp up America's rearmament.[9] In September 1939, the US Army had been the world's seventeenth largest, just behind Romania. That year America had produced almost no tanks and could field only five infantry divisions. The transform-ation had begun in the autumn of 1940 with the introduction of the draft to expand the Regular Army and the National Guard. Sixteen million men were registered, though two-fifths failed to meet the fairly rigorous physical standards of recruits needing to stand at least five feet tall and weigh 105 pounds, possess twelve natural teeth, and be free of flat feet, venereal disease and hernias. A further 2 million were disqualified on psychiatric grounds. A Gallup poll that year found a common view of American youth as a 'flabby, pacifistic, yellow, cynical, discouraged, and leftist lot'.[10]

In July 1941, Roosevelt had asked his military to estimate the resources they would need to defeat America's potential enemies. The detailed report – known as the Victory Program – concluded that America required 10 million men in uniform, 26,000 combat planes and 869 warships. It also recommended that half the total manpower would be needed to defeat the Germans in continental Europe, a campaign that could not begin until full mobilisation was complete in 1943.[11] Roosevelt read the report in September, but a final estimate could not be prepared until British and Soviet requests for military aid had been drawn up and approved. Military expenditure in 1941 was, as a result, just 4 per cent of the total amount spent between 1941 and 1945.

After Pearl Harbor, the process of transforming America's military from puny weakling to latter-day Hercules gathered pace. In 1942, American industry outproduced the Axis states combined: 24,000 tanks to 11,000, 47,000 aircraft to 27,000, and six times as many heavy artillery pieces. By the end of the war, industrial output would have doubled in size and would account for two-thirds of all Allied military equipment: 297,000 aircraft, 193,000 artillery pieces, 86,000 tanks and 2 million army trucks. It was also to produce 8,800 naval vessels and 87,000 landing craft. For every major warship constructed by Japan, America made sixteen.[12]

This was all to come. But in December 1941, when America entered the war, there 'already existed a framework for close cooperation' with Britain.[13] That framework included the secret 'ABC1' Anglo-American staff talks in March 1941 that had agreed, in the event of war, on a broad 'Germany First' strategy: that is, to defeat Germany and Italy in Europe first, before turning to deal with Japan. The strategy had first been articulated to Roosevelt in November 1940 by Admiral Harold R. Stark, the Chief of Naval Operations, who argued that without the deployment of American military force in Europe, Britain was doomed. The defeat of Nazi Germany was, therefore, to take precedence over any threat that might arise from Japan. This was now adopted as official Allied policy at the post-Pearl Harbor 'Arcadia' Conference in Washington DC in December 1941 which also set up a Combined Chiefs of Staff (CCS) Committee to direct the war.

On the question of *how* to defeat Germany, however, there was less agreement. Churchill preferred a 'peripheral' strategy whereby Germany was contained by blockade, bombing, small raids and an attack on North Africa until it was sufficiently weakened by its efforts in Russia for a knockout blow on the continent. Roosevelt was broadly in agreement. But his chief political and military advisors – notably Henry Stimson, the septuagenarian Secretary of War, General George C. Marshall Jr, the US Army Chief of Staff, and Dwight D. Eisenhower, the deputy chief of the War Plans Division (soon to be renamed the Operations Division) – were convinced that only the earliest full-frontal assault on Germany via France would keep Russia in the war. Marshall's sole slight concession was his conditional support for an Allied landing in North Africa in early 1942 if Vichy France, which controlled most of the northwest coast, was prepared to cooperate. This, he knew, would help to prevent the Germans from gaining control of the Middle East's oilfields.[14]

In the Far Eastern theatre, the initial outlook for the new alliance was grim. On 10 December, three days after Pearl Harbor, the battle-ship *Prince of Wales*, pride of the Royal Navy, and the battle cruiser *Repulse* were sunk by Japanese planes off Malaya. The Japanese advance into southeast Asia – launched on 8 December – soon seemed unstoppable: Hong Kong fell on Christmas Day, 1941; the fortress island of Singapore, at the southern tip of the Malayan peninsula, on 15 February 1942, with the loss of its 85,000 strong garrison (causing Churchill to lament that the numerically superior defenders 'should have done better');[15] and Rangoon, the capital of Burma, on 7 March. Meanwhile American troops, under General Douglas MacArthur, were hard-pressed by the Japanese in the Philippines (the last 10,000 surrendered on 8 May), British and Commonwealth troops were retreating in North Africa, and British India was being destabilised by internal dissent from Mahatma Gandhi and others in the form of the 'Quit India' movement.

For Marshall, these theatres were largely a sideshow. What mattered was continental Europe, and the obvious route into it, via Britain, was France. In early March 1942, Marshall asked Eisenhower, the new chief of the Operations Division, whose organisational genius and equable temperament marked him out as the coming man of the War Department, to draw up invasion plans. Eisenhower came up with three (in a document known as the Marshall Memorandum). First would be Operation Bolero, the shipment of thirty divisions – 500,000 men – and 3,250 aircraft to Britain over the next year as preparation for an invasion. This would be followed in April 1943 by Operation Roundup, an assault on the French coast between Le Havre and Boulogne by forty-eight Allied divisions and 5,800 planes (with the British contributing almost half the planes and a third of the troops). And if before then Germany showed signs of serious weakness, or Russia was in danger of being overwhelmed, a smaller 'emergency' assault by five to ten divisions – Operation Sledgehammer – would be launched in the autumn of 1942 to secure a beachhead in France, possibly at Cherbourg or Calais, to tie up as many German troops as possible.[16]

When Marshall presented his memorandum to the British in April 1942, Churchill responded enthusiastically. In truth, he and his Chiefs of Staff were extremely sceptical about the prospects of Operation Sledgehammer, and even an early Roundup. But he could not admit that because he feared that if the Americans knew the truth they might abandon their plans for Bolero – the build-up of troops and materiel in Britain – and concentrate instead on defeating Japan in the Pacific.[17]

Churchill preferred a joint invasion of French North Africa in 1942 because it was less risky than a direct assault on the continent but might have far-reaching consequences: the destruction of Erwin Rommel's Italo-German Panzer Army between the landing forces and the Eighth Army that was already fighting in Egypt; the reopening of the Mediterranean route through the Suez Canal, which would shorten the trip around the Cape of Good Hope by thousands of miles and save a million tons of shipping; the blooding of inexperienced American troops in a combat zone that was not expected to be as tough as northwest Europe; the potential for luring Vichy France, or at least its North African colonies, back into the Allied camp; and the denting of Mussolini's prestige to such an extent that Italy might withdraw from the war.[18]

It was unfortunate, then, that in July 1942, the month Churchill had to 'procure from the United States the decision which, for good or ill, dominated the next two years of the war', he was politically at his 'weakest' and 'without a gleam of military success'.[19] A few weeks earlier, Churchill had flown to America to discuss strategy with Roosevelt. On 20 June, during a one-to-one meeting at Roosevelt's Hyde Park estate in upper New York, Churchill gave the president a skilfully argued memorandum. It warned against a landing in France in 1942 'unless we are going to stay', adding: 'No responsible British military authority has so far been able to make a plan for [Operation Sledgehammer in] September 1942 which had any chance of success unless the Germans became utterly demoralised, of which there is no likelihood.'

In the absence of a viable plan, Churchill suggested a continuance of Bolero, which was already under way, *and* a separate operation to 'take some of the weight off Russia'. His vote was for a landing in 'French North-West Africa'.

A day later, back at the White House in Washington DC, Churchill was given the bombshell news that Tobruk in Libya had fallen to Rommel's Panzer Army with the loss of 25,000 men. The vital seaport had survived a seven-month siege in 1941, so this sudden capitulation, in the wake of the Eighth Army's defeat at Gazala, was for Churchill particularly unexpected. 'This was,' he wrote later, 'one of the heaviest blows I can recall during the war . . . I did not attempt to hide from the President the shock I had received. It was a bitter moment. Defeat is one thing; disgrace is another.'

With typical chivalry, Roosevelt asked how America could help. 'Give us as many Sherman tanks as you can spare,' said Churchill, 'and ship them to the Middle East as quickly as possible.' This

Roosevelt and Marshall were able to arrange – sending 300 Shermans and 100 self-propelled guns by fast ships – even though it meant delaying the supply of these brand new tanks to American armoured formations.[20]

Marshall was less pliable when it came to Churchill's preferred strategy. The argument came to a head in early July when Churchill reiterated his earlier point to Roosevelt that 'no responsible British general, admiral, or air marshal is prepared to recommend "Sledgehammer" as a practicable operation in 1942'. Their objections included the likelihood that a lodgement in northern France would curtail the bombing campaign of Germany, interrupt training and might even 'decisively injure the prospect of a well-organised large-scale action [Roundup] in 1943'. A landing in French North Africa, on the other hand, was both in 'harmony' with Roosevelt's ideas and the 'safest and most fruitful stroke' that could be 'delivered this autumn'.★[21]

While Roosevelt weighed up the merits of the North African landings, he faced strong opposition from his senior military advisors, Marshall and Admiral Ernest J. King, the Commander-in-Chief of the US Fleet and a member of the Joint Chiefs of Staff. Tall with thinning dark hair, a Roman nose and a cleft chin, King was fiercely intelligent and hardworking, but also rude, obnoxious and, in Marshall's opinion, a 'mental bully'. On the need to attack France in 1942, however, the pair were in agreement.[22] On 10 July, Marshall and King told Roosevelt that if the British insisted on 'scatterization' in North Africa, 'America should turn to the Pacific for decisive action against Japan'.[23] After a string of defeats, the US Navy had recently gained a hard-fought and even fortunate naval victory at Midway in the central Pacific – sinking four Japanese aircraft carriers for the loss of one of its own – and was planning to go on the offensive at Guadalcanal in the British Solomon Islands. But the threat to abandon the 'Germany

---

★ Churchill also mentioned the possibility of an 'operation in Northern Norway' (Jupiter), but that was never taken seriously by his Chiefs of Staff.

First' strategy if Britain did not step into line was a bluff by Marshall and King, and Roosevelt refused to go along with it.

To resolve the issue, he sent the two Joint Chiefs to London to consult with Churchill and his military chiefs. They were accompanied by Harry Hopkins, Roosevelt's personal envoy who, having recently survived stomach cancer, cut a sorry figure with his long neck and gaunt features. The trio's remit was to 'carefully investigate' the possibility of executing Sledgehammer; only if it was 'impossible' were they to consider the 'best methods of holding the Middle East' – including its invaluable oil – by sending troops to either the Persian Gulf, Syria, Egypt or French North Africa. What was not an option was an 'all-out effort in the Pacific'. Roosevelt ruled it out on the grounds that 'defeat of Japan does not defeat Germany and that American concentration against Japan this year or in 1943 increases the chance of complete German domination of Europe and Africa'.[24]

After consulting with Lieutenant General Eisenhower, commanding the US Army's European Theater of Operations (ETOUSA) in London, and 'anxious to go ahead' with Sledgehammer, Marshall and his staff began planning for a seizure of the Cherbourg peninsula in northern France. But this was vehemently opposed by Churchill and his Chiefs of Staff, and even King had sympathy for their argument that an autumn cross-Channel assault would face perilous weather.[25] 'We went on arguing for 2 hours,' General Sir Alan Brooke, Chief of the Imperial General Staff since the previous December, wrote in his diary, 'during which time King remained with a face like a Sphinx, and only one idea, i.e. to transfer operations to the Pacific.'[26]

When Roosevelt was informed that the talks were in stalemate, he instructed Marshall, King and Hopkins to consider another operation that would pit American troops against Germans in 1942. His preference was for a landing in 'Algeria and/or Morocco', an operation that was particularly time sensitive since the receipt of intelligence that plans were under way for the 'substantial strengthening of the coast defences and air bases' in French Morocco. The delegation was urged to reach a decision with 'our friends' as quickly as possible.[27]

This was, in effect, an order and Marshall and King took it as such. 'They all agreed to giving up immediate attack on Continent,' scribbled Brooke in his diary on 24 July, 'to prepare plans for attack on North Africa.'[28] Hopkins confirmed the decision in a cable to Roosevelt: 'We are naturally disappointed, but good will prevails . . . Now that the decision has been made we are hard at work on the next steps.' Hopkins also raised the issue of logistics, but Roosevelt was unconcerned. He could see no reason why 80,000 American troops could not be transported in ships from the United Kingdom, and also directly across from the United States. Once the original bridgeheads in Morocco and Algeria had been secured, the Americans would be in a position to drive east to Tunis.[29]

Roosevelt assumed the matter was settled. But after their return from Britain on 27 July, Marshall and King made fresh attempts to veto the North African operation (the name of which had been changed for security reasons from Gymnast to Torch). Roosevelt was having none of it. Summoning them to the White House on 30 July, he announced that, as Commander-in-Chief, his decision was final. North Africa was now the 'principal objective' and the operation would begin 'at the earliest possible date'.[30]

Roosevelt's decision has been criticised by some historians as caving in to British pressure. In fact, as Douglas Porch makes clear in *Defeat and Division: France at War, 1939–1942*, the US president and his influential chief military advisor, Admiral William D. Leahy, had long favoured an 'air-sea machinery-based war, with a remarkably small land army, all things considered', and a campaign in North Africa ticked a lot of these boxes. They had both been alarmed when, earlier that year, Vichy France handed over Indochina to the Japanese, and felt that it was only a matter of time before the North African colonies were given to Germany. Roosevelt, moreover, agreed with Churchill that it was vital to secure Egypt and Suez, the gateways to the Middle

East, and that it was foolish to risk the outcome of the war on a premature invasion of northern Europe. 'Rather than Roosevelt being "manipulated" by Churchill to support British interests as American generals complained,' wrote Porch, 'on the contrary, the invasion of the Mediterranean bought time for the United States to mobilize its industrial and military assets and so to assert its power in the alliance during the war's concluding stages.'[31]

It was one of the few major military decisions of the war that Roosevelt made against the advice of his senior military advisors. The consequences were potentially disastrous: defeat for the Soviet Union, as a result of the Western Allies' failure to open a Second Front in France in 1942, or even in 1943 (as Marshall feared). Yet, as we shall see, Roosevelt made the correct call. Sledgehammer in 1942 would have been a disaster. Only when Germany had been sufficiently weakened by air bombardment, the bloodletting on the Eastern Front, and the loss of some of its allies and most of its air force, would a full-scale invasion of northwest Europe be possible. In 1942 that was far from the case.

One last major player needed to be persuaded: Soviet dictator Josef Stalin. Churchill flew to Moscow, via the Middle East and Tehran, arriving on 12 August. After a brief rest in 'State Villa No. 7', a luxuriously appointed residence on the outskirts of the city, its sideboards 'laden with every delicacy and stimulant that supreme power can command', Churchill was driven to the Kremlin for his first meeting with the 'great Revolutionary Chief'. It did not go well. Dressed casually in a lilac tunic, cotton trousers and long boots, Stalin would not look at Churchill, preferring to gaze blankly at the wall or the floor as he listened and spoke. What the British prime minister had to say did not help. He told Stalin that there would be no Second Front in France in 1942. It could only have been on a small scale and would have ended in disaster. But they were preparing for 'a very great operation in 1943', and to that end a million American troops would be in the United Kingdom by the following spring.

A glum Stalin was unimpressed. Already that year the Germans had captured Crimea and blunted a Soviet counter-attack near Kharkov in Ukraine, two defeats that had cost Stalin half a million troops. Even more ominous was the huge new offensive Hitler had launched in late June – Operation Blue – with the oilfields of the Caucasus as its target. By the time he met Churchill, Stalin knew that Rostov-on-Don had fallen and the Germans were almost at the gates of Stalingrad on the Volga river. He was desperate for the Western Allies to open a Second Front that would force the Germans to move troops to France, and had little time for Churchill's excuses. 'A man who is not prepared to take risks,' he mocked, 'cannot win a war. Why are you so afraid of the Germans? If you do not blood your troops, you have no idea what their value is?'

To mollify Stalin, Churchill unfolded a map of southern Europe, the Mediterranean and North Africa. 'What is a Second Front?' he asked rhetorically. 'Is it only a landing on a fortified coast opposite England? Or can it take the form of some other great enterprise which might be useful to the common cause?' After mentioning various options in western France and Holland, and the strategic bombing of Germany, he revealed his big secret. 'We and the Americans have decided upon another plan, which I'm authorised by the American President to impart to you secretly.' It was, he explained, an invasion of French North Africa called Operation Torch. It would take place not later than 30 October and, if all went well, would deliver important military advantages: the freeing of the Mediterranean which, in turn, would open up the possibility of other fronts. 'If we can end the year in possession of North Africa,' said Churchill, 'we can threaten the belly of Hitler's Europe, and this operation should be considered in conjunction with the 1943 operation.'

To illustrate the point, he drew a picture of a crocodile, noting that it was their intention to attack its soft belly (the Mediterranean) at the same time as its snout (northern France) in 1943. Visibly cheered by the news, Stalin said (perhaps surprisingly): 'May God prosper this undertaking.'

The Soviet ruler immediately grasped the strategic advantages of Torch, and rattled off four reasons to the stunned Churchill: it would threaten the rear of Rommel's Italo-German Panzer army; overawe Spain and prevent it from joining the Axis; produce fighting between Germans and Frenchmen; and expose Italy to the full brunt of the war.

'Very few people alive,' noted Churchill, 'could have comprehended in so few minutes the reasons which we had all so long been wrestling with for months. He saw it all in a flash.' For good measure, Churchill added a fifth reason: the shortening of the sea route through the Mediterranean.

After three hours and forty minutes, the meeting broke up. 'He knows the worst,' Churchill signalled his deputy prime minister in London, 'and we parted in an atmosphere of goodwill.'[32]

3

Ike

UK, July–November 1942

LATE ON 25 JULY 1942, Lieutenant General Dwight D. 'Ike' Eisenhower was shown into General Marshall's suite at Claridge's Hotel in central London. There was no sign of the US Army Chief of Staff until a familiar voice hollered through the closed washroom door: 'Ike? Is that you?'

'Yes, General.'

'You're to be the Allied Commander-in-Chief of the Torch expedition. Admiral King and I both feel you're the best man for the job. The British agree. The decision has been made, but it won't be announced for a few days yet. Congratulations.'[1]

While personally gratified at the faith shown in him by Marshall and King, Eisenhower had mixed emotions. Like his chief, he preferred Sledgehammer to Torch, and felt that any 1942 operation in the Mediterranean would almost certainly 'eliminate the possibility of a major cross-Channel venture in 1943'. He also knew that an invasion of North Africa meant a 'complete reversal' in the Allies' thinking and a 'drastic revision' of their planning and preparation. He wrote later:

Where we had been counting on many months of orderly build-up, we now had only weeks. Instead of a massed attack across narrow waters, the proposed expedition would require movement across open ocean areas where enemy submarines would constitute a real menace. Our target was no longer a restricted front where we knew accurately terrain, facilities, and people as they affected military operations, but the rim of a continent where no major military campaign had been conducted for centuries. We were not to have the air power we had planned to use against Europe and what we did have would be largely concentrated at a single, highly vulnerable base – Gibraltar.[2]

It was a daunting task for Eisenhower who, at fifty, was the second youngest lieutenant general in the US Army. Only two years earlier, he had been a lieutenant colonel in command of the 1/15th Infantry. But his organisational ability and limitless capacity for work – he would go to bed late, rise early and work seven days a week, smoking incessantly – had brought him to the attention of Marshall who appointed him, five days after Pearl Harbor, as the head of the Philippines and Far Eastern Section of the War Plans Division. Two jumps of rank later, Eisenhower was to command the first Anglo-American operation of the war.

Descended from German immigrants who had settled in Pennsylvania in 1732, Eisenhower ('iron miner' in German) was born in Texas but moved with his family to Abilene, Kansas, when he was two. There his parents David and Ida eked out a modest living and invested all their hopes in their six sons' careers. Both parents were religious fundamentalists – originally Mennonites, though Ida became a Jehovah's Witness – who stressed the simple virtues of 'honesty, self-reliance, integrity, fear of God'.

Entering West Point, the United States Military Academy, in 1911, Eisenhower became a star half-back on the football team until a bad knee injury kept him on the sidelines. He only graduated halfway up the class of 1915 – known as the 'class the stars fell on' because fifty-nine graduands became general officers – but once a commissioned officer, he went from strength to strength. He commanded the US Army's first tank school and, in 1925, passed out first of the Command

and General Staff School at Fort Leavenworth, and served as chief of staff to General Douglas MacArthur in the Philippines in the late 1930s.[3]

A broad-shouldered six-footer, Eisenhower could dominate any gathering by sheer force of personality. Almost bald in 1942, he was still an exceedingly attractive man with his prominent forehead, broad, expressive face and toothy grin. His vivacious Irish-born driver Kay Summersby, a 33-year-old former couture model who had joined the Mechanised Transport Corps★ in September 1939, wrote of him: 'Brilliant blue eyes. Sandy hair – but not very much of it. A fair, ruddy complexion. A nice face – not conventionally handsome, but strong and, I thought, very American. Certainly very appealing. And I succumbed immediately to that grin that was to become so famous.'

Eisenhower had been married to his wife Mamie since 1916. The first of their two sons had died in early childhood of scarlet fever; the second was at West Point. Missing family life, Eisenhower took solace in his increasingly close relationship with Summersby who, at Ike's insistence, would accompany him to North Africa.[4]

'He had,' noted his biographer, 'a sharp, orderly mind. No one ever thought to describe him as an intellectual giant and outside of his professional field he was not well read. He was not liable to come up with brilliant insights. But he had the ability to look at a situation or a problem and analyse it, see what alternatives were available, and choose from among them.'

He was also excellent at handling people – with 'firm ideas on justice and fair play' – a vital attribute for an Allied commander.[5] 'He is noted for his informality, lack of austerity and pleasant manner', read a briefing note for the press in 1942. 'He is a leader rather than a driver of men.'[6] How he would cope with the pressure of commanding armies in the field for the first time, however, only time would tell.

Eisenhower's first task, on being given command of Torch, was to

---

★ A British women's civilian organisation, founded in 1939 by Mrs G. M. Cooke, OBE, that provided drivers for government departments and other agencies.

select the right people for what would become Allied Force Headquarters. As his deputy he chose 46-year-old Major General Mark W. 'Wayne' Clark, a brilliant planner and trainer of troops he had befriended at West Point. Tall and loose-limbed, with a long beaky nose, thick lower lip and prominent Adam's apple, Clark was 'extremely professional, with a faculty for picking fine assistants and for developing a high morale with his staff'.[7]

In one of his regular letters to General Marshall, Eisenhower admitted on 17 August that some officers of 'splendid reputation' had failed to live up to his idea of military efficiency. Clark was not among them. 'I know of no one,' he wrote, 'upon whom you can depend with greater confidence and assurance.'[8]

Colonel Paul M. Robinett, commanding the US 13th Armored Regiment, was a former War College classmate of Clark's, and thought him a 'man of great ability, drive, and initiative, but exorbitant ambition'.[9] Clark's fellow general George S. Patton Jr agreed with the last point. 'He seems to me,' noted Patton in his diary, 'more preoccupied with bettering his own future than in winning the war.'[10]

As his chief of staff, Eisenhower procured the services of the highly regarded Brigadier General Walter 'Beetle' Bedell Smith from the secretariat of the Combined Chiefs of Staff in Washington. Below Bedell Smith, Eisenhower tried to include a mixture of British and American officers. His deputy chiefs of staff were, for example, Brigadier General Alfred M. Gruenther and Brigadier John Whiteley of the US and British Armies respectively. In the early days, still unused to each other's methods, the two nationalities were 'apt to conduct their business in the attitude of a bulldog meeting a tomcat'. But as time went on, noted Eisenhower, they developed into 'a team that in its . . . absence of friction could not have been excelled if all its members had come from the same nation'.[11] When disagreements did break out, Eisenhower was quick to nip them in the bud. A drunk American officer who called his British colleague a 'son of a bitch' was sent back to the States; not for using the profanity, but for prefacing it with the word 'British'.[12]

Eisenhower was particularly impressed by Major General Humfrey Gale, his British Chief Administrative Officer, who was, he thought, 'the best man in this line in all of England'. His American supply equivalent was Colonel Everett Hughes, soon to be promoted to brigadier general. 'I have no fears,' Eisenhower told Marshall, 'that these two, with their assistants, will do a grand job. Incidentally, their job is an enormous one, even though theoretically each national force is responsible for its own logistics.'[13]

Eisenhower's initial directive from the Combined Chiefs of Staff on 13 August was to gain, in conjunction with Allied Forces in the Middle East, complete control of North Africa from the Atlantic to the Red Sea. The first stage would be to establish firm, mutually supported lodgements on the north coast, and in the Casablanca area on the northwest coast, in order to have readily available bases for continued and intensified air, ground and sea operations. A second stage was to extend control over the entire area of French Morocco, Algeria and Tunisia, and, in the event of hostile action by Franco's Spain, over Spanish Morocco also. The ultimate objective would be the 'complete annihilation of Axis forces now opposing the British forces in the Western Desert and intensification of air and sea operations against the Axis on the European Continent'.

The total area that Eisenhower had to subdue – comprising the three colonies of French North Africa – was enormous: more than a million square miles, stretching 1,274 miles from Casablanca on the Atlantic coast to Tunis in the Mediterranean. As it was mostly mountain and desert, the bulk of the 16.7 million total population – all but 1.5 million of whom were either Berber or Arab Muslims, the rest French settlers or African Jews – was concentrated in a small part of the total area, mostly at the ports. In Algeria, where there had been a French colonial presence since 1830, there were two systems of government: the northern coastal strip was fully integrated into the pre-war Third French Republic and sent representatives to the legislative assembly in Paris, while the southern provinces were directly ruled by a governor general and a French military administration. The other two colonies, by contrast, were nominally led by local rulers, the Sultan of Morocco and the Bey of Tunis. But real power lay with respective French Residents General who controlled foreign relations and supervised the civil administration. In 1942, they were both military officers: Général d'armée Auguste Paul Noguès in Morocco and Vice Amiral Jean-Pierre Esteva in Tunis. The governor general of Algeria was a civilian, Yves Chatel, but his cabinet was headed by Vice Amiral Raymond Fenard. Completing the military power structure was Général de corps d'armée Alphonse Pierre Juin, the Commander-in-Chief of all French army forces in North Africa: 55,000 in Morocco, 50,000 in Algeria and 15,000 in Tunisia.[14]

Eisenhower's planners had to decide on the location and strength of the various landings, and – crucially – how to provide adequate air cover for the convoys, particularly in the western Mediterranean where they could be attacked by Axis bombers based in Sicily and Italy. This cover, given the rarity of aircraft carriers at this stage of the war, could only be provided by land-based aircraft at Gibraltar; which in turn limited the distance to which surface ships could safely proceed into the Mediterranean.

Eisenhower and his staff knew that a direct landing in the northeast of Tunisia – where lay the two great ports of Tunis, the capital, and Bizerte, just forty miles to the north – might yield 'great results', notably the capture of that country before Axis troops could land by air or sea. But as it was too far outside the range of fighters operating from Gibraltar, and the British experience of running convoys to Malta, a little further to the east, had been, up to this point, 'only little short of disastrous', this particular project was quickly rejected as being 'beyond the bounds of justifiable risk'.

Eventually four more westerly port areas were selected as potential targets: Casablanca on the Atlantic coast of Morocco; and (from west to east) Oran, Algiers and Bône on the Mediterranean coast of Algeria. There was never any doubt that Oran and Algiers would be attacked.

Both were substantial ports, and the airfields near Oran would be essential for later operations, while Algiers was the centre of political, economic and military activity in the area. But there was only enough shipping to target either Casablanca or Bône. Both had advantages: possession of Casablanca would help to overawe Spain and the warlike Moroccan tribes; while Bône was only a short hop of a hundred miles or so from Bizerte and Tunis.

Eisenhower's preference, as it happens, was to take the 'entire force inside the Mediterranean': partly because it was better protected from tricky sea conditions on the Atlantic coast; but chiefly because 'Tunis was so great a prize' that it justified a landing as far east as possible at Bône. Unfortunately, the American Joint Chiefs of Staff disagreed. They felt that relying entirely on the Straits of Gibraltar as a line of communication was too great a risk, and that the rickety railway that ran from Casablanca to Tunis, via the Atlas mountains, would provide a vital lifeline for Eisenhower's forces if Hitler struck a deal with Franco to move his troops into Spain. They also questioned the ability of the land-based Allied fighters at Gibraltar to provide adequate air cover for a landing at Bône, which was easily within range of Axis airbases in Sicily and Italy.

When the British Chiefs of Staff agreed with their American counterparts – Brooke noting in his diary that Casablanca was a 'much wiser' choice than Bône – Eisenhower and his staff were overruled. It was, Ike remembered, the only time during the war that one of his staff's 'proposed operational plans was changed by intervention of higher authority'. The decision was 'cheerfully accepted' because 'the governing considerations were political more than tactical, and political estimates are the function of governments, not of soldiers'. Yet he was bound to inform his superiors that, as a result, the early capture of Tunis had been 'removed from the realm of the probable to the remotely possible'.[15]

French sensibilities – notably an enduring hatred of the British for, in 1940, unilaterally withdrawing from Dunkirk and then sinking French ships and killing French sailors, not to mention the ongoing struggle between pro-Vichy and pro-Allied elements – were at the forefront of the decision to make the expedition as 'exclusively American' as possible. This would, both governments believed, reduce the bad feeling that the presence of British troops on French soil would cause; but they also felt that the expedition needed to be large enough to persuade the 'French forces, officials, and population of northwest Africa' not to oppose the landings, but instead to join the fight against Germany. To that end, Allied troops were not to act as if they were 'conquering a hostile territory' unless the French put up serious resistance.[16] Moreover, all soldiers, including the British, were to wear the Stars and Stripes on a 5-inch armband.[17]

To provide an 'entirely American façade' to the attacking force was easy enough at Casablanca and Oran. The Western Task Force – made up of elements of the US 2nd Armored and 3rd and 9th Infantry Divisions – would head directly for Casablanca from the United States. Its 56-year-old commander was Major General George S. Patton Jr, a hard-charging tank expert who was desperate to prove himself in battle. 'The more I dig into this thing,' he told his former divisional commander, Major General Charles L. Scott, 'the more I am sure that the only thing that will win it will be leadership, speed and drive, plus sound tactics . . . Spiritually, I have complete confidence, in fact certainty that we shall succeed, although when one studies it logically it looks almost impossible. However, wars are only won by risking the impossible.'[18]

Eisenhower regarded Patton as a 'shrewd battle leader who invariably gained the devotion of his subordinates'. Even after Patton had used intemperate language to rile Torch naval commander Rear Admiral H. Kent Hewitt, putting in jeopardy Patton's participation in the invasion, Eisenhower asked Marshall to pour oil on troubled waters. It worked and Patton kept his job.[19]

The Central Task Force to attack Oran was also all-American, but made up of troops from the US II Corps that were already stationed in the UK: the 1st Infantry Division (or 'Big Red One', the symbol on its shoulder patch), part of the 1st Armored Division and the 1st Ranger Battalion. The II Corps had been commanded by Mark Clark since June, but his new role as Deputy Commander-in-Chief, Allied Force, meant he could not also direct a task force. Out of a list of possible replacements, Eisenhower chose Major General Lloyd R. Fredendall, the previous commander of II Corps who had been replaced by Clark. 'I am glad he has a job,' Patton noted in his diary, 'as he has been badly used.'[20] Though Ike hardly knew Fredendall, he was aware that his reputation as a 'fine trainer and organiser was unexcelled'.[21]

Since a lack of shipping did not allow more troops to be brought directly from the United States, the only American forces that could be committed to the Eastern Task Force's assault on Algiers were elements of the US 34th 'Red Bull' Infantry Division, a National Guard formation then stationed in Northern Ireland, and a regiment of the regular US 9th Infantry Division. 'British supporting units,' wrote Eisenhower, 'were so distributed in the landing tables that in only a few instances were they in actual assault waves.' To preserve the American character of the Algiers attack, command was given to Major General Charles W. Ryder of the 34th, a man of 'sterling character and great gallantry in combat' who, during the First World War, had won battlefield promotions to the rank of lieutenant colonel. Once the Eastern Task Force was firmly established, however, command would pass to Lieutenant General Kenneth Anderson whose British First Army had the task of moving eastwards as quickly as possible to secure Tunis. Anderson was, noted Eisenhower, 'a gallant Scot, devoted to duty and absolutely selfless. Honest and straightforward, he was blunt, at times to the point of rudeness, and this trait, curiously enough, seemed to bring him into conflict with his British confreres more than it did with the Americans. His real difficulty was probably shyness. He was not a popular type but I had real respect for his fighting heart.'[22]

In the unlikely event that Anderson was ordered 'to undertake an attack that would unduly imperil his troops', the British War Office wanted the First Army commander to have the same right of appeal to his own government that Sir Douglas Haig had enjoyed in the First World War. But Ike refused, arguing that it would violate 'the unity of command inherent' in the assignment of an overall Allied commander, and 'that no time should be lost during a battle by waiting for approval or disapproval of his orders by either the War Office or the War Department'. Instead, Anderson would first come to him with his concerns, and only if 'still dissatisfied' could he appeal to the War Office.[23]

The invasion was scheduled for 8 November.

Determined to leave no stone unturned, Eisenhower worked up to sixteen hours a day, seven days a week, to prepare for Torch. His duties included twice-weekly meetings with Winston Churchill 'for war-gaming sessions'. These tended to be lunch on Tuesdays at 10 Downing Street, a meal often attended by one or more members of the British Chiefs of Staff and the War Cabinet; and dinner on Fridays at Chequers, the beautiful if draughty Elizabethan manor house in Buckinghamshire, forty miles from London, that served as the prime minister's weekend retreat. Eisenhower hated going there because it lacked central heating and, even in summer, was so chilly he called it a 'damned icebox' and always wore two pairs of underwear. Other American guests felt the same. During one visit, Harry Hopkins, Roosevelt's special envoy, was found in the downstairs lavatory 'wearing his overcoat, gloves, muffler and hat, perched on the toilet reading the newspaper'.[24]

After one meeting, Eisenhower introduced Churchill to his driver Kay Summersby. 'Churchill looked just like all the photographs and cartoons,' she remembered, 'that same baby bulldog face, with eyes as blue as Eisenhower's. He wore his famous siren suit . . . The best way I can describe it is to say it was very similar to a baby's one-piece sleeping suit. He liked it because he could thrust his stubby legs into it, pull it up, push his arms into the sleeves – and zip, he was dressed.'

Churchill was absolutely charming, telling Summersby that he had heard what a good driver she was, and adding: 'Now I want you to take good care of your general. We need him.'

To give Ike a break from the incessant workload, his naval aide and good friend Lieutenant Commander Harry 'Butch' Butcher found him a hideaway called Telegraph Cottage, an 'adorable Tudor doll-house' set in 10 acres of woods and gardens near Kingston upon Thames, and just thirty minutes by car from central London. Eisenhower moved in with his immediate staff: Butcher, his army aide Colonel Ernest 'Tex' Lee, and his orderly, Sergeant Michael 'Mickey' McKeogh, who was so devoted to Ike that he would even help him on with his underpants. 'It was a very simple little house,' wrote Summersby, 'but it could not have been cozier or happier. From the first time we drove out there, the General felt at home and so did the rest of us.'

Ike spent up to four nights a week at Telegraph Cottage, and would relax by playing bridge for money, badminton, and holes of golf on the neighbouring course. He also sketched and shot tin cans with a handgun. Even Summersby was given a small Beretta pistol to fire. 'I'd prefer to see you dead,' he told her, 'than a prisoner of the Germans.'[25]

Eisenhower made a point of visiting as many UK-based units involved in Torch as he could. One of his last trips was to western Scotland to observe men from the US 1st Infantry Division assaulting a beach from landing craft. He travelled in his private railway carriage, 'Bayonet', with its little teak-panelled sitting room, private office and sleeping quarters. From the terminus he was driven by Summersby close to the site of the training exercise, and tramped the final stretch 'across fields, down cart tracks and onto the rugged beaches to talk to the men and the officers'. He wanted to 'show himself and demonstrate his concern for American soldiers', but also to assess their performance.

The exercise was not a success, with Eisenhower and his staff 'far from encouraged by the evident lack of skill, particularly among ship companies and boat crews'. Or as he put it to Butcher: 'They'll be sitting ducks if they don't sharpen up.'

As the date of his departure for Gibraltar drew nearer, the pressures started getting to Ike who became increasingly 'impatient, tired and nervous, his temper at the ready'. He was 'drinking more coffee, smoking more cigarettes and getting less sleep than ever'. He could not stay still, and would drum his fingers nervously on the table.

During a sombre final dinner at Telegraph Cottage, he and his staff raised a glass to the success of Torch, but no one felt like talking. It was almost a relief when, at 8.20 a.m. on Thursday, 5 November 1942, they took off in rain, fog and practically zero visibility from Hurn Airfield near Bournemouth in a flight of five Boeing B-17 Flying Fortresses, bound for Gibraltar.

Major Paul Tibbets,⋆ the pilot of Ike's plane 'Red Gremlin', had been wary of the weather, but Ike insisted they '*had* to go'. They flew at an average height of 100 feet, just above the waves, and 'reached Gibraltar at 4.20 [p.m.], circled for an hour, then landed'.[26]

⋆ Tibbets would go on to pilot *Enola Gay*, the B-29 Superfortress that dropped the first atomic bomb on Hiroshima on 6 August 1945.

4

'Welcome to North Africa'

Algeria and Gibraltar, October–November 1942

A FORTNIGHT EARLIER – IN THE EARLY hours of 22 October –
Major General Mark Clark and four key members of his
planning staff had been delivered to a lonely stretch of the Algerian
shore by submarine and folbots, two-man wood and canvas folding
canoes crewed by members of the British Special Boat Section (SBS).
Their mission: a secret meeting with Général de division Charles-
Emmanuel Mast, commanding the Algiers garrison, to discuss the
plans for Operation Torch.

No sooner had they reached the beach than a tall and stooped
figure, informally clad in turtleneck sweater and baseball cap,
appeared out of the shadows. Clark recognised him as Bob Murphy,
the senior American diplomat in Algiers. 'Welcome to North Africa,'
said Murphy.

'I'm damn glad we made it,' replied Clark, puffing with exertion.[1]

The risky covert mission had been Murphy's idea. On a trip to
Eisenhower's headquarters earlier that month, he had listed the French
officers with pro-Allied sympathies who were ready to offer active
assistance. They included Générals de division Mast and Béthouart, the
latter commanding the Casablanca garrison. But there were others who
would encourage their men to resist the Allies, said Murphy, particularly in French Morocco where the pro-German Général d'armée

Auguste Charles Noguès, Resident General since 1936, had happily implemented Vichy's antisemitic decrees against the will of Sultan Mohammed V. It was Murphy's job to prevent French opposition to the landings if he could.[2]

On 17 October, now back in Algiers, he had sent a cable to Washington DC suggesting an 'unbelievable plan' that would give the whole Torch operation a 'much better chance of quick success if it could be pulled off'. Murphy had spoken to Mast, who was prepared to meet senior American officers to discuss 'cooperation instead of resistance' from the Algiers garrison when the Allies invaded.

When Ike was told about the mission, he had 'wanted desperately' to be involved. But he also realised that, as the Allied Commander-in-Chief, he could not risk being interned. His deputy Mark Clark, on the other hand, was 'thoroughly familiar' with the planning for Torch and had the appropriate rank. When told he would be going, Clark was 'as happy as a boy with a new knife'. He knew all too well what was at stake. A bloodless occupation of French North Africa – or at least the Algerian part of it – was a very real possibility. But if it failed – and Clark was captured by the French with full knowledge of every aspect of Operation Torch (a position as sensitive as being 'Bigoted', or having Top Secret knowledge of Operation Overlord, the D-Day landings in 1944) – well, that did not bear thinking about.[3]

With Murphy leading the way, Clark's party carried their folbots up a steep, stony path to a white stone villa with a red-tiled roof. They were ushered inside by the owner, a 'dishevelled and rather frightened-looking Frenchman' called Henri Teissier who was risking his life by hosting the meeting. He told Clark that General Mast and his staff were coming by car from Algiers and would not arrive for a couple of hours. Clark had a nap in an upstairs room while the SBS officers stowed their folbots and hid in a separate room. The presence of British soldiers, Clark knew, would not go down well with the French.

Clark was woken at 5 a.m. and told that Mast had arrived. 'Welcome to my country,' said the French general, who otherwise spoke little English.

Mast, Clark and Murphy discussed strategy over an impromptu breakfast of coffee, bread, jam and sardines. Careful not to admit that Torch was under way – with some ships from the United States already at sea – Clark sounded out Mast as to the possible French response to the Allied landings. 'I was very impressed with Mast's sincerity,' Clark wrote. 'He certainly convinced me that he was entirely at our disposal and would do everything possible to help us carry out an operation that to him was only a hope.'

Once they had been joined by their respective staffs, Mast asked how many Allied soldiers might be involved. 'At least half a million,' said Clark, struggling to look sincere, 'as well as 2,000 planes and many US ships.'

This was a gross exaggeration: only 112,000 American and British troops would participate in Torch. But if his intention was to impress Mast, it had the desired effect. The French general suggested that an American submarine be sent to the coast of Vichy France to pick up Général d'armée Henri Giraud, a legend in the French army who had the unique distinction of having escaped from German captivity in both world wars. Fiercely anti-Nazi, Giraud would help to prevent bloodshed between the French and the Allies in North Africa, said Mast, if he were appointed Supreme Commander of Allied troops. Clark's response was non-committal: 'I will do what I can.'

After a hasty lunch of chicken in a hot Arab sauce, washed down with red wine, Mast returned to his duties in Algiers, leaving his staff officers to supply the Americans with vital information as to the 'positions and strengths of troops and naval units', the location of supplies like petrol and ammunition, and the places where resistance would be stiffest, particularly Oran and Casablanca where pro-Vichy sentiment was most pronounced.

In mid-afternoon, the phone rang. Teissier answered, and quickly announced to the room that police were on their way. Cue a major panic as French officers fled in every direction until only Teissier, Murphy and his assistant were left. Ushering the American officers and the SBS men into a wine cellar, Teissier and the others pretended to be drunk when the police arrived. 'They clanked bottles about,' wrote Clark, 'sang a little and were very jovial indeed.'

Having identified himself as the American Consul in Algiers, Murphy told the police a party was in progress and there were women in the room upstairs. He urged the police not to embarrass him. They said they were bound to search the house, as the owner's Arab servants had reported suspicious footprints on the beach.

Listening from the cellar, Clark knelt at the foot of the stairs with a carbine in his hands, fully intending to shoot his way out if the police opened the trap door. Unfamiliar with the carbine's mechanism, however, he kept muttering, 'How does this thing work?' Not long after, the trap door swung open and the eight men inside cocked their weapons. Fortunately, it was Murphy with news that the police had left but would soon be back. They needed to leave.

Retrieving the folbots, they headed for the beach where the surf was 'curling thunderously' onto the beach. It looked too rough to paddle through, but they were determined to try. After the senior SBS officer had called in the submarine HMS *Seraph* by walkie-talkie, one of his subordinates and Clark made the first attempt to reach it, with the American general stripping down to his shorts and shirt to reduce the drag in case he capsized. 'We floated the boat, waist deep,' recalled the SBS man, 'waited for the lull with the undertow tearing at our legs, and at a favourable moment made a dash for it; but just as we were almost clear an extra large wave crashed down on top of us, she rolled over, and in an instant we were struggling to free ourselves in a boiling turmoil of foam.'

The others rushed to help, pulling free both occupants and saving the paddles. But they were unable to rescue Clark's rolled-up trousers, inside which he had placed his money belt – containing several hundred dollars in gold – in case the weight caused him to drown. The money was never recovered.

After returning to the house for clothes and food, Clark made a second attempt with a different paddler. Their task was made easier when the SBS commander, remembering the technique used by inhabitants of the Gold Coast, instructed the others to carry the loaded boat through the first line of surf. It worked. Paddling furiously, they surmounted a series of waves 'by the skin of their teeth'. The others did the same and, after paddling for what seemed like hours, they finally reached the submarine. As the last SBS man climbed the conning tower, he looked towards the shore and saw headlights approaching the house. The police were back in force and they had got away just in time. Soaked and exhausted, they celebrated with a glass of whisky, while the submarine's crew were given, on Clark's authorisation, a double ration of rum.

A day later, 24 October, the *Seraph* surfaced in daylight to allow Clark and his party to be transferred by folbot to a Catalina flying boat. As the lumbering Catalina rose into the sky and turned towards Gibraltar, the SBS officers felt relieved that a 'considerable responsibility had been discharged, in spite of some extremely anxious moments'.

The Americans flew back to Gibraltar in the Catalina and, after a brief stop for a hot bath and a decent meal, they continued on to England in the B-17s. On arrival, Clark went straight to Ike's country retreat, Telegraph Cottage, where he gave a full account of the mission. Ike was delighted and phoned Churchill to tell him that Clark was back. They were both asked for supper at 10 Downing Street, but Clark was 'too tired to accept'.

A couple of days later, Clark was invited to Buckingham Palace to meet George VI. 'I know about all you,' said the King. 'You're the one who took that fabulous trip. Didn't you, by the way, get stranded on the beach without your trousers?'[4]

The dénouement of Clark's daring mission to Algeria – codenamed Operation Flagpole – was a four-hour interview that Ike Eisenhower later described as one of the 'most distressing' of the war. It took place on 7 November – just hours before the invasion of North Africa was due to begin – in the tiny office, just eight feet square, that Ike shared with Mark Clark at the end of the cold and damp 500-yard-long tunnel beneath the Rock of Gibraltar. The subject of the interview was 63-year-old Général d'armée Henri Giraud who, at Mast's suggestion, had just been picked up from the coast of Vichy France by the same British submarine, HMS *Seraph* (albeit this time skippered by an American), that had conducted Clark's mission.

Exceptionally tall and erect, 'almost stiff in carriage, and abrupt in speech and mannerisms', Giraud cut a 'gallant if bedraggled figure' in his rumpled civilian garb. With hollow cheeks, a dark growth of beard and a drooping handlebar moustache, he hardly seemed the figure of destiny who could unite Frenchmen against the Axis.

Ike opened proceedings by welcoming Giraud and explaining – via his French translator – that Operation Torch was about to begin. To that end, the Allies had prepared a message to the French people in North Africa, in Giraud's name, 'stating in rather vague terms that the United States, anticipating the plans of the Axis to seize North Africa, was intervening, and calling upon all officers and soldiers of the Army of Africa to do their duty'. The message ended: 'I resume my place of combat among you.'

The old general stiffened. 'As I understand it,' he replied, 'when I land in North Africa I am to assume command of all Allied forces and become the Supreme Allied Commander.'

Ike frowned. 'There must be,' he said cautiously, 'some misunderstanding. I will be Supreme Commander. I want you to proceed to Africa, as soon as we can guarantee your safety, and there take over command of those French that will voluntarily rally to you.'

Giraud, however, was adamant. He believed that his own and his country's honour was at stake, and that he could not accept anything less than supreme command. Ike knew, of course, that Giraud's request was impossible. No subordinate general in the expedition could legally accept an order from Giraud, and, moreover, there was not a single

Frenchman in the Allied force. All this was 'laboriously explained' to the French general who was 'shaken, disappointed, and after many hours of conference felt it necessary to decline to have any part in the scheme'.

With Giraud digging in his toes, Ike let his deputy have a go. 'We would like the honourable general to know,' said Clark, an edge to his voice, 'that the time of his usefulness to the Americans and for the restoration of the glory that was once France is *now*.'

'But what would the French people think of me?' the old general asked. 'What about the prestige of Giraud. What about my family?'

Clark said it was wrong of Giraud to let his personal ambitions 'stand in the way of the best interests of France', but this had little effect. Exasperated, he said to the translator: 'Tell him this: "If you don't go along, General, you're going to be out in the snow on the seat of your pants."'

Ike's political advisors were so worried that they suggested placing Giraud in nominal command while Eisenhower reserved for himself 'the actual power of directing operations'.

The association of the Giraud name with the Allied cause might well, they felt, mean the 'difference between success and disaster'. But Ike did not agree, and the arguments continued, back and forth, until the early hours of 8 November when the French general went to bed. 'Giraud,' he insisted, as a parting shot, 'will be a spectator in this affair.'[5]

5

'Suicidal and absolutely unsound'

Gibraltar and Algeria, 7–8 November 1942

A T 5.20 P.M. ON 7 November 1942, while Ike was still locked in negotiations with Giraud, a message was flashed to the 200 warships and 110 troop and cargo ships that made up the three task forces – one of the 'greatest fighting armadas of all time' – heading for Casablanca, Oran and Algiers: 'Warning Order. H-Hour confirmed November 8. For East and Centre 1 a.m. For West about 4.30 a.m.'

The weather and sea conditions, which had caused Eisenhower and his staff so much worry, were better than expected. 'Providence,' noted Harry Butcher in his diary, 'or one of Ike's lucky charms is effective. The high swells from the Atlantic, crashing against the shores on and around Casablanca, have been considerably nullified by ten-foot waves going southward from the area of the entrance to the Strait of Gib.'[1]

There was still plenty that could go wrong. 'Our troops,' wrote Eisenhower later, 'had only been hastily trained for this complicated type of landing operation and, for the most part, had never participated in battle. Available shipping did not permit us to carry along all the forces and equipment necessary to assure success. Of course we were tense.'[2]

A chief concern was that the convoys would be attacked by Axis bombers and submarines, particularly the two task forces – Centre and Eastern – that had already entered the Mediterranean. These fears were realised when a message reached Eisenhower's HQ on 7 November from Rear Admiral Sir Harold Burrough, the British naval commander of the Eastern Task Force, that the USS *Thomas Stone*, proceeding in convoy towards the beaches east of Algiers with a reinforced battalion of American troops (the US 2/39th Infantry), had been bombed by a German plane within 150 miles of its destination. The stricken ship was 'left with anti-aircraft and/or anti-submarine protection', noted Harry Butcher in his diary, 'but the convoy must go on if Torch is to succeed'.[3]

Details were lacking, and Eisenhower feared 'very considerable loss of life'. The incident had a happy outcome, however, when news arrived the following day that casualties were few and the ship not badly damaged, though its rudder and propeller had been wrecked. Instead of waiting quietly for the *Thomas Stone* to be towed to a convenient port, however, the 700 officers and men of the 2/39th Infantry had cheered the decision of their commander to take to twenty-four landing craft 'in an attempt to reach, on time, the assault beach to which they were assigned'. Foiled in their gallant purpose by adverse weather and mechanical breakdowns, they were rescued by the corvette *Spey*, and finally put ashore 'some twenty hours behind schedule'.

A total of 76 German planes were in the air, and 9 German and 26 Italian submarines were stationed in the supposed paths of advance, on 7 November. But, fortunately for the Allies, the ships bound for Algiers passed south of the westernmost group of submarines, and then swung towards the attack area to the east of another line of submarines, while the Oran convoy also stopped short of the submarines in the new positions to which they had moved. The only other successful Axis strike on the convoys was, therefore, an aerial bomb attack on the destroyer HMS *Panther* which was covering the Algiers landings. The explosion killed three sailors and injured ten, and forced the badly damaged warship to return to Gibraltar at low speed for repairs.[4]

At 1 a.m. on Sunday, 8 November 1942 – H-Hour for the landings at Algiers and Oran – two pre-recorded addresses were broadcast on the BBC World Service in French. The first, by President Roosevelt, proclaimed: 'We come among you solely to destroy your enemies, and not to harm you. Do not obstruct, I beg of you, this great purpose.' The second was purported to be Eisenhower. It was in fact the voice of his French-speaking head of Civil Affairs, Colonel Julius C. Holmes.

There was then an agonising wait at Gibraltar for the first news of the landings. It finally arrived at 2.38 a.m. in the form of a message from the Eastern Task Force at Algiers: 'Landing successful, A, B and C Beaches.' Forty-four minutes later, the Centre Task Force (Oran) 'reported landings at two beaches, identified as Y and Z, the latter unopposed'. At 3.32 a.m, there was news of a successful landing at the other Oran Beach, X. 'After that,' wrote Mark Clark, 'the messages came in rapidly, and most of them seemed good.'

There was a scare when three enemy planes were sighted over Gibraltar, prompting a clatter of anti-aircraft fire and the long tunnel under the Rock to fill with people. Fortunately, the planes were on reconnaissance and dropped no bombs.

Eisenhower and Clark were persuaded to get an hour's sleep on their cots, while Butcher dozed under the table. They woke to more good news. Rear Admiral Henry K. Hewitt, the Western Task Force naval commander, radioed that the attack was 'proceeding to schedule'. From Major General Fredendall, the Centre Task Force commander, came word that the Oran 'landing continues unopposed'. At 7.45 a.m., Major General Ryder, heading the Algiers assault force, reported that the vital Maison Blanche airfield had been captured.

'As anticipated,' wrote Eisenhower, 'the landings at Algiers met almost no opposition and the area was quickly occupied. This was largely due to the prior accomplishments of Mr Murphy, working through General Mast of the French Army, and to the sympathy, even if cloaked in official antagonism, of General Alphonse Pierre Juin.'

The optimistic messages continued for another hour or so. Then the tone changed as news trickled in of fierce French resistance, particularly in and around Oran.[5]

Founded in the tenth century by Moorish traders, the Algerian port of Oran had known many foreign rulers: Spaniards, Ottomans and, since 1831, the French. The bulk of its 200,000 residents were European and fiercely resentful of the British since the Royal Navy's ruthless destruction of the French fleet, which had refused to surrender, at the nearby base of Mers-el-Kébir in the summer of 1940. It was situated in the middle of three bays, subdivided by headlands, that lay between Cap Falcon on the west and Pointe de l'Aiguille on the east. Twenty miles farther east was the small secondary port of Arzew, nestled on the eastern side of a wide and hilly promontory.

Oran's bustling harbour – a narrow rectangle, a mile and a half long, lined with quays crammed with barrels of wine and crates of tangerines, and subdivided by four breakwaters – was closely defended by forts and shore batteries, totalling forty-five guns, that promised destruction to any ship that arrived with hostile intentions. Its garrison, the Oran Division, was 16,700 strong and stationed partly in barracks near the port and the main approaches to the city, and partly at inland stations within a day's march. At the western end of the harbour, and at the naval base of Mers-el-Kébir, several French warships were usually moored.

The plan for seizing Oran – as for the other French North African ports – was to land on beaches either side and to envelop from the flanks, using 37,000 American troops and 3,600 British (mostly sailors). There were, however, two other daring elements that made the Oran operation unique: the dropping of a battalion of US paratroopers on two nearby airfields to neutralise French air power; and a direct assault on the harbour itself by two former US coastguard cutters, HMS *Walney* and *Hartland*, each containing 200 men from the US 6th Armored Infantry and a detachment of SBS commandos, led by Captain Harry Holden-White, whose task was to capture or sink the Vichy French warships inside.[6]

The architect of the daring attack on the harbour – dubbed Operation Reservist – was Captain Frederick 'Fritz' Peters, a 53-year-old Canadian-born Royal Navy officer who had won a Distinguished Service Order (DSO)★ and Distinguished Service Cross (DSC) in the First World War. Thin-lipped, with high arching eyebrows and a penchant for small black cheroots, Peters was just the type of bold and determined – some might say foolhardy – leader required for such a dangerous mission. 'This,' he told a colleague, 'is the opportunity I have been waiting for.'

Others were not so convinced. 'If determined resistance is met from the French navy,' wrote Rear Admiral Andrew C. Bennett, the naval commander of the Oran task force, to Ike, 'which seems to be the general opinion, it is believed that this small force will be wiped out.' Against serious opposition, said Bennett, even 'five times the number of troops would be insufficient'. The plan was 'suicidal and absolutely unsound'.[7]

Peters thought otherwise, telling the key participants on the voyage from Scotland that they could expect opposition from the French navy, but not from the soldiers of the Oran Division. This information had come, of course, from General Mast. What Peters did not know, however, was that Mast's fellow conspirator in the Oran Division – its chief of staff, Colonel Paul Tostain – had decided at the last moment that a plot to arrest his boss, Général de division Robert Boissau, and seize key military installations was doomed to fail. The assault on Oran would, as a result, be opposed by *all* the French troops in the vicinity.[8]

As Peters's main objective was to prevent the port from being destroyed by the French, the role of the American soldiers was to occupy all tactical positions covering the docks, including the shore batteries. The naval boarding parties, meanwhile, would prevent merchant ships from being scuttled, while a demolition party, led by an SOE officer, took

---

★ After the VC, the DSO was the most prestigious gallantry award available to British and Commonwealth military officers.

care of any submarines that refused to surrender. They would hold the port, said Peters, until they were relieved by larger US forces converging from beaches to the east and west.

The two sloops left Gibraltar on 7 November and were approaching the east-facing entrance to Oran harbour in the early hours of the 8th when the shore battery at Cap Blanc opened fire on HMS *Walney*, the lead ship. Minutes later, *Walney*'s bows struck the double boom across the harbour entrance, breaking it 'without difficulty'. They were now inside the narrow harbour, subdivided by four moles, that extended along the coast for more than a mile. It was, in Harry Holden-White's estimation, 'a death-trap for a seaborne assault'.

Once opposite the first mole, du Ravin Blanc, Captain Peters ordered the launch of the folbots. The canoe containing Holden-White and his paddler, Corporal Derek Ellis, was the first to hit the water. 'Frankly,' wrote the SBS captain, 'I was so bloody glad to be away from it. Soon that feeling turned to guilt as [we] paddled off to find suitable targets for our mini-torpedoes. We had not travelled far when there was a huge explosion. We looked back. *Walney* had been hit by shore batteries and was already sinking.'[9]

A shell had struck the bridge, killing Peters's French interpreter, Lieutenant Paul Duncan. But it had not stopped the sloop which steamed on towards its objective at the far end of the harbour, the 200 American soldiers on its mess deck waiting anxiously for the order to disembark.[10]

Meanwhile, Holden-White and Ellis were paddling hard towards their primary target – a destroyer lying alongside the fourth mole, known as the Quai Centrale – at a brisk pace of 4 to 5 knots, and using the cover provided by a thin stretch of water between a block of barges and the northern arm of the harbour.[11] They could see *Walney*'s bridge and surrounding superstructure 'burning furiously' as more shells were fired at it from a French battery on the hill overlooking the eastern end of the harbour. Opposite *Walney*, alongside the northern jetty, an armed French trawler was also on fire.

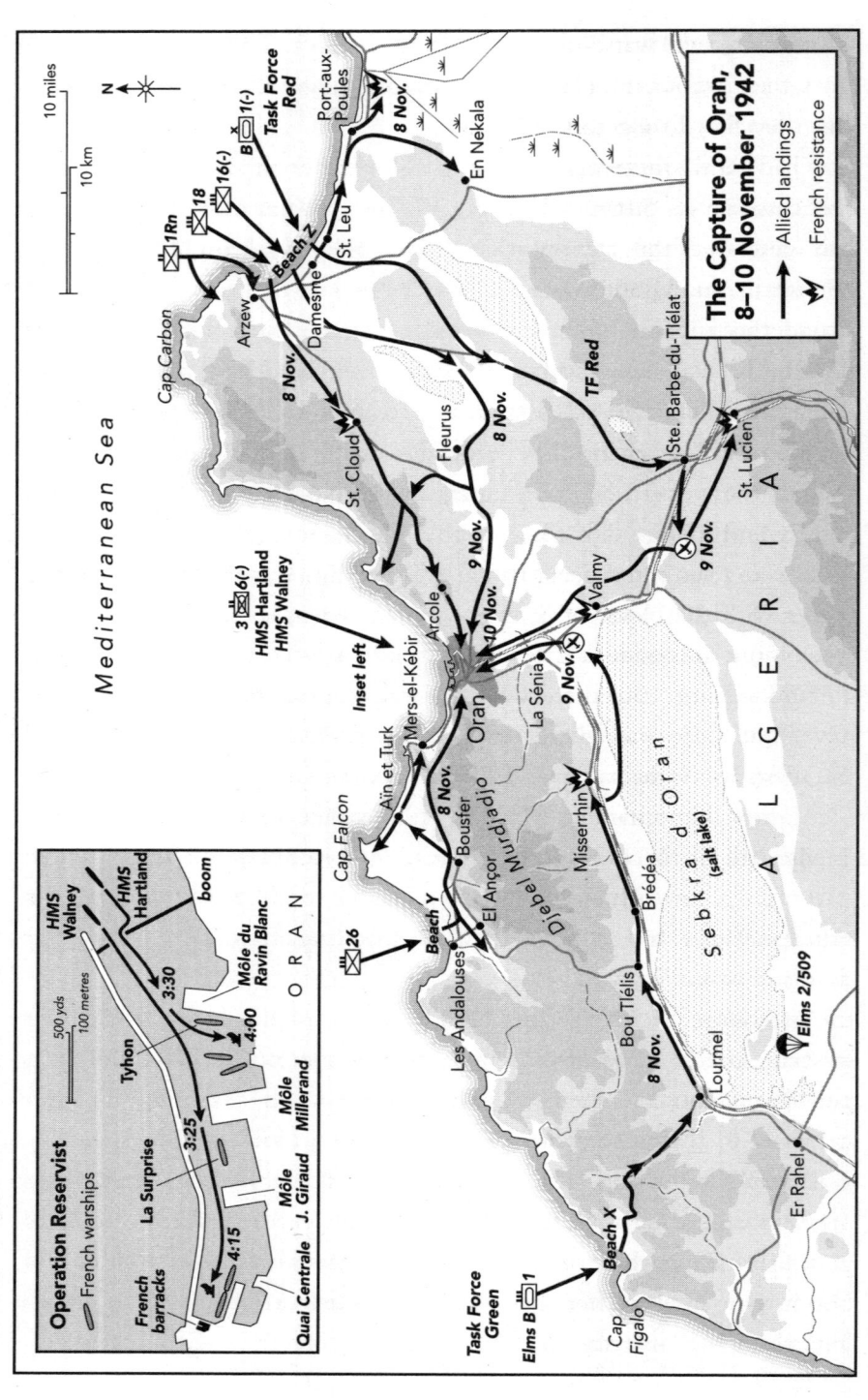

The Capture of Oran, 8–10 November 1942

→ Allied landings

⚡ French resistance

Mediterranean Sea

Operation Reservist

⬭ French warships

HMS Walney
HMS Hartland

boom

Môle du Ravin Blanc

3:30
Tyhon
4:00

La Surprise

3:25

French barracks
4:15

Môle J. Giraud
Môle Millerand

Quai Centrale

O R A N

500 yds
100 metres

N

Cap Carbon

Arzew

Beach Z

Damesme

St. Leu

Port-aux-Poules

En Nekala

8 Nov.

Task Force Red

B ☒ 1(-)

16(-) ☒

18 ☒

1Rn ☒

8 Nov.

St. Cloud

Fleurus

8 Nov.

TF Red

Ste. Barbe-du-Tlélat

St. Lucien

9 Nov.

9 Nov.

Arcole

Mers-el-Kébir

Inset left

3 ☒ 6(-)
HMS Hartland
HMS Walney

Aïn et Turk

Cap Falcon

Bousfer

8 Nov.

El Ançor

Djebel Murdjadjo

Oran

La Sénia

Valmy

9 Nov.

10 Nov.

Misserrhin

S e b k r a   d' O r a n
(salt lake)

Brédéa

Bou Tléllis

Lourmel

Elms 2/509

A L G E R I A

Beach Y

26 ☒

Les Andalouses

Task Force Green

Elms B ☒ 1

Beach X

Cap Figalo

8 Nov.

Er Rahel

10 miles

10 km

Spotting two warships – a submarine and a destroyer – trying to leave the harbour, Holden-White attacked them with mini-torpedoes. But they failed to detonate.[12] By now *Walney* was in its death throes. She had taken the worst of her punishment from deck guns on the French sloop *La Surprise*. The first salvo, at a distance of just 300 yards, had destroyed the armour plating on *Walney*'s bridge, killing the helmsman among others. Captain Peters, blinded in his left eye, shouted a rudder instruction, but no one was listening. As *Walney* drifted aimlessly past the French ship, another broadside raked its decks, peppering the defenceless infantrymen. Passing the third mole, a shell exploded in the engine room, depriving the ship of power. Momentum carried her on towards the western end of the harbour as guns on submarines, a shore battery and snipers all took their toll. 'Topside,' read one account, 'the dead were piled three-deep. Below, the deck resembled a charnel house, scarlet with the blood of butchered infantrymen.'

Coming alongside a moored destroyer, survivors on *Walney* flung a grappling iron. But there was no steam to drive the winch, and they never got close enough to board. They were cut down, instead, by the destroyer's deck guns. It was now that the *Walney*'s skipper, Lieutenant Commander Meyrick, and Lieutenant Colonel George F. Marshall of the US 3/6th Armored Infantry were killed.[13]

At 4.15 a.m., *Walney*'s magazine exploded, a shocking sight for Holden-White and Ellis. She then keeled over and sank, taking her dead and wounded with her. Peters was not among them. Shortly before the explosion, he had 'accomplished the berthing of his ship', helping to secure the fore and aft mooring lines with 'utter disregard of his own personal safety'. He then got on a raft with ten other survivors and managed to reach the shore, but soon after was taken prisoner.[14]

Walney's sister ship, *Hartland*, had not fared any better. Following *Walney* into the harbour, she was also pummelled by shell and machine-gun fire, taking three direct hits as she passed through the broken boom. One shell put her engines out of action, but momentum carried her on to her objective on the first mole. En route she was riddled by 'fire from the 5.1 [inch] guns of a destroyer on her port bow and received hits at a range of 30 yards'. By the time she reached the mole, noted an SBS officer on board, she was 'burning furiously' and 'out of control'. Efforts were made to secure her bow line, but the rope snapped and she swung out into the harbour with only her stern attached to the mole. 'In this position,' wrote Lunn, 'it was impossible for the assault troops to make a landing, but some were lowered away in two ships' boats from the starboard side.'[15]

The operation had been a disaster, and with horrific casualties. Of the 393 US infantrymen who took part, 189 were killed and 157 wounded. The rest were taken prisoner. The Royal Navy suffered a similar attrition rate with 113 dead and 86 wounded, while the US Navy suffered five fatalities and seven wounded. Only the SBS were relatively unscathed, with just one of their eleven men killed, though the rest were captured. Of the 600 or so Allied soldiers to take part, therefore, roughly half of them were killed, a death rate that far outstrips the one in six suffered by the British Army on the Somme in 1916, the gold standard for battlefield carnage.

These 300 corpses were eventually buried in communal trenches on the heights outside the town, with US engineers having to use jackhammers to break the rock-hard ground. Almost thirty bodies could not be identified, and the missing included Lieutenant Colonel Marshall, just thirty-one years old, who left behind a wife and two small children.

The Allies had also forfeited two ships, while French losses were a single armed merchantman – set on fire by *Walney* – and an estimated 165 men killed. The failure of Operation Reservist gave the French the opportunity they needed to put the harbour out of action. By the time they surrendered to advancing US troops on 10 November, they had sunk twenty-seven hulks and scuttled three floating dry docks, including the 25,000-ton Grand Dock which blocked the harbour entrance for two months.[16]

In revenge, the Allied navies sank or drove aground a number of French ships that escaped Oran, notably two destroyers and the sloop

La Surprise, the latter going down with its skipper and fifty men. To obscure the scale of the defeat, moreover, the Allied leaders resorted to a time-honoured tactic: post-facto justification, hyperbolic praise and the award of gallantry medals. An almost unprecedented thirty-eight were given for Reservist, including one Victoria Cross (for Peters), four DSOs, six DSCs, two MCs, thirteen Distinguished Service Medals (DSM) and one Military Medal (MM).★ Admiral Sir Andrew Cunningham, the Allied naval commander, insisted that the attempt to capture the harbour had been 'worthwhile', but foiled 'by the alertness of the French Navy'. He added: 'It is as well I think, to bear in mind that great achievements in war are seldom brought about without considerable risk to personnel, and that their failure is not in itself proof that the enterprise was faultily conceived or executed.'[17]

★ The DSM (or DCM for the army) and MM were British and Commonwealth gallantry awards for other ranks that were equivalent to the DSO and Military Cross respectively.

6

'I've captured *my* objective!'

Algeria, 8 November 1942

PRICKS OF DOUBT RAN through Lieutenant Colonel William O. Darby's mind as he saw lights flickering on the distant shore in the early hours of 8 November. He was standing on the bridge of HMS *Ulster Monarch*, a 3,700-ton passenger ferry that had been converted into an infantry landing ship, complete with six assault landing craft and room for 200 troops. The small Algerian port of Arzew, their target, was by Darby's reckoning some 30 miles off the starboard bow (and 20 miles east of their main objective, Oran). Did the lights signify that the French knew they were coming? he wondered. And would they fight to the finish, or give up after satisfying their honour with a token resistance?

Darby moved to the port side of the bridge and stared into the water. Close astern were the shady outlines of *Ulster Monarch*'s two sister ships, *Royal Scotsman* and *Royal Ulsterman*, carrying the rest of Darby's new and untested unit, the 1st Ranger Battalion. Suddenly, Darby stiffened with fright as he spotted two silver objects heading for the ships at terrifying speed. 'My God, torpedoes!' he cried, grabbing the master of the ship by the arm and pointing towards the streaks of foam. 'We've been discovered.'

They stared in numbed silence. It was too late to take evasive action. The streaks were just 25 yards from the ship and closing fast. Darby covered his face with his hands, to protect himself from the inevitable explosion. Then, with the objects just yards from the hull, two porpoises leapt out of the water in a fountain of spray. 'We mopped the perspiration from our foreheads,' wrote Darby, 'and laughed weakly at one another's fears.'

A handsome 31-year-old career officer with a 'high forehead, blue eyes, firm mouth and jaw, and a ready smile', Darby had grown up in small-town Arkansas. Hard-working, charming and persuasive, he had a can-do attitude that impressed his superiors. He also had an uncanny knack of being in the right place at the right time. In 1941, then a captain in the field artillery, he underwent amphibious training in Puerto Rico and North Carolina, and was about to be posted to Hawaii when Pearl Harbor was attacked. Darby was reassigned as aide to Major General Russell P. Hartle, commander of the 34th (Red Bull) Infantry Division. In late January 1942, Darby accompanied the division to Northern Ireland, the first American ground troops to arrive on British soil.[1]

Bored of staff work, and anxious to see action, Darby put in for a transfer. Before it could be arranged, another opportunity beckoned: the formation of a unit of American Commandos, based on the British coastal raiders who been raised at Churchill's suggestion two years earlier to provide 'specially trained troops of the hunter class'.[2] The new unit was the brainchild of Brigadier General Lucian K. Truscott Jr of the US Army who, in April 1942, had been attached to Vice Admiral Lord Louis Mountbatten's Combined Operations HQ in London, the organisation that controlled the Commandos. 'If you do find it necessary to organise such units,' Ike had told Truscott, 'I hope that you will find some other name than "commandos", for the glamour of that name will always remain – and properly so – British.'

On 1 June, at Truscott's prompting, the US War Department authorised the raising of a 'training and demonstration' unit to participate in actual raids under British control. It was to be composed of volunteers from elements of the US Army in Northern Ireland, notably the 34th Infantry and 1st Armored Divisions. Now commanding all US troops in Northern Ireland, Hartle told his chief of staff, Colonel Edmond Leavey: 'We need somebody good to put in charge – any ideas?'

'Why don't you give the job to Bill?' said Leavey, who knew that Darby hated being an aide.[3]

On 8 June the delighted Darby was appointed the new unit's commander.[4] Captain Henry Gardiner, a 36-year-old tank officer temporarily attached to Hartle's staff, grumbled in his diary:

> That is just the sort of job I was made for and I know I could do a better job than the man who is starting out to run it. However, the fighting they will do, while spectacular and the basis for many post war stories, will only be on the fringes. We in the outfits like the 1st Armored [Division] will really make the holes and roll up the flanks and cause whole armies to collapse while they will principally give officers of the day sleepless nights.[5]

Darby spent the next ten days interviewing officers and, with their help, 2,000 volunteers from the troops in Northern Ireland. They were looking for men in prime physical condition, but not necessarily tall. Ideally the recruits would have experience of judo, mountain climbing, small boats, scouting, demolition and mechanics. Above all they required men with good judgement, initiative and common sense. Those they hoped to weed out, wrote Darby, were 'the braggart and the volunteer looking for excitement but who, in return, expected to be a swash-buckling hero who could live as he pleased if only he exhibited courage and daring in battle'. Of the original 2,000 volunteers, 575 were selected and, of those, 107 were eventually returned to their units.

On 19 June, Darby's new command – the 1st Ranger Battalion – was activated. The name was inspired by Rogers' Rangers, the famous American unit of irregulars that Major Robert Rogers had led against the French and their Native American allies in the Seven Years' War of the mid-eighteenth century. According to Darby, 'Rangers' was first suggested as a name by General Marshall, the US Army Chief of Staff, after he had visited the British Commando Training Depot on his visit to the UK in April 1942. 'Rogers' Rangers had been famous for hit-and-run raids into enemy country,' wrote Darby. 'This, in General Marshall's eyes, was to be one of the main tasks of the new Rangers, thus giving the men experience for the greater battles to come.'[6]

Darby's battalion consisted of an HQ Company and six fighting companies (A to F), a total of 26 officers and 442 enlisted men. They ranged in age from seventeen to thirty-five, and came from across the United States and from a wide variety of backgrounds, including salesmen, boxers, police officers and industrial workers. At least two had Native American blood: Sergeant Joe Dye and the improbably named Private Sampson P. Oneskunk. Clyde Thomson, a Technician 5th Grade (or junior NCO) from Ashland, Kentucky, joined on the promise that the Rangers would 'work in small combat groups' and 'hit the enemy and run'. In the event they hit more than they ran, but he was pleased the army kept most of their promises, and they were on their own 'most of the time'.[7]

Like the British Commandos, the Rangers were essentially light troops designed for shock action. Their weapons included .45 semi-automatic pistols, Thompson sub-machine guns ('Tommy' guns), Browning automatic rifles, 60mm and 81mm mortars and, issued just before their departure from the UK, the excellent .30 M1 Garand semi-automatic rifle which had replaced the long-serving bolt-action M-1903 Springfield. Their only British weapons were the .55 Boyes anti-tank rifle, and the Fairbairn-Sykes fighting knife that had been designed by two former Shanghai policemen for the Commandos.

Their instruction mirrored that of the British Commandos, and took place at the latter's spartan training depot at Achnacarry Castle in the Scottish Highlands. There was the same emphasis on speed marches with pack and equipment, river and stream crossings, swimming in ice-cold water, rock climbing, abseiling, hand-to-hand and bayonet fighting, boxing, scouting and patrolling, small–unit tactics, map–reading and first aid. They then moved to HMS *Dorlin* in Argyll to practise amphibious landings with the Royal Navy, under live fire, navigation and night operations. At Darby's insistence, the officers received the same training as the men, and were the first to tackle each new obstacle. 'I included myself in this rule,' wrote Darby, 'believing deeply that no American soldier will refuse to go as far forward in combat as his officer.'[8]

After three months of this brutal but effective training, the volunteer Rangers had been 'welded into a close-knit unit able to operate in any kind of warfare'. Darby wrote: 'Their bodies were physically hard, wits sharp, hands firm on the trigger, bayonets and knives ready. They were not supermen but highly trained American infantrymen. They were not thugs or cutthroats . . . They wore their uniforms correctly, they saluted smartly, and they had confidence in their leaders.'

Though fifty officers and men had played a minor role in the disastrous raid on Dieppe in August 1942,* the 1st Ranger Battalion would receive its unit baptism of fire at Arzew in Algeria on 8 November.[9]

After the porpoise scare on *Ulster Monarch*, Bill Darby went below deck to make his final preparations. The Centre Task Force's overall plan was to land the US 1st Division's 16th and 18th Infantry Regiments on the beaches of Arzew Bay, to the east of Oran, while its 26th Infantry Regiment was put ashore far to the west. Supported by tanks and guns from the 1st Armored Division, the two forces would then converge on Oran and compel its French garrison to surrender.

---

* On 19 August 1942, the Canadian 2nd Infantry Division, supported by British Commandos and US Rangers, carried out an amphibious assault on the French Channel port of Dieppe. Apart from a few minor successes (such as Lord Lovat's 4th Commando knocking out the Hess Battery to the west of Dieppe), it ended in bloody failure as the attackers came up against a near-perfect system of defensive fire. Of the 6,000 men who took part, 2,010 were taken prisoner and almost 1,000 were killed. Ranger casualties included seven missing in action and seven wounded. (Patrick Bishop, *Operation Jubilee*, pp. 302–3)

The task of Darby's 1st Ranger Battalion was to go in ahead of the 16th Infantry and knock out two French gun batteries at Arzew that commanded the beaches: one in the Fort de la Pointe at the edge of the habour; and the larger Batterie du Nord, made up of four 105mm guns in concrete emplacements, on a hill overlooking the harbour and the bay to the east. Darby's plan was to assault both batteries simultaneously by splitting his force: his executive officer (or XO) Major Herman Dammer would lead two companies against the harbour fort, while Darby and the remaining four companies took on the bigger fort on the hill.[10]

Major Dammer's men were on the first landing craft lowered into the sea from HMS *Royal Scotsman*. They were quiet-running British LCA models, and each contained a platoon of Rangers and a crew of five. Passing through Arzew harbour's open boom, the vanguard scrambled onto the sloping sea wall at 1 a.m., cursing quietly as their equipment got tangled in the small buoys acting as fenders. All was quiet ashore.

While Company B established blocking positions, Company A advanced on the fort. In the darkness, the 2nd Platoon was able to enter the fort by following a French soldier with a basket of laundry on his head through the open gate. The 1st Platoon, meanwhile, had moved farther along the wall and up a grassy embankment to get at the guns. As the scouts were cutting their way through three strands of rusty barbed wire, they were challenged by a sentry. '*Nous sommes vos amis*,' responded a French-speaking Ranger.

When the sentry came to investigate, he was struck from behind and taken prisoner. The Rangers then poured through the wire, vaulted a low wall and 'after a few quick shots captured the guns and some sixty prisoners'. Those taken inside the fort included the commandant and his wife who were in bed. Dammer at once radioed Darby: 'I've captured *my* objective!'[11]

Darby's force had also landed successfully, thanks to a four-man team from Lieutenant Commander Nigel Willmott's 'Party Inhuman', a mixture of Royal Navy navigators and Special Boat Section opera-tors, who paddled in from a submarine in folbots to mark the correct beach with an infra-red beacon.[12] But Darby's force was half an hour behind Dammer and four miles from its objective: the Batterie du Nord on the hill above Arzew.

With two miles still to go, and the garrison almost certainly alerted, Darby hurried his men onwards. Leaving Company D's heavy mortars in a ditch to provide covering fire, Companies C, E and F advanced abreast up the hill towards the concentric circles of barbed wire on the north side of the battery. The point men were cutting through the last strands of wire when French machine guns opened fire, hitting several Rangers. One was pulled to safety by Lieutenant Klefman who, moments later, called for mortar support. 'Eighty 81mm shells came in a flurry,' wrote Darby, 'turning the French machine guns off as if someone had pulled a switch. Ranger riflemen sprang from prone positions close to the wire and went over the parapet, shouting as they bored in. Needing no orders, several Rangers rushed the big guns, thrusting Bangalore torpedoes – four-foot sections of steel pipe crammed with explosives – into the muzzles.'

As they did so, a larger party of Rangers stormed the battery's main entrance, shooting a sentry and forcing the remaining French soldiers to barricade themselves inside an underground powder magazine. When they refused to surrender, Rangers dropped grenades down the ventilator shafts. That did the trick. The survivors came out with their hands in the air. Sixty prisoners were taken in all, and the guns destroyed. Ranger losses in both actions were two killed and eight wounded. Darby was jubilant, but had no way to signal his success because the one boat that had been lost in the landing contained his long-range radio and white star shells.

The Ranger leader eventually got a message to the ships that the batteries had been neutralised via a British naval forward observer. But even without Darby's confirmation, Major General Terry Allen of the 1st Infantry Division had ordered his men ashore, and, despite several mishaps – strong tides and navigation errors causing many of the landing craft to arrive late and at the wrong place – by dawn the 16th and 18th Regimental Combat Teams, and elements of the 1st Armored Division's Combat Command B, were safely on to Beach Z in the Gulf of Arzew and heading inland. The Rangers' first action had been a triumph. 'They hit the ground,' wrote Darby, 'fired their weapons, crawled or ran forward without deliberate or conscious thought. Improvisation on the battlefield was not needed. Each Ranger knew his job and anticipated events.'[13]

7

Little Napoleon

Algeria, 8 November 1942

T HE BATTLE FOR ORAN would rage for two more days. At its heart was the outspoken but hugely talented 48-year-old tank officer Colonel Paul M. Robinett, who had attended the US Army's War College at the same time as Mark Clark. Hailing from Missouri's Ozark foothills, Robinett joined the 1st Cavalry as a second lieutenant in 1917. A crack shot and an expert rider, he had competed with the US Army's equestrian team, done a spell at the French cavalry school at Saumur, and worked as a strategic planner and intelligence officer for George C. Marshall.

Arrogant and querulous, and just 5 feet 4 inches tall, Robinett was known as 'Little Napoleon' or 'Robbie'.[1] He was also a keen student of military history, and a great believer that armies learn by studying their opponents. While working for Marshall, he noted that the Ordnance Department 'had no systematic way of recording the many advances then being made in armoured equipment', and contrasted that with the work in Germany by Dr Fritz Heigl who had 'made a thorough study of armored vehicles of all nations, including the United States, and had published his findings in the *Taschenbuch der Tanks*'. Heinz Guderian, one of Germany's leading tank tacticians, would acknowledge his debt to Heigl in his own post-war memoir *Panzer Leader*.

Germany's successful use of a mass armoured force in Poland, the

Low Countries and France – part of the combined arms surprise attack known as Blitzkrieg – had led, in Robinett's opinion, to 'profound diplomatic and military repercussions in the United States', notably a determined effort 'to develop weapons capable of defeating the tank'. As a result, America had produced 'inefficient' weapons such as 'the 37-mm towed gun, the 37-mm gun mounted on a three-fourth ton truck, and the 75-mm gun on half-track', and a tactical doctrine of 'Seek-Strike-Destroy'. This, in turn, had delayed the production of 'highly efficient tanks and tank guns', and the true power of massed armour was 'not fully appreciated or tested'. Even so, a new and more powerful cavalry was formed and Robinett was determined to join it. He got his way in early 1942 when he was given command of the 1st Armored Division's 13th Armored Regiment, only the second cavalry unit to be mechanised.

'The condition of the 13th is not the best in the world,' he was told by his divisional commander, Major General Orlando Ward, 'though it is a going concern and on the whole excellent.' Having inspected the unit – made up of a headquarters and three tank battalions, a total of 2,474 officers and men, 63 light and 116 medium tanks, and 390 other vehicles – Robinett took a dimmer view. The 'standards of discipline, smartness, and personal appearance were', he wrote, 'anything but impressive'. He set out to change all that with a rigorous training programme. What he could not do, however, was improve the regiment's tanks which were mostly the 'obsolete' M3 Stuart Light and M3 Lee Medium models. The 13-ton Stuart was crewed by four and armed with a 37mm cannon and three .30 machine guns; the much heavier 30-ton Lee had a crew of seven, a top speed of 26mph, thicker armour and greater firepower (including a 75mm cannon mounted on the hull *and* one of 37mm in the turret). But this was offset by drawbacks with its design and shape, including a high silhouette – making it more vulnerable to anti-tank fire – a sponson or side mounting of the main gun (which meant that it could not traverse or take a proper 'hull-down' defensive position, with only the turret visible), riveted construction and poor off-road performance.

What Robinett wanted instead was the new M4 Sherman tank with its '75mm gun mounted in a 360 degrees traversable turret, low silhouette, welded instead of riveted armor, improved power train and improved suspension'. Shermans had first rolled off the production line in February 1942, but none was immediately available to equip the 13th Regiment because they had been promised to the British who were under pressure in Egypt.

Arriving in Northern Ireland with the rest of the 1st Armored Division in May 1942, Robinett had put the 13th through a series of tough exercises. 'This stood us in good stead many times later,' he wrote, 'for we could traverse the most difficult terrain at night without lights and without getting lost.' They also practised with artillery support, but, to Robinett's disappointment, 'had no exercises with close support aviation or in tank-infantry cooperation', or any amphibious training. His other main gripe was the loss of men to the Rangers. In theory, they should have been returned to the 13th once blooded. In reality, the 13th went into battle 'with untrained replacements'.

Robinett's role in Operation Torch, as explained to him in London in early September, was to command Task Force Green – consisting of one-third of Combat Command B (CCB), 1st Armored Division, including most of Robinett's 13th Armored, a battalion of the 6th Armored Infantry, a battery of field artillery, a tank destroyer battalion, engineers, and anti-aircraft guns – which would land on Beach X, 40 miles west of Oran. At the same time the slightly larger Task Force Red, commanded by the CCB's Brigadier General Lunsford E. Oliver, would hit Beach Z in the Gulf of Arzew. Once ashore, the two task forces were to swing inland and quickly seize the important airfields of Tafaraoui and La Sénia, south of Oran, if they had not already been captured by parachute troops. They were then to make a coordinated attack on Oran, directly from the south.[2]

Task Force Green's landing on Beach X in the early hours of

8 November was unopposed, if slightly chaotic, with currents, poor navigation and accidents causing some of the second wave to arrive before the first. By the time Robinett came ashore on the 'White' (or right) part of Beach X just after 7 a.m., a 300-foot pontoon bridge had been built by engineers to transport armoured vehicles from the larger tank landing ships to the shore. Unfortunately, it was still 60 feet short of dry land, causing at least two vehicles to 'drown out', though they were later recovered. But most of the light tanks were able to negotiate the shallow water and reach the metal road mat that had been laid across the beach by engineers.

Robinett – so festooned with personal equipment that his small frame resembled a Christmas tree – found the beach a 'scene of intense activity'. Eventually, 3,242 men, 458 vehicles and 1,170 tons of supplies were landed at the 'White' end of Beach X alone.

He likened Algeria to pictures he had seen of Palestine at the time of Christ. 'It was mountainous, barren, and arid,' wrote Robinett, 'but not entirely devoid of life. Barefoot Arabs, garbed in ragged burnouses, were sitting or squatting in groups on surrounding hills, talking of the events of the morning as they tended flocks of undernourished sheep and goats . . . Some of the Arabs made a nuisance at once, begging for food or clothing and grabbing, like vultures, at anything discarded.'

At 9 a.m., Robinett despatched Lieutenant Colonel John Todd with a flying column of light tanks and half-tracks towards the village of Lourmel, 10 miles inland. Soon after, word came back of a clash near the village between a reconnaissance platoon from the 13th Regiment, sent out earlier, and a French armoured car. Todd reached Lourmel at 11.35 a.m. and quickly secured the village and the nearby airstrip. He also pushed patrols to the southwest, pending an advance on Tafaraoui airfield from the west. But at noon, Robinett received orders from Oliver to capture La Sénia airfield by the shorter northern route, and these were forwarded to Todd.[3]

In the early afternoon, Robinett moved his forward HQ to Lourmel along a black-topped road that traversed 'very rough mountainous terrain, which fortunately was not defended'. En route to Lourmel he passed a crashed RAF Spitfire and a number of abandoned parachutes, indicating that a few men from Lieutenant Colonel Edson Raff's 2/503rd Parachute Infantry were nearby. Rain, fog, faulty radio intercommunication and defective running lights caused the majority of Raff's 556 US parachutists, who had taken off from two airfields in Cornwall the night before, to be dropped or landed over a wide area, leaving the battalion 'scattered and ineffective'. Many would not reach Tafaraoui airfield until the following day.

Todd's flying column, meanwhile, had encountered and destroyed a number of French roadblocks en route to Bredeah Station, an important link in Oran's water supply. But he had lost some tanks to enemy fire in the process, and had also outrun his rear units, leaving a trail of stragglers – including tanks and 75mm assault guns – for Robinett to collect as he followed in the column's footsteps that afternoon.

By nightfall, out of radio contact with both Todd and his rear HQ, Robinett ordered his column to 'circle wagons' in a concealed bivouac between the road and the Sebkra desert to the south. Todd's reduced force spent the night close to the village of Misserrhin, which was strongly held by French infantry, artillery and anti-tank guns, and still five miles short of La Sénia airfield which remained in French hands. He hoped to bypass the strongpoint and capture the airfield the following morning.[4]

Overall, the beach landings either side of Oran had been successful,* 'although the pace had fallen behind expectations'. Thanks to the Rangers, Arzew had been captured intact, and its small port was already in use. The airfields at Tafaraoui and Lourmel were in American hands,

---

* Landing on one of Oran's beaches with the assault troops, tasked with clearing obstacles and explosives, was a section of Royal Naval Commandos led by my paternal grandfather Lieutenant Commander Aubrey David. Thereafter he acted as Beach Master (BM) with responsibility for guiding ashore troops, vehicles and supplies (see Plate section).

and La Sénia soon would be. Only at St Cloud, a village in a wide, bowl-shaped depression on the Arzew–Oran highway, had Americans faced serious resistance when the 18th Regimental Combat Team was stopped in its tracks by a combined force of the French Foreign Legion and the 16th Tunisian Regiment. Major General Allen's plan for the following day was to seal off the village and advance round it. Despite the failure of subsidiary operations – the direct assault on Oran harbour and the airborne attacks on the airfields – the American vice was beginning to tighten, and Oran's fall was just a matter of time.[5]

8

'Old Blood and Guts'

Morocco, 7–8 November 1942

FOUR HUNDRED AND FIFTY miles to the west of Oran, on the storm-tossed Atlantic coast of Morocco, lies the great port of Casablanca which at the time of the Torch landings had been a French possession for thirty years. Strongly defended by submarines, coastal guns, planes, the half-finished battleship *Jean Bart* (which was moored in the harbour) and a sizeable French garrison, it was thought by the Allies to be immune to a frontal attack. So, as at Oran, the Western Task Force – an armada of more than one hundred vessels that had sailed in nine columns from the eastern seaboard of the United States – hoped to land the bulk of its forces on either side of Casablanca and attack overland. With few suitable ports or landing places close to Casablanca, the planners chose Safi, 140 miles to the southwest, and the small fishing town of Fedala and the larger Port Lyautey, 18 and 78 miles respectively to the northeast. The main effort would be at Fedala, where the beaches were bounded by only a few low sand hills, while the bulk of the armour was landed at Safi.[1]

During the two-week crossing of the Atlantic on Admiral H. Kent Hewitt's flagship, the cruiser USS *Augusta*, the task force commander, Major General George S. Patton Jr, had kept himself busy by reading the Koran – though it 'bored the hell out of him' – shooting carbines off the fantail, and urging his officers to 'impress your men that fire wins battles . . . we are better in all respects than our enemies, but to win, the men must know this. It must be their absolute belief . . . Always attack, never surrender.'[2]

To his soldiers, he wrote:

When the great day of battle comes, remember your training, and remember above all that speed and vigor of attack are the sure roads to success and you must succeed – for to retreat is as cowardly as it is fatal. Indeed, once landed, retreat is impossible. Americans do not surrender . . .

The eyes of the world are watching us; the heart of America beats for us; God is with us. On our victory depends the freedom or slavery of the human race. We shall surely win.

Patton's hyperbole was typical, but it also betrayed his determination not to let slip this opportunity to prove himself a great commander. 'Every once in a while,' he noted in his diary on 3 November, 'the tremendous responsibility of this job lands on me like a ton of bricks, but mostly I am not in the least worried. I can't decide logically if I am a man of destiny or a lucky fool, but I think I am destined. Five more days will show . . . I feel that my claim to greatness hangs on an ability to lead and inspire.'[3]

The chance for Patton to command a sizeable force in battle had come late in life. Almost fifty-seven years old, he was descended from Scottish immigrants who had settled in Virginia and later fought for the Confederacy during the US Civil War. Patton himself had been born at St Gabriel, California, the son of a successful lawyer and businessman, but never considered a career other than the military. Graduating 46th out of 103 cadets at West Point in 1909, he had joined the US Cavalry. An expert swordsman and rider, he competed in the modern pentathlon at the 1912 Olympic Games.

In 1918, Patton had commanded an American light armoured brigade at the Battle of St Mihiel, riding fearlessly if recklessly on top of a tank, and was badly wounded in the upper thigh during the Meuse–Argonne offensive, later admitting that he might have killed with a shovel an American soldier who refused to follow orders. He was awarded the DSC for 'extraordinary heroism' and the following year, fully recovered, met the younger Lieutenant Colonel Dwight D. Eisenhower at Camp Meade in Maryland. 'On balance,' wrote Patton's biographer, 'they seemed a genuinely mismatched pair: the brash, outspoken cavalryman-tanker and the fun-loving midwesterner whose roots were in the infantry. Yet the two soon forged an enduring friendship that lasted until shortly before Patton's death.'

Eisenhower recalled: 'From the beginning he and I got along famously. Both of us were students of current military doctrine. Part of our passion was our belief in tanks – a belief derided at the time by others.' It was a relationship that would 'delight and dismay' Ike for the rest of his life. They were among a handful of officers who foresaw the importance of armoured warfare and had pushed for its development. But a limited budget, and the dominance of the infantry and cavalry branches, meant that the US Army did not create its first independent tank force – initially comprised of the 1st and 2nd Armored Divisions – until after the Germans had demonstrated the success of Blitzkrieg in the summer of 1940.[4]

Patton was one of the 'basement conspirators' who had convinced George C. Marshall that armoured divisions were necessary. 'Patton is by far the best tank man in the Army,' Marshall told his executive officer, Lieutenant Colonel Leonard T. Gerow. 'I know this from the First World War. I watched him closely when he commanded the first tanks we ever had. I realize he is a difficult man but I know how to handle him.'

With Marshall's blessing, Patton was given command of the newly formed 2nd Armored Division's 2nd Brigade – consisting of 350 officers, 5,500 men, 383 tanks and 202 armoured cars – and then the division itself when his boss Major General Charles L. Scott was made the commander of I Armored Corps. He quickly stamped his personality on the division (known as 'Hell on Wheels') – which he had found ill-equipped, understrength and low on morale – by insisting on the highest standards of discipline and dress, and inculcating the best practice in reconnaissance, refuelling, maintenance, camouflage, security, radio discipline, and manoeuvring tanks and armoured cars.

It was around this time that Patton acquired the nickname 'Old Blood and Guts', often wrongly cited by critics as an example of his huge ego and wilful disregard for his men's lives. In fact, it probably came from his habit of telling junior officers that in combat they would be 'up to their necks in blood and guts'. Within the 2nd, however, he was known affectionately as the 'Old Man'.

By the time Patton was promoted to major general in April 1941 – his second elevation in six months – his command had swelled to 14,000. His indispensability as a senior commander was confirmed during the US Army's three great exercises of 1941 – in Tennessee, Louisiana and Carolina – when his 2nd Armored Division performed brilliantly and demonstrated, among other things, its ability to advance at speed in the dark, without lights and under radio silence. In the wake of the Louisiana exercise, thirty-one of the US Army's forty-two top generals – army, corps and divisional – were replaced by a younger generation. Patton was one of the eleven who remained in place or were promoted – in his case to the command of I Armored Corps. His final act of preparation, before he was chosen to lead Operation Torch's Western Task Force, was to anticipate service in Africa. 'The war in Europe is over,' he told the staff of I Armored Corps. 'England will probably fall this year. Our first chance to get at the enemy will be in North Africa. We cannot train troops to fight in the desert . . . by training in the swamps of Georgia.'

After voicing these qualms to his superiors, he was ordered to set up the Desert Training Center, 20,000 square miles of scrub and mountains known as 'Little Libya' in southeast California and west Arizona. During his few months in charge, more than 60,000 troops passed through the centre, gaining invaluable experience of desert conditions that would serve them well in North Africa.[5]

The post-war image of George S. Patton Jr – shaped by actor George C. Scott's bravura performance in the film *Patton* – is of a scowling, irascible character who did not suffer fools, a 'brash, swash-buckling, controversial warrior'.[6] Yet this portrait is only partly true. He certainly expected a lot from his officers and men and worked them tirelessly. He was also famously profane. But when Eisenhower's driver Kay Summersby met Patton in London in the summer of 1942, she found him 'by no means coarse or crude'. She wrote:

> He was a gentleman, terribly courteous and very proper. I am not saying that the legendary 'blood and guts' Patton did not exist. He most definitely did. But there was another side to the man, a rather sweet and affectionate side. He was very strange – and very endearing. He loved the Army. He loved pomp and spit and polish. He was always ramrod stiff, whether standing or sitting, and always a military fashion plate.[7]

Woken at 2 a.m. on 8 November, Patton dressed in his trademark leather flying jacket, jodhpurs and riding boots, topped with a helmet sporting two shiny silver stars, and went on deck. He could see lights blazing on shore, marking Casablanca and, 18 miles to the north, the target port of Fedala. A day earlier the convoy had split, with twenty-six ships and 6,000 troops heading towards Safi, in southern Morocco, and another twenty-seven ships and 9,000 men making for Port Lyautey, away to the north. The USS *Augusta* was, as a result, now leading around fifty ships and 19,000 men. 'Sea dead calm, no swell,' noted Patton in his diary. 'God is with us.'[8]

His one cause of irritation was to hear over the ship's public address system President Roosevelt's BBC radio appeal to the Vichy authorities not to oppose the invasion. As the landings in Morocco were due to take place three hours after those in Algeria, he had pleaded with Eisenhower to delay the broadcast. But to no avail.[9]

Hampered by miscommunication and the tardy loading of landing craft, the first 3rd Division troops did not reach the beach at Fedala until 5 a.m., an hour behind schedule. 'The men,' noted the official history, 'in herringbone twill fatigue uniforms and with U.S. flag arm bands, were heavily laden.'

There was little opposition. But faulty navigation, caused by compass deviations and inexperienced crews, 'brought boatloads of troops to shore sometimes miles from the designated points, and onto rocky obstructions of reefs rather than at sandy beaches'. Of the thirty-one boats carrying the first four waves of the 1/7th Infantry towards Beach Red 2, some ended up in the right place, some on Beach Red 3, and some on the rocky shore in between. 'The surf swept many boats out of control, throwing them against rocks with such destructive force that they either capsized or were smashed. A total of twenty-one boats were lost. Heavily laden troops could not swim, and drowned.'

Despite these setbacks, the small garrison of Senegalese infantry in Fedala was 'quickly surprised and captured', and the port was under American control by 6 a.m.[10]

On shore, unbeknown to Patton and Hewitt, the French plot to prevent armed opposition to the landings was beginning to unravel. Mast and Murphy had enlisted as a pro-Allied conspirator Général de division Émile Béthouart, commander of the Casablanca garrison. At 8 p.m. on 7 November, Béthouart had informed ten trusted officers of the imminent landings and dispatched them to secure key locations and airfields. He himself had headed for Rabat, the seat of government, where he took over the command post of the Moroccan Army, protected by a battalion of Colonial Moroccan Infantry, in the early hours of the 8th. At the same time he had a letter delivered to Général d'armée Auguste Charles Noguès, the Vichy loyalist Resident General, informing him that Général d'armée Henri Giraud, 'aided by American troops, was taking command in all French North Africa', and had designated

Béthouart to take control of Morocco and assist the American expedition which was about to land.

It was a bluff that did not work. Noguès immediately telephoned
Vice Amiral François Michelier, commanding naval forces and the
Casablanca defence sector, to inform him of Béthouart's attempted
coup d'état. Michelier agreed to cancel Béthouart's orders for troops
to stand down, while Noguès issued a general alert that a hostile
landing was imminent. He was further emboldened by the news that
the garrisons at Oran and Algiers were resisting an Allied invasion,
and that Giraud had not been generally accepted as the leader in
North Africa. He ordered Béthouart to dismiss his Moroccan guard
and surrender. Béthouart did so, to avoid bloodshed, and was promptly
arrested, 'kept in custody until evening and then sent to Meknès to
stand trial for treason'.[11]

The Allies, meanwhile, were confident that the French could be won
over. Much to their disappointment, they heard gunfire from the shore
batteries near Fedala at 6 a.m., the first overt sign that the French
would contest the Moroccan landings. This was followed, fifty minutes
later, by French anti-aircraft guns in Casablanca shooting at American
observation planes, and the uncompleted battleship *Jean Bart* opening
up on Hewitt's naval covering force with its 15-inch guns. The
American warships – including the battleship USS *Massachusetts* –
returned fire and, within twenty minutes, had knocked out *Jean Bart's*
main armament.

At 7.13 a.m., Patton received the two-word radio message 'Play Ball'
from Major General Lucian K. Truscott Jr, the founder of the Rangers
who was commanding his Northern Attack Group. It was code for 'am
fighting'. Only later would Patton discover that the landings at Port
Lyautey had been badly bungled, with troops dropped off late and in
the wrong place.

The plan was to push six miles inland and capture the Port Lyautey
airfield. But determined opposition from planes, artillery, infantry and

even tanks meant the day would pass with the airfield still in French hands. With French hostile intentions clear, American carrier planes were launched on bombing and strafing runs, and quickly gained air superiority as far north as Port Lyautey.

The battle continued at sea when seven French destroyers used a smoke screen to leave Casablanca harbour and head north along the coast to Fedala. In an effort to get at the transports, they engaged two American destroyers and forced them to retire. But they were eventually driven off by Hewitt's cruisers, leaving one French ship 'smoking badly'.[12]

The most serious French naval attack was made by the French cruiser *Primaguet* and two destroyers at around 10 a.m. as Patton was preparing to go ashore. '[The Higgins] boat was on davits swung out with all our things in her, including my white pistols,' noted Patton in his diary. 'I sent an orderly to get them, and at that moment, a light cruiser and two big destroyers came out of Casa, tearing up the coast close to shore to get our transports. At once Augusta speeded up to 20 knots and opened fire. The first blast from the rear turret blew the [Higgins] boat to hell and we lost all our things except my white pistols.'[13]

As well as delaying his journey ashore, the blast had knocked out Patton's tactical radios and severed communication with Eisenhower in Gibraltar. Yet Patton was far from downhearted, even when a French shell struck the sea so close to where he was standing that he was splashed with yellow water (from the dye added to the shell to make it easier to observe the fall of shot and correct the range). An aide tried to wipe clean Patton's leather jacket, but was told: 'Leave it there. This will stay on the #$%&?# [sic] jacket as long as I am able to wear it.'[14]

Patton finally went ashore with his staff at 1.20 p.m., getting 'very wet' as he waded from the landing craft to the beach. Shortly before leaving *Augusta* he had received a delayed message from Major General Ernest N. Harmon, commanding the southern landing force, that the port of Safi was in his hands (and had been since 5.15 a.m.), as was 'a battalion of the Foreign Legion, three tanks, and a lot of guns'.

In Fedala, Patton was told by the captured French commandant that his army did not want to fight and that an envoy should be sent to Casablanca to demand a cease-fire. Just such a mission had already been undertaken by Colonel William H. Wilbur, a member of Patton's staff, who was repeatedly fired on as he drove in a small car sporting a huge flag of truce through 16 miles of enemy-held territory. Finally reaching the naval headquarters in Casablanca, Wilbur was told that Michelier would not see him. As he returned from his failed mission, Wilbur learned that a coastal battery was still targeting American ships offshore. Gathering four tanks and a company of infantry, he rode on the lead tank and directed the attack that led to the battery's surrender. 'From the moment of landing until the cessation of resistance,' read his citation for the Medal of Honor, the American military's highest award for valour, 'Col. Wilbur's conduct was voluntary and exemplary in its coolness and daring.'

Patton, meanwhile, had sent a second envoy – his trusted chief of staff, Colonel Hobart R. Gay – who was also rebuffed by Michelier. A French army general told Patton that he 'could do nothing' as Michelier 'was senior'. His staff were more accommodating. They 'gave us all the dope', noted Patton, 'and even suggested that Casa could be taken more easily from the rear'.

Patton spent the night in Fedala's Hotel Miramar. 'It was,' he noted in his diary, 'very nice, but it had been hit several times so there was no water nor light and only cheese and fish to eat and champagne to drink . . . God was very good to me today.'[15]

9

'France and her honour are at stake'

Algeria, 8 November 1942

VIEWED FROM ITS CRESCENT-SHAPED bay, wrote a visitor, Algiers was a 'fairy city' with its white buildings covering the high steep hills that rose almost from the sea in 'dazzling beauty'. By moonlight, it resembled something out of the *Arabian Nights*. 'A soft mist crept over the hills, swathing the snow-white buildings in a soft veil of loveliness.'[1]

A small trading port of the ancient Carthaginians, Algiers had risen to prominence with the arrival of Moors expelled from Spain in 1492. For three centuries, under the loose overlordship of the Ottomans, the city had been controlled by Barbary pirates who attacked ships and raided for slaves as far as Iceland. Among the prominent captives later ransomed was Spanish novelist Miguel de Cervantes, author of *Don Quixote*, who had spent five years in the city.

In 1830 – using an affront to their consul as a pretext – the French had captured Algiers and would later place it at the heart of their North African empire. Many Europeans settled there, and by the early twentieth century they represented a majority of the city's population. The architect Le Corbusier hoped to redesign the colonial city which he described as 'nothing but crumbling walls and devastated nature, the whole a sullied blot'. His plans came to nothing.[2]

In 1942, as the capital of Algeria and the seat of government for all

French North Africa, Algiers was the main objective of Operation Torch. Its port, railway terminal and two airfields made the city a 'prize', while its ample housing made it the obvious choice for Eisenhower's Allied Force Headquarters once the landings were complete. It was also the Allies' easternmost objective and could be used as a springboard for the subsequent seizure of Tunisia (and the two great ports of Tunis and Bizerte).

The plan was this. Spearheading the Allied landings on beaches either side of Algiers, from 1 a.m. on 8 November, would be the men of the British Nos 1 and 6 Commando. To mask their true identity from the French, they had been equipped with American uniforms and weapons, and supplemented by a detachment of 'first-rate men' from the US 34th Division's 168th Infantry. These Americans 'had been through the same concentrated training as us', remembered Corporal 'Tag' Barnes of No. 1 Commando, 'and, like us, were honed to a peak of fighting fitness'.[3]

To facilitate the capture of Algiers, Général de division Emmanuel-Charles Mast had arranged for trusted pro-Allied officers and associates to seize key installations, including the radio station and army and police headquarters, and to arrest the local corps commander, Louis Koeltz. This plan was put into action in the early hours of 8 November and by 1.30 a.m. the pro-Allied French were in control.

At around the same time, the American envoy Bob Murphy drove up in his Buick to the Villa des Oliviers, a substantial Moorish Revival house in the upmarket suburb of El-Biar that was protected by tall Senegalese sentries. In the foyer he was met by a swarthy man in pink-striped pyjamas: Général de corps d'armée Alphonse Pierre Juin, commanding the Vichy Army in North Africa.

Murphy told him that the American and British armies of liberation were about to land.

'What!' responded Juin. 'You mean the convoy we have seen in the Mediterranean is going to land here?'

Murphy nodded.

'But you only told me a week ago that the United States would not attack us.'

'We are coming by invitation,' said Murphy.

'By whose invitation?'

'By the invitation of General Giraud.'

'Is he here?'

'He will be here soon,' said Murphy, though he knew that Giraud was still sulking in Gibraltar.

Deliberately exaggerating the size of the invasion forces, Murphy reminded Juin that he had long sought the liberation of France, and could now play his part by ordering his troops not to oppose the landings.[4]

Juin paused before replying. He was torn between hatred of the Germans and loyalty to Pétain, and later explained the quandary that he and his men found themselves in:

This [North African] army did not hide its anti-German feelings . . . But overall it saw the victor of Verdun as a leader whose patriotism could not be called into question and it hoped that one day he would give the signal for the conflict to start again. Without approving all that happened in Vichy, about which it only heard vague rumours, it tended to separate the Marshal from the acts of his government.[5]

Fortunately, Juin had a 'Get out of Jail' card and he played it. Expressing sympathy for the Allied cause, he told Murphy he was constrained by the unexpected presence in Algiers of Amiral de la flotte François Darlan, the commander of all Vichy armed forces, who had come to the city to comfort his dying son Alain. 'He can immediately countermand any orders I issue,' said Juin. 'If he does, the commands will respect his orders, not mine.'[6]

Commander-in-Chief of the French navy at the start of the war – and instrumental in the decision not to allow the French fleet to submit to the British in the summer of 1940 – Darlan had since served in General Pétain's Vichy government as Minister of Marine and, for a time, as de facto prime minister. In April 1942, at Germany's insistence, Darlan had been forced to resign his political posts in favour of Pierre Laval, though he remained the commander of French armed forces. Yet Darlan's 'aversion to Britain was notorious', wrote Churchill, and he had 'for a long time been committed to the Axis', a collaboration that included the use of Tunisian ports to resupply Rommel's armies.

Called to Juin's villa to adjudicate, the small, pigeon-chested Darlan told Murphy: 'I have known for a long time that the British were stupid, but I always believed the Americans were more intelligent. I begin to believe that you make as many mistakes as they do.'[7]

Like Juin, Darlan was in an impossible position. He knew that if he sided with the Allies, he would be personally responsible for the inevitable German invasion and occupation of Vichy France. For fifteen minutes he procrastinated, pacing back and forth while Murphy urged him to act. 'The moment has now arrived!'

'I have given my oath to Pétain,' replied Darlan. 'I cannot revoke that now.'

What he would agree to do was send a message to Pétain asking for liberty of action. As he stepped outside, however, Darlan noticed that the Senegalese guard had been replaced by forty anti-Vichy Frenchmen with white armbands and ancient rifles. 'Does this mean,' asked Juin, 'we are prisoners?'

They were. Murphy's colleague Kenneth Pendar, vice consul at Marrakesh, was sent to the Admiralty office with Darlan's sealed message for Pétain. Pindar opened it on the way and, deciding it was not sufficiently anti-Axis to have the desired effect, threw it away. Returning to the villa, he told Darlan: 'The necessary has been done.'

But where were the Commandos and the other Allied troops? With dawn not far off, some of them should have landed already. As the minutes ticked by with no response from Vichy and no sign of the Allied invaders, Murphy wondered if he had got the date wrong. He had not – but the delay of two or three hours gave the loyalist forces time to recover their nerve and recapture the key installations from the rebels.

Before daybreak, a patrol of the Vichy loyalist Garde Mobile arrived at the villa, dispersed the anti-Vichy guard and locked Murphy and Pendar in the porter's lodge.[8]

Juin and Darlan then went to the army headquarters in Fort l'Empereur to decide on their next move. To reassert his authority, Juin ordered the release of Koeltz from captivity; Koeltz, in turn, sacked the arch-conspirator Mast who was on the loose in the city. Darlan sent the following message to Pétain:

> At 7.30 the situation was as follows: Landings have been carried out by American troops and British ships at Algiers and in the neighbour-hood. The defences have repulsed the attacks in several places, in particular in the port and at the naval headquarters. In other places landings have been effected by surprise and with success. The situation is getting worse and the defences will soon be overwhelmed. Reports indicate that massive landings are in preparation.[9]

Darlan could see the writing on the wall and, having made a show of resisting, was preparing to switch sides. For Pétain in Vichy, there were no good outcomes. But for German consumption, if nothing else, he sent to President Roosevelt the following brief message (drafted by Pierre Laval, his pro-German President of the Council of Ministers, the de facto prime minister): 'France and her honour are at stake. We have been attacked. We will defend ourselves.'[10]

The British Commandos, meanwhile, had been having a torrid time. Due to land at 1 a.m., their various objectives included the capture of forts, coastal batteries and an airfield. The immediate task of 'Tag' Barnes's No. 6 troop, however, was to storm a large house to the east of Algiers and capture or kill its occupants who were believed to be high-ranking members of the German Gestapo, or secret police. Barnes and half of No. 1 Commando – three British troops and two American, under the overall command of Major Ken Trevor – had sailed from

Belfast in late October on the former luxury liner *Leedstown*. Much of the voyage had been spent climbing up and down rope ladders in dark glasses 'to prepare us for scrambling down the ship's sides to assault landing craft after dark'. Barnes's troop had also studied aerial photos of the Gestapo house and gardens until 'every inch of the exterior was completely familiarised'.

Raised in 1940 to carry out seaborne raids against the coast of Europe, No. 1 Commando contained a number of veterans who had distinguished themselves in operations in France, including Chariot, the successful if costly amphibious attack on the Normandie dry dock in St Nazaire in March 1942 (for which Sergeant Thomas Durrant was awarded a posthumous VC). Barnes had only joined the unit that year, however, and Torch would be his first taste of action. Before volunteering for the Commandos, he had had a 'cushy job' training Royal Artillery recruits, but deep down he felt a desire to experience 'real action'. His applications to riskier posts were all blocked by his CO, who did not want to lose him. When an opportunity to join the Army Commandos appeared on the notice board, however, he would not be deterred.

Sent to the Commando Basic Training Centre at Achnacarry in western Scotland, he endured eight weeks of physical and mental torture. Of the original intake of 240, Barnes was one of only twenty-seven to pass the course and receive the coveted green beret. Some failed the initial tests, others were 'returned to unit' for not reaching the required standards in training.

Barnes joined No. 1 Commando at its base in Ayrshire where the work, if anything, was even more intense. The total strength of the Commando was around 450 officers and men. It was composed of an HQ, led by a lieutenant colonel, and six troops, each subdivided into two platoons, and each platoon into two sections. The men were encouraged to team up with an 'oppo', a constant companion that they could rely on when things got tough. Barnes chose Arthur Barnett, a 'big man with a heart like a lion', alongside whom he would fight for much of the next three years. 'I would have trusted him with my life,' wrote Barnes, 'and I would like to think he felt the same about me.'

Shortly after midnight on 8 November 1942, the *Leedstown's* engines were stopped and the landing craft lowered from their davits. The wind was blowing hard, and each wave sent the landing craft out from the ship by as much as six feet, before hurling them back again with a 'resounding thud as they hit the side plates'. As he peered over the rail in the darkness, loaded down with M1 rifle, ammunition and hand grenades, Barnes imagined that he might die just getting off the ship:

> The main problem was that the bottom of the ladder didn't reach the landing craft. What happened was that one climbed down, clinging on like grim death, and waited, tightly hugging the rope at the bottom, until the landing craft swung back to the ship. At this point the sailors manning the craft would shout 'Jump' and one had to let go on that precise order. A moment's hesitation would have meant almost certain death by crushing between the LCA and the ship.[11]

Incredibly there were no casualties as the five troops of No. 1 Commando were transferred to eleven landing craft. But the tricky manoeuvre took longer than expected, and the convoy was already late as it set off on its bumpy eight-mile trip to shore. It was delayed further by a bank of fog which caused the pilot of the leading craft to slow down to keep the formation together.[12]

As his landing craft approached Green Beach, 10 miles northeast of Algiers, Barnes could see beams from several searchlights on Cap Matifou scanning the waves before, thankfully, they turned upwards and lit the sky. Scrambling from the bow, he and his colleagues 'crunched ashore and deployed in a rough circle'. It was deathly quiet. Barnes, crouching behind a rock, thought: 'My God, I'm in North Africa.'

They began climbing through sweet-smelling myrtle bushes. Before long, they were observing the Gestapo house from a grassy mound. Watches were checked and the signal given to advance. Led by Lieutenant

Tim Evill, Barnes and his platoon made their way up a flight of stone steps to a set of French windows on the first floor. Someone broke a pane of glass and turned the key on the inside, allowing the windows to be opened and the Commandos to pile in. The sound of gunshots and explosions ripped through the night, though it was unclear who was shooting and at what.

Barnes and his mate Arthur Barnett stopped on either side of a bedroom door, or so they thought, and went through a drill they had practised a hundred times: 'door opened, grenade tossed inside, await explosion, charge inside and spray the room with small arms fire'. They had both emptied a magazine before they realised they were standing in an empty bathroom.

As the firing in other rooms died away, lights were switched on to reveal a deserted house. Only later did they discover that the Gestapo had left three weeks earlier. They gathered outside as dawn broke 'feeling terribly deflated and almost embarrassed', objects of curiosity for the local Arabs.

Their second objective was a coastal strongpoint known as Fort d'Estrées that lay in fairly open country, bar the odd patch of scrub and thin woodland, a short distance to the west. As they approached the 'picture-book' fort – complete with drawbridge and dry moat – shots rang out and they took cover. The firing, they realised, was coming from positions outside the battlements. Barnes crawled through a patch of scrub to the top of a small rise and peered over the top. He could see, fifty yards away and slightly below him, 'a uniformed figure firing a machine gun over a pile of sandbags'. He was side-on to Barnes who slowly raised his rifle, took aim and fired.

A second French soldier removed the body of the first and was about to start firing when Barnes shot him in the left temple. A third appeared and 'looked hesitantly around him'. Barnes was about to pull the trigger when he came under some 'well aimed' fire and was forced to move.

It took less than half an hour to subdue all resistance outside the fort and capture a number of prisoners. But those inside continued the fight. Using a loud-hailer, and speaking in French and English, their troop commander Charlie Pollitt advised the defenders that they had twenty minutes to surrender. If not, they would be bombarded by Allied warships off shore. There was no response.

Pollitt gave a second warning with ten minutes to go, and another at five. The French did not reply. By this point, Barnes and Barnett were crouching at the base of the fort's walls, weapons at the ready. They looked at each other. 'He's got to be joking,' said Barnett. 'They wouldn't shell us while we are here!'

Realising his men's predicament, Pollitt gave the order to pull back. But it was too late. The first two naval shells burst in a field nearby, sending a cascade of soil high into the sky. The next two explosions were much closer. 'The navy's finding its range!' joked a Commando. Barnes and Barnett ran down the hill and across some low ground while shells detonated all around them. They eventually took cover in a roadside ditch.

Begun at 10.40 a.m., the bombardment continued for an hour, killing a French child, whose lifeless body was carried from a small farm building by its screaming mother, and wounding two Commandos. But it failed to dislodge the fort's defenders who refused to submit.[13]

Elsewhere, the other four troops of No. 1 Commando, under the overall command of Major Kevin Trevor, had captured the village of Jean Bart, a French barracks and a signal station. But their main objective, a large fortress on Cap Matifou with four emplaced guns known as Batterie de Lazaret, was proving as tough a nut to crack as Fort d'Estrées. Trevor's new plan was for his Commandos to assault both targets after a combined air and naval bombardment. Fort d'Estrées was targeted first with shells from the cruiser *Bermuda* and bombs dropped by Albacore dive-bombers from the carrier *Invincible*.[14]

The pounding went on for more than an hour. When it was over, mortar shells put down a smoke screen to cover the Commandos' assault. The plan at the fort was for part of No. 6 Troop to cross some barbed wire, drop into the moat and use lightweight aluminium ladders to climb up the other side and over the battlements. Once in, they would lower the drawbridge to admit the rest of the troop.

Led by Captain Pollitt, and carrying their ladders, Barnes and the other attackers quickly crossed the wire and approached the moat. They were about to drop into it when machine guns opened up and Pollitt shouted, 'Get back! Get back!'

The French had built firing slits into the inner wall of the moat that would have taken a heavy toll had the Commandos gone any further. Pollitt's quick thinking had saved them. He intended to launch a frontal attack on the drawbridge after dark. But he was overruled by Trevor who ordered No. 6 Troop to assist the assault on Batterie de Lazaret, which with its sophisticated range-finding equipment and searchlights posed a serious threat to Allied shipping.

At 5 p.m., supported by an American self-propelled 105mm howitzer, and again masked by smoke, the Commandos launched a two-pronged attack on the battery. One force, including No. 6 Troop, advanced on the main gates; while a second attacked the back wall which, in places, had 'badly crumbled' and was patched with rows of barbed wire.

Barnes was scrambling up the slope towards the main gates – and wondering what he would do when he got there – when they swung open and a uniformed figure appeared with a white flag. The Commandos brushed past him and ran into the fort to find 'little resistance and in quick time the big guns were secured'. After the commandant and fifty French marines had surrendered, Trevor's men were surprised to find an even larger number of marines locked in a cellar because they did not want to fight the Allies.

The Commandos made a final attempt to capture Fort d'Estrées that evening by shooting at its drawbridge with a field gun. But the shells had little effect on the massive wooden structure and the attack was called off at 8 p.m. Barnes and his troop spent the night in a nearby village, dozing in deckchairs they had found in a cellar.[15] Meanwhile, Algiers itself had fallen back under Vichy control.

10

'Money for old rope'

Algeria and Gibraltar, 8–11 November 1942

A s at Oran and Casablanca, the Allied landings at Algiers had been only partially successful. There were three zones of attack: A and B sectors, 20 and 6 miles to the west of Algiers respectively; and C sector to the east where 'Tag' Barnes and half of No. 1 Commando had landed. In picking these sectors, the Eastern Assault Force had not been able to use the best landing beach on the eastern shore of Algiers Bay because it lay within range of coastal guns.

At A Beach, farthest from the objective, around 7,000 men of the British 11th Infantry Brigade – disguised as Americans – had taken advantage of a clear night and a moderate swell to get ashore without incident. Like the US Rangers at Arzew, they had been immeasurably assisted by the fine work of Nigel Willmott's 'Party Inhuman' which marked the beaches with beacons and piloted in the landing craft from motor launches. Before daylight, the men of the 11th had secured their main objectives: two key road bridges to the east and the settlements of Castiglione, Koléa and Zéralda. Units of the French army at Koléa barracks told the British they had been ordered not to resist.[1]

The 10,400-strong force landing at B Beach was chiefly from the reinforced US 168th Infantry, assisted by part of No. 1 Commando and all of No. 6 Commando. The former had landed and achieved their main objective – the capture of a battery in the Fort de Sidi Ferruch

on the western flank of the sector – by 3 a.m. But their comrades in
No. 6 Commando, with objectives much closer to Algiers, had not
fared so well, mainly because many of their landing craft were unsea-
worthy or broke down.

Among the troops slated to take part in the attack on No. 6
Commando's main objective, the powerful coastal battery of Fort
Duperré in the city's northern suburbs, was Private Francis Bowen, a
regular who had served in the Buffs. In fact Bowen, a French speaker,
had volunteered to accompany Captain Davis, his troop commander,
to the fort gates, under a flag of truce, to help negotiate the surrender
of the garrison. He was hoping the French would respect a white flag,
particularly after Davis had told one of his men: 'If they shoot us, you
can really let them have it.'

Bowen's landing craft had caught fire on the run in to the coast,
wasting at least an hour before the blaze was brought under control
and the engine restarted. The delay was compounded when the
Merchant Navy crew lost their way and tried to return to the troop
ship. They changed their minds when Captain Davis drew his revolver.
Bowen recorded:

Eventually landed on a rocky promontory where there was a little
fishing-harbour just as it was getting light. Landed with a view to
finding out where we were, and when we had discovered that we were
about 17 miles from where we should be, returned to where we had
left the [landing craft] to find the birds had flown! Met some French
soldiers, who offered no resistance, and whom we disarmed and told
to go home. One laughed and said he was from Montpelier, so that
he would sooner come with us, after he had discovered we were British.
Actually quite a few people mistook us for Germans at first, with these
strange American helmets we were ordered to wear.

Marching along some tramlines, they reached the cement works at
the foot of Fort Duperré at 10.30 a.m., six and a half hours late. After

a wash and a rest, they were ordered to relieve No. 3 Troop which had been besieging the fort. Before they could take up their positions, they were told to wait because 'the French had been given an ultimatum to surrender, failing which they would be dive-bombed'.

The whole bay was spread out beneath them, a 'wonderful sight, with the blue sea, big grey transports everywhere, warships in the distance, and landing-craft dashing about everywhere'. The importance of their mission was brought home to them every time the fort's big guns fired with a 'rolling barrel' type of sound as the shells passed overhead and exploded a few seconds later among the shipping. Fortunately, the accuracy of the gunnery was poor.

As elsewhere, the French ignored the ultimatum and at 4 p.m. nine Albacores of the Fleet Air Arm bombed the fort. Bowen and his troop were moving forward to attack when the garrison surrendered. 'Money for old rope,' he wrote in his diary, 'as far as our Troop was concerned, but 3 Troop apparently had a couple of casualties. Had to escort an ammunition truck into Algiers town, and spent the night at the Police Station, where I received a most friendly reception.'[2]

Two battalions of the 168th Infantry, due to reach the high ground above Algiers before daylight, were also disrupted by swells and poor navigation, and most landed much farther west than intended. Components of each battalion were scattered over 15 miles of coast.[3] Even so, Lieutenant Colonel Edward J. Doyle of the 1/168th aggressively led part of his battalion through sporadic resistance as far as the western outskirts of Algiers. Fired on from higher ground, Doyle teamed up with elements of the 2/168th and 3/168th to force back the French. While the latter were distracted, Doyle and about twenty-five of his men advanced into Algiers to capture the governor general's Palais d'Eté by 3 p.m. They went on to secure the police HQ and snare the German consul, before the intrepid Doyle was shot and killed by French snipers.[4]

The chief reason for the stiffening of French resistance in and around Algiers was, of course, Koeltz's sacking of the traitor Mast and the countermanding of his orders to assist the invasion. Mast, meanwhile, had gone to one of the B sector beaches to contact the Allies and so avoided arrest. Instead he met up with Lieutenant Colonel Tom Trevor – the commanding officer of No. 1 Commando and cousin of Major Kevin Trevor whose men, 'Tag' Barnes included, had landed to the east of Algiers – and persuaded him to divert from his original orders and use French transport to capture Blida airfield, 25 miles south of Algiers. Initially opposed by the French garrison, which was receiving contradictory orders, Trevor waited until British reinforcements from 11th Brigade had arrived before agreeing that the French would remain in possession of the airfield, but it could not be used for warlike purposes by either side: Allied planes could land but not take off again.

By the end of 8 November, therefore, the Allied forces landing west of Algiers had achieved all their major objectives bar the occupation of the great city itself. This omission had a knock-on effect on the daring if poorly planned Allied attempt that morning to capture the Algiers port by coup de main, an operation known as Terminal. It differed from Reservist, the disastrous attempt to capture the port of Oran that same day, in that the anti-sabotage force – 74 Royal Navy personnel and 662 men from the 2/135th and 3/135th Infantry, 34th Division, mostly Minnesotans led by the bullish Lieutenant Colonel Edwin T. Swenson, a craggy-faced former assistant warden of the state penitentiary – was transported in two Royal Navy destroyers, *Broke* and *Malcolm*, that were expected to pierce the barrier booms and discharge their troops and naval boarding parties at the Quai de Dieppe and the Grande Môle. Teams would then secure key points in and around the port, and thus ensure it could quickly be used by Allied shipping. The advantages Terminal had over Reservist were that its assault ships had greater firepower, and its target was not as formidably defended. But essentially it was the same plan.

As the two destroyers approached, they were spotted and targeted by coastal guns and, in the confusion, twice missed the harbour entrance.

As they came around a third time, *Malcolm* was struck by a shell and set on fire, prompting her skipper to withdraw from the fight with ten killed and twenty-five wounded. *Broke* tried a fourth time and, having easily pierced the chained timber-baulks that made up the barrier, dropped its largely unscathed complement at the Môle Louis Billiard which she had misidentified in the dark as the Grande Môle. Swenson and half his men fanned out, and within a short period of time had captured the mole (albeit the wrong one), the power station and the fuel depot. Encouragingly, the naval boarding parties could see no signs of scuttling or sabotage. But the whole enterprise depended on the early arrival of American relief troops which, for a variety of reasons, were nowhere to be seen, much to Swenson's frustration.

Under heavy fire, *Broke* withdrew at 9.40 a.m. with about sixty assault troops. The rest had either been unwilling, or unable, to respond to her recall siren. They were assisted for a time by Albacore bombers who neutralised the coastal guns at the northern end of the harbour. But gradually the pressure told as Senegalese troops, supported by Renault tanks, closed in for the kill. 'We had Bazookas,' wrote Sergeant Ralph B. Schaps, a 22-year-old machine gunner in 2/135th Infantry's H Company, 'but the tanks never came within range so they were of no help. Soon two more tanks were observed coming in our direction and still we heard no firing from other areas so it was presumed that they were running out of ammunition and something had been snafu-ed.'[*]

At 12.30 p.m, with his men almost out of ammunition, Swenson surrendered. Among the casualties was a good friend of Schaps, Private First Class Mel Lien, a medic who was killed saving a wounded officer's life. He was awarded a posthumous Distinguished Service Cross, the US Army's second highest award for valour. Schaps was among the prisoners who were surprisingly well treated. 'We stacked arms in a park,' he recalled, 'and in a couple of hours we were drinking wine in a bistro.'[5]

---

[*] SNAFU was American military shorthand for 'Situation Normal, All F****d Up'.

The other assault landings to the east of Algiers, meanwhile – by 5,700 men of the US 39th Infantry, supported by 300 men from 'Tag' Barnes' No. 1 Commando – had largely gone to plan, though various units were jumbled up and in the wrong place. Once the 3/39th had straightened itself out, however, it quickly set off along the coastal road to the resort village of Fort de l'Eau, a distance of six miles, where it was engaged by French infantry supported by three Renault tanks, and brought to a halt.

Its sister battalion, the 1/39th, had been tasked with the capture of the Maison Blanche airfield, 10 miles to the southwest. This it managed after some French light tanks had provided only token resistance. The airfield was formally surrendered at 8.30 a.m., but fog delayed the arrival of eighteen Hurricanes from the RAF's 43rd Squadron for two more hours. Even then, the airfield's use was hampered by the slow arrival of RAF support vehicles, supplies and ground crews, the victims of deteriorating weather, a pile-up of landing craft and beaches too soft for heavy equipment.[6]

Observing the chaos on one Charlie Sector beach was Lieutenant Commander Willmott, commanding the 'Party Inhuman' teams who had guided in the assault craft. Earlier he had 'spent a nightmare three-quarters of an hour threading' his pilot vessel 'through a confused swarm of lost boats, hailing and rounding up craft for his sector'. He then set a course inshore, calculating from the North Star, and eventually led the boats to the right beach at around 3.30 a.m.

Between sporadic German air attacks, the beach was invaded by Arabs on the hunt for goods and supplies. Helping themselves to unguarded stores, they carted them up the cliffs where some were intercepted by a revolver-wielding Willmott. It was, he mused, a good way of getting supplies up from the beach. Later, from the terrace of a clifftop villa, he had a bird's-eye view of the chaos below: the water-line strewn with wrecked landing craft; troops in the wrong place; and, thanks to worsening weather, support waves still to arrive. He also witnessed, later that day, a German aerial attack on Allied ships anchored off Charlie Sector that badly damaged the destroyer *Cowdray* and immobilised the troop transport *Leedstown*.★

Thank heaven, thought Willmott, the invasion was largely unopposed. If the French had defended the cliffs, it would have been a massacre. He was proud of the role his men had played in getting the troops ashore. Yet he knew they could and should have done more: particularly in the realm of pre-invasion beach reconnaissance. That would be, Willmott was convinced, a prerequisite if future amphibious operations were not to end in disaster.

A month after the Torch landings, Willmott was tasked with forming a new specialist canoe-borne unit for beach reconnaissance, marking and pilotage. It was known as the Combined Operations Pilotage Parties (COPP), and would play a vital role in the success of all future large-scale amphibious landings, including D-Day. Willmott is acknowledged today as one of the founding fathers of the modern Special Boat Service.[7]

Shortly after 4 p.m. on 8 November, with his troops holding the heights west of Algiers, the highways approaching the city from the east and west, the airfields at Blida and Maison Blanche, and many of the principal coastal batteries, Major General Charles S. Ryder, commanding the Eastern Task Force, was informed that Juin was ready to negotiate. Less welcome was the news that Juin had authorisation from Darlan to discuss a cessation of hostilities in Algiers, but not elsewhere in French North Africa.

The two generals met at Juin's headquarters in Fort l'Empereur, after Ryder and two aides had been driven through the lines at Lambiridi in the Frenchman's official car. They agreed that hostilities would cease, and control of the city pass to the Americans, at 8 p.m. French troops would return to their barracks, yet keep their arms

---

★ Crippled by this aerial attack, *Leedstown* was sunk the following day by a U-boat. She lost 59 of her complement of 163.

pending a formal armistice that would be thrashed out the following morning. Ryder then returned to *Bulolo*, his command ship, to keep Eisenhower up to date, and to request an armistice on the generous terms prepared for a token French resistance.[8]

Back in his underground headquarters at Gibraltar, meanwhile, Eisenhower and his staff had received only fragmentary news of the landings. But, as the day wore on, it became increasingly clear that the early 'encouraging reports' had been superseded by news of fierce French resistance at Casablanca, Oran and even Algiers.

On the plus side, General Henri Giraud had now agreed to participate in Operation Torch on the basis that he would assume the civil administration of French North Africa and take command of all French forces who might rally to the Allied cause, while Eisenhower retained command of all Anglo-American troops. But Giraud had also shown how completely out of touch he was with military realities by insisting that the Allies invade southern France within two months. 'He could not see,' wrote Eisenhower, 'the need of North Africa as a base – the need for establishing ourselves firmly and strongly in that region before we could successfully invade the southern portion of Europe.'[9]

The news that Amiral de la flotte Darlan was in Algiers, and wanted to negotiate, was a political complication that Ike could have done without. He had agreed to put Giraud in charge of French forces. Now there had appeared on the scene, 'suddenly and unexpectedly', a rival source of authority, second only to Marshal Pétain, 'who could in fact decide whether any French forces at all in North Africa would come over in an orderly fashion and join the Allies'.[10]

The solution was to fly Giraud and Ike's deputy Major General Mark Clark to Algiers the following morning to 'make some kind of agreement' with Darlan to end the fighting and, if possible, persuade the French to turn against the Axis. Giraud, for his part, had agreed to find a place for Darlan in his command structure if in return the admiral could get the French fleet to come over to the Allied side.

The British prime minister had emphasised the value of just such a deal before Ike's departure from England. 'If I could meet Darlan,' Chuchill told Eisenhower, 'much as I hate him, I would cheerfully crawl on my hands and knees for a mile if by doing so I could get him to bring that fleet of his into the circle of Allied forces.'[11]

Giraud departed for Algiers by plane on the morning of 9 November. Clark was due to follow in a second plane soon after, but the weather closed in and his departure was delayed until shortly after noon.[12] Giraud's frosty reception by the French authorities, meanwhile, had been a 'terrible blow' to Allied expectations. 'He was completely ignored,' wrote Eisenhower. 'He made a broadcast, announcing assumption of leadership of French North Africa and directing French forces to cease fighting against the Allies, but his speech had no effect whatsoever.'[13]

Accompanied by thirteen Spitfires, and flying at an altitude of 700 feet, Clark's plane landed at Maison Blanche airfield at 5 p.m. on the 9th, just as a dozen German bombers flew over in the direction of Algiers harbour. One was shot down by a Spitfire, but others braved a 'solid wall' of anti-aircraft fire to attack ships in the bay, the 'orange balls of fire looking like strings of Christmas-tree lights across the sky'. Soon after, a second bomber was hit by flak over the airfield and seemed to be heading exactly for the spot where Clark's ground transport had stopped when it 'exploded into thousands of pieces at an altitude of about 1000 feet'.

At the grand Hotel St George – built in 1514 as a palace for the Dey of Algiers, and surrounded by a lush botanical garden – Clark was met by a haggard and grim Major General Ryder who told him: 'I'm glad you're here. I've stalled them off about as long as I can.' Clark later spoke to Giraud who confirmed that his relations with the French officers in North Africa were 'none too good', and that he had decided to go into hiding and 'await developments'.

Next morning, 10 November, Clark met Darlan and Juin in a small room off the hotel foyer. He had stationed a platoon of American infantry outside the building, 'mostly for psychological effect' and to show the French he 'meant business'. Taking his place at the head of the table, he had to his left Darlan, 'a little man with watery blue eyes and petulant lips', and to his right Juin, who would later become one of his best friends but who, at the time, was 'no help' in his negotiations. Returning home that evening, Juin would tell his wife that he had been dealing with a 'big American who does nothing but shout and pound the table'.[14]

Before the meeting, Clark had been authorised by Ike to strike a deal with Darlan without recourse to Washington DC or London. He therefore told Darlan that he would be recognised as the chief civil and military authority in French North Africa if he agreed to an armistice. When Darlan said that only Marshal Pétain could issue such an order – the 'traditional French demand for a cloak of legality over any action they might take', as Eisenhower put it – Clark gave him half an hour to decide one way or the other. After much agonising, Darlan agreed to order a general cease-fire and, in the name of the Marshal, assumed complete authority throughout French North Africa and ordered all officials to remain on duty.[15]

In Vichy, Pétain was in two minds how to respond. Maxime Weygand, his army chief, and Amiral Auphan, his Minister of Marine, were urging him to approve the cease-fire. Taking the opposite view was Pierre Laval, his pro-German chief minister, who had been summoned to Munich for talks with Hitler and the Italian foreign minister, Count Ciano. 'If Hitler believed the French could not be trusted in North Africa,' said Captain Édouard Archambaud, one of Auphan's aides, at Pétain's post-war trial, 'Laval would have no bargaining position to prevent German retaliation against mainland France.'

Swayed by Laval's threat to resign, Pétain disavowed Darlan's actions and replaced him as head of the French armed forces with Général d'armée Charles Noguès, Resident General of French Morocco. According to Archambaud, Pétain later sent an explanatory secret message to Darlan that read: 'Understand that the order [to resist] was necessary for the negotiations that are going on [with the Germans].'[16]

In response to his sacking, Darlan tried to backtrack by rescinding his cease-fire order, but this Clark 'would not allow'. He placed Darlan under armed guard.

What simplified matters for Darlan was the news on 11 November that, despite Laval's efforts to reassure the Führer that the French could be trusted to defend North Africa, Hitler had ordered German troops to invade Vichy to protect the Mediterranean seaboard. Ten divisions swept across southern France without opposition, in accordance with plans for Operation Anton which had been prepared in May. At the same time, six Italian divisions marched into eastern France.

Because Germany had now violated the 1940 armistice agreement, said Darlan, he was ready to cooperate freely with the Americans. This included, at Clark's insistence, the issuing of an order from Darlan to the senior admiral at Toulon to bring the French fleet to North Africa. He also agreed to telephone Amiral Jean-Pierre Esteva, the Resident General in Tunisia, to instruct him to fight the Germans with all means available.[17]

Eisenhower and Clark would later be heavily criticised by the British and American press for dealing with the notorious collaborator Darlan, in preference to a true patriot like Giraud. For Clark, the explanation was simple. He wrote:

> As Ike's deputy, I was charged with fighting a war, or, more specifically with preventing a war against the French and getting on as rapidly as humanly possible with the war against the Axis in Tunisia. That meant I was trying to save American, British, and French lives – a great many of them. That meant that every day, every hour, was important . . . And to carry out this mission I was ready to deal with anybody who could do the job.[18]

Pétain, meanwhile, had responded to the news of the German invasion by issuing a message of protest that was broadcast over the radio at regular intervals. Many of Pétain's advisors now urged him to leave for North Africa. 'I shall never understand,' said Charles de Gaulle later, 'why the Marshal did not go to Algiers in November 1942. The French in Algeria would have cheered him, the Americans would have embraced him, the English would have followed him ... The Marshal would have made a triumphant return to Paris on a white charger.'

Instead, remaining in France, he doubled down on his earlier decisions to allow German planes to fly over French territory and use Tunisian airbases (8 November), and German troops to disembark at Tunis (10 November), with an unambiguous telegram to Esteva in Tunis on 11 November: 'The Marshal has decided to continue the struggle against Anglo-Saxon aggression within the limits of our possibilities.'[19]

II

'They had better hurry up'

Tunisia and Algeria, 8–16 November 1942

THE CITY-PORT OF TUNIS has long been a prize for invading armies. Nestled in the northeastern corner of Tunisia, it guards a natural choke point in the Mediterranean between the northernmost tip of the African continent and the island of Sicily. This vital strategic location, at the base of the 90-mile-wide Sicilian Narrows, the gateway to Europe and the eastern Mediterranean, is the reason this pictur-esque city, sprawled across the hilly eastern shore of Lake Tunis, a natural harbour, has been fought over since ancient times.

The city's foreign conquerors include the Phoenicians, who also took neighbouring Carthage (the ruins of which now lie in Tunis's northern suburbs), the Romans, the Ummayids, the Byzantines and the Ottomans. The varied architecture reflects all these influences. But it was the arrival of the French, who declared a protectorate over Tunisia in 1881, that led to a rapid expansion in both the size of the city and its population.

By the turn of the twentieth century, Tunis had a dual identity: at its heart was the old town or Medina, a rambling collection of mosques, palaces and narrow streets dating back to the seventh century AD; and built on reclaimed land to the east was the French-influenced Ville Nouvelle with its broad avenues and leafy suburbs inhabited by Europeans and a large Jewish community. Forming a bridge between the two, at the eastern approach to the Medina, was the French Resident General's mansion at 2 Place de la Résidence.

The occupant of the mansion in late 1942, and the man upon whose shoulders rested Allied hopes of a quick victory in Tunisia, was 62-year-old Amiral Jean-Pierre Esteva. A native of Rheims in Champagne, he had entered the French naval academy in 1898 and later fought in the Dardanelles campaign, taught at the École supérieure de la Marine and was a pioneer of naval aviation. Short and impeccably groomed, with a neat square beard, Esteva was a bachelor whose ascetic lifestyle – rising early to attend mass, and eating just toast and an orange before noon – had given rise to his nickname the Monk. Resident General since 1940, he was trusted by Pétain and regarded as a safe pair of hands, a talented if unimaginative administrator.

Like Juin in Algiers, he had been woken early on 8 November by the American consul general, Hooker A. Doolittle, and told that swarms of Allied troops would soon be in Tunis. 'They had better hurry up,' said Esteva coolly, 'because the others will be here within forty-eight hours.'[1]

By 'others' he meant, of course, the Germans. Yet Esteva, a Vichy loyalist keen to do Pétain's bidding, had underestimated the speed with which Hitler's forces would react. Early on 9 November, the Vichy government informed the Germans that French airbases in Tunisia and in the eastern department of Algeria were available to the Luftwaffe. At this stage, the invitation did not extend to the Italians, a veto reiterated by Esteva at noon. Already the first Luftwaffe fighters had touched down at El Aouina airfield, northeast of Tunis, at 10.55 a.m. Dive-bombers and air transports soon followed. The latter brought German paratroopers and the personal headquarters guard of Generalfeldmarschall Albert Kesselring, Wehrmacht Commander-in-Chief South.[2]

A jovial 57-year-old Bavarian, known by his soldiers as 'Smiling Albert', Kesselring had commanded Luftwaffe air fleets in Poland, France and Russia, and during the Battle of Britain. He had been shot down no fewer than five times. In late 1941, he was sent to Italy to command all German armed forces in the Mediterranean – bar Rommel's German-Italian Panzer Army in North Africa – and had been wrestling with the difficulties of coalition warfare ever since. He had anticipated the Allied invasion of North Africa, but his warnings, like those of Warlimont, were ignored. When he was proved right – and was given a 'free hand in Tunisia' by Hitler himself – Kesselring knew the importance of swift action. He wrote later:

If the Allied invasion army were not opposed by fresh German forces it would mean the total loss of the German-Italian army in Africa. For there would be no hope of getting them out with nothing to stop the combined forces of the Eighth Army and the invasion army with their strength in the air and their undisputed supremacy at sea. Further, it would mean the surrender of the whole of Tripolitania, the peaceful occupation of the French colonies and the capitulation without a fight of all effectives there; the Allies would capture an ideal springboard for a future landing in Sicily and Italy in the early months of 1943, and with it probably achieve the elimination of Italy as Axis partner.

With so much at stake, Kesselring realised that 'everything must be done to postpone a sequel to the invasion of a kind which might decide the war'. But as no planning had been done by either the OKW or the Comando Supremo, he had to improvise.

His first priority was to capture the harbours and airfields between Algiers and Tunis, and also to build up a bridgehead 'covering Bizerta and the city of Tunis, in which the behaviour of French troops of the Bey [of Tunisia] might prove decisive'.[3] But no sooner had Kesselring's headquarters guard and a reinforced battalion of paratroopers landed at El Aouina than they were hemmed in by a cordon of French troops and armoured cars. The standoff continued until a senior German deputation persuaded Amiral Esteva to remove the cordon. By dusk, ninety transport planes had landed and German troops were singing

'Lili Marlene' as they dug in along the Carthage road.⁴ 'To begin with,' wrote Kesselring, 'relations between the French and German troops were excellent. Our parachutists went out on patrol against the enemy in French armoured cars.'⁵

Eisenhower would later partially excuse Esteva's actions by noting that he had been placed in an impossible position because of the 'length of time consumed in the negotiations' with Darlan in Algiers. 'This created uncertainty on the part of Admiral Esteva,' wrote Ike, 'who, while informed of the nature of the conversations then going on in Algiers, was also in receipt of orders from Vichy to resist the Allies and, we were told, to admit the Germans into his area.'⁶

Further exculpation was provided after the war by Général de division George Barré, commanding the French army in Tunisia, who claimed in a letter to Eisenhower that, even before the agreement between Darlan and the Allies, he had 'disobeyed an order from Admiral Darlan received in Tunis on 9 November at 7.30 a.m . . . to collaborate militarily with the Germans', and that Esteva 'joined with me in my disobedience, without any indecision or hesitation'.★⁷

It is true that Esteva's men never fought side by side with the Germans in Tunisia; and that many of them, Barré included, would later join forces with the Allies. But they also, in those crucial early days, made only minor attempts to prevent the Germans from establishing a bridgehead in Tunisia that would prove a serious thorn in the Allies' flesh, and condemn a million men from both sides to, as one historian put it, 'seven months of torment'.⁸ Esteva's excuse at his trial in France in 1945 was that, with only 15,000 men under his command, and the Allies too far away, he was not in a position to oppose the Axis. He was found guilty of treason, nonetheless, and sentenced to life in prison with forced labour.

★ When Barré wrote this letter, in 1949, Esteva was in Clairvaux prison serving a life sentence with forced labour for treason against the French state. Terminally ill, he was pardoned in 1950 and died a few months later in Rheims.

Kesselring's determination to build up Axis forces in Tunisia as quickly as possible was supported by Hitler who told Ciano, during their meeting on 9 November, that Vichy's refusal to allow Italian forces to land was tantamount to refusing his demands per se, since Germany lacked both the materiel and manpower to do the job on its own. Moreover, he added, the Axis position in Tunisia could only be defended if a convoy was allowed to land heavy equipment, including some of the new Mark VI 'Tiger' tanks which were on their way to Italy.

The first Italian planes – a squadron of twenty-eight Macchi 202 fighters – reached Tunisia without French permission, on the morning of 10 November.[9] This breached an earlier agreement between the Germans and the French, and was done without Kesselring's approval. He complained to the Comando Supremo, and the squadron was flown back to Sardinia. But it was too late. Kesselring was convinced that, 'but for this incident, Pétain's order, which later came in to the effect that the French colonial troops should march with us, would have been implemented to our advantage.'[10]

Even so, the French did not try to prevent the arrival of more Axis troops by plane and, from 12 November, by sea when two Italian transport vessels reached Bizerte in the evening carrying 340 men, 17 tanks, 4 guns, 55 trucks, 40 tons of ammunition and 101 tons of fuel. Opposition was briefly ordered by Vice Amiral Louis Derrien, commanding French naval forces in Tunisia, who told his subordinates at Bizerte: 'The enemy is the German and the Italian . . . Blaze away with all your heart against the foe of 1940.' But he soon changed his mind when contradictory orders arrived from Vichy. 'November 10 (noon), we fight the Germans,' he wrote bitterly. 'November 11 (night) we fight nobody.'[11]

The officer chosen by Kesselring to lead Axis troops in Tunisia was 50-year-old General der Panzertruppen Walter Nehring, the son of a West Prussian landowner who had commanded a panzer division in Russia – where it was said to have committed war crimes – and, from

May 1942, the Afrika Korps in North Africa. Nehring was on his way to meet Rommel in Benghazi, having recovered from wounds sustained during the Battle of Alam Halfa in Egypt, when he was redirected by Kesselring to fly to Tunis and assess the military situation. Narrowly surviving a crash landing, he made 'a reconnaissance tour around Tunis, had conferences with the German ambassador and local commanders and Admiral Esteva'. He did not meet Général de division Barré who was in the process of withdrawing the bulk of his troops to Medjez el Bab, a dusty market town to the southwest of the capital that straddled the Medjerda river and acted as a gateway to the rugged north–south mountain chain known as the Eastern Dorsal.

During the night of 14 November, Nehring flew back to Italy and reported to Kesselring. There had been, he told the Generalfeldmarschall, no proper attempt to organise the defence of Tunis, which was easy prey to an Allied attack. Without rapid reinforcement it would soon fall. Kesselring promised 'new and sufficient' troops, which satisfied Nehring. The first emergency act was to fly out infantrymen armed only with rifles, and officers 'not fit and trained for front line service'. His 'best man', Colonel Stolz – who later became liaison officer to the Italian units – he met by chance on a train.

When Nehring returned to Tunis by air on 16 November, and set up his headquarters in the American consulate, his entire staff consisted of his aide-de-camp Salla and an orderly. The force at his disposal, meanwhile, still numbered only about 5,000 men, but it included two Italian battalions in Bizerte and Tunis (each of 800 men); two battalions of the excellent German 5. *Fallschirmjäger-Regiment* (5th Parachute Regiment), under Oberstleutnant Walter Koch, a highly decorated veteran of the Blitzkrieg and Crete campaigns; and another superb airborne unit, the 11. *Fallschirm-Pionier* (11th Parachute Engineer Battalion), commanded by Major Rudolf Witzig who, as a young *Oberleutnant* in Koch's airborne task force, had planned and led the daring capture of Fort Eben-Emael in Belgium in 1940, a feat for which he was awarded the Knight's Cross. Nehring also had the use of a fighter group in Tunisia and Stukas based in Sicily, but only a few artillery pieces, tanks and anti-tank guns.[12]

This build-up of troops and supplies had been briefly threatened by the actions of Barré and Derrien, the senior French commanders in Tunisia, who had ordered the sinking of vessels at the approaches to Tunis and Bizerte harbours to deny their use to Axis ships. But with the aid of special Italian port engineers, Bizerte had been cleared for use by 12 November and Tunis three days later. Presented with a fait accompli, Barré had authorised the use of Sidi Ahmed airfield near Bizerte, as well as the port, to prevent an armed clash.

Barré had then partly redeemed himself in Allied eyes by acting on Général de corps d'armée Juin's orders to withdraw his troops, around 9,000 in total, to defensive positions west of Bizerte and Tunis at specific places in the Tunisian hills and the Medjerda river valley. Not so Derrien – due to retire in a month after forty-two years' service – who had defied Juin by keeping a proportion of Barré's Tunis Division in Bizerte with his naval troops to defend the coast and operate the coastal batteries. As if that was not bad enough, Derrien then caved in to German threats and surrendered his 6,000-strong force on 14 November. 'I shall be known,' he had accurately predicted two days earlier, 'as the admiral who delivered Bizerte to the Germans.'[13]

Nehring estimated that an Allied force of 70,000 men with heavy equipment would soon be heading in his direction, with the more mobile elements already on the move. To counteract this, he had been promised the 10th Panzer and Hermann Göring Divisions from France and the new 334th Infantry Division, then being organised in Germany. They would be supplemented by an Italian corps headquarters and two divisions. But it would take many weeks for all these troops to arrive and, in the meantime, he knew he had to take the offensive. He therefore ordered a three-pronged advance to expand the bridgehead west towards Algeria, and the Allied forces: Witzig's 11th Parachute Engineer Battalion to seize the coastal town of Tabarka, close to the

Algerian border; the 'best Italian groups' to advance on the lateral road from Mateur, a few miles southwest of Bizerte, to Béja; and the two battalions of Koch's German 5th Parachute Regiment to move down the road from Tunis to Medjez el Bab. Nehring would also make every attempt to persuade the French troops at Medjez, under Barré, not to oppose the German advance.

The remaining Italian troops were to concentrate south of Tunis to protect Nehring's right flank, while all the planes under his command would attempt to slow the Allied advance by bombing and strafing its mobile columns.[14]

As Nehring's scratch force prepared to fight a delaying action close to the border with Algeria, Allied forces were closing in from the west. They were led by Lieutenant General Kenneth Anderson who had been tasked with moving his British First Army eastwards from Algiers without delay to secure Tunis and Bizerte. That this would be far from straightforward was brought home to Anderson on 10 November when a French air force officer, who had flown to Algiers from Tunis, informed him that '40 German bombers had landed at Tunis airport that morning'. This was confirmed the following day 'by information that Admiral Esteva had agreed in an interview with the German General Nehring not to oppose the Axis entry into Tunisia; also that further enemy transports and planes were constantly arriving in Tunis and Bizerte'.[15]

The selection of the diminutive 50-year-old Anderson for this vital mission was a curious one. A dour and dogged Scotsman with thin lips, small eyes and unkempt grey hair, he had been given the ironic nickname of 'Sunshine'. Eisenhower would later praise his 'devotion to duty' and 'readiness to subordinate himself in the common good'; he was less impressed with Anderson's tendency to get bogged down in detail, at the expense of the big picture, and his abrasive approach to subordinates.[16]

Born in India, the son of a railway engineer, Anderson had won a Military Cross (MC)★ for 'conspicuous gallantry' on the first day of the Battle of the Somme when he was shot in the leg, one of the 4th Tyneside Scottish's nineteen officer casualties (and 629 in total). He attended Staff College at Quetta in the late 1920s, but did not excel, with one instructor questioning his 'capacity to develop much'. He did better when war broke out, commanding the 11th Brigade during the British Expeditionary Force's ill-fated 1940 campaign, and taking temporary charge of the 3rd Division when the then Major General Bernard Montgomery was promoted to corps commander. He owed this promotion to Alan Brooke, the departing corps commander, who thought highly of both Monty and Anderson. After he had become Chief of the Imperial General Staff in late 1941, Brooke promoted Anderson to temporary lieutenant general and gave him the Eastern Command. But Anderson lacked experience of commanding large formations in battle, and was only assigned to the First Army for Operation Torch after the original commander, Edmond Schreiber, developed kidney disease and the first and second choice replacements, Lieutenant Generals Sir Harold Alexander and Sir Bernard Montgomery, were made Commander-in-Chief Middle East Command and General Officer Commanding (GOC) Eighth Army respectively in early August 1942.

Montgomery's switch had been prompted by the untimely death of William 'Strafer' Gott who was about to take command of the Eighth Army in Egypt when his transport plane was shot down in flames on 7 August. Only later would it occur to Brooke that divine providence was at work. 'I am convinced,' he wrote, 'that the whole course of the war might well have been altered if Gott had been in command of the 8th Army. In his tired condition I do not think that he would have had the energy and vitality to stage and fight this battle

---

★ The third-level gallantry award, after the VC and DSO, for British and Commonwealth army officers. The navy and air force equivalents were the Distinguished Service Cross (DSC) and Distinguished Flying Cross (DFC).

[Alamein] as Monty did.'[17] The Eighth Army's gain, however, was the First Army's loss: Anderson – as we shall discover – was not in Montgomery's league.

Having taken over from Ryder in Algiers on 9 November, Anderson's priority was to get his men on the move. He had, however, plenty of disadvantages: the relatively small number of troops immediately at his disposal (essentially four British brigades and a mixture of American units); a lack of transport; a small window of opportunity, as the winter rains normally began in early December; and the uncertain attitude of the French.

Small wonder that he feared the consequences if his small advance force suffered a setback. But urged on by Eisenhower – who cabled on the 12th that 'Boldness is now more important than numbers' – he knew that haste was 'the best, indeed the only course'.

The original plan had been to use parachutists and Commandos to seize the airfields at Bône, Bizerte and Tunis on 11, 12 and 13 November. But with French support uncertain, and Axis troops pouring into the area, the latter two operations were cancelled, and the former delayed for twenty-four hours. Instead, a more measured advance from Algiers to Tunis by sea and land, a distance of 560 miles, would be made by the British 78th (Battleaxe) Infantry Division, a formation created specifically for Operation Torch and comprised of three infantry brigades – the 1st (Guards), 11th and 36th – and supporting units. Its commander was 43-year-old Major General Vyvyan Evelegh, a ruddy, gap-toothed officer, known as 'Santa Claus' on account of his generous girth and ready smile, who had yet to command troops in battle. Ambitious and pugnacious, possessed of a loud braying laugh and a tendency to stutter when angry, Evelegh had selected a Crusader battleaxe as the divisional insignia.

On 11 November, part of the 36th Infantry Brigade Group landed without opposition at Bougie, over 100 miles to the east of Algiers. But a heavy swell prevented a second landing at the nearby port of Djedjelli and the airfield was not seized until the 13th by troops advancing overland from Bougie. 'This delay,' wrote Anderson, 'had serious consequences, as before our fighters with petrol and ground staff could be established the Axis bombers sunk three large ships, only partially unloaded, in Bougie harbour, causing heavy losses of equipment and stores urgently needed for the subsequent advance.'[18]

The port and two airfields at Bône, 150 miles east of Bougie, were the targets of a joint seaborne and air operation on 12 November. Transported by two Royal Navy destroyers, the men of No. 6 Commando and the 1st Ranger Battalion sang the Marseillaise as they landed in the harbour at 8 a.m. Expecting tough opposition, they were surprised to be met by a 'guard of honour, headed by a fat little man in an off-white uniform resplendent with gold braid, who insisted on making a speech of welcome'.

Given the job of securing the closest airfield at L'Alelik, in hills overlooking the town, Private Francis Bowen and his troop of No. 6 Commando were nearing the perimeter when they heard the roar of engines and saw, through the drizzle and cloud, about twenty transport planes. Warned that German paratroopers might try to seize the airfield, the Commandos took up firing positions in orange groves and ditches. But they were ordered not to shoot when a Commando spotted a white star on one of the planes and realised they were American Dakotas. 'Just as well,' wrote Bowen, 'for the Paratroops turned out to be our own C Company, 3rd Battalion of the Parachute Regiment. They were as surprised to find us there as we had been to see them dropping out of the overcast sky. The general consensus of opinion was that someone might have warned us!'[19]

The incident was typical of the muddle and confusion that afflicted these early Allied operations. The original intention had been to use only a single battalion of American paratroopers to capture airfields near Oran. But in late September, thanks to the lobbying of Major General 'Boy' Browning, the British airborne advisor to Allied commanders – who was convinced that the conflict would initially be fought 'over great distances' and against 'comparatively light opposition'– the 1st Parachute Brigade was added to Anderson's Order of Battle.[20]

Because of a shortage of aircraft, most of the brigade had gone by sea, with the main body sailing from Greenock in Scotland and arriving at Algiers on 12 November. The only parachutists to fly to North Africa were the headquarters and two rifle companies of the 3rd Parachute Battalion, under the unfortunately named Lieutenant Colonel Geoffrey Pine-Coffin. Delayed by fog, they had finally arrived at Maison Blanche airfield, outside Algiers, at 8 a.m. on 11 November. Pine-Coffin had then been briefed by Anderson himself to capture the two airfields at Bône the following day. There was no mention that Commandos might be in the vicinity.

In the event, Pine-Coffin and his men landed without opposition, though they were scattered over three miles and took time to recover their containers and head for the two airfields. One man was lost to friendly fire and three more when two Dakotas came down in the sea. The drop was far from perfect, but it was certainly timely in that the Germans, with the same idea, had also just dispatched a battalion of *Fallschirmjäger* in Junkers Ju-52 transport planes to occupy the airfields. Arriving too late, they called off their operation and Pine-Coffin and the Commandos were able to consolidate. 'In some ways,' noted the airborne official history, 'it was an example of a perfectly planned airborne operation, in that mobility was exploited to forestall the enemy.'[21]

But Bône, too, was quickly a target for German and Italian planes flying from Sicily, Sardinia and Tunisia. In the afternoon of 13 November, for example, twelve Stukas dive-bombed the town, wrecking the train station and cinema and killing 200 people. Other raids soon smashed eighteen of the port's twenty-two piers. The arrival of twelve RAF Spitfires at L'Alelik airfield threatened to turn the tide. But at least six were destroyed on the ground by German fighters on the 14th.[22]

At this early stage of the campaign, with shorter distances to fly, Axis planes dominated the air. This had tragic consequences for the men of No. 6 Commando as they moved east on a slow train, perched on top of boxes of ammunition placed in open trucks. Shortly after the departure of their two escorting Spitfires, another pair of planes appeared. 'They were optimistically referred-to as Mustangs,' noted Bowen in his diary, 'until one started diving behind the train, and the other sideways to it – by which time it was too late. They machine-gunned the whole length of the train and made a horrible mess, as the wounded and those trying to jump off fell under the moving waggons.'

This short but violent attack by German Messerschmitt Bf 109 fighters was over in seconds and, when the train came to a halt, Bowen could see dead and wounded strewn over 500 yards of track. He and the survivors were ordered to take up defensive positions in the nearby hills. Later, he helped to carry the wounded – some in a 'shocking state, with huge big holes torn in their bodies by cannon shell' – to Arab huts, and to place in sandbags the human remains that included 'legs, arms, hearts, and pieces of body carved up by the wheels just like the meat in a butcher's shop'. The final toll was ten killed and eighteen wounded. 'We were all lucky that the Germans were not firing incendiaries,' wrote Bowen, 'or the whole of that train would have blown up.'[23]

12

The Race for Tunis

Tunisia and Algeria, 16–25 November 1942

O N 16 NOVEMBER, KENNETH Anderson sent General Sir Alan
Brooke an update on the First Army's progress:

My hopes of reaching Tunis & Bizerta before the Boche were completely
dashed when Esteva let them walk in unopposed. Since then it has
been a wild race to gain as much ground to the east before the Boche
can push out to the west. In this rush I have taken great risks – both
in driving on before the French attitude here was settled & while we
were still looking askance at each other, and in running out of reach
of my supplies.

In spite of these difficulties, his advance patrols had got as far as Mateur,
in northern Tunisia, and east of Béja, on the road to Tunis. But with
his neck 'so far stuck out', he had decided to call a halt and 'wait for
the main body to follow'. To do anything else would 'risk a bad setback'. His only hope was that reinforcements would arrive by road, rail
and air 'before the Hun is strong enough to push me back – as only a
small effort on his part is needed to do so'. To confuse the enemy, he
had planned sea and parachute landings to 'give a (false!) appearance of
relentless advance & great strength'.

As for the French, the majority were in his opinion a 'bunch of useless

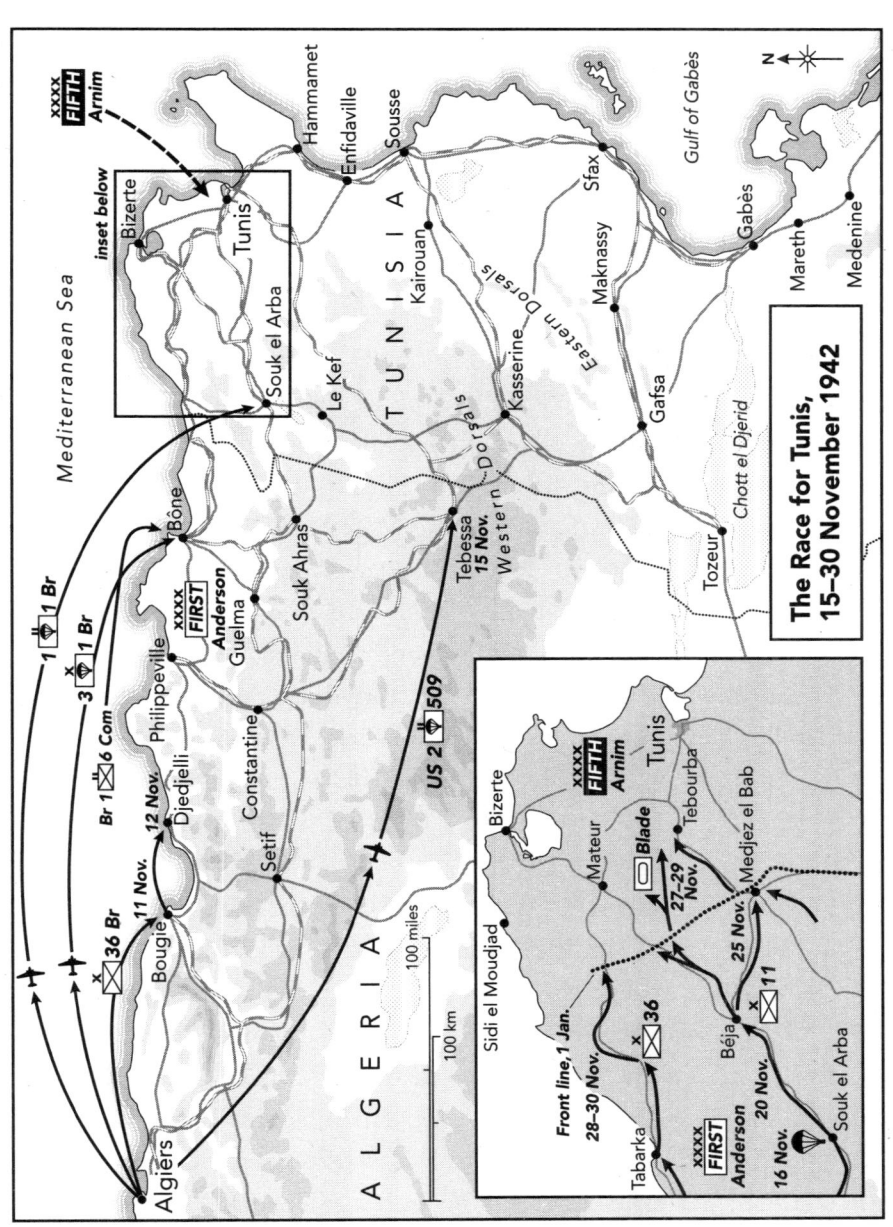

The Race for Tunis,
15–30 November 1942

Mediterranean Sea

Bizerte
Tunis
inset below
Souk el Arba
Hammamet
Enfidaville
Sousse
Le Kef
Sfax
Kairouan
Gulf of Gabès

T U N I S I A

Eastern Dorsals

Maknassy
Kasserine
Gabès
Gafsa
Mareth
Medenine

Chott el Djerid

Western Dorsals

Tebessa
15 Nov.

US 2 509

Tozeur

XXXX
FIFTH
Arnim

1 1 Br
3 1 Br
Br 1 6 Com
36 Br 11 Nov.
12 Nov.

Bône
XXXX
FIRST
Anderson
Guelma
Souk Ahras
Constantine
Philippeville
Djedjelli
Setif
Bougie

A L G E R I A

Algiers

100 miles
100 km

Inset:

Bizerte
Mateur
Tunis
Tebourba
Medjez el Bab

XXXX
FIFTH
Arnim

Blade
27–29
Nov.
25 Nov.
11

Sidi el Moudjad

Front line, 1 Jan.
28–30 Nov.
36
Béja
20 Nov.

Tabarka
XXXX
FIRST
Anderson
16 Nov.
Souk el Arba

stiffs' who were 'willing to "watch" or "keep in touch with" the Hun, but the thought of fighting fills them with terror'. Giraud was 'quite genuine', as were a few others, but the rest were 'weak, self-seeking, selfish and confused'. He would try his best to capture Bizerte 'in one rush', he told Brooke, and if he did not succeed he would pin the enemy 'into a very small bridgehead'.[1]

Tunisia's geography limited Anderson's options. Shaped like a pregnant woman, its northern and eastern boundary (the head and belly) is on the Mediterranean coast, while its inland western border (the back) lies astride the eastern fringe of the Atlas Mountains which extend for 1,200 miles to the coast of Morocco. This portion of the border is easily defensible at the few passes through the mountains. In the south, a lower range of mountains limits any advance from Libya, to the east, through the Gabès Gap. That, in turn, was protected by a series of fortifications known as the Mareth Line which the French had built in the 1930s to deter an Italian invasion. Only in the far north, above the eastern extremity of the Atlas Mountains, is the ground remotely favourable for an offensive from Algeria.

Anderson would later complain that early press communiqués about the landing and advance of the British First Army caused the public to overestimate the size of his force, and this, in turn, produced public impatience with his perceived lack of progress. In reality, 'the initial thrust in the north was made by only two reduced Brigade groups of 78 Division, each on very light scales of transport, plus one armoured regimental group of the 17/21 Lancers', a total of around 12,000 men. Or as Anderson put it: 'First Army did not spring ashore full-formed like Afrodite from the sea. Far from it.'[2]

Two days before he wrote to Brooke, Anderson had ordered Evelegh to send a mobile task force from the 36th Infantry Brigade Group – composed of infantry, supporting armour, artillery and engineers – along the coastal road from Bône to the port of Tabarka, 110 miles from Tunis. This overland advance would be supported by two airborne operations the following day: the British 1st Parachute Battalion would land near the border town and railway hub of Souk-el-Arba, 40 miles south of Tabarka; and Raff's American 2/509th Parachute Infantry, reassembled after its unfortunate experience near Oran, would be dropped on the Allies' southern flank at Youks-les-Bains airfield, near Tébessa, close to the Tunisian border. If successful, these three operations would place Allied forces 'within Tunisia at two northern points, each covering a major route from Algeria, and at the Algerian-Tunisian boundary on the southern flank'.[3]

Raff's men jumped as planned from thirty-three Dakotas on the morning of 15 November and, thanks to a friendly French reception, quickly occupied the airfield and the nearby town of Tébessa. Two days later, they seized another airfield at the oasis town of Gafsa in southern Tunisia, having driven more than 80 miles down the Roman road unopposed. 'Mobile mixed US-French patrols in requisitioned transport roamed far and wide over the whole southern area,' noted Anderson, 'mopping-up small Italian detachments.'[4] Eisenhower would later describe Raff's actions to Marshall as a 'magnificent piece of work'. He added: 'By his dash and skill, and the exemplary conduct of the US Troops, he has vastly raised the morale of the French Forces and we have derived untold benefit from the coverage we have thus secured.'[5]

Poor weather conditions, meanwhile, had delayed the British drop for twenty-four hours. Commanding the 1st Parachute Battalion was 31-year-old Lieutenant Colonel James Hill, the super-fit and charismatic son of a general who had won the Sword of Honour for best cadet at Sandhurst. Awarded the Military Cross for gallantry during the Dunkirk campaign, Hill had volunteered for parachuting a year later as a means of recovering his batman (who had done the same thing). His task, having seized the airfield at Souk-el-Arba, was to move the 500 men of his battalion 30 miles to the northeast where Vichy French troops were holding key road junctions around the town of Béja. Having done a deal with the French, he was to 'patrol east to harass the enemy, resorting to guerrilla warfare if necessary'.[6]

During the three-hour flight from Maison Blanche airfield on 16

November, the battalion's Dakotas were bounced by two Bf 109 fighters. Fortunately, both were shot down by their escort of Spitfires. Sweating in the humid heat, the men sang songs and cracked jokes to hide their nerves. At last came the time to jump. 'The order "Go" rang in my ears,' wrote 21-year-old Corporal Reg 'Lofty' Curtis, a strapping former Grenadier Guardsman from Catford, southeast London. 'Before long I was a changed man: I felt much cooler being whisked about in the air. All round me seemed hundreds of parachutes, just like a training exercise, then I realised I had dropped into action. I landed O.K.'

One man was killed when he hit a power line. Otherwise the drop was 'unopposed except for some rather excitable Arabs' who galloped towards the parachutists 'on frisky-looking Arab horses'. They fired a few shots in the air, 'more in jubilation than trying to be hostile', and then rode off.[7]

Once on the ground and formed up, the bulk of the battalion moved off in requisitioned vehicles, mostly buses, for the market town of Béja, a cluster of whitewashed buildings perched on the flank of a steep hill (close to the ancient Punic settlement of Vacca), 20 miles to the north-east. Leaving his men on high ground, Hill walked into the town with a French liaison officer to speak to Général de division Barré who had set up his headquarters there after withdrawing west from Tunis. Barré told Hill that his main concern, if he threw in his lot with the Allies, was how to combat German armour. After Hill had reassured him 'in the most glowing terms' that Allied armoured divisions were rushing to their aid, Barré agreed to let the paratroopers take over key road junctions. He had 2,500 men in the area; Hill only 525. At dusk the next day, Hill marched his battalion through the town twice to make his force look bigger. He knew that French emotions over support for the Allies (particularly the British) were running high, and that Vichy loyalists were still numerous. 'We wanted desperately to bring the French in on our side,' wrote Hill, 'and demonstrate to the local population that the Germans were not infallible.'[8]

The paratroopers got their opportunity the following day, 18 November, when Major Peter Cleasby-Thompson's mobile column – two platoons of the 1st Parachute Battalion's S Company, two sections of sappers and a detachment of 3-inch mortars – ambushed a column of German armoured cars on the highway between the village of Sidi Nsir and the town of Mateur, 35 miles northeast of Béja. There were six enemy vehicles – three heavy eight-wheeled armoured cars and three light recce cars – with 40 yards between each of them. The paratroopers held their fire until the first vehicle had detonated one of the mines laid by the sappers. This was the signal for battle to commence as men with Gammon bombs – plastic explosives wrapped in fabric that would detonate on contact, and named after an officer in the battalion – 'quickly immobilised two of the armoured cars' and the scout cars were also 'put out of action'. Those Germans not killed or wounded in the first five vehicles soon surrendered. That just left the armoured car at the rear of the column which 'opened fire with machine gun and sub-machine gun'. But it was targeted with accurate 3-inch mortar fire and eventually knocked out.[9]

An undamaged German scout car was used to transport the single British casualty and a badly wounded German back to Béja, while the rest of the force withdrew to Sidi Nsir. Overall the ambush had the desired effect of impressing the French and making them, as Hill put it, 'better disposed' to the Allied cause.[10]

That same day, 18 November, the armoured cars and trucks of B Squadron, 1st Derbyshire Yeomanry – the reconnaissance regiment of the 6th Armoured Division, and spearheading the 17/21st Lancers Regimental Group, otherwise known as Blade Force★ – rolled into Béja. Commanded by Major J. Crompton-Inglefield, a former Royal

---

★ The force was composed of C Squadron, 17/21st Lancers (medium tanks); B Squadron, 1st Derbyshire Yeomanry (armoured cars); B Company, 10th Rifle Brigade; a troop each of sappers and anti-tank guns; a section of light anti-aircraft guns; and supporting units of Royal Army Service Corps and medics.

Navy officer who was affectionately known as 'The Bo'sun', the squadron had set out from Algiers with the rest of Blade Force on 15 November with orders to press on until they encountered the enemy. 'We were tired when we started,' remembered Lieutenant Vincent Moore, commanding No. 2 Troop, 'and we pressed on for three whole days, over the Atlas Mountains, through mountain gorges and over rolling plains, with about ten hours' sleep for most of us in all that time.' They had been told to expect no French military opposition, 'but to fight it if encountered'.

Informed at Souk Ahras, 45 miles west of the Algerian/Tunisian border, that the Germans had issued an ultimatum to the French defenders of the semicircular arch bridge at Medjez el Bab to 'stop fighting' or face the consequences, B Squadron was ordered to get there as quickly as possible to stiffen French morale. Leaving the rest of Blade Force at Souk Ahras, they had set off at 3 a.m. on 18 November and covered the 100-mile stretch of twisting mountain road to Béja in darkness and pouring rain, with everyone taking a turn at driving and dying 'a thousand deaths while fighting the overpowering impulse to sleep at the wheel'. Arriving at Béja at 1.30 p.m., they linked up with Hill's paratroopers and discovered that the French were refusing to allow them 'to take over or even go near' the bridge at Medjez, built by the Bey of Tunis in the seventeenth century, because it 'would result in an immediate attack by the Germans'.[11]

Proceeding with caution, Crompton-Inglefield hid most of the squadron on a farm near Oued Zarga, five miles short of Medjez, and went forward with one of his troop leaders to contact the French. They were guided by poilus to a house 200 yards from the bridge where the French commander, Colonel Guy Le Coulteux, had set up his command post. Le Coulteux's delight at seeing Allied troops was soon dampened when he realised how few there were. His troops, he explained, were on the west bank of the river; the Germans on the east bank. The enemy had demanded free passage over the bridge and on to Béja, adding: 'Marshal Pétain, your Commander-in-Chief, orders that you put up no opposition to us but allow us to advance towards Algeria.'

'We have not received any such order,' Le Coulteux had replied. 'Show us your authority.'

'Authority from Marshal Pétain is on its way. You must assist the Axis Forces in every possible way.'

'We have seen no authority.'

Le Coulteux was explaining to Crompton-Inglefield that the wrangle was still ongoing when two junior officers burst in with news that a German delegation was at the door. Ushered hastily into a side room, Crompton-Inglefield heard the ensuing conversation between a German major, his interpreter and the colonel.

'Two envoys direct from Herr Hitler,' said the interpreter in French, 'are arriving at Medjez el Bab this evening. They have flown from Berchtesgaden to Tunis Airport. They send their compliments to General Barré and ask him to have dinner with them in Medjez el Bab at eight o'clock this evening. They will bring the authority of free passage from Marshal Pétain.'

After Le Coulteux had promised to relay the invitation to Barré, the German major left, none the wiser that two British officers were in the next room. Crompton-Inglefield was told: 'Go back and keep your squadron hidden. We will keep you as a surprise. When General Barré returns from his conversations with the envoys, you will be informed of everything that has taken place.'

He and the troop leader returned to the squadron's hiding place in the grounds of a large French farm owned by two brothers, both staunch supporters of de Gaulle, who put rooms at their disposal and entertained the officers with wine. One of them explained that Medjez was the 'key' to Tunis, and that the Arabic words 'El-Bab' meant 'The Gate'. Two thousand years earlier, the great Carthaginian general Hannibal had said: 'Medjez is the gate to Carthage. He who holds Medjez rules Carthage.'

When they turned in that night – lying on bed-rolls on the

floor – there was no word from the French. But at one in the morning they were woken by the arrival of four senior French officers. 'One', remembered Lieutenant Moore, 'was a smart, well preserved man with a grey-white mustache, wearing a khaki great-coat and khaki kepi', on which was a major general's badge of rank: Barré. The other three were colonels, 'more ornately attired, two with sky-blue kepis, gold braided and red topped, the other with a black and gold kepi'. They made the British officers, in their 'travel stained battledress and black berets', feel positively shabby.

'It is war,' said Barré, bluntly. 'The Germans give us until seven o'clock this morning. After that they warn us any attempt to prevent their advancing would be crushed by force. I would now like to discuss your resources, and our joint plans to defeat them.'

They did a quick inventory: Barré's troops were 'fairly numerous but woefully ill equipped'; B Squadron had around 150 men; there was also a company of the 1st Parachute Battalion, another 150 men, which had been sent to Medjez from Béja; and during the night a battery of American artillery had arrived.

The 7 a.m. deadline on 19 November came and went. But four hours later, a dozen Stukas dive-bombed some French positions, a mile down the road from B Squadron's laager. Soon clouds of black smoke could be seen rising from a French field kitchen and a burning lorry. Then B Squadron – which had sent out patrols of armoured cars, armoured scout cars and jeeps with anti-tank guns to watch important road junctions – was itself targeted, with shrapnel striking many of the armoured cars but causing no casualties. More Stukas flew over to bomb unsuspecting Béja which was teeming with civilians. It was, noted Vincent Moore, 'sheer murder'.[12]

In Medjez, meanwhile, the French, the 1st Parachute Battalion's R Company and a battery of American howitzers from the 175th Field Artillery Battalion had 'fought magnificently' to beat back the Germans that day, though French casualties were heavy. Barré appealed to Anderson for urgent tank and air support which, for the moment, the British lieutenant general was unable to give. So just after midnight on 20 November, the French told Crompton-Inglefield that, weakened by air attack, they were withdrawing to more easily defensible positions west of Oued Zarga, and that B Squadron would act as their rearguard. The movement took 'all morning, though it was supposed to have been completed by dawn'. Fortunately, the men from the German 3/5th Parachute Battalion made no attempt to pursue. Their seizure of Medjez and its bridge over the Medjerda river − the gateway to Tunis − was, for the time being, enough.[13]

Further north the 6th Royal West Kents and supporting guns − the forward elements of the British 36th Infantry Brigade − had been in action on 18 November as they came up against two companies of Witzig's parachute engineers, backed by tanks, armoured cars and artillery, at the village of Djebel Abiod, sited on a key road junction 20 miles east of Tabarka. 'When the Royal West Kents, with three companies, moved in they were immediately attacked by three German battalions and twenty tanks,' wrote John D'Arcy-Dawson, the Military Correspondent for the *Daily Sketch* and *Sunday Graphic*. 'Rising behind the village are high hills with a flat plain carrying, on the bed of a valley, the road north-east to Mateur. Faced with overwhelming odds and the necessity to watch in three directions, our men put up a magnificent show.'[14]

For forty-eight hours they held off a series of determined and furious German attacks, knocking out eight tanks and inflicting heavy losses on enemy infantry. The British lost, in turn, five field guns, most of their anti-tank guns and a large number of Bren gun carriers and other vehicles. The battle ended in stalemate. 'Despite unbelievably unfavourable positions (with no covered approaches, no covered artillery positions, no favourable terrain of attack or attack zone for our tanks),' reported Witzig, 'the Kampfgruppe held its ground until 25 November 1942, some 50 kilometres forward of friendly lines with no other German or Italian units on its flanks.'[15]

The standoff meant that the First Army's sudden dash for Bizerte and Tunis had been stymied here and at Medjez el Bab, away to the south, and Anderson – who had done his best with limited resources – knew it. 'It was now evident,' he wrote, 'that we would have to fight seriously for any further advance and it was decided to wait until 78 Division (still less one Brigade Group) had closed up and a very small forward reserve of supplies was established before striking at Tunis.'[16]

13

'A Herculean task'

Algeria and Tunisia, 23–26 November 1942

ON 23 NOVEMBER, ANXIOUS to speed up the eastward advance of his troops, 'Ike' Eisenhower moved his Allied Force HQ from Gibraltar to Algiers. At Oran airfield, en route, he got his first taste of the difficult weather conditions that were to plague Allied troops 'throughout that bitter winter' when his plane blew a tyre and was dragged off the hard airstrip into a sea of 'bottomless mud'. While repairs were under way, he lunched with Major General Fredendall who explained that the port was still 'clogged with sunken ships' and would take some time to clear.

At Algiers, he was driven to the Hotel St George where a corner suite of three bedrooms and a parlour on the upper floor had been reserved for him and his personal staff. He got to work immediately, querying why orders he had issued to support Anderson 'with whatever American contingents could be brought up to him from the Oran area' had not been 'clearly understood nor vigorously executed'. He spoke to Brigadier General Lunsford E. Oliver of the US 1st Armored Division's Combat Command B, and discovered that his offer to march his half-tracks the full 700 miles from Oran to Souk-el-Arba had been refused by a well-meaning but short-sighted staff officer on the grounds that the journey would consume half the useful life of the vehicles. Eisenhower was astounded. 'What are we saving them for?' he asked. 'Now's the time to use them, before the Germans can further reinforce their rapidly mounting forces.' Within five minutes, Oliver 'was on his way with the orders he sought'.[1]

That night, the old hotel 'quivered and shook' as anti-aircraft guns fired incessantly at German planes overhead, and the odd bomb exploded nearby. 'No one slept much,' wrote naval aide Harry Butcher in his diary. 'Ike was in the corner bedroom and I in the one next to him. In the morning, he was fuming about the effect of the bombing and what he thought of our inadequate defence, particularly absence of night-fighters. Worried about effect psychologically on French and Arabs. Little damage to shipping.'

Next day, having moved their sleeping quarters to two rented villas, Ike's staff replaced the beds in the hotel suite with desks and chairs, rigged up some telephones, and were 'almost in business'. It was bitterly cold, but fortunately there was a fireplace in Ike's office. Elsewhere, soldiers slept in the hotel's hallways, out of the rain, and corridors were 'gritty with mud which becomes dust when the bare-footed Arab women wield their brooms'.

After three days of intensive work, galvanising the staff and the widely separated commanders into coordination – during which he received the joyous news that the French had chosen to scuttle their fleet at Toulon rather than hand it over to the Germans (though Ike would always wonder 'why in the world' the French naval officers had not answered the call to join the Allies immediately after Operation Torch) – Eisenhower decided to visit the front with his deputy Clark. They were driven in Ike's semi-armoured Cadillac, with a jeep and a scout car leading, and followed by a quarter-ton truck with their batmen and a scout car bringing up the rear. They had quite a few .50 calibre machine guns, but no anti-aircraft protection, and the appearance of any plane 'was the signal to dismount and scatter'.

They met up with Anderson beyond Souk Ahras, but still in Algeria and 150 miles on difficult roads from Tunis, and entered a zone where 'all around was evidence of incessant and hard fighting'. One American colonel they encountered was angry at the lack of air support, albeit prone to wild exaggeration. British soldiers were being murdered, he said, and Béja had been 'bombed to rubble'.

Eisenhower put this down to inexperience and thought that, on the whole, morale was good. 'The boldness, courage and stamina of General Anderson's forces,' he wrote later, 'could not have been exceeded by the most battle-wise veterans. Physical conditions were almost unendurable. The mud deepened daily, confining all operations to the roads, long stretches of which practically disintegrated. Winter cold was already descending upon the Tunisian highlands. The bringing up of supplies and ammunition was a Herculean task.'

Ike was warned that the American public might not take kindly to the 'dissipation' of its army. But so determined was he to strengthen Anderson, even at the risk of weakening his rear areas, that he was 'quite willing to take all later criticism if only the Allied forces could turn over Tunis to our people as a New Year's present'. The gamble, he knew, was great, but the prize was such a 'glittering one' that he was prepared to 'abandon caution in an effort to bring up to General Anderson every available fighting man in the theater'.[2]

By 24 November, Eisenhower's efforts were bearing fruit. The concentration of the 78th Infantry Division and Blade Force, on a light scale, was 'complete'; the leading elements of the 6th Armoured Division were moving up to the Téboursouk area, 20 miles southeast of Medjez; and the spearhead of Oliver's Combat Command B was on its way from Oran to Souk-el-Arba. With more troops available, Anderson resumed the offensive on the 25th with a three-pronged attack towards the towns of Mateur and Tebourba, gateways to Bizerte and Tunis respectively.

The terrain Anderson's men were attempting to traverse in northeastern Tunisia is rugged and of 'great topographical complexity'. Both Bizerte and Tunis are situated in coastal flatlands fringed by hills. Bizerte's basin is relatively small and covered in lakes. Tunis's is bigger, but bounded on the northwest, west and south by the eastern extremities of high mountain ranges. Only in the southwest, between the Medjerda and Miliane rivers, does a fringe of low hills allow easy access to Tunis by road and rail.

The mountainous region north of the Medjerda, and southwest of Bizerte, is 50 miles wide and 40 deep, and separated by four lesser streams: the Sedjenane, Malah, Djoumine and Tine. The high ground between each river is covered with a dense scrub in the northern belt, but elsewhere its upper portions are 'rocky and bare, dark gray in color, speckled with shadows, with a trace of green along the brooks nearer the bases'. The terrain favoured the defence, with excellent observation, good cover for mortars and only a few routes suitable for tanks (and easy to mine).[3]

The 36th Infantry Brigade Group began the northern attack after dark on 25 November. But it soon discovered that Witzig's parachute engineers had withdrawn from their position west of Djebel Abiod. So began a cautious if uncontested pursuit, slowed by mines and booby traps, until contact was re-established near Djefna, 10 miles west of Mateur, where the enemy were in a 'very strong natural position on commanding ground'. Witzig had prepared a near-impregnable position with sheltered gun pits, interlocking fields of fire and excellent camouflage. Minefields had been laid on both sides of the road, and the high ground was protected by wire and S-mines, deadly 4kg anti-personnel devices that, when activated by pressure or remote control, would leap from three to five feet into the air before exploding and spreading steel balls across a killing ground of 50 yards. American troops dubbed them 'Bouncing Betties'.

Repeated attempts by 36th Brigade to take this strongpoint on 29 and 30 November were repulsed with heavy casualties. In one of the first attacks, two companies of the 8th Argylls lost thirty men killed, fifty wounded, eighty-six taken prisoner and eleven carriers. But the Germans also suffered. 'It was terrible,' remembered young Rifleman Bohn of Witzig's 3rd Company. 'The khaki uniforms worn by the soldiers of both sides were mixed in the battlefield. Our small group numbered only 28 men and so was grossly outnumbered by the foe. Fighting petered out about 4 p.m.' Bohn was among the casualties. Captured with two wounded comrades, he was surprised when the British, despite their heavy losses, observed the rules of 'fair play' and tended their injuries. He wrote: 'It seemed to me that the British regarded us as gallant and loyal soldiers, certainly among the bravest they had to contend with.'[4]

A coordinated attempt by the six British and four American troops of No. 1 Commando to turn 'the enemy's sea flank' by landing on the coast to the west of Bizerte on 1 December also failed to have much effect. Various key road junctions were occupied by the Commandos, and the enemy was 'harried for three days' and 'forced to draw on his reserves'. But ultimately the operation was a failure because it failed to dislodge the Germans from Djefna and the Commandos eventually withdrew, footsore and hungry, and with heavy casualties of 6 officers and 128 men, back along the coast to the British lines at Cap Serrat. Among the dead was 28-year-old Captain John Bradford from Swansea in Wales, a bank employee before the war, who led his men 'to within four miles of the centre of Bizerte' before he was killed by machine-gun fire on 2 December.[5]

The central attack by Colonel R. A. Hull's Blade Force was more successful. Leaving its assembly area northeast of Béja at 7 a.m. on 25 November, the column of more than 100 tanks – mostly 16-ton British Valentines and 13-ton American M3 Stuarts – soon reached the junction on the Sidi Nsir–Tebourba road that branched northeast to Mateur. After capturing two nearby farms from a German-Italian detachment, Hull moved part of his force closer to Mateur. The rest, including the US 1/1st Armored Regiment under Lieutenant Colonel John K. Waters (Patton's son-in-law), were sent east to create a 'tank-infested area' in the Tine Valley, southeast of Mateur, and to reconnoitre the bridges across the Medjerda river at El Bathan and Djedeïda, towards which the 11th Brigade Group would advance after it had captured

Medjez el Bab to the south. Waters's battalion included a Headquarters Company and three other companies of M3 Stuart light tanks, an 81mm mortar platoon, and an assault gun platoon with three 75mm pack howitzers on half-tracks. But it had no artillery, infantry or engineers in support, and only intermittent air cover.

Approaching the three-mile-long Chouïgui Pass, Waters's vanguard came up against a company of Witzig's parachute engineers and an Italian anti-tank gun platoon that had been sent down from Mateur that morning to support the troops at Tebourba. Warned that Allied tanks were in the vicinity, the German force had set up a strong defensive position in a walled farm two miles from the northwestern entrance to the pass. Repeated efforts to capture the farm were made by Waters's Company A, and later by other American and British units, but they all failed because of a lack of infantry and artillery support.

The seventeen light tanks of Waters's Company C, meanwhile, had overrun an enemy detachment of Volkswagens and motorcycles on the far side of the pass, and, bypassing the German garrison in Tebourba, destroyed a defensive position on the bridge over the Medjerda at El Bathan. The company then moved east along the left bank of the river to Djedeïda where, behind a low ridge, it discovered an Axis airfield 'packed with planes'. Major Rudolph Barlow, the company commander, immediately deployed for battle, with two platoons in front and one in the rear, and charged. 'The German planes,' wrote Colonel Paul M. Robinett, 'like "fat geese on a pond", were blasted and riddled with high explosive and canister and machine gun bullets and physically crushed in a wild orgy of destruction which only a few managed to escape.'

Company C lost two men killed, and one tank and its crew missing, while several other tanks were damaged. But they destroyed thirty-six planes and shot up buildings, supplies and defending troops, before withdrawing at dusk to the west.[6]

The third attack that day was made by the reinforced 11th Infantry Brigade Group along the Béja–Tebourba highway, with the bridge at

Medjez el Bab its immediate objective. The defenders at Medjez included the 3/5th Parachute Battalion, an Italian anti-tank company, two 88mm dual purpose guns, and tanks of the Panzer-Battalion 190. To outflank this powerful force, the 11th's commander, Brigadier Edward Cass, had decided to use a reinforced infantry battalion to approach the town from each side of the river, while a third element came from the west to seize commanding ground.

The northern force – the 2nd Lancashire Fusiliers – was spotted by the enemy in bright moonlight as it tried to cross the bare and level plain towards Medjez during the night of 24/25 November, and targeted by machine-gun and mortar fire. The initial burst killed the commanding officer and his deputy Major S. J. L. Kelly took over. Tall, slim and softly spoken, Kelly was an insurance broker in civilian life and an unlikely hero. Yet he displayed outstanding leadership qualities as he urged his men over a ford in the 100-yard-wide Medjerda river. 'Holding their guns over their heads,' wrote John D'Arcy-Dawson, 'the men waded into the saffron-coloured river. Shoulder-high in water, they got across and scaled the steep, slippery bank. They reached the top and were met with a hurricane of machine-gun fire followed by heavy and accurate mortar fire.'

Two companies got within yards of the defensive position taken up by the *Fallschirmjäger*, but were pinned down by heavy fire. They withdrew back to the river after a forward artillery observer had called down accurate fire on the German machine-gun nests. At 4 p.m., with their position untenable, the surviving Lancashires were pulled back across the river. They were reorganising along the Tebourba road when they were counter-attacked by enemy tanks and infantry from the town, and driven back into the hills with heavy casualties.

The other reinforced battalion – the 5th Northamptons, supported by the US 175th Field Artillery Battalion – attacked from the southwest and seized the heights of Djebel Bou Mouss, later known as 'Grenadier Hill'. But they, in turn, were driven off the ridge by German tanks debouching from Medjez.[7]

Both flank attacks had failed. Yet, that night, General Nehring chose to withdraw his men from Medjez rather than commit more troops to its defence. It was a decision that mystified the British. 'What caused them to go like that?' wrote Lieutenant Vincent Moore. 'Had the Germans believed our news stories about the First Army being in Tunisia? If so, it was a wonderful bluff. We were not an Army, not a Corps, scarcely a division. Whatever the reason, Germany has so often spoiled a fine military achievement – garrisoning Tunisia so quickly – by one stupid incredible blunder.'[8]

Nehring's decision to withdraw his troops closer to Tunis had been partly prompted, of course, by the shocking news that American tanks had shot up the Stuka airfield at Djedeïda, and a subsequent report – false as it turned out – that Allied forces were within nine miles of the Tunisian capital. This had caused panic at Nehring's HQ, and a flustered call to Kesselring in Rome. 'Nehring rang me up in a state of understandable excitement,' remembered Kesselring, 'and drew the blackest conclusions from the raid. Unable as I was to share his worst fears, I asked him to be calm and said I would arrive the following day.'[9]

Nehring wanted to consolidate his forces for a close-in defence of the Tunis bridgehead. Kesselring overruled him. He was convinced that the Allied advance would continue to be 'cautious and tentative', and that Nehring's troops needed to take the initiative. On 26 November, therefore, Oberst Friedrich Freiherr von Broich – who had taken command at Bizerte eight days earlier – sent a small force of engineers, infantry and tanks (the latter composed of a company of the 190th Panzer Battalion) from Mateur to Tebourba. En route, the German panzers – including thirteen Mark IV models with long 75mm high-velocity guns, and three or more Mark IIIs with 50mm cannon – clashed with Colonel Waters's 1/1st Armored Regiment at the entrance to the Chouïgui Pass in what became the first American/German tank battle of the war.[10]

For tank crews, armoured warfare was a hellish experience. There were typically four or five per tank: commander, main gunner, loader, driver and machine gunner who doubled as the radio operator. In combat, with the hatches sealed, the tank was roasting hot, claustrophobic and very noisy – a squeaking washing machine on full spin. The main fear was that in the event of a hit, the vehicle would catch fire – 'brew up', in military slang – igniting the ammunition, in which case it was a desperate lunge to get out through the top or an escape hatch below. Some crews would be burnt alive.

In this action, Company B, under Major William R. Tuck, was on a reverse slope covering, from a distance of 50 to 100 yards, the Mateur–Chouïgui road as it went through the pass, while Company A was on the slope of a hill on the far side the road. The approaching panzers were engaged first by a section of American 75mm assault guns whose shells were not armour-piercing and had little effect. Company A was next into action, but its M3 Stuarts were easily outgunned by the Mark IV panzers, and six were quickly put out of action, including the command tank of Major Siglin who was killed instantly when an armour-piercing round entered his turret. An American tank commander described the unequal contest:

The 37-mm gun of the M3 light tank popped and snapped like an angry cap pistol . . . Tracer-tailed armor piercing bolts streaked out of the American muzzle and bounced like a mashie shot from the plates of the Mark IV. The German shed sparks like a power-driven grindstone. In a frenzy of desperation and fading faith in the highly-touted weapon, the M3 crew pumped more than eighteen rounds at the Jerry tank while it came in. Through the scope sight the tracer could be seen to hit, and glance straight up. Popcorn balls thrown by Little Bo Peep would have been just as effective.

As the Mark IV approached to within 30 yards, the M3 began to reverse. But it was too late. A 75mm round hit the 'vertical surface of the heavy armored driver's door and literally caved in the front of the M3', killing the driver and blinding the bow gunner. Only the commander got out of the burning tank, but he was cut down by machine-gun fire and killed as he tried to escape.

The rest of Company A might have shared this M3's fate had not the German panzers, in engaging the American tanks, exposed their sides and rear to Company B. Firing at close range, Tuck's 37mm guns riddled nine German tanks – including at least six Mark IVs – 'through their engine doors and decks'. Companies A and B then 'hunted down the accompanying infantry' and turned the walled farm that had held out the previous day 'into a death trap for those who sought shelter there'. When the survivors withdrew the following night, the position was occupied by a company of the 1st Parachute Battalion, under Major Vic Coxen, and known thereafter as 'Coxen's Farm'.[11]

Other Allied successes on 26 November included the 11th Infantry Brigade's bloodless recapture of Medjez el Bab, where a Bailey bridge span was quickly erected over the broken gap in the original bridge, and a subsequent advance by the 1st East Surreys and a small artillery group to Tebourba, which was occupied the following morning. On 27 November, the troops at Tebourba were reinforced by the 5th Northamptons and the bulk of the US 2/13th Armored Regiment.

Despite the odd setback, Anderson's forces were in a strong position and closing in on the twin prizes of Bizerte and Tunis (the latter just 20 miles east of Tebourba), possession of which would cut Rommel's land supply lines and allow the Allies to reopen the sea lanes to Alexandria and the Suez Canal. One more determined push might do it. The scene was set for the battles to the west of Tunis that would determine the course of the campaign.[12]

14

'Cut to pieces'

Algeria and Tunisia, 24 November–3 December 1942

A KEY COMPONENT OF THE First Army's renewed attempt to capture Tunis and Bizerte with fresh forces advancing on three axes was Brigadier General Lunsford E. Oliver's Combat Command B, the balance of which had finally left Oran for Tunisia, with Eisenhower's blessing, on 24 November. The wheeled vehicles took the easier, but longer, east–west coastal highway; all the half-tracks, by contrast, went by the shorter, inland route across several rugged mountain passes.

Two days in, the half-track column led by Colonel Paul Robinett could see, away to the south, the snow-covered Atlas Mountains glistening under a bright sun, 'a most beautiful sight'. Later, the column halted beside the road at dusk to celebrate Thanksgiving Day – 26 November – with a 'C-ration supper: hash, beans, or stew'. Reaching Constantine – the 'City of Bridges', named after Rome's first Christian emperor – the following day, Robinett learned that Lieutenant General Anderson, commanding the First Army, was with his forward headquarters at Ain Seynour, close to the Tunisian border. He decided to pay him a visit.

Shown into Anderson's office in a French house off the main highway, the American saluted and said: 'Colonel Robinett, 13 Armored Regiment, reporting.'

'No, general!' replied Anderson.

A little confused, Robinett repeated his introduction, and got the same reply.

'I've just received a message,' explained Anderson, 'that you've been promoted to brigadier general and Oliver to major general. Congratulations, now put on the star.'

Anderson then welcomed Combat Command B to the front and said that he was convinced they would 'soon end the campaign in Tunisia'.[1]

His plan was to renew the multi-pronged attack against the Axis troops defending Tunis and Bizerte. This would include an assault on Djedeïda by the 11th Infantry Brigade Group and, once the town and bridge were in Allied hands, an advance northwest towards Mateur. This move, in turn, would cover the northern flank of the main attack on Tunis by Blade Force, using the Djedeïda crossing to strike eastwards, while Oliver's Combat Command B would cross the Medjerda at El Bathan, swing through St Cyprien, on the road from Massicault just 12 miles from Tunis, and head towards the capital from the southwest.

To assist these attacks, and cause havoc behind enemy lines, the 2nd Parachute Battalion was scheduled to drop on 29 November near Oudna airfield, south of Tunis, destroy any enemy aircraft and then strike northwest to 'protect the southern flank of the advance on Tunis, joining up eventually with the armoured force near St Cyprien'.[2]

It sounded credible on paper. But airborne operations are inherently risky – particularly if parachute troops are dropped too far ahead of ground support (as the British would learn to their cost at Arnhem in September 1944) – and Anderson had not factored in the possibility that the Germans might have plans of their own. The cracks in his leadership were beginning to show.

Robinett came away with an impression of the British general as 'something of a juggler, playing with three balls representing Tunis, Bizerte and Tunis/Bizerte, who could not decide whether to concentrate on one or the other or try for them both at the same time'.

While Anderson's 'personality and manner were good', he was also 'a dreamer' who had not quite realised that he would have to 'get along with available means, not being able to order additional resources to the front'. It did not help that his advanced HQ was 'far behind the front', nor that the chain of command in Tunisia already included a corps and a divisional HQ.[3]

Even as the Allies rushed troops to the battlefield, the Axis was preparing its own attack. Thanks to the emergency arrival of rein-forcements by air and sea, Nehring now had at his disposal up to 15,500 men, including elements of both the German 10th Panzer and the Italian 1st Infantry ('Superga') Divisions, the 190th Panzer Battalion, Witzig's 11th Parachute Engineer Battalion and Koch's 5th Parachute Regiment. It was a small if formidable array of veteran troops, bolstered by 60 field guns and up to 130 tanks, including four of the new and gigantic Mark VI ('Tiger') tanks with 88mm guns that had been rushed into production, months earlier than planned, on Hitler's orders. These 54-ton monsters had made their battlefield debut near Leningrad, Russia, in September 1942, but this would be the first time they had met Western armour.[4]

Nehring also had the advantage of airfields 'with concrete runways close behind his front and only half an hour's flight from Sicily'. The few Allied fighters, by contrast, 'had to work from Bône (114 miles to the rear), with a very muddy emergency landing at Souk el Arba, and could only remain over the battle zone for ten minutes before returning to refuel'. Yet the attrition rate for both was high.[5]

Major Werner Baumbach, twenty-seven, a veteran Luftwaffe dive-bomber pilot who had flown countless sorties in the Low Countries, Norway and Russia, before taking over a wing of thirty-nine Junkers Ju-88 bombers at Comiso airfield in Sicily on 10 November, was shocked by the rapid destruction of his command in the skies over North Africa. 'The Angel of death cast its shadow over us immedi-ately on our arrival,' he noted in his diary.

Dante's Hell is a reality here. Roth's crew gone, Lieutenant Grigoleit shot down, little Quisdorf missing, Stoffregen down and mortally wounded, Metzenthin's and Lieutenant Harmel's Ju 88s shot down in flames over Algiers . . . Since we have been here I have stopped talking to the men. I could not find anything to say which would lessen the feeling of hopelessness. They understand me. No one is quicker on the uptake than the man in the ranks.

The German bomber squadrons in Sicily had begun the battle with 200 aircraft. Within a few short weeks, that figure had been reduced to 'barely fifty operational aircraft and crews'. The odd replacement plane did little to change the picture. Before long, noted Baumbach, 'we had only the staffs and skeleton organisations on the airfields – without aircraft, crews or hope'.[6]

On 29 November, with Axis forces still enjoying air superiority over Tunisia, Nehring discussed the coming battle with Generalleutnant Wolfgang Fischer, the grizzled 53-year-old commander of the 10th Panzer Division. A veteran of countless campaigns in both world wars, and the holder of the German Cross in Gold, Fischer was given a simple assignment: 'annihilate the enemy in the Tebourba area' and extend the perimeter around Tunis from just west of Tebourba to Massicault, eight miles to the southeast, 'with cover to the south'. Supported by combat units already in Tunisia – including elements of the 5th Parachute Regiment, the 190th Panzer Battalion, the 501st Heavy Panzer Battalion (two Tigers), and anti-tank and flak battalions – he was to execute his attack by 1 December 'at the latest'.[7]

A day earlier, Cass's 11th Infantry Brigade – supported by the medium Lee tanks of the US 2/13th Armored Regiment – had tried and failed to capture the village of Djedeïda on the left bank of the Medjerda river, five miles northeast of Tebourba.[8] The attack was poorly planned, with Lieutenant Colonel Hyman Bruss, the 30-year-old commander of the 2/13th, directing a suicidal charge across an open plain with men from the 5th Northamptons clinging to his tanks. As predicted by Bruss's XO, Major Henry Gardiner (the aspiring Ranger), it had ended in disaster as concentrated German anti-tank fire knocked out four M3 Lees, while the others fled back over a nearby ridge. 'I went up to take a look,' wrote Gardiner, 'and could see the four tanks burning with a dense black column of smoke pouring out of the turrets of each of them. Much confusion. There were men lying around the tanks, most of them apparently dead. We could observe a few crawling and could hear some cries for help.'

Ignoring heavy small-arms fire, Gardiner and a medic went forward in a half-track to try to recover the wounded. They picked up one casualty with a 'huge chunk torn out of his back and part of his shoulder' as bullets rattled off the half-track 'like hail on a tin roof'. Attempting to rescue others, they were waved away and eventually withdrew. 'We really didn't profit much by that trip,' admitted Gardiner, 'for both the sergeant and the half-track driver were wounded in the process, the driver rather badly.'

Two tanks were sent along a railway track to try to outflank the German position. Only one came back, along with part of the crew from the other. An anti-tank gun had knocked out their tank and killed its commander, Lieutenant Eugene Jehlik, one of the battalion's 'best officers and finest men'. A successful infantry attack on the next ridge allowed Jehlik and the other casualties – dead and wounded – to be recovered by the light of the burning tanks. Pausing to rest and eat a high-energy D bar, Gardiner could 'still hear some of the wounded moaning and smell the odor of burnt flesh from the tanks that had served as crematories for some of the crews'.

At dawn the following day, 29 November, after a thirty-minute bombardment of high-explosive and smoke shells, the 5th Northamptons and twelve of Bruss's tanks attacked again, but were repulsed by heavy anti-tank and machine-gun fire, and by Stukas swooping from the sky. The dive-bombers were so destructive that Gardiner – in Bruss's absence – pulled the tanks off the ridge line and into cover.

After dark, the 'weary and badly beaten Northamptons' were relieved by the 2nd Hampshires of the 1st Guards Brigade. The new arrivals were fortunate that their attack, scheduled for the following morning, was postponed by Major General Evelegh until the arrival of more ground and air reinforcements.[9]

Evelegh's decision came too late to halt an ill-conceived airborne operation that would, to all intents and purposes, destroy one of the finest combat units in the British Army. The original plan had been for the 2nd Parachute Battalion, a troop of airborne sappers and a section of a parachute field ambulance – 600 men in all – to drop near the town of Pont du Fahs in northern Tunisia, 'destroy enemy aircraft, stores and petrol there', and then move in two 12-mile jumps northeast and do the same at the airfields at Depienne and Oudna, the latter just 15 miles south of Tunis (and close to the site of one of the largest preserved amphitheatres of the Roman world, built during the reign of Emperor Hadrian in the second century AD). With that accomplished, they would link up with advance elements of Anderson's First Army at St Cyprien. But last-minute intelligence had indicated that there were no Axis planes at either Pont du Fahs or Depienne, so the revised operation was a drop at Depienne and a march to Oudna where they would deal with the enemy aircraft and then link up with the First Army.[10]

'It was,' noted Anderson, 'a risky mission, ordered in the hope that it would confuse the enemy and induce him to dissipate his strength in the very fluid and confused situation still existing, when bluff could still play a good dividend.'[11]

Commanded by Lieutenant Colonel John Frost, the 29-year-old son of a general who had made his name leading the daring and successful Bruneval Raid to capture part of a German early warning radar from the coast of France earlier that year, the 2nd Parachute Battalion had arrived at Algiers by sea on 12 November. Just over two frustrating weeks later, it became the last of the 1st Parachute

American troops in a landing craft heading for the beaches at Oran, Algeria, on 8 November 1942.

British troops landing on a beach near Algiers, 8 November 1942.

Allied troops enter Oran, Algeria, on 10 November 1942.

Generalfeldmarschall Albert Kesselring (centre), Wehrmacht Commander-in-Chief South, discusses strategy with Generalfeldmarschall Erwin Rommel, commanding the Italo-German Panzer Army, in North Africa in late 1942.

Rommel welcomes Ugo Cavallero, the head of the Italian armed forces, to Libya in late 1942. Rommel's immediate superior, Maresciallo Ettore Bastico, the Commander-in-Chief of Axis forces in North Africa, is to Cavallero's left.

Lieutenant General Charles Allfrey (centre), commanding the British V Corps, a 'tall, lean, handsome fellow with a fine sense of humour and one of the keenest officers in Africa', at his headquarters in northern Tunisia on 5 December 1942.

Major General George S. Patton Jr beside an M3 Stuart light tank during his tour of the front line in northern Tunisia in mid-December 1942.

Men of the German 5th Parachute Regiment – 'Koch Kampfgruppe' – on the move in Tunisia.

US president Franklin D. Roosevelt ('FDR'), British prime minister Winston S. Churchill (right) and their respective chiefs of staff pose for the cameras in front of the president's villa at the Casablanca Conference in January 1943. Standing (from L to R): Lieutenant General Henry H. 'Hap' Arnold, Admiral Ernest J. King, General George C. Marshall, Admiral Sir Dudley Pound, General Sir Alan Brooke, Air Chief Marshal Sir Charles Portal.

FDR (left) inspecting Patton's troops in Morocco in late January 1943. His plan to visit the front line in Tunisia had been stymied by General George S. Marshall, the US Army Chief of Staff, who said it was 'out of the question'.

General Sir Harold Alexander (right), commanding the 18th Army Group, discusses future operations with the Allied Commander-in-Chief, General Dwight D. 'Ike' Eisenhower.

PFC Philip L. Mahoney (driver) and T/5 R. R. Pollard (left) were among the handful of Americans to escape encirclement at Sidi Bou Zid and reach the safety of American lines at Kasserine on 17 February 1943.

A knocked-out German Panzer III, with the body of one of its crew lying on the hull, 24 February 1943.

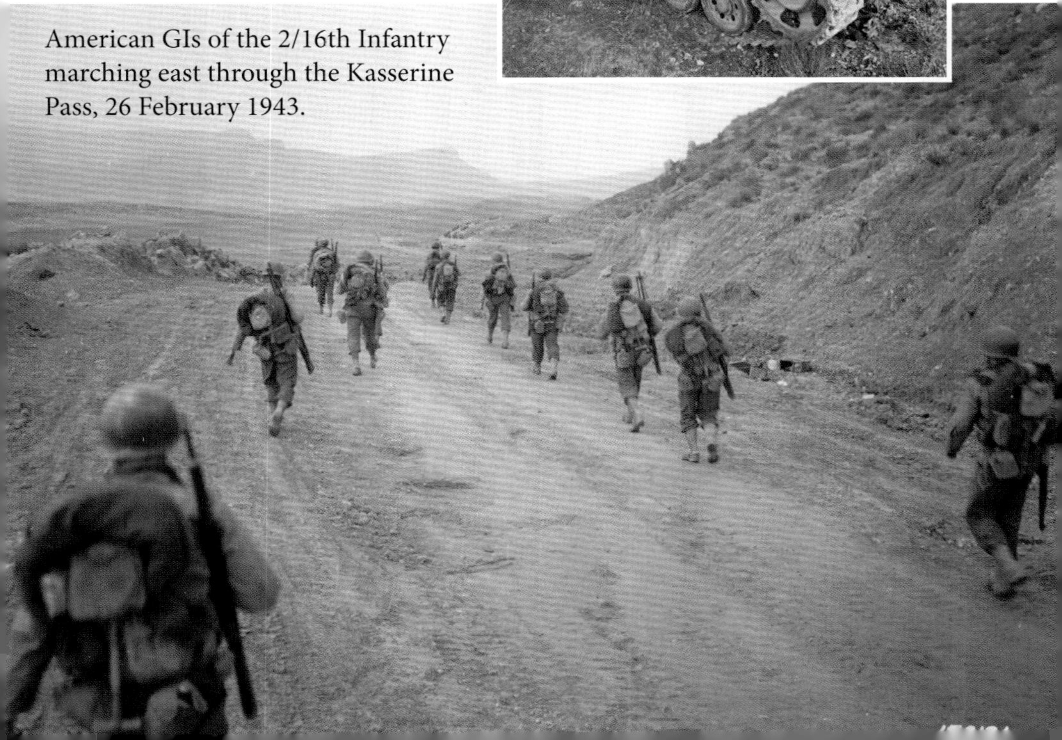

American GIs of the 2/16th Infantry marching east through the Kasserine Pass, 26 February 1943.

British troops search a German prisoner, February 1943.

A British 17-pdr anti-tank gun in action on the Medenine front in Tunisia, 11 March 1943.

Lieutenant General Patton discusses II Corps' future operations with Eisenhower in mid-March 1943.

Patton observing enemy positions in March 1943.

A wounded soldier from the Durham Light Infantry shares a cigarette with a German prisoner during the fighting for the Mareth Line, 22 March 1943.

Monty congratulating some of the troops who took part in his operation to outflank the Mareth Line, 2 April 1943.

Wadi Akarit, seen from the direction of the Allied attack on 6 April. *(courtesy of the A. A. Blackwell Archive)*

Captain Alan Blackwell (left), commanding HQ Company of the 5th East Yorks, with his command truck in the desert. A veteran of countless North African battles, he was killed at Wadi Akarit on 6 April 1943. *(courtesy of the A. A. Blackwell Archive)*

Blackwell's temporary grave (left) at Wadi Akarit. His wife Marjorie heard the news of his death from a fellow officer, Major Andrew Edgar, who wrote to sympathise with her 'tragic loss'. *(courtesy of the A. A. Blackwell Archive)*

Brigade's three battalions to drop into battle. Frost's men were transported to the target by forty-four Dakotas of the US 60th and 64th Transport Groups. They took off from Maison Blanche airfield near Algiers at noon and flew due east across the Atlas Mountains in a 'clear and cloudless' sky, and with an escort of long-range fighters for company.

It was, Frost knew, an extremely hazardous mission. They would have no transport on the ground, unless they captured some, and 'had a long way to go carrying all the ammunition, food, batteries, and other stores we needed for at least five days'. He was, however, reasonably optimistic. There was talk of a combined thrust towards Tunis and he had visions of himself and his men arriving 'Primus in Carthago',* the heroes of the hour. They had no information about the local inhabitants, but assumed they would be friendly and were taking along a large quantity of francs to ease their passage. More worrying was the lack of intelligence on the size and strength of the opposition. They could only hope, remembered Frost, that the enemy 'would not be able to spare any armour'.

Approaching their target after a three-hour flight, the country 'appeared to be smooth and level with no obstacles except an odd dried up watercourse and a few clumps of cactus'. As soon as they had passed over Depienne, Frost jumped, the signal for the other sticks to follow.[12]

They landed without opposition – though one man died when his parachute failed to open, and six were injured – and quickly secured the drop zone. Soon after, three armoured cars appeared on the road running north from Depienne. Fortunately, they were British, part of the 1st Derbyshire Yeomanry – an encouraging sign as Frost had not expected Allied forces 'in the area so soon'. The troop commander

---

* A reference to the ancient city-state of Carthage, located in modern Tunis's northern suburbs, that was destroyed by the Roman general Scipio Africanus in the 3rd Punic War in 146 BC.

said he was patrolling as far north as Cheylus, part of the way to Oudna, 'where a German road block was suspected'. He returned an hour later with the news that the obstruction was south of Cheylus at a place called Djebel Oust.

This convinced Frost to use a country track to bypass the German roadblock en route to Oudna. His force set off at midnight, using mules and carts to transport some of the heavier equipment. It was slow going across difficult, hilly terrain, and they were still well short of the airfield when Frost called a halt before dawn. The soldiers grabbed what rest they could in deep heather beside the track. Frost was too cold to sleep.

At 7 a.m. on 30 November, with the sun warming their shivering bodies, they set off again and were soon spotted by Arabs who gave away their progress by shouting from village to village, and lighting fires. Before midday, the battalion was deployed in low hills near Prise de l'Eau with a commanding view of Oudna airfield. Apart from one crashed German aircraft, there was no sign of enemy planes. Civilians confirmed that the strip 'was not being used by the Axis and that all the enemy troops were withdrawing to Tunis'. To make certain, Frost ordered A Company to move by the most direct route to Oudna 'with the object of making a complete recce', while the rest of the battalion kept to the high ground.[13]

As they approached the airfield – empty but for a few abandoned 50-gallon oil drums – A Company was engaged by long distance small-arms and mortar fire. They took a few Germans prisoner, while C Company moved forward in support on its left. But they had a nasty surprise. 'Tanks had been lurking near an old Roman viaduct,' wrote Frost, 'and as soon as our men left the rocks and boulders on the slope of the hill this unwelcome column trundled into action.'

Ken Morrison, C Company's intrepid second-in-command, crawled forward with a handful of volunteers to knock out the tanks with Gammon bombs. But he was killed, and only one volunteer survived. German Bf 109 fighters then appeared, and made several low strafing runs. But, thanks to their smocks and camouflage nets, the paratroopers were hard to observe from the air and no casualties were inflicted. By 9 p.m., aware that the battalion was very vulnerable to counter-attack, Frost ordered his men back to their original positions near Prise de l'Eau, which most of them reached an hour later.

Next morning, 1 December – after an uncomfortable night lying back-to-back with his deputy Philip Teichman for warmth – Frost decided that his next move should be towards the First Army. 'We had been told to make for St Cyprien,' he remembered, 'which was well to the north and not many miles from Tunis. However, bearing in mind the armoured thrust which we were expecting, and encouraged by the contact we had with our own armoured cars on the day we landed, I felt that we should stay where we were for the time being, and continue to try and get in touch with First Army by wireless.'

It was a mistake. From 10 a.m, they were shelled and machine-gunned from a range of 2,000 yards. They responded with 3-inch mortars, landing one bomb 'slap in the middle of a group of vehicles and men' and forcing them to withdraw to a safe distance. A report came from C Company, facing south, that two tanks and an armoured car were approaching, and that they were displaying yellow triangles, the First Army recognition sign. Frost heaved a sigh of relief. 'All our troubles seemed over,' he wrote, 'and we should soon be on our way with more ammunition, our wounded taken care of, and with the tremendous moral support of some of our own armour.'

Then came the crushing news that the armour was, in fact, German and must have picked up the yellow triangles from the party left at Depienne. Soon after, Frost received a dispiriting wireless message from the First Army: the armoured thrust on Tunis had been postponed. He felt a mixture of 'sickness, rage, and utter weariness'. Their only hope now, he knew, was to move to high ground a mile to the north, and then head west across the plain as soon as it got dark. Having destroyed the wireless sets and mortars – which were respectively out of batteries and ammunition – and informed the medic Jock McGavin that he and his ambulance section would have to remain behind with the wounded, they set off for the hills.

The Germans responded by shelling their line of march, and rock splinters caused terrible wounds. Gradually, heat, thirst and exhaustion took their toll as the men climbed the steep hillside on their hands and knees. Frost called a halt when they reached the northern slopes of Sidi Bou Hadjeba where they were fortunate to find a well. Deploying the men on two summits, Frost could see enemy activity on the plain below and knew an attack was imminent.

It began at 3 p.m. with infantry and light tanks assaulting uphill. The paratroopers held their ground, and even managed to disable a couple of tanks with Gammon bombs, but their casualties steadily mounted. They included the dependable Major Frank Cleaver, the 33-year-old commander of B Company from Essex, who 'was suddenly struck down while he was talking to some of his HQ'.

With the enemy pressure at its height, and Frost wondering how much longer they could hold on, enemy fighter planes appeared overhead. But instead of attacking the embattled paratroopers, they mistakenly opened fire on their own side in the valley, giving Frost's men just enough breathing space to survive the day.

They set off after dark, heading west in company groups to reduce the risk of detection. One platoon was left behind to collect the wounded, and was later captured. 'The coming cold of the night,' wrote Frost, 'and the uncertainty of the behaviour of the local Tunisians, required that our men be collected and protected despite the cost. "C" Company had practically ceased to exist.' Since the drop, the battalion had lost a quarter of its men.[14]

Battalion HQ and A Company found refuge in a farm 'on the southern slopes of a gentle rise, surrounded by thick cactus hedges which as obstacles were as effective as barbed wire'. There was 'plenty of cover, abundant water and fairly solid buildings'. Their main issue, now, was an acute shortage of ammunition.

That afternoon, German troops were observed setting up machine guns and mortars on a ridge a few hundred yards to the north. They attacked at 3 p.m. and, despite taking several casualties, moved steadily closer to the farm perimeter. As the light began to fade, Frost blew his hunting horn: the signal for the battalion to withdraw southeast to a rise known as Djebel El Mengoub where they would rally before continuing their march westwards. But not everyone was able to disengage. Lieutenant Dennis Rendell, commanding 1st Platoon, was wounded by mortar fragments and lost consciousness. He was captured the following morning.[15]

Of the original 200 defenders of the farm, only 110 made the rendezvous. They headed in the direction of Medjez el Bab and, after more close shaves, encountered half-tracks from the US Combat Command B on 3 December. The Americans agreed to take Frost's walking wounded and a small recce party with them back to Medjez and to report their whereabouts. Frost went with them and eventually reached the headquarters of the British 78th Division at Oued Zarga where he spoke to Major General Vyvyan Evelegh. Frost was told that the main battle was being fought further north at Tebourba, on a separate axis of advance, which was probably why so little interest had been taken in his 'abortive mission'. Yet Evelegh reassured him that if the paratroopers had achieved nothing else, they had 'at least drawn off a considerable number of enemy mobile and armoured troops from the main battle'.

The survivors of Frost's battalion were moved back to the village of Sloughia where they were joined by a few C Company men. Both Major Philip Teichman, Frost's deputy, and the adjutant Jock Short had been killed with that company 'when they were isolated and attacked by an armoured column'. There was hardly anyone left from B Company.

Army commander Kenneth Anderson later praised Frost and his men for returning to Allied lines 'after an epic adventure and great physical endeavour, sadly depleted in strength'. But this was little consolation for Frost whose greatest regret was having to abandon his wounded. He could understand the difficulty of finding a worthwhile mission for his battalion when the situation in Tunisia was so fluid, and intelligence was incomplete. What he could not forgive, however, was the failure to support his men once the mission was under way. His battalion had, as a result, been 'cut to pieces' on a pointless venture.[16]

15

'A nasty setback'

Northern Tunisia, 1–4 December 1943

A T 7.45 A.M. ON I December – three days after Kesselring had flown to Tunis and ordered Nehring to regain lost ground – Generalleutnant Wolfgang Fischer launched a four-pronged attack on Tebourba with elements of the 10th Panzer Division attacking from the north, Koch's parachute regiment from the south, and Group Djedeïda, reinforced by two Tiger tanks, in the centre.[1]

The heaviest blow fell on Blade Force, close to the village of Chouïgui, in the form of two V-shaped panzer formations advancing from the north (led by Fischer in person) and northeast. In danger of being cut off, the supply and service units of Blade Force, screened by B Squadron of the 1st Derbyshire Yeomanry, fell back towards the Tebourba Gap, south of Chouïgui. En route, some soft-skin vehicles were shot up by German paratroopers who had infiltrated behind Allied lines to set up an ambush on the Tebourba–Medjez road.[2]

By noon, Blade Force had been 'largely overrun, its headquarters dispersed, and the remainder driven back on Tebourba'. An attempt by Crusader tanks of the 17/21st Lancers to counter-attack from the Tebourba Gap was foiled by long-range fire from German guns concealed in trees. Five Crusaders were knocked out, and the rest withdrew to a knoll northwest of Tebourba in support of the 11th Brigade Group.

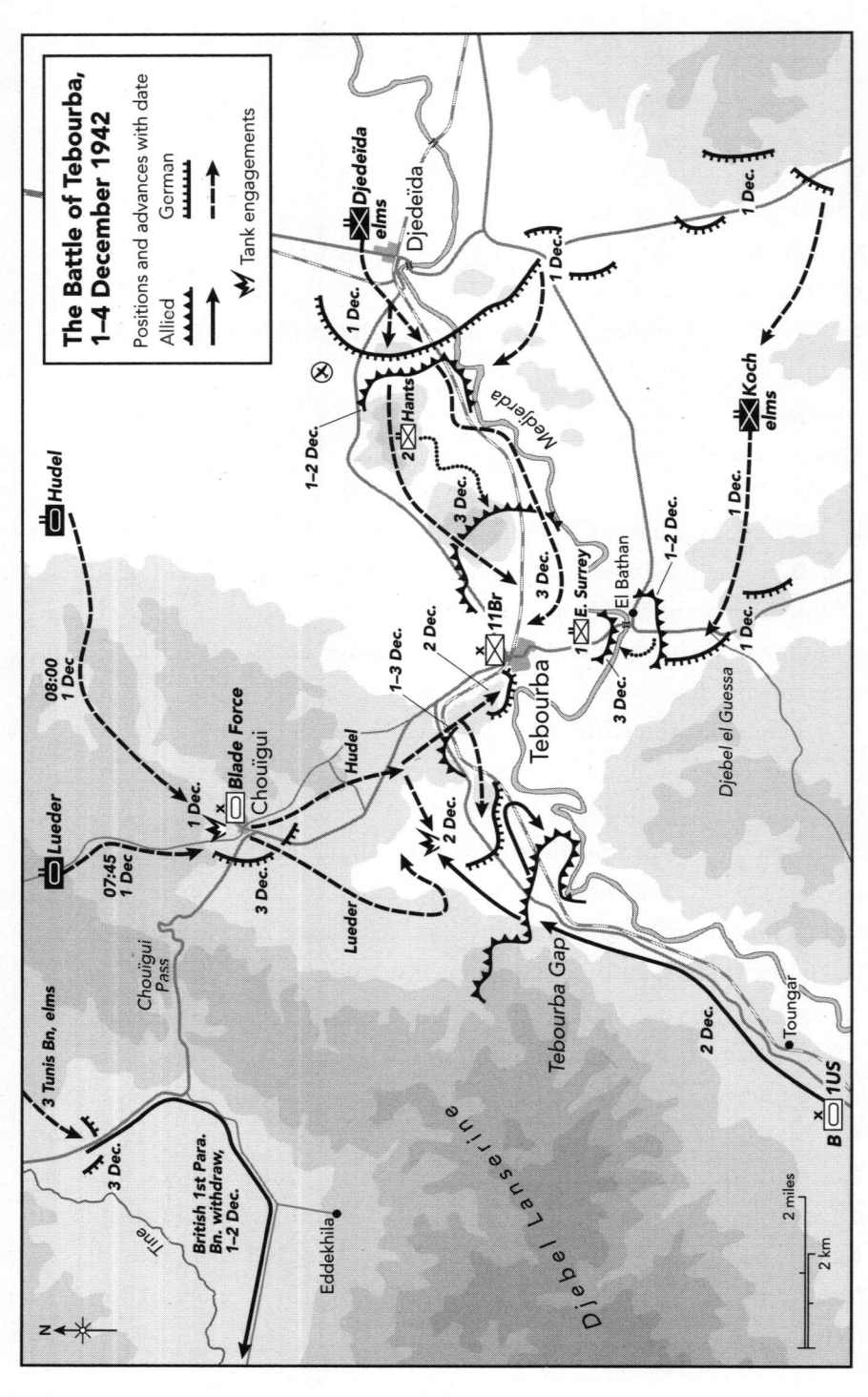

The Battle of Tebourba,
1–4 December 1942

Positions and advances with date

Allied
German

Tank engagements

Hudel

08:00
1 Dec

Lueder

07:45
1 Dec

3 Tunis Bn, elms

3 Dec.

British 1st Para.
Bn. withdraw,
1–2 Dec.

Eddekhila

Chouïgui Pass

Blade Force
Chouïgui

1 Dec.

Hudel

Lueder

3 Dec.

Tine

N

Djedeïda
elms

Djedeïda

1 Dec.

1 Dec.

2 Hants

1–2 Dec.

3 Dec.

3 Dec.

3 Dec.

Medjerda

11Br

2 Dec.

1–3 Dec.

E. Surrey

El Bathan

1–2 Dec.

3 Dec.

Tebourba

1 Dec.

1 Dec.

Koch
elms

1 Dec.

Djebel el Guessa

Tebourba Gap

2 Dec.

Toungar

B 1US

2 km

2 miles

Djebel Lanserine

That afternoon, Fischer's men made two follow-up attacks on Tebourba from the east and southeast. The first assault, from the direction of Djedeïda, was stopped in its tracks by the stubborn resistance of the 2nd Hampshires who had replaced the depleted 5th Northants two days earlier. Fischer, who had raced south in his scout car after the fall of Chouïgui to supervise the attack in person, was horrified by the infantry's lacklustre performance. 'Not the slightest interest existed,' he told Nehring, 'no aggressive spirit, no readiness for action, so that I was forced to lead some companies, platoons, even squads, and to assign them a sector on the battlefield . . . It is impossible to fight successfully with such troops.'

The last attack, by Koch's men, reached points south and east of El Bathan, but failed to capture the stone bridge over the Medjerda which was held by the East Surreys. The supporting 155mm howitzers of the American 5th Field Artillery Battalion, meanwhile, had been withdrawn to Medjez el Bab without authority because they were out of ammunition.

By nightfall, therefore, German forces had closed in on Tebourba from three sides, and only Highway 50, which led southwest to Medjez, offered a possible means of escape for the three battalions of Cass's 11th Infantry Brigade and the remnants of Blade Force. To keep it open, and prevent disaster, Major General Evelegh ordered the tanks and infantry of Combat Command B of the US 1st Armored Division to counter-attack the German panzers northwest of Tebourba.[3]

The meeting between Evelegh and CCB's senior officers – Oliver and Robinett – took place at the former's HQ in a farm well to the rear of the battle line. 'Although friendly and comradely,' wrote Robinett, 'Evelegh's explanation of the situation and the disposition of his troops was vague. Long after the war, I learned the facts and was amazed at the shotgun fashion in which he had scattered his troops in quest of the Germans, who failed to disperse like quail but, instead, concentrated their meager forces on vital terrain features and managed to secure and hold a Tunisian bridgehead against a preponderance of force.'

Robinett would later criticise the Allied generals' habit of siting their command posts 'miles behind the scene of action', whereas the German commanders were right up at the front and 'better situated to bring into play all available means in the Tunis area'. This factor, in his view, 'undoubtedly had a decisive effect on the outcome of the initial battle for Tunis'.[4] Another was the tangled chain of command, and the myriad of different personalities: Evelegh, the pugnacious but relatively inexperienced boss of the British 78th (Battleaxe) Infantry Division; Oliver, the chief of Combat Command B, who had done well in the Oran landings but, like Evelegh, was still undercooked when it came to directing troops in battle; Robinett, the talented but self-regarding leader of the 13th Armored Regiment; and above all the disastrous Bruss, the young commander of one of Robinett's two tank battalions who, as it turned out, had been promoted way beyond his ability.

Another disaster in waiting was Oliver's plan, scheduled for the morning of 2 December, to use three tank battalions – Todd's 1/13th, Waters's 1/1st (which had narrowly avoided destruction, as part of Blade Force, the previous day) and Bruss's 2/13th – to outflank and destroy the enemy armour. This flew in the face of existing American tank doctrine, which held that tanks should not fight tanks, but should rather destroy enemy defences and infiltrate to the rear. Stopping enemy armour was the job of anti-tank guns and specialist tank destroyers. Yet Oliver's tanks would be supported by only a single battery of field artillery. The rest of the guns and both battalions of armoured infantry would not be involved. 'Available information,' wrote Robinett, 'the lack of coordination of British and American troops present on the same ground, and the improbability of the various arms being employed so as to afford mutual support made me rather pessimistic of the outcome. Certainly, our prospects were not very propitious.'

At 9 a.m. on the 2nd, Robinett went forward with a small staff in his command vehicles – a quarter-ton car known as a 'Peep', the command half-truck and an escort of light tanks – to coordinate the attack. After just a few miles their movement was betrayed by smoke rising from the far bank of the Medjerda river, 'put out by enemy agents or subverted natives', and minutes later they were strafed by enemy planes and forced to take cover in ditches beside the highway. A truck nearby received a direct hit from a bomb and 'started to burn, increasing the number of derelicts already obstructing traffic'.

At noon, close to where the Medjerda river turns east towards Tebourba, Robinett dismounted from his 'Peep' and climbed a steep ridge. He had a bird's-eye view of some of Waters's tanks on the forward slope and a company of British infantry in slit trenches. On the far side of the valley, at a distance of about 1,500 to 2,000 yards, were at least twenty-five German Mark III and Mark IV panzers 'widely deployed' and apparently preparing to attack.

Speaking to each of his battalion commanders in turn, Robinett realised they were in 'no condition to fight offensively' and that a proper command structure was vital. Bruss explained that he had lost radio contact with most of his battalion which was down to about twenty-five medium tanks and still in the vicinity of Tebourba. He was, thought Robinett, acting 'like a beaten man'. Waters's light tank battalion had also suffered heavy losses, while Todd had only two companies of light tanks present. They had attempted to advance at 9.30 a.m., but were beaten back. As it was clear to Robinett that the American armour was no match for its opponents, he called off any further attacks.

What he did not realise until later was that Bruss had already ordered the medium Lee tanks of his E Company to attack Tebourba from the west with a view to extricating the rest of his battalion. The company commander, Captain Mayshark, had questioned the sense of such an order without proper reconnaissance. But Bruss insisted and, in the space of barely twenty minutes, eight of the Lees were knocked out by German

88mm anti-tank guns. 'Some of the men died in those tanks,' wrote Robinett, 'and others, badly burned and wounded, were saved by their comrades under enemy fire in total disregard of their own safety.' Mayshark's tank was among those hit.[5]

Bruss had also contacted his XO, Major Gardiner, on the 1/1st Battalion's radio net, and instructed him to make a simultaneous attack from the east with the surviving tanks of D and F Companies. 'He said,' recalled Gardiner, 'that the plan was to have us attack from one side and E Company, which was now back with the CCB, was to come on from the other flank, and we were to "destroy" the enemy in this area.'

Gardiner had a low opinion of Bruss who, he noted in his diary, 'isn't the easiest to get along with'. He was surprised when Robinett made him a battalion commander. 'Our Colonel,' wrote Gardiner, 'knew him as a sergeant and had a high regard for his ability and has been responsible in a large measure for his rapid advance.'

Robinett was generally a good judge of character, but he badly misread Bruss who was not up to the job of commanding a tank battalion in action. He had already shown signs of over-confidence – telling Gardiner in late November that they would 'soon be in Tunis' – and tactical naivety, as evidenced by his insistence on the costly all-out attack on German positions at Djedeïda on the 30th. He also had an alarming habit of going walkabout, and for blaming others for his inadequacies. After Gardiner, in his absence, withdrew the battalion closer to Tebourba on 1 December, Bruss had all but accused him of 'being yellow'.

The orders for Mayshark and Gardiner to attack without support on the 2nd were yet more examples of Bruss's incompetence. During the advance in his M3 command tank, Gardiner spotted a German panzer at a distance of 300 yards. Out of 75mm ammunition, he engaged the tank with his 37mm gun and hit it twice with armour-piercing rounds. The enemy crew baled out and tried to flee, but were forced back to the cover of their burning tank. Focused on their victims, Gardiner and his crew failed to spot another German panzer take aim. 'There was a blinding flash in the tank,' he wrote, 'a scream and I realized I had been hurt. I jumped out of the tank and ran back a short distance and crouched. There had been seven of us in the tank and I saw four get out.'

As more shells came in, Gardiner moved into a gully to take stock of his injuries. He had a slight cut on his right wrist, but a more serious one on his elbow that was 'bleeding quite freely'. From his first-aid kit he got out some sulfanilamide anti-bacterial powder and sprinkled it on the wound. But he was too weak and light-headed to apply the bandage, and put this down to exhaustion and loss of blood. Eventually another tank stopped and the commander helped him fix the bandage. Feeling a little better, he climbed back up the hill to take stock: the other American tanks had halted and backed up a short distance, but were well deployed to handle a frontal attack. The German tanks were in their original positions. In the valley beyond them, burning fiercely, were at least six of E Company's tanks. Others appeared to be disabled.

As darkness fell on 2 December, he left the tanks on the hill covering the road out of Tebourba, but moved them closer together for mutual protection, and put the half-tracks in a hollow to the rear. He also sent word to the CCB headquarters that his 'position would be untenable by daylight with the enemy apparently advancing steadily on both sides'.[6]

Robinett had come to the same conclusion. After postponing any further attacks by CCB, he had gone to consult Brigadier Cass at his command post in a nearby ravine. Cass told him that his brigade was 'tired and too thinly spread', and that he needed the CCB to bolster his left flank which 'he thought was threatened'. Cass's positioning of his forces appeared to Robinett to be 'most peculiar'. The only connection between the two elements of his command were the tanks of Bruss's 2/13th Armored Regiment, 'against which the Germans were bringing terrific pressure west of Tebourba'. It was clear to Robinett that Cass's brigade was in grave danger unless the Allies could bring up more troops to resume the offensive. If they could not be brought up promptly, he told Cass, Tebourba 'should be abandoned'.

Cass agreed, and said he would point out the situation to his divisional commander, Major General Evelegh.[7]

Despite Robinett's advice, Cass's brigade was still holding Tebourba when German panzer grenadiers (motorised infantry) attacked a vital ridge east of the town at 10 a.m. on 3 December. In the savage fighting that followed, 26-year-old Major Wallace Le Patourel of the 2nd Hampshires and four volunteers managed to knock out several enemy machine-gun posts. With all his men casualties, Le Patourel continued the assault, and was last seen clutching his pistol and throwing grenades. Assumed to have been killed, he was later awarded a posthumous Victoria Cross. This was corrected to a living award when Le Patourel turned up in an enemy prisoner-of-war camp, wounded but alive.[8]

The loss of the ridge was decisive. At 7 p.m., the senior officer in Tebourba gave orders for the remnants of the 2nd Hampshires, 1st East Surreys and supporting troops to evacuate the town and withdraw south along the river bank. It was a nightmare retreat, as vehicles at the head of the column were hit and set on fire. With all movement stopped, and progress impossible, the vehicles – including field guns, tractors and motor transport, along with much ammunition – were abandoned and the troops made their way cross-country as best they could. Fortunately, the hills to the south of the river had been cleared earlier that day by the US 6th Armored Infantry, thus sparing the fugitives harassing fire from the flank. They were thankful for small mercies.

At 11 a.m. on 4 December, Tebourba fell to the Germans. 'Heavy losses inflicted on the enemy,' reported Generalleutnant Fischer. 'Valuable booty.' His estimate of Allied losses in the four-day battle was 55 tanks, 4 armoured cars, 4 anti-tank guns, 6 100mm guns, 6 120mm guns, 13 smaller guns, 38 machine guns, 40 mortars, 300 motor vehicles, 1,100 prisoners and huge quantities of ammunition.[9]

In a letter to Eisenhower, Anderson described the defeat as 'a nasty setback' that had cost the Allies heavy losses in tanks, men and guns. The 11th Infantry Brigade, in particular, had exhausted its 'fighting value' and would not be in a position to re-enter the fray until it had been rested, reinforced and refitted. The 1st East Surreys and 5th Northamptons were both down to about 350 all ranks (less than half a typical infantry battalion's strength of 800), the 2nd Lancashire Fusiliers was 450-strong, while the 2nd Hampshires (lent by the 1st Guards Brigade) had been, to all intents and purposes, 'wiped out'.

How had this happened? Anderson cited a number of factors that included the enemy's air superiority; the failure of the local commander, Evelegh, to appreciate the danger to his troops in Tebourba after the enemy had captured the Chouïgui ridge; the faulty use of field artillery in penny-packets (small groups, rather than concentrated in large formations); the poor handling of American medium tanks which had counter-attacked without any support from field artillery and tank destroyer guns; and the most important factor, which was that 'after such a long advance and a series of successful minor clashes, there was almost a sense of careless "dash" and a failure to adopt proper action and tactics when faced by a serious assault by tanks, until too late'.

Under the circumstances, said Anderson, it would be impossible to launch any follow-up attack until 9 December at the earliest, by which time the 1st Guards Brigade would have relieved Cass's 11th. In the interim, he hoped to continue armoured probes towards Tunis 'to keep the Hun busy and guessing'. Nowhere were First Army troops to be allowed to adopt an attitude of passive defence. Aggressive patrolling was to be the order of the day.

He ended the letter by stating that the enemy's control of the air was an 'increasingly unhappy' situation that could not continue indefinitely, and that ongoing problems with resupply would inevitably limit the size of the force that he could put into the field. Worried that his tone was overly pessimistic, he added a handwritten postscript that there had been 'many gallant deeds and there is no loss of spirit'.[10]

Anderson made no mention, of course, of his own failings, which included a tangled and inadequate command structure, the setting up of his command post too far from the scene of battle (a problem that extended down the chain of authority), and an inability to intervene decisively when disaster beckoned, as it had after the defeat of Blade Force near Chouïgui on 1 December.

Ike, it should be said, was well aware of the difficulties facing Anderson's First Army. He told Marshall on 30 November:

When I made the decision to rush our forces into Tunisia as rapidly as possible, I did so in full realization that we were assuming the inescapable risk of having bases damaged, particularly by night air attack, of sabotage on lines of communication, and of having some of our small columns get into bad tactical situations. However, I felt that the Axis was startled and upset by our initial landing and that I was perfectly justified in assuming any risks that did not actually jeopardize seriously what we had already gained.

On the 30th, he had still been hopeful of pinning the enemy into the twin fortresses of Bizerte and Tunis, and 'confining him so closely that the danger of a break-out or a heavy counter-offensive will be minimized'. Ike's plan then was to use air and artillery to pound the Axis troops 'so hard that the way for a final and decisive blow can be adequately prepared'. As for his field commander Anderson, he seemed to be 'imbued with the will to win, but blows hot and cold, by turns, in his estimates and resulting demands'.[11]

Three days later, while the battle at Tebourba was still raging, Eisenhower had informed the Combined Chiefs of Staff that the Allies had now 'gone beyond the sustainable limit of air capabilities in supporting ground forces in a pell-mell race for Tunisia'. With Allied air operations close to 'complete breakdown', they needed a breathing space of at least a week to provide airfields closer to the front, maintenance troops and spares, and early warning radar and anti-aircraft facilities. Only then could they continue their advance with the 'principal objective' being the capture of Tunis; that, in turn, would 'throw the enemy back into the Bizerte stronghold' where they could be confined while additional means were brought forward for the 'final kill'.[12]

Ike's letter to the Combined Chiefs of Staff was written after a conference at Algiers with his senior commanders, including Anderson (army), Admiral Sir Andrew Cunningham (navy) and Air Marshal Sir William Welsh, Lieutenant General Carl 'Tooey' Spaatz and Major General Jimmy Doolittle★ (all air force). They concluded, wrote Ike's naval aide Harry Butcher, that the First Army had reached, at least for the moment, a point of 'diminishing power', being at the end of a long and tortuous line of supply. Axis planes, tanks and mines had stopped Anderson's advance 'within twenty-five miles of Tunis and Bizerte'. Butcher added: 'Overnight it looked to Ike as if we would be stalemated and would have to begin the slow process of methodically building up, just as Generals Alexander and Montgomery had to do at El Alamein.'[13]

Ike never mentioned it, but a key factor in the Allies' failure to win the 'Race for Tunis' was faulty intelligence. Prior to the landings, the Joint Intelligence Committee (JIC) – set up in the 1930s as a subcommittee of the British Chiefs of Staff to assess military intelligence – had correctly estimated the Axis strength immediately available in the western Mediterranean. But in forecasting the Axis, primarily German, ability to deploy reinforcements to North Africa once the landings had begun, Allied intelligence judgement 'proved badly flawed'.

JIC expected 515 aircraft to be deployed by the Luftwaffe against Torch forces within a month. The actual figure was 850 and, according to Andrew Boyd, author of *British Naval Intelligence Through the Twentieth*

★ Doolittle had won the Medal of Honor and national fame for leading the so-called 'Doolittle Raid' on 18 April 1942, four months after Pearl Harbor, when sixteen B-25 bombers with reduced armament to lighten their weight and no fighter escort had struck Tokyo. The raid was a major morale booster for the United States.

Century, many planes 'were operating from Tunisia, which the JIC had discounted as a base for German air operations'. Boyd added:

> Within days the Germans increased transport aircraft numbers by an astonishing factor of three, and had an armoured division transported and operational in Tunisia by end November, a month before the JIC had judged this feasible. This underestimate of German reinforcement capacity had serious consequences. It meant Allied forces were too weak, and deployed on too narrow a front, to take Tunisia before the Germans could deploy major forces there.[14]

16

'My word still counts for something'

North Africa, Germany and Italy, 20 November1–2 December 1942

'Dearest Lu,' wrote Erwin Rommel to his wife on 11 December from the Libyan coast, 700 miles southeast of Tunis. 'Not much news. Things have livened up a little at the front. Our supply troubles are as bad as ever and are causing me a lot of headaches ... Nehring has been relieved of his command and a Colonel-General has taken over. I wonder if he'll do any better.'[1]

The *Generaloberst* in question was 53-year-old Hans-Jürgen von Arnim, a hawk-nosed scion of an old Prussian military family and veteran of both world wars who, until recently, had commanded a panzer corps in Russia. Diligent and hard-working, but lacking in charisma, he was seen by Hitler as a safe pair of hands who would secure Tunisia while Rommel regrouped in Libya.

The Axis had done well to win the 'Race for Tunis', but the broader outlook was far from rosy. Though Rommel had saved his Panzer Army from destruction in Egypt, it was outnumbered and outgunned by Montgomery's Eighth Army and, with supplies hard to come by, the imbalance would only get worse. The same could be said for the troops rushed to Tunisia to forestall the Allies. They had performed miracles thus far. But sooner or later – unless Rommel or Arnim could conjure a crushing battlefield victory from somewhere – the Allies' superiority in men and materiel was bound to tell.

Kesselring had forced the issue by insisting that Axis forces in Tunisia needed to be coordinated by an army HQ. Hence the formation of the Fifth Panzer Army in early December, though its initial strength 'consisted of little more than a number of hastily collected units, the equivalent of one or two German divisions with very little transport or heavy weapons'.[2] Despite his successful defence of Tunis, Nehring had paid the price for losing Medjez el Bab and his persistent pessimism. He wrote:

On the 7th [December] I was informed . . . that General von Arnim had to take over my command. Arnim arrived on the 9th December at noon; we met for four hours and at dusk I started back to Sicily. I had the impression that Arnim had the same optimistic ideas about the situation as Hitler. We had a discussion, but he had fixed orders. They were: to make a decisive breakthrough in the general direction Algiers![3]

Ultimately, Arnim was expected to coordinate his offensive with Erwin Rommel who, until his unauthorised withdrawal from El Alamein, had been Hitler's favourite field commander. But, unbeknown to the Führer, Rommel no longer believed that a successful Axis defence of North Africa was possible.

Born in the relative backwater of Swabia, Württemberg, in November 1891, the son of a schoolmaster, the young Rommel – small, pale-faced, fair-haired and blue-eyed – did not seem destined for the military. He was neither particularly academic nor sporty, and there was no tradition of soldiering in his family. He possessed, however, extraordinary physical toughness and courage. It helped, too, that his mother was a 'von', a member of the minor nobility, which opened doors when Erwin said he wanted to become a soldier.

He joined the Württemberg infantry as a cadet in 1910, and was commissioned two years later. But he first came to national prominence in 1917 when he was awarded the *Pour le Mérite* (or 'Blue Max', Imperial Germany's highest gallantry medal) for outstanding leadership during the Battle of Caporetto. Between the wars he wrote an infantry training manual, commanded a battalion of elite *Jäger*, and taught at the War Academy in Potsdam. His memoir *Infantry Attacks* became an international bestseller and brought him to the attention of Adolf Hitler who gave him the command of his escort battalion. He was, at this stage, an uncritical supporter of the Nazi regime, though he never joined the party.

In the summer of 1939, Rommel was promoted to *Generalmajor* (major general) in charge of Hitler's special field headquarters, and was responsible for the Führer's personal security during the six-week Polish campaign. The experience made him, if anything, even more of an admirer, as his biographer David Fraser wrote:

> He had been comforted by the immense restoration of national morale Hitler had brought about. He had marvelled at what seemed the diplomatic skill by which Hitler had achieved so many patriotic ends with (until now) so little international opposition; and he had turned his attention away from the excesses, the blemishes, as things typical of some of the undesirables who had always attached themselves to Hitler but utterly untypical of the Führer himself. With Hitler, Rommel's relations were now easy, friendly and gratifying. He had, he recorded during the campaign, frequent chats with him, and even a talk of about two hours on military problems.[4]

In early 1940, without any experience of armoured warfare, Rommel requested and was given command of a panzer division – the 7th – which he led with distinction during the Blitzkrieg campaign in Belgium and France. Nicknamed the *Gespensterdivision* ('Ghost Division'), because of its ability to appear where least expected, the 7th was the first German formation to pierce the French defences on the River Meuse and later took the surrender of the British 51st (Highland) Division at Saint Valery-en-Caux in Normandy, for which Rommel was awarded the Knight's Cross, Nazi Germany's equivalent of the Blue Max. Unusually for a divisional commander, Rommel led from the front, giving verbal orders and exposing himself to enemy fire. He was, noted Fraser, an 'individualist, his opponents said an egomaniac and ungenerous about others (as some were to say about Montgomery), a commander with absolute faith in himself and his guiding star, of iron will'.

That faith was tested by the huge challenge of his next appointment, in February 1941, to command the two-division Afrika Korps sent to Libya to assist the Italians whose North African empire, thanks to the catastrophic recent defeat of Graziani's Tenth Army by O'Connor's Western Desert Force, was hanging by a thread. Displaying his customary boldness and tactical brilliance, Rommel led the Afrika Korps and, later, the Italo–German Panzer Army to many victories over British and Commonwealth forces in Libya and Egypt, earning him the respect of friend and foe and the nickname 'the Desert Fox'. His high-water mark was the capture of Tobruk after a long siege on 22 June 1942, a feat for which he was sent a field marshal's baton and Hitler's customary signal of thanks: '*Vorwarts zum Sieg, fur Führer, Volk und Reich!*'[5]

But after defeats by Montgomery at Alam Halfa and El Alamein – thus shattering his dream of reaching the Suez Canal and controlling the oilfields of the Middle East – Rommel lost confidence in himself and faith in Hitler's strategy. His uncharacteristic refusal to obey the Führer's express order 'not to yield a step' on 4 November was done to save his Panzer Army from destruction. It worked. But his relationship with Hitler never recovered.

Thereafter, starved of supplies and physically exhausted, Rommel had the demeanour of a beaten man. 'Rommel was continuing his retreat,' remembered Kesselring, 'and bombarding me with impossible demands for reinforcements, which I could not even begin to satisfy. The oversea supply lines had been curtailed, communications through Tunisia had not yet been organised and I had no justification for robbing my own air-transport formations.'[6]

There was also the issue of Rommel's deteriorating relationship with his Italian superior Maresciallo (Marshal) Ettore Bastico, the Governor-General of Libya and Commander-in-Chief of Axis forces in North Africa. On 12 November, four days after the Allied landings, Bastico had been ordered by Ugo Cavallero, the head of the Italian armed forces, to defend the Marsa el Brega line near El Algheila, on the border between Cyrenaica and Tripolitania. Bastico agreed to do so, but on condition that Rommel, whom he considered 'morally beaten' since his defeat at El Alamein, was sacked. Cavallero refused.[7]

Bastico, however, was right to suspect Rommel of defeatism. On 20 November, as his Panzer Army continued its long retreat from El Alamein, Rommel confided his fears to one of his favourite officers, 31-year-old Major Hans-Ulrich Freiherr von Luck. The two had met in 1931 when the then Captain Rommel was an instructor at the infantry school in Dresden and Luck an officer cadet. In 1940, during the invasion of France, Luck had commanded the 7th Panzer Division's armoured reconnaissance battalion. The young officer had gone on to fight in Russia but in April 1942, at Rommel's request, transferred to North Africa where he assumed command of the 21st Panzer Division's 3rd Reconnaissance Battalion. In November, Luck was flown from his base at the Siwa Oasis to meet his old boss at an airfield in Libya. 'Rommel looked exhausted,' wrote Luck. 'His uniform was worn and dusty. The hard withdrawal actions, his deep disappointment, and his fitness, not yet fully cured, had left their mark on him.'

What shocked Luck the most, however, as the two men walked arm in arm beside the airfield, was Rommel's deep pessimism for the future. 'Luck, it's the end!' said Rommel, his face lined and shoulders drooping. 'We can't even hold Tripolitania, but must fall back on Tunisia. There, in addition, we shall come up against the Americans and, possibly, also the French. What I was afraid of weeks ago will then occur: our proud Africa Army, and the new divisions that have landed in northern Tunisia, will be lost.'

'Generalfeldmarschall,' responded Luck, 'we still have a chance. The men are behind you, their morale is first-class. If we can get sufficient supplies, we're bound to pull it off.'

Rommel smiled. 'I know,' he said, 'and I'm proud of the men. But the supplies will not be forthcoming. Hitler's HQ has already written off this theatre of war. All he requires now is that the "German soldier stands or dies." What we need is to create a German "Dunkirk"; that means flying out as many officers, men and specialists as possible to Sicily, while leaving the materiel behind. We need the men for the decisive struggle in Europe.'

'How will you ever put that to Hitler?' asked Luck.

'After consulting Kesselring and the Italians, I shall fly to Hitler and make my opinion clear to him, beyond all doubt. My word still counts for something; I am still respected among the people and by my men. I don't believe anymore that we shall get what we need in further divisions, aircraft, and supplies, in order to turn the wheel yet again.'

Rommel paused, his face a picture of dejection, then said: 'Luck, the war is lost!'

The young officer was appalled. 'We're still deep in Russia,' he protested. 'Half Europe is occupied by us. Bitter though the loss of North Africa will be, we can carry on the fight in Europe and bring about a change of fortune.'

Rommel slowly shook his head. 'Luck,' he said, 'we've got to seek an armistice, precisely because we still have a lot of pawns in hand. If possible, an armistice with the Western Allies. We still have something to offer. This assumes, of course, that Hitler must be forced to abdicate; that we must give up the persecution of the Jews at once and make concessions to the Church. That might sound Utopian, but it is the only way of avoiding further bloodshed and still more destruction in our cities.'

This was dangerous talk – or so Luck reported it in his post-war memoir – and Luck held his tongue as they walked back to Rommel's command post.[8]

The Desert Fox's immediate priority was to avoid the destruction of his army at Marsa el Brega, the southernmost port in the Mediterranean, by Montgomery's Eighth Army, which was pursuing them from Egypt. This could only be achieved, he told Bastico, by withdrawing another 200 miles west to the port of Buerat, which would allow more time for reinforcements and supplies to reach him.

Even Mussolini recognised the importance of resupplying Rommel's Italo-German army and securing the Axis presence in North Africa. If it fell to the Allies, Italy could do nothing but wait passively for an Allied invasion which might take place on any part of its coast between southern France and Greece. It would be impossible to defend. Yet resupplying North Africa was a major problem. The sea route to Tripoli was now threatened by Allied planes and vessels based at both Malta and Algeria. Italy had only five fast merchant ships left, and few escorts. The vast majority of supplies, therefore, had to come by air.[9]

To discuss the situation, Kesselring and Cavallero flew from Rome and met Rommel and Bastico at Arco di Fileni (known to the Allies as 'Marble Arch'), close to the Tripolitania/Cyrenaica border, on 24 November. Rommel opened the meeting by describing the course of the fighting since Alamein, the poor supply situation and the fact that his army had lost most of its heavy equipment. The remnants represented in fighting strength 'approximately one weak division', while the armament of three Italian infantry divisions was practically unusable. It was, therefore, impossible to hold Marsa el Brega and the best option, in his opinion, was to evacuate Libya entirely and withdraw to Gabès, inside Tunisia, where the terrain favoured the defender. It would be, he added, too late to make such a withdrawal in two or three weeks when the British attacked the line with 800 armoured vehicles, 400 pieces of artillery and 550 anti-tank guns. To hold the Marsa el Brega line, said Rommel, would require the delivery within a week of at least 50 75mm anti-tank guns, 50 long-barrelled Panzer IVs, 78 field guns of at least 100mm calibre, and 4,000 tons each of petrol and ammunition.

Such a rapid resupply was, both Kesselring and Cavallero knew, impossible. But nor would they agree to Rommel's request to evacuate Libya. The former 'looked at everything from the standpoint of the Luftwaffe, and thought principally of the consequences which the move would have on the strategic air situation'; the latter thought too rapid a retreat to Tunisia would simply lock the troops up in a 'surrender citadel'. Their solution was a compromise: the Marsa el Brega line would be held for as long as possible, but in the event of a 'preponderant enemy attack' Bastico and Rommel could withdraw to Buerat.

Two days later, they received additional instructions from Rome: they were to detach some troops to protect Tripoli, but the majority would defend the Marsa el Brega line as Mussolini had requested. But Il Duce also wanted them to launch an attack on the pursuing British 'as soon as possible', using Luftwaffe reinforcements that were on their way. Only in the 'direst emergency', insisted the Comando Supremo, was Bastico to order a retreat.

Their meagre forces would thus be split three ways. A furious Rommel decided to bypass Rome and appeal directly to the Führer, as he had threatened to Luck he would. 'I wanted to ask him personally for a strategic decision,' wrote Rommel, 'and to request, as a long-term policy, the evacuation of North Africa. I intended to lay before him the operational and tactical views of the Panzer Army.'[10]

Unfortunately for Rommel, his timing could not have been worse. Since returning to the Wolf's Lair field headquarters at Rastenburg, East Prussia, on 21 November, Hitler had been preoccupied with the effort to relieve Paulus's Sixth Army encircled in Stalingrad. Having rejected the request by Kurt Zeitzler, the Chief of the Army General Staff, for the Sixth Army to be allowed to fight its way out, he had ordered Generaloberst Hermann Hoth's 4th Panzer Army to advance from Kotelnikov, southwest of the city, and break through the Russian siege lines. But Hoth needed at least ten days' preparation, and in the meantime Paulus had to hold his ground, while his troops were supplied by air. Luftwaffe chief Reichsmarschall Hermann Göring had assured

Hitler that such an expedient was possible; Generaloberst Wolfram Freiherr von Richthofen, commanding Luftflotte (Air Fleet) 4, disagreed on the grounds of worsening weather and an inadequate number of aircraft. But Hitler sided with Göring.

Hitler's decision was backed, curiously enough, by Generalfeldmarschall Erich von Manstein who, on 24 November, had been given command of the new Army Group Don, including the trapped Sixth Army. As one of Hitler's most trusted generals, his opinion mattered.[11]

This frantic debate about the fate of Paulus's Sixth Army at Stalingrad was still ongoing when Rommel reached Rastenburg during the afternoon of 28 November, having flown that day from North Africa. He was driven by staff car from the airfield to the Wolf's Lair, built in 1941 in the gloomy Masurian woods as Hitler's temporary field headquarters for the invasion of Russia.[12]

Having passed through the inner security checkpoint, Rommel was dropped outside the long, narrow conference room,* close to the guest bunker in the western half of the compound, where he met Keitel, Jodl and Generalmajor Rudolf Schmundt (Hitler's chief military adjutant). The first two he found 'extremely wary and reserved'. At 5 p.m. he was taken to speak to Hitler. 'There was,' recorded Rommel, 'a noticeable chill in the atmosphere from the outset. I described all the difficulties which the army had had to face during both the battle and the retreat. It was all noted and the execution of the operation was described as faultless and unique.'

Rommel then came – rather 'too abruptly', as he acknowledged later – to the crux of the matter: as he did not anticipate any improvement in the supply situation, 'the abandonment of the African theatre of war should be accepted as a long-term policy'. He told Hitler: 'There should be no illusions about the situation and all the planning

---

* The same conference room in which, twenty months later, Oberst Claus von Stauffenberg would attempt to assassinate Hitler by detonating a briefcase bomb in the so-called July Bomb-Plot. Hitler was wounded but survived.

should be directed towards what was attainable. If the army remained in North Africa, it would be destroyed.'

Expecting a 'rational discussion', Rommel was shocked when Hitler 'flew into a fury' and directed a 'stream of completely unfounded attacks' on him and his Panzer Army which included, among other calumnies, that they had thrown away their weapons. Rommel tried to defend his men by saying that their weapons had simply been 'battered to pieces by the British bombers, tanks and artillery and it was nothing short of a miracle' that they had been able to escape with all the German motorised forces, particularly given the 'desperate petrol shortage'. But Hitler refused to listen, preferring to argue that his decision to stand firm on the Eastern Front in the winter of 1941–2 had saved Germany's Russian conquests. The same was now necessary in North Africa where there was a 'political necessity' to maintain a major bridgehead – presumably to bolster his fellow dictator and ally Mussolini – and 'there would, therefore, be no withdrawal from the Marsa el Brega line'.[13]

Hitler's one concession was that he would do everything possible to get supplies to Rommel. It was, after all, only 'a short hop' to Tunis from Italy, and to expedite the process Göring would accompany Rommel back to Rome with 'extraordinary powers' to negotiate with the Italians.

The abusive tone adopted by Hitler at this meeting was proof that Rommel's unauthorised withdrawal from the Alamein position in early November had not been forgiven. Far from it. Nor was the dictator sincere in his promise to get Rommel the supplies he needed. According to Warlimont, Hitler told the OKW Operations Staff on 7 December that he considered it 'a positive advantage that for the moment Rommel's Army has insufficient fuel to enable it to withdraw further'.

A few days later, however, while briefing Generaloberst Hans-Jürgen von Arnim, who was about to take command of the newly formed Fifth Panzer Army in Tunisia, Hitler was far more optimistic about Axis prospects. His idea, according to Warlimont, 'was that, after driving the enemy from port to port as far as Casablanca', Arnim's army 'should finally throw him out altogether'. He was, needless to say, heavily influenced by Kesselring's optimism with regards to 'future developments both in Tunis and as regards the sea situation'.[14]

Warlimont's boss Jodl had also got the message. Asking his staff to produce a three-page strategic summary, he anticipated it with his own thesis that North Africa was the 'glacis of Europe' and needed to be held 'under all circumstances'.

Yes-men like Keitel and Jodl were telling Hitler what he wanted to hear. On 30 November, the OKW Operations Staff war diary had recorded that the Führer was 'confident regarding Sixth Army's situation at Stalingrad'. Meanwhile Vichy France had been occupied without incident and Italo-German forces had successfully formed a bridgehead around Tunis. 'So by the end of November,' wrote Warlimont, 'there was once more a deceptive atmosphere of confidence in German Supreme Headquarters.'[15]

Rommel, on the other hand, was acutely aware of the difficulties his and von Arnim's troops were facing in North Africa, a situation that the puffed-up Göring did nothing to improve when the pair reached Rome on the latter's special train. The Luftwaffe chief possessed, wrote Rommel, 'inordinate ambition and had no scruples about the means he used to advance it.

Thus he thought there were easy laurels to be earned on the African front and was angling to manoeuvre the Luftwaffe into control of it. Units of his Praetorian Guard, the Panzer Division 'Hermann Göring', were already on their way to Tunis. His estimate of the possibilities offered by the African theatre was a disastrous fallacy. I do not think that there has been any other front where we have been opposed by a command with such excellent qualities and by such well-trained troops – not to mention their equipment and armament . . . Our only advantage over them was our modern conception of war, and this was of no avail once the material conditions for it no longer existed.

Aware that the Italians also had a say in strategy, Rommel had worked hard on the journey to Rome to convince Göring to back his plan to withdraw the Panzer Army to Gabès in southern Tunisia, from where it could join with the motorised forces of Arnim's rapidly forming Fifth Panzer Army and attack the Allied forces in Algeria. But no sooner had they reached the Eternal City than the slippery Göring, influenced by Kesselring, did a U-turn. The Reichsmarschall now felt that to gift Libya to the Allies – thus giving them a Malta–Algiers–Tripoli air triangle that would pose a serious threat to Axis forces in Tunisia – 'outweighed the advantages' of Rommel's plan.

Later that day, all three met with Mussolini, Cavallero and Ammiraglio (Admiral) Arturo Riccardi, the head of the Italian navy. It got off to a bad start when Göring, out of the blue, accused Rommel of leaving the Italians in the lurch at Alamein. Before he could respond to this 'outrageous statement', Mussolini said: 'That's news to me; your retreat was a masterpiece, Marshal Rommel.'[16]

Cavallero also had a bone to pick with Rommel for going over Bastico's head and appealing to Hitler directly. Had an Italian general done such a thing, said Cavallero, 'he would be put in front of a military tribunal for abandoning his post in the face of the enemy'.[17] Yet the Italians also knew that a last stand at Marsa el Brega would mean the destruction of the Panzer Army, which was why Mussolini gave Rommel permission to begin building a new defensive line at Buerat, 200 miles to the west, and to 'take steps to move the non-motorised Italian infantry back there in good time'. In the event of a British attack, the motorised troops could also withdraw. 'That was,' wrote Rommel, 'at least something.'

What the Desert Fox could not forgive, however, was Göring's constant undermining of his position. He was convinced that the Reichsmarschall wanted to get him sacked 'in order to realise his own plans in North Africa'. To this end, he dismissed every report Rommel sent to the Führer's HQ as 'mere pessimism', and promoted the idea that he 'was governed by moods and could only command when things went well'; if they went badly he 'became depressed and caught the "African sickness"'.

Flying back to Africa on 2 December, Rommel realised that he and his army were effectively on their own, and that to prevent its destruction 'as the result of some crazy order or other would need all our skill'.

It did not help that, after Arnim had set up his new Fifth Panzer Army HQ in Tunis on 10 December, there was very little coordination between his command and Rommel's. They were equals, but also rivals, competing for reinforcements and supplies. 'We badly felt the need during this period,' wrote Rommel, 'of a single authority on African soil which could have welded together under a single common command the two armies whose fates were so closely dependent on each other.'[18]

Rommel felt, needless to say, that he – and not Bastico or Arnim – was the obvious choice to command both armies. In the meantime, his priority was to prevent his Panzer Army from being overwhelmed by superior enemy forces. To that end, he began withdrawing his Italian infantry from the Marsa el Brega position to Buerat on 10 December, before Montgomery could attack in earnest, and the rest of his troops followed on the 12th. 'There was,' wrote Rommel, 'no hope of opposing a British outflanking thrust with the motorised forces; we had too little petrol. It would therefore have been suicide to have remained in the position any longer.'[19]

When Hitler learned of Rommel's withdrawal on the 12th, he told a meeting of his top commanders that it had been a mistake to abandon the Alamein position which could have been held 'by a couple of divisions', some tanks and artillery. Instead they had moved back a thousand miles with their 'household stuff and everything else they could lay their hands on' and, as a result, had suffered half their casualties 'during the retreat'.

This was nonsense, but nobody had the courage to challenge the Führer in mid rant. He partly blamed himself for Rommel's failings by admitting that it was counter-productive to leave a man 'too long in a position of such heavy responsibility' because, sooner or later, he was bound to crack up. He added:

It's different if one's in the rear. There of course one keeps one's head. [But] these people can't stand the strain on their nerves . . . I am therefore determined that as soon as the first rush is over we will relieve a number of generals who in themselves are perfectly all right – even field marshals – we'll simply order them to take so-and-so many months' leave so that they can return to the front completely recovered . . . That's Göring's impression too. He says that Rommel has completely lost his nerve.[20]

17

'It was all so utterly pointless'

North Africa, 6–14 December 1942

G EORGE S. PATTON, MEANWHILE, WAS bored. Since his eventful landing a month earlier at Fedala on 8 November, followed by the surrender of the French defenders of Casablanca three days later, he had been kicking his heels in Morocco, waiting anxiously for the order to march east. 'We have been here for a month today,' he wrote on 8 December to Major General Thomas T. Handy, head of the Operations Division in Washington DC, 'which means that for 26 days we have not had any fighting. This is regrettable . . . From what I can hear we are losing quite a few tanks in Tunisia, and I have gotten permission from General Eisenhower to take a private voyage to that front in order to learn at first-hand how the Germans succeed in smashing our tanks.'

His duties hitherto had been mostly diplomatic as he used his fluent French to work with Noguès, the French Resident General, and Sultan Mohammed V of Morocco – a 'very handsome young man, extremely fragile, with a highly sensitive face' – who on 18 November had celebrated the fifteenth anniversary of his accession to the throne in Rabat. Not to be outdone by Noguès, Patton made an impromptu speech at the ceremony that promised 'certain victory against our common enemy the Nazi' and reminded the sultan that his predecessor had given 'the beautiful building which houses the American mission in Tangier to General [George] Washington as a token of friendship and respect'.

Patton loved the pomp and ceremony at Rabat, but he had come to North Africa to fight and the fact-finding mission to the front was the next best thing. On 9 December, he flew to Algiers and narrowly survived a friendly fire incident as anti-aircraft guns mistakenly opened fire on his plane, shaking the fuselage and damaging one wing.[1] Despite the incident, Patton was 'full of his usual pep', noted Ike's aide Harry C. Butcher, 'and spent the night with us' at Villa dar el Ouad, Eisenhower's modest private residence perched high on a hill above the city.[2]

He made a good impression on Ike, who wrote a day later that, of his generals, 'Patton I think comes closest to meeting every requirement made on a commander.' He added: 'Just after him, I would, at present, rate Fredendall, although I do not believe the latter has the imagination in foreseeing and preparing for possible jobs of the future that Patton possesses. Clark is an unusual individual and is particularly strong in his organizational ability and orderliness of his mind.'[3]

Patton was driven 250 miles in an open-top scout car, through the cold and rain, to Anderson's headquarters in Ain Seynour, close to the Tunisian border, where the First Army Chief of Staff provided him with a map of the area and lunch. He motored on to the head-quarters of the British V Corps, commanded by Lieutenant General Charles Allfrey – a 'tall, lean, handsome fellow with a fine sense of humour and one of the keenest officers in Africa' – who gave him the first details of another recent setback involving American troops.[4]

On 6 December, German panzers, Stukas and paratroopers had attacked Oliver's Combat Command B along a one-mile front southeast of Tebourba, turning the flank of the 1/6th Armored Infantry and pinning a battery of field artillery into a rocky amphitheatre to the east of the Medjerda river. The key German objective was to drive the Allies back across the river and ultimately retake Medjez el Bab, the gateway to Tunis. 'For Christ's sake,' radioed the battery commander, 'isn't

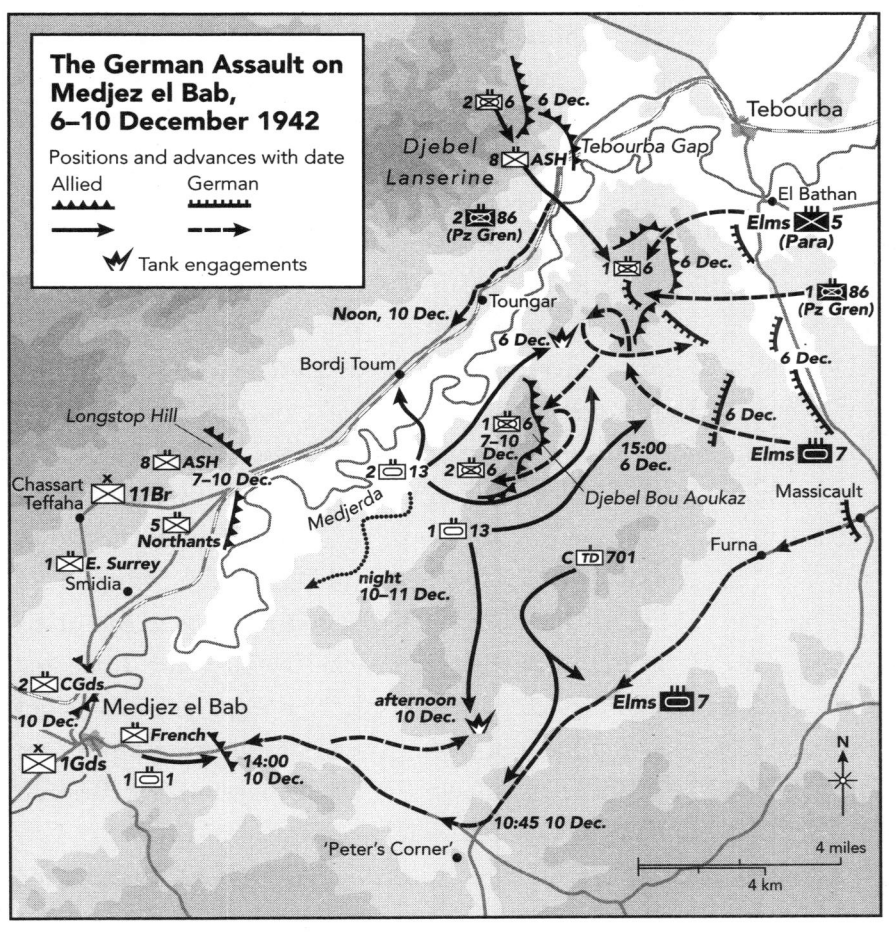

The German Assault on Medjez el Bab, 6–10 December 1942

Positions and advances with date

Allied   German

Tank engagements

2⊠6   6 Dec.   Tebourba

Djebel   8⊠ASH   Tebourba Gap
Lanserine

2⊞86   Elms⊠5
(Pz Gren)   (Para)   El Bathan

1⊠6   6 Dec.

Noon, 10 Dec.   •Toungar   1⊞86
                                        (Pz Gren)

Bordj Toum   6 Dec.   6 Dec.

Longstop Hill   6 Dec.   6 Dec.
                1⊠6   Elms⊟7
8⊠ASH   7–10
7–10 Dec.   2⊞13 2⊠6   Dec.
Chassart ⊠11Br   15:00   Massicault
Teffaha   6 Dec.
        5⊠Northants   Medjerda   Djebel Bou Aoukaz
1⊠E. Surrey   Furna
Smidia•   1⊟13

                C⊞701

2⊠CGds   night
10 Dec.   Medjez el Bab   10–11 Dec.   Elms⊟7

⊠1Gds ⊠French
        1⊟1   14:00
            10 Dec.   afternoon
                    10 Dec.
                                N

'Peter's Corner'•   10:45 10 Dec.   4 miles

                            4 km

there anything besides C Battery in this First Armored Division? We're putting up a helluva fight, but we can't hold out all day. Please, *please* send help!'[5]

From Combat Command B's headquarters at St Eloi farm, Major General Oliver had ordered Bruss's 2/13th Armored Regiment to counter-attack. But it was not until 1 p.m., five hours later, that Bruss's force – including four Shermans attached to the battalion from the 2nd Armored Division – arrived on the scene. True to form, Bruss split up his command, made no reconnaissance, and left the attack to his subordinates while he established a command post on high ground. 'Without communication,' wrote Robinett, 'he lost control of his battalion . . . In the attack that followed, which was made without supporting artillery, all the attached M-4 [Sherman] tanks, in addition to several others, were knocked out by concealed anti-tank guns.'[6]

One platoon commander remembered German shells 'cutting through the wheat on either side' as he 'walked from tank to tank trying to make them fire and retire'. They seemed 'petrified'. As he climbed on a tank, shouting insults, an exploding shell peppered his arm, eyelid and right temple with shrapnel. 'I was swearing and crying from frustration and pain,' he recalled. 'Took a shot of morphine and felt better.'[7]

The one benefit of this poorly coordinated attack was that it so confused the Germans that the survivors of the 1/6th Armored Infantry could withdraw to a new defensive position. That night, the rain pelted down and did not stop for four days.[8] Aware that his troops were out on a limb, and that Evelegh had already pulled back the 11th Brigade to Djebel el Ahmera – a large hill feature northwest of Medjez el Bab that would become infamous as Longstop Hill – Oliver asked for permission to move his CCB to a more favourable position.

Anderson wanted to withdraw his forces from the Medjerda valley altogether, to give them time to rest and refit.[9] But Eisenhower would not hear of it. He was convinced – as were the French generals, Juin and Barré – that the loss of Medjez el Bab would end any lingering hopes of an early capture of Tunis.[10]

Instead, a new plan was worked out: Anderson's army would defend, with French support, a line which ran east of Medjez el Bab, from Tamera in the north through Sidi Nsir to Bou Arada. From this new – and slightly more conservative – base line, the attack would be resumed when more troops were available and the weather had improved.

Orders were issued for the 1st Guards Brigade to move to Medjez el Bab during the night of 10/11 December, while the 11th Infantry Brigade and Combat Command B were withdrawn through the town to take up positions farther west. But before the move could take place, the Germans launched a two-pronged offensive along both sides of the Medjerda river with tanks and infantry. It crashed into positions held by the CCB which, for much of the day, was leaderless as Major General Oliver had gone forward earlier to reconnoitre and was out of radio contact. It was left to Brigadier General Paul Robinett to fight the battle from the CCB's new command post in another farmhouse three miles southwest of Medjez.

The biggest threat came from a flanking attack by artillery and thirty tanks of the 7th Panzer Regiment against the rear of Medjez. Smashing through John Waters's 1/1st Armored Regiment, which was driven back across the Medjerda with the loss of five Stuarts and five half-tracks, the German column next encountered a French blocking position, held by a company of the 4th Zouaves and some artillery, two miles west of Medjez. With the situation critical, and the French at risk of being overrun, Robinett ordered the 1/13th Armored Regiment to attack due south from its position on Djebel Bou Aoukaz. Nineteen M3 Stuart light tanks were lost in the unequal fight, with one American company commander noting that 'in spite of their hopeless plight, every tank fought until it burned or until casualties disabled the crew'. Led by the gallant Captain Hatcher, twenty-five fugitives hid in a ditch and later swam the Medjerda to reach the safety of American lines. Others were 'killed in their tanks or machine-gunned to death as they emerged from burning hulks'. One crewman was deliberately crushed beneath a panzer's tracks, but survived because the mud was so deep.

At 4.30 p.m., Robinett issued orders for the remnants of the CCB to withdraw over the Bordj Toum bridge – the only crossing north of Medjez still in Allied hands – after dark. Minutes later, Oliver appeared at the command post, muddy and exhausted after a harrowing day. 'My God,' he said, with tears in his eyes, 'why did you attack with the light tanks? You have ruined me?'

'No, General,' replied Robinett, jaw set and eyes unblinking, 'I have saved you.'

Told there was no time to lose to extricate his men, Oliver arranged to meet British V Corps commander Allfrey and Evelegh on the road west of Medjez to discuss measures to keep the remaining Allied Medjerda crossing open. In contrast to Evelegh's indecisiveness – which had cost the 11th Brigade so many casualties at Tebourba – Allfrey was 'every bit the soldier', remembered Robinett, 'calm and firm'.

Returning to his command post, Oliver lay down to sleep while Robinett coordinated the withdrawal. But, as Robbie acknowledged later, the command post was 'too far to the rear' and he quickly 'lost the thread of events shaping up'. The man on the spot was Lieutenant Colonel John R. McGinness, a 43-year-old West Pointer from Ohio, commanding the 2/6th Armored Infantry. By length of service and training, he 'should have been equal to the task'. Sadly he was not.

Told by a panicky officer that the Germans had 'broken through' to the bridge – when, in fact, the British were still in control – McGinness failed to verify the report and instead gave orders for the battalions east of the bridge to withdraw to Medjez by an unpaved goat track on the south bank of the river. It ended in disaster as the lead vehicles quickly became bogged down in knee-deep mud.[11]

A shocked General Anderson wrote to Alan Brooke, Chief of the Imperial General Staff (CIGS),

They then abandoned [all the] vehicles, panicked and rushed back – not stopping at the position they were told to take but going past it for miles. The Hun must have been astonished next day when he saw his prize! And I was in tears. It was all so utterly pointless. Fortunately for me, General George Patton was visiting Oliver from the Central Task Force. His comments were lurid in the extreme (he is a Texan): the b[attalion]n commander was placed under arrest etc. But the damage is done. This fine C[combat] T[eam] can now muster only one weak battalion of light tanks and one weak battalion of medium tanks (including all the replacements the US can scrape up in Africa) and one battalion of infantry with enough transport.[12]

Anderson wrote later that Oliver's command had needlessly lost in this debacle alone 'well over 100 light and medium tanks, 15 field guns, and much transport and equipment', all of which fell into enemy hands. Combat Command B, as a result, was 'temporarily withdrawn from the battle'.[13]

Even allowing for exaggeration, it was a devastating blow as the 2/6th Armored Infantry, the 1/13th Armored Regiment and a company of the 701st Tank Destroyer Battalion 'lost the greater part of their remaining vehicles and heavy weapons'. Overall, the CCB had lost 40 medium tanks, 84 light tanks, 22 self-propelled 75mm guns, 13 105mm howitzers, 210 half-tracks, 66 2½-ton trucks and 72 1-ton trailers. This represented nearly three-quarters of its tank strength 'and the ones remaining were badly worn'.

McGinness was relieved of his command by Oliver when he turned up at the CCB's command post, 'muddy and bedraggled', at noon on 11 December. Bruss was also sacked, and replaced by Gardiner. The setback was proof, for Robinett, that the Allies had 'lost the snail-like race for Tunis and Bizerte by the narrowest margin'. The 'prizes were firmly in the hands of the Germans who, nevertheless, needed much more terrain before they could consider their hold on Africa secure'.[14]

Patton was given the bad news as he stopped off at Allfrey's command post during his tour of the front. He quickly concluded that the chief problem was not American failings per se, but poor leadership by the British generals. Arriving at the 78th Division's headquarters at 8.30 a.m., for example, he was disgusted to find the erratic and eccentric Evelegh rising from his bed.

He next visited the 1/1st Armored Regiment, commanded by his son-in-law Lieutenant Colonel John K. Waters, which had lost 39 tanks, two-thirds of its original strength. Two of Waters's three captains had been killed, while Waters himself had a bullet hole through his clothes, but no injury. 'I was very much pleased with his attitude,' wrote Patton, 'and also the behaviour of his men, who were glad to see me.'

Waters told Patton that at one point he wanted a nearby Royal Artillery battery to fire on German guns, but was told he needed permission from the brigade artillery officer. This caused a delay of two and a half hours. When Patton visited the commander of the British 11th Infantry Brigade, Cass, he found him 'trembling all over'. Cass said he was tired. Patton could smell alcohol on his breath and knew that was the reason.

The men of the 1st Armored Division told Patton that he was the first general officer they had seen in twenty-four days at the front. This was not strictly true, as both Oliver and Robinett had been out and about. But Patton took the claim at face value and thought it reflected badly on the British generals *and* Eisenhower and his deputy Clark. '[They] have no knowledge of men or war,' he noted of the American commanders in his diary. 'Too damned slick, especially Clark.'

Patton also spoke to Oliver and Robinett at Combat Command B's new bivouac at Souk el Khemis, 12 miles southwest of Béja. Robinett, who had instructed Patton at the Cavalry School at Fort Riley, Kansas, in 1923, remembered his former student arriving in an 'armoured scout car with machine guns manned fore and aft'. Wearing 'two bone-handled revolvers in the best Hollywood style', Patton jumped from the scout car and shouted in a high, shrill voice: 'Where are the damned Germans, I want to get shot at!'

Patton looked 'hard and fit' and was 'full of enthusiasm and good cheer as he greeted everyone in the most friendly and comradely fashion'. Later, joining Robinett in his 'drab little room' where they shared a 'warming drink' from a flask of whisky, Patton remarked: 'I'm glad you're here. There is a lot to be done before we are through and I expect you to be in it.'[15]

It was from Robinett that Patton got much of the detail about the inadequacy of American armour that he included in his report for Eisenhower on his return to Algiers. The light tanks were too light and the 37mm gun on the Stuart lacked the power to penetrate German armour. The M3 Lee was higher than German tanks and thus presented a better target, while their 75mm guns were side-mounted and lacked all-round traverse. Even the 75mm gun's armour-piercing ammunition lacked the punch of its German counterpart: penetrating steel plate to a depth of 3.5 inches at 1,000 yards, whereas the German shell could cut through 4.1 inches to 5.9 inches of armour. American instruments, such as field glasses and tank sights, were also inferior to those of the enemy, making American tactical doctrine and training out of sync with reality.[16]

He also noted with approval in the report the German ability to coordinate the use of infantry, tanks, artillery and dive-bombers. He was less enamoured with the British habit in Tunisia of relinquishing the high ground to the Germans, taking defensive positions in front of rather than behind rivers, and failing to carry out adequate air and ground reconnaissance. Patton had held his British brothers-in-arms in high esteem during the First World War. That changed in Tunisia as he formed a negative opinion of British officers and soldiers that would last for the rest of the war.[17]

After delivering his report to Ike, Patton was anxious to return to Casablanca. Though air officers advised against the trip because the weather was bad, he insisted and soon regretted his decision. 'We struck a terrific rain and wind storm,' he wrote, 'and could see nothing at all. This had the advantage of preventing the anti-aircraft from seeing us. It was violently rough, and we had to use our safety belts.'

Unable to identify the airfield, the pilots circled the city for an hour, hoping for a break in the weather. As the fuel tanks ran dry, they decided to 'make a bellylanding on any piece of ground we could find, or if we could not see the ground – which was most of the time – we would have to jump'. Fortunately, the rain stopped briefly at 8.20 p.m. and the pilot 'practically dived into the field through a hole in the clouds', making a 'perfect landing'. It was, Patton noted in his diary, 'the most dangerous experience I have had in this war'. Had God, he asked himself, 'saved me for something'?

To his wife Beatrice, he admitted the flight was 'an error in judgement' that had 'nearly ended fatally'. Next time, he would 'listen to advice'. He also mentioned visiting their son-in-law John Waters – married to their beautiful eldest daughter Bee – who was fine. A day later, he changed his tune: 'I am very worried about John, as I fear he will be cut off and captured.'[18]

Patton's negative feeling towards his Allies was reciprocated by senior British commanders. On 14 December, in the same letter that he had informed General Brooke about the McGinness fiasco, Anderson noted that while Eisenhower was a 'real "white man" and 100% straight', he was 'not a practical soldier and, quite frankly, understands little or nothing of the foundations of battle'. Clark was 'much the same'. As for Oliver's CCB, it was a 'fine outfit' but 'tragically "green" and quite unwilling to listen to advice'. Oliver himself was a 'good man', but the tactics of his units 'were quite deplorable' and the 'mis-use of his tanks just suicidal'. There were 'no co-ordinated plans, no artillery support, always late, infantry not digging in, transport put in the front line, etc. etc.' His men were keen, and showed 'plenty of guts', but were poorly trained.

Anderson was gloomy about their prospects. He wrote:

And now I've got to have another shot at getting Tunis before the heavy rains and before the Hun gets stronger than I am. He is nearly as strong now. And in tanks is stronger. It is indeed tragic in the 4th year of war to find myself with thin-skinned, mechanically unreliable Crusaders to match against his [Panzer] III, IV and a few VI [Tigers]. The few remaining US Grants* and Shermans are all I've got to match the panzers. The US light tanks are of course useless except for recce and in any case have lost enormously already.'

He had failed to persuade Ike to pause operations until the First Army had concentrated enough men and materiel to overwhelm the Germans. 'He is determined,' wrote Anderson, 'to have a shot at Tunis even at a big risk of failure, as he cannot contemplate the alternative of sitting down and building up another front here.'[19]

The date tentatively set for the renewed offensive was 22 December. That it would be far from a foregone conclusion was obvious from Eisenhower's naval aide Harry Butcher's estimate of each side's strength. 'Our ground forces in the battle,' he wrote in his diary on the 16th, 'now number about 20,000 British, 11,000 Americans, and 30,000 French, although the latter are poorly equipped and couldn't withstand tank attacks.' The assessment of the enemy strength, meanwhile, was '19,500 German and 11,250 Italian combat troops, with about 2,500 German Air Force and 5,000 service troops, total about 38,500'. He added: 'Fighting value of German armour described as high, morale of remainder of ground forces not high.'[20]

The Allies had a numerical edge in troops and tanks, but most were inferior in quality. While the number of planes was almost equal, Axis air power was much closer to the battlefield and operated from bigger and better airfields. The Allies, for example, had 'no tarmac runways'. Small wonder that Anderson put the odds on the offensive succeeding at 'no more than 50-50, though of course I don't say so to anyone except "Ike"'.[21]

---

* The British name for the M3 Lee, after Ulysses S. Grant the US Civil War general.

18

'Sit still in the middle, goddammit, or we'll all drown!'

Mediterranean Sea and North Africa, 20–25 December 1942

O N 20 DECEMBER, THE night before they were due to disembark at Algiers, Kay Summersby celebrated with her fellow passengers. 'In our joy at the prospect of landing,' she recalled, 'we forgot the crowding, the petty gossip, the discomfort and the dreary boredom of life on a troopship.'

Nine days earlier, Summersby had embarked on the SS *Strathallan*, a 23,000-ton former P&O liner and, in her eyes, a 'hideous tub', at Greenock in Scotland for the voyage to North Africa where she would resume her duties as Eisenhower's driver. Also on board were 248 American WACs (members of the Women's Army Corps) and nurses, 4,408 British and American officers and men – mostly destined for the First Army's rear echelon – and a crew of 466. The ship, as a result, was crammed to the gunnels and Summersby found life afloat 'so awful that it was funny'.

She was fortunate to share a cabin with two good friends – Ethel Westermann and Jean Dixon – who, like the rest of the passengers, were told to pack a 'torpedo bag' with essentials that included warm clothes and medications. Summersby, for one, could not imagine abandoning ship without her nylons, her grandmother's diamond earrings and her wedding trousseau* of two satin nightgowns and silk underwear. They passed the time by eating, sleeping, gossiping and playing cards, their bridge four completed by Margaret Bourke-White, the celebrated *Life* magazine photographer, who had taken pictures of Ike and his staff a couple of months earlier. The ship was so crowded there were three sittings for each meal, all of which had to be queued for, as did the toilets.

It was a rough trip, with southwesterly gales lasting four days as the convoy of troopships and their destroyer escorts ploughed through the stormy grey Atlantic. Once into the Mediterranean, however, the wind died down and Summersby and her pals raced on deck to enjoy some fresh air and the unusual sight, after three years of blackout, of city lights twinkling along the African coast 'like clusters of diamonds'.

Approaching Oran, the all-American section of the convoy broke away, while the British/American section, including the *Strathallan*, continued steaming east for Algiers. As enemy submarines were reported to be in the area, the ship was zigzagging. Conditions – bright moonlight and smooth seas – were ideal for a U-boat attack.[1]

Kapitänleutnant Horst Hamm could hardly believe his luck when he spotted just north of Cap Ferrat, in serene weather and perfect visibility, a large Allied transport through *U-562*'s periscope at 1.16 a.m. on 21 December.

Born in the Ruhr city of Düsseldorf, Hamm had joined the Kriegsmarine in 1935 and served as First Watch Officer on the famous *U-96*,† skippered by submarine ace Heinrich Lehmann-Willenbrock,

---

* Summersby was engaged to marry Colonel Dick Arnold of the US Corps of Engineers, then serving in North Africa. He was killed by a land mine in June 1943.
† War correspondent Lothar-Günther Buchheim accompanied *U-96* on one of its later patrols, and used the experience to write his bestselling novel *Das Boot* ('The Boat'). Lehmann-Willenbrock, who was awarded the Knight's Cross with Oak Leaves, served as the model for Buchheim's fictional commander.

during three successful Atlantic patrols that accounted for more than 80,000 tons of Allied shipping in the early years of the war. Hamm was rewarded with the Iron Cross 1st Class and his own command, the small training boat *U-58*, in the spring of 1941 when he was just twenty-five years old. That September he got his second boat, the larger *U-562* – a Type VIIC model, like the *U-96*, and the workhorse of the German submarine force with more than 500 constructed during the war – weighing 1,070 tons, and with a crew of forty-nine and five torpedo tubes.

Germany had begun the war with just fifty-seven U-boats, mostly the small and short-range Type II. But when Admiral Karl Dönitz, commanding the U-boat fleet, suggested that Britain could be brought to its knees by deploying 'wolf packs' of the latest Type VII long-range submarine to throttle commercial trade, a huge programme of expansion was authorised by Hitler. The strategy almost succeeded. In the first half of 1942, German U-boats sank more than 320 Allied ships (weighing 2,250,000 tons). But, gradually, Allied tactics and innovations – including the use of protective convoys, long-range aircraft and flying boats, and the breaking by Bletchley Park of the German naval Enigma cipher – began to turn the tide as U-boat losses climbed: sixty were sunk in the Atlantic in August and September 1942, almost as many as in the previous two years.

When *U-562* departed its base at La Spezia on the northwest coast of Italy on 22 November 1942, Hamm was embarking on his seventh patrol in just over a year: one in the Atlantic and six in the Mediterranean. Yet in that time he had torpedoed and sunk only three British cargo ships, weighing a total of 13,000 tons, and all those successes had come in the first two patrols in late 1941. Since then, all he had to show for his efforts were damage to a Dutch oil tanker and two small British vessels sunk by mines laid by *U-562*.

On 9 December, two weeks into his seventh patrol, Hamm had fired at and missed a British destroyer. The sighting of the huge *Strathallan* in the early hours of 21 December was, therefore, an opportunity to redeem himself and, in the process, more than double the tonnage of enemy shipping sunk by *U-562*. Once in position, Hamm ordered the firing of two torpedoes at the former liner. In the minute or so it took the torpedoes to reach the target, *U-562* dived to avoid retaliation, and so Hamm was unable to witness the outcome. He later reported (not entirely accurately): 'At 0223 hours, two hits after 61 seconds on a large transport, eastern area. Sinking noises – the steamer is presumed sunk.'[2]

Kay Summersby had just kicked off her shoes, loosened her tie and was preparing for bed when a 'tremendous explosion' threw her off the bunk. She landed beside her two companions as the lights flickered and went out. The ship began rocking ominously. 'This is it,' said Ethel Westermann. 'Let's get going.'

A single torpedo had struck the ship below the waterline on the port side, tearing a jagged hole and damaging the bulkhead between the engine and boiler rooms, blasting a huge column of water over the ship, and knocking No. 8 lifeboat 'over the heads of the davits, from where it could not be dislodged'. With the loudspeakers out of action – probably because the amplifier had been damaged in the explosion – 'Boat Stations' were sounded on the alarm gongs.

Grabbing her shoes, life preserver and handbag, Summersby followed the others to their lifeboat station, a drill they had practised so often they could have performed it in the dark. Fortunately, Jean Dixon had a flashlight. They clambered into the lifeboat and, with the ship listing dangerously fifteen degrees to port, the order was given to 'lower the boats'.

As the lifeboat descended, some of the occupants leaned over the edge to look down. 'Don't do that!' shouted Summersby, who had been around boats all her life. 'Sit still in the middle, goddammit, or we'll all drown!'

The boat reached the water safely. Others had capsized, and the water was alive with soldiers and nurses trying to find something to cling to. A good number were pulled into Summersby's boat where Ethel, a nurse, got to work on the casualties, several of whom had broken legs or arms.

'We could see the convoy silhouetted against the sky,' wrote Summersby, 'our sister ships streaming past, seemingly aloof and uncaring. I felt very much alone. The *Strathallan* was in the distance now, settling lower and lower into the water.'

She thought of all the possessions she had left behind and would soon be at the bottom of the sea: her trousseau, the precious diamond earrings, snapshots of her family. A British destroyer appeared and, through a loud-hailer, told them that they would all be picked up in the morning as it was too dangerous, with German submarines in the area, to rescue them in the dark.

Eight hours later, by which time they were using handkerchiefs to shelter from a fierce sun, the same destroyer – HMS *Verity* – returned to collect Summersby and the 1,300 or so occupants of the lifeboats. Only after she had scrambled up the rope ladder, and could feel *Verity*'s solid deck beneath her feet, did she realise how terrified she had been. She burst into tears.

The remaining 3,300 troops were taken off the *Strathallan* by other warships, one of which took the troopship in tow. With most of the ship's bulkheads still intact, and its pumps holding their own, Captain J. H. Briggs thought they might make it as far as Oran. But they were unable to put out a fire started by the explosion and, at 2 p.m. on the 21st, Briggs gave the order to 'Abandon ship'. Early the following morning, while still under tow, the stricken ship rolled onto its port side and sank, 12 miles from Oran. The casualties were six dead and many more wounded.

Summersby and her colleagues, meanwhile, had been landed at Oran. Despite her dishevelled appearance – her uniform skirt was stained by salt water, her shirt torn and her hair a mess – she made her way to Fredendall's headquarters and explained that she was a member of Eisenhower's staff and, having survived the torpedo attack on the *Strathallan*, needed Ike to know that she was safe. Mention of

Eisenhower's name had the desired effect: she was ushered into an office, given coffee and put through to Algiers.

Ike came on the line. 'Thank God you're safe. Are you all right?' She said she was fine, if short on clothes.

'Great. Now you tell headquarters to find a place for you to spend the night and I'll send a plane for you and Ethel tomorrow.'[3]

Following U-562's successful torpedoing of the *Strathallan*, Horst Hamm set a course for his home base of La Spezia, reaching it on Christmas Eve. On 7 February 1943, after a lengthy interval for repairs, Hamm and U-562 left Italy on their eighth and last war patrol. Twelve days into the voyage, in a position northeast of the Libyan port of Benghazi, U-562 was spotted by an RAF Wellington bomber on convoy escort duty and attacked. Two Royal Navy destroyers, also on escort duty, joined in the assault with depth charges and U-562 was sunk with all hands. Hamm was twenty-six years old when he and his crew of forty-eight officers and ratings were killed. He was posthumously awarded Italy's *Medaglia di bronzo al valor militare* (Bronze Medal of Military Valour).[4]

U-562 was one of 757 German submarines – out of a total combat force of 859 – that were sunk at sea by Allied ships and aircraft during the Second World War, a shocking loss rate of 88 per cent. Of the 39,000 officers and men who took part in the U-boat offensive, 32,000 – or 82 per cent – were killed or missing.[5]

By the time Kay Summersby arrived at Allied Force Headquarters in the St George's Hotel in Algiers, on 23 December, Eisenhower had already left for a tour of the front with his naval aide Harry Butcher. Travelling as before in his semi-armoured Cadillac, with scout cars as an escort, Eisenhower reached Lieutenant General Anderson's command post at Ain Seynour in the early morning of Christmas Eve, and they continued on together to Souk el Khemis, a few miles inside the Tunisian border, where Lieutenant General Allfrey's V Corps was headquartered.

Before consulting Allfrey on V Corps' all-out push on Tunis – now scheduled for the night of 26 December – Eisenhower and Anderson walked through deep mud and persistent rain to meet Oliver and the officers of Combat Command B who were stationed in a nearby farmhouse. Ike also spoke to a number of GIs who, Butcher told his wife, 'were living in conditions which only a mudhen could enjoy'. Their two-person pup tents were pitched in thick mud, 'but as many had received mail and packages from home shortly before General Ike's visit they were very happy'. Not so the four soldiers they observed trying to extricate a motorcycle from the 'sticky clay' of a wheat field. Eventually conceding defeat, they left the bike 'more deeply bogged than when they started'.

Later, at the conference at Allfrey's headquarters, Anderson told Ike that as it was almost impossible to move vehicles and supplies in the mud, it would make sense to postpone the attack until 'there was a good chance of continuing favourable weather'. Even a short window of dry weather would not help, said Anderson, because it would inevitably be followed by a wet spell which would allow the enemy to counter-attack with infantry and capture V Corps' stranded vehicles. He had consulted the locals who insisted 'the rains would get worse through January and much of February'. For that reason, 'discretion ruled against attempting another attack for probably six weeks'.

Bitterly disappointed, Ike agreed to postpone the attack on Tunis 'for a minimum of 14 days and probably for 6 weeks or more'.* Despite the weather, he 'wanted to keep on the offensive, so the enemy couldn't get too well set', and had been exploring the possibility of supplying

---

* When word of the postponement reached London, Churchill suggested replacing Anderson with Alexander. Brooke convinced him not to. Influenced by Anderson's dispatches, he considered the real villain to be Ike. 'I am afraid,' he noted in his diary, 'that Eisenhower as a general is hopeless. He submerges himself in politics and neglects his military duties, partly, I am afraid, because he knows little if anything about military matters. I don't like the situation in Tunisia at all!' (Alanbrooke, *War Diaries 1939–1945*, p. 351)

a force 'to push from the south to cut the enemy's supply line from Tunis to Tripoli, possibly at Sfax or Gabès'. It was agreed at the conference, therefore, to shift Combat Command B 95 miles southwest, and back over the border into Algeria, at Tébessa, where it would be joined by the rest of the 1st Armored Division. 'The game,' noted Butcher in his diary, 'was to have a hard-hitting mobile force that could rush into Gabès, Sousse, or Sfax, play hell with supplies and lines, and then retire to Tebessa, or whatever point was ultimately selected for the garrison.'

They also discussed the issue of command. The French, said Anderson, would not serve under him, although cooperation with Juin was 'harmonious and satisfactory'. A possible solution was for Ike himself to take personal command at the front, 'leaving Anderson in charge of the First Army in the north, the French with their own forces in the centre of hilly terrain', and the American force in the south. This was the solution eventually agreed, with Eisenhower setting up a forward command post at Constantine. 'It is clear,' wrote Anderson to Brooke on 25 December, 'that there can only be one Commander in Tunisia – for many crudely obvious reasons, not least of which is the logistical one.' Ike's solution, therefore, was to retain overall command, but give Anderson authority over both the US II Corps in the south and the French XIV Corps in the centre of the Allied line.[6]

The American force would be commanded by Major General Lloyd R. Fredendall who was ordered to move his US II Corps headquarters from Oran to Tébessa, an 'enchanting' walled Roman city close to the Tunisian border. 'Much of its ancient golden-stoned bastions are intact,' wrote war correspondent Philip Jordan in his diary. 'It has an airy, almost fluid appearance as you first glance at it as though it were Greek. Aristocrat rather than bourgeois.'[7]

Under Fredendall's control would come the 1st Armored Division, the 1st Infantry Division (once it could be assembled from its scattered positions across the front), the 34th Infantry Division and part of the 9th Infantry Division (less the combat team that had landed at Algiers).

All this would take time. Meanwhile, Fredendall's instructions were 'to provide a flank guard' for the main forces in the north, hold the mountain passes and attack any hostile column that might try to advance. Once his corps was assembled, he was to take offensive action over the border in Tunisia in the direction of Sfax or Gabès, to try and sever Rommel's line of communication from Libya.

Eisenhower's defensive line – now that the plan for the immediate capture of Tunis had been given up – was to include the forward airfields at Thelepte in the south, Youks-les-Bains (west of Tébessa) and Souk-el-Arba. 'As long as these fields were in our possession,' wrote Ike, 'we could, with our growing air forces, constantly pound away, at least in decent weather, at Axis communications.'[8]

Eisenhower's intention had been to dine on Christmas Eve with Allfrey and his officers at their farmhouse headquarters, but he received a call from his deputy Mark Clark. 'Ike,' he said, 'there is serious trouble in Algiers and you must return immediately.'

Clark spoke 'in terms so guarded that Ike suspected, but wasn't sure', that Amiral de la flotte Darlan, now the High Commissioner for French North and West Africa (a title bestowed by the Allies), 'had been shot'. They packed up immediately and left Allfrey's farmhouse at 10 p.m. on Christmas Eve, driving through rain, snow and sleet that night and most of the next day, Christmas Day, stopping only to refuel and to eat breakfast in Constantine. There they received confirmation that Darlan had been assassinated at his headquarters in Algiers by a young anti-Vichyiste and monarchist Frenchman, Fernand Bonnier de la Chapelle. 'It solves one problem,' said Eisenhower, 'but no doubt creates many more.'[9]

Eisenhower – his face 'a grey pall of exhaustion' – reached Algiers at 6 p.m. on Christmas Day and was briefed by Clark who explained that, on hearing of Darlan's death, he had told General Giraud that he was Eisenhower's preferred successor as High Commissioner for French North and West Africa. Though Giraud still wanted a military appointment, he agreed to take over immediately, and the appointment was later confirmed by other senior French officials in North Africa. Prompted by Churchill, Clark also arranged for the news of Darlan's murder to be broadcast on Radio Algiers and Radio Morocco. The announcement ended: 'The examination of the murderer is now taking place. It is not yet known from preliminary investigation of the assassin whether the assassination was of German or Italian inspiration.'

This was a deliberate muddying of the waters by Clark to prevent the Axis from gaining any political capital from Darlan's death. Bonnier de la Chapelle was quickly tried by the French and executed on Boxing Day. Clark came to see Darlan's death as 'an act of providence'. He wrote: 'His removal from the scene was like the lancing of a troublesome boil. He had served his purpose, and his death solved what could have been the very difficult problem of what to do with him in the future.'[10]

At the time, however, Darlan's assassination – coming so soon after the decision to postpone the attack on Tunis – was a hammer blow for Ike who feared that Axis agents or anti-Allied elements might try to overthrow Giraud's cooperative arrangement with the Allies. 'Only the inner circle was allowed to see how depressed he really was,' wrote the newly arrived Kay Summersby, fresh from her brush with the torpedo. 'To the rest of the world, he was his usual brisk, charming and confident self – just a bit weary, that was all.'

At around 9 p.m., Ike ordered Summersby to get the car.

'Where is it?' she asked.

He leaned back in his chair and laughed. 'My God, welcome home, Kay. It seemed so natural to have you here and I had so much on my mind that I forgot you just arrived. Let me take a look at you.'

He got up, put his hands on her shoulders and turned her around. 'Well, no damage that I can see. When the news came through that the *Strathallan* had been hit, well, I don't mind telling you I never did get to sleep that night. Now let's forget this mess for a few hours. Even a general is allowed to celebrate Christmas.'

They had been invited for Christmas dinner by Eisenhower's chief of staff, Brigadier General Walter 'Beetle' Bedell Smith, whose villa, wrote Summersby, was 'gorgeous – practically a palace, with gardens and terraces and two vast drawing rooms', its floors covered with mosaics and oriental rugs. The usual suspects were there – Harry Butcher, 'Tex' Lee and Ethel Westermann – and Summersby was in her element. 'We talked a mile a minute,' she wrote, 'busy trying to catch up with all that had happened. Ethel and I described how it felt to be torpedoed, and we heard how Ike had caught a terrible cold in Gibraltar because his headquarters, deep inside the Rock, was cold and damp.'

Bedell Smith, normally so stern and harassed at work, was the perfect host: 'witty, thoughtful, kind and with as much charm as Ike'. It was a proper American Christmas dinner – 'George Patton sent him two turkeys,' Eisenhower told Summersby, 'God only knows where he liberated them from' – with all the trimmings, plum pudding and champagne.

Eisenhower was in great spirits, singing carols and wishing everyone 'Merry Christmas'. Asked by Summersby if his villa was as splendid as Beetle's, he replied: 'God, no! But it's still too splendid for my taste. You will see it tomorrow. You'll be over for breakfast, won't you?'

'Yes, thanks,' she said, 'I'll be over for breakfast.'[11]

19

Longstop Hill

Northern Tunisia, 22–25 December 1942

SEVEN MILES NORTHEAST OF Medjez el Bab, jutting into the Medjerda valley and creating a bottleneck through which pass Highway 50 and the railway to Tunis, lies the low, hogback ridge called Djebel el Ahmera. It is separated from the higher ground to the west by a saddle or col; and from a loop in the Medjerda river on its eastern flank by a gap, less than half a mile wide, that contains the railway station Halte d'el Heri. To the British in late 1942, in a nod to the cricket fielder of last resort, the hill became known as Longstop.

At first glance, Longstop is not particularly forbidding. Scented with thyme, and covered with heather, scrub juniper and, along its lower flanks, olive groves, it could be mistaken for the verdant landscape of Corfu. Closer up, its many rocky folds, dips and crevices make orientation almost impossible. It features a succession of knolls, the highest being Point 290,★ at 900ft, near the centre of the two-mile-long hill. From its crest, moreover, it dominates the Medjerda valley, through which nothing can move without being detected.[1]

Longstop had been ceded to the Germans on the same night – 10/11 December 1942 – that Oliver's Combat Command B had lost much of its transport during the disastrous retreat along the southern bank

---

★ Points were identified as such by their height in metres.

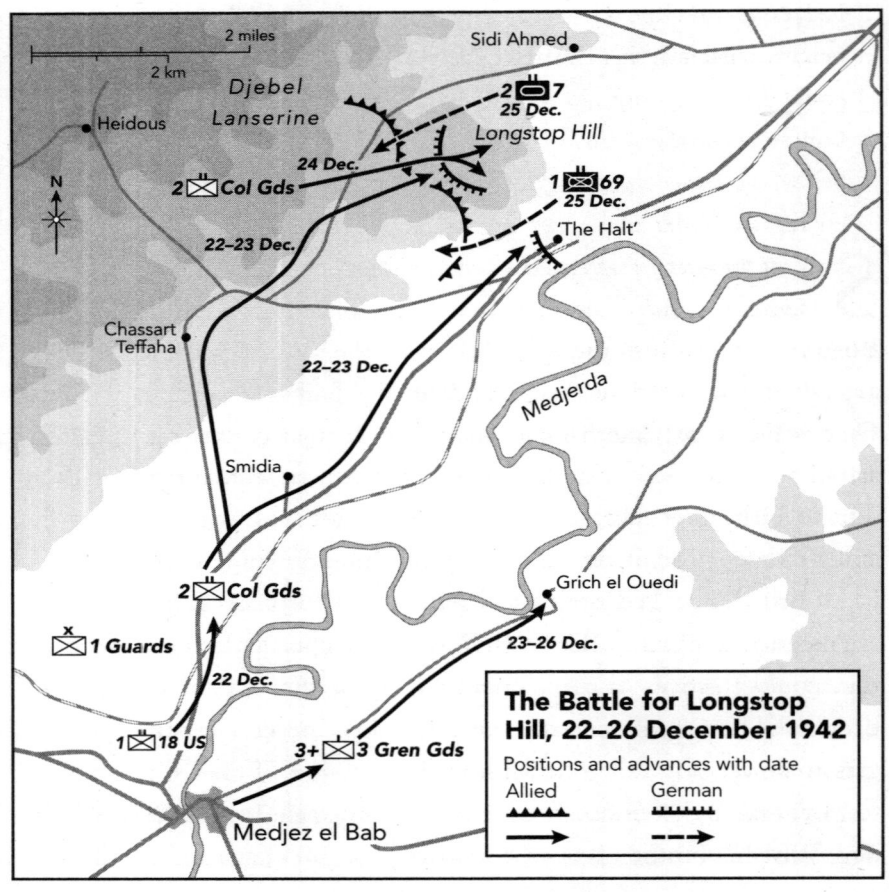

The Battle for Longstop Hill, 22–26 December 1942

Positions and advances with date

Sidi Ahmed

Djebel Lanserine

Heidous

2 ☐ 7
25 Dec.

Longstop Hill

24 Dec.

2 ⊠ Col Gds

1 ⊠ 69
25 Dec.

22–23 Dec.

'The Halt'

Chassart Teffaha

22–23 Dec.

Medjerda

Smidia

Grich el Ouedi

2 ⊠ Col Gds

23–26 Dec.

x
⊠ 1 Guards

22 Dec.

1 ⊠ 18 US

3+ ⊠ 3 Gren Gds

Medjez el Bab

Allied   German

▲▲▲▲▲   ▪▪▪▪▪▪▪▪

⟶   ⤍⤍⤍⟶

of the Medjerda. Eleven days later, as a precursor to the Allies' renewed assault on Tunis, the 2nd Coldstream Guards were given the unenviable task of retaking this vital feature. As Lance Sergeant Derrick Jackson wrote,

> It was no use ignoring Longstop or going round it. Even if your forces had done this, the Germans would still command the surrounding heights, enabling them to shell the two roads leading to Tunis. They could break up our convoys and also launch counter-attacks. On Longstop, the Germans had dug trenches which had deep shelves well below the surface. During a barrage from our 25-pounder guns, the enemy lay under these shelves in safety. It was only in the very last stage of an attack that they had to put their heads out.

Born in Nuneaton in the Midlands, Jackson was married and working as a milkman when he was called up in May 1940 and sent to the Guards Depot at Caterham in Surrey. There recruits were taught the art of spit and polish, and drilled relentlessly for two months, then sent to Pirbright where they went on regular route marches at night, and practised live firing on the open ranges. In double quick time, Jackson had mastered both the Bren gun and the Lee-Enfield rifle.

Assigned to the 2nd Battalion, The Coldstream Guards – a regiment that could trace its history to 1660 when the 2nd Foot Guards had been raised from former units of General George Monck's Scottish garrison – Jackson was a model soldier who quickly earned promotion to corporal and then lance sergeant. In early 1941, he received the news that his brother Roy, a Royal Navy telegraphist serving on the destroyer HMS *Jaguar* in the eastern Mediterranean, was missing and presumed killed.[2]

His battalion – part of the 78th Division's 1st Guards Brigade – had landed at Algiers on 22 November because Bône harbour was too damaged to receive ships. For ten days, Jackson and his colleagues had camped in a tangerine grove on the edge of the city, waiting impatiently to begin the 500-mile journey to the battlefront in Tunisia. When the order came in early December, Jackson was left behind at Algiers with a platoon of reinforcements.

By the time he rejoined his company, No. 4, it was defending trenches on a ridge line to the north of Medjez, 500 yards from the enemy's position across a narrow valley. As he peered into the valley, he could see 'bodies dotted all over the lower slopes', grey as well as khaki. Ten yards in front of his section position lay a British corpse, its face exposed to the sun. He wondered why it had not been recovered. The answer was provided by a volley of German mortars, the shell bursts deafening as scrub was set on fire and rocks and dirt rained down. One mortar killed four men in the neighbouring section. Jackson had one fatality – blown to pieces by a direct hit – and three wounded. That night, they were relieved by the 2nd Hampshires.[3]

After two days' rest, the 2nd Coldstream Guards returned to the front line. Their task was to seize Longstop Hill during the night of 22/23 December and to hand it over before dawn to a battalion of the US 18th Infantry, part of Terry Allen's 1st Infantry Division, which had been lent to Allfrey's V Corps. The battalion plan was to execute a pincer attack: No. 4 Company would advance on the left, via the village of Chassart Teffaha, two miles southwest of the hill, and capture the col, allowing No. 1 Company to pass through it, climb the hill and secure the crest; at the same time, No. 3 Company would move along Highway 50 and take the railway station, Halte d'el Heri, while the reserve company, No. 2, assembled at the southern base of the hill close to battalion headquarters.

Defending the hill was a German force commanded by Oberst Rudolf Lang, a grizzled veteran of the Polish, French and Russian campaigns, and the holder of the Knight's Cross. As well as his own regiment, the crack 69th Panzer Grenadier (part of the 10th Panzer Division), Lang had been given command of two companies of the 754th Infantry Regiment which he used to relieve outposts of the 69th on the hill and at the railway station during the night of 21/22 December. Only recently arrived in North Africa, the 754th lacked special equipment, transport and reserve ammunition.[4]

If the relative weakness of the 754th benefited the attacking British, this was counter-balanced by the 2nd Coldstream Guards' failure to appreciate that Longstop Hill was, as their second-in-command Major Roddy Hill wrote later, 'in fact, a double feature, the part that we could see on the ground and which was marked on the map' as Djebel el Ahmera, and a smaller and slightly lower feature to the northeast, Djebel el Rhar, which was 'separated from it by a deep gully'. During the reconnaissance for the attack from Grenadier Hill, a dominating feature to the southeast of Medjez and seven miles from Longstop, they could not see Djebel el Rhar and thus 'failed to realize its tactical importance or even its existence'.

The battalion had also underestimated the number of German defenders – they thought the hill was defended by a single company with four to eight machine guns, rather than the two companies of the 754th in position, with more from the 69th Panzer Grenadier Regiment in reserve – and was unaware that the vital position of Halte d'el Heri was protected by minefields. Collectively these omissions would have disastrous consequences.[5]

After a brief twenty-minute bombardment by a battery of field artillery, the 2nd Coldstream Guards began their moonlit attack at 11.35 p.m. on 22 December and, for a time, all went well. 'The ground,' remembered Lance Sergeant Derrick Jackson, 'was hard and slippery from the rain, the hillsides were covered with scrub and boulders. Then suddenly all hell let loose. I felt the sing of bullets whizzing past and, half crouching with my section, we carried on up the slope.'

Once Jackson's No. 4 Company had captured the col, No. 1 Company advanced up the hillside and took the summit as far as Point 290, though both the company commander and his sergeant major were mortally wounded. Meanwhile No. 2 Company had stormed the railway station.

Both here and on the hill, the inexperienced German troops of the 754th Infantry had fled after exhausting their ammunition.

The tide began to turn when a company of the 69th Panzer Grenadiers managed to retake Halte d'el Heri. The commander of No. 2 Company, Captain the Earl of Devon, ordered his reserve platoon to respond. But it ran into an undetected anti-personnel minefield and the railway station remained in German hands.

On hearing this the battalion commander, Lieutenant Colonel W. S. Stewart-Brown, should have committed his reserve company, No. 3. But, under the mistaken impression that his men possessed the whole of the hill's summit – when in fact they were only holding the western half as far as Point 290, and were unaware of the deep gully between them and the second summit – he held No. 3 Company back.

The US 1/18th Infantry, meanwhile – a unit that could trace its history back to 1861 when it was raised in Columbus, Ohio, to fight on the Union side in the US Civil War – had set off late and with its companies mixed up. The plan had been for two companies to advance on the left, and two on the right with battalion headquarters. In the event three companies (including the heavy weapons company) and battalion HQ struggled up the dirt track that led to the col, while only a single company and the anti-tank platoon used Highway 50 to head for Halte d'el Heri. The confusion got worse when the guides left by the Coldstream Guards either missed the Americans in the dark rainy night, or did not know where to lead them. The end result was that the commander of the 1/18th, Lieutenant Colonel George Fricke, lost his way near the railway station and was pinned down for a time by enemy machine-gun fire. He eventually found his way to the Coldstream command post, a small white mosque at the southern foot of Longstop, but without his headquarters staff.

At 4.30 a.m., Stewart-Brown handed control of the hill to Fricke and ordered his Guardsmen to withdraw. 'We marched away from the hills,' wrote Lance Sergeant Jackson, 'towards the Medjez-Tebourba road, whistling and full of the fruits of victory ... The Regiment was in high spirits. Although we had suffered severe casualties, we had won a victory, the taking of the legendary Longstop Hill.'[6]

Not quite. At dawn on the 23rd, Fricke's men were shocked to discover that they held only half the hill, and that the railway station was still in German hands. To rectify the situation, Fricke ordered his Company A, reinforced with armour, to advance between the road and Longstop's eastern slopes and assault the station. En route, Company A was ambushed by a reinforced panzer grenadier company and all but destroyed: only one officer and thirteen men avoided death or capture.

Elements of the 69th Panzer Grenadiers had also counter-attacked the top of the hill and driven the Americans off Point 290. By 3 p.m., Oberst Lang reported to his superiors that he had recaptured the whole of his original main line of resistance. An hour later, the Americans tried to regain the high point with British artillery support, but failed. By 6 p.m., they had taken up defensive positions to the west and south, with Company B on the knob closest to Point 290, and Companies C and D in support. Communications between the companies were almost non-existent. Telephone lines were frequently cut by shell and mortar fire; radios failed because of the heavy rain. Those that did work were ineffective in such hilly terrain.[7]

Earlier that day Colonel Frank Greer, commanding the 18th Infantry, had requested reinforcements in case the hill was lost. The only reserve available was the 2nd Coldstream Guards, then eating a well-deserved breakfast near Medjez el Bab. 'The men hurriedly stamped out their fires,' wrote the war correspondent for the *Express* newspaper, 'drained off their tea, crammed down bully beef and biscuits. Within five minutes they were marching down the Medjez road.'[8]

In fact, only a single company – No. 4 – and the carrier and anti-tank platoons were sent at first. But as the situation worsened, the rest of the battalion was ordered to return to Longstop, with Stewart-Brown told to assume command of all troops on the hill. He did so early on Christmas Eve and quickly devised a new plan. Advancing from the col, where the bulk of the battalion was concentrated, No.

4 Company would pass through the 1/18th's Company B, still clinging tenaciously to the hill opposite Point 290, and attempt to clear the rest of the ridge from west to east. No. 3 Company would follow in support, while No. 1 was in reserve.

The attack began at 5.30 p.m., two hours before dark, and made rapid progress.[9] When the spearhead of No. 4 Company reached the final peak, wrote Major Roddy Hill, 'they saw in the failing light what had never previously been appreciated – Djebel el Rhar staring at them across the gully'. They at once attempted to deal with this 'new objective' by inclining to the right, descending into the gully and up the other side. But the objective was 'strongly held' and much larger than one company could cope with. A small group captured Djebel el Rhar's highest peak, Point 243, for a time. But the platoons lost contact with each other in the darkness and, with most of their leaders killed, the survivors withdrew back to the western part of Longstop.[10]

For the second time in three days, the Guardsmen were in control of Djebel el Ahmera, but not the neighbouring Djebel el Rhar from where the Germans were able to direct mortar and machine-gun fire on to their hastily dug positions. 'We kept our heads down,' wrote Lance Sergeant Jackson, 'and were lucky to come through again. Our rations now were very small as we had eaten most of them during the march back.' At stand-to on Christmas Day, he thought about his wife and parents celebrating in Nuneaton. 'Here I was on a hillside seven hundred feet up in the Tunisian mountains,' he wrote, 'with one tin of sardines and a bottle of rain water. However, I still had my life, which was more than the rain-washed bodies had which lay out in front of us.[11]

A day earlier, Generaloberst von Arnim and Generalleutnant Fischer had visited Lang's command post to watch the battle. Aware it was balanced on a knife edge, Arnim sent Lang reinforcements, including tanks, which were used on Christmas Day to attack and disperse a company of French colonial troops who were defending the col. The Germans' main effort, led by Oberst Lang in person, was an assault on the Americans holding the southern slopes from both the flank and the rear. This isolated the Guardsmen on the top of Longstop who were cold, hungry and almost out of ammunition. At 10 a.m., shortly after the Germans had retaken Point 290, Lieutenant General Allfrey ordered the survivors to withdraw.[12]

Both battalions were badly depleted: the Coldstream Guards had lost 178 men (including Lance Sergeant Jackson who was shot in the ankle as he came down the hill); the 1/18th Infantry more than 350. Second Lieutenant Franklyn A. Johnson, commanding a platoon of the 18th's Cannon Company, spoke to one of the limping survivors who told him: 'We took Longstop three times, but the Germans took it four.'

The battle would go down in history, wrote Johnson, as 'one of the worst for the 18th Infantry': a 'calculated risk which failed – too little and too soon'.[13]

Inevitably there were recriminations with the British criticising the Americans, and vice versa. Certainly errors were made: insufficient reconnaissance meant that Longstop was 'never completely captured'; requiring one battalion 'to secure the objective and perfect the transfer in the same night was asking the impossible'; communication within the battalions, and between them, was patchy at best; mules should have been provided to bring forward rations and ammunition; and artillery support was 'highly unsatisfactory' on Christmas Day, during the decisive German counter-attack, because forward observers had been withdrawn the night before.[14]

In difficult terrain and appalling weather, both the American and the British troops had fought magnificently, but, ultimately, Lang's superior battle management was decisive. 'We had to recognise,' wrote Lieutenant General Anderson, 'that all our efforts to reach Tunis had failed. It was a bitter disappointment to everyone after coming so near to success. Although this original failure enhanced our ultimate success in North Africa, the consequent delay in liquidating Rommel was serious. Had we got to Tunis in December, the whole subsequent course of the war might have been speeded-up.'[15]

Maybe, but one junior officer had noticed failings among the German troops that still gave him cause for optimism. To all outward appearances, 25-year-old Lieutenant Nigel Nicolson was a typical product of the British upper class. The son of politician Sir Harold Nicolson and writer Vita Sackville-West, and raised amidst the Jacobean splendour of his mother's ancestral home of Knole, and later at Sissinghurst Castle, he had been educated at Eton and Balliol College, Oxford, and in 1939 joined the Brigade of Guards. But Nicolson was also a deep thinker with a social conscience – he had spent a year prior to the war as a voluntary social worker in Newcastle upon Tyne – and would later co-found, with George Weidenfeld, the famous publishing house that took their names.

Nicolson had been keen to serve because, as he put it, young men of his generation 'felt wanted, even perhaps a little heroic simply being in the army'. He also believed that a uniform made him more attractive to the opposite sex. The fact that he might be killed in action never crossed his mind; nor did the pressing need to fight for King and Country to defeat the evil of Nazism. 'You were given a designated enemy,' he said, 'the Germans, the Italians, the Japanese – it could've been anyone. You were pointed in the right direction and your main motivation after that is really not to disgrace yourself.'[16]

Rejected by the RAF, he had joined the Grenadier Guards instead, and became the 3rd Battalion's intelligence officer. He was with the battalion during its skirmishes in and around Medjez el Bab and Longstop Hill in December 1942, and remembered quite a lot of bullets 'flying about' but not feeling scared. Because he was one of the few officers in North Africa who could speak German, he tended to have 'first go' at any prisoners taken in the divisional area. This had caused him to conclude, he told his mother in a letter from Tunisia, that the Germans were 'extraordinarily poor soldiers – or at least the ones we have had opposite us so far'. He added:

They will tell you anything you want to know without the slightest hesitation. One of them, when he had finished telling me exactly where

all his troops were situated, told me that he had given me this information because I was an officer and he was only a Gefreiter [lance
corporal]. They are just as simple as children. They don't think they
have much hope in Tunisia, but I wouldn't say that they were fed up.
They are just rather low and rattled.

This poor first impression was confirmed when a German patrol
approached the Grenadiers' position by walking down a road in broad
daylight. 'We waited for them in the trees,' wrote Nicolson, 'closed
behind them, and captured fifty without a single casualty on our side.
It is that sort of thing which gives confidence to our men. They are
at the top of their form. The First Army is all at the top of its form:
they are really first rate, and I do hope people at home are not comparing
them unfavourably with the Eighth Army. It is a question of opportunity and strength.'

Commanded by the celebrated Sir Bernard Montgomery, and with
a string of victories over Rommel's Panzer Army dating back to Alam
Halfa in July 1942, the Eighth Army was the darling of the newsreels
back in the UK. The First Army, by contrast, had yet to win its first
major battle. But Nicolson had no doubt that it would soon do so, and
prove itself every bit as good as its more experienced counterpart.

He was, he concluded his letter, particularly looking forward to the
imminent juncture of the two Allied armies, 'for even Daddy's witnessing
of the Versailles treaty will be as nothing compared to the *stimmung*
[charged atmosphere] of that occasion'.[17]

20

'It is killing that animates them'

North Africa and Germany,
December 1942–January 1943

'IKE' EISENHOWER WAS NURSING a severe cold in his hilltop villa in Algiers when word reached him on 30 December 1942 that the Allied leaders, President Franklin D. Roosevelt and Prime Minister Winston Churchill, and their senior military and civilian advisors, planned to hold a conference near Casablanca, Morocco, in January. Ike's staff was to make the necessary arrangements.

This was not what the ailing Eisenhower wanted to hear. Not only would preparations for the conference require a 'very considerable amount of work', they would be hard to keep secret. Casablanca, moreover, was still receiving occasional visits from Axis bombers and the local population included many 'fanatics' who might be capable of assassination attempts. It seemed to Ike a 'risky thing to do'.

Harry Butcher agreed. 'The President's winter vacation?' he noted in his diary. 'Imagine it will be ultra-secret, and the press at home will be amazed when they are eventually told where the President has been sojourning.'[1]

Roosevelt had cabled Churchill in late November to suggest that representatives from the American, British and Russian General Staffs should meet at the end of the Tunisian campaign to discuss future Allied strategy. Churchill had agreed, but felt that the leaders themselves, Stalin included, should be present, and that Iceland was a possible location in January 1943, by which date – optimistically – he declared: 'Africa should be cleared and the great battle in South Russia [Stalingrad] decided.'

Warming to the idea, Roosevelt told Churchill on 3 December that he had sent an invitation to Stalin and was convinced the Soviet dictator 'will accept'. His preferred date for the conference was 'January 15, or soon thereafter' by which time 'Tunis and Bizerta should have been cleared up and Rommel's army liquidated'. As to the venue, he preferred 'a secure place south of Algiers or in or near Khartoum [in Sudan]' to Iceland, and suspected that might suit Stalin too. 'I don't like mosquitoes,' he had cabled Churchill. 'I think the conference should be very secret and that the Press should be excluded.'

The proposal had 'delighted' Churchill who felt the sooner they met with their respective staffs – in his case that meant the Secretary of State for War, Anthony Eden, and the Chiefs of Staff – the better as 'all prospect of an attack in Europe in 1943 depends on early decision'. He had offered Khartoum and Marrakesh (in Morocco) as possible venues, and could personally vouch for the latter 'as regards accommodation, climate and, barring any extraordinary lapse, weather'. It all now hinged, said Churchill, on whether 'Barkis [Stalin] is willin'. This was a playful reference to Mr Barkis, a character in Charles Dickens's novel *David Copperfield*, who uses the phrase to hint that he wishes to marry Clara Peggotty.

In the event, Stalin was not. In response to Churchill's invitation, sent soon after Roosevelt's on 3 December, he said that he had welcomed the idea of a meeting between the three leaders 'to fix a common line of military strategy', but to his 'great regret' was not able to leave the Soviet Union in January because 'operations in the Stalingrad area as well as on the central front are developing'. At Stalingrad, he said, 'we are keeping a large group of the German troops surrounded' and 'hope to annihilate them completely'. He added: 'I am waiting your reply to the paragraph of my preceding letter dealing with the establishment of the Second Front in Western Europe in the spring of 1943.'

With Stalin a no-show, Roosevelt had told Churchill on 14 December that the two of them should still 'get together as there are things which can be definitely determined only by you and me in conference with our Staff people'. He now suggested a meeting at either Algiers or Casablanca as it would give him the opportunity to meet Eisenhower and the other senior commanders in northwest Africa, and inspect some American troops. In a follow-up telegram, the president had narrowed the option to a 'satisfactory and safe place just north of Casablanca'. Churchill was delighted. 'Yes, certainly,' he wrote. 'The sooner the better. I am greatly relieved.'

The conference, at Churchill's suggestion, was codenamed Symbol, and set for 'about January 15'. A huge barbed-wire enclosure, a mile square, was constructed around a large white four-storey hotel in Anfa, a well-heeled suburb of Casablanca. Within the lush grounds that stretched down to the sea were eighteen 'extremely comfortable' villas that were reserved for Roosevelt, Churchill, Giraud and their advisors. The grandest, Dar es Saada – allocated to the American president – boasted a living room with a 28-foot vaulted ceiling and zebra-hide sofas, steel shutters to protect the windows, and a swimming pool converted into a bomb shelter.[2]

Meanwhile, both sides in Tunisia tried to take advantage of the lull in ground fighting to bring in more troops. Yet the air war, if anything, increased in tempo as the Axis forces sought to exploit their relative advantage. As Lieutenant General Anderson admitted,

Our troops were badly harassed by the German Air Force. Forward units were dive-bombed without mercy, and day movement on all roads in the forward area was continually strafed and harassed by low flying machine gun attacks. Owing to his nearness to the concrete runways at Tunis and Bizerte, the enemy had an enormous advantage over our own aircraft striving to operate from muddy airstrips or at long range from Bône, over the mountains.[3]

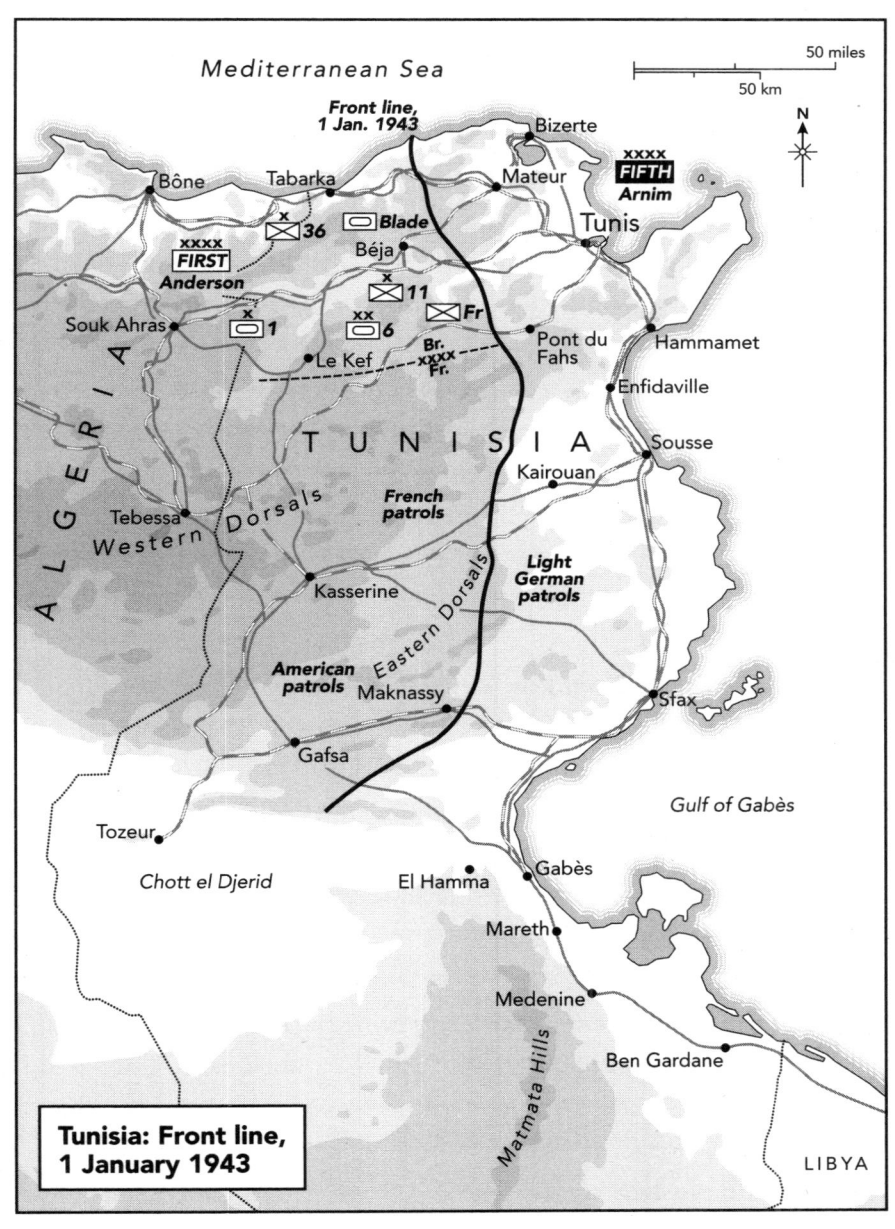

Tunisia: Front line,
1 January 1943

It was during a visit to one of those muddy airstrips – at Biskra in northeast Algeria – in January 1943 that veteran newspaperman Ernie Pyle came under fire for the first time. Forty-two years old, a troubled soul with a scrawny frame and thinning grey hair, Pyle was an unlikely war correspondent. He had served briefly in the First World War as a petty officer in the US Navy, before attending Indiana University where he edited the student newspaper, and then had made his name as a roving correspondent for the Scripps-Howard newspaper chain, reporting on the lives of ordinary people in rural America in the 1930s.

He now planned to do something similar for American servicemen, and his daily column about life at the front was eventually syndicated to more than three hundred newspapers. Since arriving in Algiers on the troopship *Rangiticki* on 22 November, he had spent much of his time with Fredendall's men bivouacked near Oran. 'The American soldier is quick in adapting himself to a new mode of living,' he wrote on 1 December.

> Outfits which have been here only three days have dug vast networks of ditches three feet deep in the bare brown earth. They have rigged up a light here and there with a storage battery. They have gathered boards and made floors and sideboards for their tents to keep out the wind and sand. They have hung out washing, and painted their names over the tent flaps. You even see a soldier sitting on his 'front step' of an evening playing a violin.

His Christmas Eve column noted, somewhat provocatively, that 'Oran, as a city, is not a bad place at all . . . It has palm-lined streets, broad sidewalks, outdoor cafés, a beautiful harbour, restaurants with soft-colored lighting, and apartments with elevators.' At the same time, he wrote, it had 'Arabs dressed in ragged sheets, garbage in the gutters, dogs that are shockingly gaunt, and more horse carts than autos . . . most Americans would trade the whole layout for the worst town in the United States, and throw in a hundred dollars to boot'. Why? Because 'that's the way Americans are, including me'.

Commenting on the campaign in Tunisia in early January 1943, Pyle acknowledged that 'we seem to be stalemated for the moment' for two reasons: the Allied army was 'green', and most of its troops were 'in actual battle for the first time' against seasoned opponents. It would, therefore, take months of fighting for the Allies 'to gain the experience our enemies start with'. Pyle had hit upon an important point: it was not only the American component of Eisenhower's force that was inexperienced and had to learn on the job; so too were most of the British, only a few of whom had seen action in the ill-fated Dunkirk campaign.

At that time, he was reporting from American field hospitals that the only deaths in the original invasion of Algeria and Morocco were 'those killed outright and those so badly wounded nothing could have saved them'. Almost nobody had died from infection – one of the biggest killers in all previous wars – because of the miracle drug sulfanilamide, an antibiotic developed in the 1930s, that was issued to each soldier in the form of twelve tablets and a small sack of powder for sprinkling on wounds. The result was that hardly anyone died of an infected wound. 'Hundreds are alive today,' wrote Pyle, 'who would have been dead without it. Men lay out for twenty-four hours and more before they could be taken in, and the sulfanilamide saved them.'

The first of Pyle's many flirtations with danger – war reporting proper – was at the desert airfield at Biskra in Algeria, dubbed the 'Garden of Allah', in mid-January 1943. He had been there barely three hours when German planes arrived at dusk, flying 'arrogantly low' – for which some 'must have regretted their audacity, for they never got home' – and dropped bombs on several parts of the airfield. Fortunately, no one was injured, partly because the air-raid trenches were so deep. 'The officers don't have to hound their men,' wrote Pyle. 'They dig with a will of their own, and with a vengeance.

Nowhere on the field – and it is a huge one – do you have to run more than fifty yards to drop into a trench.'

Among the pilots he met at Biskra was 22-year-old Lieutenant Jack M. Ilfrey from Houston, Texas, the 'leading American ace in North Africa'. It was, for Pyle, hard to imagine that the baby-faced Ilfrey – nicknamed 'Happy Jack' for his cheerful disposition – had ever killed anybody. Softly spoken, he had a 'very slight hesitation in his speech that somehow seems to make him a gentle and harmless person'. He was, noted Pyle, 'wholly thoughtful and sincere' with 'not the least trace of the smart aleck or wise guy about him'. Yet, in the air, he was a stone-cold killer.[4]

The son of a cashier at Houston's First National Bank, Ilfrey had learned to fly at the Civilian Pilot Training Program at Texas A&M University in 1939. Two years later, he joined the US Army Air Corps as an aviation cadet and was commissioned five days after Pearl Harbor. He was assigned to the 94th Fighter Squadron, 1st Fighter Group, equipped with the Lockheed P-38 Lightning, a single-seat, twin-engined fighter that could be used in multiple aerial combat roles: fighter-bomber, night fighter, aerial reconnaissance and long-range escort. Robust, nimble and fast – its twin supercharged engines were capable of a top speed of 360mph – and armed with four Browning machine guns and a 20mm cannon, it could take on the best Axis fighters.

So keen was Ilfrey to prove himself in combat that he had almost caused a diplomatic incident in mid-November 1942 when one of his long-range drop tanks failed en route to North Africa and he was forced to land in Portugal. Informed that he was in a neutral country and would be interned for the duration of the war, Ilfrey had somehow persuaded the Portuguese to refuel his plane before removing an officer from the wing and taking off without permission. His commanding officer had been furious; but not Major General Jimmy Doolittle, commanding the US Twelfth Air Force, who felt Ilfrey had shown the right qualities to be a successful fighter pilot. He was correct.[5]

Twice Ilfrey had shot down two enemy fighters in a single day: on

2 December when he destroyed a brace of Messerschmitt Bf-109s near Gabès in southern Tunisia; and again on Boxing Day when his victims, over the port of Bizerte, were two Focke-Wulf Fw 190s. The fifth confirmed victory that Ilfrey needed to call himself an 'ace' had been, according to Pyle, a 'twin-motored Messerschmitt 110, which carries three men'. In fact, Ilfrey had shared that 'kill' with another pilot, and still needed the same again. He would go one better, destroying a third Focke-Wulf 190 near Tunis on 3 March.

Ilfrey, whose plane was nicknamed 'Texas Terror', did not have it all his own way. On one occasion he was isolated by enemy fighters and narrowly escaped with his plane riddled by 268 bullets, at least a dozen of which would have killed him if they had not been stopped by the armour plate behind his seat. Another time he almost collided with an enemy fighter as it exited from cloud cover. 'They both kicked rudder violently,' wrote Pyle, 'and they missed practically by inches . . . Jack says he was weak for an hour afterward.'

Having spoken to both bomber and fighter pilots, Pyle realised that the latter were typically younger and inclined to be 'more harum-scarum'. Yet their work was 'so deadly, and the sobering dark cloud of personal tragedy is over them so constantly', it had made them humbler. Few had felt much personal animus towards their Axis opponents before they arrived in North Africa. That changed as they had lost 'too many friends, too many roommates'. Now, noted Pyle, 'it is killing that animates them'.

Most of their missions were as escorts for bombers. Their prefer-ence, however, was for freelance work 'to shoot up whatever they see, and going in enough force to be pretty sure they'll be superior to the enemy – that's Utopia'. They 'laughed and got excited' as they told him about a strafing run earlier that day on a German convoy that had resulted in men flying out of trucks 'like firecrackers', and motor-cyclists skidding forty feet along the ground. Two German fighters tried to intervene but were shot to pieces. As Pyle looked into these young men's excited eyes, he felt oddly concerned. As he wrote,

They were all so young, so genuine, so enthusiastic. And they were so casual about everything – not casual in a hard, knowing way, but they talked about their flights and killing and being killed exactly as they would discuss girls or their school lessons.

Maybe they won't talk at all when they finally get home. If they don't it will be because they know this is a world apart and nobody else could ever understand.[6]

On Christmas Eve, 1942 – the fourteenth birthday of his only child Manfred – Erwin Rommel wrote to his wife: 'To-day my thoughts are more than ever with you two at home. Kesselring was here yesterday. New promises were made, but it will be the same as it ever was. They can't be kept because the enemy puts his pencil through our supply calculations.'

Rommel was at Buerat in Tripolitania where he had been ordered to make his last stand. To that end, 80,000 mines had been laid and several anti-tank ditches dug. Yet he was convinced the position would not survive a full-scale attack by the British Eighth Army, particularly an outflanking manoeuvre to the south, and had asked Mussolini for permission to move his non-motorised troops to Homs, 1,000 miles to the west, before it was too late. The Duce had responded on 19 December: 'Resist to the uttermost, I repeat, resist to the uttermost with all troops of the German-Italian Army in the Buerat position.'[7]

The Italian dictator should have been attending a three-day conference with Hitler at Rastenburg in East Prussia that had begun on the 18th. Too ill to attend in person, he had sent Ugo Cavallero, the head of his armed forces, and his foreign minister (and son-in-law) Count Ciano to try to persuade Hitler to conclude a peace with Stalin – or at the very least to set up a defensive line in western Russia – and concentrate his military effort against Britain and the US in the Mediterranean. As part of Italy's contribution, Ciano told Hitler, the Duce intended to call up four classes of recruits in 1943, making a million men in total, along with arms and equipment.

Ōshima Hiroshi, the Japanese ambassador in Berlin, had come to the same conclusion. In late November, he told a meeting of his ambassadorial colleagues in Europe that it was time for Japan, Germany and Italy to coordinate their strategic planning, which meant joint operations against India and a possible link-up with Axis forces in the Middle East. Convinced that it would be 'practically impossible for Germany to overthrow the Stalin regime', he hoped Hitler would make peace with the Soviet Union so that a larger 'Four Power Pact' could confront the Anglo-Saxon powers.[8]

Hitler was not swayed. A deal with Stalin could never be more than temporary, he told Ciano (and later Hiroshi),* and within a short period of time they would be fighting a reinvigorated Soviet Union not for the existence of their regimes but for the future of their nations and for world civilisation. Turning to North Africa, the Führer insisted that the 'dominant problem' was transportation. If that could be solved, he would send the 'best German divisions' to Tunisia, and use them to capture Algeria and French Morocco. That, in turn, would intimidate the Spanish and encourage them to close the Mediterranean to Allied ships, forcing them to use the longer Cape Town route.

That this was all pie in the sky was brought home to the Italian delegation when Cavallero's request for another 500 German planes to safeguard the supply routes to Tunisia was turned down flat. Instead, the Germans promised to bring those air units already in the Mediterranean up to full efficiency as soon as possible, and to convert old French 75mm field guns for anti-tank use. Was it any wonder that a depressed Ciano felt the Germans had lost the war? 'There's nothing to do,' he told his entourage, 'but wait for the collapse.'[9]

Walter Warlimont, the OKW's Deputy Chief of the Operations Staff, also saw the contradiction in Hitler's determination 'to hold

---

* In July 1943, with the defeat of the Soviet Union still his priority, Hitler assured Ōshima that the Germans and Japanese would surmount every obstacle. (Overy, *Blood and Ruins*, p. 237)

North Africa' while refusing to devote enough resources to make that possible. He blamed Kesselring who had a 'considerable influence on Hitler's attitude'. The Commander-in-Chief South was, wrote Warlimont, 'optimistic about future developments both in Tunis and as regards the sea supply situation'.[10]

Rommel was optimistic about neither, and on New Year's Day 1943 – after extensive lobbying by him and his superior Bastico – finally received permission from Cavallero and Kesselring to begin the withdrawal from Buerat along the Libyan coast to Khoms. But there was a caveat. They were to hold a defensive line at Khoms for at least six weeks, and block the Eighth Army from getting past it to Tripoli, 70 miles farther west. Eventually, Libya would be evacuated, Cavallero told him, 'because of the impossibility of re-supply'. But until then, the Eighth Army had to be held at bay long enough to build up sufficient forces and supplies in Tunisia.

Rommel knew that it was pointless to commit himself to 'definite dates', and said as much. The length of their stay in Tripolitania would be decided, he told Bastico, not by the Comando Supremo but by Montgomery. He expected the commander of the Eighth Army to launch an attack on the Buerat position any day. As ever, Monty would not be rushed. While he brought more troops and supplies forward, Rommel was running through his own meagre stockpile. Between 1 and 8 January, Rommel's men fired off 50 tons of ammunition, and received only 30 tons; during the same period, they used 1,900 tons of fuel, less than half of which was replaced.

Finally, on 14 January, Rommel discovered through wireless intercepts that the British would attack with overwhelming force the following day. The imbalance in tanks, alone, was almost five to one. In danger of being outflanked to the south, and with neither the petrol nor the ammunition required to fight a defensive battle, Rommel ordered his troops 'to retire to the west'. He wrote to his wife on the 15th: 'Our movement has begun. How fast it will go will depend on the pressure. I'm not feeling too good, for obvious reasons.'[11]

21

Desert Raiders

Libya and Tunisia, 8–23 January 1943

O N 8 JANUARY 1943, a small British convoy – two heavily armed jeeps and five 30-cwt trucks – left Zella oasis in western Libya on a secret mission: to reconnoitre the mountain passes west of the Mareth Line in southern Tunisia. The orders had come directly from General Sir Bernard Montgomery who knew that, once Tripoli had fallen, the Mareth Line – a system of fortifications built by the French in southern Tunisia in the 1930s – would be the Eighth Army's next major obstacle. The main defences at Mareth extended southwest from the Gulf of Gabès to the edge of the Matmata hills, a distance of 30 miles. West of the hills, however, there was a less heavily defended gap from Djebel Nefusa to Djebel Tebaga. Montgomery hoped to threaten this gap, and thus outflank the Mareth Line proper, with a strong diversionary force. But to achieve this 'left hook', he needed to find a pass through which the diversionary force could advance.[1]

The man given this vital task was Major Vladimir 'Popski' Peniakoff, a Belgian-born Russian Jew who had created one of the most remarkable yet little-known irregular units of the war. 'He was a small squat man,' recalled Brigadier Edgar 'Bill' Williams, Monty's intelligence chief, 'with a rubber face banked by heavy eyebrows, eyes that shone with his slow broad smile, indeed the figure of a music hall comedian, with all the likeability of that tribe and with much of its essential seriousness too.'

Williams had first come across Popski when a report arrived at GHQ Cairo about enemy transport in the Libyan Desert. 'Who's Peniakoff?' he had asked. 'And why do we use such unconvincing codenames?'

'He's a Belgian,' the staff officer in the know had replied, 'who sends in very objective reports. You can believe them.'[2]

The son of wealthy Russian émigrés, Peniakoff had been reading Engineering at the Free University in Brussels when his studies were interrupted by the outbreak of the First World War. He moved to the UK and read Mathematics at St John's College, Cambridge. At first this self-confessed 'intellectual prig, with high scientific ambitions', had conscientious objections to war. But these faded and, in 1915, he had enlisted as a gunner in the French artillery, and was later badly wounded and invalided out of the army with 80 per cent disability.

In 1924, the restless Peniakoff had emigrated to Egypt where he worked as an engineer for a sugar manufacturer, married and had two children, and learned to sail, fly and navigate a Model A Ford known as 'the Pisspot' through the desert. He was a polyglot who could speak six languages, including Arabic, and thanks to his incessant exploring was elected a fellow of the Royal Geographical Society. 'Desert travelling,' he wrote, 'had for me ceased to be an adventure. My navigation was sufficiently reliable to give me at all times the feeling that I knew roughly where I was.'

A fervent Anglophile since his youth, Peniakoff volunteered for service with the British Army in 1939 and was commissioned a year later. He was forty-three years old, of medium height and overweight. He had high blood pressure and became breathless if he walked too far. Yet his poor physical condition was counterbalanced by his linguistic and navigational talents, and he was accepted into the British-officered Libyan Arab Force (LAF) in October 1940. Most of the rank and file were semi-nomadic Senussi tribesmen from Cyrenaica, refugees of Italian repression, who neither drank, smoked nor blasphemed. Peniakoff did all three.

In March 1942, Peniakoff came up with the idea of creating a small guerrilla unit to collect intelligence over the whole of Axis-occupied Cyrenaica. It would do this, he promised, by forging links with local Arabs and building up a network of surveillance across the huge Djebel el Akhdar, a range of mountains that runs for 170 miles parallel with the Mediterranean coast from Derna to Benghazi, rising abruptly from the sea in precipitous rocky cliffs, reaching a height of 3,000 feet, and then dropping in a succession of peaks of decreasing height to the great inland desert plain. As a useful sideline, Peniakoff's unit would also destroy enemy fuel dumps.

Tapping local Arabs for information was not a new idea. The Long Range Desert Group – a reconnaissance and raiding unit of the British Army that had been formed by Major Ralph Bagnold in June 1940 – ran regular motor patrols to the south of Djebel el Akhdar, and would leave Arabs at various spots to glean what information they could. But this intelligence was 'necessarily fragmentary and frequently out of date'. Peniakoff's, on the other hand, would be collected continuously, and he would be on the spot to evaluate its worth. 'I wanted to present Eighth Army Headquarters,' he wrote, 'not with disconnected pieces of information, but with a co-ordinated picture of the enemy position in Cyrenaica kept up to date day by day.'[3]

It was an ambitious plan that, according to Williams, he pulled off with gusto.[4] He did this by forming a small LAF 'Commando' – himself, two British signallers to operate the wireless sets and a few Arab bodyguards – to roam Djebel el Akhdar. Transported on his initial trip by the LRDG, he lived happily among the Senussi. 'Although I never really behaved like an Arab,' he wrote, 'in a way I thought and felt like one.'

He was informed of his nickname 'Popski', a popular cartoon character in the *Daily Mirror*, by Guy Prendergast, Bagnold's successor, who told him: 'We call you Popski. Nobody can understand Peniakoff on the phone. Do you mind?'

He did not. He knew his cartoon namesake to be a 'comical hairy little bolshy' and revelled in the comparison. He had become Popski, and would remain so for the rest of his life. The staff officers at Eighth Army HQ were so impressed with the quality of intelligence that Popski brought back from his first trip to the Djebel that he was given carte blanche to arrange another. His only instructions were to spread 'alarm and despondency' in the enemy rear areas, destroy fuel dumps and forge political alliances with the tribal sheikhs. Without an official title, his unit was known colloquially as Popski's Private Army (or the PPA) and the name stuck.[5]

The value of so-called 'mosquito' units like the PPA, LRDG and Special Air Service (SAS) – buzzing about the Middle East at a time when the Allies could do no more than play 'tip-and-run' – have often been questioned. But Brigadier Bill Williams, Monty's intelligence chief who worked with Popski from August 1942, was convinced of their worth. He wrote:

> When the British forces were getting stick from the enemy, to hear that David Stirling [of the SAS] had been off on some coup . . . that Jake Easonsmith [of the LRDG] had 'done it again' . . . or that Popski had another whimsical success: it was heartening. Somebody was laughing at the enemy we feared. We could laugh too. The value of the Popski legend to our own troops was, I think, prodigious . . . Militarily he did his most effective work after we were winning; he helped us to win more easily – by leading us round the enemy, by scaring the enemy, by telling us about the enemy. But I think sometimes his most remarkable work was wrought among us, and earlier.[6]

Popski's task in early 1943 was to lead the Eighth Army, as Williams put it, 'round the enemy' defences in Tunisia. But before he could do that, he needed to discover if the 'left hook' route past the Mareth Line was suitable for tanks and trucks, hence the reconnaissance mission to Djebel Nafasa. On the day his convoy left the Zella Oasis, 8 January, he and his four men were in the two jeeps. The five 30cwt trucks each contained five men from a Rhodesian patrol of the LRDG, led by Captain Lazarus, a young New Zealand surveyor who had worked in southern Africa before the war.

They spent the night of 12 January in the 'upper reaches' of Wadi Zem Zem, a broad ravine close to Rommel's position at Buerat, where they were entertained by a friendly sheikh of the Fezzan Arabs. 'We were the first British troops they had seen,' wrote Popski, 'a momentous break in the monotonous round of their pastoral lives; the party went well and they told us that there had been considerable enemy traffic moving northwards on the Shweref-Mizda road, twenty-two miles to the west.'

Next morning they drove cautiously up the wadi, stopping a mile from the coastal road on which they observed a steady stream of Italian military traffic. They decided to disperse the vehicles and wait for a break in the traffic which would typically come at noon when the Italians enjoyed a siesta. In the meantime, Popski and Lazarus climbed a hummock and took down details of the vehicles in their notebooks. They were 'well hidden under bushes, seated on comfortable sand and commanded a long stretch of road'.

Suddenly they heard gunfire to their rear and, soon after, saw a column of black smoke rising. Returning on foot, they discovered one of Lazarus's trucks bogged down in the sand, a German armoured car burning fiercely, and no sign of Lazarus's men who had taken to their heels. Later, having changed position, Popski and Lazarus spotted five German armoured cars and two lorries with three captured LRDG trucks in tow. They knocked out one armoured car with a road mine, and briefly opened fire on the others before 'dashing away madly, zigzagging down the road'. Since his jeeps were equipped only with light machine guns, Popski knew he was outgunned and that it was better to live to fight another day. They retraced their steps, as per standard operating procedure, and in the early hours of the 14th spotted a glimmer of fire among rocks to the right. They shouted a greeting, and out popped one of Popski's men, a Sergeant Waterson. 'All nice and snug, sir,' he said with a smile. 'Come in and have a look.'

Inside the natural cave they found nineteen of their men asleep, 'comfortable on beds of twigs and leaves, round a smouldering fire'. Waterson explained that they had had to escape on foot after their last truck got jammed against a rock. They had left behind two men: Lazarus's navigator who had been shot in the stomach, and Binney, Popski's 'cheerful Cockney, usually full of banter and brave words', who 'lost his nerve and refused to face the dash in the open to the hilltop under the German bullets'. Another three Rhodesians had been separated from the party as they headed back down the wadi.

Popski did a quick mental sum: two German armoured cars 'burnt out', but at a cost of two men captured, three missing, five trucks lost (three of them captured) and the trip to Tunisia 'cancelled'. It was not the PPA's finest hour, but Popski still saw positives: Waterson 'had proved himself to be a tower of strength' and he had 'got rid of a weak reed, Binney'. He concluded: 'Thus, by slow degrees, would PPA be built up.'

They headed for the nearby wadi at Schweref 'to find a kind of general assembly of LRDG'. Prendergast appeared a day later to commiserate – 'it was rather unfortunate, wasn't it?' – and inform Popski that 'Eighth Army was attacking Rommel at Buerat that very day, expected to be in Tripoli a fortnight later, and wanted urgently information about the Mareth Line'.

The good news was that a separate LRDG patrol – with two of Popski's jeeps and a handful of his men attached – had found a pass through the Nefusa range suitable for Montgomery's left hook. But that still left the ground leading north from this gap to the Mareth Line to be scouted, to see if it was suitable for an armoured division, and also the defences between Matmata and Djebel Tebaga, which were more than 300 miles away from their current position. This was Popski's new mission, with a start date of 18 January. To assist him, fuel dumps had been established near the Tunisian border and in southern Tunisia. When and if he completed his mission, he would have a 'free hand to operate in any area *behind* the Mareth Line' and do what harm he could to the enemy.

There was just one word of warning: the SAS would probably be operating in the same area, but 'their movements and indeed also their aims remained obscure', for their commanding officer David Stirling 'kept his own counsel and preferred not to disclose his plans to possible rivals'.

Popski was slightly in awe of the 'young, tall, good looking and dashing' Stirling, even forming the charitable view that it was against Stirling's 'naturally modest disposition' that he had become 'the romantic figure of the war in the Middle East'. Having raised and trained the 1st SAS Regiment for parachute operations behind enemy lines, Stirling had then switched to 'land fighting in jeeps', and in that capacity, and assisted by his deputy Paddy Mayne, 'had ravaged the German airfields before El Alamein and spread panic amongst the defeated troops after the battle'. Popski wrote generously: 'With a light heart and a cool courage he inspired in his men a passionate devotion and led them to thrilling adventures. Where we plodded, he pranced.'[7]

Popski, like many others, had fallen for the Stirling legend. Certainly, the SAS, like his own unit, had played its part in turning the tide of the Desert War. Yet Stirling's personal contribution was never quite as significant as he liked to insist. Born in late 1915, the younger son of a wealthy Scottish landowner (and related by his mother to the Lovats of Clan Fraser), Stirling was a sickly child who did his best to avoid sport at Ampleforth College, the Catholic boarding school to which he was sent at the age of eight. Yet he kept growing and, by the age of seventeen, was 'nearly 6 feet 6 inches tall, a gangly bean-pole, wilful, reckless and exceptionally polite'.[8]

Stirling would later claim that when war broke out in 1939 he was training in North America for an attempt on Mount Everest. In fact, as a recent biography reveals, he was working as a ranch hand in the United States because his exasperated parents were hoping it might give their feckless son – who had been sent down from Cambridge University after just one year – some focus and direction. He joined the Scots Guards, his father's regiment, but soon tired of the discipline and repetitive drill and volunteered for No. 8 (Guards) Commando instead.

By the summer of 1941, Stirling was in the Middle East with Jock Lewes, another Commando officer who had come up with the idea of creating a small raiding unit that would parachute behind enemy lines. Stirling asked to join the experiment. 'He persuaded me to let him in on it in the last days,' wrote Lewes to his father, 'when all arrangements were made. I let him come reluctantly . . . I resented the strength of his persuasion and despised a little his colossal confidence.'

Herein lies the secret to Stirling's success: an ability to bend people to his will. It helped, too, that he was born into Scottish upper-class privilege and extremely well connected. His first parachute attempt was a disaster and he badly injured his back. Following his convalescence, so the story goes, he broke into GHQ in Cairo in July 1941 to deliver a memorandum about his parachute raiding force that eventually led to the formation of the SAS (or L Detachment, 1 Special Air Service Brigade,* as it was originally known).[9]

After a slow start – the initial parachute operation, Squatter, was a disaster with only twenty-one of the fifty-four men returning to British lines – Stirling's SAS refined its tactics by teaming up with the Long Range Desert Group to attack enemy airfields and other targets. Over the next twelve months, chiefly thanks to Lewes's organisational brilliance (before he was killed on an operation in early 1942) and the daring pugnacity of another founding officer, Blair 'Paddy' Mayne, the SAS destroyed 320 enemy aircraft and was expanded in size to

---

* 1 SAS Brigade did not exist. It was a cover name for nefarious activity, the invention of Lieutenant Colonel Dudley Clarke who ran a branch at Middle East HQ in Cairo that was responsible for deception and intelligence gathering.

two regiments: Stirling's 1st SAS and the 2nd SAS, formed in late 1942 and commanded by David's elder brother Bill.

But not all Stirling's operations were successful – an ambitious raid on Benghazi in September 1942, codenamed Bigamy, led to the loss of many men and achieved nothing – and his attempt to recruit 150 Eighth Army veterans soon after was vetoed by Montgomery himself. 'In all honesty, Colonel Stirling,' said Monty, 'I am not inclined to associate myself with failure.'

Even Monty was prepared to admit later that the string of SAS behind-the-lines raids in late October and early November – disrupting communications, sowing confusion and sapping German morale – had made an important contribution to the success of his Alamein offensive, Operation Lightfoot. The reality, however, was that most of this havoc was coordinated by Mayne and not Stirling.[10]

In January 1943, as the Desert War drew to a close, Stirling plotted his 'most hare-brained scheme yet': a daring mission that would, he hoped, 'guarantee the future of his regiment and ensure a major role for the SAS in the next phase of the war in Europe'. He proposed to lead a small raiding party deep into enemy territory in Tunisia to attack lines of communication, reconnoitre the terrain and become the first Eighth Army unit to link up with Eisenhower's forces advancing from the west.

Suffering from desert sores, migraines and an eye infection that required dark glasses, Stirling was in no fit state to undertake such an arduous trip. But, tired of being overshadowed by Mayne, he was determined not to miss out and, at dawn on 16 January, departed his forward base at Bir Zelten with fourteen men in five jeeps. Six days later, having negotiated boggy marshes, furrowed sand dunes and steep, boulder-filled ravines, they were nearing the German-held Gabès Gap in Tunisia, a natural bottleneck five miles wide between the Mediterranean and the impenetrable salt marshes to the west, when they were spotted by two German reconnaissance planes. They pressed on and, in the early hours of 23 January, passed through the gap unchallenged.[11]

Soon after, they passed a German armoured division – almost certainly Rommel's 21st Panzer – camped on both sides of the road. 'We're going to bluff it,' Stirling told his men. 'Just look straight ahead.'

Nobody challenged them and, a short while later, they turned into open country and headed for the foothills of Djebel Tebaga to find somewhere to lie up. Spotting a long narrow ravine dotted with bushes, Stirling gave the order to drive in and camouflage their vehicles. Before bedding down, two of his men – the navigator Mike Sadler and Johnny Cooper – climbed to the lip of the ravine from where they spotted through binoculars a convoy of enemy vehicles halted on the track below them. 'We assumed they were all getting out to just pee,' recalled Sadler.

He was woken, a couple of hours later, by the crunch of footsteps. Two blue-clad *Fallschirmjäger* were standing over him with Schmeisser sub-machine guns. Indicating that he and Cooper should stay where they were, the Germans moved off down the gully to help round up the rest of the party. No sooner were the enemy out of sight than Sadler and Cooper legged it up the hillside and hid in some camel scrub.

Stirling and the others were captured without a fight. A rotund, red-faced officer – who turned out to be the unit dentist – led Stirling down the gully, Luger pistol at the ready, where they encountered a couple of hundred armed Germans and an armoured personnel carrier, part of a special company of Luftwaffe paratroopers that had been tasked with tracking down the British raiders.

That evening, after his preliminary interrogation, Stirling was allowed outside to pee and ran off. The guards fired shots after him, but missed. He had covered about 15 miles and was hiding in some acacia scrub when he was discovered by an Arab herder who offered to bring him water. Instead the herder returned with Italian soldiers who, taking no chances, tied up the SAS leader and escorted him to their nearby headquarters.

Flown back to Rome for interrogation, Stirling was cautious when speaking to the Italians, but much more voluble in conversation with a fellow captive, Captain John Richards of the Royal Army Service Corps. Unbeknown to Stirling, 'Richards' was actually Private Theodore Schürch, an Anglo-Swiss deserter from the British Army who was working for fascist intelligence. He managed to wheedle out of Stirling vital details about SAS operations, including the location of patrols and their missions, and the name of his probable successor: Paddy Mayne.[12]

News of Stirling's capture, meanwhile, had spread like wildfire among the delighted Axis troops. The version of events told to Rommel was that the SAS commander had offered some Arabs a reward if they could get him back to the British. 'But his bid must have been too small,' wrote Rommel, 'for the Arabs, with their usual eye to business, offered him to us for 11 pounds of tea – a bargain which we soon accepted. Thus the British lost the very able and adaptable commander of the desert group which had caused us more damage than any other British unit of equal strength.'[13]

22

The Casablanca Conference

Morocco, 13–24 January 1943

AT 11 A.M. ON Tuesday, 13 January 1943, a modified B-24 Liberator bomber – call sign 'Commando' – touched down at an airfield near Casablanca, after a long flight from Oxford in the UK. The senior officer on board, according to the manifest, was 'Air Commodore Frankland'. Yet the officer's distinctive figure and eccentric behaviour quickly gave the game away. 'Any fool can see,' muttered Major General Hastings 'Pug' Ismay, Churchill's chief military assistant, also on the flight, 'that is an air commodore disguised as a Prime Minister.'[1]

Winston Churchill loved subterfuge and sometimes, to hide his appearance, wore a false beard. This time he had settled for an RAF uniform, but no one was fooled. It did not help when he ignored security officers trying to hustle him into a car, and strode around the airfield, smoking a cigar and shaking hands with well-wishers.[2]

During the flight itself, wearing only a silk vest, he had been woken up somewhere over the Atlantic by a burning sensation in his toes. As B-24s were unheated, the technicians had tried to make the journey more comfortable for the prime minister and his entourage by rigging up a petrol heater in the bomb bay. The result was petrol fumes and very hot pieces of metal, one of which had singed Churchill in his bunk. Deciding that it was 'better to freeze than to burn' he ordered all heating to be turned off and went back to bed 'shivering in the ice-cold winter air about eight thousand feet up'.[3]

Driven to the conference compound in Anfa, Churchill was delighted with the arrangements in general, and the Villa Mirador in particular. He cabled his deputy Clement Attlee: 'Conditions most agreeable. I wish I could say the same of the problems.'[4]

Those problems were not confined to Anglo-American relations. Even the British were uncertain as to the best grand strategy for 1943; Churchill argued in early December that, with the race for Tunis lost, they needed to stop the Mediterranean operations by mid-summer at the latest and concentrate instead on a cross-Channel invasion of Europe.[5] This is what the American Chiefs of Staff wanted too.

Churchill's Chiefs of Staff did not agree, particularly General Sir Alan Brooke who noted in his diary on 15 December: 'We finished off our paper refuting PM's argument for a western front in France and pressing for a Mediterranean policy aiming at pushing Italy out of the war and Turkey into it. By these means we aim at relieving the maximum possible pressure off Russia.'[6]

Brooke's argument was that the rate and scale of the American build-up in Britain were not sufficient for a successful cross-Channel invasion – Operation Roundup – in 1943. The Germans had forty divisions to oppose it and there was, in any event, still a serious shortage of landing craft and other shipping. In the Mediterranean, on the other hand, there was the possibility – as Major General John Kennedy, Brooke's chief of operations, put it – to 'waste' German strength and 'tackle him on equal or better terms in outposts like Sardinia, Sicily, tip of Italy, Crete'. Kennedy added: 'We cannot develop an offensive on both fronts. The essential condition for France is still a crack in German morale and strength. Italy may be knocked out of the war by a combination of landing attacks and bombing. The Balkans are a weak spot for the Axis. If we can get near enough to bomb the Roumanian oilfields and cut the Aegean and Turkish traffic . . . we can go far to hamstring the Germans.'[7]

Brooke had his work cut out because he knew that Churchill's thinking was similar to that of General George Marshall, the US Army's Chief of Staff, who wanted to close down all offensive operations in the Mediterranean once the Germans had been expelled from North Africa, and concentrate everything on Roundup in 1943. But gradually he won Churchill over, prompting one historian to speculate that 'all the Prime Minister was really doing was making the CIGS check and sharpen his arguments, the better for them to prevail when next they met Marshall'.[8]

That meeting between the British Chiefs of Staff and their American counterparts – the first day of the high-level staff talks at Casablanca – took place on 14 January. The Americans – Marshall, Admiral King and Lieutenant General Henry H. 'Hap' Arnold, the Chief of the US Army Air Forces – had flown in via Puerto Rico, Trinidad and Bathhurst in Gambia. At the latter venue, Marshall had bemused his British hosts by disembarking from the plane in gloves and a beekeeper's hood to ward off mosquitoes. The British were wearing shorts and shirtsleeves.[9]

The 14th was, wrote Brooke in his diary, 'a very long and laborious day'. He explained that the British Chiefs wanted to overthrow the Nazis completely before tackling the Japanese, and to erode German morale and resources in the Mediterranean before launching a cross-Channel invasion (for which sufficient landing craft were, in any case, not yet available). They preferred to attack Sicily next because it would safeguard Mediterranean shipping, tie down German troops and threaten mainland Italy, possibly driving Hitler's Axis partner out of the war.[10]

But the Americans Marshall and King both opposed the 'interminable operations in the Mediterranean' and wanted instead 'to conduct a strategic offensive directly against Germany and to aid the Soviet Union', while simultaneously keeping up a 'constant unremitting pressure against the Japanese to prevent them from digging in and consolidating their gains'.[11] When Brooke asked King to be more specific, the US naval chief proposed that '30 per cent of the war effort should be directed to the Pacific and 70 per cent to the rest'. There was deadlock – but Brooke hoped the Combined Planners, to whom the problem was passed, would side with him.[12]

Waiting for Roosevelt to arrive, Churchill had spent the day going for 'nice walks' on the cliffs and the beach. 'Wonderful waves rolling in,' he wrote, 'enormous clouds of foam, made one marvel that anybody could have got ashore at the landing. There was not one calm day. Waves fifteen feet high were roaring up terrible rocks.'[13]

Roosevelt and his entourage, meanwhile, were nearing the end of their epic journey from Miami to Morocco in a Pan American Boeing 314 Clipper flying boat. The president was accompanied, as ever, by his special advisor Harry Hopkins, Admiral William D. Leahy, the de facto chairman of the US Joint Chiefs of Staff, a doctor, a butler and six Secret Service men. They had left the White House in the evening of 9 January for a thirty-hour journey by bullet-proof train to Miami in Florida. Boarding the huge flying boat, they lumbered into the air at 6.05 a.m. on 11 January, and finally reached the airfield near Casablanca – after stopovers in Trinidad, Brazil and the Gold Coast – in the afternoon of the 14th. 'The President's son [Lieutenant Colonel] Elliott [Roosevelt] was there to meet him,' wrote Hopkins. 'Much "hush hush", and the President, Elliott, and I were hustled into a car blacked-out with mud to drive to our Villa. It is a lovely modern California bungalow – part of an hotel – taken over by the Army.'

Hopkins found the British prime minister 'in fine form' but looking older. Roosevelt and Churchill discussed the military situation – particularly Montgomery's scheduled assault on Rommel's position at Buerat that evening – before they were joined for dinner by both the British and American Chiefs of Staff.[14] Brooke's overarching memory is of King having one drink too many. 'He got more and more pompous,' noted Brooke in his diary, 'and with a thick voice and many gesticulations explained to the President the best way to organise the Political French organisation for control of North Africa! This led to many arguments with PM who failed to appreciate fully the condition King was in! Most amusing to watch.'

At around 1 a.m., an air raid siren caused the lights to be switched off and candles lit. The leaders of the Free World 'in that light and surroundings' would have made, Brooke thought, 'a wonderful picture'.[15]

Later that morning, 15 January, Eisenhower flew to Casablanca for his only day at the conference. It was almost his last on earth as first one of his B-17 Flying Fortress's four engines gave out, and then another. The pilot was sufficiently anxious to order Ike and his aides to put on parachutes, stand by the nearest exit and get ready to jump. They eventually reached the airfield safely, gliding in the last few hundred yards and ending, as Harry Butcher put it, 'a hundred miles of misery'.

As he took off his parachute, Eisenhower dislodged one of the three stars – denoting his lieutenant general's rank – on his shoulder strap. Butcher tried to re-attach the star, but his hands were shaking so much after the engine issues that he kept dropping it. 'Haven't you ever fastened a star before?' asked Ike.

'Yes, sir, but never with a parachute on, sir.'

Eisenhower briefed the Combined Chiefs of Staff on the military situation in North Africa, explaining why he had been forced to suspend the offensive in northern Tunisia and instead establish US II Corps further south in the inland Tébessa area of eastern Algeria, on the Tunisian border. As long as he could maintain an entire corps there, he said, and the enemy chose not to interfere, there would be an opportunity to advance east towards Gabès or Sfax on the Tunisian coast. But his chief concern 'was and would remain' the safety of his 'exposed right flank', which would be vulnerable to attack from Rommel's forces in Libya.

What Ike did not say was that the plans for a southern offensive were already well advanced: Major General Lloyd R. Fredendall hoped to launch it between 20 and 24 January, and to take Gabès and Sfax within ten days. It was, in Ike's view, a 'daring plan' that called for a 'quick armoured thrust to Gabès' and the 'sowing of mine-fields to help protect his right flank on the south in case Rommel tries for a quick dash northward to take Sfax'.

Even without realising the urgency, the mere existence of the plan – which had been discussed with neither Anderson nor Montgomery – ruffled a few British feathers. Ike was ticked off by Brooke for not having coordinated 'with either 1st Army or 8th Army operations'.[16] General Sir Harold Alexander, the urbane Commander-in-Chief of the Middle East Command (and Monty's boss), interrupted Ike to say that II Corps 'could drop consideration of the offensive move because the British forces [under Montgomery] would be quickly in Tripoli and, if that port was at all usable, the British Eighth Army would be at the southern border of Tunisia in the first week of March'.

The news of Montgomery's rapid progress was music to Eisenhower's ears. But the Desert Fox's accelerated retreat meant that Fredendall's plans to capture Gabès and Sfax were dangerously 'premature'.[17]

Ike would leave the conference feeling a little disgruntled and undervalued. noted Butcher in his diary later:

His bosses hadn't been at all effusive in his praise. Of course, I had heard a lot of good words for him and his forces from the so-called lower levels, but it seemed to me clear that the absence of clear-cut words of thanks from the President or Prime Minister showed they had their noses to the political winds, and weren't going to be caught holding the bag for a general who had made an unpopular decision [to keep Darlan in a position of authority] and hadn't yet got Tunisia.

Harry Hopkins thought that Ike's unpopularity in the US press over Darlan was nothing to worry about, and that if he took Tunisia he would be regarded as 'one of the world's greatest generals'. But if he did not, or took too long to do so, he was for the chop. Butcher repeated the warning to Ike: 'I told him his neck is in a noose, and he knows it, but such is the life of generals.'[18]

But Eisenhower had also been cheered by a long talk with Roosevelt, whose 'optimism and buoyancy,' wrote Ike, 'amounting almost to lightheartedness, I attributed to the atmosphere of adventure attached to the Casablanca expedition. Successful in shaking loose for a few days many of the burdens of state, he seemed to experience a tremendous uplift from the fact that he had secretly slipped away from Washington and was engaged in a historic meeting on territory that only two months before had been a battleground.'

Roosevelt insisted that the final Axis collapse in North Africa should only take a couple of months. When Ike said that might be 'too sanguine by many weeks', the President demanded a date.

'May 15,' blurted out Eisenhower. (When Ike told Alexander about his prediction, the British general smiled and said his answer to the same question had been 'May 30'.)

For Ike, the 'most gratifying' part of their conversation was Roosevelt's assurance that, whatever his chiefs' misgivings, he 'firmly adhered to our basic concept of European strategy, namely the cross-Channel invasion'. He was 'certain that great results would flow from the spring and summer campaigns in the Mediterranean but he properly continued to look upon these as preliminaries to, and in support of, the great ventures which had been agreed before as the true line of Allied effort for accomplishing the defeat of Germany'.

Churchill, too, told Eisenhower that Operation Roundup – or Overlord as it was to become – would not be scuttled. 'I have given my word,' said the British prime minister, 'and I shall keep it. But we now have a glorious opportunity before us; we must not fail to seize it. When the time comes you will find the British ready to do their part in the other operation.'[19]

Over dinner in his villa, Roosevelt expressed a wish to visit the troops at the front. He had done so in the previous war, he reminded Ike and Marshall, and intended to go 'up front in this one too'. In fact, as Assistant Secretary of the Navy, he had visited the Western Front for only a short period in the Great War, mostly behind the lines, and his generals were not prepared to take the risk with their wheelchair-bound Commander-in-Chief.

'It's impossible, sir,' said Eisenhower.

'Out of the question,' agreed Marshall.

When Roosevelt pressed the issue, Marshall responded: 'Orders are orders, sir. But if you give them, nobody in the US Army from us on down will take responsibility.' The compromise agreed was that the President would review Patton's troops near Rabat.[20]

Between 14 and 23 January, the Combined Chiefs of Staff held no fewer than fifteen meetings in the conference room at the Anfa Hotel in Casablanca. Slowly but surely the British brought the Americans round to their way of thinking with regard to more operations in the Mediterranean at the expense of Roundup in 1943. It helped that Roosevelt was already on board, and that the line taken by the US Joint Chiefs was far from unanimous. Admiral King, wrote Robert E. Sherwood, 'as a sea-power man saw the enormous advantage of increased security in the Mediterranean', whereas Arnold, Chief of the US Army Air Forces, 'as an air-power man could not fail to be tempted by the prospect of obtaining such advanced bases as Foggia in Italy'.

By Monday, 18 January, the Combined Chiefs had agreed on the decision to attack Sicily, an operation codenamed Husky, in the summer of 1943. Marshall was persuaded by the British Chiefs' insistence that, as he put it, 'we will have in North Africa a large number of troops available' and that possession of the northern coast of Africa and of Sicily would 'release approximately 225 vessels which will facilitate operations in Burma, the Middle East and the Pacific'. The occupation of Sicily, in particular, would 'deprive the enemy of the base from which to attack Allied shipping in the Mediterranean at its narrowest point', and give the Allies a base for the establishment of 'much broader air coverage for their shipping'.

It meant, of course, a further postponement of Roundup which 'disappointed and depressed' Harry Hopkins as much as it did Marshall. They both believed that there was 'no really adequate substitute for the opening of a Second Front in France'. But as a quid pro quo, the British were persuaded to back American objectives in the Far East and the Pacific that included retaking Burma, via a land operation in the north to reopen the Burma Road to China, and an amphibious strike in the south to recapture Rangoon; seizing the huge Japanese naval base of Rabaul on the island of New Britain in the south Pacific; recovering Kiska and Attu, the two Aleutian Islands in the north Pacific that had been occupied by the Japanese in the summer of 1942;[*] and advancing west through the Gilbert and Marshall Islands in the central Pacific towards Truk and the Marianas.[21]

American planners would long resent their 'defeat' at Casablanca, blaming superior British preparation and staff work. 'It taught us a lesson,' wrote one. 'Never go to a meeting like that without plenty of help because you need it.' Even Marshall admitted later that 'there was too much anti-British feeling on our side, more than we should have had.'[22]

After hosting two of the British Chiefs at dinner, Patton wrote: 'Brooke is nothing but a clerk. Pound slept most of the time. The more I see of the so-called great the less they impress me – I am better.'[23] This was unfair on Sir Dudley Pound, Britain's First Sea Lord, who was suffering from an undiagnosed brain tumour that would kill him later that year.

In his own diary, Brooke was almost as dismissive. 'I did not form any high opinion of [Patton],' he wrote, 'nor had I any reason to alter this view at a later date. A dashing, courageous, wild and unbalanced

---

[*] Situated off the southern coast of Alaska, Kiska and Attu were the only slivers of the USA occupied by Japan during the war. Attu was retaken, after a bloody fight that cost the Americans 3,500 casualties, in May 1943. By the time an American and Canadian force landed on Kiska, in August 1943, the Japanese had already withdrawn.

leader, good for operations requiring thrust and push but at a loss in any operation requiring skill and judgment.' His estimation of Marshall was, if anything, even more damning: 'It was almost impossible to make him grasp the true concept of a strategic situation. He . . . preferred to hedge and defer decisions until such time as he had to consult his assistants.'[24]

At the concluding press conference, on 24 January, Roosevelt announced that the Allies were demanding unconditional surrender from the Germans and the Japanese – much as the Union general Ulysses S. Grant had insisted during the US Civil War with the Confederates – but not Italy. This had been agreed in advance with Churchill who, four days earlier, ran the idea past his War Cabinet. 'The omission of Italy would be to encourage a break-up there,' he wrote. 'The President liked this idea, and it would stimulate our friends in every country.'

As for the demand itself, it would ensure, Churchill explained in a speech later that year, that the Axis 'will-power to resist' was 'completely broken, and that they must yield themselves absolutely to our justice and mercy'. Only then would the Allies be able to take 'all those far-sighted measures which are necessary to prevent the world from being again convulsed, wrecked, and blackened by their calculated plots and ferocious aggressions'.[25]

23

Victory or Destruction

North Africa, Germany and Stalingrad,
December 1942–February 1943

NEWS OF THE ALLIES' demand for unconditional surrender
reached Hitler at the Wolf's Lair in East Prussia as yet more
disasters were playing out on the battlefield. On 23 January, Tripoli
fell to the Eighth Army after Rommel had withdrawn the Panzer
Army from the Tarhuna–Khoms line to save it from destruction. 'You
can either hold on to Tripoli a few more days and lose the army,' he
had told Ugo Cavallero on the 20th, 'or lose Tripoli a few days earlier
and save the army for Tunis. Make up your mind.'

Cavallero's response, on behalf of the Duce, did not mention Tripoli.
Instead he told Rommel to preserve the army, but also to gain as
much time as possible to fortify the Mareth Line in Tunisia. This gave
Rommel licence to move the Panzer Army back to the Tunisian
border, abandoning Tripoli in the process, after Montgomery had
attempted to outflank the Tarhuna–Khoms line on the 21st. Rommel
had few regrets. Had they stayed, 'as the Duce was insisting from his
seat in Rome,' he wrote later, 'the army with all its infantry would
have been surrounded and destroyed'.[1]

All eyes at Rastenburg, however, were focused on the catastrophe
at Stalingrad where Paulus's Sixth Army was on its last legs. A month
earlier, the attempted relief by Hoth's Fourth Panzer Army had got
within 40 miles of the Stalingrad pocket before it found itself 'heavily

outnumbered and had to give up' on 21 December. At that point Manstein ordered Paulus to break out of the *Kessel* (cauldron) within twenty-four hours. Impossible, he replied, his tanks only had enough fuel to drive 20 miles. His generals then urged him to abandon his transport; but without a direct order from Hitler he would not budge. By Christmas Day, with Manstein's Army Group Don in full retreat, the fate of the Sixth Army was sealed.

Nicolaus von Below, Hitler's Luftwaffe Adjutant, had with mounting dread been following events at Stalingrad since the initial Russian breakthrough north of the city on 19 November. On 1 December, he had received a letter from Generalleutnant Arthur Schmidt, Paulus's chief of staff. 'Now we have our ardent all-round defence,' wrote Schmidt. 'I have enough weapons but little ammunition, little bread and spirit, no wood for burning or building materials to go below ground and keep warm, and the men, who remain astonishingly confident of victory, are daily losing strength.'[2]

By Christmas 1942 – a festive twenty-four hours that saw the death of 1,280 German soldiers – all optimism at Stalingrad had vanished.[3] A day later Hauptmann Behr, Schmidt's orderly officer, informed Below that 'we think ourselves at the moment a bit betrayed and sold down the river'. There was, he added, 'simply nothing more to eat here . . . the black bread stocks have run right down'. It was inevitable, under the circumstances, that the average soldier's 'physical will to resist will become weaker in the cold and the moment will come when . . . he simply allows himself to freeze to death or lets the Russians overrun us'.

On 11 January, two days before he had the good fortune to be flown out of Stalingrad with the Sixth Army's war diary, Behr wrote: 'It has become so bad that German soldiers are going over to the other side.'

Hoping to provoke a reaction, Below read out to Hitler some of the more graphic extracts from these letters. The Führer's only response was that 'the fate of the Sixth Army was for us all a profound duty in the struggle for the freedom of our people'. Below felt that Hitler knew a two-front war against the Americans and the Russians could 'no longer be won'. Hitler even considered pursuing Ribbentrop's suggestion of 'driving a wedge between his two major enemies' by negotiating a peace treaty with the Soviets. Ultimately, he decided 'that that solution was not yet to be pursued'. Instead it 'remained his intention to mobilise the entire German people' to win the war.

Soon after Behr – Below's future brother-in-law – arrived at Rastenburg, as one of two emissaries sent by Paulus to report to Hitler, and delivered a 'clear and simple picture' of conditions in the *Kessel*. 'According to him,' wrote Below, 'there was no hope. A man fought and fell where he stood . . . Supply to the units was no longer possible as there was no means of transportation. It was the absolutely unequivocal picture of a lost battle.'

Hitler, though, was unmoved. He 'never betrayed a sign of weakness nor indicated that he saw any situation as hopeless', remembered Below. On the contrary, he let it be known that he was confident in ultimate victory, and 'ensured by his attitude, mood and appearance that none of his visitors nor his trusted companions should infer from his demeanour how he really judged the war situation'. He gave the strong impression that one day the tide would turn in Germany's favour, and it fascinated Below 'to see how he contrived to put a positive value on setbacks and even succeeded in convincing those who worked most closely with him'.

His Luftwaffe adjutant, however, was not among them. Below no longer believed that victory was possible, but nor did he think that Germany would lose the war. 'I envisioned', he wrote, 'a sort of compromise European peace solution which, despite everything, seemed to be still attainable with a little goodwill.'[4]

On 15 January, Hitler ordered Generalfeldmarschall Erhard Milch, his Luftwaffe transportation chief, to fly in 300 tons of supplies a day to the besieged Sixth Army. It was wishful thinking, particularly as snow and ice on the runways, and sub-zero temperatures, were preventing many planes from landing. After 22 January, when the last airfield was overrun, supplies could only be dropped from the air, and most were lost to the enemy.

Still Hitler insisted that all was not lost. He told Goebbels, who visited the Wolf's Lair on the 22nd, that parts of the Sixth Army could hold out until relieved. Of course he knew, better than anyone, that would never happen. The same day, Paulus requested permission to surrender. It was rejected. The army would stand fast, said Hitler, 'to the last soldier and the last bullet'.

By 26 January, the remnants of the Sixth Army had been reduced to two small pockets, one in the north of the city, one in the south. Paulus was in the latter, with his headquarters in the basement of the Univermag department store. Such was the shortage of food that he now forbade the issuing of rations to the 30,000 sick and wounded.

On 30 January, the tenth anniversary of Hitler's accession to power, Paulus sent a perfunctory telegram of congratulations. 'The swastika flag is still flying high above Stalingrad,' he wrote. 'May our battle be an example to the present and coming generations, that they must never capitulate even in a hopeless situation, for then Germany will emerge victorious.'

The following day, to stiffen Paulus's resolve, Hitler promoted him to Generalfeldmarschall. It made no difference. That afternoon, the Sixth Army's headquarters sent its final message: 'The Russians are before our bunker. We are destroying the station.'[5]

Paulus then capitulated with the rest of the southern pocket. Friedrich Roske, acting commander of the 71st Infantry Division, wrote: 'Since we were to lose our weapons anyway, we rendered them useless and threw parts of them into the fire, which was busy consuming my personal papers, photographs, identity documents and money. Our army doctor then provided me with a phial of cyanide, which I could take with me "just in case".'[6][*]

---

[*] Choosing not to take the poison, Roske spent almost thirteen years in captivity. A year after returning home, he committed suicide.

On 2 February, the northern pocket surrendered and the epic five-month Battle of Stalingrad was over. 'Dead bodies, frozen stiff, were lying everywhere,' wrote a German artillery officer, 'completely emaciated, unshaven, often curled up in agony. In some places the corpses lay entwined in large mounds, as if a crowd had been driven together and cut down by automatic weapons. Other bodies had been mutilated until they were no longer recognisable.'

During 150 or so days of combat, 2.9 million bombs and shells had destroyed a million square yards of the city, including 126 factories, 110 schools and 15 hospitals. The total casualties were more than 2 million, including 64,000 Russian civilians and 110,000 German soldiers killed. A further 113,000 German and Romanian soldiers were taken prisoner. Only a few thousand would return to their homes.

Hitler expressed no sympathy for the victims. He was far more interested in the loss of prestige and shame that Paulus's surrender had inflicted on Germany. 'How can he give himself up to the Bolsheviks?' he asked, almost speechless with anger. 'What sort of cowardice does it take to pull back from [shooting yourself]?' He had, he added, 'no respect' for a soldier who was too afraid to kill himself, 'but would rather be taken prisoner'. Paulus's betrayal meant there would be no more field marshals. 'I won't go on counting my chickens before they're hatched.'

On 3 February, the German people were mendaciously informed that the men of the Sixth Army had fought to the last and 'died so that Germany might live'. This was little consolation to the families of the victims who raged at the leadership's lies. Why hadn't the Sixth Army been pulled back while there was still time? they asked. Why were earlier reports so optimistic? For almost the first time since his accession to power, Hitler himself was criticised. 'To this extent,' wrote Ulrich von Hassell, a senior German diplomat who opposed the regime, 'there is a genuine leadership crisis . . . The sacrifice of most precious blood for the sake of pointless or criminal prestige is again plain to see.'[7]

Critics of the Allies' demand for unconditional surrender at the

Casablanca Conference have argued that it made it impossible for the Germans and Japanese to pursue a negotiated peace and, as a result, they fought more fanatically. But were negotiations with Hitler ever a realistic option? We know that by late 1942 elements within the German High Command and Foreign Office, notably Foreign Minister Joachim von Ribbentrop, were urging him to consider a separate peace with Stalin so that he could concentrate his forces against the Western Allies. But he had rejected those proposals even before the discussions at Casablanca and the surrender at Stalingrad.

In truth, wrote Hitler's biographer Ian Kershaw, the Allies' demand 'altered nothing', and merely confirmed that the Führer's 'uncompromising stance was right'. He told party leaders in early February that the demand had 'freed him completely' from any need to consider a negotiated peace. 'It had become,' argued Kershaw, 'as he had always asserted it would, a clear matter of victory or destruction. Few, even of his closest followers, as Goebbels admitted, could still inwardly believe in the former. But the compromises were ruled out . . . For Hitler, closing off escape routes had distinct advantages. Fear of destruction was a strong motivator.'[8]

On Monday 18 January, two days after returning to Algiers from Casablanca, 'Ike' Eisenhower had flown to his advanced command post – operating under Major General Lucian K. Truscott Jr, his deputy chief of staff, in an orphanage at Constantine – for a conference with his senior commanders Anderson, Fredendall and Juin. He told them that II Corps' plan to cut Rommel's supply lines at Gabès and Sfax would have to be postponed because 'of the information obtained at the Casablanca meeting from General Alexander as to the rapidity of the Axis retreat' in Libya. With the Eighth Army not due at the Mareth Line until the first week of March, it was inadvisable, said Ike, for Fredendall's 'smaller force' to be exposed to 'flank attacks' from Rommel in the south and Arnim in the north. Instead it should be 'held as a mobile reserve, with occasional pokes at the enemy to keep him upset and guessing, but must not jeopardize itself by undue risk until the Eighth Army has chased Rommel into the Mareth line and begins its assault there'.

In other words, the operations of the two Allied forces needed to be 'carefully co-ordinated', which would be his and Alexander's responsibility. Fredendall could 'conduct raids' and even 'take vantage points', but he was to stay back from either Sfax or Gabès. 'It is imperative,' said Ike, 'that you hold as much of the II Corps as possible in mobile reserve, especially the US 1st Armored Division. Defences in the southern sector should be impregnable.' This was to prevent Axis forces from breaking through and outflanking Ike's forces in the south.

Turning to Juin, he promised to 'scrape the bottom of the barrel' to get the French troops the equipment they needed to take on the German paratroopers, including Sten guns, machine guns and 37mm anti-tank guns with armour-piercing ammunition. Juin also asked for wireless sets, so that his battalions could keep in contact with their outposts, and Truscott and Anderson said they would do their 'utmost to supply them'.[9]

Henceforth, the Allied strategy in Tunis was, wrote Anderson, 'to build-up strength for a major assault on Tunis when the rains stopped, to improve our positions by limited attacks and to hold on to what we had got'. The First Army was also to support the French 'as far south as Pont du Fahs with artillery, transport and signals, without which aid they could not have endured the strain; and push on with the construction of airfields and improvement of communications'. Yet it was obvious to Anderson that the 'Allied front was very extended and weakly held, thus offering many hostages to fortune'.[10]

Since late December, the Fifth Panzer Army had been occupying much of Tunisia's coastal plain, while the Allies were strung out along the Grande or Eastern Dorsal, the mountain range that runs from the northern coast to the salt marshes in the south. The only way for Arnim's Fifth Panzer Army to break out of the coastal plain was round the Eastern Dorsal's southern tip, at Gafsa, or by surging through the mountain passes at Pichon, Fondouk, Faïd and Maknassy. All four were defended by French troops, though their garrisons at Faïd and Maknassy came under the command of the US II Corps.

The Allies were also astride the Petite or Western Dorsal, a smaller range of mountains that joins with the Eastern Dorsal in the north, but diverges further south so that the two ranges form an inverted 'V'. It has passes at Maktar, Sbiba, Kasserine and Fériana. In effect, the Allies had a double defence line of mountains; to reach the Allied rear, an attacker would have to penetrate passes on both the Eastern and Western Dorsals – a daunting task.

Arnim began the process when his troops captured the Fondouk Pass in the Eastern Dorsal on 2 January. Just over two weeks later, while Eisenhower was postponing II Corps' drive on Sfax and Gabès, Arnim launched a much larger offensive – codenamed Eilbote (Courier) I – against Bou Arada and the gap between Djebel Mansour and the high massif at the northern end of the Eastern Dorsal. The Bou Arada assault was parried by elements of Allfrey's British V Corps, notably the 38th (Irish) Infantry Brigade. 'These attacks were properly dealt with,' noted Allfrey in his diary. 'Tanks withdrew, coming in again later and again were dealt with. Small packets of fighting all day, rather confused but everywhere situation completely in hand.'

The second Axis attack, using Tiger tanks of the 501st Panzer Battalion against Barré's Division du Maroc, had more success. Barré called in at Allfrey's command post at 2 p.m. to say that all was well. He returned six hours later with the alarming news that a battalion of the Foreign Legion at Oued el Kebir had been 'pierced' by a German tank attack and needed assistance. Allfrey promised to send a battery of 25-pounders and as many 6-pounders as he could spare. But they arrived too late to make a difference. French resistance crumbled and by late on the 19th the enemy advance had 'cut off seven battalions in the mountains and captured many guns'. With the route now open to the Ousseltia valley behind the Eastern Dorsal, Anderson ordered V Corps to send troops and requested II Corps to move a Combat Command from the 1st Armored Division north to the Maktar area to cover the French right.[11]

From his bomb-proof command post at Speedy Valley, a 'narrow, pine-dotted slash in the hills near Tebessa, on the Tunisian border', Fredendall selected Robinett's Combat Command B, in bivouac near Sbeitla, to assist the French.[12] (Robinett had taken over CCB from Major General Lunsford E. Oliver who had returned to the United States in early 1943 to command the 5th Armored Division). Given over an open phone line, Fredendall's instructions to Robinett were confusingly enigmatic: 'Move your command, i.e., the walking boys, pop guns, Baker's outfit and the outfit which is the reverse of Baker's outfit and the big fellows to "M" which is due north of where you are now, as soon as possible. Have your boss report to the French gentleman whose name begins with "J" at a place which begins with "D" which is five grid squares to the left of "M".'

Robinett admitted later that it took him as much time to interpret the message as it would have taken a German commander had he intercepted it. 'M' was identified as Maktar, 'J' was Juin, commanding general of French forces in Tunisia, and 'D' was Juin's headquarters in Djerissa. The march began at 9.35 p.m. on 19 January and was completed by 9 a.m. the following morning. In all, Robinett moved tanks, tank destroyers, infantry and artillery, with engineers, medics and maintenance companies – a total of over 3,400 men – over 'difficult mountainous terrain under blackout conditions'. A fine effort.

En route Robinett met Juin – 'short and stocky with keen black eyes', a 'ready smile and a good sense of humour' – who showed him Ike's instruction that the CCB would serve as a unit under his direct orders, and not be split into detachments. In the event, the distance between Robinett's command post and Juin's headquarters, and the lack of radio equipment, made this order redundant. The CCB was placed instead under the orders of Louis Koeltz, commanding the French XIX Corps. Moved by Koeltz into positions north of the town of Ousseltia, CCB counter-attacked towards the Kairouan Pass on 21 January and helped to cover the withdrawal of the French infantry isolated on the Eastern Dorsal.

Meanwhile, elements of Major General Charles Keightley's British 6th Armoured Division and the 36th Infantry Brigade had moved down from the north in support of the French, with some of Keightley's men advancing nine miles east of Bou Arada and threatening the German flank.[13] 'Went again to 6th Armoured after lunch,' noted Allfrey in his diary, 'and found Charles a different man after one night's rest. Much more cheerful, which he probably would not have been had he known that the LIR [2nd London Irish Rifles, part of the division's 38th Brigade] had legged it that day.'[14]

More Allied reinforcements poured in to the Ousseltia valley – including units of the US 1st Infantry Division, which were attached to Robinett's CCB – and by the time the fighting died down on 28 January, and the Americans began redeploying to the south, the French had established a new defensive line which ran from Djebel Bargou on the Western Dorsal, and across the Ousseltia valley to Pichon on the Eastern Dorsal. Robinett's command had lost five dead, fifty-four wounded and twenty-five missing, yet had killed an estimated 205 of the enemy, and destroyed nine tanks and eight 88mm anti-aircraft guns.

French losses, however, were much more serious, with 3,449 men taken prisoner. Materiel captured or destroyed included 87 machine guns, 16 anti-tank guns, 36 artillery pieces, 21 tanks, 4 armoured cars, 4 self-propelled guns and 200 other vehicles. 'Allied aviation and artillery had inflicted considerable damage on the enemy,' wrote the US Army's official historian, 'but control of the passes west of Kairouan was worth this price to the Fifth Panzer Army.'[15] The Axis forces now had a foothold in the Eastern Dorsal and a springboard for further attacks on the Western Dorsal where the Allies had their fallback position.

On 21 January, while Arnim's attack was under way, Ike had flown back to Constantine for a second conference with his senior commanders.

The emergency had shown that control of the entire Allied battle-front from his advanced command post was not practical. So instead, with Juin's agreement, he appointed Lieutenant General Anderson to coordinate operations in the three national sectors.

It sounded fine, in theory, but so great were the distances, and so difficult the terrain, that simple 'co-ordination' of forces was not enough; what was needed was direct command. During a four-day period, Anderson motored more than 1,000 miles to visit his three corps commanders and set out a general plan of action. It was a pace that was not sustainable. Eisenhower recognised this and, at a meeting with Anderson at Télergma airfield near Constantine on 24 January, he made the First Army commander 'responsible for the employment of American troops' as well, in accordance with general directions from Allied Forces Headquarters (AFHQ). A day later, after a lengthy discussion with Juin, Anderson was given command of Koeltz's French XIX Corps with effect from 3 February.

Eisenhower's directive to Anderson, dated 26 January, noted that as commander of all Allied forces in Tunisia – including the British First Army, the US II Corps and the French XIX Corps (with US troops attached) – Anderson's task was to re-establish a general defensive line that included the eastern exits to the passes on the Eastern Dorsal, including the Fondouk Pass that had been lost to the Germans earlier in the month. He was, moreover, to pay particular attention to the defence of his right (southern) flank, and to the airbases in the Tébessa area, by keeping the bulk of the US 1st Armored Division 'well concentrated' and available to counter-attack. The ultimate aim was to facilitate 'the launching of a powerful coordinated attack as soon as the weather will permit and the necessary forces and supplies can be assembled in position'.[16]

Anderson had got what he wanted: field command over all Allied troops in Tunisia and eastern Algeria. But with that responsibility came the urgent need for Anderson to prove himself by straightening out the kink in the Allied defences at Fondouk, and the sooner the better. The clock was ticking, and the British general knew it. He wrote later:

> Thus, at long last, there was (under Eisenhower) one commander of the battle-front; though the decision when it came was made on faulty premises and too late for it to be really effective, since First Army HQ and signals were already so located as to confine any effective control to the northern portion of the line and there was insufficient spare equipment to establish an efficient new lay-out or a properly equipped tactical headquarters.

As a result, the task of controlling the whole of this 300-mile-long front would be, admitted Anderson, 'too much for the commander of First Army'.[17]

24

'Save yourselves! Save yourselves!'

North Africa, 24 January–3 February 1943

A T THE CLOSE OF the Casablanca Conference, Admiral King and General Marshall flew to Algiers to discuss the next stage of the campaign with Eisenhower. They told Ike that the failure of his 'all-out gamble' to take Tunis might have had dangerous consequences, but that it had been a risk worth taking. 'We've seen what happens when commanders sit down and wait for the enemy to attack,' said King. 'Keep slugging!'

While at Casablanca, Ike had been informed of a 'general plan' to put both the Eighth Army and the Desert Air Force under his command once they had entered Tunisia. Marshall now confirmed that the new arrangement had been approved by the Combined Chiefs of Staff, and that General Alexander would become Ike's deputy 'in executive command of land operations'. The British Admiral Sir Andrew Cunningham would remain as his naval chief, while Air Chief Marshal Sir Arthur Tedder controlled all Allied air forces.

With Britain still providing the bulk of men and materiel in the Mediterranean, Marshall had assumed that the British Chiefs of Staff would insist on subordinating Eisenhower to Alexander. They did not because they were impressed with the smooth running of AFHQ in Algiers – there was, noted Brooke, 'remarkably little friction . . . between the staff of the two nations' – and preferred to confine Eisenhower to a role where his perceived inadequacies as a field commander would not be exposed. As Brooke put it: 'We were pushing Eisenhower up into the stratosphere and rarefied atmosphere of a Supreme Commander, where he would be free to devote his time to the political and inter-allied problems, while we inserted under him one of our own commanders to deal with the military situations and to restore the necessary drive and co-ordination which had been so seriously lacking.'[1]

It was a smart move. As war correspondent Philip Jordan wrote in his diary,

> E's genius seems to be that of a good chairman. By his personality he has drawn together all the contending elements, British and American, who warred in the early days. He has managed to achieve something more than co-operation here: single-mindedness, and there is no doubt that he has brought his own men more and more towards our point of view . . . I have changed my view of this man: he has something.[2]

The new organisation would become effective in early February, and was 'extraordinarily pleasing' to Ike 'because it meant, first and foremost, complete unity of action in the central Mediterranean' and provided the necessary 'machinery for effective tactical and strategical co-ordination'. The other major decision of the conference that Marshall and King passed on to Eisenhower was 'to prepare to attack Sicily as soon as Africa should be cleared'.[3]

This was not what Ike wanted to hear. Like Marshall, he supported the earliest possible assault on northwest Europe as the shortest route into Germany. He was delighted to learn from his boss, however, that he would soon be awarded a fourth star – promoted to full general – and from Major General Brehon Somervell, Marshall's supply chief (who had also come to Algiers), that the first of 5,000 trucks would begin arriving in North Africa within three weeks. This would, Ike knew, go a long way to easing the supply difficulties for troops at the front.[4]

To accommodate the two Joint Chiefs, Ike gave up his spacious bedroom to Marshall, and Butcher did the same for King. Eisenhower's generous gesture almost backfired when Telek, the little Scotch terrier he had gifted to Kay Summersby, peed on the bed's luxurious maroon cover. Ike was furious. 'Get that goddamned dog out of here!' he yelled.

If Marshall already suspected that Ike's regard for Summersby was not merely professional, this incident hardened his dislike for the former couture model. She, in turn, found him cold, austere and formal, and one of the few senior officers who refused to call Eisenhower by his nickname 'Ike'.

Harry Butcher saw a very different side of Marshall: a father figure who wanted the workaholic Ike to take time off to recharge his batteries. To that end, Butcher was told to arrange regular massages for his boss and to find a place outside the city where he could ride. 'You must look after him,' said Marshall. 'He is too valuable an officer to overwork himself.'

At 5.15 p.m. the following day, as per instructions, Butcher told Ike that it was time to go home to meet the masseur.

'Holy smoke,' said Ike, 'a masseur?'

'Yes, sir, my orders from your superior, sir, General Marshall.'

Ike found his first massage 'very relaxing indeed'. But it was the only one as, in future, he could never find the time. When it came to 'sissy stuff', wrote Summersby, 'Ike simply dug his heels in'.[5]

While the Allies looked forward to the junction of their forces in Tunisia, Kesselring was doing all he could to prevent such an outcome. 'Our strategic objective,' he had told Hitler during a visit to the Wolf's Lair in mid-January, 'must be to keep the two armies apart and to attack and defeat them, one after the other, from an interior line.' Hitler approved of this strategy, and 'gave wholesale promises that reinforcements would be forthcoming'.[6]

Back in Africa, Rommel had already transferred the veteran 21st Panzer Division to southern Tunisia 'to rest there and to ward off a possible American attack'.[7] He himself crossed the frontier on 26 January, intending to make a stand on the Mareth Line. But that same day he was informed by the Comando Supremo that, on account of his ill health, he would soon be released from his command and replaced by the Italian Generale d'Armata Giovanni Messe who, until late 1942, had led Italy's contingent in Russia. Messe would take over Rommel's Panzer Army which – because it had more Italian troops than German – would be renamed the First Italian Army. 'Of course,' he informed his wife Lucie, 'it's really for quite other reasons, principally that of prestige. I have done all I can to maintain the theatre of war, in spite of the indescribable difficulties in all fields. I am deeply sorry for my men.'

Yet he also told Lucie he was 'not well', with 'severe headaches and overstrained nerves, on top of circulation trouble', allowing him little rest. What he needed was a few weeks to recover. But given the situation 'in the East' – Stalingrad – that was unlikely.

His inspection that day of the Mareth Line – a chain of 'antiquated French block houses which in no way measured up to the standards required of modern warfare' – led him to conclude that only the southern sector was tank-proof, and that, overall, the siting was bad because it lay 'immediately behind some high ground' (the Matmata hills) which denied any long-range artillery observation and required, to hold them, a 'serious division' of Axis strength. The line could also be outflanked, which was why Rommel had demanded the occupation of the more easily defendable Akarit Line in the Gabès Gap, 40 miles to the rear. But that request was refused.[8]

About to be sent home, Rommel was reprieved by a wholesale changing of the guard in Rome as Ciano was sacked as Foreign Minister (Mussolini took over his responsibilities), and Cavallero was replaced as head of the armed forces by Vittorio Ambrosio, a 'cool and somewhat austere' general with a 'clear, panoramic and synthetic' view of Italy's war effort. His unambiguous strategic assessment, produced for Ribbentrop's forthcoming visit to Rome, was in line with the dismissed Ciano's: the Germans should adopt a defensive strategy in Russia and devote more resources to the Mediterranean theatre where Tunisia needed to be held for as long as possible because North Africa was bound to be the Allies' springboard for future operations in southern Europe. If they did not change their attitude and help Italy, Ambrosio told Mussolini, 'we shall no longer be obliged to follow them in their mistaken conduct of the war'.

Ambrosio's views were reciprocated by Arturo Riccardi, the Chief of the Italian Naval Staff, who regarded the retention of Tunisia as 'extremely important'. Without it, Axis forces would find it impossible to seal the Sicilian Straits and force the Allies to send supplies the long way around the Cape of Good Hope. With it, enemy landings in southern Europe – Provence, Sicily, Sardinia, Greece and the Aegean – were 'improbable'.[9]

In no doubt that Rommel was more of an asset than a liability, Ambrosio would eventually give the German field marshal the command of a new Army Group Afrika, comprising Messe's First Italian Army and Arnim's Fifth Panzer Army. In the short term, Rommel would stay in command of the Panzer Army until, as he put it, he could 'feel that its position was reasonably firm for some time ahead'.

As far as Rommel was concerned, Cavallero's dismissal had not come a moment too soon. He was more ambivalent about the news that Marshal Bastico had been recalled. Despite some friction between them, they had 'worked well together' and Bastico often supported him. It was largely thanks to Bastico that the army had managed to get back to the Mareth Line 'reasonably unscathed'.

When Messe arrived in Africa, he projected an air of 'considerable optimism' that was, thought Rommel, fairly typical of those who 'came from Russia' (as Arnim had).[10] His First Italian Army would eventually consist of four Italian infantry divisions (Trieste, Pistoia, Spezia and Giovani Fascisti), two German infantry divisions and what remained of the Deutsche Afrika Korps, including the 15th Panzer Division, the Sahara group – a weak division alongside various artillery and engineer units – and the skeletal remains of the Centauro armoured division, a total of 77,000 men. It was woefully under-equipped with only 80 tanks,

87 armoured cars and 400 field guns. Air support was almost non-existent. There was also the issue of morale: most of these men had retreated more than 1,500 miles since Alamein, and were tired and depressed. To enforce discipline, a private Italian soldier had been shot for desertion in late December. Yet many were going on duty improperly dressed and few saluted their officers.

Before leaving Rome, Messe had been assured by Mussolini: 'You are taking over an army that is in good order; it is still well armed.' The reality was very different, as Messe soon found out, yet he was expected to use this underpowered and demoralised force to check the enemy advance from the west and south which threatened to crush the Axis forces in Tunisia in a vice. 'In the summer,' promised Mussolini (who was even more hopelessly deluded than Hitler), 'we'll retake the initiative with a great offensive push towards Algeria [and] Morocco and to reconquer Libya.'[11]

The Axis strategy in Tunisia was coordinated by Kesselring who planned to attack and defeat the two converging Allied armies in detail (one after the other), 'beginning in the west, with a series of thrusts intended to delay their offensive at least for some weeks or even months'. He would do this by inflicting such heavy losses on the Allies that replacements would have to be brought in from overseas. The terrain that offered the greatest opportunity for an outflanking movement was, in his opinion, the middle sector of the Allied defensive line in Tunisia occupied by the Americans and the French, particularly the terrain to the south of the Fondouk Pass that was already in Axis hands. A sweep northwest from there – with its immediate objective the rail and road hub of Tébessa in Algeria – might yield important strategic results because it would 'pave the way for a drive across the [Allies'] lines of communication, involving a perilous situation for the enemy's young and inexperienced troops'.[12]

Arnim's Fifth Panzer Army began the next phase of Kesselring's offensive against the French defenders at the Faïd Pass in the Eastern Dorsal – barely 500 yards deep and half a mile wide – on 30 January.

Using the tanks and infantry of the 21st Panzer Division – temporarily detached from Rommel's army – and the Italian 50th Special Brigade Imperiali, the plan was to 'gain the defile, annihilate the enemy units in line there and block the mountain ridge on both sides of Faïd and toward the south in the Gafsa direction to prevent at that point any enemy drive in the direction of the sea'. Its ultimate aim, according to Rommel, was to capture a 'starting point for a thrust on Sidi Bou Zid and Sbeitla, 15 miles west and 33 miles north-west of the Faïd Pass respectively'.[13]

The attackers successfully infiltrated the pass, and by the evening of 30 January the 1,000 or so French defenders were surrounded. Repeated French requests for assistance had prompted Fredendall to order Brigadier General Raymond E. McQuillin, commanding the 1st Armored Division's Combat Command A, to restore their ally's positions but without weakening defences around the town of Sbeitla. McQuillin sent a modest force forward. But reports that German panzers were in possession of Faïd village, on the western side of the pass, caused him to postpone his counter-attack until early on 31 January. Launched at 7 a.m., it was repulsed by well-sited anti-tank fire which knocked out at least eight American tanks. By early afternoon, the Axis troops had captured the Faïd Pass, much to the fury of General Giraud who complained to Fredendall about the slowness of the American relief effort, and the ineffectiveness of their aerial and artillery support.

When subsequent counter-attacks failed to regain possession of the high ground on either side of the Faïd Pass, McQuillin set up a new defensive line on Djebel Ksaira and to the east of Sidi Bou Zid.[14]

Fredendall's hesitant response on the 30th had been partly because he was planning a simultaneous raid against the road and rail hub of Maknassy, 50 miles south of Faïd, that would threaten the rear of the Germans and so relieve pressure on the French. Ignoring Eisenhower's insistence that he keep the 1st Armored Division together, he used parts of Combat Command C (which was orginally sent north to assist McQuillin) and Combat Command D (with elements of the 168th Infantry attached) to advance on Maknassy on 31 January. Held up that day by enemy air attacks and stronger than expected resistance, CCD eventually captured Sened Station, 20 miles west of Maknassy, in the afternoon of 1 February. 'It is of vital necessity for you to get forward and place the infantry on its objective *four* (4) miles east of Sened Station,' Fredendall cabled CCD's commander at 6 p.m. 'Too much time has been wasted already. I shall expect you to be on the objective not later than 1000hrs, 2 February. Use your tanks and shove.'

Back at Telergma airfield that day, at a stand-up conference around the bonnet of an automobile, Eisenhower told Anderson that Fredendall had to conserve his strength. 'If Maknassy is not taken by tonight,' he insisted, 'the whole [1st Armored] division should be withdrawn into a central position and kept concentrated.' Ike was insistent, wrote Butcher, 'that there must be a large, central, and powerful reserve, mobile so it can strike in any direction on short notice, held in the central part of Tunisia'.

That never happened. Instead, in line with Fredendall's orders, CCD and the 168th Infantry continued to advance on Maknassy and by noon on 2 February were in position on the ridge east of Sened. Four hours later, dive-bombed by Stukas and assaulted by panzers, some men from the 1/168th fled in disorder. 'There has been a break-through!' shouted an officer. 'Save yourselves! Save yourselves!'

The stampede was eventually halted and turned around, while American tank destroyers drove off the panzers that had infiltrated the main position. Next morning, they continued the advance, and came within six miles of Maknassy. But orders from II Corps put an end to the raid: they were to withdraw to Gafsa.

It was another confused and unsatisfactory fight that had cost the Americans 4 tanks, 9 half-tracks and 3 self-propelled guns, as well as 51 killed, 164 wounded and 116 missing. The enemy had lost 7 tanks, 4 artillery pieces and 160 prisoners. 'The extent of the front,' noted a 1st Armored Division report, referring to the 100 or so miles that was the responsibility of the US II Corps, 'made a concentration of force impossible.'[15]

25

Monty

Libya and Algeria, 3–6 February 1943

A T 4.30 P.M. ON 3 February 1943, even as Fredendall's failed raid on Maknassy was petering out, Winston Churchill and his CIGS, Sir Alan Brooke, landed at Castel Benito aerodrome outside Tripoli where they were met by Generals Alexander and Montgomery ('a victor at the end of his historic march'). With the Casablanca Conference over, Churchill had spent thirty-six hours in Marrakesh with President Roosevelt, before flying to Cairo to meet General Alexander, and then on to Adana in Turkey for discussions with the prime minister and the president. The next stops were Cyprus, Cairo (again) and finally Tripoli. Brooke noted in his diary: 'We drove off to Monty's camp, where Monty gave the PM and me a long talk on the situation. He then paraded the whole of his HQ which was addressed by the PM on a loudspeaker.'[1]

Speaking to about 2,000 officers and men, Churchill quoted a line from Franklin L. Sheppard's popular hymn 'Forever with the Lord':

> Yet nightly pitch our moving tent,
> A day's march nearer home.

He knew, of course, that they were 'still a long way from home' and that the route was unlikely 'to be direct'.[2] He ended his speech with words of consolation: 'In days to come, when asked by those at home what part you played in this war, it will be with pride in your hearts that you can reply, "I marched with the Eighth Army."'[3]

They dined that evening in Monty's mess which was, noted Brooke, 'the same tent we had dined with him in before the battle of El Alamein!!'[4] Before and during the dinner, they spoke at length about the Tunisian campaign, and Monty, for one, was doubtful that Anderson was the right man to lead the First Army. 'It seems to me,' he wrote to Brigadier Frank 'Simbo' Simpson, his former brigade major who was Deputy Director of Military Operations, 'the whole show wants some inspiration and uplift; unless morale is high, and you have the initiative, you can achieve nothing in war.'

He said much the same thing to Brooke in a letter sent after the visit. According to a 'very great personal friend' of Monty's on Anderson's staff, First Army HQ was 'not a happy party; there is no pep or up-lift, the show does not run smoothly'. Montgomery added: 'Anderson insists on going himself personally into every detail and no one is left alone to run his own show. I will pass this on to Alex and I expect he will investigate.'[5]

Since beating Rommel at Alamein – a victory that Churchill heralded on 10 November with the words: 'Now this is not the end. It is not even the beginning of the end. But it is, perhaps, the end of the beginning'* – Montgomery had become the most celebrated general in the British Army. The capture of Tripoli eleven days earlier by his Eighth Army, thus fulfilling Churchill's directive of 10 August 1942 for Alexander to 'take or destroy at the earliest opportunity the German-Italian army commanded by Field Marshal Rommel, together with all its supplies and establishments in Egypt and Libya', had only

---

* In the same speech to the annual Lord Mayor of London's Banquet, he fired a mild shot over Roosevelt's bow by saying he had 'not become the King's First Minister in order to preside over the liquidation of the British Empire'. (Roy Jenkins, *Churchill*, London: Macmillan, 2001; repr. 2002, p. 702)

added to Monty's laurels. Yet, for all his success on the battlefield (perhaps because of it), he was never popular with his fellow generals and has divided opinion among historians ever since.

To many of his colleagues, Montgomery was insufferably arrogant and high-handed. When Ike lit a cigarette during their first meeting in England in 1942, Monty snapped: 'I don't permit smoking in my office.'[6] Eisenhower put it out, but never quite forgot or forgave. Monty's idiosyncrasies can be traced, at least in part, to his difficult childhood. Born in Surrey in November 1887, the fourth child of a Church of Ireland minister of Ulster-Scots heritage, young Bernard spent his formative years in Tasmania where his father was the bishop. Neglected by his self-centred mother Maud, he became a difficult and irascible character. 'I was a dreadful little boy,' he wrote later. 'I don't suppose anybody would put up with my sort of behaviour these days.'[7]

Educated at King's School, Canterbury, and St Paul's School in London, he entered the Royal Military College, Sandhurst, in 1906 and only narrowly avoided expulsion for rowdiness and violence. Once in the army, however, Montgomery thrived and his courage in battle was legendary. In October 1914, he was shot through the right lung and almost killed leading a counter-attack of the 1st Royal Warwicks. He was appointed a Companion of the Distinguished Service Order, Britain's second highest award for gallantry.

Back on his feet, he shone in a series of staff appointments and ended the First World War as Chief of Staff to the 47th (London) Division with the temporary rank of lieutenant colonel. The conflict, moreover, had a profound influence on his theory of leadership, the need to limit casualties and the primacy of firepower (chiefly artillery). He wrote:

There was little contact between the generals and the soldiers. I went through the whole war on the Western Front, except during the period I was in England after being wounded; I never once saw the British

Commander-in-Chief ... and only twice did I see an Army Commander.

The higher staffs were out of touch with the regimental officers and with the troops ... My war experience led me to believe that the staff must be the servant of the troops, and that a good staff officer must serve his commander and the troops but himself be anonymous.

The frightful casualties appalled me. The so-called 'good fighting generals' of the war appeared to me to be those who had a complete disregard for human life. There were of course exceptions and I suppose one was Plumer.★[8]

He took a hard line against Irish rebels during the Civil War of the early 1920s – telling a colleague that 'Oliver Cromwell, or the Germans, would have settled it in a very short time'[9] – and he later helped to write the Infantry Training Manual and became an instructor at the Indian Army Staff College at Quetta. He also married Betty Carver, the widow of an officer who had died in the Great War, and became stepfather to her two teenage sons. His only child, David, was born in 1928. Tragically, Betty died in 1937 after contracting septicaemia from an infected insect bite, and a grief-stricken Montgomery found solace in his work. His stepson John would later insist that Betty had done the country a favour by keeping Montgomery's personal oddities – his extreme single-mindedness and intolerance of others[†] – within reasonable bounds for long enough for him to reach high command.[10]

He led the 3rd Infantry Division with distinction during the Dunkirk

---

★ This was Field Marshal Herbert Charles Onslow Plumer, commander of Second Army and victor of the Battle of Messines in June 1917.

† It is possible that Monty had Asperger's syndrome, known today as high-functioning autism spectrum disorder (ASD), whose symptoms include good language and cognitive skills, but difficulty with social interaction and communication. People with ASD often exhibit repetitive behaviour, such as hand flapping, and have a narrow range of interests, rigid routines and an exceptional attention to detail.

campaign – having trained it to be agile and flexible – and by early 1942 had infused the South-Eastern Army, Britain's first line of defence, with an offensive spirit. He did the same thing for the demoralised Eighth Army when he replaced William Gott, killed in a plane crash, as its commander in August 1942. A few weeks later he defeated Rommel at the defensive Battle of Alam Halfa, telling his officers: 'There will be no retreat. If we cannot stay here alive, then we will stay here dead.'

One of the best pen portraits of Monty was provided by Alan Moorehead, the Australian-born war correspondent for the *Daily Express*, who described him as 'a slightly built man with a thin nervous face, an ascetic who neither drank nor smoked'. Moorehead added:

> He was a military scholar who had cut away from himself most of the normal diversions of life, and this left him with a fund of restless energy, part of which he expended in a religious faith in himself and his God and part in a ruthless determination to make battle. Like most missionaries he was flamboyant, and there was in him an almost messianic desire to make converts and to prove his doctrines were right ones. An unusual man, not an easy companion.

Monty tried to meet as many of his soldiers as possible, giving impromptu speeches and doling out cigarettes. 'Follow me,' he cried, 'and we will smash Rommel.' Since he believed this, it was not long before the men began to believe it too.[11]

In the early years of the war, the British Army had been characterised by an 'amateur spirit' and 'club ethos' that put it at a disadvantage. It was this lack of dedication and hardness that Monty was determined to change. 'There was,' admitted Brigadier Eric Dorman-Smith, the architect of O'Connor's destruction of Graziani's Italian army in the winter of 1940–1, 'not the same savage professionalism as existed in the Afrika Korps ... We were an unaggressive, unassertive lot, rather too polite & gentle, perhaps lacking in drive ... We were ultra-detached, recognising nothing as a crisis. Odd to say about a British regular officer, but we were too civilised. Montgomery's vinegar-and-gall was necessary when it came . . . Something was wrong with us, not just our tanks.'[12]

Prior to the Second Battle of El Alamein, Monty prepared meticulously and refused Churchill's pleas to attack before he was ready. The subsequent twelve-day battle was a slogging match that ended with one of the most decisive Allied victories of the war, although the historian Correlli Barnett tried to belittle Montgomery's achievement by pointing out he had a marked superiority in men and heavy weapons – 195,000 troops to 116,000, 1,029 tanks to 547, and 900 artillery pieces to 552 – and yet was unable to prevent Rommel's battered Panzer Army from escaping.

Air Vice-Marshal Arthur 'Mary' Coningham, who as commander of the Desert Air Force had done so much to revolutionise close tactical air support for the Eighth Army, agreed with Barnett that an opportunity was lost. '[Monty] was a competent general in positional warfare,' said Coningham in 1947. 'But he never exploited his victories. He wouldn't fight until he had everything . . . He won at Alamein, but he didn't follow it up. It was almost a defeat that he let Rommel get away. He could have cut across in front of Rommel, but no, despite my advice to use his air, he pushed along, pushed along . . . Some day the truth will be written about him, and the legend will be dispelled.'[13]

Monty's own explanation was that the battle went entirely to plan, and the pursuit was delayed because he wanted to avoid over-reaching himself. 'I am determined that this time there will be NO setbacks,' he had told his friend Brigadier Frank Simpson on 19 November. '. . . I have now got to pause, to collect my scattered forces, and get my administration on a firm basis – it is stretched almost to breaking point at the moment.'[14]

Montgomery's predecessors had tried and failed to beat Rommel in the desert by attacking en masse with armoured brigades. What they did not appreciate, however, was that Rommel's panzers fought in an offensive/defensive mode and were always protected by anti-tank guns – particularly the excellent 88mm anti-aircraft gun deployed in a ground role – which took a heavy toll of British armour. Montgomery solved this problem by 'the old style, methodical, carefully choreographed application of firepower'. Rob Lyman and Lord Dannatt put it best:

> If the British Army couldn't out-manoeuvre the Desert Fox, it could bludgeon him. In Monty's view, crushing tactical attrition was the only solution to the operational manoeuvre deployed by his opponent . . . With the massive quantities of new American weapons and equipment flooding in to North Africa, materiel superiority made Monty's task possible, in a way denied to Auchinleck and Cunningham before him. It was the approach adopted for the remainder of the war in Europe . . . Monty's success lay in imposing an approach to warfighting that, in the absence of any other doctrinal templates, enabled Britain's citizen army to use its increasingly dominant materiel strength and far greater firepower to win its battles.[15]

A similar point was made by Field Marshal Lord Carver who, in 1942, as the 7th Armoured Division's Chief of Staff, took part in both the planning and the execution of the battle. 'It may have been expensive and unromantic,' he wrote, 'but it made certain of victory, and the certainty of victory at that time was all important. Eighth Army had the resources to stand such a battle, while the Panzerarmee had not, and Montgomery had the determination, will-power and ruthlessness to see such a battle through.'[16]

Alan Moorehead, who reported on El Alamein, felt that while Monty's 'battles lacked genius at least they were fought brilliantly and with good sound logic'.[17]

Yet, for all his pragmatism on the battlefield, Montgomery was his own worst enemy off it. His lack of diplomacy and charm was not lost on one of his greatest admirers and patrons, General Sir Alan Brooke, who noted in his war diaries: 'A difficult mixture to handle, brilliant commander in action and trainer of men but liable to commit untold errors in lack of tact, lack of appreciation of other people's outlook. It is most distressing that the Americans do not like him and it will always be a difficult matter to have him fighting in close proximity to them. He wants guiding and watching continually and I do not think that Alex is sufficiently strong and tough with him.'

On a separate occasion, Brooke wrote: 'I had to haul him over the coals for the trouble he was creating through his usual lack of tact and egotistical outlook which prevented him from appreciating other people's feelings.'[18]

Kay Summersby, Ike's driver, considered Monty to be 'the only person in the whole Allied command in North Africa' that she 'disliked'. She explained: 'Not only was he a supercilious, woman-hating little martinet, but he did things that used to make me so indignant that I would say to the General, "How can you stand it? Why don't you tell him off?"'

Ike responded: 'Don't let him bother you. He just can't help it.'

Monty was, Ike later admitted, 'a thorn in my side'.[19] He put up with his antics because he respected his outstanding ability as a battle-field tactician and his unmatched ability to connect with the ordinary soldier (the 'greatest personal asset a commander can possess').[20]

But when Churchill and Brooke visited him in Tripoli in early 1943, Montgomery was basking in the glory of his victories over Rommel in Egypt and Libya, and could do no wrong. On 4 February, he and his guests drove into Tripoli where security was tight with 'streets and housetops . . . lined with sentries' to hold back the locals. At the main square they reviewed the bulk of the 51st Highland Division. 'The last time we had seen them,' wrote Brooke, 'was near Ismailia just after their arrival in the Middle East. Then they were still pink and white, now they were bronzed warriors of many battles and of a victorious advance. I have seldom seen a finer body of men or one that looked prouder of being soldiers.'[21]

Taking up their position on a dais, they watched the whole division march past. It was, remembered the prime minister, a 'magnificent' sight. 'At their head,' he wrote, 'were the pipers of the 51st Highland Division. Spick and span they looked after all their marching and fighting.'[22] Watching the Highlanders, 'with the wild music of the pipes' in his ears, Brooke 'felt a large lump' in his throat and a tear run down his face. Churchill was also crying.[23] So moved was the prime minister by the sight of these veterans that, according to Monty, he 'could hardly trust himself to speak'. The parade and march past in the main square was a 'wonderful sight', wrote Monty, by 'magnificent fighting men' who would compare with any in the world. As proof of their high morale, he noted that only one man in a thousand was off sick. 'You cannot want anything better than this.'[24]

Churchill had planned to visit the besieged island of Malta next. But he was dissuaded by Monty who said the proposed journey in a small two-seater plane with an escort of six Spitfires was too dangerous. Instead, on 5 February, Churchill and Brooke arrived in Algiers in two Liberators – after an overnight flight from Tripoli – for talks with Eisenhower. The prime minister stayed in Admiral Cunningham's villa, which was next door to Ike's. 'Both are surrounded by barbed wire and heavily guarded and patrolled,' Churchill informed his deputy Attlee. 'We came here by circuitous route in bullet-proof car. I do not propose leaving precincts.'[25]

One of the first people Churchill bumped into was Kay Summersby. 'Well, Kay,' he said, waving a big cigar, 'I thought I might find you here. How do you like driving on the wrong side of the road?'

Ike and Churchill jointly hosted a lunch for twelve, including de Gaulle, Giraud, Anderson and Cunningham. 'Do you realize, Kay,' Eisenhower had said to Summersby, 'that almost all my guests will outrank me?'[26]

Later, during a smaller dinner at Cunningham's villa, Churchill and Ike discussed the campaign, and the political difficulties with the French. This led to discussions the following morning with Noguès and Peyrouton, the Governors General of Morocco and Algeria respectively. 'I told them,' wrote Churchill, 'that if they marched with us we would not concern ourselves with past differences. They were dignified, but anxious.'[27]

Before Churchill's arrival, Ike had been warned 'that the Germans or somebody were going to assassinate the Big Cigar Man while in Algiers'. He was, therefore, keen to get him 'out of town' as soon as possible.

To fool any potential assassins, a fake cavalcade was sent to the airport with Butcher impersonating Churchill in Ike's semi-armoured car. It was a nervous ride, particularly when they were stopped in a narrow street by an 'Arab traffic jam'. At the airfield they 'made signs of loading people aboard [Ike's B-17], watched it take off, waving farewell as it zoomed, actually with only the crew aboard'.

Departing a few hours later, Churchill's actual plane 'Commando' never took off, because of engine failure, prompting Churchill to tell a small assistant secretary: 'Your light weight is a great advantage in flying, but if we come down in the desert you will not keep us going very long.'

To avoid arriving in Britain in broad daylight and without an escort, they delayed the flight by twenty-four hours and by 1 a.m. on 6 February were back at Ike's and Cunningham's villas. 'I put Sir Alan Brooke in my bed without changing sheets,' wrote Butcher in his diary, 'he being dead tired from sleep lost the previous night . . . My bedsheets were still warm.'

One member of the party did not return from the airfield: Sir Charles Wilson, Churchill's personal physician. He had taken some sleeping tablets and was lost to the world when the trip was abandoned. 'He did not hear us leave', remembered Churchill, 'and was locked up for the night in the plane. He was only liberated at daybreak.'

Before leaving the following evening, Churchill told Ike that he 'must take care of himself, that he was doing a magnificent job, that he should be careful that nothing should happen to him, all because the PM didn't see a man in sight, except General Marshall, and he couldn't be spared from his present job, to be Allied Commander'. He 'emphasised that the Allied Command was held together by dint of personality of the Commander-in-Chief', and that he was 'very happy with Ike'.[28]

Eisenhower's disarming response was that the prime minister was worth two armies to the Allies when in London, but in Algiers or any other unsafe place he was just a liability. Churchill appreciated that.

With Churchill's departure, the last of the Casablanca visitors were gone and, by and large, Ike was pleased with the results. Well aware that, as Butcher had put it, his neck was on the block if he did not capture Tunisia quickly enough, he had at last been given the tools to do the job. They included a new command structure – with Alexander, Cunningham and Tedder all operating under his overall direction – more transport (in the form of Somervell's 5,000 trucks) and a force swelled by the inclusion of the veteran Middle East troops.

But he was also concerned: that II Corps' defences in the mountains of southern and central Tunisia were stretched too thin; and that an Axis counter-attack, using the combined strength of Rommel's and Arnim's forces, would take advantage of this weakness to force the passes of the Western Dorsal and dismantle the Allied defences from south to north.[29]

26

'Let's give Rommel this one last chance of glory'

Tunisia, 4–14 February 1943

'I 've decided only to give up command of the army on orders,' wrote Erwin Rommel to his wife Lucie on 8 February 1943, 'regardless of the state of my health. With the situation as it is, I intend to stick it out to the limit, even against my doctor's advice. You will understand my attitude. The successor that Rome has sent for me [Messe] will have to wait his time.'

Rommel's determination to stay in North Africa was partly because he sensed an opportunity to strike a decisive blow. As he put it:

> By exploiting our 'interior lines', we were now in a position to concentrate the mass of our motorised forces for an attack on the British and Americans in Western Tunisia, and possibly to force them to withdraw. We had no need to expect any effective diversionary attack by Montgomery during this operation, for any such attack, launched without powerful artillery and bomber support, was certain to come to a halt in the Mareth line, with a heavy cost in casualties to the British.[1]

The presence of this strong defensive position in southern Tunisia allowed Rommel to leave only a screen of Axis troops to oppose the vanguard of the slowly advancing British Eighth Army while he and Arnim used the rest to try to defeat Anderson's forces – including the British First Army, the US II Corps and the French XIX Corps – sprawled across the Algerian/Tunisian frontier. If successful, he could then turn on Monty's men.

His initial plan, proposed to the Comando Supremo in Rome on 4 February, was to leave his infantry divisions at the Mareth Line, and use his motorised formations to strike Gafsa from the southeast, while Arnim's panzers attacked from the northeast. The situation, Rommel believed, was uniquely auspicious. Given that units from both the Fifth Panzer Army and the First Italian Army would be involved, it would have made sense to bring forward OKH plans to establish a unified Axis command in the form of an Army Group Afrika under Rommel. This did not happen, and the command responsibilities were shared by Arnim and Rommel, with predictable results.

By 9 February, when Kesselring met Rommel and Arnim at the Luftwaffe base at Rennouch in Tunisia to thrash out the final details, intelligence reports indicated that American units were leaving Gafsa for more northerly stations. This prompted the two army commanders to revise the weight and direction of their assaults to take advantage of this relative Allied weakness. The attack would now consist of an initial operation – *Frühlingswind* ('Spring Breeze') – by the Fifth Panzer Army, using the 10th and 21st Panzer Divisions, and supported by strong elements of the Luftwaffe, to advance west of the Faïd Pass and destroy the 'comparatively weak' American forces defending Sidi Bou Zid and Sbeitla. If successful, it would be followed a few days later by a joint attack under Rommel's command against Gafsa – Operation *Morgenluft* ('Morning Air') using elements of the Afrika Korps and the 21st Panzer Division which had redeployed from the north.[2]

The overall plan at this stage, according to Rommel, was 'first intended to eliminate the threat of the two armies being divided by an Anglo-American thrust from Gafsa to the sea, by smashing the enemy assembly areas. This done, our striking force was to double back to Mareth to attack Montgomery.' But there was also the possibility, if all went well, of a thrust as far as II Corps' headquarters at

Tébessa in Algeria; and from there a drive to the Algerian port of Bône, thereby cutting the First Army's lines of supply.

To encourage both generals, Kesselring told them: 'Meine Herren, after Stalingrad our nation is badly in need of a triumph.' Arnim was enthusiastic, but pointed out that there was not enough fuel for such an ambitious scheme. However, they could inflict large losses on the French and Americans and force them to withdraw. If Kesselring agreed, he would attack on the 14th.

Rommel was happy to go along with this, despite his personal distaste for Arnim, a poker-faced Prussian aristocrat of the old school. 'What counts,' he said, 'isn't any ground we gain, but the damage we inflict on the enemy.'

Kesselring assented, telling Rommel that if he was successful he would be placed in command of all the forces in Tunisia with Arnim as his subordinate. But this was a hollow promise because he knew that Rommel's doctor had recommended a rest cure for his ailing chief. 'Let's give Rommel this one last chance of glory,' Kesselring told Arnim, 'before he gets out of Africa.'[3]

While the final details of *Frühlingswind* were being worked out by Generalmajor Heinz Ziegler, Arnim's deputy who would have operational command, and the leaders of the Air Corps Tunis and the 10th and 21st Panzer Divisions – Hans Seidemann, Friedrich Freiherr von Broich and Hans-Georg Hildebrandt respectively – a brilliant young staff officer who would play a key role in the offensive was hurrying out to North Africa. Oberstleutnant Claus Graf von Stauffenberg was replacing Major Wilhelm Bürklin, the 10th Panzer Division's chief of operations, who had been badly wounded by the same exploding mine that killed the commander Generalleutnant Wolfgang Fischer near the Mareth Line on 1 February.

Stauffenberg is best remembered as the man who so nearly assassinated Adolf Hitler in the 'Bomb Plot' of July 1944. But his early views on Nazism in particular, and the rejuvenation of Germany in general, were more ambivalent. Born in the ancestral Stauffenberg Castle at Jettingen, Bavaria, in October 1907, the third son of the last *Oberhofmarschall* of the Kingdom of Württemberg, young Claus had an idyllic and cultured childhood, moving from one great house to another, holidaying by the North Sea and in the Alps, and learning to play the violin, cello and piano. All this changed with defeat for the German Empire in 1918, and the abdication of King Wilhelm II of Württemberg, effectively putting his father out of a job. 'My Germany cannot perish,' implored Claus, 'if she goes down now, she will rise again strong and great. After all, there is still a God.'

Abhorring the economic and political instability of the early 1920s brought on by hyperinflation and the clash between Communists and the far right, the strikingly handsome Claus dedicated his life to the service of the nation by joining the Weimar Republic's small regular army, the *Reichswehr*, as an officer cadet in the 17th Cavalry. A model soldier and a devout Roman Catholic, he preferred reading history and writing poetry to the typical pursuits of a young officer: dancing, drinking and hunting parties. 'Stauffenberg's charm, directness and brilliance,' wrote his biographer, 'tended to dominate conversations. He liked to talk, to examine all the arguments, even to play devil's advocate against the views of his interlocutor. In 1930, his squadron commander paid tribute to his initiative, judgement, above-average tactical and technical competence, exemplary treatment of subordinates, love of horses, and interest in social, historical and religious matters.'[4]

Stauffenberg welcomed Hitler's appointment as Chancellor of Germany in 1933 – not least because the Nazis had promised to rearm and increase the size of the army – and claimed, along with his brother Berthold, that the idea of 'the Führer principle . . . bound together with a Volksgemeinschaft, the principle "The community good before the individual good", and the fight against corruption, the fight against the spirit of the large urban cities, the racial thought, and the will towards a new German-formed legal order appears to us healthy and auspicious'.[5]

If his enthusiasm cooled as Hitler appropriated dictatorial powers and began his persecution of the Jews, he remained a keen nationalist who supported the Nazis' broader foreign policy goal of uniting the German people within the borders of a greater Reich. That he had the military talent to play a significant personal role was underlined by his performance at the prestigious War Academy where he wrote a prize essay on 'Defence against Enemy Parachute Troops' and passed out first in his class in 1938.

Appointed to the elite *Generalstab* (General Staff) – whose members were easily recognisable by a broad red stripe down the outer seam of their trousers – he was made quartermaster of the 1st Light – later 6th Panzer – Division and fought with it in Poland in 1939, a war of conquest that he supported wholeheartedly. In letters to his wife Nina, he described the Poles as 'an unbelievable rabble' and a 'people which surely is only comfortable under the knout'. The 'thousands of prisoners-of-war', he added, 'will be good for our agriculture'. A few days later, with the campaign as good as won, he wrote: 'It is essential that we begin a systematic colonisation in Poland. But I have no fear that this will not occur.'

Clear in his mind that the post-First World War Versailles Treaty – which had taken territory from Germany and imposed crippling reparations – was an injustice, and that the Western powers had declared war on Germany (and not the other way around), Stauffenberg believed the purpose of the conflict was 'the high aim of self-preservation' which could be attained 'only in a good long fight'. He did more excellent work as quartermaster of the 6th Panzer Division during the victorious Blitzkrieg campaign in the Low Countries in the spring of 1940 – forcing the British Expeditionary Force to evacuate from Dunkirk – and was rewarded with the Iron Cross First Class and a posting to the Second (Organisation) Branch of the Army General Staff. For the defeated British, he felt only mild sympathy. 'If they do not give in,' he wrote, 'there will be more hard fighting, for we shall have to make ready for the battle of annihilation against England.'

Stauffenberg would later condemn Hitler for halting his panzers short of Dunkirk and allowing the British to escape. Yet, in general, he recognised the Führer's 'flair for military matters' and the fact that he had got most of his strategic calls right. Hitler was struggling for Germany's future and, at this stage, Stauffenberg felt it was his duty to support him. What turned Stauffenberg from an admirer to an implacable and dangerous opponent of the regime was his growing realisation that Hitler had authorised the mass murder of Jews and the intelligentsia in the East: first in Poland and then, after the launch of Operation Barbarossa in June 1941, in the Soviet Union.

Initially, when asked by anti-Hitler plotters to join them, he said it was necessary to 'win the war first'. But afterwards, he promised, 'when we come home, we shall clean up the brown plague'. This all changed in 1942 as the atrocities in the East mounted and the hope of victory in the Soviet Union receded. On hearing an eyewitness report of the execution of Jews in Ukraine after they had been made to dig their own graves in May 1942, he said that Hitler must be removed, and that senior commanders had a duty to act.

He grew even more disillusioned after Hitler sacked the Army Chief of Staff, Franz Halder, in September 1942, and redoubled his efforts to find someone to lead the revolt. His approaches, however, were all rebuffed. Generalfeldmarschall Erich von Manstein – who had his own concerns about Hitler's generalship, but stopped well short of open rebellion – threatened to have Stauffenberg arrested if he did not cease his traitorous talk. This faint-hearted response was not what Stauffenberg expected of such a senior officer. 'Those chaps have their pants full or straw in their skulls,' he told a like-minded friend, 'they don't want to do anything.'

Stauffenberg was playing a dangerous game and, the longer this went on, the more likely he was to be denounced. Which might explain why, in early February 1943, his request to join a panzer division on active duty was granted by his superiors. Appointed the replacement operations officer for the 10th Panzer Division in Tunisia, he flew from

Munich to Naples on 10 February and, a day later, arrived in Tunis where he visited his wounded predecessor, Major Bürklin, in the military hospital. He finally reached the 10th Panzer Division's command post on the 14th – the day Operation *Frühlingswind* was launched – and told Generalmajor von Broich, his new boss, that he had got into hot water at General Headquarters and was glad to be far away in Africa.

He was fortunate that the 47-year-old Broich – an experienced veteran of the French and Russian campaigns, and the holder of the Knight's Cross – was, like him, an aristocratic former cavalryman, and an opponent of the regime.★ For his part, Broich was delighted to have as senior staff officer 'an upright man, an anti-Nazi, and a very capable General Staff officer'. They would sit up late at night, drinking Tunisian wine and discussing philosophy, literature, poetry and Hitler's removal.[6]

The noble commander of the crack 164th Light Division, Oberst Freiherr Kurt von Liebenstein, was similar to Broich in that he had no time for the Nazis and detested dictatorship 'in all its forms'. He was, in addition, a talented artist, a great lover of horses, fluent in English and French, and sympathetic towards the Italians who were 'despised by the Germans more than they deserve'.[7]

But not all German forces in North Africa were led by such cultured anti-Nazis. The Afrika Korps' 15th Panzer Division, for example, was commanded by Generalmajor Willibald Borowietz, a committed Nazi and former Silesian border guard who had lost an eye in the First World War. Bizarrely, Borowietz had married a Jewess, Eva Levin. But in October 1938, 'to make life easier for him and their three children', she committed suicide in Berlin. Her self-sacrifice had the desired effect because, after their mother's death, the children were recognised as 'honorary Aryans' and Borowietz's career flourished.[8]

★ After his capture and incarceration at Trent Park in the UK with other senior German officers, Broich was part of the Thoma group that 'considered the war lost, condemned the atrocities in the East and spoke detrimentally about Hitler and Nazism'. (Neitzel, *Tapping Hitler's Generals*, pp. 36–7)

Many of Borowietz's staff were also pro-Hitler. His ordnance officer, Leutnant Klaus Hubbuch, was later described by British intelligence as a 'typical Nazi product' who, if Germany 'should lose the war' will 'try to join a "Freikorps" on the lines of those in existence after the last war, and strive for revenge'. He would make 'an implacable and cruel enemy'.[9]

Blissfully unaware of Axis plans, Fredendall's US II Corps had aggressive intentions of its own. They centred on the 1st Ranger Battalion which, since its excellent work neutralising French batteries at Arzew the previous November, had not been deployed. That was about to change. Flown in thirty-two Douglas transports on 3 February from Oran to Youks-les-Bains, near Tébessa, the battalion was trucked to Speedy Valley where its commander Lieutenant Colonel William O. Darby was briefed by Fredendall. Darby wrote:

> This time there was to be no spearheading of strong US formations; rather the opposite. We were to give the impression that Allied strength in central Tunisia was greater than was actually the case. Night missions with fast movement, darting, pinpricking raids, and heavy firing of weapons were to be our job. Secondly we were to capture prisoners for identification of the steady flow of German and Italian troops then moving into Tunisia and Tripolitania.

They were also to inflict as many casualties on the enemy as they could. They could write their own ticket, as long as they did their job.

Three raids were planned. The first, for the night of 11/12 February, would be against an enemy position five miles northwest of Sened Station, the settlement taken and then relinquished in the aborted attempt to capture Maknassy at the start of the month. After surveying the ground from an observation post manned by the 1st Derbyshire Yeomanry, Darby discovered that the troops holding the high ground were from the Italian Bersaglieri Corps, elite mountain troops who wore wide-brimmed hats with black feathers. Expert shots, mobile and highly aggressive – the Axis equivalent of the Rangers – they were arguably the best Italian troops in North Africa.

Darby assigned half his battalion – A, E and F Companies, supported by the 81mm mortars of HQ Company – to the raid. Each man would carry, as well as his personal weapons, a C ration, a canteen of water and a shelter half. They left their bivouac at Gafsa in the early hours of 11 February and were trucked 20 miles east to a French outpost. From there they marched at speed another eight miles over rugged terrain to their lying-up point just four miles from the objective. 'Out came the shelter halves,' wrote Darby, 'and the men hid away in the mountains for the day, watching their objective like a cat ready to spring on its prey.'

At midday Darby and his XO, Major Dammer, led a reconnaissance party closer to the Italian position and made their final plans. At around midnight, as the moon began to set, the Rangers – with faces blackened, equipment tied down, and wearing woollen caps – 'swung across the intervening miles and crawled up the rocky hill where lay the Italian camp'. At a distance of 600 yards, they fixed bayonets and formed into a skirmish line, with Company A on the left, Company E in the centre and Company F on the right.

Advancing with stealth, they were just 200 yards from the camp when a spooked sentry opened fire, his blue tracers arcing above them and hitting no one. They sank to their bellies and continued to inch forward. More Italian shots rang out. Still the Rangers held their fire. Finally, Darby gave the order to charge. 'We went in that last 50 yards,' he remembered, 'making all the noise possible and firing heavily. Italians streamed out of tents, some trying to jump on motorbikes, others realizing they were caught begging for mercy in high-pitched Italian. But some of the Italians reached the 50-mm antitank gun and began dropping shells around my command post.'

Darby radioed the company commander whose objective included the gun, and asked: 'When are you going to reach it?'

'Objective reached, sir,' came the reply.

'Well, when are you going to knock out that blasted gun?'

There was a pause, then two explosions as Ranger grenades detonated.

'Fifty millimetres reached and destroyed, sir,' said the captain.

The raid, Darby remembered, was 'clockwork precision, and rough going'. He called up another company commander to find out how many prisoners he had taken.

'I think I have two, sir.'

The connection was bad and Darby asked for confirmation.

Before the captain could reply, the prisoners tried to escape and two shots rang out. 'Well, sir,' said the captain, 'I *had* two prisoners.'

With support from the 81mm mortars, which fired on the rear of the Italian position, the Rangers took the camp in under thirty minutes, killing fifty Italians, wounding 'many others' and taking eleven prisoners. They were, they confirmed later, from the 10th Bersaglieri Regiment.

Darby's casualties were one man killed and eighteen wounded. With only two and a half hours of darkness left, he quickly formed his men into two columns, fast and slow (the casualties in the latter). The former reached the trucks before dawn; the latter hid in the hills en route, keeping the more serious casualties alive with morphine and sulfanilamide drugs. Jeeps and trucks carried the slow column out the following night.

The raid had been a brilliant success. A delighted Fredendall awarded the Silver Star to Darby, four of his officers and nine of his men. Another two received battlefield commissions. But a second raid, planned for the night of 14 February, was postponed when the enemy struck first.[10]

27

'I've got a hunch this is the dance'

Algeria and Tunisia, 12–14 February 1943

EARLY ON FRIDAY 12 February – warned by his British intelligence chief, Brigadier Eric Mockler-Ferryman, that a major Axis attack through the Fondouk Pass was imminent – Ike left Algiers by car to spend a few days at the front and assure himself that all was well.[1] He was driven by Kay Summersby who found it a very different experience from their carefree drives through the British countryside. She remembered:

> Now we travelled in convoy – a scout car leading, then the General's big car with the flag flying, a weapons carrier, a backup car in case something happened to the General's car and finally a second scout car bringing up the rear. The highway was two lanes wide, and the traffic was remorseless, all of it military. Trucks high-balling it up to the front with supplies; more trucks racketing back empty to pick up more supplies. Coping with those trucks on that narrow, potholed highway was an exhausting experience ... I was constantly terrified of being forced off the road and either being up to my axles in mud or tilted at a forty-five-degree angle in a ditch.

There was also the ever-present danger of strafing attacks, prompting Summersby to warn the newly minted four-star general – the news of

Ike's promotion to full general had arrived before their departure – that if it happened it was 'every man for himself' and she would not wait to hold the door open for him. 'Fine,' Ike replied, trying hard not to laugh. 'Agreed.'

He was less amused by the antics of truck drivers coming the other way who, on spotting Summersby behind the wheel, saluted her 'with whistles, wolf calls and all kinds of interesting proposals', completely uninhibited by the presence of a senior officer. She found it flattering, not least because – in contrast to the trim, tailored uniform she had worn in England – she was clad in boots, slacks, a battle blouse and an old Air Corps flying jacket she had managed to scrounge. Ike teased her that she was trying to look like General Patton.[2]

Ike's destination was Fredendall's II Corps Headquarters which was sited in the 'deep and almost inaccessible ravine, a few miles east of Tebessa' codenamed Speedy Valley. It was, remembered Fredendall's aide Captain James R. Webb, 'not a pleasant spot in February, being subject to rain and flurries of wet snow, but the mountains on either side made it cosily proof against low-level air attack'.[3] This was why Fredendall had chosen the location and, moreover, had directed two hundred of his corps engineers to work for three weeks to build a narrow, twisting access road and underground bomb shelters for himself and his staff. 'Most Americans who saw this command post for the first time,' an observer wrote, 'were somewhat embarrassed, and their comments were usually caustic.'

They included Ike who might have expected Fredendall to adhere to army doctrine by placing his command post near a crossroads and not too far from the front. But preferring hints to compulsion, he had simply told his corps commander that he was concerned about 'the habit of some of our generals staying too close to their command posts' and that he was to 'please watch this very, very carefully among all your subordinates'. Clearly this had had no effect on Fredendall.[4]

★

Next morning, with Ike still on the road, Fredendall was warming himself beside a stove in his operations tent – filled with 'several field tables and a great many maps' – when the Chief of Staff of the Twelfth Air Support Command appeared. He headed straight for Fredendall, 'a compact, alert-eyed man who somehow contrived to look erect while huddling over the stove, and spruce while wearing muddy boots and a blackened combat jacket'. The corps commander, like everyone else, was wearing a knitted cap over his shaven head, his jacket fastened tight at his neck, and boots.

'What's the matter Pete?' Fredendall asked. 'Did you get lonesome or is there something on your mind?'

'I don't know, sir. Maybe this means something, and maybe it's just another target.'

Fredendall read the message: 'Approximately three hundred trucks, in groups of thirteen, proceeding southwest . . .' The time and position followed. His grin faded. American pilots had spotted a huge enemy truck column on the far – hostile – side of the Eastern Dorsal, heading for Maknassy.

He called for his intelligence chief or G-2. 'Okay, Dickson,' he said, handing him the message. 'This is what you get paid for.'

Colonel Benjamin A. Dickson knew, by listening in on the German communications net and from other sources, that the 15th Panzer Division was at Mareth, the 21st Panzer Division farther north at Sfax, on the coast, and the 10th Panzer Division still farther north at Kairouan. They were likely to be used offensively by Arnim and Rommel against II Corps and the British First Army. Was this the moment?

'General,' said the G-2, 'you remember the report we got on February fifth of a large number of enemy vehicles fifteen miles east of Gafsa on the road from Gabès? . . . I think this is what we've been expecting, sir. Of course, these three hundred trucks may be a feint . . .'

'They may be,' responded Fredendall. 'But ever since I got off that banana tramp at Arzew back in November, I've been sure that one of these days I'd have a real waltz with Rommel. Those little bows and scrapes at Faïd and Ousseltia were just the polite preliminaries. I've got a hunch this is the dance.'

He telephoned Anderson at First Army headquarters and, in view of the latest intelligence, requested the release of Robinett's Combat Command B which was covering the Fondouk Pass in the British sector. Anderson refused. There were indications that the enemy might attack there, too, and he did not want to let CCB go until Rommel and Arnim had definitely committed themselves against the American front.

Fredendall put down the receiver and turned to his map. Those trucks, he knew, could continue down towards Gafsa or make a sudden dart through the Faïd Pass and hit the soft centre of II Corps' defences at Sbeitla. Then he remembered the reports of more trucks near Gafsa. That isolated oasis – garrisoned by a mixed force of Americans, British and French – and incapable of sustained defence, was surely the Axis target. 'With Gafsa in his pocket,' noted Webb, 'Rommel could roll north, capture the immense Thelepte airfields near Feriana, and menace Tebessa. To strike directly at Sbeitla and Kasserine Pass meant trying to crash the center, normally more difficult than a flank attack.'

This was the conclusion that Fredendall came to. 'It looks like a two-pronged attack on Gafsa,' he told the G-2. 'Northwest from the Gabès area, and southwest from Faïd Pass-Sidi Bou Zid. Gafsa's going to be like the girl who married three sailors. I'm going down there.'[5]

By the time Ike reached Speedy Valley in eastern Algeria during the afternoon of 13 September, after a gruelling thirty-six-hour drive, Fredendall and his senior staff officers had already left for Gafsa. Stepping out of his car, Ike could hear the 'din of hammers and drills'. On asking the cause, he was told that corps engineers were tunnelling into the sides of the ravine 'to provide safe quarters for the staff'.

Were the engineers not needed, Ike asked, to prepare front-line defences? 'Oh,' responded a young staff officer, without a hint of irony, 'the divisions have their own engineers for that!'

Ike was shocked. 'It was the only time, during the war,' he wrote later, 'that I ever saw a divisional or higher headquarters so concerned over its own safety that it dug itself underground shelters.'

Unable to confer with the absent Fredendall, Ike and Major General Lucian K. Truscott (who had joined the party at Constantine) set off on an all-night inspection of the front lines with Lieutenant Colonel Akers of Fredendall's staff, while Summersby got some rest at Speedy Valley. The trip was an eye-opener for Ike. The first cause for alarm was a worryingly complacent attitude among front-line troops, 'illustrated by an unconscionable delay in perfecting defensive positions in the passes'. At one location mines had not been laid because, he was told, the infantry unit had only been there two days. His curt response was that the enemy were able to prepare a strong defensive position to resist a counter-attack within two hours of arriving. 'These tactical lessons had apparently been ignored by commanders,' wrote Ike, 'even by those who had been in theater for three months. I gave orders for immediate correction.'

But 'by far the most serious defect' he found was the fact that the US 1st Armored Division 'was still not properly concentrated to permit its employment as a unit'.[6] As recently as 2 February he had told Anderson to ensure that the whole of the 1st Armored Division was available as 'a large, central, and powerful reserve' so that it could 'strike in any direction on short notice'.[7] That had not been done because, as Ike acknowledged later, 'General Anderson had such meagre reserves throughout his long line that he felt compelled to station half the division near Fondouk, where he expected the main enemy attack to fall, and he held this force in army reserve by keeping in his own hands the authority to commit it to action'. The rest was scattered in penny-packets along the whole of II Corps' front. 'As a result,' wrote Ike, 'the 1st Armored Division commander, Major General Orlando Ward, had nothing left under his own command except minor detachments of light tanks.'[8]

During his nocturnal tour of the front, Ike visited Major General

Ward's command post in a large cactus patch near the town of Sbeitla. There he met, among others, his old friend Robinett who had come down from Maktar 'to learn at first hand the true state of affairs which then appeared to be serious'. Robinett told Ike that, contrary to the intelligence reports, he did not believe the enemy would attack at Fondouk. He had conducted a number of reconnaissance patrols close to the pass and found no evidence of enemy activity. These facts had been reported 'several times to his superiors', said Robinett. Ike's response was that he 'would take the matter up the next day with the corps and army commanders'.

Ike then discussed with Ward, Truscott and General Schwartz, the local French commander, the situation at the Faïd Pass which was in German hands. Schwartz seemed confident. 'Now that General Eisenhower is here and the Americans are in force,' he said, 'the situation will be restored.'

But Robinett, for one, was not convinced, and the full gravity of the Allied position at Faïd became 'even more apparent' as he heard details of the troop dispositions.[9] Guarding either side of the road that runs from the Faïd Pass to Sbeitla are two prominent features: the 640m Djebel Lessouda to the north and, at 560m, the slightly lower Djebel Ksaïra to the south. In accordance with Fredendall's orders, Brigadier General Raymond E. McQuillin, commanding Combat Command A, had placed a 900-strong force of infantry, tanks, artillery and tank destroyers, under Lieutenant Colonel John K. Waters, now the XO of the 1st Armored Regiment, on and near Lessouda. It was expected to block any Axis attack until a mobile armoured reserve of about forty tanks (from the 3/1st Armored Regiment) counter-attacked from the village of Sidi Bou Zid, six miles to the south. A separate force of 1,000 men – made up of the 3/168th Infantry and a platoon of engineers, under Colonel Thomas D. Drake, the 168th's regimental commander – was holding Djebel Ksaïra to the east of Sidi Bou Zid and 10 miles southeast of Lessouda. They were supported by two battalions of field artillery and a unit of anti-aircraft guns. 'I want a very strong active defense and not just a passive one,' Fredendall had insisted on 11 February. 'The enemy must be harassed at every opportunity. Reconnaissance must never be relaxed – especially at night. Positions *must* be wired and mined *now*.'[10]

The issue for Robinett was that Djebel Lessouda and Djebel Ksaïra were 'so far apart that the troops on those features were not mutually supporting'. He also felt that McQuillin's reserves near Sidi Bou Zid, between the two mountains, 'were inadequate'. This was because the enemy already had control of the Faïd Pass and the high ground on its shoulders. Its armour, moreover, had already passed through the pass into the broken cactus-covered area east of Sidi Bou Zid 'where it stood on commanding ground prepared for offensive action to the west'. Despite his relatively junior status, Robinett was given the opportunity to speak his mind. He pointed out the lack of evidence that an attack would come through Fondouk, and the 'superiority of German tank and anti-tank guns'. It was, he concluded, futile to attempt to hold the Eastern Dorsal position with the men and weapons available and recommended that it be 'given up immediately'.

The generals listened but made no comment. Truscott's 'glowering face registered his disapproval', wrote Robinett, 'as well it might, for long afterwards it became clear that he had a lot to do with the disposition of the Allied forces on the Eastern Dorsal'. When the conference finally broke up, 'no decision had been made', though Robinett 'fully expected that the high command would try to hold on'.[11]

He was right. Ike went next to McQuillin's command post in Sidi Bou Zid where he decorated Colonel Thomas D. Drake, commanding the 168th Infantry, with a Silver Star for gallantry at Sened Station two weeks earlier. McQuillin informed Ike that there were indications that an attack might be imminent. Outposts had spotted hostile vehicles moving in the direction of Maknassy, and listening posts had heard the 'noise of large tank formations in our front to the east'. But McQuillin was not particularly concerned because, he insisted, his troops were well positioned and prepared to meet any eventuality.[12]

Making a mental note of the matters he intended to take up with Fredendall, Ike headed back to Speedy Valley. After several hiccups – notably when Ike's substitute driver fell asleep and the car 'ended up in a shallow ditch, but with no casualties' – he finally reached Speedy Valley in the early hours of the morning, and declared his intention to get a couple of hours' sleep in the VIP guest tent before returning to Algiers. 'Your driver's in there,' he was told. 'We'll wake her.'

'Jesus Christ, don't do that. Let her sleep,' growled Ike, before entering the tent and laying out his sleeping bag on a neighbouring cot. In minutes he was snoring 'like a one-man artillery bombardment'.[13] He wrote later: 'Upon arrival at corps headquarters I found that the German attack had already struck. It was too late to make changes in dispositions.'

That was not strictly true. He had seen for himself the weakness of the front-line defences and could have acted on Robinett's advice to abandon the Eastern Dorsal and withdraw to the west before it was too late. But he chose not to – because, thought Robinett, the yielding of 'even worthless, untenable' ground would involve too embarrassing a loss of face. Many of the front-line troops would pay the price.[14]

28

Sidi Bou Zid

Tunisia and Algeria, 13–14 February 1943

FOR THE AMERICAN TROOPS dug-in on Djebel Ksaïra, the first sign of a possible attack came during the night of 13/14 February when they spotted column after column of enemy trucks 'with their lights on!' The Germans had learned, noted 23-year-old Corporal Wade Nyquist, a machine gunner with M (Weapons) Company of the 3/168th Infantry, 'that a truck without lights can be more dangerous than our artillery' because it ran the risk of crashing in the dark.[1]

Descended from Swedish immigrants, Nyquist had been born in Neola, Iowa, where his father ran a bakery. He was in his third year of college when his National Guard unit was activated in February 1941. A year later, he was shipped across to Northern Ireland with the rest of the 34th Division and eventually assigned to Operation Torch.

After landing on a beach to the west of Algiers, Nyquist and his unit faced only light opposition and, once the fighting had ended, were used to guard a bank in the city from looters. In early February 1943, they were issued with new air-cooled Browning .30-calibre medium machine guns and trucked east to Tunisia where, with the rest of the 168th Infantry, they were attached to Combat Command A of the 1st Armored Division.[2] On 8 February, Nyquist's 3rd Battalion relieved a unit of the 26th Infantry on Djebel Ksaïra, and spent the next five days putting up wire entanglements and laying mines. Each night, on Brigadier General McQuillin's orders, patrols were made into no-man's-land and prisoners captured and sent back.[3]

For front-line GIs like Nyquist, it was a miserable existence that journalist Ernie Pyle described as 'only slightly above the caveman stage'. Pyle wrote:

> They have not slept in a bed for months. They've lived through this vicious winter sleeping outdoors on the ground. They haven't been paid in three months. They have been on British rations most of the time, and British rations, though good, get mighty tiresome.
>
> They never take off their clothes at night, except their shoes. They don't get a bath oftener than once a month. One small detachment acquired lice and had to be fumigated . . . Very few of the front-line troops have ever had any leave. They never go to town for an evening's fun. They work all the time.[4]

After dark on 12 February, Nyquist's battalion had been bolstered by the arrival of 200 replacements. Many were clutching two heavy barrack bags of clothing but no weapons or entrenching tools, and admitted they had never fired a rifle in their life. They were mostly medics, artillerymen and tank crew – 'everything except infantrymen'. Nonetheless Colonel Drake, the regimental commander, assigned them to the companies holding Ksaïra.

The following day, six truckloads of a new hand-held anti-tank rocket launcher known as a 'Bazooka' – weighing just 13lb and firing a 2.36-inch high-explosive projectile that could penetrate two inches of armour plate – were distributed to Drake's men. Instruction in their use was scheduled for 14 February, but events intervened. 'Every effort had been made to get just one "bazooka" in the regiment for instructional purposes,' wrote Drake, 'but without success. They had been systematically forwarded to front line units where they were just as religiously thrown away.'[5]

Wade Nyquist's first few days on Ksaïra were quiet. Then the Germans started shelling the hilltop, but because they were using flat-trajectory field guns – and not high-angle howitzers – and the Americans were mostly hiding in ravines and folds in the ground, little damage was done. More worrying were the signs of 'heavy traffic in the German area' during the night of 13/14 February.[6]

Unbeknown to Nyquist and his buddies, this movement of vehicles heralded the start of Operation *Frühlingswind*.

At 4 a.m. on St Valentine's Day, 1943, more than two hundred German tanks, half-tracks and self-propelled guns of the 10th Panzer Division left their assembly area in an olive grove and entered the Faïd Pass which was guarded by Italian troops. 'Engineers had cleared a mine field during the night,' wrote Major Hudel of the 7th Panzer Regiment, 'and signalled with dimmed lights the route to be taken. Beyond the pass the battalion turned north. Despite darkness and the continuing sand storm it advanced with the highest possible speed.'

Hudel's combat group emerged from the Faïd Pass in two parallel columns, one heading for the northern side of Djebel Lessouda, and the other for Sidi Bou Zid. The growl of their diesel engines and the tell-tale clanking of their tracks was masked by a fierce sandstorm. At the same time, motorised elements of the 21st Panzer Division moved forward on two roads from Maknassy to Sidi Bou Zid. Dive-bombers supported the advance.

Three miles beyond the mouth of the pass, the lead panzers overran an unsuspecting squad of the 2/168th Infantry that had been ordered to watch the road and report any movement by radio or rocket signal. Some were crushed to death in their foxholes; the lucky ones were captured. Two miles further on, the panzers surprised ten Shermans of G Company, 1st Armored Regiment, under Major Parsons, who had driven from their laager in a ravine near Sidi Bou Zid to an observation point on a squat hillock east of Djebel Lessouda known as the Oasis, as they did every morning. It emerged later that some crews had dismounted and were making breakfast when the panzers

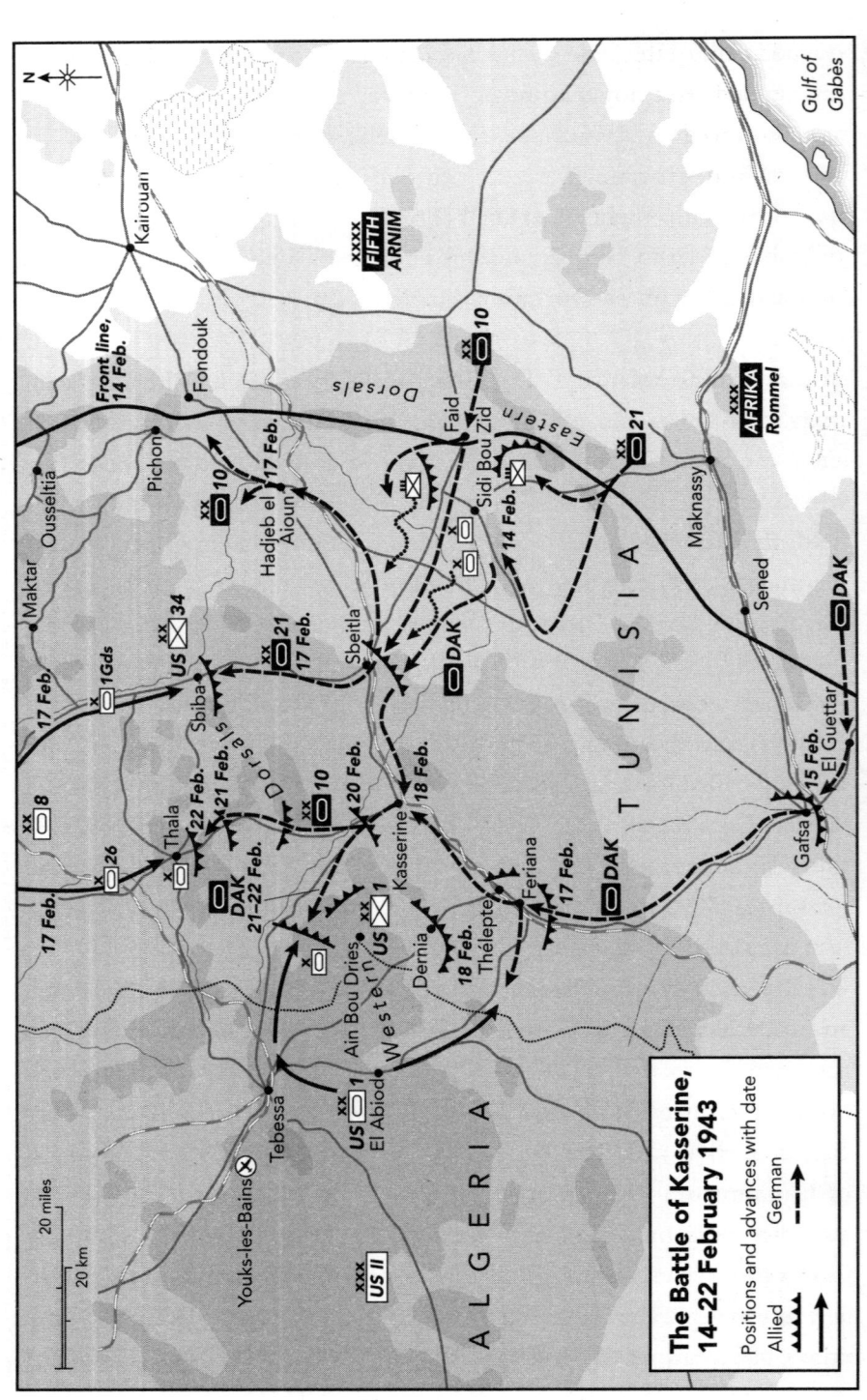

The Battle of Kasserine,
14–22 February 1943

Positions and advances with date

Allied

German

opened fire. All ten tanks were soon ablaze and most of their occupants incinerated. According to some of the survivors, Parsons' tank was hit and destroyed early in the battle. As he had the only radio, news of the attack never reached Lieutenant Colonel Waters, commanding the 900-strong mixed force on Djebel Lessouda from his command post in a ravine on the south slope of the feature. The pre-arranged artillery bombardment on the mouth of the Faïd Pass was, as a result, never requested.[7]

The remaining five tanks of G Company were knocked out by concealed German anti-tank guns as they went to the assistance of their colleagues from a wadi just west of Djebel Lessouda. Most of their crews were killed. 'Each tank,' wrote a colleague who visited the battlefield months later, 'had from one to three [corpses] inside, except for one, Dick Richards, who had dismounted from his tank and come out fighting. He had been shot down near his tank and buried by the Germans.'[8]

Hearing the sound of gunfire, Colonel Peter C. Hains III of the 1st Armored Regiment called Waters from McQuillin's CP and was told that, while it was still too dark to see what was going on, it was obvious that 'a battle had started on the plain between Lessouda and Faïd, apparently between our tanks and hostile tanks'. This prompted McQuillin to order 33-year-old Lieutenant Colonel Louis V. Hightower, a West Point classmate of Waters, to 'clear up the situation' with the mobile reserve: 47 M4 Sherman tanks (recently arrived in North Africa) and 12 tank destroyers, supported by 2 battalions of artillery.

As Hightower's tanks and tank destroyers set off, Sidi Bou Zid was hit by the first of a series of enemy bombing and strafing attacks which temporarily disrupted McQuillin's command post. Repeated requests were made for air support, but only a single flight of four American planes appeared over the battlefield that day.

Hightower's Shermans engaged a superior force of German tanks – including Mark IVs and at least four Tigers – near Poste de Lessouda, where the road forked southeast to Sidi Bou Zid, and began to suffer casualties. 'Sometimes two or three men got out,' reported a sergeant. 'Sometimes no one got out. Most of the tanks burned when hit.'

By 9 a.m., a report reached McQuillin's command post that a second force of German tanks and mobile infantry – including, the report insisted, thirty-nine Mark IV panzers and some Tigers – was moving south, 'from an area just west of Lessouda'. This was passed on to Hightower who, realising it might threaten his flank, sent a company of his tanks to oppose it.[9]

In fact, this force of tanks from the 7th Panzer Regiment was mostly composed of Mark IIIs, with 50mm guns, and only a few Mark IVs with the longer 75mm gun. Harassed only by long-range artillery and small-arms fire, it had just come around the northwest side of Djebel Lessouda when it encountered a detachment of American tank destroyers which, according to Major Hudel, 'tried to escape through open terrain, but got stalled in swampy ground'. They were put out of action.

Having reached the Faïd–Sbeitla road, due north of Sidi Bou Zid, Hudel's battle group came under intense gunfire from the south. 'The red flashes of shells could be seen whizzing through the brown and black clouds of smoke.' He and his men expected a counter-attack. But while the gunfire did not move any closer, 'it was increasing and getting more accurate'. The panzer crews' tension was 'nearing the breaking point' when the order came over the radio from division HQ: 'Advance of 21 Panzer Division from south has been delayed; tank battalion is to continue attack and to capture Sidi Bou Zid.'

Moving south, they could see the flashes of tank cannon and artillery pieces in a cactus grove to the northeast of Sidi Bou Zid. Aware that a frontal attack would have meant 'certain destruction' for the outgunned Panzer Mark IIIs and IVs – which were vulnerable to the Sherman's high-velocity shell at a distance of up to 1,500 yards – Hudel's battalion dispersed widely to the west and east, so as to attack the Americans in the cactus grove from multiple directions. 'The enemy fought back tenaciously,' remembered Hudel, some of the American tanks firing from distances as short as five to yards. But they were quickly over-whelmed as panzers appeared from nowhere.[10]

Hightower's remaining Shermans, meanwhile – supported by the guns of Lieutenant Colonel Charles P. Summerall's 91st Field Artillery Battalion – attempted to force back the original force of panzers with fire and movement. They failed and, as casualties mounted, the tanks and guns withdrew to the southwest, harried by German Stukas and fighter-bombers. By mid-afternoon, only seven of Hightower's Shermans were still intact.

While the battle around Lessouda was at its height, Colonel Drake of the 168th Infantry spotted a separate enemy force of tanks and motorised infantry approaching Sidi Bou Zid from the southeast. It was a battle group from the 21st Panzer Division that had come through the Maïzala Pass with the intention of catching the American defenders in a pincer attack. Drake immediately radioed for air support, but nothing materialised. Instead, American artillery and tank destroyers directly in the path of the panzers 'left their positions and began to withdraw to the rear'.

Drake's command post was in an olive grove a mile and a half east of Sidi Bou Zid. From there, he telephoned McQuillin to let him know that the troops were beginning to panic. 'You're on the spot,' said McQuillin. 'Take command and stop it.'

As the CCA commander had previously stripped Drake of command responsibilities by insisting that he, McQuillin, had to approve any orders issued to the 3/168th Infantry on Djebel Ksaïra, four and a half miles east of the regimental command post, Drake sought clarification. 'You mean for me to take command of all the troops in the area?'

'Yes,' said McQuillin.

Armed with this new authority, Drake took immediate steps to halt the panic by sending out officers to cease the unauthorised withdrawal at gunpoint. It worked, and the troops rushing to the rear were 'stopped and held in a state of readiness'.

Half an hour after their first conversation, Drake was told: 'General McQuillin is on the telephone and said he is pulling out and for you to stay here.'

Drake's instructions had been to hold his position to the last man. Was that still the case? he wondered. He went to the phone, but the line was dead. McQuillin had left.

Some of Drake's officers suggested that they, too, should pull back. He replied that, on the contrary, he intended to attack and take the high ground at Garet Hadid, a feature that, with Djebel Ksaïra, commanded the road from the Maïzala Pass. He and his men – a mixed force of HQ Company, E Company, engineers and artillerymen (not all of them armed) – got there just before the German armoured column which was immediately engaged and stopped in its tracks. The skirmish continued into the afternoon, by which time McQuillin and the remnants of his CCA had withdrawn to a crossroads 11 miles northwest of Sidi Bou Zid on the Sbeitla–Faïd road. The junction was being held by Lieutenant Colonel Kern's 1/6th Armored Infantry and a company of light tanks, sent there by Ward that morning from divisional reserve near Sbeitla. That still left Drake, his two battalions – 2/168th and 3/168th – and assorted stragglers isolated on Djebel Lessouda, Djebel Ksaïra and Garet Hadid.[11]

By nightfall, Sidi Bou Zid was in German hands and American troops had suffered their first major defeat of the campaign. The Americans were guilty of inexperience, poor troop deployment and failed communications, while the German commanders had used classic Blitzkrieg tactics: a pincer attack by veteran panzer troops, supported by air power, to infiltrate weak points in the enemy defences and envelop the strongpoints left behind. For the Germans, it was a much-needed boost. Rommel wrote later:

With the enemy formations pinned down frontally, one armoured group advanced round the northern sector deep into the American flank, while another went forward to Sidi Bou Zid and attacked them in the rear, thus forcing the enemy into an extremely difficult tactical situation. A violent tank battle developed in which inexperienced Americans were steadily battered down by my tankmen – veterans of hundreds of desert battles – and soon large numbers of Grants, Lees and Shermans were blazing on the battlefield. The bulk of the American force was destroyed and the remainder fled to the west.[12]

CCA had lost 54 tanks, 59 half-tracks, 26 artillery pieces and 22 trucks. Its casualties were 6 killed, 22 wounded and 139 missing. A further 1,600 or so were stranded on the three hills.[13]

Ike woke at around 11 a.m. on 14 February and was informed by Major General Fredendall, who had returned to Speedy Valley from Gafsa, that the Germans had attacked at the Faïd Pass with a strong armoured force. Information was incomplete, Ike was told, but there was no reason to believe that McQuillin could not 'hold his own'.[14]

But as the morning wore on, the constant stream of yellow message slips from Major General Ward at Sbeitla made it increasingly clear that the defenders at Sidi Bou Zid were being overwhelmed. 'We've had fifty per cent tank casualties already,' announced Fredendall's operations chief.

'How about the infantry?' asked Fredendall.

'Djebel Lessouda is entirely surrounded, but it's managed to beat off about thirty enemy tanks.'

'And Djebel Ksaïra?'

'No definite information, sir.'

Fredendall had already ordered a battery of armoured field artillery and two platoons of a tank destroyer battalion to move from Fériana to Sbeitla. But tanks were needed to relieve the infantry marooned at Sidi Bou Zid, and Ward did not have any in reserve. 'Get me First Army,' demanded Fredendall. 'I want to speak to General Anderson.'

It took a while for Fredendall to be put through to First Army HQ, via the Signal Corps net, French commercial lines and finally the British net. Anderson came on the line. 'Sir,' said Fredendall, 'the situation at Faïd is deteriorating. I'd like to request the release of our armor, Combat Command B.'

Anderson had his own troubles. He could not be sure that the German thrust at Faïd was not a feint, with worse to come in the north, and wanted to wait until the picture was clearer before sending the CCB south. In the meantime, he did agree to release one of Robinett's medium tank battalions.[15] He also ordered the withdrawal of the mixed force from Gafsa, which was too exposed, to the more defensible foothills of the Eastern Dorsal.

But it was the fatal delay in sending help to Ward that would, Ike wrote later, have serious consequences:

> Although . . . very accurate reports were submitted by the American troops to General Anderson concerning the strength and direction of the German attack through Faïd, these reports were discounted by the Army and AFHQ Intelligence divisions as the exaggeration of green, untried troops. The belief that the main attack was still to come through Foundouk persisted, both at Army headquarters and, as I later learned, in the G-2 Division at AFHQ.

After the battle, Ike sacked Mockler-Ferryman, his head of intelligence: 'The G-2 was a serious error.' But the damage had been done. 'The result of this misconception,' wrote Ike, 'was that the [German] penetration gained a tremendous headway before General Anderson could understand what was actually taking place.'[16]

Dashing off a quick note to Marshall, Ike tried to stay upbeat. 'I really believe,' he wrote, 'that the fighting of today will show that our troops are giving a very fine account of themselves even though we must give up part of our extended line.'[17]

In reality, Ike was sick with worry that the German breakthrough was more serious than anyone realised, and that Anderson's failure to heed his warnings about keeping a strong armoured force in reserve was about to backfire. As he prepared to leave Speedy Valley for his advanced command post at Constantine – from where he would hurry to the front as many reinforcements from Morocco and Algeria as possible – Ike cut a forlorn figure. He was wearing, wrote Kay Summersby, 'his heavy cold-weather gear and a wool hat pulled down over his ears, but he looked pinched with cold. He was very tired and depressed.' Fredendall had suggested that Ike fly back to Algiers rather than risk driving along roads that might at any time be severed by German panzers. He refused, saying: 'We need all our aircraft for fighting, not for ferrying generals about.'[18]

29

'We are going to kick hell out of him today'

Central Tunisia, 15–17 February 1943

NEWSPAPERMAN ERNIE PYLE WAS with American troops in the Ousseltia valley when he heard about the German breakthrough at Sidi Bou Zid. It was just after noon on 14 February. He immediately packed his jeep and drove 70 miles to Major General Ward's command post in Sbeitla. 'It was a bright day,' he wrote, 'and everything seemed peaceful. I expected to see German planes as I neared Sbeitla but there were none, and I drove into my cactus-patch destination about an hour before sundown.'

Told by some intelligence people that the battle was 'dying down with the coming of dusk', Pyle pitched his tent and went to sleep. Next morning, just after dawn, he caught a ride in a jeep with two officers to Ward's new forward command post in yet another cactus patch, sited just off the Sbeitla–Faïd road and about 10 miles from the front line. The site also contained the remnants of McQuillin's Combat Command A command post which had fled Sidi Bou Zid the day before. This amounted to half-a-dozen half-tracks, a couple of jeeps, three light tanks and a couple of motorcycles – 'all that was left of the impressive array' that Pyle remembered from his visit a few days earlier. McQuillin himself 'had already gone forward again, in a tank, to participate in the day's coming battle', leaving behind his surviving staff members who, with nothing to do, were sitting around aimlessly.

Invited into Ward's operations tent, Pyle was given a personal briefing on the plan to rescue the two battalions cut off near Sidi Bou Zid. 'Here', said Ward, pointing to a spot on the map, 'would be a good spot to watch the fighting. The only danger is being cut off and encircled if the battle goes against us. But it won't, for we are going to kick hell out of him today and we've got the stuff to do it with.'[1]

Ward sounded more confident than he felt. The order to counterattack had come from Anderson, who had messaged Fredendall the night before:

> As regards action in the Sidi Bou Zid area, concentrate tomorrow on clearing up situation there and destroying enemy . . . Army Commander deeply regrets losses suffered by CCA, but he congratulates them on their fine fight, is confident they will decisively defeat the enemy tomorrow, and is sure that the enemy must have suffered losses at least as heavy as their own.

This was wishful thinking, as was Ward's claim to Pyle that he had enough men and tanks to do the job. In reality, Anderson had released only a single medium tank battalion from Robinett's CCB for the counter-attack. It would be joined by a battalion of armoured infantry – the 1/6th – a company of tank destroyers and some artillery, a combined force that was weaker than the one defeated the day before. Ward confided his true feelings to his diary: 'I didn't like it much.'[2]

Unable to cadge a lift to the front line, Pyle spent the morning talking to dozens of traumatised CCA men who had narrowly avoided capture at Sidi Bou Zid by fleeing in command cars, half-tracks and jeeps across the semi-cultivated desert, harried all the way by German armour. It should have been a newspaperman's dream. 'There were fantastic stories of escape,' he wrote, 'intimate recountings of fear and elation. Any one of them would have made a first-page feature story . . . Yet I was defeated by the flood of experiences. I listened until the

stories finally became merged, overlapping and paralleling and contra-
dicting until the whole adventure became a composite.'

He was doubly relieved when, just after noon, a young lieutenant
'dug up a spare jeep' and offered a lift to the front. They drove east
for a couple of miles to a crossroads that, only minutes before, had
been bombed by German planes. There was a large crater in the road
and, close by, the hulk of a burning tank. Pyle looked around. They
were in the centre of a 'huge semi-irrigated desert valley' that reminded
him of Phoenix, Arizona – 'not trees but patches of wild growth,
shoulder-high cactus of the prickly pear variety'. In other parts of the
valley were cultivated fields and the tiny square adobe houses of Arab
farmers. The whole vast scene was 'treeless, with slightly rolling big
mountains in the distance'. It was perfect country for armour.

They had arrived just in time because, as far as the eye could see,
were American tanks, half-tracks, artillery pieces and troops, waiting
for the order to advance and rescue the men trapped on high ground
beyond Sidi Bou Zid. The lieutenant put the jeep into low gear and
drove slowly across the sandy desert towards the tanks.[3] They were all
the latest M4 Shermans from Lieutenant Colonel James D. Alger's 2nd
Battalion, 1st Armored Regiment, which had been ordered down from
near Maktar the night before. Witnessing its departure, Robinett wrote:

> Alger himself was in a tank near the head of the column. He saluted
> and smiled broadly as he passed. All tank leaders seemed equally serene
> and confident . . . The outfit was most impressive, but I felt sorry for
> the men as they moved out toward their first battle with the enemy's
> clever veterans established in positions of their own choosing. I very
> earnestly asked a special blessing for them as they sped along.[4]

Alger's battalion had reached the area just before Pyle arrived in his jeep.
'As we drove past tank after tank,' noted Pyle, 'we found each one's crew
at its post inside – the driver at his control, the commander standing with
head sticking out of the open turret door . . . silent and motionless.'

They stopped and asked several what they were doing. Nobody seemed to know – they were 'merely ready in place and waiting for orders'. Suddenly, 'out of this siesta-like doze' came the order to advance over their radios. With engines belching blue smoke, they poured forward. 'There weren't lines or any specific formation,' noted Pyle. 'They were just everywhere. They covered the desert to the right and left, ahead and behind as far as we could see, trailing their eager dust trails behind. It was almost as though some official starter had fired his blank pistol. The battle was on.'

Pyle's driver headed for a nearby rocky hill – known as Djebel el Hamra – from where they could watch the fight. There, in a hidden gully, they found Colonel Robert E. Stack of Combat Command C who was directing the attack from a radio half-track. Using binoculars, Pyle could see the 'fantastic surge of caterpillar metal move forward amidst its own dust'. Far ahead – at a distance of 13 miles – stood the oasis town of Sidi Bou Zid, its green trees standing out against the bare brown of the desert. Beyond that were the high hills where thousands of American soldiers were trapped.

As the tanks advanced, they were followed by other armoured vehicles with self-propelled guns and towing artillery, and armoured infantry in half-tracks and jeeps. The desert, wrote Pyle, was 'surging in one gigantic movement'.

Over Stack's radio, Pyle could hear Alger, a 29-year-old West Pointer from Massachusetts, reporting: 'We're at the edge of Sidi Bou Zid, and have struck no opposition yet.'

It sounded encouraging. But the faces round the command truck were grave, as if expecting a trick. They were right. Suddenly a bright flare 'blazed' in a sky already aglow with the afternoon sun. Seconds later the desert erupted in 'brown geysers of earth and smoke', and from far off 'came the sound of explosions'.

Alger spoke again, his voice more anxious now. 'We're getting shelled, but can't make out where it's coming from.'

More silence, then: 'I'm not sure, but I think it's artillery along the road north of the town . . . Now there is some from the south.'[5]

On the northern flank, an enemy battery of four 88mm and two 47mm anti-tank guns were concealed in a cactus patch. But before their fire could take deadly effect they were spotted and overrun by the advance platoon of Alger's D Company.

The main body of Alger's tanks had to cross a series of wadis, forcing them to concentrate at pinch points. This was where they were engaged by enemy artillery and anti-tank fire, particularly from the south. As the Shermans tried to outflank them they were engaged by more hidden batteries.[6]

Enemy tanks now appeared on both flanks, all part of a pre-arranged scheme to envelop the attacking force. Pyle noticed tell-tale 'dust plumes extending and pushing forward' – a sure sign that German panzers were advancing – and persuaded his driver to take him closer to the scene of the action. As their jeep bounded forward across the plain, they noticed the incongruous sight of Arabs herding their livestock and ploughing their fields. 'Children walked along,' wrote Pyle, 'driving their little sack-laden burros, as tanks and guns clanked past them. The sky was filled with planes and smoke bursts from screaming shells.'

They passed relics of the previous day's battle – including a trailer still full of ammunition, charred half-tracks and a burned-out tank named *Temes* – before wisely stopping half a mile short of the tank fight. Even so, it was a mad manoeuvre that might have been fatal. Pyle discovered later that German tanks had got around behind them and shot up some half-tracks and jeeps. At the time, they had no idea and, having been joined by American light and field artillery, considered the main threat to be incoming artillery shells.[7]

Slowly but surely, the pressure from enemy tanks on both flanks began to tell. At 4.45 p.m., Colonel Stack reported to Ward that it was doubtful they would reach Djebel Ksaïra before sundown. A few minutes later, Stack asked Alger to report his situation and state what help he could use. 'Still pretty busy,' the tank commander replied. 'Situation in hand. No answer to second question. Further details later.'

Alger's radio then went silent. Only after the war would he explain that he had been withdrawing to the village of Sidi Salem when his tank was hit by a shell that killed his radio operator and forced Alger and the remaining crew to bale out. All were later captured. Alger's command, meanwhile, was disintegrating. Attempting to escape encirclement, the surviving tanks ran the gauntlet of enemy anti-tank fire and only four escaped.

Unsure of the outcome, Ward messaged II Corps at 10.45 p.m.: 'We might have walloped them or they might have walloped us.'

It was definitely the latter. In successive days, an American tank battalion had been decimated by German armour, leaving the enemy masters of the field. Total American losses were 2 light and 46 medium tanks, 130 vehicles, and 9 105mm self-propelled guns. Alger's battalion had lost 15 officers and almost 300 men killed and captured.[8]

Even before news of this latest disaster reached him, Lieutenant General Anderson had made the decision to withdraw all troops to the more defensible Western Dorsal, thus abandoning Pichon, Sbeitla and the newly constructed air base at Thelepte. The attempt to hold on to forward positions had been too ambitious, he concluded, and the whole Allied force was in danger of being outflanked and cut off from the south. Ike agreed and the first warning order to pull back was sent out at 5 p.m. on 15 February.[9]

To cover the withdrawal, Anderson agreed to release the rest of Robinett's Combat Command B to II Corps, which ordered it to move at once to Sbeitla. 'Move the big elephants to Sbeitla,' instructed Fredendall, 'move fast, and come shooting!'[10]

Anderson also insisted that the vital pass of Kasserine in the Western Dorsal, 15 miles southwest of Sbeitla, must be defended, and that II Corps should do everything it could to extricate the infantry from the hills around Sidi Bou Zid before it was too late.[11]

It nearly was. Watching the failed counter-attack with dismay from his mountain-top eyrie on Djebel Lessouda was Major Robert Moore, commanding the 2/168th Infantry. At dusk, not long after the last of the American tanks had been driven off to the south and west, Moore was handed a message that had been dropped by a P-40 Warhawk. It was from Major General Ward to Lieutenant Colonel Waters (whose fate was still unknown), and urged him to withdraw the men on Lessouda that night to a position nine miles to the west where they would be met by guides. It ended: 'Bring everything you can.'

Taking the wounded and some German prisoners with them, Moore's men set off from the southwestern edge of the mountain at 10.30 p.m. in two files, each man a yard apart. They carried only personal weapons; the heavier kit and vehicles had been sabotaged and left behind. Leading one column, Moore passed so close to a German 88mm gun position he could have reached out and touched it. There was a heart-stopping moment when they were challenged by a member of the gun crew. No one responded and, fortunately, the gunner lay down and went back to sleep.

Close to the point where they were meant to meet the guides, they were once more challenged in German. 'Since we did not answer this time either,' recalled Moore, 'they immediately opened fire with their machine guns on the head of the column. I gave the order for all to scatter and run like hell.' Many of the Americans were killed, injured and taken prisoner in the confusion. But Moore and several members of Company F got away and eventually reached the safety of 'Kern's crossroads' at 5 a.m. on 16 February where they met guides from the 6th Armored Infantry. More stragglers – mainly from Companies H and G – came in that day, bringing the total number of escapees to 432 out of Moore's original command of 904 men. There was no sign of Lieutenant Colonel Waters.[12]

Incredibly, the 1,600 Americans on Djebel Garet Hadid and Djebel Ksaïra did not receive the order to withdraw until late on 16 February, by which time it was much too late. Twice as far from safety as those on Lessouda, they had been forced back into ever-shrinking perimeters and were out on their feet.

Of the two, the slightly larger garrison on Garet Hadid, under Colonel Drake, had suffered the most. A third had arrived without weapons, and had been forced to scavenge what they could from shot-up half-tracks and dead comrades. They also faced multiple attacks by German panzer grenadiers and tanks which, on three separate occasions on 15 February, had penetrated as far as Drake's command post before they were beaten back. Drake reported: 'Due to the rough ground and the several pieces of artillery picked up in the move to Garet Hadid, the enemy tanks could not get into the American forces to overrun them. All of the artillery was knocked out by the 16th of February by direct fire. Casualties were heavy and finally the enemy pushed in the right flank.'

So desperate did the fighting become on the 15th that Drake sent an officer and six members of the regimental band to retake a key piece of ground. They succeeded and thereby 'saved the entire position'. But by the following day Drake's 'entire rear and right flank' had been 'driven in' and the situation was becoming critical. There were no medical supplies to treat the wounded. The men had not eaten or drunk for three days and, thanks to the 'hot weather and nervous exhaustion', many were in a 'pitiful state'.

At 2.30 p.m. on the 16th, Drake received a cryptic radio message in clear from Ward: 'We can do no more for you. The decision is yours. I will try to have supplies dropped to you.'

No supplies arrived, and Drake was uncertain what to do. He had been ordered to hold the position to the last man. Now it seemed that Ward was letting him decide whether to surrender, withdraw or fight on. There was, in his own mind, only one option. He prepared to leave that night, and sent a coded message for Lieutenant Colonel John H. Van Vliet, Jr, commanding the 3/168th Infantry on Ksaïra, to do likewise.

The move was confirmed by a message from Ward to Drake that

was mistakenly dropped on Ksaïra. They were to head for Sbeitla, a total distance of almost 30 miles, by a route of Drake's choosing. An air umbrella would be provided. Fully aware that he could not reach Sbeitla in a single night, Drake decided to make for Djebel el Hamra, en route, and lie up there during the day. Like Moore, Drake ordered the destruction of all vehicles and heavy equipment: tyres were slashed, magnetos and radio parts buried, and heavy machine-gun bolts hidden. But unlike Moore, Drake wisely decided to leave the wounded behind with some medical volunteers: the more serious cases placed in ambulances; the others under canvas.

With the farthest distance to cover, Van Vliet's men left first at 9.50 p.m. As the column crossed the plain it was spotted and challenged by a German scout car which was promptly blown up by an American grenade. Incredibly the burning wreck 'did not excite the Germans', wrote Drake, 'as there was a great deal of confusion in the area'.[13]

They linked up with the men from Garet Hadid and continued at a fast pace over broken ground with Drake in the lead. It was particularly tough for men like Corporal Wade Nyquist who were carrying light machine guns and mortars. 'We were tired,' he recalled, 'had not slept for 24 hours because of the mortar barrage, had been on short rations and were carrying no food. As the night went on, we became thirsty and drank the water from the machine guns, then disassembled the guns and tossed the pieces as we walked. Our new guns would kill no Germans!'

Nyquist remembered passing one American vehicle after another – half-tracks, tanks and trucks – and assumed they were in friendly territory. It was too dark to see the vehicles had been knocked out and abandoned. Later Nyquist noticed camouflaged tanks. They had stumbled into a German tank park and bivouac, but were not discovered.[14]

At dawn, the head of the column was still five miles short of Djebel el Hamra and cover. To give them a better chance of defending themselves, Drake ordered the units to split into two files, 50 yards apart, and they pressed on. But as they attempted to cross the Sbeitla–Faïd road, a machine gun opened up on them from the foothills of Djebel el Hamra, and a convoy of enemy trucks appeared to their left, stopped and dropped off scores of panzer grenadiers. At the same time German panzers raced around their right flank in an attempt to encircle them.

Drake ordered the men to deploy and return fire. But they lacked heavy weapons and were hopelessly outgunned. 'After three and one-half hours of fighting,' wrote Drake, 'the American fire power diminished and then practically ceased as the men were out of ammunition or had become casualties. Finally a German armored car bearing a white flag came dashing into the American circle.'

Drake – perhaps mindful of his instructions to fight to the finish – ordered his men to wave the car away. When it did not respond he told them to fire on it. But by then German tanks had infiltrated the defensive perimeter from multiple directions, cutting Drake's forces into small groups, and those 'who did not surrender were killed'.

Drake was captured by a German major who told him, in perfect English, that he had once practised law in Chicago and was pleased to meet him. He was driven in a staff car to the headquarters of Generalmajor Ziegler, Arnim's deputy, who was commanding Operation *Frühlingswind*. Saluting Drake, Ziegler said: 'I want to compliment your command for the splendid fight they put up. It was a hopeless thing from the start, but they fought like real soldiers.'

Ziegler then assured Drake that all the wounded POWs would be taken care of, and that he was to leave American medical personnel to assist their German counterparts. This promise was not kept. The medics were taken away with the rest of the prisoners, leaving the American dead and wounded to be looted by local Arabs. If any of the living objected, they were beaten insensible.

A total of 1,400 American officers and soldiers – most from the 168th Infantry – were captured with Drake near Djebel el Hamra. After being systematically stripped of watches, rings, pocketbooks, pens and other valuables, they were assembled into a huge column of fours and marched back to Djebel Lessouda through the heat of the day. Armed guards flanked the column, and three tanks brought up the rear. 'Those Americans who were slightly wounded,' wrote Drake, 'or who became ill because of fatigue, lack of food and water and could not keep up with the column were ruthlessly bayoneted or shot. Many were walking barefooted because the Arabs had taken their shoes from them under the supervision of German soldiers.'

All day they were marched through the arid landscape until their thirst became unbearable. Colonel Drake, who was at their head, appealed to the senior German officer in the name of common humanity to give them water. He replied: 'We only have enough for our troops.'[15]

Shuffling along with his fellow prisoners, weak from fatigue and hunger, was Corporal Wade Nyquist. It was dark when they were led into a field and ordered to lie down. He wrote:

> The Germans passed out cans of sardines to be shared – several men to a can – it was delicious! At daybreak a column of trucks (captured American) were stopped on the road and we were loaded up and moved out. Later that day we arrived at Sfax on the Tunisian coast and our first barbed-wire enclosure, which was just that – a piece of desert with slit trenches for latrines. No structures or vehicles, just a teeming mass of men. We slept on the ground under one blanket, if we were lucky enough to get one. We dug shallow depressions to get out of the cold desert wind.

They were then taken by cattle truck to Tunis, and from there in Ju-52 transport planes and boats to a transit camp in Capua, southern Italy. After two weeks they were moved again by rail to permanent POW camps in Germany and Poland where most of them would see out the war. 'So ended our African experience,' wrote Nyquist. They had trained for two years, suffered an 'ignominious defeat' in their first serious action, and would spend twenty-seven months in captivity.[16]

The senior American officers captured were Colonel Thomas Drake, and Lieutenant Colonels John Van Vliet and John Waters. Patton's son-in-law had been taken on 14 February after a 'heroic stand' that earned him a Distinguished Service Cross. 'He personally maintained radio communications with his headquarters,' read his medal citation, 'reporting enemy movements until his command vehicle was hit and destroyed by fire and repeatedly exposed himself to enemy fire to encourage and control his troops.'[17] Approving the award, Ike told Patton that Waters's action was 'one of the finest performed in this war'. What exactly had become of him at this point, however, no one yet knew.

'There is still a chance he may have escaped,' Patton informed his brother-in-law Frederick Ayer on 2 March. 'Personally knowing John, I do not think that he surrendered, but it is very important to make little Bea and also Bea senior believe that he did.' The whole family had to wait another nerve-wracking two weeks before word arrived that 'John is safe' but in captivity.[18]

For the inexperienced Americans, the battle had been a chastening experience. They were providing the Western Allies with quantity, but not quality. That would change, as they learned from their errors. But not before more disasters had unfolded.

Before the action at Sidi Bou Zid, the 168th Infantry had numbered 189 officers and 3,700 men. Now it was down to 50 officers and 1,000 men. Among the few to avoid capture were Lieutenant Colonel Gerald C. Line, Drake's deputy, and Lieutenant Harry P. Hoffman, a 3/168th company commander. Hiding by day, Hoffman eventually made his way back to the Kasserine–Thala road where he flagged down an American vehicle and got a ride back to the 48th Hospital in Tébessa. Line staggered into an American camp, after days sleeping rough and scavenging food, and wrote to his wife: 'I haven't found out for sure whether I am sane or insane.'[19]

30

Kasserine Pass

Southern Tunisia, 15–21 February 1943

I F IT HAD BEEN up to him, Generalfeldmarschall Erwin Rommel would have exploited the capture of Sidi Bou Zid on 14 February by pushing on that night to 'keep the enemy on the run and capture Sbeitla'. This is where he differed from Monty. 'Tactical successes must be ruthlessly exploited,' he wrote. 'A routed enemy who, on the day of his flight, can be rounded up without much effort, may reappear on the morrow restored to his full fighting power.'

With this in mind, he urged the Fifth Panzer Army to keep attacking on the 14th. But Generalmajor Ziegler preferred a more cautious approach and, even after defeating the American counter-attack on the 15th, did not resume his advance on Sbeitla until the night of the 16th. This gave the Americans time, wrote Rommel, 'to organise some sort of a defence and they now fought back skilfully and bitterly'.[1]

It was a missed opportunity. Late on 14 February, Major General Orlando Ward, commanding the 1st Armored Division, had only a small force available to defend Sbeitla: the remnants of Combat Command A and his divisional reserve, which included an armoured infantry battalion (1/6th), a half-strength light tank battalion (1/1st), a company of armoured engineers and a handful of anti-aircraft guns.[2] A determined attack by the combined forces of the 10th and 21st Panzer Divisions would have destroyed this force. Kesselring claimed it would have taken place had he still been in Rome. 'Unfortunately,' wrote Kesselring, 'on the two most important days [14/15 February] I was absent at the Führer's GHQ so that I was unable to find the remedy in time.'[3]

Rommel's own attack on Gafsa – Operation *Morgenluft* – was not scheduled to begin until the 21st Panzer Division had been returned to his control. But when advance units of his Afrika Korps, under Oberst Kurt Freiherr von Liebenstein, discovered that the Allies had already evacuated the oasis town in southern Tunisia, they occupied it without a fight during the afternoon of 15 February. As Rommel drove into Gafsa the following day, he 'passed long columns of Arabs driving pack animals laden with loot'. They had taken advantage of the Allied withdrawal to carry away 'everything moveable that could be stripped from the abandoned houses and buildings'. Anything made of wood was 'particularly prized'.[4]

Before their hurried departure, the Americans had blown up six tons of ammunition in the cellars of the town's citadel, a botched operation that destroyed neighbouring houses and killed more than a hundred Arabs. This made the locals 'very bitter' towards the Allies and, conversely, well-disposed to the Axis troops whom they saw as liberators and presented with chickens and eggs. Arriving in the town square in his staff car, the Desert Fox was greeted by large crowd of Arabs chanting 'Hitler!' and 'Rommel!'

Abandoned supplies that did fall into Rommel's hands included 200,000 tons of phosphate – which 'could no doubt have been put to good use in Europe if only we could have got it there' – a 'considerable quantity of petrol' and an entire freight train which had to be left by the Allies when a railway bridge north of Gafsa was destroyed prematurely.[5]

That evening, 16 February, Rommel phoned Arnim and persuaded him to continue the Fifth Panzer Army's advance from Sidi Bou Zid to Sbeitla. But that was as far west as Arnim was prepared to go. Having destroyed the Allied supply dumps at Sbeitla, Arnim intended to shift his axis of advance to Fondouk in the northeast where he hoped to destroy the Allied forces south of the gap. Arnim was, of course, unaware that Anderson had already made the decision to withdraw all Allied forces back to the Western Dorsal.[6]

Rommel's plan was to capture Fériana, 40 miles northwest of Gafsa, and then persuade Arnim to join him in a joint operation through the passes of the Western Dorsal and on to the major American base of Tébessa across the Algerian border. He accomplished the first part of this mission during the morning of 17 February when the Afrika Korps took Fériana and the nearby airfield at Thelepte. Before leaving, the Americans had set fire to their stores in the town, as well as thirty planes at Thelepte that they had been 'unable to get off the ground because of a lack of parts or repairs'. Rommel's men were able to capture intact some 75mm tank destroyers that did not receive the order to withdraw.[7]

With the Americans seemingly in disarray, and their commanders 'jittery' and 'showing the lack of decision typical of men commanding for the first time in a difficult situation', Rommel sensed an opportunity. He wrote:

> I wanted to push forward with all our strength for Tebessa, take possession of this important airbase, supply and transport centre, and strike on deep into the Allied rear. The situation in Africa had always been implicit with very great risks for me, because of the constant inferiority of my force. But I had never gambled; even in the most daring operations, I had always kept enough in hand to deal with any situation, and had never had to fear losing everything. But in the position as it was now, a rather greater risk had to be taken.

Just after midday, he wired a proposal to Kesselring who was now back in Rome. If all three panzer divisions – the 10th, 15th and 21st – were placed under his orders in the vicinity of Fériana, he would head for Tébessa with a view to invading Algeria and overrunning the Allied rear areas. The opposition was in disarray and a better opportunity might never present itself. 'I was convinced,' Rommel wrote later, 'that a thrust beyond Tebessa by the combined armoured and motorised forces of the two armies would force the British and Americans to pull back the bulk of their forces, thus greatly delaying their offensive preparations. The essential conditions for the stroke to succeed were that it should be made at once and that the striking force should be strong enough to overcome any reviving enemy resistance rapidly and break through to the open road.'

The proposal was music to Kesselring's ears and he wired back his approval. Rommel celebrated with a bottle of champagne – a rare indulgence – and told Leutnant Berndt, his chief of publicity, that he felt 'like an old warhorse that had heard the music again'.

Next morning, however, Generaloberst von Arnim voiced his objection to the plan. Having occupied Sbeitla – which the Americans had abandoned on 17 February – he now hoped to use the 10th Panzer Division to launch a separate and more limited attack further north in the Tunis sector. Rommel's proposed operation was, in his view, far too ambitious. In an effort to break the deadlock, Rommel appealed to both Kesselring and the Comando Supremo in Rome. The Duce, he knew, 'badly needed a victory to bolster up his internal political position'.

Rommel waited for the Comando Supremo's response in a 'fever of impatience'. It finally arrived at 1.30 a.m. on 19 February: the operation could go ahead, but with the 'all-important modification' – suggested by Arnim – that the axis of advance would be from Fériana and Sbeitla north towards Le Kef in northern Tunisia, via Thala, and not west towards Tébessa in Algeria.

The alteration was, in Rommel's opinion, 'an appalling and unbelievable piece of shortsightedness'. It meant that instead of a executing a sickle-stroke deep into the enemy's rear, the thrust would be 'far too close to the front and was bound to bring us up against the strong enemy reserves'. But there was 'no time for argument' if he was to achieve even his limited aim of 'breaking up the American assembly areas'. Consequently, he issued orders for an advance on two main axes: the Afrika Korps' combat group would lead the advance on Thala, and ultimately Le Kef, through the Kasserine Pass, 20 miles northwest of Fériana (and the same distance from Sbeitla); while the 21st Panzer Division attacked north up a neighbouring valley from Sbeitla to Sbiba, a distance of 25 miles. Units of the 10th Panzer Division, meanwhile, would be brought forward to Sbeitla 'from where they could either be thrown in to join the 21st Panzer Division at Sbiba or to help the Afrika Korps' group at Kasserine, according to how the situation developed'.[8]

The Kasserine Pass – Rommel's immediate objective on 19 February 1943 – is one of three major gaps in the southern section of the Western Dorsal (the others are at Sbiba and Dernaïa). It is hemmed in by two 4,000ft mountains, Djebel Chambi (to the south) and Djebel Semmama (to the north), and from the air resembles a huge X: broad, almost four miles wide at both entrances, but narrowing to just a mile at its pinch point in the centre.

A road and narrow-gauge railway climb up the pass, over gently undulating ground, to the hamlet of Bordj Chambi in the Foussana Plain, a basin surrounded by wooded hills. There the road forks, the main route heading north to Thala and a subsidiary route, then a dirt track, that winds its way northwest to Tébessa. Flowing down the pass, from northwest to southeast, is the Hatab river.[9]

On 16 February, in line with Anderson's orders, II Corps had put the Kasserine into a state of defence. 'We may hold 'em at Kasserine,' Fredendall told his chief of staff, 'but not before.'[10]

In fact, the troops sent there were far from adequate. They included the US 19th Engineer Regiment, under Lieutenant Colonel Anderson T. W. Moore, whose original task had been to lay almost 3,000 mines along the road that sloped uphill from the village of Kasserine to the entrance of the pass. Moore's engineers had then withdrawn through the pinch point and, by the 18th, were in positions covering the exit into the Foussana Plain. They were on low ground to the right, covering the Tébessa track; the 1st Battalion of the 26th Infantry Regiment (acting under Moore's orders) was on the left, astride the Thala road. Each had placed a platoon on the heights above. Dividing the two forces was the Hatab river, requiring a ten-mile detour to the nearest bridge if Moore wanted to shift troops from one side to the other. In all, 2,000 men were guarding a front of about three miles. Supporting them were two batteries of American 105mm howitzers, a battery of horse-drawn French 'seventy-fives' (75mm field guns) and a battalion of tank destroyers. Their intention was to destroy the Germans as they became bunched together in the pass.

But Moore's engineers, in particular, were of doubtful fighting ability. They were not trained to hold defensive positions and only one officer had combat experience. When a German reconnaissance unit probed the pass on the 18th, wounding one man, some engineers left their posts and fled to the rear. A few were rounded up, but others could not be found. With the inexperience of the engineers in mind, Fredendall put Colonel Alexander N. Stark of the 26th Infantry Regiment in overall command. 'Alex,' said Fredendall, 'I want you to go to Kasserine right away and pull a Stonewall Jackson. Take over up there.'

'You mean tonight, General?' asked Stark.

'Yes, Alex, right away.'[11]

Stark reached the pass at 7.30 a.m. on 19 February as the first serious assault was made by the armoured cars of Major Hans Freiherr von Luck's 3rd Reconnaissance Battalion. Luck's vanguard was able to negotiate the minefield at the entrance to the pass because Moore's men had helpfully marked it with 'mounds of earth, red flags, and simple plain flags, and clearly outlined by barbed wire' (probably to assist the passage of American troops).

'With the motorcycle escorts in front, I moved off before dawn in the hope of catching the Americans unawares,' recalled Luck. 'They were on the alert, however, and straddled us with heavy artillery fire, which was directed by observers stationed on the heights on either side of the way through the pass. I couldn't get through. Neither could a rifle regiment that was sent in . . .' Luck's men did manage to take some prisoners, and were surprised by their 'first-class equipment' and daily ration of chocolate, chewing gum, butter and cigarettes which for the Germans were 'unaccustomed treats'.[12]

Meeting stiff resistance at the end of the pass, German infantry began to climb the heights. Then panzers were brought up to assist the infantry, but a combined attempt to rush the pass was broken up by artillery and machine-gun fire.

All the while, Stark was gaining in confidence, particularly when reinforcements arrived in the shape of a battalion of the 39th Infantry and some British mortars and reconnaissance troops. He was now considerably stronger than the Afrika Korps combat group attacking him (three weak battalions – one panzer and two infantry).

To strengthen the line, Stark placed one company of the 39th on either flank. But the Germans continued to infiltrate along the heights and behind the defensive positions. At dusk, they captured 100 men from the company guarding the engineers' flank. This, and the sudden withdrawal of their supporting tank destroyers, caused the neighbouring company of engineers to abandon their positions. The Germans promptly occupied them.[13]

At the Sbiba Gap, meanwhile, the advance elements of the 21st Panzer Division had been held up by waterlogged roads, a dense minefield and a strong Allied defending force that included units from the 1st Guards Brigade, the 18th Regimental Combat Team and supporting artillery and anti-tank guns. Commanding a platoon of the 18th's Anti-tank Company – having transferred from the Cannon Company – was Lieutenant Franklyn A. Johnson, a 'spoiled only child' from New York who had attended the prestigious Rutgers University in New Jersey. Johnson's unit – composed of four truck-drawn 37mm anti-tank guns – had been rushed down from its bivouac near Maktar during the night of 17/18 February, and ordered to defend a valley three miles east of the oasis village of Sbiba. 'Don't call me for help,' they were told by the regimental commander Colonel Greer, 'I haven't any. If they attack us in force we cannot hold, but by God, we will. We must!'

It was terrain that, in Johnson's opinion, was perfect for attack, not defence. 'Between us and Kasserine Pass to our right rises a frowning Djebel, or mountain, many hundreds of feet high,' he wrote, 'and to the left a low sloping hill of a hundred feet or so. The flat valley stretching eastward before us is a mile wide and down the middle extends the natural channel for Germany's panzers, the hard surface highway which links their headquarters in Sbeitla and the thin Allied line.'

Johnson had sited his guns to best support the men of the 1/18th Infantry – the unit so badly battered at Longstop Hill – who were dug in across the valley. His diary for 19 February noted:

Rained half the goddam night, but strangely my tent stood up. Rain and wind until 1030 [hrs], when a German tank attack came at the English, about 1 mile from our position, on our right flank. Biggest damn tank in the world, a Mark VI (63 tons), appeared on a hill. Unbelievably huge. Proceeded to shell the English area; joined by second Mark VI. The British sent up 5 tanks – 2 knocked out before they even got close, others withdrew.

German infantry tried to advance, but Coldstream Guards held. Then I saw our left being approached, standing on my ammo box, using glasses. 8 Mark VI's, but 2 were suddenly destroyed by a mine-field we didn't know was there. They attempted to pick out the mines, but our artillery drove them back.

Johnson's command post took three direct hits from 88mm shells that killed two of his men and mortally wounded another. Johnson was unharmed and the position held, but only just. That night they were ordered to pull back to a new defensive position at Rohia, north of Sbiba. Unbeknown to them, the Germans had also withdrawn to Sbeitla. 'Why?' asked Johnson. 'That is a complete mystery. Perhaps they did not realize how relatively weak we were, and how little additional pressure might outflank the 18th and penetrate the passes.'[14]

Rommel's assessment of the 21st Panzer Division's failed assault was scathing. 'They had made', he wrote, 'the same mistake of attacking frontally in the valley instead of striking across the hills.' Convinced the Allies were weaker at Kasserine than at Sbiba – which they were – he decided to use the 10th Panzer Division to focus the weight of his attack there.[15]

Early next morning, 20 February, Rommel drove to Kasserine in his armoured scout car and met Generalmajor von Broich, the 10th's commander, at the railway bridge over the Hatab river. 'Unfortunately,' recalled Rommel, 'he had brought only half his force, von Arnim having held back part of it in the north for his own purposes. The division's motorcycle battalion was already on the move and I passed it on the way.'

Rommel's instructions to Broich were to deploy his spearhead battalion behind parts of Panzer Regiment 'Afrika' and the crack mountain troops of the Italian No. 7 Bersaglieri Regiment (one of the few Italian units in which Rommel had any faith), both under the command of Oberst Menton. But as the hours ticked by there was still no sign that Broich's 10th Motorcycle Infantry Battalion (K10) was in action. 'When I inquired from von Broich what all the delay was,' recalled Rommel, 'he told me that he had detailed a different unit for the assault, as he wanted to reserve the motor-cycle battalion for the pursuit. The assault unit was still on its way.'

Furious that precious time was being wasted, Rommel told Broich to move closer to the front. He also ordered the motorcycle battalion to attack immediately 'for the Americans were growing stronger every hour'. Rommel's insults had the desired effect. 'From midday onwards', he wrote, 'the attack was 'resumed in fierce hand-to-hand fighting.

Nebelwerfer' – a multiple rocket launcher that could send its 210mm high-explosive missiles up to 8,000 yards – 'were brought into action for the first time in Africa, and proved very effective.'[16]

Moore's engineers were the first to crack and by 5 p.m. the whole defensive line had disintegrated. Hundreds surrendered; the rest scarpered to the rear. The only effective resistance was from a detachment of the British 6th Armoured Division – a tank squadron, an infantry company and a field battery, and known collectively as 'Gore Force' after its commander Lieutenant Colonel A. C. Gore of the 10th Rifle Brigade – that was covering the road behind the pass. The end came when the veteran 8th Panzer Regiment drove the British squadron's 11 tanks back against the mountain and destroyed them, the survivors abandoning their vehicles and fleeing on foot over the hills. In all, some 20 tanks and 30 armoured troop-carriers (most towing 75mm anti-tank guns) were captured, causing Rommel to marvel at how 'fantastically well equipped' the Americans were.

That night, Rommel sent reconnaissance groups northwards along the Kasserine–Thala road and westwards to Tébessa, but they saw no sign of Allied troops. Expecting a counter-attack nevertheless, he held the bulk of his forces at Kasserine on the defensive. Only when the Allies failed to appear during the morning of 21 February did he order Broich's 10th Panzer Division – now reduced to 30 tanks, 20 self-propelled guns and two panzer grenadier battalions – to push on up the road to Thala, 35 miles from Kasserine, while the Afrika Korps combat group was told to capture the pass near Djebel el Hamra on the track to Tébessa.[17]

Rommel accompanied the 10th Panzer Division's advance, driving on the left side of the leading tanks in his armoured car, while Broich drove on the right side in his jeep. Following not far behind, with a battalion of panzer grenadiers (II/86th), was Oberstleutnant von Stauffenberg, Broich's operations chief. Held up by heavy artillery fire in one Arab village, Rommel and his chief of staff, Oberst Fritz Bayerlein, went forward on foot to find the lead scouts taking cover in a cactus grove. 'Confusion was complete,' wrote Rommel, 'with every living creature, bird and beast, scattering in all directions. Bayerlein collected up eggs which some hens had dropped. Then we, too, had to get into cover, and Bayerlein crawled amongst the cacti carrying his precious booty. We came to no harm – neither, fortunately, did the eggs.'

About 10 miles on from Kasserine, having already overrun a British anti-tank company, Broich's panzers came up against the rest of the 26th Armoured Brigade Group – consisting of two armoured regiments and two infantry battalions, under Brigadier Charles Dunphie – spread across three successive lateral ridges. They were part of 'Nickforce', led by Brigadier Cameron Nicholson, the deputy commander of the 6th Armoured Divison, who had opened his HQ in Thala at 6 a.m. on 21 February.

Once again, the panzers prevailed by outflanking and enfilading the British positions. Seventeen of the 2nd Lothians' Mark VI Crusader tanks, armed with powerful but short-range 3-inch howitzer guns, were destroyed at the first ridge. At dusk, as they withdrew through the last defensive line held by the 2/5th Leicesters on a ridge two miles from Thala, the remnants of Dunphie's force were closely followed by Broich's armour. Led by a captured Valentine tank, the German panzers were mistaken for stragglers and allowed to enter the British lines. They quickly wheeled round and opened fire on the Allied rear, forcing two companies of infantry from their shallow slit trenches and taking hundreds of prisoners. But a desperate defence by the remaining Leicesters, some anti-tank guns and the rest of Dunphie's force prompted Broich to withdraw. For the loss of 12 tanks, Broich's division had knocked out or captured 38. It had also destroyed 28 artillery pieces and taken 'nearly a battalion of prisoners'.[18]

Second Lieutenant Peter Moore, a 22-year-old platoon commander in the 2/5th Leicesters, narrowly avoided capture when six Germans stopped to smoke a cigarette in front of his slit trench. Fortunately, it was dark and, after taking off his greatcoat and webbing, including his .38 pistol, he slithered out of the trench and wormed his way down the hill. 'I felt no exhilaration at having escaped death or capture,' he recalled. 'My feelings were of shame for having been overrun in our first battle . . . My brain remained detached and interested but, above all, impressed by the sheer professionalism of the German army.'

Taking a wide detour across rough and rocky ground, Moore eventually ran into a group of British soldiers hiding in a cactus grove. They told him the survivors of his battalion had reformed further down the road. Among the Leicesters' 300 casualties – many of them missing in action – was Second Lieutenant Jim Pickard who had joined the battalion at the same time as Moore. Before Pickard's body could be recovered, it was stripped by Arabs who also cut off a finger to steal his ring. 'Poor Jim never had a chance,' noted Moore. 'He was well over 6 feet tall and it had been impossible to dig a slit trench deep enough to protect him before his company was overrun by tanks.'[19]

What mattered, however, was that Thala, 35 miles north of Kasserine and a keystone in Anderson's defences, remained in Allied hands.

31

'The enemy has broken through'

Southern Tunisia, 21–23 February 1943

A T DAWN ON 21 February, Brigadier General Paul Robinett climbed to a vantage point near his command post in the Djebel el Hamra Pass, a natural pinch point on the track that led westwards from the Kasserine Pass to Tébessa in Algeria. From there he should have had an unobstructed view of the entire Foussana Plain, 'but a low fog filled the valley and denied all observation'. Later that morning, after the clouds had lifted, he looked down on a 'vast bowl dominated in all sides by mountains and split down the middle by the sharply cut' Hatab river.

On the far side of the plain stood a seemingly unbroken line of barren mountains. It was hard for Robinett to make out the entrance to the pass at Kasserine through which the tanks, artillery, armoured infantry and tank destroyers of his Combat Command B had passed three days earlier as they withdrew from Sbeitla, and which was now in the hands of Rommel's troops. Yet he knew the Hatab flowed through the pass, and the trick was to follow its course. There, where the river met the base of the mountains, the terrain was 'broken and partially covered with cactus patches and scrub growth'. Numerous Arab huts, some made of concrete, dotted the landscape.[1]

For the diminutive Robinett, it had been an eventful few days. On 15 February, after one of his tank battalions had been cut to pieces in the doomed counter-attack at Sidi Bou Zid, he had been ordered to move the rest of CCB to Sbeitla to cover II Corps' withdrawal to the Western Dorsal. There, on 17 February, Lieutenant Colonel Henry Gardiner's battalion of medium tanks had fought the advance elements of the 21st Panzer Division to a standstill, thus enabling the rest of the command to get away. 'With a display of the finest discipline,' read the unit citation, 'superb leadership, and unflinching courage, the battalion stood like an iron wall to the last vehicle, under perfect control of its commander, with no other order than, "When they are close enough, boys, let them have it!"' The hard fighting of the battalion prevented the enemy from bypassing Sbeitla on the south and permitted the orderly withdrawal of the entire command.[2]

Gardiner's tank had been one of nine destroyed. As usual, the battalion commander had stayed to the very end and it almost cost him his life. Two of his crew were killed – including his driver, Corporal Orvis Carlock, who was awarded a posthumous Silver Star – and two seriously wounded, by the shell that knocked out his tank. He removed one of the casualties, amidst a hail of machine-gun fire, and gave him first aid. In a letter to his father, Gardiner described the hour lying in an exposed position, with enemy tanks passing on either side of him, as the 'longest' of his life. He eventually escaped and made his way back to American lines, a distance of 25 miles. For his outstanding leadership that day, he was awarded the Distinguished Service Cross.[3]

The remnants of Robinett's CCB, meanwhile, had withdrawn back through the Kasserine Pass and, on 18 September, were sent to join the rest of the 1st Armored Division in a defensive position south of Tébessa. Robinett considered the move an error. The most likely direction of an Axis attack, he thought, would be further north against Kasserine and Sbiba, and he was soon proved right. Fredendall – who, following the withdrawal from Gafsa and Fériana, had moved his command post from Speedy Valley to a schoolhouse in Le Kouif, a tiny mining village in the mountains 20 miles to the northeast – warned Robinett in the early hours of 20 February that if the situation at

Kasserine got any worse, he would have to counter-attack with a 'portion of your division'. That became necessary at 10.30 a.m. when Robinett received orders from II Corps to 'march without delay on Thala, by way of Tebessa and Haidra, and to assume command of all troops defending Kasserine Pass'. He was to report to Fredendall on the road south of Thala.

Hurrying ahead of his command, Robinett met Fredendall and his staff on a ridge beyond Thala. 'Robby, am I glad to see you,' said the corps commander. 'The enemy has broken through Kasserine Pass and is advancing north on Thala and west on Tebessa. The British will cover Thala. Head your column off at Haidra and move south-east and secure the passes of Djebel el Hamra, stop the enemy advance in that sector, drive him out of the valley, and restore our position in Kasserine Pass.'

Robinett nodded. 'I understand, sir.'

'Good. If you get away with this one, Robby,' said Fredendall grinning, 'I will make you a field marshal!'

'I will do my best, sir.'

They shook hands. 'Good luck!' said the corps commander, before mounting his vehicle and speeding away.

Robinett dispatched a staff officer to redirect his men and vehicles to the Djebel el Hamra Pass. Then, having taken a moment to study the map and gather his thoughts, he set off in pursuit. It was dark and raining steadily by the time he reached the assembly area in a pine wood. He called in his unit commanders and gave them their instructions: stragglers from the front were to be intercepted, reorganised and placed in a defensive position on the heights dominating the Djebel el Hamra and neighbouring Bou Chebka passes. The remaining tanks, tank destroyers, infantry and artillery pieces were to be dug in to cover the mouths of both passes.[4]

Robinett then drove back to Thala for a midnight conference with Brigadiers C. V. McNabb, Anderson's chief of staff, and Dunphie, commanding the British 26th Armoured Brigade, in the latter's command post in the French post office. In the dimly lit hallway he passed Colonel Stark, a 'tired and bedraggled-looking man' who had just returned from Kasserine.

As they sipped hot tea, seated around a table on which a large map of the area was spread, the well-groomed and no-nonsense McNabb gave his assessment. Speaking slowly and with measured words, he said the situation was 'desperately critical'. Save those of Robinett's CCB, the 1st Armored Division had lost most of its tanks. Under the circumstances, there could be no question of retaking the Kasserine Pass. Only with difficulty could they maintain a presence in Tunisia at all.

Robinett suggested a spoiling attack by his units to discourage any further Axis gains, while Dunphie held on in front of Thala. When the tide had been turned, they could advance together to eject the enemy from the Foussana Plain.

After a brief discussion, McNabb ruled that they should wait for the next German attack, probably against Dunphie at Thala. Then, having held it, they could counter-attack as Robinett had suggested. Their priority, McNabb insisted, was to conserve their forces, particularly tanks. Anderson had earlier appointed Brigadier Cameron Nicholson, second-in-command of the 6th Armoured Division, to coordinate Allied forces in the area. But as he had still not arrived, McNabb gave the job to II Corps instead, which effectively meant Robinett was the senior American officer present.

Armed with this new authority, Robinett returned to his command post which, in the interim, had been moved to a new location in the Djebel el Hamra Pass. It proved to be the most picturesque of the entire campaign. Robinett wrote:

We were in mountainous terrain of outcropping stone, loose boulders, and precipitous cliffs. Much of the area was covered by scrub pine and bushes, which furnished excellent cover. The Tebessa-Djebel el Hamra-Kasserine road passed by the command post and furnished good communications to the front and to the rear. Engineers of some other outfit had set demolition charges along the cliffs of defiles and had prepared the road for mines. They would not be needed.

During the morning of 21 February, while fog obscured his view, Robinett was kept abreast of Rommel's activity by the 13th Armored Regiment's reconnaissance company which was operating in the plain. At dawn he was told that the enemy was 'advancing on Thala as well as on the Tebessa road'. Just after 8 a.m. a large German force, including more than eighty vehicles, was reported directly to his front.[5]

These were the advanced elements of the Afrika Korps, under Generalmajor Karl Bülowius, whose task it was to 'throw back the enemy at El Hamra and take the summit of the pass on the road to Tebessa'. But slowed by incessant rain, which had reduced the single track to a quagmire, they did not begin a full-scale attack on the pass with the tanks of the Italian Centauro Division, supported by infantry and artillery, until mid-afternoon.[6]

It was fortunate for Robinett that the weight of the attack fell on Gardiner's 2/13th Battalion, whose tanks were cleverly concealed in hull-down positions near the entrance to the pass. 'The artillery forward observers soon had the enemy under fire,' wrote Robinett, 'while the 894th Tank Destroyer Battalion manoeuvred into position to engage him from the high ground to the south.'[7]

The Italian tanks were, as a result, caught in crossfire and brought to a standstill. Ten tanks and another ten armoured vehicles were knocked out, for the loss of one American tank. At one point, Gardiner's own tank came under long-range fire from what he assumed was a heavy German tank. He gave his 75mm gunner – who was an excellent shot – a range of 2,000 yards and ordered him to fire a round of high explosive. 'It looked like a hit,' wrote Gardiner to his father, 'so we put in another and then one round of AP [armour-piercing]. The next day, when we took that position, we found we had been firing on a 75-mm anti-tank gun, had hit it squarely near the shield, wrecking it completely and scattering three members of the crew about the immediate vicinity.'[8]

Early on, guns of the 27th Armored Field Artillery Battalion were attacked by ten Stuka dive-bombers, killing two men and wounding eight. But the planes were driven off by devastating fire from an M15 half-track armed with a 37mm anti-aircraft gun and two .50 calibre machine guns on a single mount. Two Stukas left trailing smoke, and their crashed remains were later discovered farther down the valley. Thanks to this new anti-aircraft weapon, it would be the last time that CCB was seriously troubled by dive-bombers.[9]

Rommel, who witnessed the tail end of the defeat as he drove back to Kasserine from the 10th Panzer Division's failed assault on Thala, was critical of Bülowius's tactics. 'After some initial success,' he wrote, the Afrika Korps combat group's advance 'had steadily slowed down in the face of continually stiffening resistance. Unfortunately, it, too, had kept to the valley bottom and had not simultaneously advanced over the hills on either side in order to reduce the positions in the pass by an attack round their flank.'

And yet, he conceded, the Americans' defence had been 'very skilfully executed'. After allowing the attacking column to move peacefully up the valley, they had 'suddenly poured fire on it from three sides, forcing the column to a halt'. Bülowius's men had then been 'astounded at the flexibility and accuracy of the American artillery, which had put a great number of tanks out of action'.[10]

By nightfall on 21 February, Robinett's CCB had accomplished the first part of its mission. The enemy had been stopped with the loss of a 'very few men and one tank'. Robinett was tempted to launch a vigorous counter-attack, but McNabb's words of caution were ringing in his ears. After the battle, Robinett would see plainly that 'the enemy's tactics were designed to draw CCB's tanks into pursuit. Had this happened, they would have run into well-emplaced 88-mm guns which would have reversed the entire situation in a few minutes.'[11]

★

Next morning, 22 February, Rommel drove back to the 10th Panzer Division's command post near Thala to consult with Broich. The divisional commander wanted to resume the attack on Thala at 1 p.m. and requested air support. But Rommel felt the enemy had grown 'too strong' for the attack to be maintained – more artillery from the US 9th Division had arrived overnight after a forced march from Algeria – and eventually Broich agreed. Without adequate infantry – two of the 10th's four battalions of panzer grenadiers had been held back by Arnim in northern Tunisia – Broich knew the isolation of the division was inevitable.

Bülowius, on the other hand, did make a second attempt to break out of the Foussana basin by capturing the Bou Chebka Pass that morning. Assaulting the junction of two battalions of American infantry, his tanks and infantry were able to get through and overrun a battery of artillery. But they were counter-attacked and driven back by Robinett's tanks and armoured infantry mounted in half-tracks. Among the three hundred or so Axis troops taken prisoner were the vaunted mountain troops of the Bersaglieri Regiment. 'We didn't have any infantry with us,' wrote Henry Gardiner to his father, 'so herded them back to the rear with a tank in the lead and one in the rear . . . It has been raining a lot lately and the roads behind us are a mess, so it was nice to have a labor pool to draw from.'[12]

Returning to his headquarters near Kasserine, Rommel met Kesselring who had flown over from Rome. 'We agreed that a continuation of the attack towards Le Kef held no prospect of success,' wrote Rommel, 'and decided to break off the offensive by stages. Accordingly, the 10th Panzer Division and the Afrika Korps' group were drawn back to Kasserine during the night, where they took up positions north-west of the pass. The 21st Panzer Division was to remain at Sbiba for the moment, but was to be prepared to receive orders to mine the road and withdraw.'[13]

Kesselring's recollection of their meeting is very different:

I had a long talk with Rommel and found him in a very dispirited mood. His heart was not in his task and he approached it with little confidence. I was particularly struck by his ill-concealed impatience to get back as quickly and with as much unimpaired strength as possible to the southern defence line, where Generale d'Armata Messe had been in command since the beginning of February. His apathy betrayed his reluctance or inability to grasp the significance of the operation which was then in progress towards Tebessa.[14]

This does Rommel a disservice. The original plan to strike through Tébessa and deep into the Allied rear had been his. The fact that it had been watered down by Arnim and the Comando Supremo, and then undermined by a divided command structure and lack of resources, was not his fault. He had inspired his men by leading from the front, at considerable personal risk to himself, and they had responded by capturing the Kasserine Pass and almost getting as far as Thala. But when the Allies got their act together – holding him at Thala and the Djebel el Hamra Pass – he was right to call it a day.

Was he really 'dispirited' when he met Kesselring? He was certainly disappointed, tired and physically unwell. But he was also, as he told Kesselring, determined to execute the second part of his strategy: a surprise strike on Montgomery's Eighth Army before it was ready to attack the Mareth Line. It was now, according to Rommel, that he was offered the command of a new Army Group Afrika by Kesselring. 'Apparently,' wrote the Desert Fox, 'as a result of the Kasserine offensive, I had ceased to be *persona non grata*, and had become acceptable again, in spite of my defeatism.'

Rommel declined the verbal offer. He was convinced that Hitler had already earmarked Arnim as Army Group commander, and had 'no great wish to hold a command under the Luftwaffe and Comando Supremo and to have to go on suffering their interference in tactical questions'. Kesselring, he felt, 'his undoubted merits aside, had no conception of the tactical and operational conditions in the African theatre'. Instead, the Luftwaffe man 'saw everything through rose-coloured glasses' and, since the successes at Sidi Bou Zid and Kasserine, this optimism had been bolstered. Many more victories were possible, thought Kesselring, because the 'fighting value of the Americans was low'.

This was, thought Rommel, to underestimate American troops. While they could not yet match the veterans of Montgomery's Eighth Army, they 'made up for their lack of experience by their far better and more plentiful equipment and their tactically more flexible command', which meant, in effect, an ability to adapt to changing circumstances. They also had far more tanks and anti-tank weapons than their opponents, which meant that the Axis forces had 'but small hope of success' in the mobile battles to come.

Rommel had also been impressed by the speed at which the Americans had recovered after the 'first shock' by 'grouping their reserves to defend the passes and other suitable points'. Their stubborn defence of the Kasserine Pass, and the tardy arrival of Arnim's units, had prevented him 'from making a surprise break-in to the enemy hinterland'. Yet not all the Allied troops had 'come up so quickly', and Rommel remained convinced that had they stuck to his original plan to go straight for Tébessa they might have been able to 'thrust far beyond it to the north before meeting any serious opposition'.

As the last of Rommel's troops were being pulled back through the Kasserine Pass on 23 February, the skies cleared and Allied aircraft pounced. 'Aircraft of all kinds', wrote the Desert Fox, 'maintained a ceaseless attack by cannon fire and bombs against my troops retreating through the valley bottoms, and observation planes directed the fire of numerous batteries on all worthwhile targets.' In the space of fifteen minutes, more than a hundred Allied planes were seen over Kasserine alone. Rommel was lucky to survive a bombing attack as he arrived at his forward HQ.

That evening, against his wishes, he was ordered by the Comando

Supremo in Rome to take command of the new Army Group Afrika. He had mixed feelings. On the one hand, he would call the shots in Tunisia and be able to have some 'wider influence' over the fate of his men; on the other, he would remain the 'whipping-boy' for the Führer's HQ, the Comando Supremo and the Luftwaffe. He also doubted, he wrote to his wife Lucie on 24 February, that it was a 'permanent solution'.[15]

32

Alex

North Africa, 14–23 February 1943

'THE ENEMY HAS MADE an advance into Kasserine Pass,' wrote Ike to General Marshall on 22 February. 'We are supposed to be counter-attacking as quickly as possible. Evidence increases that he may try a major stroke attempting to get in rear of 5th Corps. We have enough to stop him – or at the very least to foil such purpose – if we can only use it effectively.'

It was, for Ike, the low point of the nine-day seesaw fight for the passes of Tunisia's Western Dorsal that would come to be known, somewhat misleadingly, as the 'Battle of Kasserine'. In fact, the action had ranged across a much wider area, and included clashes at or near Sidi Bou Zid, Sbeitla, Sbiba, the Kasserine Pass, Thala and the Djebel el Hamra and Bou Chebka passes. Ultimately, Ike's men had checked Rommel in the Foussana Plain on 21 February and forced him to withdraw. But it had nevertheless been a close-run thing.

For the first two days of the battle – 14 and 15 February – Ike had carried the heavy burden of high command almost alone: Bedell Smith and Patton were visiting Montgomery in Tripoli, Clark was ill, and Alexander and Tedder had not yet assumed their new commands. He told Marshall: 'I was really busy!'[1]

Ike's priority at this early stage – which he spent at his forward HQ in Constantine – was to advance as many reinforcements as possible, including the 9th Division artillery which he sent from Algeria, as well as trucks, tanks and ammunition from the US 2nd Armored and 3rd Infantry Divisions that were training for the Sicily landings. He told Fredendall 'that every position to be held must be organized to max. extent – at once – mines, etc. *Emphasize reconnaissance.*'[2]

On 17 February, having returned to Algiers from Constantine, Ike told Harry Butcher that defeat in the initial engagement at Sidi Bou Zid had cost 'four or five thousand men and considerable equipment, including tanks (fifty Sherman replacements were requested), self-propelled artillery, numerous trucks, half-tracks and guns'. It was, noted Butcher in his diary, the 'worst walloping we have taken in this fight, and perhaps the stiffest setback of our ground forces in the war [thus far]'.

Later that day, General Sir Harold Alexander flew in from Tripoli to take up his new job as Deputy Allied Commander-in-Chief and commander of the new 18th Army Group (to include the British First and Eighth Armies, US II Corps and French XIX Corps). Ike was hugely relieved, and told him that 'he could write his own orders at the front, that he was proud to have Alex serve under him and to let him know what was needed at the front in men, supplies, or what-ever, and the C-in-C would do his best to get it from the rear, from the UK or from the US'.

Alex thanked him and said he had been disappointed when his first assignment to serve under Ike in Operation Torch had been cancelled after just twenty-four hours. He fully recognised that Tunisia was an 'American sphere' and it was 'not only necessary but a privilege to come under the American C-in-C'.

After more mutual back-slapping, they turned to strategy. Alex said he was pretty convinced that the Germans were heading for Tébessa in eastern Algeria (which had, of course, been Rommel's original objective before it was altered by the Comando Supremo, at Arnim's behest, to a more significant breakthrough towards Le Kef in eastern Tunisia).

Ike agreed with Alex, adding that Fredendall was not given the reserves he needed because Anderson had been overly influenced by faulty intelligence that the main weight of the attack would be further north at Fondouk.

'My fear now,' said Alex, 'is that our units are too dispersed and the Hun is going to gobble them up one by one, which is already happening. The solution, I think, is to give Anderson one sector, as the long front is too much for one man to handle, Fredendall another, and then soon we'll have Montgomery advancing from Tripoli.'

Alexander left the meeting to fly to his new HQ in Constantine, leaving Ike to brief journalists 'off the record' that the British general had gone to the front 'to take charge'. Ike was also man enough to take 'full responsibility' for the defeat at Sidi Bou Zid, ascribing it principally to the miscalculation he had made as to the 'ability of the French troops, with their poor equipment, to hold the central front'. When they collapsed, and their 60-mile front had to be taken over by American and British troops, the line could only be 'thinly held'. American armour was in 'small packets', which allowed the German panzers to overwhelm them. However, said Ike, the American troops had shown great fighting spirit.

Not surprisingly, Ike made no mention to the press of the real reason they had been caught on the hop: the misinterpretation of intelligence regarding the direction of the Axis attack by both his own G-2, Mockler-Ferryman, and Anderson's. Mockler-Ferryman was replaced by another Briton, Brigadier Kenneth Strong, who remained with Ike through the rest of the war.[3]

Ike also had doubts about Fredendall, not helped by the latter's attempt to replace Orlando Ward as commander of the 1st Armored Division while the battle was still raging. 'At present,' Fredendall wired Ike on 19 February, '1st Armored in bad state of disorganization. Ward appears tired out, worried and has informed me that to bring new tanks in would be the same as turning them over to the Germans. Under the circumstances do not think he should continue in command.'

Unwilling to sack Fredendall or Ward in the middle of the battle, Ike sent Major General Ernest N. Harmon, commander of the 2nd Armored Division, to II Corps HQ. Fredendall was to use him in any way he saw fit. But when Harmon reached Le Kouif, via Tébessa, in the morning of 23 February, a few hours after Rommel had begun his withdrawal, but before the Americans knew he was pulling out, Fredendall assumed he was being replaced, and that defeat was only a matter of time. He gave Harmon a letter, saying: 'Here it is. The party is yours.'

Harmon opened it, and found a typewritten order placing him in command. The exhausted Fredendall then went to bed and slept for twenty-four hours straight. When he woke up, the Battle of Kasserine was over, thanks in no small part to Harmon.[4]

Ike would later give a lot of the credit for forcing Rommel back to his start line to the unflappable Alexander who, for the last few days of the Battle of Kasserine, was 'on the ground and in command of the battle line'. Ike wrote: 'I quickly formed a great respect and admiration for his soldierly qualities, an esteem that continued to grow throughout the remainder of the war.'[5]

Even Alex had feared the worst at one point, telling Ike on 21 February that he was heading down to II Corps because he was worried that Rommel might pierce the southern end of the line before attacking northwest towards the coast. In fact, Rommel's offensive – the last great Axis opportunity to turn the tide in Tunisia – was hindered from the start by inadequate resources and a fatal switch in the direction of the Axis attack from a deep incursion via Tébessa to a shallow breakthrough towards Le Kef. Ziegler, commanding the northern prong, might have done more to press home his advantage after the stunning capture of Sidi Bou Zid on the first day. But Rommel, his brilliant victory at the Kasserine Pass notwithstanding, was always likely to run out of steam sooner or later given his supply difficulties.

Colonel Stark's men of the 26th Infantry at Kasserine had played their part by holding up Rommel for two days before they cracked under the pressure. Ike left 'no stone unturned' to get men and equipment to the front so that the gaps in the line could be plugged. Even Fredendall, oscillating from panic to calm, had the good sense to move Robinett's CCB to the Foussana Plain in time to meet the Afrika Korps' attack on 22 February. But the best work was done by Robinett and Dunphie, and the men under them, whose stoic defence of the Tébessa road and Thala respectively stopped Rommel in his tracks.[6]

There was, however, no hiding the shame of the early setbacks and the scale of the losses. On 20 February, even before the battle was over, Harry Butcher did the sums in his diary: 117 medium and light tanks, 80 half-tracks, 21 tank destroyers, 22 anti-tank guns, 15 scout cars, 200 trucks, and 'such things as sub-machine-guns, mortars, rifles, pistols, telescopes, twenty-nine binoculars, and even forty watches'.*[7]

Ike told Marshall that 'most of this stuff was destroyed in battle and that we took a heavy toll from the enemy'. But he also admitted that 'some of it was overrun through surprise action', and that the transport would be 'particularly valuable to the enemy'.[8]

American casualties, alone, were 192 killed, 2,624 wounded and 2,459 prisoners and missing. To have so many captured was, Ike knew, often indicative of a breakdown in morale, though in this instance poor leadership was more to blame.

How had these setbacks come about? Ike put the 'embarrassment' down to four principal causes: failure to capture Tunis quickly, which left units dispersed and unable to resist strong counter-attacks; misinterpretation of intelligence, which caused the army commander to make faulty dispositions; underestimating the enemy's capabilities; and the 'greenness' of the American troops and their commanders.

Ike admitted later that the week of the German offensive was a

---

* The Germans would later claim to have destroyed 235 tanks, 110 self-propelled guns and reconnaissance vehicles, and to have taken more than 4,000 prisoners in the battle. They put their own losses at just under 1,000 men – 201 killed – 20 tanks, 5 anti-tank guns and 61 vehicles. (Howe, *Northwest Africa*, p. 477)

'wearing and anxious' time. He added: 'Whenever the initiative is lost to the enemy there is bound to be tension and worry, because it is always possible for anything to happen. No one escapes; in spite of confidence in the overall situation and eventual outcome, there is always the possibility of local disasters.'[9]

Even at the height of the crisis, when news reached Algiers that Rommel had captured the Kasserine Pass, Butcher felt that Ike's worries were 'not because he feared our ability to handle the newest break-through', but rather a concern that forces in the rear were not doing everything they could to get armour, supplies and men to the front. It had been, nonetheless, a humbling experience. As Butcher noted in his diary on 23 February,

> The outstanding fact to me is that the proud and cocky Americans today stand humiliated by one of the greatest defeats in our history. This is particularly embarrassing to us with the British, who are cour-teous and understanding. But there is a definite hangheadedness. Fortunately, this is being followed by a determination to profit from our mistakes, to make definite suggestions to the War Department to improve and intensify training, and to get in there and beat the hell out of the Axis.[10]

The one British commander who was neither 'courteous' nor 'under-standing' was Monty. Instead he shamelessly tried to take the credit for Rommel's withdrawal. In a letter to his confidant Brigadier Frank Simpson, he said that he had received a 'cry for help' from Alexander on 20 February: the Americans 'were being pushed back', the situation was 'very critical' and 'a major disaster was possible'. What Alex wanted was for Monty to threaten the Mareth Line and thus relieve the pres-sure in central Tunisia.

'At that time,' Monty explained, 'I was pressing in slowly and making good progress, being careful not to get unbalanced. But on receiving the cry for help I at once took out the whip. I "drove" forward hard.

I took every sort of risk; and by 25 February I had got right forward to within a few miles of the Mareth position proper. I think there is no doubt that this pressure exerted by me did definitely make Rommel draw off in central Tunisia.'[11]

This was nonsense. Rommel had decided to pull back before he knew about Monty's advance. But Monty was never averse to stealing someone else's thunder, or denigrating other commanders and armies to enhance his own reputation. He repeated the 'I was the saviour' claim in a letter to Major General John Harding, the former commander of the 7th Armoured Division, who was recovering from shell splinter wounds in Cairo. Monty wrote on 25 February:

The real trouble is the low fighting value of the troops in Central Tunisia. Alexander tells me the situation there is quite frightful. There was no plan, no system, no guidance from above, no policy, and no one knew what do. The whole thing was a complete 'dog's breakfast'. They very nearly had a real disaster, and would have done so if I had not driven forward hard and, by creating a strong thrust at Mareth, forced the Bosche to pull out from Kasserine and Tebessa.[12]

Alexander may well have been shocked by what he found when he toured the front line in Tunisia. But it was incredibly indiscreet, not to say inadvisable, of him to share his thoughts with the egotistical Monty. Nor did Monty's criticisms take account of the unique diffi-culties faced by the Allies in the mountains of Tunisia, including resupply, poor communications and adverse weather.

In the end it was troops from the US II Corps and the British First Army, and they alone, who restored the situation, whatever Monty cared to believe. On 23 February, Alex told Monty that the situation at Kasserine was improved and, as a result, he was to keep up a 'display of force' but not take any undue risks. This did not prevent the Eighth Army chief from pressing his claims. 'I hope my pressure this side,' he replied to Alex on 27 February, 'was of value in making Rommel break off the battle your side. We went all out, but I was careful to keep balanced and I am sitting very pretty now.'[13]

General the Honourable Sir Harold Alexander, Ike's new ground forces' commander, was a sound choice. Born in 1891, the third son of an Ulster earl, he had shown early promise as an artist. But in 1911, after Harrow and Sandhurst, this most unlikely army officer joined the Irish Guards. The outbreak of war revealed his latent martial talents, and by 1915, aged just twenty-three, he was an acting battalion commander. Thrice decorated for gallantry (two DSOs and an MC) and thrice wounded, his only respite from four years at the front was the odd training course and to convalesce.

Unlike many other outstanding combat soldiers, Alexander's career prospered between the wars, with service in the Baltic and on the Northwest Frontier, and a stint at staff college where he impressed many of his fellow (and younger) students. The two exceptions were Bernard Montgomery and Alan Brooke, the latter concluding that Alexander was not a 'big man'. However, in 1937, aged just forty-five, he became the youngest major general in the British Army.

This faith was justified by his skilful handling of the 1st Infantry Division during the BEF's retreat to Dunkirk in May 1940. Promoted to command I Corps, he refused to be evacuated until he was certain no more British troops remained. Back in England, with this experience in mind, he set up battle schools to teach simple drills – 'Down, crawl, observe, fire' – to which soldiers would react automatically in times of stress. He also introduced live firing, to prepare soldiers for the shock of combat, and insisted on minimum levels of fitness.

In early 1942, with the Japanese pouring through Southeast Asia, he was given the unenviable task of commanding the Anglo-Indian Army in Burma. Again, he displayed composure in a tight spot by narrowly evading the encircling enemy and supervising an orderly withdrawal back to India. He was rewarded by Brooke, his former critic, with the Middle East Command in August 1942. Churchill had wanted his CIGS to take the job for himself – predicting a 'wonderful future' for him if he 'succeeded in defeating Rommel' – and Brooke was certainly tempted. But he eventually persuaded the prime minister that Alexander was a 'better selection' and he could 'do more by remaining as CIGS'.

Brooke still had doubts about Alex, and thought he needed an able chief of staff 'to think for him'. On the other hand, Harold Macmillan, the British minister in Cairo, was impressed by Alex's urbane manner and ability to maintain inter-Allied cooperation. It had, moreover, worked out well. The dapper and charming Alexander devised the broader strategy, and left Monty, four years his senior, to fight the battles. 'They made an unlikely couple, Alex and Monty,' wrote James Holland in *Together We Stand*, 'yet their backgrounds, experience, and differing skills complemented one another perfectly.'[14]

In truth, the secret of their close relationship is that Alex managed Monty with a light touch. 'Intellectually [Alex] was unimpressive,' wrote the editors of Brooke's *War Diaries*, 'although whether this stemmed from genuine stupidity or an Edwardian desire not to appear too keen is open to doubt. His amiability and desire to be agreeable to all often gave the impression that he lacked "grip", but may on occasion have made him a suitable candidate for high command over an army which contained numerous and fractious allies. If his personality hindered victory, it prevented disintegration.'[15]

Brooke was convinced that Alex could only be successful if he had talented generals under him. He noted in his diary on 22 February:

Alexander . . . has many fine qualities, but no very great strategic vision. He had been carried by Montgomery through North Africa as regards strategy and tactical handling of the situation. Monty was now far from him, and Anderson certainly had not got the required qualities to inspire Alex. It was very doubtful whether he was fit to command his Army. The only comfort rested in the fact that Dick McCreery was still Alex's Chief of Staff and I had the greatest confidence in his ability.

The issue now was Anderson. Brooke had approved his appointment to First Army partly because he remembered how well Anderson had performed during the retreat to Dunkirk. As he was not 'living up to that reputation' in Tunisia – having made a bad call on the Axis attack coming through the Fondouk Pass, rather than the Faïd Pass to the south, not to mention his tendency to micromanage and lose sight of the bigger picture – Brooke had sent a 'wire to Alex telling him to get rid of [Anderson] if he thinks he is no good'. He secretly doubted that Alex would have 'enough grit' to wield the axe, and he was right.[16]

On taking over 18th Army Group, Alex made it clear to London that the leadership in Tunisia was in disarray. 'I am frankly shocked,' he wrote, 'at the whole situation as I have found it . . . Real fault has been the lack of direction from above from [the] very beginning resulting in no policy and no plan.' His priority was to restructure the forces and set out his strategic objectives. On 20 February, he laid down the following five organisational principles:

1. Separate British, American and French sectors were to be organised forthwith under their respective commanders.
2. The 'bits and pieces' were to be collected and reorganised into their proper formations.
3. The front was to be held by static troops, and armoured and mobile forces withdrawn and grouped to form a reserve striking force.
4. All troops were to be extensively trained and re-equipped where necessary.
5. Immediate plans were to be prepared to regain the intiative, starting with carefully planned minor operations to force the enemy to react. But . . . there must be no failures.

A day later, Alex announced his plan to destroy all enemy forces in Tunisia by advancing the Eighth Army north of Gabès, while the First

Army mounted attacks to draw off reserves. The coordinated land, sea and air power of the Allies would draw the net round the Axis forces in Tunisia by mid–May, to meet the timetable set at the Casablanca Conference to invade Sicily during the favourable weather of July 1943.[17]

33

Operation *Oschenkopf*

North Africa, 26 February–7 March 1943

O N 26 February, while General Alexander was still settling into his new role, Generaloberst von Arnim's Fifth Panzer Army launched Operation *Oschenkopf* (Ox-head). Arnim's initial plan had been to launch a spoiling attack near Medjez el Bab, and Rommel, as the commander of the new Army Group Afrika, gave his blessing to this on the 24th. But that same day, Arnim flew to Rome where Kesselring persuaded him to expand the attack across the Fifth Panzer Army's entire front from the coast to the Bou Arada valley.

The strategic objectives were two-fold: to expand the Axis bridge-head in northern Tunisia westward to a line that would run from Djebel Abiod, via Béja, to Testour and El Aroussa; and to keep the Allies under pressure in the north while Rommel's forces were preparing to assault Montgomery's Eighth Army in the south. The main effort, using the only armoured force available (77 tanks, including 14 Tiger tanks), would be directed at Sidi Nsir with Béja as its final goal.[1]

Though unable to dissuade Kesselring from going ahead, Rommel did refuse his request to hold on to rearguard positions at Kasserine 'for another few days and to co-operate if required with Fifth Army in its advance on Béja' because the 10th Panzer Division's withdrawal had already begun. It was an operation, he felt, that 'should have been started on the day we attacked Thala'.[2] Rommel feared this new operation would fritter away resources better used in his attack on the Eighth Army, planned for early March. His failure to prevent it underlined the limitations of his authority as army group commander when both Kesselring and the Comando Supremo chose to overrule him.

The offensive opened on 26 February with multiple axes of attack from Jefna in the north to Bou Arada farther south, a total distance as the crow flies of more than 70 miles. Major Rudolf Witzig's 11th Parachute Engineer Battalion – which had got as far as Djebel Abiod three months earlier – was part of the main attack in the north as eight battalions attempted to advance from Jefna into the Sedjenane valley. His men, flanked by Italians of the 10th Bersaglieri Regiment to the north, and the paratroopers of the Barentin Regiment to the south, pushed back the British 139th Brigade and two battalions of the Corps Franc d'Afrique to within two miles of the mining hamlet of Sedjenane before they were halted. 'We attacked under the cover of darkness,' remembered Witzig, 'and took the place without losses.'

Follow-up attacks forced the 139th Brigade (and later the 1st Parachute Brigade, which had been moved up from its position south of Bou Arada) to relinquish both Sedjenane and Tamera, and eventually withdraw more than 20 miles to positions close to Djebel Abiod. In just a few days of fighting, the inexperienced 16th Durham Light Infantry was decimated, its colonel sacked and its survivors merged into two composite companies. Lieutenant General Allfrey, commanding V Corps, was appalled. He noted in his diary on 1 March:

The pull out of 139 Brigade last night was very badly done. It appears that they continued firing with 25-pounders until midnight and so gave themselves no chance of pulling out and having to destroy them. In addition [Brigadier] Chichester-Constable refused to allow transport to move east of the main rear position, with the result that the Lincolns left some stuff which they could easily have taken away. A sickening business really, as it is the only bad show in what has otherwise been a good party so far.

A day later, Allfrey sacked Chichester-Constable because his men were 'worried about his decisions', and replaced him with acting Brigadier Bernard 'Swifty' Howlett who had been commanding 36th Brigade since December. This helped to steady the ship.

The Axis troops came within two miles of Djebel Abiod, but no further. In three weeks of fighting in the northern sector, they captured 1,600 Allied prisoners, and took or destroyed 17 guns, 16 tanks, 13 anti-tank guns and 70 vehicles.[3]

The main Axis attack by Oberst Rudolf Lang's battle group (*Kampfgruppe Lang*) – including the Tigers of the 501st Heavy Panzer Battalion, part of the 7th Panzer Regiment and units of panzer grenadiers and armoured reconnaissance troops – was down the Mateur road towards Sidi Nsir, a small agricultural village in the Bou Oissa river valley that was defended by the 5th Hampshires and eight 25-pounders of the 155th Field Battery (part of the 172nd Field Regiment RA). The Hampshires were disposed on the high ground above the railway station, with E and F Troops of the 155th on either side of the Mateur road. Battalion HQ was in the railway station. The main line of defence by the rest of the 128th Infantry Brigade was 12 miles to the southwest, halfway to Béja, in a long defile the British had named 'Hunt's Gap'.

The battle opened at 6.30 a.m. on 26 February with a mortar bombardment on the Hampshires' forward positions. Forty-five minutes later, German tanks drove down the road from Mateur but were driven off by artillery fire. A second German attack was made on the left flank at 11 a.m., and this time repulsed by the guns of E Troop which left four panzers ablaze. Taking fire orders for the troop's No. 4 gun was signaller Frank Read, a 23-year-old Cockney who had worked as an apprentice tailor before the war. After he shouted the elevation and range, the gun would be adjusted, loaded and then fired. 'As the tanks were coming up,' he recalled, 'you could see smoke [from] where some had been hit.'[4]

By 1 p.m., German tanks, self-propelled guns and infantry had worked round both flanks and were within 600 yards of the position. An observation post on the neighbouring Hill 609 had been overrun and, soon after, German planes strafed the British positions, inflicting casualties and setting fire to supply vehicles with reserve ammunition. At 3 p.m., the road to the rear was cut by German infantry, meaning no more reserve 25-pounder shells could be brought forward in carriers. About this time, Corporal George Vaughan of HQ Company came across the 5th Hampshires' commanding officer, Lieutenant Colonel Newnham, and the RSM at the back of the railway station and 'could tell by the expression on their faces that the prospects were not very hopeful'.[5]

Not long after, a column of German tanks came racing down the road towards the heart of 155th Field Battery, while other tanks gave covering fire from hull-down positions. The gunners, firing over open sights, knocked out three panzers and halted the attack. But from stationary positions the tanks were able to take out one gun at a time.

F Troop was overrun first. The Germans then concentrated on E Troop until only one gun, Frank Read's, and one Bren were still firing. The order came: 'Every man for himself and God bless you!' Read smashed his signalling kit. They were about to fire a final round at a Tiger tank 200 yards away, by lifting up the trail and pointing the gun, when there was a sudden 'bang!' and the muzzle 'opened up like a great big tulip'. It had received a direct hit from the Tiger, the explosion wounding many of the crew. Read dragged one casualty to a nearby little slit trench, got into it and pulled the wounded man on top of him. They were both taken prisoner.[6]

Back at the Hampshires' HQ, George Vaughan had heard the firing of the guns die away and knew it was 'only a matter of time'. Soon after, they received the order to break out after dark and make their way back to the main British line at Hunt's Gap. As the light was failing, a single Tiger tank rumbled down to the station. It was, remembered Vaughan, 'an awesome sight, at close quarters, when one is caught in the open'.

The Tiger opened fire on the Signals' wagon, the station buildings and the pillbox in which Vaughan was positioned. It was, he decided, time to go. Exiting the pillbox, he, a sergeant and two privates began crawling down the railway line towards Mateur. Once clear of the fires in the village, they climbed to their feet and headed for high ground to the west. At 3 p.m. the following day, having survived on emergency chocolate rations and water, they reached a tarred roadway where they were picked up by a truck from the battalion's B Echelon and taken back to Battalion HQ at some farm buildings in the new front line.[7]

Led by the commanding officer, Lieutenant Colonel Newnham, ninety men of the 5th Hampshires and a further nine men from the 155th Battery, 'cold, wet, hungry and tired', arrived back at the command post of the 2/4th Hampshires in Hunt's Gap at 8 a.m. on 27 February. They were joined there, over the course of the day, by another hundred or so fugitives, mostly from C and D Companies, bringing the total number of survivors to eight officers and two hundred men.

It had not been in vain. Their gallant defence of Sidi Nsir had, wrote V Corps commander Charles Allfrey in his diary, 'resulted in the enemy being unable to [reach] Hunt's Gap for at least 24 hours after he had anticipated'.

This gave the rest of the 128th Brigade Group time to prepare a 'hot reception' for the Germans at Hunt's Gap where a tank-killing zone was prepared with minefields, anti-tank guns, hull-down Churchill tanks and direct fire areas for medium and heavy artillery. By 3 March, as a result, Lang had only five tanks fit for action and was forced to call off the attack. The plan to capture Béja had failed.

Newnham was awarded the DSO, while a platoon commander and a private got the Military Cross and the Military Medal respectively. Newnham wrote of his men: 'These lads were tougher than anything I have ever served with or hope to serve with. There was no suggestion of a waver; every man stood to his rifle, his Bren, his mortar, until the end . . . The way back was long and arduous, but nobody lost heart and they were soon back in battle helping another Battalion in the Brigade.'

Newnham and the brigade commander, Manley James (himself a VC winner in 1918), recommended balloted awards of the Victoria Cross for members 'of this very gallant Battery'. They were never given – possibly because so many survivors were taken prisoner and not able to support the recommendation – and instead six lesser gallantry medals were awarded: a Military Cross for the battery commander, Major John Raworth; two Distinguished Conduct Medals; and three Military Medals. Of the battery's original complement of 130 men (9 officers and 121 other ranks), only nine escaped to join the rest of the regiment. One of them, Private J. G. Bryce, wrote to his wife:

> We withstood the brunt of a powerful German attack – all on our own, with no support whatever, under continuous dive-bombing, mortar fire and eventually tanks (the last German Mark VI). We knocked out seven of them. Everyone showed perfect calm and coolness, even when the end was in sight. One gun crew were actually singing that song 'Praise the Lord and Pass the Ammunition' when their gun was hit. But we held them all until our guns were knocked out, and we were finally overrun by the enemy.[8]

The southern prong (or 'horn', named after the Zulu tactic of encirclement known as the 'horns of the buffalo') of Arnim's offensive was aimed at Medjez el Bab and Bou Arada, the former guarded by the 11th Infantry Brigade, and the latter by the 38th Infantry Brigade and the 1st Parachute Brigade.[9] It was even less successful than the attacks further north. 'The attack on Medjez itself, south of the river,' wrote General Alexander, 'was repulsed with heavy losses after small initial success. The attack further south penetrated deeply into our lines but was beaten back north of El Aroussa while our defences round Bou Arada, some 10 miles to the west, held firm in spite of being threatened from three sides.'[10]

The main blow south of Bou Arada fell on Pine-Coffin's 3rd Parachute Battalion, with Frost's 2nd Parachute Battalion in action soon after. 'We all knew,' wrote Frost, 'we were as fully prepared as possible, plenty of ammunition had been stocked, the defensive fire-plan had been carefully worked out and neatly fitted in, the positions had been properly dug, revetted and concealed. Moreover, the men were fit, fresh and should know exactly what to do.'[11]

In the event, the 2nd and 3rd Parachute Battalions held all their positions, inflicted 400 casualties and took 200 prisoners, at a cost of 18 killed and 54 wounded. Though the 38th Brigade to the north had given ground, it counter-attacked on 28 February and was able to restore its original positions.[12]

Yet the ill-timed withdrawal of four French battalions from high ground overlooking the Béja–Medjez road, to rejoin the main body of French troops further south, left the town of Medjez itself 'in a dangerous salient' – an exposed bulge in the line – 'and completely overlooked'. Assuming its fall was 'almost inevitable', Anderson advised a withdrawal from Medjez into the mountains to the west where the Allies would be 'in a stronger defensive position' and able to economise their troops. But Alexander was having none of it. Determined to retain the 'gateway into the Tunis plain' for future operations, he ordered the town to be held 'at all costs'.[13]

Overall, Arnim's offensive had failed to achieve its main objective: possession of a new front line that ran from Djebel Abiod in the north, via Béja, to El Aroussa in the south. Worse than that, it had cost Arnim the bulk of his armour, a frittering away of a precious resource that Rommel found hard to forgive. The offensive, he wrote,

could never, at the best, have achieved any major success, and the losses suffered by our forces were of greater moment than those we were able to inflict on the enemy . . . It made me particularly angry to see how the few Tigers we had in Africa, which had been denied our offensive in the south, were thrown in to attack through a marshy valley, where the principal advantage – the long range of their heavy guns – was completely ineffective . . . I very soon gave orders to Fifth Army to put a stop to the fruitless affair at the earliest possible moment.[14]

On 3 March, with Operation *Oschenkopf* running out of steam, Ike wrote to General Marshall about the commander of II Corps. 'As you know,' he explained, 'I have had my moments of doubt about Fredendall and I have spent much time in travelling just to assure myself that he was doing his job successfully.' He continued:

> Alexander likes him, and by every yardstick that can be produced for measuring an officer, he is tops – except for one thing. He has difficulty in picking good men and, even worse, in getting the best out of his subordinates; in other words, in handling personnel. He is too good to lose; but his assignment is critical at this moment because Alexander is depending on the II Corps as an *independent* American organization, to conduct a speedy attack.

Ike had discovered, he added, that 'a man must take the tools he has and do the best he can with them', which left him two options: find a 'good substitute' for Fredendall or 'place in his command a number of assistants who are so stable and sound they will not be disturbed by his idiosyncrasies'.

In reality, Fredendall was not 'tops' by many other yardsticks – and Ike knew it. For some days he been canvassing opinon about Fredendall and most of it was negative. On 28 February, for example, he had asked Major General Ernest Harmon – back from his stint as temporary commander of II Corps – his opinion of the American generals at the front. Ward was all right, said Harmon, but Fredenhall had to go.[15] Ike next spoke to Truscott and Bedell Smith, who said much the same thing.

Still Ike hesitated. What started to tip the balance for him, even before he dispatched the letter to Marshall, was the receipt of a message from Alexander's chief of staff, Dick McCreery, expressing concern at 'Fredendall's apparent inability to plan the next operation'. II Corps' commander seemed incapable of developing a team, wrote Ike, 'and in this war the team must be developed before any of these large organizations will work'. To 'settle the matter once and for all', Ike flew to the front on 4 March.[16]

Asked to meet Ike at Youks-les-Bains airfield, near Tébessa, Fredendall drove down from Le Kouif in his French Buick. He assumed the meeting was 'pure routine', and that Ike would want to discuss the forthcoming operation to retake Gafsa and Maknassy that was due to begin on 10 March. Ike told him instead that, as the 'coming operation would be primarily an armored show', he was replacing him with Patton, a tank man.[17] It emerged later that Ike had already offered II Corps to Ernest Harmon, another armoured specialist, who had refused it because, he said, it would be unethical to step in after recommending Fredendall's relief.[18]

To sugar the pill for Fredendall, Ike told him that he was not being blamed for the initial defeats in the Kasserine battle. But morale in II Corps had been 'shaken', nonetheless, and the troops needed to be 'picked up quickly', a job for which Patton was uniquely qualified. Fredendall, meanwhile, would return to a training job in the United States with the rank of lieutenant general. Marshall had personally requested his recall, and it was Ike's hope, he said, that he would eventually be given the command of an army.[19]

Later on the afternoon of 4 March, George S. Patton Jr returned from a 'nice ride' on a horse loaned by General Noguès, the French Resident General of Morocco, to find a message from Ike. He was to be ready to leave Rabat the following day 'for extended field service, and to pack tonight'.

Excited, but unsure exactly what this meant, he phoned Bedell Smith for clarification. 'You may be about to relieve Fredendall,' said Ike's chief of staff.[20]

It was the news he had been waiting for. He had been bitterly disappointed not to be given field command in December, telling Harry Butcher on a visit to Algiers a few weeks earlier that he was the 'logical man to chase Rommel' and, if circumstances allowed, to shoot him dead. Now, it seemed, he would have that opportunity.[21]

'Well,' he noted in his diary, 'it is taking over rather a mess but I will make a go of it. I think I will have more trouble with the British than with the Boches. "God favours the brave, victory is to the audacious."'

To his wife Beatrice, he wrote: 'I think I am to replace Lloyd [Fredendall] but don't know and anyhow it may not happen . . . Of course I don't expect to be killed but one can never tell. If I am, I will take lots with me.'

Was Patton surprised by the news? Probably not. Two days earlier, Ernest Harmon had visited Rabat on his way back from the front to tell Patton that his son-in-law John Waters was missing. But it was his damning assessment of Fredendall that hinted at a change. The commander of II Corps was, in Harmon's opinion, 'a physical and moral coward' – about the harshest criticism you can make of a soldier – who 'never went to the front at all and tried to make Harmon the goat'. It backfired because Harmon then 'won the battle'.[22]

On 5 March, Patton met Ike at Maison Blanche airfield near Algiers, the two having flown in from opposite directions. It was, remembered onlooker Harry Butcher, an informal thirty-minute chat as the two generals and their respective Chiefs of Staff – Brigadier Generals Walter Bedell Smith and Hugh J. Gaffey – stood together in a huddle on the tarmac.

'George,' said Ike, 'you're going to replace Lloyd as commander of II Corps because the fighting in Tunisia is primarily a tank show and you know more about tanks. But it's also true that Lloyd's relations with the British were less than harmonious, and that has to stop. It's vital that we create a feeling of partnership. II Corps will take orders as an American unit direct from the 18th Army Group, commanded by General Alexander. You are to respond to General Alexander's orders exactly as if they were issued by me. I want no mistake about my thorough belief in unity of command.'

'I understand, sir.'

'Good,' said Ike, before scribbling a note in pencil and handing it to Patton. 'This is your authority to assume command of II Corps as soon as you arrive. Fredendall has been notified of his impending release.'

Patton's first and most important task, said Ike, was to help the British Eighth Army 'get through the Mareth Line' by retaking Gafsa and tying up as much German strength as possible. He was, moreover, to 'rehabilitate, re-equip and train his troops to take advantage of lessons so far learned' in the recent humiliations. If he needed any help, Major General Omar N. Bradley – whom Ike had appointed as his 'eyes and ears' across the whole front – was available for 'any duty you may desire'.

As for weapons, Patton was to ignore reports that the 37mm anti-tank gun was worse than useless. The latest tests with new armour-piercing ammunition had shown that it could penetrate a German Mark IV tank at a range of 800 yards, 'except for a very small band around the middle'. At close range it was deadly.

Ike continued: 'You must not be personally reckless, George. I need a corps commander, not a casualty. I understand that you must visit all your troops, and the positions they occupy, but you should never forget that, in an actual battle, a commander can best direct his outfit from a command post where he can be in touch with all of his staff and subordinates.'

Patton nodded, but, as Ike must have feared, this was one piece of advice he would repeatedly ignore.

'One more thing, George. You are to be cold-blooded about the removal of inefficient officers. If a man fails, send him to me and I will deal with him. We cannot afford to throw away soldiers and equipment out of a reluctance to hurt the feelings of old friends. Success for the rest of the Tunisian campaign will, I am certain, have a far-reaching effect on the progress of the war.'

Naturally, Ike did most of the talking. Patton's main contribution, according to Butcher, was to curse the Germans three times 'so violently and emotionally that tears came to his eyes'. He 'normally hates the Hun', noted Butcher, 'as Ike says, like the devil hates holy water', but now was 'all the more embittered because his son-in-law, Johnnie Waters, is reported missing in action' and probably dead.[23]

An emotional Patton flew on to Constantine to meet Alexander who, he thought, 'seems competent'. He later told Beatrice that the army group commander was 'very quiet and good looking' and had impressed him 'a lot'. Alexander, in turn, told Patton that he 'wanted the best corps commander he could get and had been informed that I was the man'. Patton was to command a separate and wholly independent sector, under Alexander's 18th Army Group, 'much like Pershing under Foch'.

Patton stayed the night in Constantine, and continued on to II Corps headquarters at Le Kouif the following morning. It might have been an awkward encounter, but Fredendall, still breakfasting at 10 a.m., was 'very nice and conducted himself well – very well'.

Patton wrote to his wife: 'Fredendall is a great sport and, I feel sure, is a victim largely due to circumstances beyond his control. He says he is sure John [Waters] is alive, a prisoner, and Omar Bradley who is here feels the same. So I am much more encouraged.'

Less to his liking was the relaxed atmosphere at Corps HQ. He thought the staff in general were 'poor', as was their discipline and standard of dress. Henceforth, insisted Patton, officers and soldiers would salute their superiors and wear helmets, ties and leggings at all times. 'It is absurd to believe,' he noted in his diary, 'that soldiers who cannot be made to wear the proper uniform can be induced to move forward in battle.'[24]

The new regime was not well received. 'A tie had become a vague memory to us,' wrote Fredendall's aide Captain James R. Webb, 'and helmets were cumbersome things that you wore only when something nasty and solid was flying around.'

Fredendall and his inner circle left for Algiers by car at 3.30 a.m. on 7 March, having distributed the former commanding general's stock of alcohol to 'soften the blow' for staff members left behind. Fredendall had refused to fly and the early start was because, noted Patton, it was 'the safest time on the road'. Patton concluded: 'Fredendall is either a little nuts or badly scared.'[25]

34

Medenine

Southern Tunisia, Italy and Ukraine, 5–10 March 1943

'IF ONLY WE COULD win a major victory here,' wrote Rommel to his wife Lucie from southern Tunisia on 26 February. 'I rack my brains night and day to find a way. Unfortunately, the conditions for it don't exist. Everything depends on supplies – and has done for years.'

All his hopes now rested on one last throw of the dice: Operation Capri, scheduled for 4 March. The intention was to launch a surprise attack by three panzer divisions – the 10th, 15th and 21st – on Montgomery's Eighth Army before it had time to concentrate properly in front of the Mareth Line. His plan, authorised by the Comando Supremo on 23 February, was to assault the Eighth Army's assembly area near Medenine, a town 20 miles southeast of the Mareth. It was, he knew, a particularly difficult operation. If successful it would gain time by postponing Montgomery's attack on the Mareth Line; but it if failed 'the end of the army in Africa would be close'.

He hoped to strike before Montgomery was ready, using tactics suggested by Generale d'Armata Messe: one panzer division, the 15th, would advance down the Mareth–Medenine road; another, the 21st, would cross the mountains and attack the Eighth Army from the west; and the third, the 10th, would appear from behind Djebel Tebaga and try to outflank the Medenine position, though Rommel conceded that the ground here was 'too open for tanks to attempt a breakthrough'. Most full-strength panzer divisions at this stage of the war had at least 145 tanks in a single panzer regiment, two regiments of panzer grenadiers and supporting units of engineers and artillery. At the start of Operation Barbarossa – the invasion of the Soviet Union – the 10th Panzer Division had deployed 182 tanks. For Operation Capri, Rommel's three panzer divisions numbered 160 tanks in total.

Several members of Rommel's staff suggested postponing the attack until the next full moon. He refused because he knew that, by then, Montgomery's preparations 'would be certain to be complete'. He did, however, authorise a two-day delay to give the panzer divisions enough time to get into position. On 5 March, Rommel moved up to his forward HQ on Hill 715 at the southern end of the Mareth Line, and 20 miles inland, to brief his senior commanders. From the hill, with its remarkable views 'ranging far beyond Medenine', he would observe the battle.[1]

The commanders included Generalmajor von Broich and his operations chief, Oberstleutnant Claus von Stauffenberg, whose 10th Panzer Division had had to travel the furthest to be in position. Stauffenberg had done a brilliant job organising the hazardous march, along narrow roads 'full of curves and inclines'. So slow was their progress that they had had to 'move in daylight, exposed to aerial observation'. The gorges and high cliffs had protected them from fighter-bomber attacks, but not from accidents. On 5 March, the division was in position at Ksar el Hallouf, close to Djebel Tebaga, waiting for the order to advance.

Broich and Stauffenberg knew the situation was hopeless for Axis forces in Tunisia. They were receiving very few reinforcements and supplies, while the enemy grew stronger by the day. Their suggestion for Operation Capri was to concentrate all 160 tanks of the three panzer divisions against the left flank and rear of the Eighth Army. But Rommel preferred Messe's three-pronged attack along the length of the British position. It was, Stauffenberg felt, a senseless plan. Yet he had to go along with it by issuing an order for the 10th Panzer

Division to attack 'the enemy forces between Medenine and the Mareth position, and annihilate them'.[2]

Monty admitted after the battle that had Rommel attacked four or five days earlier he would have had a 'great chance as I was rather weak in the forward area and might have been in difficulties'.[3] Responding to Alexander's 'cry for help', at Kasserine, he had pushed two divisions – the 51st Highland and 7th Armoured – to within a few miles of the Mareth position by 25 February. But this had left him dangerously unbalanced and with a tank strength of just 120. To rectify this, he rushed forward tanks, artillery, anti-tank guns and the 2nd New Zealand Division, but most would not arrive until 4 March. 'I must admit,' he told his friend Brigadier Frank Simpson, 'that for about 3 days I was on a very sticky wicket. But I had to go on and help Alex.'

He knew from Ultra intercepts that an attack was imminent. By 5 March, however, his fears were over. He had in position three veteran divisions, 360 field and medium guns, 467 anti-tank guns (many of them excellent 6-pounders) and nearly 400 tanks. 'I am in fact,' he told Simpson, 'sitting "very pretty", and Rommel can go to hell. If he attacks me tomorrow (as he looks like doing) he will get an extremely bloody nose; in fact it is exactly what I would like him to do. The situation has great possibilities and I may possibly be able to write off a good bit of Rommel's army.'[4]

Monty's confidence was justified. The ensuing battle was, wrote Lieutenant Colonel David Belchem, commanding the 1st Royal Tank Regiment, 'an excellent example of Montgomery's command system, and a technical triumph of artillery command, deployment, flexibility and discipline, in the desert conditions of the 1940s'.

Belchem was in a perfect position to know. From December 1941 until he was sent back to Cairo with suspected appendicitis a year later, he had served as Monty's operations chief (GSO1). A brilliant staff officer, fluent in three languages (French, Russian and Italian), he had helped to plan all of Monty's major victories. The only reason he did not return to Eighth Army HQ on recovering from illness in January 1943 was because Monty wanted all staff officers to do a stint with a fighting unit before taking up a new appointment. Belchem was sent first to 2nd Armoured Brigade HQ, and then given command of the 1st Royal Tank Regiment (RTR), part of the 7th Armoured Division's 22nd Brigade, which he joined on the outskirts of Tripoli.

As a former tank officer, Belchem settled in quickly. He had fifty-two tanks under his command: a squadron each of Shermans, Grants and Crusaders. The other vehicles included ten two-man armoured reconnaissance 'Dingos' and 100 trucks and lorries to ferry ammunition, fuel and rations. At night they would close up into a box formation – or 'leaguer' – and were often supported by a company of motorised infantry and a battery of Royal Horse Artillery.

At or just before dawn, the regiment would disperse to avoid air attack. At first light, the crews boiled water ('brewed up') for tea and made porridge from army biscuits. When in action, their only food by day were biscuits and a minute piece of cheese. But there was always a nightly rum ration and, if possible, hot stew brought forward in water containers. This, wrote Belchem, usually 'did the trick'.

At Medenine, Belchem's regiment was in the centre of the British line. To the north, holding a front of 20,000 yards on the line of the Wadi Zessar, an anti-tank obstacle that had been sown with mines, was the 51st Highland Division. Next came the 7th Armoured Division, with the 131st and 201st (Guards) Brigades holding a frontage of 13,000 yards that included the Tadjera hills, and supported by the 22nd Armoured Brigade (including Belchem's 1st RTR). Further south, protecting a front of 14,000 yards, was the 2nd New Zealand Division, with a single brigade forward and one in reserve around Medenine, but also ready to extend its front along the open southern flank. The armour was all in reserve, waiting to pounce.

Monty's plan at Medenine – perfected from previous engagements – was for the anti-tank guns to hold their fire until the panzers came within optimum killing range which, in some cases, was as little as 300 yards. When the anti-tank guns did come into action, the artillery would also open up on the assault infantry which followed the armour.[5]

The attack began at dawn on 6 March. 'The sky was cloudy,' wrote Rommel, 'and the whole battle ground was shrouded in mist. Like a hammer blow the artillery opened fire on the stroke of six. *Nebelwerfer* bombs lobbed through the layers of mist into the valley below. The 10th Panzer Division had meanwhile moved up through Hallouf without interference from the enemy.'[6]

In fact, it had proved impossible to remove all the mines the British had sown at the exit to the Hallouf valley and this prevented the 7th Panzer Regiment from storming out at full speed. The panzers had to wait while the mines were detonated and, even then, were forced to proceed in single file along narrow channels so that the British guns could concentrate on each panzer in turn. Even so, the tank attack continued, as it did in the two sectors to the north.[7]

At 6.40 a.m., the 131st Brigade reported 'the characteristic thump and squeak' of armoured vehicles out to the west. The mist was beginning to clear, but visibility was still difficult because of sand churned up by tank tracks and gunfire. At 7.20 a.m. the first tanks came into view. 'Progressively,' wrote David Belchem, 'the enemy closed on 131 Brigade, 201 Guards Brigade and the New Zealand Division; in each sector there were battle-groups of tanks, with Panzer Grenadier infantry (debussed at a prudent distance from armoured half-tracks) following behind the tanks. 15 Panzer Division attacked 131 Brigade, 21 Panzer Division was directed on the Tadjeras, and 10 Panzer Division assaulted the New Zealand Front.'

The leading wave comprised 80 tanks and three battalions of panzer grenadiers. By 9.30 a.m., reserve battle groups had been committed in all three sectors. By around 9.45 a.m., the Germans had lost – set on fire or immobilised – 28 of the 115 tanks committed. A single anti-tank 6-pounder in the 131st Brigade had destroyed 5 enemy tanks in the first hour of battle, and the 73rd Anti-Tank Regiment had accounted for at least 4 on the New Zealand front.

Once the assault infantry had disembarked from their armoured vehicles, they were engaged by Allied artillery fire, 'pinned down, dispersed, and suffered very heavy casualties'. In no section were they able 'to get to grips' with the Allied infantry in their well-concealed Forward Defended Localities (or FDLs). Opposite the New Zealand Division, the panzer grenadiers of the 10th Panzer Division withdrew nearly three miles before digging in.

Fresh assaults, supported by Stuka dive-bombers, continued throughout the day, but none breached the Allied front line. The 2.30 p.m. assault, supported by infantry from the German 164th Light Division and the Italian 136th Giovani Fascisti 'Young Fascists' Armoured Division, saw the tanks of the 15th and 21st Panzer Divisions (by this time at half strength) advance in the 'face of withering defensive fire'. It was now that a squadron of Belchem's tanks were ordered forward to 'give close support' to the 131st Brigade. 'Some eleven German tanks had launched a thrust against 1/7 Queen's Royal Regiment,' he recalled. 'Eventually seven enemy tanks were knocked out, but a more anxious moment occurred on the front of the 1/6 Queen's RR when eight German tanks found a run-in to our positions. Fortunately, we came upon them at the right moment, and they were destroyed.'

During one of the 'pauses' in the main battle, two German armoured reconnaissance battalions attempted to get around Monty's open southern flank, but were repulsed by Free French forces under Général de brigade Philippe Leclerc.[8]

Broich and Stauffenberg did everything they could to break the deadlock. At one point, the commander of the 10th Panzer Division went forward in an armoured car and found three of his Mark IVs and a battalion of panzer grenadiers pinned down in a wadi. He reformed them for a fresh assault. Meanwhile, Stauffenberg was issuing orders at the divisional command post 'with exemplary composure'.[9]

The 10th Panzer Division's final attack in late afternoon got as far as the Metameur hills. It was now that Rommel, who had come forward to see for himself, issued orders 'to discontinue the action, hold the captured territory and recover damaged vehicles'. His initial intention was to continue the battle the following day. But after consulting with Generalleutnant Hans Cramer, commanding the Afrika Korps, he decided to cut his losses and 'break off the operation altogether'.[10]

The 10th's successful retreat along narrow mountain roads owed much to the organisational brilliance of Stauffenberg and the leadership of Broich – both of whom waited at the entrance to the Hallouf valley until all the men were clear – and the failure of the British to pursue.[11]

Acknowledging that the attack had got 'bogged down in the break-in stage' and 'never had a chance of becoming fluid', Rommel gave due credit to Monty. 'The British commander,' he wrote, 'had grouped his forces extremely well and had completed his preparations with remarkable speed. In fact, the attack had been launched about a week too late. The operation had lost all point the moment it became obvious that the British were prepared for us. We had suffered tremendous losses, including 40 tanks totally destroyed.'

The 'cruellest blow', however, was the knowledge that he had failed to 'interfere with Montgomery's preparations' to overcome the Mareth Line. For the Army Group to remain any longer in Africa was, in his view, 'plain suicide'.[12]

Monty, needless to say, was elated. On 7 March, he crowed to Alex:

Rommel absolutely bought it yesterday. He lost over 30 tanks knocked out,* many more hit and damaged, and had heavy casualties in his infantry. His troops were much shaken by my concentrated artillery fire. My tank losses are nil and my casualties in personnel are negligible.

---

* He later upgraded this number to 52 destroyed: 45 by 6-pounder anti-tank guns and 7 by Belchem's squadron of Shermans.

Only effect of his attack has been to increase the confidence of my troops in their ability to be able to stand no nonsense from Rommel at any time and they see that Rommel can never regain the initiative from Eighth Army. All signs point to fact that enemy has had enough and is pulling out.[13]

Rommel *was* pulling out, and not just from Medenine. At the end of February, he had asked his two army commanders, Arnim and Messe, to write an assessment of Axis prospects in Tunisia. He summarised their reports – both of which emphasised the untenability of the positions the army group was having to hold – by noting that the front was 400 miles long, with two centres of gravity: one west and southwest of Tunis, and the other on the Mareth Line. The other 350 miles were 'only very lightly held and, in some places, owing to our lack of troops, not held at all'. Yet the two armies would soon have to face attacks by a combined Allied force of at least 1,600 tanks, 1,100 anti-tank guns, 850 artillery pieces and 210,000 fighting troops. If the Allies attacked simultaneously, the Axis forces – which only had a fraction of this firepower – would be quickly overwhelmed.

Rommel's advice, therefore, was to shorten the front to just 100 miles by confining the bridgehead to northern Tunisia from a line running from Djebel Mansour across the mountains to Enfidaville near the coast. Ideally its western extremity would include Bou Arada and Medjez el Bab, which would have to be wrested from the enemy. Lastly, monthly shipments would need to increase to 140,000 tons: in January and February, by contrast, they had received supplies of 46,000 and 53,000 tons respectively (though these figures, including 100 tanks, 3,300 vehicles and 320 guns in total, were well up on previous months).

Hitler's delayed response to his proposal arrived the day after the battle. It came via Kesselring who noted that the Führer was 'unable to agree' with his judgement of the situation. Attached to the message was a statement comparing the forces on either side, 'irrespective of their state of motorisation, equipment or strength of personnel'. The intention was to prove that the Axis forces in Tunisia 'were nowhere near as inferior in strength' as Rommel was claiming. This massaging of the figures infuriated the Desert Fox, and as he made his way back to Beni Zelten on 7 March he knew what he had to do: fly once again to the Führer's HQ to speak to Hitler in person and 'rouse a true understanding in the highest quarters of the practical operational problems of Tunisia'. He hoped, at the very least, 'to see to it that the troops were saved'.[14]

Before departing, Rommel spoke to Major von Luck whose 3rd Reconnaissance Battalion had missed Medenine because it was down to its last few armoured cars. 'Rommel sat in his "Mammoth"* as always, with his campaign maps before him,' wrote Luck. 'I hadn't seen him for some weeks and was shocked at how unwell he looked. He was visibly weak, suffering from tropical disease, and completely worn out. Still, he had that unique sparkle in his eyes.'

Luck had heard that Rommel was about to leave Africa and wanted to say goodbye, on behalf of all his men, 'till we meet again, some-time, somewhere'. He added: 'We'll hold out here for as long as we can, always after the example you have given us.'

With tears in his eyes, Rommel went to a cupboard and came back with a large photo of himself in better times. He signed and dedicated it, before handing it over. 'Here, Luck,' he said, 'take this in gratitude and appreciation of your brave battalion. Keep well; I hope we shall see each other again at home. God be with you.'

He turned around, and Luck departed, 'deeply moved'.[15]

On 9 March, leaving Generaloberst von Arnim in temporary command of Army Group Afrika, Rommel flew to Rome to report to Ambrosio at the Comando Supremo. He got the impression from

---

* The 'Mammoth' was one of three 20ft British armoured command vehicles, with room for eight people, that Rommel had captured from the Western Desert Force in April 1941. He used two of them as his own mobile command post until he left Africa in March 1943.

Ambrosio that the Italians were not expecting him to return to Africa as Hitler would order him to take sick leave. 'This was far from being my idea,' he wrote, 'for I hoped to get my plans accepted and then to continue for some little time yet while in command of the Army Group.'

He then spent twenty-five minutes with Mussolini, explaining the situation in Tunisia and what he hoped to do next. Like Hitler, the Duce seemed incapable of confronting reality and spent the whole time 'searching for arguments to justify his views'. His main anxiety was the inevitable shock to public opinion in Italy 'if Tunis were to fall'. He offered to send another Italian division to Tunisia, but Rommel declined, saying he would prefer to re-equip those already there. Their discussion, for the most part, was cordial, though it got 'more acrimonious towards the end'.

Rommel learned later from his publicity chief, Leutnant Berndt, that Mussolini had planned that day to award him the *Medaglia d'Oro al Valor Militare* (Gold Medal for Military Valour), but changed his mind because of the German's 'defeatist' attitude.

Next day, Rommel flew on to Vinnitsa in Ukraine where Hitler had his southern 'Werewolf' HQ.[16] It was a depressing, cramped location in damp huts that were chilly in winter and stiflingly hot in summer. 'The countryside is fairly awful,' noted Goebbels in his diary. 'Everywhere there is poverty and neglect. The clothes and especially the shoes in which the natives present themselves are indescribable.'[17]

Hitler had arrived there, at Generalfeldmarschall von Manstein's request, on 19 February to observe Army Group South's latest counter-offensive. It was worth the trip as Manstein's forces — notably the 1st and 4th Panzer Armies and the SS Panzer Corps — recaptured Kharkhov and Belgorod, and eventually drove the Soviets back as far as the River Donets. When Hitler returned to Rastenburg in East Prussia on 13 March — flying via Army Group Centre's HQ at Smolensk where Oberst Henning von Tresckow, a co-conspirator of Stauffenberg's, placed a bomb on his plane that failed to detonate — he did so, according to Walter Warlimont, 'with the air of a victorious warlord, clearly considering himself and *his* leadership primarily responsible for the favourable turn of events in the East which had temporarily ended the withdrawal after Stalingrad'.

Manstein's success might also explain Hitler's bullishness when he heard of Rommel's defeat at Medenine. 'Tunis', he announced, 'is a strategic position of the first order. It is of decisive importance for the outcome of the war and all available resources must be used to hold it.'[18] With this 'refusal to contemplate any withdrawal', wrote Hitler's biographer Ian Kershaw, 'military disaster beckoned'.[19]

Hours after his arrival at Vinnitsa, Rommel was granted a private audience with Hitler. It did not go well. 'He seemed very upset and depressed about the Stalingrad disaster,' recalled Rommel. 'He said that one is always liable to look on the black side of things after a defeat, a tendency which can lead one into dangerous and false conclusions.'

Undeterred, Rommel insisted that the Axis position in North Africa was hopeless. He added: 'The "African" troops, mein Führer, must be evacuated to Italy and re-equipped so that they can defend our southern European flank. I give you my guarantee that, with these troops, I will be able to beat off any Allied invasion in southern Europe.'

Hitler was unconvinced. He considered Rommel to be far too pessimistic, and discounted his arguments as a result. 'You are to take some sick leave and get yourself put right,' said the Führer, 'so that you can take command again later for operations against Casablanca.'

It seemed astonishing to Rommel that Hitler, in his delusion, still considered the possibility of conquering North Africa as far as Morocco. 'It never occurred to him,' wrote Rommel, 'that things could go wrong in Tunisia. Nor would he hear of the front being shortened, for then it would be impossible to take the offensive again.'

Hitler also refused Rommel's request to remain in command of Army Group Afrika until it was clear if the Americans 'really were going to take the offensive' or not. His one concession was to allow

Rommel to begin moving the infantry from the Mareth Line to the Gabès Gap where a new defensive position was being constructed.[20]

After their talk, to sweeten the pill, Hitler pinned on Rommel the Knight's Cross with Oakleaves, Swords and Diamonds, the Third Reich's highest gallantry award and only given to twenty-seven people (including fighter ace Werner Mölders and Albert Kesselring).[21] It was little consolation to Rommel as he flew back to Wiener-Neustadt in Austria for his enforced convalescence. 'All my efforts to save my men and then get them back to the Continent,' he wrote, 'had been fruitless.'[22]

35

'We beat the living hell out of them'

Southern Tunisia, 15–29 March 1943

'G ENTLEMEN,' GEORGE S. PATTON JR told his staff on 15 March, 'tomorrow we attack. If we are not victorious, let no one come back alive.'[1]

The task given to Patton's II Corps by General Alexander, the Allied ground forces commander, was to attack the Axis flank to draw off reserves that might otherwise be used by Arnim to check the Eighth Army's assault on the Mareth Line, Operation Pugilist, scheduled for 20 March. Patton was, therefore, to 'exert pressure on the right rear of the enemy defending the Mareth positions, and to be ready to open an alternative line of supply for Eighth Army after they had broken through the Gabès Gap'.

Patton would do this by attacking Gafsa with the US 1st Armored and 1st Infantry Divisions 'on or about 15 March' (in the event, bad weather forced a postponement until the 16th). Once he had secured Gafsa and built up a dump of petrol for the Eighth Army, he was to move on two axes: southeast down the Gabès road to the El Guettar defile, but no further; and northeast towards the Maknassy Pass 'in order to draw the enemy's attention and provoke counter-attack'. Alexander's directive that II Corps was not to advance beyond the Eastern Dorsal was a clear indication that Montgomery's Eighth Army offensive took precedence.[2]

Writing to his wife Beatrice on 15 March, Patton noted that 'Alexander is o.k., though naturally selfish for his side as I would be in his place'. His positive first impression of Alexander had been confirmed when the latter visited his headquarters on 9 March to discuss the battles to come. 'I was very much taken with Alexander,' he wrote in his diary. 'He is a snob in the best sense of the word – very alert and interested in all sorts of things including genealogy . . . He seemed to agree with most of my [military] ideas. I really think he is a good soldier and much more talkative than he is supposed to be.'

Patton's main concern, before his men went into battle, was to improve morale. He went about this by visiting all four divisions, delivering pep talks and ruthlessly enforcing discipline. If any officer was improperly dressed, he was fined $25; men too. 'Discipline consists in obeying orders,' he wrote in his diary. 'If men do not obey orders in small things, they are incapable of being led in battle. I *will* have discipline – to do otherwise is to commit murder . . . I cannot see what Fredendall did to justify his existence. Have never seen so little order or discipline.'

Out at all hours in the cold and rain, plastered with mud that was 'blue clay so that it sticks like cement and won't brush off', Patton appreciated what the men were going through. They are, he told Beatrice, 'taking an awful beating from the weather' and 'if we can get out of these mountains onto the coastal plain it will be warmer.'[3]

To prepare the men for battle, he issued a typically forthright call to arms. Their task, he wrote, was to 'utterly defeat the enemy'. He added: 'We must be eager to kill, to inflict on the enemy – the hated enemy – wounds, death and destruction. If we die killing, well and good, but if we fight hard enough, viciously enough, we will kill and live. Live to return to our family and our girl as conquering heroes – men of Mars.'

Meeting the men face to face, Patton mixed bloodcurdling statements with profanities. This was too much for Major General Omar Bradley, Ike's 'eyes and ears' and a product of a devout Christian and strict teetotal Midwest upbringing, whom Patton had appointed as deputy commander of II Corps (and likely successor when Patton returned to II Armored Corps to prepare for the Sicily landings). 'Whenever he addressed the men,' Bradley wrote later, 'he lapsed into violent, obscene language. He always talked down to his troops . . . Yet when Patton was hosting at the dinner table, his conversation was erudite, and he was well-read, intellectual and cultured. Patton was two persons: a Jekyll and Hyde.'

Even senior officers were not immune to Patton's tirades and humiliations. Visiting the command post of the 1st Infantry Division, Patton demanded to know why so many slit trenches had been dug.

'For protection against air attack,' replied Major General Terry Allen, an old friend of Patton's from their time as instructors at the Cavalry School.

'Which one is yours?'

When Allen pointed it out, Patton walked over, undid his fly and urinated into it. 'There, now try to use it.'

If Patton's methods were extreme, they seemed to have the desired effect. 'The old soldiers,' wrote Paul Robinett, 'who knew him as *Gorgeous Georgie* or *Flash Gordon*, rejoiced at his coming, even though they feared his rashness. They knew he would demand much, but that there would be a pat on the back for every kick in the pants and that their interests would be his interests.' Patton's success as a commander was, in Robinett's opinion, thanks to his 'unrelenting application' of US Civil War General William T. Sherman's principle: 'No man can properly command an army from the rear, he must be at the front . . . [He] must be seen there, and the effect of his mind and personal energy must be felt by every officer and man present with it.'[4]

When he finally learned, many weeks later, that Rommel had returned home to recuperate, and that their long hoped-for showdown – 'Let me meet Rommel in a tank,' he had told Bradley, 'and I'll shoot it out with the son-of-a-bitch' – would not now take place, Patton was consoled by the news that he had been promoted to lieutenant general. 'When I was a little boy at home,' he wrote in his diary on 12 March,

'I used to wear a wooden sword and say to myself, "George S. Patton, Jr, Lieutenant General." At that time I did not know that there were full generals. Now I want, and will get, four stars.'[5]

The evening before the Gafsa operation, Patton invited British war reporter John D'Arcy-Dawson for dinner in his mess. During a hearty meal of Viennese steak and tinned apricots, Patton was cautious about II Corps' prospects, but thought 'the enemy would go back to Maknassy and beyond El Guettar'. He had, wrote D'Arcy-Dawson, a 'charming manner, talked freely, and had unbounded confidence in his troops'. When the meal was over, he gave everyone present a packet of cigarettes and some 'lifesavers – glucose sweets with a hole through the centre'.[6]

Early on 17 March, Gafsa was recaptured without a fight by two battalions of the US 18th Infantry. On marching in, the GIs gasped in surprise as it was clear, from the defences, that the place could have withstood many days of assault. 'A fortified series of bare conical hills four hundred feet or so high,' noted Second Lieutenant Frank Johnson, 'and a ring of three or four rows of barbed wire converging on coordinated machine gun emplacements of concrete, rise sheer from the flat desert. Emplacements for a score of big guns, stores of ammo, food, and water, and elaborate communications.'

Nestling at the base of this 'citadel' was the town and oasis of Gafsa. It had been abandoned by the enemy because, Johnson was told, the Italians had overestimated the strength of the approaching Allied troops and departed as soon as they began to feel their 'pincer grip'. Johnson and the rest of the 18th's Anti-tank Company were ordered to site their guns on a highway to the northeast, towards El Guettar and Maknassy.[7]

Ignoring the advice of Ike and Alex to stay back, Patton had followed close behind the infantry until his scout car, proudly if unwisely displaying the three stars of a lieutenant general and the II Corps' flag, was held up by a minefield. 'We took a famous town and had practically no casualties,' he told Beatrice. 'It was a very well run show . . . The Dagoes beat it and I fear we got few prisoners, but the air and artillery killed a lot of them.'[8]

With the town secured, D'Arcy-Dawson and some other British correspondents set up shop in a deserted villa in the main square. 'In a little paved courtyard protected from the sun by a grapevine trained on wires overhead,' he wrote, 'we put out a table and brought out our typewriters. Masses of bougainvillea hung from the walls, while in the small garden tall, swaying palmtrees with young clusters of golden dates completed a charming vista.'[9]

The 'victory' at Gafsa received wide media coverage in the United States, with one radio show telling its listeners that 'a hard-hitting, fast-thinking American hero is tonight planning his next move'. It added: 'Certainly the prayers and best wishes of every American are with that six foot, lean, determined tank expert, on whose shoulders has fallen the task of helping to bring the battle of Africa to a head . . .'[10]

A day later, the 1st Ranger Battalion, working with the 1st Infantry Division, took El Guettar village. But minimal progress was made towards the Maknassy Pass, Patton's other objective, because incessant rain had left the 1st Armored Division 'largely stuck in the mud'. To speed things along, Patton paid a visit to Ward's HQ on the 19th, driving down the new road built and maintained by US engineers. En route he stopped and complimented each 'wet, dirty and isolated' group.

He reached CCB's command post first and was surprised by Robinett's 'mental attitude – he is defensive and lacks confidence'. Moving on to divisional HQ, he was no more impressed by Ward. 'He fears that tanks can't move due to mud, but I told him to do it with [his] infantry . . . I want to hit Rommel before he hits us, also to help Eighth Army, which attacks tomorrow.'

Returning that night to Gafsa, Patton was reminded by Major General Dick McCreery, Alexander's chief of staff, that he was to take Maknassy and the heights immediately beyond, and then stop. This meant, in effect, that as soon as the Eighth Army passed Maknassy, Patton's II Corps would be out of a job. 'In brief,' he noted in his diary, 'this is to pinch us out so as to ensure a British triumph. I kept my temper and agreed. There is nothing else to do, but I can't see how Ike can let [the British] pull his leg so. It is awful.'

He got better news late that evening, from Bradley, that his son-in-law John Waters was captured and 'safe'. On 21 March, with both divisions advancing, he went forward to El Guettar to see how Allen's men were getting on. It almost cost him his life as he rather unwisely sat on the 'forward face of a hill', stars easily visible on his helmet, and shortly afterwards the exact spot was hit by a salvo of 150mm shells.[11]

As Ward's 1st Armored Division had, once again, made little progress at Maknassy, Patton wrote him a strongly worded message 'to use more drive and keep his command post at the front'. It did not have the desired effect. 'Ward simply dawdled all day,' wrote Patton, 'finally capturing the town of Maknassy, but has not taken Maknassy heights.' Spurred on by Alexander, who wanted II Corps to take the pressure off Monty's Eighth Army – which was struggling to break through the Mareth Line – Patton issued new orders for the 1st Infantry and 1st Armored Divisions to 'seize and hold' the defiles on the Gafsa–Gabès and Gafsa–Maknassy roads respectively.

Ward was instructed to launch a night attack against the hills beyond Maknassy, but it failed, as did two follow-up assaults on 23 and 24 March (the latter by three battalions of infantry, supported by two companies of tanks, some 75mm tank destroyers and four battalions of artillery). Frustrated, Patton got Ward on the phone and ordered him 'to personally lead the attack on the hills and take them' the following morning, 25 March. He noted in his diary: 'Now my conscience hurts me for fear I have ordered him to his death, but I feel that it was my duty. Vigorous leadership would have taken the hill the day before yesterday. I hope it comes out alright.'

It did not. Led by Ward, and with no artillery preparation, three battalions of the 6th Armoured Infantry took and briefly held Hill 322, the key objective. But, assailed by German mortars, machine guns and artillery, and unable to dig in through solid rock, they could not maintain their foothold on the ridge. 'I, therefore, ordered the 1st Armored Division to quit attacking and consolidate,' noted Patton in his diary. 'In the course of the above attack, Ward received a slight wound. He showed good personal courage.'[12]

Further south, at El Guettar, the 1st Infantry Division had made better progress by capturing a series of low ridges at the entrance to the long El Guettar plain, four to five miles wide, and confined by mountain ranges on the northern and southern flanks. Thanks to good work by the 1st Ranger Battalion, which climbed the high ground, and the 26th Infantry which moved along the road, 700 prisoners from the Italian Centauro Division were taken during the night of 20/21 March, and the forward troops gained control of the Djebel el Ank defile and reached the village of Bou Hamran. By noon the following day, the 18th Infantry on a separate axis to the southeast had advanced the front line to a road junction east of Djebel el Kheroua, 14 miles southeast of El Guettar.

The 22nd was spent consolidating and probing east of Bou Hamran, while two battalions of the 18th Infantry occupied heights south of the Gabès road, at the northeastern tip of Djebel Berda. At 5 a.m. the following day they were attacked by the tanks of the 10th Panzer Division, supported by infantry, artillery and dive-bombers.[13] Watching the battle from a nearby ridge was war reporter John D'Arcy-Dawson. 'The German tanks burst into view in the distance,' he recorded, 'advancing rapidly up the flat plain ablaze with yellow daisies and poppies. They advanced steadily, the lorried infantry bringing up the rear. Overhead, dive-bombers swept down through a hail of light flak to bomb American gun positions. From behind me salvos of shells from American heavies whined through the air.'

Before long, having isolated the American infantry on the heights, the German tanks and self-propelled guns overran some artillery positions before they were stopped by a combination of American field artillery, tank destroyers and a hidden minefield. 'The plain', wrote D'Arcy-Dawson, 'was dotted with huge columns of smoke going up from wrecked tanks.' Thirty were lost to enemy fire; another eight in the minefield.[14]

After a pause, the Germans attacked again with more than thirty tanks at 4.45 p.m.[15] D'Arcy-Dawson recorded: 'Right through the curtain of artillery they went, losing many, but the survivors came on until self-propelled guns rolled towards them, blazing away. The leading German tanks were knocked out and were out of sight and the Americans left triumphantly in possession of the battlefield. On the plain, under the burning sun thirty-five enemy tanks were lying blazing or disabled.'

Returning to Gafsa after the battle, D'Arcy-Dawson met Patton and congratulated him on the victory. 'Yes,' said Patton, beaming. 'You've got a good story today. We beat the living hell out of them.'

No one was happier than Major General Terry Allen, the Big Red One's commander, who told the newspaperman a day later that his men had come up against the same panzer grenadiers who had handled them so roughly at Medjez el Bab earlier in the campaign. This time his men had killed hundreds of panzer grenadiers and taken nearly three hundred prisoners. Allen, wrote D'Arcy-Dawson, was a 'slim man with tanned face and unruly, grizzled hair . . . Vital and alert, he commands the best trained infantry division in Tunisia'.[16]

Oddly, Patton made no mention of the victory in his diary – maybe because it was a defensive action which had gained no ground. He was more concerned with the 1st Armored Division's perceived failures in attack, telling Ward on 27 March that 'he lacked drive and trusted his staff too much in that he presumed orders were carried out and did not take the trouble to find out that they were'. Ward 'admitted this', according to Patton, who then warned him that if he 'failed in the next operation', he would be sacked. All this Ward took 'very well', and was mollified a little when the corps commander decorated him with a Silver Star for leading the attack on the 25th. It would have merited the Distinguished Service Cross, wrote Patton in his diary, 'except for the fact that it was necessary for me to order him to do it'.

In truth, Patton had lost confidence in both Ward and the 1st Armored Division. 'Ward lacks force,' he wrote on the 28th. 'The division has lost its nerve and is jumpy. I fear that all our troops want to fight without getting killed.'[17]

Alex mirrored Patton's concerns when he told Monty, in a private letter on 29 March, that the Americans were 'proving to be most disappointing'. He had worked hard, he said, to gain the American commanders' trust, and also their friendship. But this had not resulted in better combat performance. 'They willingly accept my plans,' he explained, 'and my suggestions for carrying them out . . . But I have grave doubts that [American] soldiers are really doing their duty as we understand it.' They were, he added, 'mentally & physically rather soft and very green'. It was the 'old story again – lack of proper training allied to no experience of war – and too high a standard of living'.[18]

This was unfair. Learning from their earlier mistakes, the Americans (particularly Robinett's CCB) had fought well at Sbeitla, Djebel el Hamra and near El Guettar. As for Alex's charge that Americans were 'soft' because they were too wealthy and pampered, it was nonsense. Most of the servicemen were from blue-collar families that had struggled to make ends meet during the Great Depression. They were, as a result, physically and mentally tough, qualities that would serve them well once they gained more combat experience.

Even Alex, in his summary of the campaign, acknowledged the 'solid contribution to the success of operations in southern Tunisia' made by II Corps at El Guettar and Maknassy. Although they had been 'denied the pleasure of a spectacular advance into the enemy's rear', they had 'kept in play the whole of the 10th Panzer Division while the decisive battle was being fought and won by the Eighth Army'.[19]

36

Monty's Left Hook

Southern Tunisia, 20–29 March 1943

'ALL AT ONCE,' WROTE 21-year-old Lieutenant Lionel 'Doughy' Baker, 'the inferno of the 8th Army's massed artillery burst over the desert. A great segment of the darkness erupted in a furious storm of explosions and darting flashes, which leapt in myriads against the night sky. The battle was on.'[1]

It was 9.30 p.m. on 20 March 1943, and Monty's long-awaited assault on the Mareth Line in southern Tunisia had begun. His plan, as he explained in a letter to Major General John Harding, was for three infantry divisions – the 4th Indian, 50th Tyne Tees and 51st Highland – to attack the 'extreme enemy left flank, near the sea'. The initial assault would be by a single brigade, the 151st (of 50th Division), explained Monty, but 'the hole will be widened, and exploited; the tactics will be to roll up the enemy from the sea, working south-westwards'. His intention was to 'continue this thrust, and nourish it, almost indefinitely'.

At the same time, he would send the New Zealand Corps of 27,000 men and 200 tanks around the right (or land) flank of the Mareth Line, west of the Matmata hills, taking a route scouted by Major Vladimir Peniakoff ('Popski') of the PPA★ and a patrol of the LRDG. His last

---

★ Peniakoff had set out from Shweref in Libya on 18 January to reconnoitre the 'going leading up to the Mareth Line; then to get information concerning the

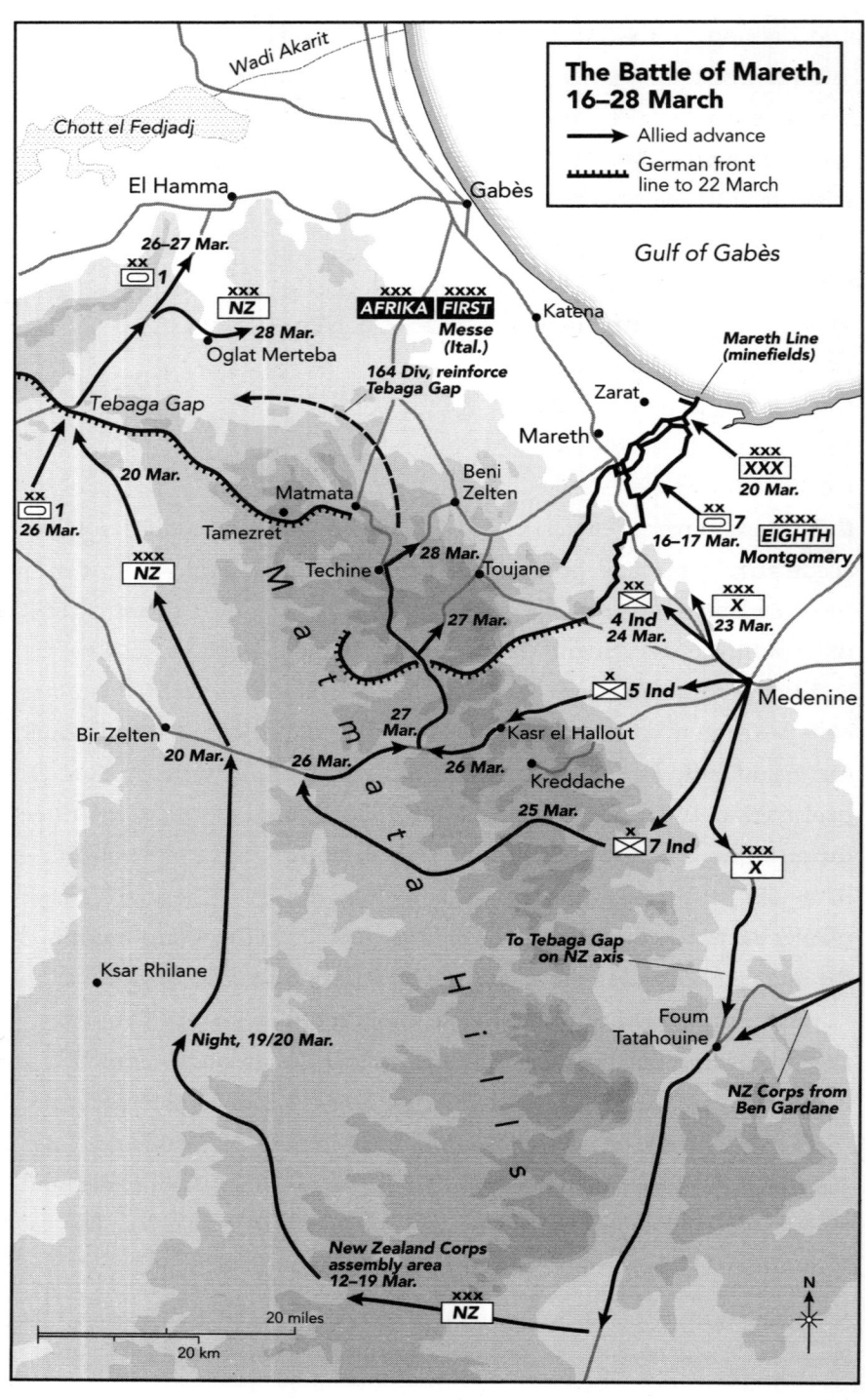

The Battle of Mareth, 16–28 March

→ Allied advance

⋯⋯ German front line to 22 March

Wadi Akarit

Chott el Fedjadj

El Hamma

Gabès

Gulf of Gabès

26–27 Mar.

xx ⌷ 1

xxx NZ

xxx AFRIKA   xxxx FIRST
Messe (Ital.)

Katena

→ 28 Mar.
Oglat Merteba

164 Div, reinforce Tebaga Gap

Mareth Line (minefields)

Zarat

Tebaga Gap

Mareth

Beni Zelten

20 Mar.

Matmata

xxx XXX
20 Mar.

xx ⌷ 1
26 Mar.

Tamezret

Techine

28 Mar.

Toujane

xxx NZ

27 Mar.

xx ⌷ 7
16–17 Mar.

xxxx EIGHTH
Montgomery

27 Mar.

xx ⊠ 4 Ind
24 Mar.

xxx X
23 Mar.

Bir Zelten

M
a
t
m
a
t
a

27 Mar.

x ⊠ 5 Ind

Kasr el Hallout

Medenine

20 Mar.

26 Mar.

26 Mar.

Kreddache

25 Mar.

x ⊠ 7 Ind

xxx X

Ksar Rhilane

H
i
l
l
s

To Tebaga Gap on NZ axis

Night, 19/20 Mar.

Foum Tatahouine

NZ Corps from Ben Gardane

New Zealand Corps assembly area 12–19 Mar.

xxx NZ

N

20 miles

20 km

two divisions – the 1st and 7th Armoured – would hold the centre ground while the 'two flank thrusts' were developed. 'I do not know what the enemy will do about it,' Monty wrote to Harding. 'He is not strong enough to hold off both thrusts simultaneously . . . If he concentrates against one, then the other will progress.'[2]

During the night of 16/17 March, to improve his forward positions for the main attack, Monty had ordered his 201st (Guards) Brigade to advance on both sides of the Medenine–Mareth road and clear enemy outposts from a collection of hills known as 'the Horseshoe' that were held by the veteran German 90th Light Division. The inexperienced 201st was selected for the task because, according to XXX Corps' commander Lieutenant General Oliver Leese, it would give them 'a comparatively easy period of quiet operations in order to acclimatize the many newcomers to warfare'.

The planners were aware of a large wadi, or dried-up watercourse, with banks 35 feet high, that ran along the foot of the Horseshoe, and knew that vehicles could only cross it after special entrances and exits had been constructed. But it was assumed that infantry could carry and hold the heights without the support of tanks and other heavy weapons. In the event, the enemy got wind of the attack – by capturing an artillery officer with a marked map – and the two attacking battalions, the 6th Grenadier and 3rd Coldstream Guards, took so many casualties as they crossed two unsuspected minefields and assaulted the high ground that they left behind large pockets of defenders.

Just before dawn, assailed by mortars and with their position untenable, the surviving guardsmen were ordered to withdraw. For some, it was too late. 'The Germans start closing right in, and some bitter

---

defences of the line itself between Matmata and El Hamma' to assist Monty's left hook. Having completed the reconnaissance, and lost their vehicles, Peniakoff and his men walked for six days across the Grand Erg desert to reach the oasis town of Tozeur in southern Tunisia. Six weeks later, the New Zealand Corps used the route he had reconnoitred to outflank the Mareth Line. (Peniakoff, *Popski's Private Army*, pp. 238–49)

close-quarter fighting takes place with grenades,' recalled Major Butler, a Grenadier company commander. 'I decide that the time has come to try to fight our way out rather than be massacred in our trenches. In order to do so, it is first necessary to destroy a particularly trouble-some machine gun very near our position. A few of us make the attempt, only to be shot down within a couple of yards of our trench.'

Butler found himself lying in the open with a bullet through the knee, watching in horror as a stick grenade rolled towards him and exploded, the shrapnel penetrating his chest and face. He was later dragged back into the trench by German stretcher-bearers and taken prisoner, as were the remnants of his company. Butler's battalion, alone, lost 24 officers and 255 men killed, wounded and captured; the 3rd Coldstream Guards another 10 officers and 160 men.[3]

Generale d'Armata Messe's First Italian Army was holding the Mareth Line, from the sea to the Matmata hills, with six understrength divisions: from east to west, the Young Fascists, Trieste, German 90th Light, Spezia, Pistola and German 164th Light. In immediate reserve was the 15th Panzer Division, with the 21st Panzer Division stationed further back to cover the Tebaga Gap. The assault by the 50th Division's 151st Brigade during the night of 20/21 March, therefore, fell on the Young Fascists closest to the coast. Their defences were protected by a 'very deep and steep-sided' wadi – Zigzaou – whose bottom was 'everywhere muddy' and in places filled with standing water. In his dispatch of the battle, Alex wrote:

> Our troops advanced to the assault carrying fascines and scaling-ladders as though at the storm of Badajoz. The enemy's fire, both frontal and enfilade, was very heavy and it was only by the greatest dash and courage that our advanced troops succeeded in crossing the wadi and establishing themselves on the far bank. Three of the powerful enemy strongpoints were captured and the infantry were firmly established. Unfortunately, it was proving impossible to reinforce them, for the wadi which they

had crossed on foot was quite impassable for wheels and almost impassable for tanks.

After dark on 21 March, the two assaulting battalions of the 151st Brigade were reinforced on their right (coastal) flank by the 5th East Yorkshires of 69th Brigade. More strongholds were captured that night. But a heavy downpour of rain on the following day added to the difficulties – not least because it prevented close air support – and, when Messe put in a heavy counter-attack later that same day with the 15th Panzer Division and part of the 90th Light, knocking out more than thirty Valentine tanks which had crossed the wadi to support the 151st Brigade, the position became increasingly untenable.[4]

Even getting rations and ammunition to the isolated troops on the west side of the wadi was a hazardous business. Captain Alan Blackwell, commanding the 5th East Yorkshires' HQ Company, went forward with food for his battalion's B and C Companies at 7 p.m. on the 22nd. Still only twenty-six years old, twice wounded and a veteran of numerous battles – including Gazala, Mersa Matruh and El Alamein – Blackwell kept his composure when his party was fired on by machine guns as they retraced their steps. He told his parents:

The Hun had the ford covered by the time we were ready to come away, and 53 men with 1 pistol and 1 Tommy-gun are more of a target than an offensive force so I had to sneak back across country – a minefield – getting potted at from all over the ruddy place. It was a rotten to-do, and I had 3 men blown up on a mine, but that was their own fault: [they] walked abreast instead of in my footsteps – or knee-prints rather as I did ¾ mile on hands and knees finding my way around the 'gift-parcels'. Rotten things. I hate 'em.[5]

During the night of 22/23 March, convinced his men were about to be overrun, Major General John Nichols, commanding the 50th Division, asked his corps commander Lieutenant General Leese for permission to abandon the bridgehead and withdraw his men back across the Wadi Zigzaou. After checking with Monty, Leese issued the necessary orders and the withdrawal took place that night 'under cover of artillery fire'.[6] The last troops back across the wadi were from the 5th East Yorkshires. 'B & C [Companies] got back under a barrage,' noted Alan Blackwell in his diary, 'with few casualties . . . Had put up a terrific show.'[7]

Monty did not agree, and put the blame for the setback on Nichols and his brigade commander, Daniel Beak (VC, DSO, MC and Bar), both of whom were sacked. Monty wrote to Alex on 23 March:

> There is no doubt that Beak (151 Bde) let the party down by not having his front ready to receive a counter-attack, with 6-pdr guns ready, and so on – in spite of repeated enquiries from above as [to] whether this was being done. So the Boche counter-attack drove the 50 Div back a bit, though we still hold the main obstacle. But the enemy had stiffened the front there so much that to go on would mean very heavy casualties . . . Therefore I have decided to hold on my right.[8]

Monty had hoped to widen the 151st Brigade's initial incursion into the Mareth Line and 'roll up the enemy from the sea'. That was no longer possible and, according to Alex, 'the original plan for "Pugilist" had therefore to be abandoned'.[9] Yet Monty deserves credit for rapidly devising an alternative. 'I shall now nourish my left hook,' he told Alex on the 23rd, 'and I am sending HQ 10 Corps, with 1st Armoured Div complete, to join the NZ party and push in towards Gabes from the SW. The left thrust (or hook) will now be very strong and will have over 300 tanks.'[10]

Already, by the evening of 22 March, Freyberg's New Zealand Corps – made up of the British 8th Armoured Brigade, the 2nd New Zealand Division and Leclerc's Free French – had used the reconnaissance report sent back by Popski and the LRDG to get around the Matmata hills and was engaged with the 21st Panzer Division at the Tebaga Gap, having broken through one line of minefields the night before.[11] The following day, Howard Marshall of the BBC told his listeners that 'a British armoured column has outflanked the entire Mareth position after a forced march of over 100 miles over the desert'. Alex was apoplectic at this breach of operational security. 'This is very wrong after what I had told the Press,' he wrote to Ike, 'and makes one despair that they will ever have any sense. How can any intelligent man give out the whole plan as Howard Marshall has, without realising that he was giving the whole show away?'[12]

To bolster his defences, Messe had sent the German 164th Light Division and some Italians to reinforce the 21st Panzer. But they would be heavily outnumbered and outgunned when Monty's own reinforcements reached Freyberg on 25 March. The latter now included the 4th Indian Division which had been ordered to support the left hook by thrusting into the mountains to the west of the Mareth Line and opening the road from Medenine to Bir Soltane via Ksar el Hallouf, as a 'shorter route of supply for X Corps'. Once that had been done, it was to advance along the spine of the Matmata hills and descend from there to the Mareth–Gabès road – thus executing, in effect, a smaller left hook. The plan, noted Alex, with its 'reminiscences of El Alamein, was christened "Supercharge"'.

By 26 March, the 4th Indian Division had cleared the road through the Ksar el Hallouf Pass and turned north to work towards Cheguimi. But the advance of X Corps had taken longer than expected, and Monty had to postpone the attack on the Tebaga Gap – between Djebel Tebaga and Djebel Melab – until the 26th. By then the defences in this 6,000-yard bottleneck had been strengthened by mines and the arrival of the 15th Panzer Division, giving a total of two German panzer divisions and one infantry division.

Aware that getting through the gap would not be easy, Monty arranged with Air Marshal Harry Broadhurst, commanding the Desert Air Force, for a huge air attack to precede the ground offensive in the afternoon of 26 March. It was an inspired move. For two and a half hours prior to the ground attack, Broadhurst's planes – including twenty-two squadrons of Spitfires, Curtiss P-40 Warhawk fighter-bombers (known to the British as 'Kittybombers') and Hurricane 'tankbusters' (armed with two 40mm anti-tank cannons) – pounded the German positions with bombs and machine-gun fire, 'creating great destruction among his guns and transport and having a most serious effect on morale'.[13]

In his diary notes of the battle, Monty wrote: 'These fighter aircraft operated beyond the barrage, and in that area every vehicle, and anything that appeared or moved, was shot to pieces. Brilliant and brave use of our air superiority combined with the fire of 200 guns, completely stunned the enemy. The attack was an amazing success.'[14]

Spearheaded by the 8th Armoured Brigade's 150 tanks – most of them Shermans – and three battalions of Kiwi infantry, the ground attack was made with 'great ferocity' at 4 p.m. as a dust storm was blowing. The German positions were quickly penetrated, though the fighting continued on the high ground for much of the night. During the bitter struggle for Point 209, Second Lieutenant Mo Ngarimu of the 28th (Maori) New Zealand Battalion personally destroyed two machine-gun points and inspired his men to beat off several German counter-attacks. Twice wounded, he refused to be evacuated and was killed in the final action the following morning. He was awarded a posthumous Victoria Cross, the first Maori recipient of the medal.

Meanwhile the vanguard of the British 1st Armoured Division, navigating by moonlight, had driven past the bulk of the enemy's armour and by dawn was close to El Hamma and just 15 miles from Gabès. There it was stopped by a strong German anti-tank screen and adverse weather conditions. Fighting ferociously, the remnants of three German divisions – the 15th and 21st Panzer, and the 164th Light – bought the rest of the First Italian Army enough time to withdraw back down the narrow coastal corridor from the Mareth Line to a new defensive position at Wadi Akarit, north of Gabès. On 29 March, the New Zealanders entered Gabès but the bulk of their quarry had slipped away.[15] As at Alamein, Monty would face accusations of winning a battle, but failing to destroy an enemy army that, for a brief moment, was at his mercy.

In his 'Reflections on the Battle', Monty described Mareth as his 'toughest fight' since Alamein. The enemy position was 'very, very strong', he wrote, and to have turned them out in the space of a week was 'a truly amazing performance'. Yet it was also the 'most enjoyable' battle he had fought as it 'gave considerable scope for subtlety, and for outwitting an opponent'. It ended with the capture of 7,000 prisoners – many of them German – and gave the enemy a mauling it 'could never have contemplated'. Of the six enemy divisions, the 164th Light 'lost most of its heavy weapons and vehicles'; the 21st Panzer 'took a tremendous knock'; the 15th Panzer 'had only 3 runners the next day'; and the three Italian divisions 'lost so many prisoners that they could be of little fighting value'.

He explained away the defeat on the coast – which, in effect, forced him to abandon his initial plan to roll up the Mareth Line from the sea – by noting that it served its purpose by drawing in enemy reserves. He had then resorted to Plan B by dropping the frontal assault and reinforcing the left hook with the 1st Armoured Division. 'This refusal to waste effort at Mareth,' he wrote, 'and the speedy change of the schwerpunkt, was the turning point of the battle . . . There were some unpleasant moments and the issue hung in the balance for several days. But we never once lost the initiative, even when the situation appeared very bad, and the enemy danced to our tune the whole time. By sticking to it, we won through.'[16]

That was true, up to a point. In Monty's telling, the reinforcing of the left hook was all part of his flexible plan. In reality, he did not fight that way. He liked to prepare a battle to the minutest detail. That way, he thought, he could control the outcome. But Mareth, like most battles, did not go to plan. If Monty deserves credit, it is for recognising that, as Field Marshal Lord Carver (who fought in the battle) put it, his initial plan had 'failed miserably' and 'for rapidly devising an alternative which succeeded'.[17]

In his official dispatch, written after the campaign, Alex gave an account of the battle that was both accurate and fair. He noted Monty's change of the plan and the lost opportunity at El Hamma. But at the time, in a private letter to Monty, he had only praise for the Eighth Army commander. 'Let me congratulate you on your magnificent exploits about Mareth,' he wrote on 29 March. 'It is very fine indeed.'

He then went on to update Monty on a possible replacement for Anderson as First Army commander.[18] Alex had first raised the issue of sacking Anderson by asking Monty, two weeks earlier, if he thought Lieutenant General Oliver Leese, commanding the British X Corps, could do the job. Monty said that he would 'do it well' because he had had a 'very good grounding' in the desert and has 'learnt his stuff'. But he added that to take Leese away from the Eighth Army 'at this juncture would prejudice the success of Pugilist'. Leese, therefore, remained.[19]

By the 29th, Alex's solution to the Anderson problem was not to sack him, but to force him to replace his chief of staff, C. V. McNabb, with Brigadier Cameron Nicholson, the deputy commander of the 6th Armoured Division, whose 'Nickforce' had prevented Rommel from capturing Thala. 'Of course,' wrote Alex to Monty, 'if he refuses I shall call on you for Oliver [Leese]★ – but now he has been given a clear directive from me how to organise his front and what operations to carry out, he is doing satisfactorily. I have considered the whole thing very carefully – I don't want to upset things at this stage – they are going very well. He knows the French and gets on extremely well with them. He knows a very intricate front and all his people. All things considered I feel it best to leave alone.'

Only if things got 'held up', he added, would he make a change.[20]

★ Sensibly, Anderson did not refuse Alex's instruction to 'get rid of his BGS and take Nicholson', who performed well in his new role as Anderson's chief of staff.

37

'The Führer is not ready to think of retreat'

Tunisia, Italy and Germany, 28 March–6 April 1943

WITH HIS NECK ON the line, Lieutenant General 'Sunshine' Anderson was fortunate that the First Army's next offensive – designed to push back Arnim's forces in northern Tunisia – yielded instant results. The advance was made over boulder-covered mountains and through dense scrub by three British brigades – the 36th and 138th Infantry, and the 1st Parachute – supported on the left flank by the Corps Franc d'Afrique and a unit of Moroccan Goumiers, and was helped by the fact that the German defenders had been thinned out to reinforce other sectors.[1]

Before the attack, corps commander Lieutenant General Charles Allfrey had issued a call to arms. 'I told you some time ago,' he said, 'that we were pulling back to our present position in order to get a firm base from which to strike back at the enemy. We are just about to do so, and it is vital that all of you should realise the importance of your part in this offensive.' Assailed on all sides, the enemy's ultimate defeat was, said Allfrey, 'absolutely certain'. But to bring it about quickly, it was essential that every member of V Corps was 'prepared to fight to the limit of his endurance and with the utmost display of guts'.[2]

The attack began in the early hours of 28 March. The night before, the men of the 2nd Parachute Battalion – whose objective was the village of Tamera – had attended a church service in a big machine shed. 'The men sat on shelves,' remembered their CO John Frost, 'in tiers round the sides of the building, and Padre Watkins officiated from a table in the middle. Everyone who could, went, and everybody sang, led by a small harmonium. Now that the hour of fresh battle approached, there were many amongst us who wondered what really happened if our number came up.'

When the service was over, Frost said a few words of encouragement and concluded: 'I don't know what you think of us, but I know I speak for all my officers when I say we have nothing but the highest possible regard for every single one of you.'

Advancing behind a creeping barrage, the forward companies of the 1st and 2nd Parachute Battalions were able to capture much of the high ground that marked their initial objective, and a number of German and Italian prisoners, before dawn. But a fierce counter-attack by Witzig's parachute engineers was only narrowly stopped by the 2nd Battalion's C Company, an action that cost the life of 21-year-old Lieutenant Dickie Spender, a renowned poet, who fell riddled with bullets, having killed four of the enemy.

Before his death Spender – described by the *Daily Telegraph* as the Rupert Brooke of the Second World War – wrote 'Parachute Battalion':

> And, with the night, perhaps some God looking down
> With dull, cold eyes, by the near stars, will see
> One lonely, grim battalion cut its way
> Through agony and death to fame's high crown,
> And wonderingly watch the friendless strength
> Of little men, who die that the great Truths shall live.[3]

By the evening of the 28th, the 1st Parachute Battalion – attacking on the left – had taken its second objective and six enemy guns. At one point during the assault, the paratroopers were advancing so fast they were hit by their own artillery. Corporal Reg Curtis saw his CO Alistair Pearson crouched by a rock, bellowing into a radio handset: 'What do you think you're doing? You're killing all my bwoody men!'

Meanwhile Frost's battalion, facing stiffer opposition, was down to the strength of a single company. Reinforced by two companies from the 3rd Parachute Battalion, Frost agreed to continue the attack after dark. When his men moved forward at 3 a.m., there was little opposition as the bulk of the enemy had withdrawn. 'By the time we reached our old positions in Cork Wood,' wrote Frost, 'we had collected no less than 50 [prisoners], together with a great deal of booty.'[4]

The Battle of Tamera ended with the 1st Parachute Brigade in possession of all its objectives. Allfrey was delighted but not surprised. The parachutists, he noted in his diary, 'as usual have done a magnificent job, and throughout the day pressed on, and at 1630 hrs beat off a counter-attack personally led by [Major Rudolf] Witzig' and his crack battalion of German parachute engineers. They had, added Allfrey, in conjunction with French colonial troops on their left, captured 'about 800 Italians, 150 Germans and 5 guns . . . Sent Para Bde a "Hurrah" notice in the evening which they richly deserved'.[5]

The neighbouring brigades also did well, recapturing Sedjenane on 31 March. 'By this advance of eighteen miles,' wrote a delighted Alex, 'we won back all the ground which the enemy had taken three weeks to capture.'[6]

But when the journalist Philip Jordan visited the British parachutists on 6 April in a corkwood near Sedjenane – where bodies unburied by the Germans had left the air 'beastly with the sweet smell of decay' – he found them 'discontented and furious' at the way they had been used as infantry 'without adequate equipment' since the middle of December, and without a break since the end of January. They had repeatedly 'saved the day' against vastly superior forces, noted Jordan, but had been given 'no credit for it' because journalists were banned from mentioning their name. Why? He could think of three reasons: to stop questions being asked in the House of Commons 'about the way their talents have been wasted'; the truth would 'discourage recruiting'; and somebody's reputation would 'suffer'.

Jordan and others had written that day to ask Alex to remove the ban, but were not holding their breath. He noted in his diary: 'Since January 26 the parachutists have captured more German prisoners than they have men when at full strength. They rank with the Hampshires as the heroes of this campaign; and it is high time they were recognised as such. We owe them much.'[7]

In late March, while Allfrey's troops were attacking in northern Tunisia, Major Hans Freiherr von Luck of the 3rd Panzer Reconnaissance Battalion was ordered to report to Army Group Afrika's forward headquarters in the south of the country. He was greeted by Generalleutnant Alfred Gause, Arnim's chief of staff who had long served Rommel in the same role. 'Rommel has got nowhere with Hitler,' said Gause. 'We shall neither receive supplies, nor does the Führer want to know anything about a German Dunkirk. Rommel has been sent for treatment and forbidden to return to Africa as planned. Come, the Commander-in-Chief is expecting you.'

Luck had never met Arnim and was at a loss to know why he had been summoned from his reconnaissance battalion guarding the western flank of Messe's army at Wadi Akarit. Shown into Arnim's command truck, he saluted and said: 'Here to report, Generaloberst.'

'Good to meet you, Luck,' said Arnim, a tall, slim man with a hatchet face. 'I have the pleasure of presenting you with, in the name of the Duce, the *Medaglio d'Argento*, the equivalent of our Knight's Cross. Congratulations.' He pinned the simple round medal – stamped with the words 'Al Valore Militare' and set on a blue ribbon – on Luck's chest.

'Thank you, Generaloberst.'

After a pause, Arnim explained the real reason for their meeting. 'Luck, I have decided, in agreement with Rommel and Gause, that you will fly, at once, to Führer HQ to lay before Hitler and explain a detailed plan for the evacuation of as many elements as possible of the Africa Army. For this you will first fly to Rome and have the plan countersigned by Generalfeldmarschall Kesselring. You will then fly on to Berlin and report to Generaloberst Guderian and Generalleutnant Schmundt, for countersigning. And finally you will fly to Berchtesgaden, and report to Keitel or Jodl, to be given an appointment with Hitler. Seidemann will let you have his Heinkel 111.* You must leave as soon as you can.'

'I am honoured to be entrusted with this task, Generaloberst,' replied Luck, 'but how should I, an insignificant frontline soldier, get anywhere with Hitler? Besides, I should be with my men in the final phase.'

Arnim explained that Hitler was suspicious of the generals, even Rommel, so they had decided to send an 'insignificant' major, straight from the front. 'He might listen if you give him a clear idea of the situation and the feeling among the men. You will travel, and appear before him, in your dusty faded uniform. That can't fail to have an effect. The plan you are taking with you was worked out some time ago and provides for the proportional evacuation of the most important officers, frontline soldiers, and technicians. Gause can discuss the details with you. I wish you, and us, complete success; report daily by radio.'

Two days later, the 'plan' safely stowed in his briefcase, Luck flew from the Cap Bon peninsula to Sicily in a Heinkel 111 bomber, and then on to Rome in a shuttle plane. A room had been reserved for him in the Hotel Excelsior on the Via Veneto where he had his first bath in almost a year. He ate a superb dinner of spaghetti and a flaming *omelette surprise* at Chez Alfredo.

Next morning, he met Generalfeldmarschall Kesselring – a 'charming man of medium height with warm and sympathetic eyes' – at his Frascati headquarters. 'How was the flight?' asked Kesselring. 'Did Seidemann's Heinkel bring you safely over the pond?'

---

* Generalmajor Hans Seidemann was *Fliegerführer Afrika* and the senior Luftwaffe officer in Tunisia.

After signing the plan, 'Smiling Albert' said: 'I haven't much hope that Hitler will agree to this, but we must try, and the signatures of Schmundt and Guderian will help. You can still fly to Berlin today, by courier plane. Every day counts. Good luck.'

That evening, still wearing his dusty desert uniform, Luck landed in Berlin and was shocked by the sight of houses 'now just in ruins', thanks to recent Allied bombing raids,★ and the grey faces of 'once busy Berliners' who 'no longer believed in the "Final Victory" of Hitler and Goebbels'. The destruction was in stark contrast to the beauty of Rome which had seemed, by and large, untouched by war.

He was taken to meet Generalleutnant Rudolf Schmundt, head of the German Army Personnel Office, who signed the plan without reading it. The following morning, he saw Generaloberst Heinz Guderian, the revered panzer leader who had just been appointed Inspector General of Armoured Troops. Guderian looked tired, and 'only his eyes had their old sparkle'.

'Luck,' said the Generaloberst, 'I'm glad to see one of the old hands of the panzer force again, alive and well. How many from the early days of our proud force have already gone! We've just lost Stalingrad. And now the same thing is looming in Africa. I can't even think about the seasoned members of the three divisions of the old Afrika Korps with their desert experience, or the new divisions sent into Tunisia. That is why I agreed at once to the evacuation plan, which had, of course, already been drawn up by Rommel, though we all had little hope that Hitler would agree to it. The idea of sending you to him, as an old trooper from the front, carries more weight, at any rate, than our opinion, which is regarded by Hitler as "defeatist".'

Guderian suggested that he take the night train. 'You will be in Berchtesgaden tomorrow morning.'

★ On 1 March, for example, a raid by 250 RAF heavy bombers dropped 600 tons of explosives on the capital, destroying 20,000 houses and making 35,000 homeless. Seven hundred were killed.

A day later, Luck was standing before Alfred Jodl, the OKW Chief of Operations. He explained his mission and why he had been chosen by Arnim as an intermediary. 'Things look very bad, Generaloberst. The long front from Gabès to Tunis cannot anywhere near be covered by us. To prevent a disaster as many men as possible should be evacuated at once, to be available on fronts where the Western Allies are sure to land. For this purpose, I have an evacuation plan to deliver which has been carefully worked out by Rommel and Arnim, and countersigned by Kesselring, Guderian and Schmundt.'

He handed Jodl the envelope, adding: 'I have been sent here as an insignificant field officer in the hope that this would make an impression on the Führer.'

Jodl stared at him, but did not open the envelope. 'Listen, Luck,' he said at last, 'there is absolutely no question of evacuating elements of the Africa Army. The Führer is not ready to think of retreat. We won't even let you see him personally. He would have a fit of rage and throw you out. Besides, we're glad to have the Führer on the political tack for a few days, as he is just having a state visit by Antonescu of Romania. Your "mission" is of no avail. Inform Arnim to that effect.'

A despondent Luck went to the radio office and messaged Arnim: 'Not admitted to the Führer, plan rejected by Jodl, flying back to Rome and from there to Tunisia.'

Luck was mistaken. He would not return to Africa.[8]

A few days earlier, even as Luck was flying to Europe on his ill-fated mission to save Army Group Afrika, Oberst Nicolaus von Below, Hitler's Luftwaffe adjutant, was heading in the opposite direction to report on conditions at the front. He flew first to Taormina in Sicily where Kesselring spoke in a 'very optimistic vein about holding Tunis', but was 'pessimistic about everywhere else'. He did not think, he told Below, that Tunisia could be held 'much longer'.

Below then flew with Kesselring to the southern front in Tunisia where Arnim said much the same thing. He spent an evening with an old Luftwaffe colleague, Generalleutnant 'Beppo' Schmidt, the commander of the Hermann Göring Division, who told him that his defences were spread far too thin and he could not hold off the Americans alone. Back in Sicily, Kesselring's staff were even more pessimistic: an invasion of the island was inevitable once North Africa had fallen, and there was 'no possibility' of holding it off in the long run.

When Below delivered the bad news to Hitler at the Berghof, the Führer took the news 'calmly and said very little'. It seemed to Below that Hitler had 'already written off North Africa' and was preparing himself mentally for the eventual defection of his Axis ally. 'Hitler was angry,' wrote Below, 'when he thought of the uselessness of the Italians. Basically the Italian forces did not want to fight. They would rather throw away their arms and go over to the enemy *en masse* – and today was better than tomorrow to do it.'[9]

38

Wadi Akarit

Southern Tunisia, 5–7 April 1943

'I HAD EISENHOWER HERE FOR a night,' wrote Monty to his confidant Brigadier Frank Simpson on 5 April. 'A nice chap and probably quite good in the political line. But his knowledge of how to make war, or how to fight battles, is definitely NIL. He must be kept away from all this sort of thing – otherwise we shall lose the war.'[1]

It was a typically mean-spirited and unjustified comment from Monty after Ike had visited Eighth Army HQ on 30 March. Ike's own account of the trip – written years later – mentioned the 'very colourful' and 'cosmopolitan' make-up of Monty's Eighth Army which included, 'in addition to English units, Highlanders, New Zealanders, Indians (including Gurkhas with their *kukris* – long, curved knives with which they beheaded their enemies), Poles, Czechs, Free French, Australians, and South Africans'. He also had a chance to talk with the pilots and crews of the American air squadrons that were supporting the Eighth Army, and later sent them 'some of the soldier luxuries that they had been denied during the long trip across the desert'.[2]

To Marshall, Ike was more explicit. '[Monty] is unquestionably able,' he wrote, 'but very conceited. He is so proud of his successes to date that he will never willingly make a single move until he is absolutely certain of success.'[3]

That same day, 30 March, X Corps had come within sight of the

First Italian Army's new defensive position at Wadi Akarit in the Gabès Gap. After inspecting the position which was 'dominated by some steep-sided hills', Lieutenant General Brian Horrocks, the commander of X Corps, was ordered to report to Army HQ where he was introduced to Ike and asked to explain the situation at the front. Assuming this was part of an act to impress the inexperienced Commander-in-Chief, Horrocks gave a 'short, snappy, military appreciation in the approved Staff College manner'. It concluded: 'The Wadi Akarit position is too strongly held to be bounced and we shall have to stage a proper set-piece attack before we can break through.'

As he spoke, Horrocks was sizing up Eisenhower, the virtually unknown American general who was in overall command. Was he a military genius? he wondered. Obviously not, but he had something. 'The contrast between these two men could hardly have been greater. Monty, the commander, the complete master of the art of war: the man who made it his business to win battles; small, alert, tense, rather like an intelligent terrier who might bite you at any moment. Eisenhower, a large, friendly, shrewd person with a broad grin, who was a co-ordinator rather than commander.'

By the time he left Monty's command caravan – captured from its original owner, Generale di Corpo d'Armata Annibale 'Electric Whiskers' Bergonzoli, at Beda Fomm in Libya in February 1941, and remounted on a British Leyland truck chassis – Horrocks had 'already partially succumbed to the Eisenhower charm'. What struck him most forcefully was Ike's complete selflessness. 'It was obvious even then,' wrote Horrocks, 'that he was concerned with only one thing – to win the war – and that the last person to count with him was General Eisenhower.' It was, Horrocks felt, the perfect combination: at the top the coordinator; in the field the commander. Neither would have suited the other's job. He doubted, moreover, 'whether anyone but Ike could have succeeded in driving his difficult team of Monty, Patton and Bradley to final victory'.[4]

Monty was much less appreciative of Ike's value, as his letter to

Sergeants Brown (left) and Randall (1st US Armored Division) embrace during the link-up of the Eighth and First Armies on the Gabès-Gafsa road in southern Tunisia, 7 April 1943.

Oberstleutnant Claus Graf von Stauffenberg, Operations Officer of the 10th Panzer Division, who lost his left eye and right hand in a strafing attack by a P-40 Kittyhawk fighter-bomber in Tunisia on 8 April 1943. His injuries would hinder his failed attempt to assassinate Hitler in the 'Bomb Plot' of July 1944.

Lieutenant General Kenneth 'Sunshine' Anderson (left), commanding the First Army, with Major General Omar N. Bradley who replaced Patton as commander of the US II Corps in mid-April 1943.

Sherman tanks advance past a knocked-out German 88mm anti-tank gun, 23 April 1943.

A Douglas Boston light bomber of the RAF's No. 114 Squadron, based at Souk el Khemis ('Kings Cross'), flies north of the Medjerda river (top right) to attack enemy airfields in northern Tunisia on 23 April 1943.

Stretcher bearers of the East Surrey Regiment, with a Churchill tank of the North Irish Horse in the background, during the attack on Longstop Hill, 23 April 1943.

Generaloberst Hans-Jürgen von Arnim, who succeeded Rommel as commander of the Italo-German Army Group Afrika on 9 March 1943, inspecting German positions near Tunis.

A German Mark VI 'Tiger' tank – part of Panzer-Abteilung 501 – captured intact by Allied forces near Tunis and later shipped to the Aberdeen Proving Ground, Maryland, where it resided in the US Army Ordnance Museum until 1989. It is currently part of the private Wheatcroft Collection in Leicester, UK.

German troops surrender to the crew of a British tank near Frendj, 6 May 1943.

British troops enter Tunis on 7 May 1943, almost six months to the day since the Torch landings.

German prisoners being processed by American troops, 8 May 1943.

Field Marshal Giovanni Messe (centre), commanding the Italian Tenth Army, surrenders to Major General Bernard Freyberg of X Corps on 13 May 1943, marking the final phase of the fighting in North Africa.

Generaloberst von Arnim (left foreground) leaves North Africa for captivity in England after surrendering to Tuker's 4th Indian Division near Sainte Marie-du-Zit on 12 May 1943.

Spahi light cavalrymen, recruited from the Berbers and Arabs of North Africa, and part of the 10,000-strong French contingent that led the Allied victory parade in Tunis on 20 May 1943.

Winston Churchill leaves the old Roman Ampitheatre at Carthage in Tunisia with Lieutenant General Anderson, after addressing 3,000 Allied troops on 1 June 1943. 'Not even Scipio Africanus,' wrote Anderson, 'addressing his victorious Legions could have received a more tumultuous welcome.'

The Axis in happier times: (from L to R) Reichsmarschall Hermann Goering, Count Ciano, Adolf Hitler and Benito Mussolini.

The dead bodies of Mussolini (second left), his mistress Claretta Petacci (centre) and three fellow fascists on display in the Piazzale Loreto in Milan on 29 April 1945. Captured by partisans as they attempted to flee to Switzerland on the 27th, Mussolini and Petacci were executed a day later.

Simpson makes clear. He also woefully underestimated the combat capability of the American troops, telling Simpson they 'won't fight' and 'have not got the light of battle in their eyes'. The reason, he added (without any evidence), was that they had 'no confidence in their Generals'. The best way to get the American army ready for battle was 'to teach *the Generals*', a point he had made to both Ike and Alex. 'If they know their stuff,' he insisted, 'they will teach the soldiers.'[5]

Clearly, Monty had been influenced by Alex's unfair criticism of the Americans in his letter of 29 March. But even Alex had not singled out the American commanders. That was Monty's reading of the situation, and, bar Fredendall, it was way off the mark.

None of this overt criticism had been made to Ike's face, of course. But he was able to surmise from Alex's outline plan for the conclusion of the campaign – which contemplated the 'eventual pinching out of the US II Corps' – that American troops were not trusted by British commanders. That was unacceptable to Ike, both from the political and the military point of view, and he insisted on Alex employing 'the entire II Corps, as a unit'.[6]

Messe's defensive position at Wadi Akarit at the northern end of the Gabès Gap was, in Monty's opinion, 'extremely strong'. It measured just 12 miles from the sea to the edge of the impassable salt marsh known as the Chott el Djerid, and comprised a coastal plain five miles wide that rose to a series of mountains: first Djebel Roumana, a 500-foot flat whale's-back hump; and then a series of jagged peaks known as the Zouai heights and the Fatnassa hills that towered as much as 900 feet over the plain below. The coastal belt, meanwhile, was protected by minefields, an anti-tank ditch and the steep-sided Wadi Akarit.

Monty, however, saw an opportunity. '[The enemy] had not had time to strengthen it,' he wrote, 'by means of deep minefields, defence works, wire, and so on. Therefore I must attack quickly, before he has time to make the position too strong.'[7]

His initial plan was to attack with two divisions: the 51st Highland advancing on to Djebel Roumana and over the Wadi Akarit, and the 4th Indian taking the saddle between Roumana and the Zouai–Fatnassa massif. But the two divisional commanders, Major Generals Francis Tuker and Douglas Wimberley, argued successfully that it was necessary and possible to take high ground in a night assault, and that an extra division should be involved. The plan was changed accordingly. 'Eighth Army,' noted Tuker, 'conceded all our points, so we set off to rehearse on sand models.'[8]

Now, three divisions would attack abreast (from right to left): the 51st Highland, across the anti-tank trap and up Djebel Roumana; the 50th Tyne Tees, between Djebel Roumana and the neighbouring height of El Hachana; and the 4th Indian, across the Zouai heights. Monty was confident of gaining surprise because never before had he attacked the centre of an enemy position, and certainly not in the dark with no moon. He also knew that the sectors of the front line due to be attacked were held by Italians of the 80th La Spezia and 101st Trieste Divisions. That, he felt, was the enemy's 'weak point'.[9]

The assault was due to be launched in the early hours of 6 April, supported by 450 guns, and with the US II Corps providing 'flanking pressure'. Once a breach had been made, Horrocks's motorised X Corps would pass through and head for Sfax and Sousse. This second phase would coincide with two simultaneous offensives to the north: one by an Anglo-American force, commanded by the newly arrived commander of the British IX Corps, Lieutenant General John Crocker, with orders to secure the Fondouk Gap and send the 6th Armoured Division east towards Kairouan, where it would threaten the withdrawal of Messe's army; and the other by the British V and French XIX Corps which would 'tie down the enemy on their front by thrusts aimed at the capture of important features'.[10]

At 4.15 a.m. on 6 April, Lieutenant Lionel 'Doughy' Baker of the 1/7th Middlesex Regiment had just crossed the Wadi Akarit and was driving slowly forward in his 15cwt truck when he heard a single gun fire behind him. Then came 'a rumble of explosions and the air above us moaned with shells in flight', wrote Baker, as 450 artillery pieces opened up. He added: 'Gently we moved on at our scheduled pace, which now felt slower than ever. The dark cloud was coming unexpectedly up the sky towards us. I noticed bursts of sparks in it: German ack-ack shells? – or were they our own? Then the cloud, right above us, threatening and heavy, began to look solid and jagged: it was a mountain. With a leap of my heart I realised that we were right beneath Roumana!'

The night-time assault on the Axis position at Wadi Akarit had begun. The task of Baker's platoon of machine gunners was to support the advance of a company of the 5th Camerons up Djebel Roumana, the main objective for the 51st Highland Division's 153rd Brigade. As he climbed, Baker was struck by the 'fresh rosiness of the air, the strange, soft, brown colouring on the rocks around me, the glorious, silver aura of morning light that seemed to enfringe them'. Reaching the crest, he 'caught a glimpse of pink, morning peaks beyond, and hastened to join, map-case in hand, the line of riflemen spread just forward of the summit'.

To his right, the ridge rose to the mountain's peak, Point 122, on whose steep slopes he could see the leading platoons of 5th Seaforths, the neighbouring battalion, 'scrambling spiritedly'. Above them, 'ignoring or unaware of their approach, some Italians seemed to be sheltering behind rocks'. They were members of the Italian 126th Regiment, part of the air-transportable 80th 'La Spezia' Division which had suffered severe casualties at the Mareth Line. This might explain why, when the Seaforths reached the summit, the defenders meekly 'surrendered without resistance'.

Thus far, things had gone without a hitch. From the desert, Roumana had appeared to be an isolated crag. Having reached its left shoulder, Baker could see that it was 'the outpost of a range of peaks now lying before us, bathed in the pearly, pink light of the sunrise'. While Baker positioned his guns, the company of 5th Camerons descended the hill to their next objective. Baker then returned to the trucks at the base of the mountain to get more ammunition. He struggled back up the hill to join his machine-gun platoon and, as he neared the top, mortar bombs were exploding on the ridge. 'Keeping low,' he recalled, 'I moved forward till I could see over the summit. There was not a soul there! What the HELL had happened!'

He called out. There was no reply. The gun positions that should have been occupied by his Middlesex boys were empty. Had his platoon moved forward to support the Jocks? he wondered. If so, they had gone against his express orders. Maybe they were ordered to. The only way to find out was to return to the Camerons' HQ which was in contact with the forward companies. 'With my heart in my boots,' wrote Baker, 'I hurried down the long, steep, craggy, boulder-strewn, damnable mountainside once more.'

At the bottom he admitted to the Camerons' commanding officer that his platoon was 'no longer carrying out the role he had given it in his orders', and had effectively vanished. After trying and failing to contact his forward companies by radio, the colonel told Baker to go forward in person and find out what had happened. Pausing only to wolf down a ration of bully-and-biscuit, and to take a swig of water, he struggled back up the hill with more ammunition. Dodging mortar explosions on the crest, he found a dead Cameron with a 'healthy young face, wide blue eyes, and the high, girlish cheekbones that many Scots boys have'.

He carried on down the escarpment, following the advance of the Camerons, and at the bottom found his platoon and some Italian prisoners taking cover behind a little ridge. 'Where were the guns?' he wondered. 'Not one was in action. Most of the men were crouching in holes.'

Many had been wounded by enfilade fire. The rest were so demoralised they had failed to mount the guns or even to hoard the ammunition. Baker was furious. Further along the depression he found the Camerons' company commander, Donald Watson, who had lost contact with his forward platoons. 'Why are my men down here?' asked Baker.

'I'm sorry,' replied Watson. 'One of my sergeants exceeded his authority by ordering your men down the mountain.'

Baker got his four guns into action in time to engage a German counter-attack which, nevertheless, worked its way round his flank and up the slopes of Roumana. Eventually a German machine-gunner opened up on them from the rear, the bullets kicking up sand in front of Baker's face. He rolled onto dead ground, 'shaken, but at the same time strangely elated', realising that he, Watson and a handful of their men were the 'only troops left in front of Roumana who had not been overrun by the German counter-attack'.

After one of Baker's guns was knocked out by mortar fire, and the gunner killed, Watson made the decision to withdraw behind Roumana. Baker ordered his men to leave the guns, and sent them off one by one. He and Watson were the last to leave. 'Never had I felt so exposed!' remembered Baker. 'The muscles of my back braced themselves against bullets that at any moment would be piercing them.'

Stopping to help one of his men, who had been shot in the hip, Baker eventually reached the relative safety of the Camerons' HQ. He had lost three men killed, two missing, three badly wounded (and left on the other side of the mountain), and four more wounded and evacuated. Though 'sick with fatigue', he agreed to the colonel's request to take his surviving men back up the mountain to hold it 'with rifle and bayonet'. It never came to that, however, as the German counter-attack had run out of steam. Later, Baker led two patrols that brought back the wounded and, as it was getting dark, retrieved the guns.

It had been, for him, a day of 'danger, defeat, disappointment, distress, failure, frustration and repeated weariness', yet he would remember it as one of the 'most exciting and eventful' of his life.[11] Fortunately, the setback in their sector was not decisive for the battle.

Elsewhere, XXX Corps' offensive had done slightly better, achieving mixed results as 'attack and counter-attack clashed in the hills and both

Germans and Italians showed a quite reckless determination and unimpaired morale'.[12] Tasked with crossing a minefield and an anti-tank ditch — 10 feet deep and with smooth sides — to the right (east) of Roumana, and forming a bridgehead, the 7th Argylls of 154th Brigade had captured all their objectives by dawn, albeit with 'a considerable number of casualties'. Thereafter the battalion was subjected to incessant bombardment and a number of savage counter-attacks by infantry and tanks; one of these penetrated to within yards of C Company HQ before the OC, Major John Macdougall, shouting 'No surrender!', led his remaining five men in a bayonet charge that routed the enemy. That the battalion held its ground was largely thanks to the outstanding leadership of the CO, 40-year-old Lieutenant Colonel Lorne Campbell, DSO and Bar, for which he was awarded the division's only Victoria Cross of the conflict. Part of his citation read:

> When his left forward company was forced to give ground he went forward in a hail of fire, and personally reorganised their position, remaining with the company until the attack at this point was held.
>
> As reinforcements arrived on the scene he was seen standing in the open, directing the fight under close-range fire of the enemy, and he continued to do so although already painfully wounded in the neck by shell-fire. It was not until the battle died down that he allowed his wound to be dressed.[13]

The day had started promisingly for the 51st Division, but ended with it being forced to relinquish some of its gains. At one point, divisional commander Douglas Wimberley had ordered Lieutenant Colonel David Belchem of the 1st RTR to take his tanks up the hill to assist the Scots. When Belchem radioed his brigade commander for clearance, however, he was told to stand fast. It was a close shave for Belchem. As he discovered later, the Germans had sited anti-tank guns along the top of the ridge that would have decimated his armour during the long climb.[14]

The neighbouring 50th Tyne Tees Division, in the centre, meanwhile, had been 'seriously delayed by resistance on the line of the wadi'. This left Tuker's 4th Indian Division to achieve the most significant breakthrough as it stormed up and captured the rugged Zouai heights. 'The 7th Indian Brigade,' wrote Alex, 'led by the Royal Sussex and the 2nd Gurkhas, captured all their objectives by dawn and the 5th Indian Brigade, which then passed through, completed the mopping up and was in a position to take in rear the defences which were holding up the Corps' centre and right.'[15]

Only rarely is a battle 'won' by a single officer. This, however, was the feat of Subedar Lalbahadur Thapa of the 1/2nd Gurkhas. During the uphill assault, he led two sections into a gully 'thickly studded' with machine-gun posts and anti-tank guns. Using their kukris, bayonets and small arms, Thapa and his men fought their way uphill, neutralising one strongpoint after another. Reaching the crest with just two men, Thapa killed two Italians with his kukri while the others fled. 'The chimney between the escarpments was open,' noted the divisional history, 'and with it the corridor through which 5 Brigade might pass.' For this astonishing feat, Thapa was awarded the Victoria Cross.

With his men in control of the Zouai heights, Tuker urged Horrocks to attack with his armour and turn a promising situation into a rout. But Horrocks dithered, and it was not until noon, many hours later, that the tanks moved forward. Even then they were halted by Horrocks at the furthest point of XXX Corps' advance, and not ordered to push on through, for fear of anti-tank guns. It was a wasted opportunity.[16]

Alex put the near miss down to fierce counter-attacks by the two German divisions in reserve, which was partly true. 'It looked like a complete debacle for the enemy,' he wrote, 'but the 15th Panzer and and 90th Light Divisions, fighting perhaps the best battle of their distinguished careers, counter-attacked with great vigour and by their self-sacrifice enabled Messe to stabilize the situation.'[17]

It had been, wrote Monty, 'the heaviest and most savage fighting we have had since I commanded the Eighth Army'. Many key positions had 'changed hands several times', and by his 'immense endeavours' the enemy had prevented the Eighth Army 'from breaking out into the open before dark'. He had lost 600 men killed and another 2,000 wounded.[18]

One of the last Britons to die on 6 April was Captain Alan Blackwell, commanding the 5th East Yorkshires' HQ Company, who had not seen his wife Marjorie since departing the UK for foreign service almost two years earlier. Typically, a close relative would be informed of an officer's death by War Office telegram. But, in this instance, Marjorie heard the news she had long been dreading from a fellow officer, Major Andrew Edgar, who wrote to sympathise with her 'tragic loss'. Too distraught to call on or write to Alan's parents, she left the unpleasant task to her own father who informed them, in as sensitive a manner as possible, that Alan had been 'killed instantaneously by a bomb in the advance of 6 April'.[19]

Eager for more details, Mr Blackwell wrote to Edgar and received the following reply:

The battalion had taken part in a particularly 'sticky' attack on the enemy's positions on the Wadi Akarit in Tunisia, just north of Gabes. Eventually the attack was successful, but the enemy did his best to drive us off the ground we had taken. We were shelled and counter-attacked and late in the evening he sent his aircraft over to bomb us. It was a bomb from one of these aircraft that killed your son along with three other officers with whom he was talking at the time. He was buried the next morning in a small regimental cemetery close to the spot where he fell and together with his comrades who also fell in that action . . .

I would like to say how very much we miss 'Blackie' and how much we all admired his spirit, courage and personality when he was with us. He was a fine officer and a sterling example.[20]

Marjorie, meanwhile, had received a heartfelt letter of condolence from Alan's batman, Private Leslie Binns:

> I was close by him when he was killed. I am pleased to be able to tell you that he didn't suffer at all . . . The following day, after Jerry withdrew, I spent a few hours making his grave as presentable as I could. He was more than an officer to me, he was a friend. And I feel his absence very deeply. His most treasured possession was a photograph of yourself. As soon as we had pitched his tent, my first duty was to place it on the box by his bed. And three hours before he was killed he asked me to get it out of his pack and put it inside his jacket pocket . . . I have lost a pal, if I may say so, you have lost a devoted husband, and England has lost both a gentleman and an officer of courage.[21]

Despite heavy losses, Monty had captured 6,000 prisoners – mostly Italian – in the first day's fighting at Wadi Akarit, and planned to complete the breakthrough the following morning, using all his artillery and air power 'in a blitz attack'.[22]

It was not needed. That night, encouraged by his German divisional commanders, Messe ordered the remnants of the First Italian Army to withdraw to the north. The two panzer divisions fighting on the El Guettar road also broke contact with the US II Corps and drew off to the northeast.[23]

But not all the Axis forces got away unscathed. Oberstleutnant Claus von Stauffenberg, the 10th Panzer Division's operations officer, was in his Horst jeep trying to direct traffic through a narrow defile west of Mezzouna when the column was attacked by P-40 Kittyhawk fighter-bombers of the Desert Air Force (possibly from No. 3 Squadron, RAAF). Chaos descended as vehicle after vehicle was set on fire, and ammunition exploded, making it impossible to rescue the wounded. Stauffenberg was standing up in his jeep, directing survivors to safety, when his vehicle was targeted by 20mm cannon fire. He threw himself from the jeep onto the ground, but was seriously wounded in the head and both hands by shell fragments.

His injuries were dressed by a passing medical officer who directed an ambulance to take Stauffenberg to the No. 200 Field Hospital at Sfax where his right hand was amputated at the wrist; also removed were his left eye and the little and ring fingers on his left hand. Three days later, he endured another painful ambulance journey, again disrupted by fighter-bomber attacks, to No. 950 Base Hospital in Tunis. From there he was evacuated by boat to Livorno in Italy, and then put on a hospital train to Munich in Bavaria, arriving at the First General Military Hospital on 21 April. It was during his lengthy recuperation that he began plotting Hitler's assassination in earnest.[24]

Also ambushed during the retreat – this time by the 1st Royal Tank Regiment – was a mobile column of German armoured troops near Agareb, west of Sfax. The British tanks destroyed six panzers, sixteen anti-tank guns and fifty-six armoured half-tracks and vehicles. They also disabled a Tiger. For these combined actions, CO David Belchem was awarded a DSO.[25]

George S. Patton Jr, meanwhile, had followed close behind a task force of the 1st Armored Division – a battalion of tanks, and a company each of tank destroyers and armoured infantry, under Colonel C. C. Benson – as it pursued the retreating Germans up the Gabès road on 7 April. 'We found Benson eating lunch,' noted Patton in his diary, 'not much, so I told him to stop eating and get out in front, and he moved out. He was delayed by a mine field. We drove through the mine field.'

At this point, Patton's jeep was almost at the tip of the spear, with only a single jeep and a scout car ahead of him, and 'everyone told me I was going to be killed'. Reaching the 70km marker from Gabès, he reluctantly decided to turn around and met Benson coming the other way. Keep pushing, he told him, 'for a fight or a bath' in the ocean.

Soon after Patton gave his parting instruction, Benson's vanguard crossed into the Eighth Army's zone of operation where it met troops from Tuker's 4th Indian Division.[26] 'Hello, Limeys!' the Americans shouted, unaware that these Eighth Army men were from the sub-continent.

As other British and American troops met, they grinned and shook hands. 'This is certainly a pleasant surprise,' said a British sergeant.

'Well,' replied a private from Kentucky, 'it's good to see somebody besides a Nazi.'

Patton told his wife Beatrice: 'It is just as well that I was not there, as it would have looked theatrical.'

Almost five months to the day since the Torch landings, the two Allied forces in North Africa had joined hands. Ike was overjoyed. 'We are at last operating on a single battle line,' he told his son John, 'and have placed the enemy in a position that, to say the least, is highly embarrassing for him. I have been aiming for this for a long time and, frankly, I must say that I experience a definite feeling of happiness and delight.'[27]

39

Mission Impossible

Tunisia and Austria, 7–22 April 1943

O N 7 APRIL, AS part of his plan to hit the withdrawing Axis
forces in the flank, Alex ordered Lieutenant General John
Crocker, commanding the British IX Corps, to capture the Fondouk
Pass. Crocker was a conscientious if unimaginative commander who
had followed an unusual career path. Brought up in a modest house
in Catford, southeast London, and known as 'Honest John', he had
joined the British Army as a private in 1914, and only gained his
commission three years later. After a post-war stint as a trainee solicitor,
he joined the army as a regular in 1920 and was posted to the Royal
Tank Corps. He later attended the Staff College at Quetta in India
and graduated with a rare A grade and a rating of 'exceptional merit
and outstanding ability'.

He was an excellent staff officer – Brooke, under whom he served
as GSO1 of the Mobile Division in the 1930s, could not 'speak too
highly' of him – and commanded a brigade of the 1st Armoured
Division during the disastrous 1940 campaign in France. Since then,
thanks to Brooke's patronage, he had led the 6th Armoured Division,
the 2nd Armoured Group and the XI Corps, the latter at the relatively youthful age of forty-six. But none of these roles were on
operations and Crocker was distinctly undercooked as a battlefield

commander when he arrived in North Africa with IX Corps head-quarters in March 1943.[1]

He planned to use the British 128th Brigade (part of the 46th Division) and two regiments of the US 34th Division, loaned from Patton's II Corps, to clear the heights to the north and south of the Fondouk Gap respectively. Once the defile had been secured, he would send the British 6th Armoured Brigade into the Kairouan plain to intercept and destroy the retreating Axis forces. But Crocker's inexperience showed when he ordered the 128th Brigade to secure first the heights east of Pichon, before it moved south to capture the high ground north of Fondouk. The end result was that the 34th Division's left flank was dangerously exposed as it began its own attack during the early hours of 8 April. The commander of the 34th, Major General Ryder, had raised the issue with Crocker but nothing was done.

'Progress was slow,' remembered Sergeant Ralph Schaps of the 2/135th Infantry, 'and soon got bogged down because of the intense mortar and Spandau fire. That evening it was decided that the 2nd Battalion would make a night attack. It was unsuccessful as we had no training in night fighting. Another Army SNAFU. On all of our attacks we had some tank support. However, the problem was that they would send up 2 or 3 tanks at a time and the Krauts would quickly knock them out with their "88s".'[2]

The 128th Brigade, meanwhile, had managed to capture all of its objectives near Pichon. But in doing so it fell behind schedule and was unable to conquer the heights north of the Fondouk Gap. At all points, therefore, the first day's attack at Fondouk 'had been thwarted'.

Crocker's solution – suggested by Alex – was to order the 6th Armoured Division to send its tanks through the minefields of the Fondouk Gap while the entire 1st Guards Brigade, supported by the 128th Infantry Brigade, took the heights to the north. 'This gallant attack,' wrote Alex, 'went in on the afternoon of the 9th. The motor battalion of the armoured brigade advanced into the throat of the defile under heavy cross fire to make a gap in the minefield and two armoured regiments then plunged through. Unswept mines and anti-tank guns in enfilade took a toll but our tanks pressed on undeterred and the pass was forced.'[3]

The following day, having destroyed a strong force of enemy tanks and anti-tank guns to the southeast, the vanguard of the 6th Armoured Division entered the holy city of Kairouan at 10.15 a.m. Major General Keightley's tanks had shot up the rearguard of the retreating panzer divisions, but the bulk of Messe's First Italian Army had escaped.

Among the first British journalists to enter Kairouan – founded by the Ummayads after the death of the Islamic prophet Muhammad in the late seventh century – was John D'Arcy-Dawson of the *Daily Sketch*. He wrote:

> Before us as we crossed the crest of the ridge lay the softly tinted white walls of the Holy City of Tunisia . . . On either side of the road enemy tanks were still smouldering . . . Passing Sappers with mine detectors searching the road verges, we were soon close to the city. Outlines became clearer and at the entrance we could see a large crowd of black-clothed figures. We drew closer, slowed down and were greeted with cheers and hand-clapping by the Jewish population. Joyfully tearing from their breasts the yellow Star of David which they had been forced to wear by the Germans, they surrounded us.

One Jew, clapping the journalist on the back, said: 'Oh this is a happy moment. We Jews have been in servitude. Now you have delivered us. Thank you.' It was not just the Germans who had persecuted Tunisia's Jews. The Vichy government of France, at Nazi Germany's request, had passed a series of laws that effectively banned Jewish children from school, appropriated Jewish property, prevented Jews from working as lawyers and doctors, and revoked their French citizenship. These laws were overturned by a committee set up by General Giraud.[4]

Locating the Gendarmerie off the main square, D'Arcy-Dawson

and his colleagues were given a short speech of welcome by the French mayor. They then celebrated with a glass of wine, before touring the city. 'We rode on a wave of gratifying enthusiasm,' wrote the Briton. 'Wherever we went the crowd followed us. At street corners little girls came forward shyly, curtsied and presented us with bouquets of mimosa sprays.'

The Germans had left a few hours before the first Allied troops – a patrol of the 1st Derbyshire Yeomanry – drove in. As usual, Arnim's men had hogged the best transport, leaving their Italian allies to make do with what was left. The last truck to leave had Italians clinging to the sides, sitting on the bonnet and jammed in like sardines.[5]

When Lieutenant Vincent Moore's troop of the Derbyshire Yeomanry was quartered in the city a day or two later, he and his men visited the abandoned workshops of the 10th Panzer Division and gazed in wonder at the Great Mosque, which covered an area of 10,000 square yards and was reputed to have more than 500 pillars to support its roof. Through the city passed an endless column of vehicles as the Eighth Army advanced on Messe's new defensive position at Enfidaville. 'It was', remembered Moore, 'a great thrill to see these conquering men of the Eighth Army, tanned several shades darker than us, and looking magnificently fit.'[6]

In reality, another opportunity to press home an advantage against retreating Axis forces had been missed and the fallout severely dented Anglo-American relations. John Crocker made ill-judged comments to journalists, severely critical of the US 34th Division's failure to take its objectives at Fondouk. When adverse stories concerning American units began to appear in the United States, Ike was furious. 'I had foreseen', he wrote to Marshall, 'the effect at home of discouraging reports and had been working like a dog to insure a reasonable utilization of American troops and the presentation of a proper perspective in reports. Moreover, I have made Alexander and others concerned see the great damage that would result from unfair or caustic criticism of any tactical failure of the kind indicated.'[7]

Ike was not blind to American shortcomings. But he also knew, as did Patton, that the 34th Division had not been given a fair crack of the whip. It had had, he wrote later, 'only sketchy training and had been involved for many weeks in protection of our line of communications, thus missing the opportunity to work together as a unit'. The task it was given at Fondouk was a 'difficult one and the attack failed', and even though a breakthrough was eventually accomplished by British formations, it was 'not particularly effective' because the Germans had 'made good their retreat to the northward'.[8]

In his diary, Patton also acknowledged that the 34th 'did not do too well, but that was largely because Crocker sent it on an impossible mission with both flanks open'. Once the American troops had 'drawn off the Germans, the British came in and took their hill'. He was convinced there would be a 'showdown' with the British and that he might be 'one of the victims'.[9]

He was right about a showdown. Ike read the riot act to Alex who 'quickly took steps' to ensure that no British commander repeated Crocker's mistake of criticising American troops in public. A similar veto was placed on American generals. Ike, meanwhile, tried to repair some of the damage by doing a little bit of 'propagandizing' – in other words, lauding the achievements of American troops thus far in the campaign.

He was acutely aware that it was not only II Corps that felt undervalued. Units of the British First Army, he told Marshall, 'feel that their efforts have been minimized in the press and that all the glory has gone to the more spectacular advances of the Eighth Army'. During a recent visit to the front, he had accepted Anderson's offer to drive him in a jeep to the site of the fighting at Hunt's Gap, east of Béja, where he counted '27 completely destroyed German tanks, including, in one spot, three of the big Mark 6s [Tigers]' with their huge 88mm guns. It was, Ike noted, a 'lovely sight'.

Anderson explained that the pre-registered pattern of British artillery fire on this stretch of road had been so heavy that many of the attacking panzers were hit and the crews of the Tigers forced to abandon their 'mobile fortresses'. With evidence of the 'fiercest kind of fighting' all around, Ike could understand why members of the First Army felt that 'full credit has not been given to them'.

As for American troops in the Gafsa operations, they had taken 'something over 5000 prisoners, damaged at least 60 tanks, of which almost half were completely destroyed, captured over 100 guns of various calibre, and inflicted many other casualties on the forces opposing them'. It was an impressive achievement, given their lack of experience, and compared favourably to the patchy British performance during the first two years of the Desert War. Ike's priority now, he told Marshall, was to get the American units 'the finest possible leadership that we can produce'.[10]

That would not include Major General Orlando 'Pinky' Ward, the commander of the 1st Armored Division, who had been sacked by Patton on 4 April. Alexander had wielded the knife by telling Ike he had no confidence in Ward. Ike agreed he must go, and Alex had informed Patton. Impressively, Patton did not use Alex 'as a cloak' for sacking Ward. 'I should have relieved him on the 22nd or 23rd,' he wrote in his diary, 'but did not do so as I hate to change leaders in battle, but a new leader is better than a timid one.'

That new leader was Ernest Harmon who had impressed as acting commander of II Corps after Kasserine. Harmon, in turn, fired the supine Brigadier General McQuillin as boss of Combat Command A, replacing him with Colonel Kent C. Lambert, Patton's former operations officer. At 6.30 p.m. on 13 April, on the slope of a hill near Djebel Lessouda, Harmon gathered all his officers for a pep talk. The location was deliberate. Clearly visible were the 'silent, blackened wrecks of American vehicles' destroyed by Arnim's panzers on 14 and 15 February. 'Some of the tanks had been blown up,' wrote Brigadier General Robinett, the pugnacious commander of CCB. 'Others had their turrets blown away.'

What the officers – some of whose friends had died in those

tanks – needed to hear from Harmon was a promise that such disasters were a thing of the past, and that he believed in them. Instead, he said almost the opposite.

After castigating those who had arrived a little late, recalled Robinett, 'he launched into a sharply worded speech which damned all past performance, sparing none'. A deathly silence fell over the assembly which 'only accentuated Harmon's rattling, angry voice'. Someone had told him, he said, the division was 'not battle-worthy'. It was unacceptable. 'This outfit,' he shouted, 'will have a resurrection on the ground where it was defeated. Lieutenants are expendable and may expect to die and others as well.'

Robinett was horrified by this example of poor leadership. Harmon was berating men 'who had endured hardships and battle for several months, many of whom had been wounded'. As he spoke, the men gazed on 'the blackened tanks of a battalion that had charged to its destruction in a vain effort to relieve other American troops cut off by the enemy'. The backdrop added insult to injury and, after Harmon had left, the officers 'filed away silently and dejectedly'.

If Harmon's intention had been to develop a better fighting spirit in his command, his rebukes and threats had signally failed. As the Unionist commander William T. Sherman in the US Civil War had said: 'No general can accomplish the full work of his army unless he commands the soul of his men, as well as their bodies and legs.' Harmon's 'Resurrection' address became infamous, and thereafter Robinett reported a 'noticeable loss of morale'.[11]

The biggest change in leadership – for the second time in six weeks – was at the top of II Corps. Patton suspected as much as he prepared for a conference at Alexander's HQ in the morning of 14 April. 'I think it probable,' he wrote in his diary, 'that he may send me back to work on "Husky"' – planning for the invasion of Sicily. 'I would like to finish this fight but shall not argue, as it seems to me that I am in the hands of fate, who is forging me for some future bigger role.'[12]

His intuition was spot on. At the conference, Ike told him that he was to be relieved of command of II Corps so that he could continue planning Husky. His deputy, Major General Omar Bradley, would replace him. Ike made it clear that it was not 'indicative of failure', and that he had 'done his stuff', and he wrote Patton a letter of commendation to be distributed across the Corps, congratulating him on the 'outstanding example of leadership you have given us all'. He even got a personal note of thanks from Marshall.

Alexander acknowledged that Patton had transformed the morale of the troops of II Corps from the 'natural depression caused by the early setbacks'. Alex added:

> They had absorbed with great rapidity the benefits of the intensive training to which they had been subjected and were now showing in the hard mountain fighting that they had added the skill of the trained soldier to those excellent natural qualities which had been previously in part obscured by their inexperience. General Patton was to score other triumphs in the Mediterranean and in Northwest Europe, but I think this was not the least of his achievements.

In truth, Patton was a little disillusioned with coalition warfare. He dreamt of battlefield glory, but Alex had been unwilling to let him launch a devastating attack into the flank of the withdrawing Axis forces – and Patton was convinced that Bradley would fare no better. 'I hate to quit a fight,' Patton wrote in his diary, 'but feel that I had best do so as I fear that on the north flank, where Alexander has put us, there is no future . . . I have been very fortunate so far.'[13]

Built in the early eighteenth century as a summer residence for the prince-archbishops of Salzburg, the Baroque palace of Schloss Klessheim boasts an entrance with a magnificent Triton fountain, a loggia and a grand staircase. Since the Anschluss – the bloodless union of Austria and Germany in 1938 – Hitler had used Klessheim for high-level conferences and to host official guests when he was staying at his nearby Berghof residence.

Several meetings between Hitler and Mussolini had been cancelled in the early months of 1943 because the Italian dictator was unwell. Finally, a four-day conference was arranged at Klessheim from 7 to 10 April. Before arriving, the Duce was briefed by his armed forces chief, Ambrosio, who stressed the need for a single vision on how to conduct the war, and Italy's desperate requirement for weapons and munitions to defend its coast.[14]

Mussolini arrived in Austria a shadow of his former self, worn down by the 'strain of war and depression', and had to be helped from the train. He would spend much of his visit in bed. When he did attend Hitler's noon military briefing, he was not fooled by the usual exaggeration of good news and suppression of bad. It was vital, he told Hitler, to conclude a compromise peace in the east in order to bolster Axis defences in the west. One way to do that, said Mussolini, was to construct a political 'New Order' in Europe with like-minded states that would counter-balance the Western Allies. An alliance with Franco's Spain, for example, might turn the tide in North Africa by allowing an attack across the Straits of Gibraltar and into the rear of the Allied armies. But the USSR, he insisted, could not be defeated on the field of battle. 'Mussolini was not interested in anything else,' noted Nicolaus von Below, 'and was very quiet. It was obvious that he considered the war to be lost and in his opinion Italy had no further role to play.'[15]

As before, Hitler rejected out of hand a peace deal with Russia. But he also tried to shore up Mussolini's battered morale by reminding him that the fall of Tunis would pose a mortal threat to Italian fascism. Ultimately, his only hope of salvation, said Hitler, was 'to achieve victory with us or to die'. To that end, it was vital that the Italian navy should ship as many supplies to Tunisia as possible.[16]

Privately, at least, Hitler's closest advisors knew the game was up in North Africa. 'We must not deceive ourselves,' wrote Goebbels in his diary, 'but realise that our situation [in Tunis] is almost hopeless.

The enemy press is now attacking Rommel in an infamous and shameless way. That is too bad, especially since he has had nothing whatever to do with Tunisia recently . . . Our North Africa undertaking has cost us much equipment and blood. When all is said and done, the Italians are really responsible . . . Our allies are certainly the worst in the world!'[17]

According to Walter Warlimont, the OKW's Deputy Chief of the Operations Staff, the only military man at Klessheim who was prepared to 'look facts in the face' was Mussolini's military chief, Ambrosio, much to Hitler's fury. But he was drowned out by Kesselring who, as usual, told the Führer what he wanted to hear by giving 'optimistic forecasts' and making 'proposals for the movement of the reinforcements'.[18]

The real lesson of the conference for Ambrosio was that the Germans regarded the Mediterranean as a 'war theatre of secondary importance', and that while they feared a future landing in Sicily or Sardinia, they were not prepared to send weapons to any sector that was not yet a combat zone. Even those that were would not get what was needed. Of the 500 German aircraft that Mussolini had asked for, only 100 would arrive – and those not until the summer. The army's request for 1,250 German tanks went unheeded, as did the navy's demand for 70,000 tons of fuel oil to power its ships.

Kesselring explained that, after Stalingrad, Germany was using all its reserves to hold back the Soviets. Even so, it had given Italy 500 88mm anti-aircraft guns and 180 searchlights. This was still not enough, said Ambrosio. 'The size of your requests,' Kesselring countered, 'are enough to kill the strongest man.'[19]

By 11 April, Alex had completed stage one of his mission to destroy all Axis forces in North Africa: the capture of the entire coastal plain, and the confinement of Arnim's Army Group Afrika to the northeast corner of Tunisia. As the sea blockade had tightened, the Axis resorted to air transport to get supplies and men to Tunisia, but so many transport aircraft were shot down by British and American fighters – on

19 April, twenty-one German six-engined transport planes, each carrying 120 troops, went down off Cape Bon in northern Tunisia, and on 22 April, wrote Churchill, 'a further thirty, including many laden with petrol, went flaming into the sea' – that the effort failed and no more supply planes 'dared fly by day'.[20] Yet despite their desperate prospects, wrote Alex, it was clear 'that the enemy, so far from thinking of evacuation, was using every available means to rush troops into his now much diminished Tunisian bridgehead'.[21]

Alex's new task was the complete destruction of the remaining Axis forces as quickly as possible, 'in order to obtain the use of the ports of Tunis and Bizerte for the invasion of Sicily'. There were two main axes of defence, facing west and south, with the salient angle 'protected by the tangled mountain country' of Djebel Mansour. He decided, therefore, for topographical reasons, to make his main attack on the western face, so that a breakthrough as far as Tunis would split the Axis forces into two. They could then be defeated in detail.[22]

It was not a strategy that found favour with Monty who hoped his Eighth Army would 'play the major part' in the final assault. But to do that, he told Alex, he would require 'all the resources in northern Tunisia' while the First Army sat tight and exerted pressure. 'Whoever does the business,' added Monty, 'must have the resources in Divisions, men, artillery, and ammunition, to be able to carry on day after day, and night after night.' Only by blasting them with artillery and bombs from the air, and attacking them daily, 'can you defeat the Germans'.[23]

While largely agreeing with these tactics, Alex insisted the main effort would be made by the First Army. This was partly because a successful attack by the Eighth Army 'would drive the enemy in on themselves rather than split them', and partly because the terrain in the First Army's sector was less mountainous and therefore more favourable for armour. There were three possible routes to Tunis from the west. The first ran from Bou Arada to Pont du Fahs 'and thence northeast', but this could be blocked 'fairly easily' at the Pont du Fahs defile and 'commanded from the mountains at the south side of the

Bou Arada plain'. The second ran northeastwards from the Goubellat plain, skirting the salt marshes of Sebkret el Kourzia, and into the plain of Tunis by minor roads, but the difficulty was a 'belt of broken country without roads which interposes to the northeast of the salt marshes'. The third followed the Medjez–Massicault road, the main route to Tunis from the west, which offered the best opportunities for the use of tanks, but was, as a result, the most heavily defended. All three routes would be attempted.

To give Anderson's First Army the best chance of breaking through, Alex had decided to relieve the British 46th and 4th Infantry Divisions in its northern sector with two American infantry divisions from II Corps, the 9th and 1st. Once in position, II Corps would command the area north of the Oued et Tine, and would conduct operations towards Bizerte, while the First Army concentrated on Tunis. The Americans, at Ike's insistence, would remain an independent formation, four divisions strong, and under army group command and not that of Anderson.²⁴

Ike had several reasons for insisting that Alex use II Corps as a unit: the bulk of the ground forces needed to defeat Germany in the west would come from the US Army, and battle training was urgently required; II Corps had yet 'to exert its power' in battle as a unified force; and, thanks to Patton, the morale of the Corps had improved so much since early March that it had earned the right 'to prove its own effectiveness as well as the quality of American arms'. He also had the American public to consider: if II Corps were not involved in the final operations, they would want to know why.

After discussions with Monty, Anderson and Patton (before his relief), Alex directed his staff to devise a final plan of attack against an enemy front 120 miles long and defended by an estimated 200,000 men. It would begin on the night of 19/20 April with pressure by the Eighth Army on the enemy's southern flank at Enfidaville. Koeltz's French XIX Corps, meanwhile, was to be ready to attack three mountain positions commanding Pont du Fahs from the south, the first of the three routes to Tunis, but not until Anderson gave the word. His First Army would start its broad offensive in the morning of 22 April with Crocker's IX Corps launching attacks on the enemy positions west of the salt marshes at Sebkret el Kourzia. If successful, these would allow the tanks of the 6th and 1st Armoured Divisions (the latter transferred from the Eighth Army) to advance on and capture Djebel Mengoub, an 800-foot feature that was 15 miles from the north end of the marshes and the same distance from Tunis, following the second of the three routes.

That evening, Allfrey's V Corps would join in the offensive with the 1st and 4th Infantry Divisions attacking towards Massicault, the third route to Tunis, and the 78th Division advancing in the mountains north of the Medjerda river with Djebel el Ahmera (the aforementioned 'Longstop Hill') as its first objective.

The final attack, by II Corps, was scheduled for 23 April, with the 1st Infantry Division ('Big Red One') attacking down the Sidi Nsir road towards the pass above Chouïgui, and the 9th Division from Sedjenane to Mateur. This attack, it was hoped, would eventually allow the Allies to capture the port of Bizerte. Alex would command the battle from his new army group HQ in a wood near Le Kef.[25]

40

'They were bunched like a herd of cattle'

Northern Tunisia, 15 April–1 May 1943

F OUR DAYS BEFORE THE start of the Eighth Army's final battle in North Africa at Enfidaville, Monty complained to General Sir Alan Brooke, the CIGS, that Alex's plan to end the campaign was flawed. He wrote on 15 April:

> I have an unpleasant feeling in the pit of my stomach that we may make a mess of it. The attack plan for the major effort, on the First Army front, is NOT the way that I fight the Germans. My experience is that the way to beat him is to concentrate all your strength and hit him an almighty crack; then through that place, whilst the enemy is reeling under the blow, you burst with armoured and mobile forces. But the big plan for the big blow up north, on First Army front, does not do this.

He would do his best, he told Brooke, to draw the enemy strength down on to the Eighth Army and 'away from the main attack – and this may turn the scale'. Yet he feared that the First Army attacks would fail because they had dispersed rather than concentrated their strengths. He added, with more than a touch of melodrama, that he would 'burst into tears if, having come 2000 miles and got the enemy cold, we mess it up in the end'.[1]

As the campaign neared its climax, Monty's arrogance and sense of entitlement was becoming insufferable. Six weeks earlier, he had asked Walter Bedell Smith, Ike's chief of staff, what his reward would be for getting to Sfax by early April.

'Anything you like,' said Smith unwisely.

'In that case,' said Monty, 'I'd like a B-17 Flying Fortress and crew for the duration of the war.'

Smith agreed and quickly forgot about the 'deal', but Monty did not. On 10 April, he wired Ike: 'Have captured Sfax. Send Fortress.'

Ike was furious at being 'bounced in this way by Monty' – not least because, in his eyes, Bedell Smith's comment was made 'more as a joke than a real promise' – but eventually acquiesced to keep the peace. Monty, meanwhile, blithely unaware of the furore, boasted to Brooke that the Americans 'have played up well, and I have my Fortress – my own personal property!! I shall come home in it!'[2]

But first there was a battle to fight and this time, as it happened, it was Monty who messed things up. The Axis positions at Enfidaville were undoubtedly formidable. 'Ideal for defence,' noted journalist Philip Jordan, who viewed them three days before the battle. 'You approach them across an absolutely flat plain, some twelve miles wide. It is devoid of cover. Then, quite suddenly, the hills rise up like a wall. The enemy sits on top of them . . . He can see every move we make; we can see none of his.'

Jordan went to visit Freyberg, the commander of the 2nd New Zealand Division, whom he had last seen in 1940, and found him 'fatter, quieter' and 'less apt to jump to conclusions'. He also 'looked worried', and with good reason.[3]

The battle began at 9.30 p.m. on 19 April when elements of the 50th Tyne Tees Division attacked and eventually captured the town of Enfidaville. The New Zealanders advanced to a point three miles northwest of the town, and the 4th Indian Division had a fierce struggle for the high ground of Djebel Garci that, by morning, had only yielded a toehold. 'It was noticed,' wrote Alex, 'that the Italians fought particularly well, outdoing the Germans in line with them.'

The New Zealanders had an 'equally bloody struggle' to capture the rocky peak of Takrouna, 'a pinnacle not unlike the Athenian Acropolis, rising to a height of over 600 feet and standing like a grim forbidding sentinel, nearly four miles to the west of Enfidaville'. Over the course of forty-eight hours, Lance Sergeant Haane Manahi of the 28th (Maori) Battalion performed prodigious feats of valour: first leading a small party up the steep cliff to overwhelm the Italian defenders on a ledge near the summit; and later, after this foothold had been lost, going back up with a group of volunteers to recapture the ledge and, a few hours later, the hilltop village.[4]

'This courageous action,' noted Manahi's medal citation, 'undoubtedly led to the ultimate collapse of the enemy defence and the capture of the whole Takrouna feature with over 300 prisoners, two 25-pounder guns, several mortars and 72 machine guns.' His Victoria Cross recommendation was rubber-stamped by, among others, Horrocks, Monty and Alex. But when it reached the Army Council in London it was downgraded to a Distinguished Conduct Medal, possibly because of reports that surrendering Italians had been 'shot, bayoneted or thrown over a cliff' after wounded Kiwis had been killed by a grenade. The award of a VC three weeks earlier to Lieutenant Ngarimu, a member of the same battalion, might also have been a factor.[5]

Manahi's heroics notwithstanding, the offensive as a whole had not gone as planned. 'In spite of severe losses from our massed artillery fire,' noted Alex, 'the enemy kept up his policy of continuous counter-attacks and it became clear that it would cost us heavily to advance further into this tangled mass of mountains.'[6]

Monty therefore decided late on 21 April to abandon the attacks on the high ground in the centre in favour of a breakthrough near the coast. But it would take time to realign his divisions – the exhausted 50th Tyne Tees, for example, was being withdrawn for the Sicily operation and replaced by the inexperienced 56th London – and the next 'big blow' did not take place until the night of 24/25 April.[7] 'This suspension at the very time the other attacks were beginning,' noted the US Army's official history of the campaign, 'was a serious departure from the army group's general plan.'[8]

When the first stage of the renewed attack did go in late on 24 April, the New Zealanders and the 201st Guards Brigade were able to capture Djebel Terhouna, an important piece of high ground over-looking the coast, five miles north of Enfidaville. But the main attack, scheduled for 29 April, with the object of establishing all three divisions – the 2nd New Zealand, 4th Indian and 56th London – in the area of Hammamet, at the base of the Cape Bon peninsula – was cancelled. 'On the 29th,' explained Alex, 'I received a signal from General Montgomery saying that, as a result of a failure by the 56th Division on that day when coming under artillery fire as it was about to take up positions for the attack, he now felt unhappy about the possibilities of success. As this was not going to interfere with the plans I was already forming for finishing off enemy resistance in the Tunis plain I authorised the abandonment of the attack.'[9]

True to form, Monty blamed the Eighth Army's failure to break through the Enfidaville position on Alex. He wrote to Brooke on 30 April:

Today I told Alex it was just madness to go on as we are doing and that he must re-group. My front should be a holding one; the real blow should go in on First Army front. In fact, that which should have been done some weeks ago, *must* be done now. He agreed and I have sent across two Divisions, some artillery, Gds Bde, etc., ammu-nition, hospitals, labour coys, and so on . . . We have lost a great opportunity, and we have lost a lot of good chaps.[10]

This was disingenuous. Alex had always planned to use the First Army to deliver the strongest blow. The subsidiary attacks, including the Eighth Army's, were designed to take the pressure off the main effort. But by postponing operations on 21 April, after just two days of combat, and then cancelling them entirely after limited gains on the night of the 24th/25th, Monty had made it harder for Anderson's offensive to succeed. In his official dispatch of the campaign, Alex glossed over this failure by bigging up the Eighth Army's overall contribution:

> The Enfidaville line thus marked the culmination of Eighth Army's great advance across Africa. This holding and diversionary role was not indeed its sole contribution to the final victory, for three and a half divisions were transferred to First Army to give weight to the main attack on Tunis . . . In six months, [the men of Eighth Army] had advanced eighteen hundred miles and fought numerous battles in which they were always successful. This would be an astonishing rate of progress even in a civilized country with all the modern facilities of transport . . . but in a desert it is even more remarkable.[11]

The question is: would Alex have ended the campaign sooner had the Eighth Army not been rebuffed at Enfidaville? The answer is almost certainly yes. As it was, Anderson began his offensive on 22 April after Monty had paused his. This 'cessation of pressure' was even more harmful to the First Army's prospects than a spoiling attack put in by the Hermann Göring Division against the heights to the southeast and south of Medjez el Bab, in the Goubellat sector, on the night of the 20th/21st. Taking the defenders of the British 4th and 1st Divisions by surprise, five German battalions and seventy tanks penetrated the Allied lines along a twelve-mile front to a depth of five miles, some getting as far as the gun lines and 4th Divisional HQ. But, at daybreak, the Germans ran up against the main British position and were forced to retire. By evening, they were back at their starting point, having taken 300 prisoners – they claimed – and destroyed five batteries of artillery, eighty trucks and motor vehicles, and seven tanks. Their own losses, according to Alex, were 450 POWs and thirty tanks. 'Nor were our plans for the offensive upset or delayed,' he wrote, 'except to a minor degree on IX Corps front, where the 46th Division attack had to be postponed four hours.'

Even so, the attacks to the north – which journalist Philip Jordan hoped would lead to the fall of Tunis within four days – were only partially successful. IX Corps, for example, was stopped by dense minefields and well-sited strongpoints to the southwest of the Kourzia salt marshes on 22 April. But further north the 46th Division made better progress and, by late afternoon, Crocker had committed the 6th Armoured Division to try to reach the Pont-du-Fahs–Tunis road.

Arnim responded by ordering the Afrika Korps, facing the French XIX Corps to the south, to withdraw closer to Pont-du-Fahs, and to extend its front to cover the crumbling Hermann Göring Division on its right. He also put the 10th Panzer Division, the Fifth Panzer Army's only mobile reserve, into the breach created by the 6th Armoured Division, thus beginning an attritional tank battle that lasted for three days and drew in, as reinforcements, the 21st and 15th Panzer Divisions on the German side, and the 1st Armoured Division on the British.

The occasional rivalry and bad feeling between elite German units was revealed by Oberst Hans Raumann, commanding the 10th Panzer Division's 86th Panzer Grenadier Regiment, who said of Göring's Praetorians: 'A lot of swine, nothing but puffed up . . . They were so loud-mouthed that you simply didn't know what sort of people they were; at the first attack they were scattered and ran away so fast from the tanks that we had to stop them!'[12]

The end result of this latest Allied offensive was that, by 26 April, Arnim had stabilised his front in the broken ground northeast of the Kourzia salt marshes, but at a heavy cost to both sides. From 20 to 26 April, Army Group Afrika claimed to have destroyed 162 British tanks, 24 guns, 67 motor vehicles and 23 planes. Yet its own serious losses could not be as easily replaced: the 10th Panzer Division, for example, was down to just twenty-five operational tanks after two days of battle; and, even after the First Italian Army had provided reinforcements, the total number was still only fifty-five German and ten Italian tanks. 'It was', noted Alex, 'a good preparation for the final blow.'[13]

Further north, V Corps' offensive opened on 22 April with the 78th Division's attack on Longstop Hill, the 'left hand bastion of the Medjez gate' which had defied the Allies since the previous December. The German defenders from the 756th Mountain Regiment resisted with fierce determination for the first thirty-six hours. 'The hill', noted onlooker Philip Jordan on the 23rd, 'was an infernal sight, smoking and reeking, exploding and shrieking, for two hours. Then the barrage lifted a little and left the base alone. The Argylls moved on to it; and so went up the hill behind its climbing terror. At 2.10 the barrage ceased and at 2.25 the hill was ours except for a small and unimportant tip which we shall soon engulf.'[14]

Jordan's account of the attack on Djebel el Ahmera failed to mention Major Jock Anderson, who took command of the 8th Argylls after his commanding officer was killed by shellfire. For reorganising his battalion, inspiring his men and personally leading an assault on 'at least three enemy machine gun positions', Anderson was awarded the Victoria Cross.[15]

But Djebel el Rhar still held out, and it was not until the morning of 26 April that the whole hill mass was in Allied hands, thanks to a bold combined-arms assault by the 5th Buffs and two squadrons of the North Irish Horse's Churchill tanks that scaled the hill and knocked out a ring of German strongpoints. 'Like beetles trying to climb an inverted ice-cream cone,' noted the *Belfast Telegraph*, 'they slipped a little, hung suspended and then went onwards towards the top. The behaviour of these tanks upset the Germans.'[16]

Though ultimately unsuccessful, the defence of Longstop was typical of the stubborn resistance put up by Axis troops everywhere as each yard of ground was contested.

South of the Medjerda, the British 1st and 4th Divisions attacked on 23 April and made slow but steady progress towards Massicault.[17]

One previously unblooded participant was 22-year-old Lance Corporal John Kenneally of the 1st Irish Guards. He remembered:

> We moved out at night. It was 23rd April, Good Friday, and an eerie experience as we moved in single file across the minefields through which the engineers had cleared paths marked with thick white tape. Stealth was of the essence and the only sounds we heard were the creak of equipment and the muffled curses as someone stumbled on the rocky ground. At regular intervals illuminating flares went up from the German defences. We would hit the ground and wait.

Kenneally's battalion had only been in North Africa with the rest of the 24th Guards Brigade – part of the British 1st Infantry Division – since mid-March. On 17 March, St Patrick's Day, it had received a personal message from Alex, himself a former Irish Guardsman, who wrote: 'Welcome to the Micks. Now we will get cracking.' Kenneally and his colleagues had celebrated in time-honoured manner by drinking gallons of alcohol and fighting the military police in the Algerian port of Bône. It was, he noted, the last St Patrick's Day that many of them would see.

The battalion's objective on Good Friday – its baptism of fire as a unit, though a company had been cut to pieces the day before in a failed preliminary attack on the nearby 'Recce Ridge' – was to capture, with the rest of the 24th Guards Brigade, a series of hills to the northeast of Medjez from units of the elite Hermann Göring Division. The Guardsmen's first objective was Point 151.[18]

For Kenneally, soldiering had offered an escape from a murky past. Christened Leslie Jackson, the illegitimate son of a Blackpool schoolgirl and a married Mancunian businessman (who paid maintenance but denied paternity), he had been brought up in Birmingham where his mother earned a living as a dance hostess and occasional prostitute. In January 1939, he had joined a Territorial battery of the Royal Artillery, and was later transferred to the Honourable Artillery

Company. But he gradually fell out of love with the gunners and, after various misdemeanours, including a spell of Absence without Leave (AWOL) for which he was given one month's military detention, he deserted in February 1941 and worked for a time as a casual labourer.

Ashamed at what he had done, he used another man's identity card to join the Irish Guards – a unit that had impressed him when he was serving time – with the suitably Celtic-sounding name of John Patrick Kenneally, and readily embraced the strict discipline, tough training and pride in appearance that were the hallmarks of the Brigade of Guards. Promoted to lance corporal, he was posted to No. 1 Company of the 1st Irish Guards, 1st British Infantry Division. 'My dream had come to fruition,' he wrote. 'I could go no higher. These new comrades of mine were something else. They were mostly aged from 25 upwards, all well over six feet tall. At 6ft 1in I was amongst the smallest. They were big on ability too. The drill was smooth and effortless, one had to be part of it to believe that such precision was possible. Their confidence and skill at arms was outstanding. They were real professionals.'[19]

The opportunity to put that skill into practice was the attack on 23 April 1943. It started well, and Point 151 was taken without firing a shot. Before dawn, Kenneally and his colleagues set out to take the slightly higher next objective, Point 187. On the way they passed the remnant of a company of the 1st Scots Guards that had been in action on their left flank. 'We exchanged banter with them as only soldiers can,' wrote Kenneally. 'Their Company Commander, Lord Lyell, had been killed in action' – he would later be awarded a posthumous Victoria Cross for leading an attack that knocked out an enemy post containing a German 88mm anti-tank gun and a heavy machine gun – 'They were in good order considering the fight they had been in and many had picked up souvenirs of the battle: Luger pistols, Nazi forage caps, binoculars, etc.'

The sheer fact that these Guardsmen had fought and survived gave Kenneally and his colleagues confidence as they moved on towards Point 187 which had also been evacuated before they got there. While his section started to dig in and prepare for a possible counter-attack,

Kenneally foraged around and found, in a concealed German weapon pit, a bottle and a half of white wine and some hunks of stale brown bread. He and a mate, Mick Dempsey, spent one of their last nights together 'under the African stars, chewing the brown bread and toasting the previous occupants in Tunisian wine'.

In the morning of 27 April, while the battalion officers attended an Operations Group, Kenneally and his section cleaned their weapons, drew extra ammunition and filled their water bottles. Some of the men then settled down to write their last letters. The battalion's task, their captain explained on his return, was to attack at dusk the western end of a commanding ridge known as 'the Bou' – Djebel Bou Aoukaz – on the far side of a deep valley. It was 1,500 yards long, with two high points, 214 and 212, at its western extremity. Kenneally's company – No. 1 – would be responsible for taking Point 212. Without the ridge, they were told, the enemy could not control the valley or the plains beyond. The route to Tunis would be open.

They set off in broad daylight at 4 p.m. – a little earlier than planned – and were at once targeted by German guns, mortars and *Nebelwerfers*. Kenneally remembered,

> As we entered the cornfield, the fire seemed to intensify. We plodded on grimly, our eyes fixed on Captain Chesterton and Lieutenant [Michael] Eugster, who was leading. I was dazed and shocked: the noise was devastating; hot blasts from explosions were scorching my face; patches of corn were burning fiercely; stones and earth thrown up by shell bursts were rattling down on my steel helmet; machine gun bursts were scything down the corn like a reaper and down with the corn went officers and men alike. It was a bloody massacre.

Kenneally stopped to help one Guardsman with a shattered arm and a gaping wound in his side. He gave him a swig of water and stuck his rifle in the ground to mark his position. He would not live long.

Soon after, Captain Chesterton was hit but, helped by his batman, kept going as far as an olive grove where the survivors from Nos 1 and 4 Companies regrouped. Eugster, just twenty-one years old, was killed as he led the next advance up the hill. That left Chesterton as the only officer still on his feet. Wounded a second time, he carried on. Kenneally was convinced that had he stayed down, the rest of the men would have 'hightailed it back to safety'. As it was, they followed him as he plodded slowly up the ridge, his tunic torn, his battledress trousers slick with blood, and his arm hanging limply by his side. With dusk falling, Chesterton ordered the men to fix bayonets. Spotting this, the defenders fired a few shots and fled over the ridge. Point 212 was theirs.

The western end of the 'Bou' was now in British hands. But the cost to the Micks had been heavy: only 5 officers and 168 men had survived the advance. No. 1 Company – after Captain Chesterton's evacuation – was down to a single sergeant and 16 men. Over the next three days, they would be counter-attacked five times, reducing their numbers to just 80. In one action, Point 214 was overrun by Germans who began advancing along the ridge towards Kenneally and the handful of men on 212. The Germans were stopped in their tracks by a barrage of 3-inch mortar bombs fired by a gunner who had lugged his heavy weapon up from the foot of the Bou. That same day, 28 April, Kenneally's best friend Mick Dempsey, also just twenty-one, was killed when his slit trench received a direct hit from a German shell.

When one of the biggest German counter-attacks was put in, Kenneally was on outpost duty on the forward slope. He spotted the arrival of the German reinforcements in trucks and armoured vehicles and, losing sight of them during a barrage, decided to crawl forward. 'The ground fell away into deep gully,' he wrote, 'and there they were. Most of them were squatting round a German officer. Some were lying down taking a breather and they were bunched like a herd of cattle. What an opportunity.'

He crawled back to collect his Bren and two magazines, took a deep breath and said, 'Here goes.' Then he 'belted forward, firing from the hip'. The Germans, taken by surprise, were knocked over like ninepins. He even had time to load and fire a second magazine before deciding enough was enough. Diving behind two boulders, he was pinned down until his mates came to the rescue.

Two days later, by which time No. 1 Company was down to ten men, Kenneally and a sergeant foiled a second enemy counter-attack. Though wounded, Kenneally refused to hand over his Bren gun and seek treatment because, as he put it, he was the only one who knew how to use it. It was thanks in no small part to his 'initiative and extraordinary gallantry in attacking single-handed a massed body of the enemy and breaking up an attack on two occasions' that the Irish Guardsmen were able to hold on to the western extremity of the Bou, though the Germans remained in control of the rest of it.

Alex sent his congratulations to the whole battalion for their 'magnificent fight, which has not only added fresh laurels to the illustrious name of your regiment, but has also been of utmost importance to our whole battle'. He added: 'I am immensely proud of you all. I am very sorry for your losses.'

When the first medals were handed out – including a Military Cross for Captain Chesterton – Kenneally was slightly disappointed not to be on the list. 'I thought,' he wrote, 'I might have got a Military Medal.' His consolation prize, he thought, was promotion to sergeant. Months later, while attending a course at the Allied School of Infantry in Constantine, he was astonished to hear on the radio that His Majesty King George VI had awarded the Victoria Cross to Lance Sergeant John Patrick Kenneally of the 1st Battalion Irish Guards. 'I listened to the citation in a daze,' he remembered. 'I just did not believe it. I had had to learn all the names of the Guards VCs at the Depot [all four previous awards were from 1914–18]. Now my name would be added to them, and it was not really my name – I had adopted it.'

Returning to his battalion, he was given a 'wonderful reception' with men slapping him on the back and shouting congratulations. The party in the sergeants' mess lasted three days. Kenneally wrote:

'There was no envy – infantrymen know better than that. It was not I who had won the medal: it was an Irish Guardsman. We were all Irish Guardsmen and we had all played a part.'[20]

Kenneally's heroics had helped the 24th Guards Brigade hang on to part of the Bou, though fierce German counter-attacks did force the British to relinquish some ground at the junction of the 1st and 4th Infantry Divisions near Ksar Tyr between 27 and 30 April. Enemy 'losses were heavy', noted Alex, 'but his troops continued to show an excellent spirit'.

In a letter to Churchill on 30 April, Alex wrote: 'On V Corps front fighting has been particularly fierce and bitter. Localities have changed hands several times . . . As an instance of the desperate nature of the enemy's resistance, fifty men of the Hermann Göring Division had just surrendered, when one of them persuaded them to take up arms again, and the whole party started fighting, and had to be shot to a man.'

It was the same story in the north where Bradley's II Corps attacked on two axes towards Mateur on 23 April, but made only limited progress. After five days of heavy fighting, however, the ridge of hills west of Sidi Nsir was cleared, as was the high ground east of the village. The 9th Division was held up just in front of Djefna on the northernmost road. But the most noteworthy success was the capture of Point 609 – Djebel Tahent – a 'commanding dome-shaped hill' to the northeast of Sidi Nsir by the much-maligned 34th Division on 30 April. The feat was all the more impressive because the hill was defended by parachutists from the Barenthin Regiment who were, in Alex's opinion, 'perhaps the best German troops in Africa'.[21]

After climbing the hill a few days later, the journalist Philip Jordan noted in his diary:

Because its summit rises above all others in this thick northern range it was the keystone of the German defence ring around Bizerta. You would have said looking at it, that no such fortress could fall to the assault of infantry. Yet it fell, and to-day it is a hallowed place where the wind blows above the graves of those who fell there.

It rises from a deep valley in whose sheltered folds corn is now ripening. Beneath its summit there are olive groves and a little Arab village of stone huts and dirty bare places, deserted now because the echoes of battle still linger in its squalid corners and beneath its broken roofs.[22]

Ike, who was visiting the front and saw the start of the battle from a nearby vantage point, described 609's capture as 'final proof that the American ground forces had come fully of age'.[23] Their casualties for the previous week's fighting were 2,500; First Army losses, in the same period, were 4,400.

Despite the heavy losses, noted Harry Butcher in his diary on 30 April, there was an 'air of confidence at headquarters of both the II Corps and the First Army'. They were making inroads into the Axis defences and, more importantly, the Allies enjoyed almost complete control of the air and sea. Carl 'Tooey' Spaatz, commanding the US Twelfth Air Force, told Butcher that the Allies now had 3,000 planes in Tunisia, including 200 Flying Fortresses. 'The air', concluded Butcher, 'is really coming into its own; nearly a thousand sorties a day are being flown, and medium and heavy bombers are socking everything from gun frontiers to barges, with good effect.'[24]

At sea, as Allied ground forces closed in on Tunis and Bizerte, night-time destroyer and motorboat patrols in the Sicilian Narrows were 'intensified'. In daylight, when warships were vulnerable, the task of sinking any Axis shipping that evaded submarine patrols and offensive minefields was the responsibility of Allied planes.

For the most part this division of responsibilities worked well. As Admiral Sir Andrew Cunningham wrote to Dudley Pound, the First Sea Lord, on 28 April,

With the air, we seem to have pretty well stopped shipping going to Tunisia, but there is a stream of Siebel ferries [motorised barges] and lighters that we have not hit hard yet, though the MTBs [motor torpedo boats] have had some little success.

I am moving up a division of 'Hunts' [a class of destroyer] on each flank, who I hope, when the enemy air is a little more tamed, will be able to look after themselves in daylight and at any rate increase the threat to the line of supply. The mines are, however, a nuisance.[25]

Three days later, Bedell Smith gave Ike the excellent news that, thanks to the interception of 'low-grade ciphers used at the front', they knew that some German units were almost out of ammunition. In a desperate attempt to 'fill the urgent demand', the Italians had sent three ships loaded with ammunition. But all had been intercepted by Cunningham's ships and sent to the bottom. Ike was also told that 'of two enemy destroyers bound for Tunisia with some 1600 replacements on each, one had been sunk and the other was burning from stem to stern'. This failure to get through much-needed ammunition and replacements would be, Ike felt, a 'serious blow' to Axis morale.[26]

41

Operation Strike

Northern Tunisia, 30 April–7 May 1943

THE CLIMACTIC BATTLE OF the campaign – Operation Strike – began at 3 a.m. on 6 May when 400 Allied guns 'flamed into action' on a 3,000-yard stretch of enemy front on both sides of the Medjez–Massicault–Tunis highway. Journalist John D'Arcy-Dawson described the scene:

> The gunners sweated as they thrust shells into the guns. The noise mounted in volume as the pace of the barrage increased. Then as the first streaks of light appeared over the far horizon the noise of a multitude of planes could be heard above the thunder of the guns.
>
> Over they came, dim black shapes in the steely light. They dropped their bombs behind the limit of shellfire, deepening the barrage. In front of them clouds of fighters and fighter-bombers scoured the roads and fields, destroying every living thing that moved.[1]

The plan of attack, devised by Alex, was for the British IX Corps to make a 'sudden, powerful stroke' south of the Medjerda river, where the Axis defenders had been stretched 'almost to breaking point', and into the Plain of Tunis. To help deliver it, Alex had asked Monty to transfer to IX Corps – which until then had been composed of the 4th and 46th Infantry, and the 6th Armoured Division – the best formations he could spare. Monty had sent his two most experienced and freshest divisions, the 4th Indian and 7th Armoured, along with the 201st Guards Brigade. These divisions had helped to win the first British victory at Sidi Barrani in 1940 and it was 'particularly appropriate', noted Alex, that they 'should be chosen for the main role in our last victory, the battle of Tunis'.[2]

With Crocker wounded and out of action, Alex had originally thought of Bernard Freyberg as the man to command the final thrust. But Monty was adamant that it should be Lieutenant General Brian Horrocks and Alex had acquiesced. 'The whole weight of the final attack is being shifted from here round to the First Army front,' Monty told Horrocks on 30 April, 'from where the final *coup de grâce* will be administered. You will go off today and assume command of IX Corps in General Anderson's army. You will then smash through to Tunis and finish the war in North Africa.'

Horrocks could not have been happier. 'This was the real art of generalship,' he wrote later, 'a quick switch, then a knock-out blow. How much better than battering our heads against the strong Enfidaville position. And what luck for me that I should be selected for the job.'

Taking a small staff with him, Horrocks reached IX Corps HQ that evening and 'entered a new world, because the First and Eighth Armies were as different as chalk from cheese'. Having served with the Eighth since July 1942, he was used to the 'scruffiest-looking army you could imagine'; its battered vehicles hung with old tin cans to make the 'now famous desert brew', and uniforms, when they were worn, that were 'patched and old'. The First Army, by contrast, had fairly new vehicles, painted green and not yellow, headquarters that were camouflaged, and everyone wore uniform.

Horrocks knew, too, that there was no love lost between the rival armies, and that Anderson's men resented the fact that the Eighth Army got most of the headlines. To address the elephant in the room, he assembled as many people as he could at IX Corps HQ and told them: 'I have not come here as a superior being from a superior army to teach you how to fight. I know very well the difficulties you've been through. I can't help the fact that I'm from the Eighth Army and I'm probably not as bad as you think. Anyhow, here I am and you'd better make the best of me.'

This raised a laugh and relieved the tension. It also helped that General Anderson – said to be a 'dour Scot and a difficult man to serve' – could not have been nicer to Horrocks. He said his task was simple: 'Capture Tunis'. To do the job he would have under his command two infantry divisions with 160 Churchill tanks, and two armoured divisions, supported by the whole of Coningham's tactical air force and an 'immense weight of artillery'. Hearing this, Horrocks's heart soared. 'If I failed to break through with this immensely powerful force under command,' he recalled, 'then I deserved to be shot.'

Looking at a map, it was clear to Horrocks that the 'obvious place to launch the assault was from Medjez el Bab, up the valley, via Massicault, and St Cyprien, straight through to Tunis twenty-five miles away'. But as this was the sector currently occupied by V Corps, he went to call on its commander, Charles Allfrey, another ex-instructor from the Staff College that he knew well. Allfrey could not have been 'more helpful', wrote Horrocks, and the two cooperated closely for the coming attack – now involving four divisions, two infantry and two armoured, under Horrocks's command.[3]

Allfrey might reasonably have asked why he had not been given the job. After all, he had commanded both the 4th Infantry and 6th Armoured Divisions, and knew the terrain. But Alex was heavily influenced by Monty (who later told Brooke that Allfrey did not know his 'stuff' and should be sent home) in choosing Horrocks instead. This was grossly unfair. By and large, Allfrey had done well in difficult circumstances and was one of the better corps commanders in the British Army. In time, both Alex and Monty would come to acknowledge as much.[4]

Though relegated to a supporting role, Allfrey did not blame Horrocks, and instead gave him a guided tour of the forward positions overlooking the Medjerda valley which, to the Eighth Army man, looked far more like England, 'with its growing crops and small hills broken by the mountains on either side', than the desert he was used to.[5]

The final plan of attack was heavily influenced by Francis Tuker, the commander of the 4th Indian Division, who, after a lengthy reconnaissance of the battlefield, insisted that the start time should be moved from dawn to 3 a.m. when it would still be dark. He also lobbied for pinpoint artillery fire, after the initial bombardment, onto specific targets (identified by air reconnaissance) using 1,000 rounds per gun. After much persuasion, Horrocks agreed. 'We would have preferred another hour or two so that we could smash right through into the rear areas before the light came,' wrote Tuker, 'but this timing would be enough and it would not matter if our colleague division did not get off before dawn, for we should have all that was important by then.'[6]

On 5 May, with the planning complete, Allfrey and Horrocks briefed journalists at IX Corps headquarters in a wadi close to a ripe field of wheat. 'Behind, on a low hill,' wrote John D'Arcy-Dawson, 'I could hear the musical sound of a tractor cutting the wheat. Small birds darted about. Except for the burning heat of the sun we might easily have been standing in an English field at harvesting time.'

Standing before a large colour map on an easel, Allfrey explained that he and Horrocks were 'old friends, and in this battle we will be sitting in each other's pocket'. Then Horrocks, his face tanned by service in the desert, outlined the battle plan. The main operations would begin at 3 a.m. with a huge barrage by 400 guns. After five minutes, many of the guns would switch to targeting the enemy's artillery. Meanwhile, the two infantry divisions – the 4th British on the right and the 4th Indian on the left – would assault two 350-foot hills which constituted the enemy's first positions on either side of the Massicault road. These were to be taken by 5 a.m. After a pause of forty minutes, two objectives further on were to be attacked with heavy artillery support.

At 7 a.m., all being well, the 4th Infantry would hold its ground while the 4th Indian wheeled left to tackle three small hill features masking Djebel Bou Aoukaz to the left of the road. Finally, the 4th

Infantry would capture the hamlet of Frenj, a total distance from the start line of 6,000 yards.

The armour was not to move until 7 a.m. when it would push forward on either flank: the 7th Armoured Division on the left to St Cyprien; and the 6th Armoured Division, supported by the 201st Guards Brigade, on the right to the hills south of La Mornaghia.

Altogether, said Horrocks, hundreds of guns and tanks – the greatest armoured force yet seen in Tunisia – would be hurled against an Axis force that was thought to number five battalions and thirty tanks in the front line, and another five battalions and forty tanks in reserve near Massicault. A similar force of Axis infantry was stationed to the south in the Ksar Tyr area. Meanwhile, V Corps would 'hold the corridor open' and be ready to support IX Corps, while the French XIX Corps and II Corps mounted coordinated attacks to the south and north respectively, and the New Zealanders created a diversion near Enfidaville.

Horrocks paused and smiled. 'Those are the paper objectives,' he said. 'If by tomorrow night the infantry objectives have been gained and the tanks level or a little beyond them on each flank, we shall have done very well.'

The sight of the two commanders 'standing together in the sunlight on the eve of battle upon which great events depended', calm and confident, was one D'Arcy-Dawson would never forget. He had seen and spoken to Allfrey many times when 'our line was holding by a thread'. The general was 'always calm and unflurried, always courteous, never allowing worry and anxiety to betray itself by sharp words'. And now Allfrey's men were to help 'strike this great hammer-blow'. 'The immense concentration of force on a narrow front must burst through,' wrote D'Arcy-Dawson. 'A surge of excitement swept me. We would be in Tunis within a few hours.'[7]

After the press briefing, Horrocks moved into a small command post dug into the side of a hill not far from the start line. He was sitting with his feet on the table, sipping a drink and reading a novel, when the canvas screen which served as a door was pushed aside and in came Alex, tired and dusty after a long drive. 'You don't seem to have much to do,' said the army group commander testily.

Horrocks frowned. 'If I had anything to do now, sir,' he replied, 'we should have lost tomorrow's battle before it even started.'[8]

Brigadier General Paul 'Little Napoleon' Robinett was told about Combat Command B's role in the coming battle by his divisional commander, Major General Ernest Harmon, on 5 May. In a wheat field close to Robinett's advanced command post, on a ridge south of Mateur, Harmon announced that all Allied forces would attack simultaneously at 4.45 a.m. the following morning. At that very moment, visible to the east, a reconnaissance in force by some of Robinett's armour was being checked by enemy artillery and anti-tank fire. Harmon was not impressed. Swinging round to face Robinett, he asked in a provocative, rasping voice: 'Will the damned tanks fight?'

Robinett had been shocked by Harmon's 'Resurrection' speech, but this was worse, a 'stab straight to the heart', questioning the courage of Robinett's men even as they were engaged in a 'death grip with the enemy'. He did not hold back. 'Damn right they will fight as some are doing now,' he spat. 'They have always fought and will fight again!' Throwing judgement and self-control to the winds, Robinett told his boss he was sorry he had previously questioned the courage of these men 'on the basis of secondhand reports'.

Harmon bristled. 'May I remind you that the remarks are mine and I'm present.'

'Well, sir,' responded Robinett, 'it would have been much better for yourself and others concerned had you not made them.'

Harmon turned on his heel and left, though the fight below them continued 'with increasing fury'. Spotting enemy tanks flanking his own, Robinett tried to warn the company commander. But it was too late. 'Before our artillery had fired a round,' wrote Robinett, 'the flash of guns could be seen and the bright orange flames of exploding tanks announced the results.' Three American tanks were knocked out, killing an officer and some crewmen. Lieutenant Dwight S. Varner was wounded and captured, but later escaped and returned to American lines in a German vehicle he had hijacked. He was awarded the Distinguished Service Cross.

As if the day could not get any worse, Robinett was taking a short cut back to his main command post on foot when he and his driver Corporal Robert Lee were hit by shrapnel from a shell burst. Robinett felt little pain at first, but could not move his left leg which was bleeding. Lee was more seriously injured, and did not answer when his boss called to him. Both were treated in North Africa and eventually evacuated back to the US. Robinett's only regret: that he did not have the opportunity to lead his men to their final victory in North Africa.

Before leaving, Robinett wrote a last message to his men. He reminded them that, despite fighting with 'mediocre, half-wornout American equipment', they had stopped or thrown back the enemy 'on every occasion', and that the names of Oran, La Senia, Bredeah Station, Tebourba, Medjez el Bab, Ousseltia, Sbeitla, Kasserine Pass and Maknassy were forever associated with their exploits. He added:

> Toward the rear anonymous individuals have said that we are 'not battle-worthy'. For my part, I do not doubt the determination of the men who have followed such leaders as Marshall, Todd, Gardiner, Kern, Wrockloff, Ringsak and Cosby. You will win again and seal anew the comradeship of battle.
>
> May God bless each of you.[9]

Watching the start of the battle from the same Grenadier Hill that he and his men had contested five months earlier was Captain Nigel Nicolson, now Intelligence Officer for the 1st Guards Brigade (part of the 6th Armoured Division). He wrote to his parents,

At 3 exactly, the appalling artillery barrage came down on the Hermann Göring Division facing us. These barrages are quite extraordinary. The shells whistle over your head at the rate of eight or ten a second. The gun flashes jump out of the darkness and the exploding shells on the crest of the enemy position flower a few seconds later into a ruby tulip. When dawn broke you could see through your field glasses the infantry swarming all over their objectives and the Churchills lurching up behind them . . . At the same time the wirelesses which have been discreetly dumb for the last week, burst into life, and have not stopped since.[10]

Also watching the attack was journalist Philip Jordan whose view was mostly obscured by dust churned up by hundreds of fighting vehicles. 'You could distinguish the tanks only by the flames when they fired,' he wrote in his diary. 'There was no wind to blow the dust away. Every one in high spirits to-night, for we may be in Tunis tomorrow.'[11]

That confidence was also felt by Lieutenant General Horrocks, commanding the battle, who thought the attack 'went like clockwork'. The two infantry divisions 'punched the initial breach', he wrote, 'and at 7.30 a.m. I was able to order the two armored divisions forward'. By midday, IX Corps was through the crust and the tanks were 'grinding their way forward down the valley towards Tunis'. It was a perfect use of armour – to exploit a breakthrough 'deep into the enemy's heart' – and Horrocks noted with satisfaction the all-arms nature of the battle as aircraft, guns, tanks, infantry and vehicles worked in close coordination.

Other commanders – certainly Monty – would have claimed the victory as 'a great feat of generalship'. Not Horrocks, who was honest enough to admit that it was 'nothing of the sort'. He added, with no hint of false modesty: 'I was merely fortunate to be in command of a battle in which victory was a foregone conclusion.'[12]

By evening, the 6th and 7th Armoured Divisions had reached their objectives of La Mornaghia and St Cyprien respectively. During the attack, two battalions of the 115th Panzer Grenadier Regiment had been overrun and the remainder of the 15th Panzer Division driven back past Massicault which was occupied in late afternoon. Generalmajor Willibald Borowietz's battered units had then attempted to establish a new defensive line from Djedeïda to St Cyprien, but were unable to do so. 'St Cyprien,' noted John D'Arcy-Dawson, 'which had earlier been prepared for defence by a series of trenches along the hills, was not defended although it was a strong natural position. We were now only about 12 miles from Tunis and our armour was twenty miles in front of the infantry.'[13]

Horrocks and Allfrey met at the end of the day to discuss their next move: as agreed beforehand, the 4th British and 4th Indian Divisions now reverted to V Corps' control, giving Allfrey five infantry divisions with which to hold the bridgehead; this left Horrocks free to press on to Tunis with the two armoured divisions, the 6th and 7th.

Bypassing St Cyprien early on 7 May, the 6th Armoured Division engaged the remnants of the 15th Panzer Division to the southeast of the village and forced them back to Sebkret es Sedjoumi. This allowed elements of the 7th Armoured to overcome the remaining defenders and take St Cyprien. Away to the northwest, the Germans abandoned Tebourba, while more tanks and armoured cars from the 7th Armoured Division entered Le Bardo, a suburb of Tunis.[14]

The armoured cars of the 11th Hussars − veterans of the desert fighting since late 1940 − would claim the honour of being the first Allied troops into Tunis, a full five months after the last serious attempt had come within a few miles of the city. Horrocks was standing by a road near Tunis when a soldier wearing the famous brown beret of the 11th leant out of his vehicle and said, with a grin, 'First in again, sir!'

In truth, the armoured cars of the 1st Derbyshire Yeomanry had entered Tunis by another route at almost exactly the same moment, if not slightly earlier, as Horrocks himself acknowledged.[15] An eyewitness to the historic moment was Australian war correspondent Alan Moorehead who followed the 11th Hussars in and came across 1st

Derbyshire Yeomanry vehicles carrying the mailed fist symbol of Keightley's 6th Armoured Division. 'It is', he wrote, 'useless and stupid to argue which of these units was the best or debate who got into Tunis first. They arrived together. They were representatives of the two most famous British divisions, the 6th and 7th Armoured. They were both magnificent reconnoitring units. It was almost poetic that the Hussars and the Yeomanry should have come up to Tunis together.'[16]

Free at last from Axis control, the French inhabitants of Tunis greeted their liberators with 'hysterical delight'. Some jumped onto the running-boards of Moorehead's car, and one girl threw her arms round the driver's neck. Many of the women were clutching flowers hastily picked from their gardens which they threw at the Allied vehicles. Moorehead was hit full in the face by a 'clump of roses' and there were flowers all over the car bonnet. 'Everyone was screaming and shouting,' he recalled, 'and getting in the way of the vehicles, not caring whether they were run over or not.'

On the right side of the street he saw the double doors of a big red building burst open and scores of men in British battledress emerge. They were prisoners of war who had taken advantage of their guards' disappearance to escape from captivity. Spotting the column of armoured and civilian cars – the reason for their deliverance – they cheered until they were hoarse. One man, overcome with emotion, burst into tears.

So unexpected was the arrival of Allied troops that hundreds of German soldiers were walking the streets, some arm in arm with girlfriends, while others were sipping aperitifs in roadside cafés, when three British armoured cars appeared in the city centre. The Germans stared in amazement. Mostly unarmed, they were in no position to resist; but nor could such a small force of armoured cars handle so many prisoners. The British drove on. Moorehead wrote:

> In this mad way, Tunis fell that night. Here and there a German with desperate courage emptied his gun down on the streets and hurled a grenade or two. But for the most part these base troops in Tunis were

451

taken entirely off guard and there were thousands of them. All night there was hopeless confusion in the dark, Germans and British wandering about together, Italians scrambling into civilian clothes and taking refuge in cellars, saboteurs starting new fires and igniting more dumps.[17]

A short, sharp skirmish between German and British troops was witnessed that evening by journalist John D'Arcy-Dawson as he entered Tunis with the tanks of the 6th Armoured. The Germans had barricaded themselves in a large white building in the grounds of the Bey of Tunis's palace. D'Arcy-Dawson watched as British soldiers fired shots and hurled hand grenades, setting off a large dump of Very lights. For the next twenty minutes, the flashes of blue, green, pink and white gave a 'creditable imitation of the Crystal Palace fireworks'. Suddenly, ten Germans scrambled out of second-floor windows and jumped to the ground. 'Several broke their ankles,' wrote D'Arcy-Dawson. 'Others leaped from a lorry with their hands up. The little battle was over. While it was still going on we walked about shaking hands with the French, who swarmed over the road indifferent to bullets whizzing over their heads.'[18]

When Horrocks heard at 4 p.m. that Tunis had fallen, he made straight for Major General Charles Keightley's HQ. There he ordered Keightley to turn his tanks to the southeast through the town of Hamman Lif and down the road that ran along the neck of the Cap Bon peninsula to Hammamet. As the Allies now had complete air superiority, Keightley was to 'forget all about open spacing' and drive his vehicles nose to tail, two abreast if necessary, 'as long as he got there quickly'. By reaching Hammamet, Keightley's armour would trap any Axis troops who had escaped into the Cap Bon peninsula and prevent them from linking up with Messe's army to the south at Enfidaville.

This movement of Keightley's 6th Armoured Division was in accordance with the pre-arranged plan to mop up the remaining enemy forces once Tunis had fallen. It also required the 7th Armoured Division to be sent north up the Bizerte road towards Protville, on the Medjerda;

while the US 1st Armoured Division moved east from Mateur towards the same area. The intention was to trap the northern remnants of the 5th Panzer Army – including the Manteuffel, 15th Panzer and 334th Infantry Divisions – in a pocket north of the Protville marshes.[19]

Choosing to follow Keightley's spearheads, Horrocks reached the town of Hamman Lif, flanked by the sea on one side and towering hills on the other, in time to witness the Welsh Guards assaulting one of the nearest peaks. He and his ADC continued on foot, and were fortunate not to be shot when they blundered into no-man's-land and were approached by eight frightened Italians with their hands up. 'Had they been stalwart members of the Afrika Korps,' wrote Horrocks, 'it would have been different; we could have escorted them back proudly into our new lines. But for the corps commander to return with eight weedy, miserable Italians in tow would have made me the laughing stock of the entire corps. So, feeling rather ashamed of myself, I handed them over to my ADC and went back alone by another route.'[20]

The day ended on a slightly sour note when Keightley's tanks failed to force the pass at Hamman Lif. Barely 300 yards wide at its narrowest point, it was stoutly defended by the remnants of the Hermann Göring Division and a strong force of 88mm dual-purpose guns, withdrawn from airfield defence. But its significance was summed up by war reporter Philip Jordan who noted in his diary: 'These words are written in Tunis. The great expedition that began in wind has finished in rain; and at long last – 181 days, six months in all but a day – so much patience and fortitude have had their reward. It has been a wonderful day.'[21]

In a neat touch of symmetry, men of the US 9th Infantry Division and armour from the 751st Tank Battalion entered Bizerte ninety minutes after the first British troops had reached Tunis.

The foot soldiers included Second Lieutenant Orion C. Shockley who earlier that day had used powerful binoculars to observe from a ridge east of Mateur the road that led to Bizerte, eight miles in the distance. Spotting no enemy activity, he and a sergeant set off on foot up the road.

A former member of the Missouri National Guard, Shockley had married his college sweetheart Helen just before he was shipped to North Africa as a replacement officer in late 1942. On arrival, he was assigned as a platoon leader to D (Cannon) Company, 47th Infantry, 9th Division, but did not see action until February 1943 when his three half-tracks mounted with 75mm pack howitzers helped to persuade Rommel to pull back from Thala to the Kasserine Pass, for which they and the rest of the 9th Division's artillery were awarded a Distinguished Unit Citation.

More recently, on 3 May, now serving as a forward observer for Cannon Company, he had been awarded the Soldier's Medal for risking his life to rescue five men wounded by German S-mines in a railway tunnel near Djefna. He had carried one man with a broken leg to safety, and then returned in an ambulance to pick up the others. Reversing over a mine, he suffered shrapnel wounds to his back and jaw. But he spent only a couple of nights in the 77th Evacuation Hospital — where one of the head nurses had been in his graduating class at Jefferson City High School — before checking himself out and hitchhiking back to his unit.[22]

Shockley rejoined Cannon Company in time for II Corps' final push on Bizerte on 6 May with all four divisions in line: from north to south, the 9th Infantry, 1st Armored, 1st Infantry and 34th Infantry. They made solid progress that day, with two battalions of the 60th Infantry capturing Djebel Cheniti, a dominating 650-foot feature just 15 miles from Bizerte, after the 47th Infantry had seized adjacent ridges to the north. Next morning, the 9th Reconnaissance Troop and supporting armour approached Bizerte along the road to the east, spurred by orders from Major General Bradley that an early capture of the port was vital to forestall sabotage.[23]

Also heading into Bizerte, but in their case on foot, were Shockley and his sergeant. Near the abandoned airfield, they heard the distinctive clank of tank tracks and, unsure of their provenance, hid in a culvert. Relieved to see white stars on their turrets, the marking for American armour, they flagged the tanks down and hitched a lift into the city. 'As we neared the center of town,' wrote Shockley, 'we asked to get off. I had looked at my map and noticed there was a channel to our right that led from the ocean to Lake Feriana. I was suspicious that there were Germans on the other side of the channel.'

He was right. Moments after they jumped down, the tank was hit by anti-tank fire from across the channel and knocked out. The crew, however, managed to bale out and get to safety. Shockley and the sergeant took refuge in the four-storey Hôtel de la Marine and raced up the stairs to the top floor where they gained access to the roof through a trap door. Peering over a low parapet, they could see a battery of four artillery pieces, one of which had destroyed the tank.

'It began to get dark,' wrote Shockley. 'Our regiment was undoubtedly surprised that the enemy had not mounted more of a defense of the city. Had they crossed the channel? We did not see any boats.' Unable to contact their company, and with snipers still active, they withdrew to the edge of the city and spent a 'cold and miserable' night beneath a large truck.[24]

Under the cover of darkness, units of US combat engineers cleared away wreckage and removed mines and booby-traps in the city.

'It was', wrote a delighted Alex, 'a happy coincidence that we should have gained our two main objectives simultaneously and that both the major Allies should have won a notable victory on the same day. I had of course planned this division of the spoils but I had not expected so dramatic a climax.'[25]

42

'We are masters of the North African shores'

Germany and North Africa, 7–13 May 1943

ADOLF HITLER WAS IN Berlin for the state funeral of SA-Chief Viktor Lutze – killed in a car accident – when the bad news arrived from North Africa on 7 May. 'We talked about the military position,' noted Joseph Goebbels in his diary. 'The Führer, too, regards the situation in Tunis as pretty hopeless. It is simply impossible to transport reinforcements there. If we could regularly deliver supplies to Tunis we might possibly hold on for a long time. But this is prevented by the watchfulness of the English, who won't let our ships get through.'

Goebbels's chief concern was German morale. He therefore urged Hitler to prepare the ground by allowing language to be used in the High Command's public broadcasts 'that will give some intimation that the end is in sight'. The other issue was how to explain to the public that Rommel was no longer in North Africa. 'He has been', wrote Goebbels, 'on the Semmering for several weeks and . . . nobody has the faintest idea of it! Everyone thinks he is in Africa. If we now come out with the truth, when catastrophe is so near, nobody will believe us.'

The silver lining for Hitler was that Mussolini now understood 'there can be no other salvation for him except to win or die with us'. He told Goebbels that the Duce had arrived at the Klessheim Conference, a month earlier, looking like a 'broken old man'. But after putting 'every ounce of nervous energy into the effort', he had succeeded in pushing the Italian leader back on the rails and, by the time of his departure, he was in 'high fettle, ready for anything'.[1]

This was wishful thinking. It also assumed that Mussolini's position as Italian leader was unassailable. It was not. After the defeat at El Alamein, a succession of former high-ranking servicemen had urged King Vittorio Emanuele III to intervene and 'end the madness'. He was not yet ready to do so, and instead had told Cavallero early in the New Year that Italy's war efforts needed to be prolonged for as long as possible because there was little to be gained from a compromise peace. This calculation could – and would – change, both for the King and for his armed forces' chief, Ambrosio. The latter came back from Klessheim convinced that if Germany did not do more to support Italy, then a change of policy was necessary. That, in turn, required the removal of Mussolini who would never separate himself from Hitler. To prepare the ground, Ambrosio ordered his military assistant to work out a plan for Mussolini's arrest.[2]

Though unaware of these machinations, Goebbels understood – in a way that Hitler did not – that the unfolding disaster in North Africa could have consequences for Germany every bit as significant as the recent loss of the Sixth Army on the Eastern Front. 'When you think,' he wrote in his diary, 'that 150,000 of our best young people are still in Tunis, you rapidly get an idea of the catastrophe threatening us there. It'll be on the scale of Stalingrad, and certainly also produce the harshest criticism among the German people.'[3]

Hitler preferred to bury his head in the sand. When he spoke to a meeting of the entire Nazi leadership on 8 May – the Party, SA, SS and Hitler Youth – he gave a detailed survey of the war in the east, and referred only briefly to events in Tunisia. German forces had lost Stalingrad, he insisted, 'because of the impossibility of mastering the problem of movement'. The very same issue meant they were 'now passing through a serious military crisis in North Africa'. He was not, however, downhearted. 'Whoever has the organisational power to solve the problem of movement,' said Hitler, 'will be victor in this war. In this respect we have the advantage over our adversaries, for they must attack on exterior lines whereas we can defend ourselves on interior lines.'

There was, he argued, 'practically no possibility of a compromise with the Soviets' who 'must be knocked out, exactly as we formerly had to knock out the Communists to attain power ourselves'. There would be many battles to come, said Hitler, and many 'magnificent victories'. When it was over, 'the Reich will be the master of all Europe' and, by extension, the world.

These stirring words seemed to stiffen Goebbels's backbone. 'Events at Tunis cast a heavy shadow over the whole day,' he wrote in his diary on 8 May. 'Special bulletins issued during the evening by the English portend evil. We shall have to prepare ourselves for extremely heavy blows. Nevertheless I believe we can and will survive them.'[4]

The simultaneous fall of Tunis and Bizerte to Allied forces was front-page news in Britain and the United States. 'We came into North Africa on a shoestring when we waded ashore at Algiers six months ago to-night,' wrote Bill Stoneman of the *Chicago Daily News*. 'We entered Tunis on the tail of an avalanche.'

Ike heard the glad tidings during dinner at his villa in Algiers with, among others, Major General Tom Handy, his successor as head of the Operations Division. He had just returned from a flying visit to Bradley's HQ at the front, where such a rapid advance had not been anticipated. 'Surprisingly,' noted Butcher in his diary, 'there was no jubilation. I had to emphasize that I, for one, was impressed, but Ike said he wasn't interested in the capture of mere geographical locations – he would be satisfied only when all the Axis forces were cleared from Africa.' Ike's biggest fear was a 'long drawn-out affair in the [Cap] Bon peninsula, which would be costly to us, especially in time'. He was hopeful, therefore, that Alex 'would keep the enemy upset and on the run, so they could not reorganize to furnish opposition'.

Ike was encouraged, however, by the receipt of ULTRA decrypts from Alex that included 'the "good-byes" of the 15th Panzer Division to the homeland' and a statement from the German High Command that Africa would now be abandoned and 'the 31,000 Germans and 30,000 Italians remaining' would be withdrawn by sea. Alex was quick to reassure Ike that the navy and air forces would interfere with this programme which, in any event, depended on the enemy holding a firm bridgehead in Cap Bon. He also reminded him of Churchill's words as Britain faced invasion in 1940: 'We are waiting, so are the fishes.'[5]

Alex was fairly confident that the end was near. 'The Axis front has completely collapsed and disintegrated,' he wrote to Churchill on 8 May. 'We shall have to mop up pockets of Germans, but to date probably 20,000 prisoners have been taken, besides many guns, lorries, and dumps. Our casualties both in men and tanks are light.' He and Air Vice Marshal Coningham, he explained, had been given a hero's welcome in Tunis that day. He had reciprocated by sending a French regiment into the city 'to take over the guards and to run up the Tricolour'. He ended the letter: 'Our main object now is to cut off as many enemy as possible from gaining the Cap Bon peninsula. RAF work has been quite magnificent, and all troops are in terrific heart.'[6]

At noon on 9 May, the Axis forces in the Protville pocket, north of Tunis – mostly from the Manteuffel and 15th Panzer Divisions – agreed unconditional surrender with the US II Corps. Six generals were among the prisoners, including both divisional commanders, Generalmajors Karl Bülowius and Willibald Borowietz, and General der Panzertruppe Gustav von Vaerst, who had succeeded Arnim as commander of the 5th Panzer Army in February. At 9.30 a.m., Vaerst had sent his last situation report to Arnim: 'Our armour and artillery have been destroyed; without ammunition and fuel. We shall fight to the last.' But when it came to it, he capitulated meekly to Major General Harmon's 1st Armored Division.[7]

Master Sergeant Thomas Riggs of Divisional Intelligence was an eyewitness to the surrender. 'At noon,' he wrote to his family, 'a small cavalcade of German staff cars rode into the wheatfield – two hotshot generals and accompanying minnesängers [minstrels], down to privates. There were two Volkswagens with the cavalcade – miniature station wagons with a two-cylinder engine behind. This was the car, you remember, that every German family was going to have, paid for, and of course never saw.'

Among the generals was Borowietz, 'an old enemy, out of one of the Panzer divisions of Sbeitla days', who didn't appreciate having his picture taken by Riggs and others. Riggs then used his schoolboy German on a 'runty little gefreiter' who had driven one of the cars. He was wearing the Iron Cross, Second Class, and the 'three-times-wounded badge', yet seemed 'rather glad to be out of it'. He said to Riggs: 'Your artillery, oh!'

He also wanted to know how many American armoured divisions were in Tunisia. When Riggs said only one, he didn't believe him. 'This was very flattering,' wrote Riggs. 'He had been told eleven. General Borowietz went off into the middle of the field and squeezed out a tear, then said goodbye to his officers and took off under escort.'

As the day wore on, more prisoners appeared. With not enough American trucks available, 'they drove their own vehicles, or walked in, with maybe a couple of doughfeet with tommy guns for four or five hundred prisoners'. Riggs added: 'There were reports of barns full of stores, of fields stacked with untouched munitions, of olive groves with unopened crates *aus Deutschland* parked under every tree. The men who had been in at the kill began to trickle in to head-quarters with fine lies and fine souvenirs: lugers, field glasses, cameras, German insignia of all kinds.'

When the 'souvenir lust' hit division headquarters, Riggs chose not to partake. 'I wish now,' he told his parents, 'that I had picked up anyway a handful of Afrika Korps insignia, which were going begging by the roadside, or some swastikas. The only thing I ever did acquire for myself was a set of collapsible T-poles for my mosquito net, which I am using now.'[8]

Journalist Ernie Pyle was also a witness to the generals' surrender, having spent the previous week attached to a unit of the 1st US Infantry Division. He found them 'meticulously correct in their military behaviour, but otherwise standoffish and silent'. Not so the common soldiers who were friendly and inquisitive. 'It made you a little lightheaded,' he wrote, 'to stand in the center of a crowd, the only American among scores of German soldiers, and not have to feel afraid of them. Their 88s stood abandoned. In the fields dead Germans still lay on the grass. By the roadside scores of tanks and trucks still burned. Dumps flamed, and the German command posts lay littered where they had tried to wreck as much as possible before surrendering.'

Pyle was typically a 'sucker for the guy who loses', but he did not feel sorry for the low-ranking German POWs. 'They didn't give you the feeling they needed any sorrowing over,' he wrote. 'They were loyal to their country and sorry they lost but, now that it was over for them, they personally seemed glad to be out of it.'

Pyle allowed himself one memento: a tiny 'topless two-seater' Volkswagen that the Germans used instead of a jeep. It was given to him by the staff of the 1st Armored Division for, as they put it, 'sweating it out with us at Faïd Pass all winter'. Pyle was delighted, and enjoyed the reaction of Allied servicemen as he drove back from the front line. They 'would stare, startled-like and belligerent', he wrote, 'then, seeing an American at the wheel they would laugh and wave'. He had owned half a dozen cars in his life, 'but never been so proud of one as of my clattering Volkswagen'.[9]

An unexpected bonus for the Allies was the release on 9 May of 700 American and British POWs at La Goulette, Tunisia, from an Italian ship that had run aground under heavy air attack while heading for Italy. 'Now,' wrote Second Lieutenant Frank Johnson of the 18th Infantry, 'Captain McGregor and all our other men lost as prisoners are on their way back to us. Our cup of good news is filled to overflowing when, with victory in view, we joyously turn over our area to a unit of the 3rd Infantry Division. No longer will that exhausting cry of "Over just one more hill to the coast!" ring in our ears.'[10]

The main obstacle to total victory was the stubborn defence of the Hermann Göring Division at Hamman Lif which was finally overcome during the morning of 10 May. Witnessing the denouement was Captain Nigel Nicolson, the 1st Guards Brigade's Intelligence Officer, who wrote to his parents:

> Late that night [9 May] one of our battalions took the heights overlooking the town and gazed down into the streets and pinpointed the position of every 88–mm [gun]. At dawn all the tanks drew themselves up about half a mile north of the town, and waited there for an hour . . . The whole mass then moved slowly forward, closely followed by my own battalion [3rd Grenadier Guards] on foot . . . The 88s, to do them justice, opened up as soon as we were in range and continued firing until each individually was knocked out by the tanks themselves or by infantry firing from the heights above. The position was finally turned . . . by the left hand regiment taking all their tanks along the beach and actually through the sea itself, the one avenue of approach which the Germans had overlooked.

When the infantry streamed in, Nicolson went with them to witness the French emerging from their places of refuge as Sherman tanks thundered through the streets. Dead Germans were still lying beside their guns; hundreds more were taken prisoner. Relieved the fighting was over, the civilians 'brought out wine and pastries and pressed them on the guardsmen'. They draped roses on guns and vehicles, and hugged soldiers who were 'reloading their Bren guns for the continuation of the battle'. Nicolson, meanwhile, was 'dragged off into a lovely villa and plied with questions about some subaltern in Giraud's Army, whose whereabouts I was surely bound to know'. He ended the day by driving a wounded German officer back to the advanced dressing station in his car.[11]

With the forcing of the Hamman Lif defile – a feat Generalmajor von Broich described as the 'most remarkable event of the campaign' – the 6th Armoured Division had a clear route down Highway 1 and by the early hours of 11 May had reached Hammamet on the eastern coast, thus sealing the base of the Cap Bon peninsula. The only hold-up was at the Wadi Tamed, eight miles short of Hammamet, where the Germans had blown the bridge. But the scout cars of the 1st Derbyshire Yeomanry found an alternative route along a barely discernible track, at about the same time the engineers repaired the crossing, and the advance continued.

Lieutenant Vincent Moore of 2 Troop recalled 'the memory of that hectic dash, lorries three and four abreast, doing a sort of cavalry charge in the dark – a conception of warfare that had never been explained in my training'. It was made possible by the wide sandy verges the French had built to accommodate the hundreds of Arab carts, travelling to and from the market, that typically used the road.[12]

Later on 11 May, the British 4th Division swept round the Cap Bon peninsula, encountering no serious opposition, while the 6th Armoured Division moved south from Hammamet to Bou Ficha. Contrary to expectation, the Axis forces had not planned a last redoubt in the peninsula. Instead the bulk were still facing the Eighth Army at Enfidaville, or were trapped in pockets to the northwest. The first group to surrender, to General Mathenet's French Moroccan Division, were the 10,000 men of *Kampfgruppe Pfeiffer* (mainly elements of the 21st Panzer Division), east of Pons du Fah.[13]

The biggest catches, however, were Generaloberst Hans-Jürgen von Arnim, commanding Army Group Afrika, and Generalleutnant Hans Cramer of the Afrika Korps. They were the senior German officers in Tunisia, hugely experienced and with a large force of veteran soldiers under their command. Had they insisted, those soldiers would have fought to the last bullet. Yet at noon on 12 May they surrendered to the 4th Indian Division near Sainte Marie-du-Zit, in the hills west of Hammamet. When Francis Tuker and his corps commander, Charles

Allfrey, arrived to conduct negotiations, they found Arnim's HQ in a 'deep and well-protected gorge in the mountains', with German troops standing about unarmed, and men of the Royal Sussex keeping an eye on them. Arnim and Cramer were immaculately dressed in 'their best suits, and wearing their decorations and iron crosses'. They gave, wrote Tuker, 'an agreeable impression of green, scarlet and gold' that contrasted starkly with his own shabby appearance in a pair of 'much worn drill trousers, no medal ribbons and a threadbare battle dress, with our usual reversed hide desert boots'. The comparison between loser and winner struck Tuker as 'quaint'.[14]

The negotiations were conducted in Arnim's caravan by Tuker and Allfrey. The latter noted in his diary,

> I asked him whether he was in a position to offer surrender of the fighting forces in North Africa – land, sea and air. He said he was not in such a position. I pointed out that his troops to the south were completely surrounded and that there were two alternatives, either to surrender – in which case we should treat them like ordinary POWs – or to fight on, in which case we should simply surround them with guns and blow them off the map.

Arnim's response – through his interpreter – was that he had orders to fight until the ammunition was exhausted, and that he had neither the power nor the wish to change them. He had, in any event, no means of getting orders through to his outlying commanders.

In that case, said Allfrey, he would accept the unconditional surrender of Arnim's headquarters. The *Generaloberst* was to be ready to leave in a quarter of an hour, and he could take with him his chief of staff, his ADC and a servant. Generalleutnant Hans Cramer could do the same. They must go in their own cars. After taking his leave, Allfrey sent a message that no one was to be armed. Arnim took this badly, 'pulling out his automatic and throwing it down on the table in a temper'.

Arnim was insistent that on no account would he and his men be handed over to French African troops 'because he feared what they might do to him'. Tuker's cool response was that their guards would be British, Indian or Gurkhas, and they had 'no choice' in the matter. This prompted Cramer to suggest that the onlooking Royal Sussex might do the job because they, like German soldiers, were 'white people'. Our soldiers, said Tuker firmly, are 'all the same – all white'.

When the cars and escort were ready, Arnim gave a short speech to his staff who had lined up to say goodbye. He was very emotional, and only just got through it. 'He then got in his car,' wrote Allfrey, 'and stood up in front, saluting his men as he was driven off. A dignified performance, and the men gave him a very good send off.' Allfrey thought him an 'arrogant Prussian' and was glad to see the back of him.[15]

En route to First Army headquarters, as he passed the thousands of Germans heading into captivity, he stood up in his car and saluted them. They did the same, raising their right arms and shouting 'Von Arnim! Von Arnim!'[16]

To Anderson, however, Arnim appeared 'very dazed and on the verge of a breakdown'. The reason why became clear when Arnim admitted to the British lieutenant general that he had 'expected to hold out and to deny us the use of Tunis and Bizerte until August'. The enemy was, Anderson concluded, 'prepared to pay a very high price to delay our invasion of Southern Europe until the autumn or winter, when the weather would at best be unfavourable and at worse enforce further delay until the next spring'.

After a cursory interrogation, Arnim was moved to Alex's HQ at Le Kef where, according to the British general, he 'still seemed surprised by the suddenness of the disaster'. From there Arnim was flown to Algiers where a prison camp, built on a muddy football field, was waiting to receive him. Ike sent his intelligence chief, Ken Strong, to interview Arnim, but refused to go himself. 'His hatred of the Germans, and particularly of the Nazi ideology,' noted Butcher in his diary, 'being so strong, he does not trust his own reactions before a representative of the Prussian and Nazi regime.'

Ike confirmed this in his war memoir. 'Because only by the utter destruction of the Axis was a decent world possible,' he wrote, 'the war became for me a crusade in the traditional sense of that often misused word . . . I was interested only in those not captured. None would be allowed to call on me. I pursued the same practice till the end of the war. Not until Field Marshal Jodl signed the surrender terms at Reims in 1945 did I ever speak to a German general.'

Ike raised a glass to Arnim's capture, but was far from 'jubilant' because he was anxious to complete preparations for the next campaign: the invasion of Sicily. 'All the shouting about the Tunisian campaign leaves me utterly cold,' he told Marshall. 'I am so impatient and irritated because of the slowness with which the next phase can unfold that I make myself quite unhappy.'

For commanders closer to the front, however, the excitement was palpable. 'It was an astonishing sight,' wrote Alex, 'to see long lines of Germans driving themselves, in their own transport or in commandeered horse-carts, westwards in search of prisoner of war cages. Men who had, so short a time before, been fighting like tigers now seemed transformed into a cheerful and docile crowd, resigned to the acceptance of their fate.'[17]

A couple of hours after Arnim's capture, Generalmajor Theodor Graf von Sponeck surrendered his German 90th Light Division to Pat Gardner, the Intelligence Officer of the British 26th Armoured Brigade. Gardner had arrived at the divisional HQ in a jeep flying a flag of truce, and was taken to Sponeck's command caravan. 'Two days ago,' Sponeck told him, with tears in his eyes, 'General Freyberg asked me to surrender. I refused because my men still had the means to fight with. Now their munitions are exhausted and I have no choice. But I should like to say that during the three years I have been fighting the British in Africa, I could not have wished to meet a finer enemy.'

He took out his revolver from its holster, emptied it of cartridges and passed it across the table. Gardner handed it back. Sponeck was taken to IX Corps HQ where he asked Brian Horrocks if he might be allowed to continue in his own car. 'I cannot grant your request,' said Horrocks. 'Your people have been responsible for the death of millions, for the destruction of our homes and untold misery throughout the world. You are a leader of these people, and it is you that must bear this terrible responsibility. You are a German soldier, and you live only for militarism. You have failed. And a German general who fails is worth less to me than the meanest soldier in our army. You will therefore travel back in a truck, with your private soldiers.' And he did.[18]

The only Axis troops still holding out were the rump of Giovanni Messe's First Italian Army – mostly men of the German 164th Light Division and the Italian XX Corps – in the hills north of Enfidaville. They capitulated the following day after Messe had received word from Mussolini of his promotion to *mareschiallo d'Italia* (field marshal). The message added: 'As the aims of your resistance can be considered achieved, your Excellency is free to accept an honourable surrender.'

Ten minutes before the British deadline to surrender unconditionally or face annihilation, Messe and the anti-Nazi commander of the 164th, Generalmajor Kurt Freiherr von Liebenstein, gave themselves and their troops up to Bernard Freyberg, commanding the British X Corps. It was perhaps fitting that the final surrender was to a unit of the Eighth Army which, until its final check at Enfidaville, had had an unbroken run of success against Rommel and his successors, and, in the process, had done more than any other formation to ensure the total defeat of Axis forces in North Africa.

'We have been fighting continuously for almost a year,' wrote Freyberg to Peter Fraser, the prime minister of New Zealand, 'battle after battle, with little respite, on hard rations and short supplies of indifferent water. The endurance and courage of all ranks under conditions of great discomfort and peril have been beyond praise and their resources, good humour, and wisdom have made them ideal material for a fast-moving, hard-hitting force such as ours.'[19] Freyberg was referring to his own 2nd New Zealand Division, but the eulogy could have applied just as well to any number of Monty's formations, including the 1st and 7th Armoured, 4th Indian, 50th Tyne Tees and 51st Highland Divisions.

At 1.16 p.m. on Thursday, 13 May, Alex gave Churchill the good news:

Sir, it is my duty to report that the Tunisian campaign is over. All enemy resistance has ceased. We are masters of the North African shores.[20]

43

'We have struck a blow equal to Stalingrad'

USA, Italy and Germany, 13–19 May 1943

A LEX'S TELEGRAM REACHED WINSTON Churchill at the White House in Washington, DC, where he was the guest of President Roosevelt for the latest inter-Allied conference, codenamed 'Trident'. The British premier had argued long, hard and in the end successfully for the 'peripheral' strategy of an attack on North Africa, rather than an immediate attack on northwest Europe, and here was his vindication. He wrote later:

> No one could doubt the magnitude of the victory of Tunis. It held its own with Stalingrad. Nearly a quarter of a million prisoners were taken. Very heavy loss of life had been inflicted on the enemy. One-third of their supply ships had been sunk. Africa was clear of our foes. One continent had been redeemed. In London there was, for the first time in the war, a real lifting of spirits. Parliament received the Ministers with regard and enthusiasm, and recorded its thanks in the warmest terms to the commanders.

He had ordered the ringing of all British church bells to salute the victory, and was sorry not to be present to hear their chimes. But he had 'more important work to do on the other side of the Atlantic'. His original plan had been to fly to the United States, but as his doctors did not want him to travel at the great height required of a bomber, and Clipper planes flying the northern route could not take off until 20 May on account of ice, he instead went by sea, leaving Scotland with a huge entourage of senior military and political advisors in the *Queen Mary* liner on 5 May. During the six-day voyage, they discussed how to best take advantage of the North African victory. 'Were its fruits to be gathered only in the Tunisian tip,' wrote Churchill, 'or should we drive Italy out of the war and bring Turkey in on our side? These were the questions that could only be answered by a personal conference with the President.'

It had been agreed at Casablanca, of course, that the next target in the Mediterranean was Sicily and preparations for that campaign were already far advanced. But what should come after that? Churchill and his military chiefs were not in any doubt. 'The Chiefs of Staff', he wrote, 'were convinced that an attack upon the mainland of Italy should follow, or even overlap, the capture of Sicily. They proposed the seizure of a bridgehead on the toe of Italy, to be followed by a further assault on the heel as prelude to an advance on Bari and Naples.'[1]

Two big decisions were made at the conference: a definite date, 1 May 1944, was set for the invasion of northwest Europe (Operation Overlord), which satisfied the American Joint Chiefs; and, much as the British had hoped, Ike was given *carte blanche* to exploit victory in Sicily in ways that 'are best calculated to eliminate Italy from the war and to contain the maximum number of German forces'. Though not quite a definite commitment to invade Italy after Sicily, it was the next best thing because everyone knew the only way to force an Italian surrender was to land troops. The delighted Brooke recorded it as a 'triumph' because earlier the Americans had 'wanted to close down all operations in Med after capture of Sicily'.[2]

On 19 May, the same day the Combined Chiefs of Staff reached agreement on Operation Overlord and Italy, Churchill addressed a joint session of Congress. It was seventeen months since he had last spoken to this 'august assembly' – in the wake of Pearl Harbor – and he began by noting that, for over five hundred days, Britain and America had 'toiled, suffered and dared, shoulder to shoulder, against a cruel and mighty enemy'. He promised that British forces would wage war against Japan 'side by side with you . . . while there is a breath in our bodies and while blood flows in our veins'; that the U-boat danger in the Atlantic would be overcome; and that the bombing campaign against Germany, which had already reduced the enemy's war industry to 'unparalleled devastation', would continue.

But the heart of his speech was about the victory in Tunisia, where 'we have struck a blow equal to Stalingrad and most stimulating to our heavily engaged Russian allies'. He continued:

All this gives the lie to the Nazi and Fascist taunts that the parliamentary democracies are incapable of waging effective war. We destroyed or captured over 250,000 of the enemy's best troops, together with a vast mass of material . . . A proud German army by a sudden collapse, a sudden crumbling, a breaking up unexpected to all of us, once again proved the truth of the saying 'The Hun is always either at your throat or at your feet', and that point may have a bearing upon the future. The African campaign, particularly the Tunisian climax, was the finest example yet seen of the cooperation of the troops of three countries and a combination of sea, land, and air forces under a supreme commander.

Churchill compared this to the 'military intuition of Corporal Hitler'. The same 'insensate obstinacy' which had condemned Paulus and his Sixth Army 'to destruction at Stalingrad has brought this new catastrophe upon our enemies in Tunisia'. In total, the African excursions of Mussolini and Hitler had cost their countries 'in killed and captured 950,000 soldiers'. In addition, 2,400,000 gross tons of Axis shipping had been sunk and 8,000 aircraft destroyed, as well as 6,200 guns, 2,550 tanks and 70,000 trucks. 'Arrived at this milestone in the war, we can say, "One continent redeemed".'

Churchill finished by drawing a parallel between the present position of the Allies and that of the Union after Gettysburg in 1864, the decisive battle of the US Civil War. No one then had 'doubted which way the dread balance of war would incline', yet far more blood was shed after Gettysburg than before. He suspected – correctly, as it turned out – that a similar story would unfold in the current conflict, which was why the Allies needed to search their hearts and brace their sinews 'in order that the favourable position which has already been reached both against Japan and against Hitler and Mussolini in Europe shall not be let slip'.[3]

The reaction of the two fascist regimes to the news that Tunisia had fallen – with the loss of two Italo-German panzer armies, including many veteran troops – was very different. In Rome, there was at least a public acknowledgement of the disaster as Mussolini authorised the armed forces' chief Vittorio Ambrosio to take to the airwaves on 13 May and explain what had happened. The withdrawal after the Battle of El Alamein, said Ambrosio, was 'one of the most perfect manoeuvres of retreat' in military history. But the Anglo-American landings in Morocco and Algeria had only increased the numerical and material disadvantage of Axis forces and, from that point on, the 'great function' of the fight for Tunisia was to delay the Allied victory.

The Italian navy and air force, said Ambrosio, had fought 'valorously' to protect the supply convoys in the face of huge enemy superiority. The First Italian Army, meanwhile, had battled heroically at the Mareth Line, Wadi Akarit and Enfidaville. But up against vastly superior Allied forces – who enjoyed a twenty-to-one advantage in tanks, seven to one in armoured cars and three to one in artillery – it was impossible to hold out for ever. Even the Germans had been impressed by the Italians' spirit, and particularly that of their commander Messe, whose determination to fight on had been 'the ultimate expression of manly courage'. Only when further sacrifice was pointless had the Duce ordered the fighting to cease.

Ambrosio rallied the Italians to fight on with the same faith. Clearly it would be Italy's turn next. But his words would fall on deaf ears.[4]

In Berlin, by contrast, Hitler ordered a news blackout. He had flown back to the Wolf's Lair in East Prussia on 12 May and, a day later, received Arnim's report from Tunis that all German forces in North Africa had capitulated. Hitler had 'seen it coming', noted his Luftwaffe adjutant Nicolaus von Below, and in private 'criticized the Italian supply organisation which in the final months had got out of control'.[5]

In public, however, he chose not to speak about Tunisia. All his hopes were now invested in 'Operation Citadel' – a huge armoured pincer attack on the Soviet salient at Kursk, originally planned for May, but postponed until July to build up the supply of panzers – that would, he believed, turn the tide on the Eastern Front. 'It must be a quick and conclusive success,' he had declared on 15 April. 'The victory of Kursk must shine like a beacon to the world.'[6]

Goebbels also prayed for a victory that would 'attain tangible results in the East'. But he did not agree with Hitler's decision to hide the truth about Tunisia from the German public. 'We should not suddenly introduce new methods into our news policies,' he wrote in his diary. 'In a military crisis like this they lead people to think that we must have a bad conscience!'

He particularly resented the triumphalism in the Allied press, and could hardly bear to read the 'exaggerated Anglo–American accounts', full as they were of insults to German soldiers who had, Goebbels insisted, 'fought with legendary heroism to their last round of ammunition'. In reality, many of the commanders, like Generalleutnant Hans Cramer, commanding the Afrika Korps, had chosen to surrender their troops while they still had bullets in their guns because, as Cramer put it, the battle had been decided from a tactical perspective. This willingness to capitulate in North Africa, rather than the more typical fight to the finish on the Eastern Front, came down to the fact that German soldiers knew 'that to be a POW in England is bearable in contrast to being killed in Russia', thought Cramer.

Goebbels drew comfort from the notion that 'if the English want to measure their strength against us again, they will have to step on to European soil' where they would be given 'the reception they deserve'. In another diary entry, however, he was more honest about Germany's prospects in the wake of the Tunisian defeat. 'During the past five months the enemy has had the upper hand almost everywhere. He is defeating us in the air, he has inflicted heavy wounds on us in the East, he is beating us in North Africa, and even our submarine warfare is not as successful as we really expected.'[7]

The sense that the war had reached a tipping point from which Germany could not recover now pervaded much of Führer HQ and the OKW. When Walter Warlimont, the OKW's Deputy Chief of the Operations Staff, tried to report at the daily briefing conference 'on the latest events and the losses sustained' in Tunisia, he was prevented from doing so by Generalfeldmarschall Wilhelm Keitel, the chief of staff. 'The Supreme Commander of the Wehrmacht,' wrote Warlimont, 'had apparently to be spared even a sober military report of the results of his leadership.'

Prior to the Battle of Kursk, in July 1943, Hitler tried to justify the loss of men and equipment in Tunisia to senior commanders on the Eastern Front by insisting that the campaign had 'succeeded in postponing the invasion of Europe by six months' and, more importantly, Italy 'is as a result still a member of the Axis'. He added: 'If we had not done this, Italy would almost certainly have defected from the Axis. The Allies would at some stage have been able to land in Italy unopposed and push forward to the Brenner and as a result of the Russian breakthrough at Stalingrad, Germany would not have had a single man available.'

For Warlimont, who was present, this was nonsense. None of Hitler's 'statements corresponded with the facts as we knew them at the time', he wrote, 'and in the light of subsequent events and the plans of the Allies as we know them today, none of them were correct'. Far from helping the Axis, the 'end of North Africa put an exceptional strain on relations with Italy'.

Nor was the OKW in any doubt as to the significance of the loss of North Africa. 'Now that the Tunisian bridgehead had gone,' wrote Warlimont, 'the theatre of war was no longer a comparatively restricted area of the North African coastline but the entire sweep of the Mediterranean. Major Allied forces had become available for employment elsewhere. The opening of the main and feeder lines of communication through the [Mediterranean], which had been closed for so long, was calculated to be tantamount to a gain to the enemy of about two million tons of shipping for the movement of troops and supplies.'[8]

The dire consequences of 'Tunisgrad' were summed up by Ian Kershaw, Hitler's prize-winning biographer:

On 13 May, almost a quarter of a million [Axis troops] – the largest number taken so far by the Allies, around half of them German, the remainder Italian – surrendered. The catastrophe left the Italian Axis partner reeling. For Mussolini the writing was on the wall. But for Hitler, too, the defeat was nothing short of calamitous. One short step across the Straits of Sicily by the Allies would mean that the fortress of Europe was breached through the southern underbelly.[9]

Epilogue

Destroying the Axis

North Africa and Italy, May–September 1943

A T NOON ON THURSDAY 20 May, under a scorching sun and a cloudless sky, the boom of cannon fire signalled the start of the Allies' victory parade in Tunis. 'Every street was packed,' noted Harold Macmillan, the British Minister Resident in North Africa. 'Every window in every house was packed; every roof was packed . . . It was a magnificent progress. Troops presenting arms; people cheering.'

Standing at the front of the reviewing stand, immaculate in riding breeches and knee boots, was Ike and, next to him, the French Commander-in-Chief, General Henri Giraud. In the row behind were Ike's principal lieutenants: Cunningham, Tedder, Alexander and Anderson. Macmillan and Robert Murphy, the political envoys, were in the final rank. Of the senior commanders, only Monty was missing. He had flown back to England on 17 May for a brief period of leave and would return a week later to prepare for Operation Husky, the Sicily invasion.[1]

The lesser lights had been relegated to platforms on the flank. 'Bradley and I,' noted Patton sourly, 'were put in a stand . . . largely occupied by French civilians and minor military officers'. For the next 'triumphal procession' they hoped to have a 'more conspicuous role'.[2]

Ike was not a fan of victory parades, and had tried to persuade the British and French to agree to a 'combination of victory and commemoration of those who sacrificed their lives'. But he did not succeed, and the commemoration services were held separately on Sunday 23 May.[3]

The first troops to appear, marching twelve abreast, and led by the band of the Foreign Legion, a colour guard, and their diminutive commander Alphonse Pierre Juin, were 10,000 men of the French army, a contingent deliberately inflated to overawe the Arab residents. They were mostly 'native troops', noted Charles Allfrey – Moroccans, Algerians and Senegalese in a variety of colourful uniforms that included scarlet pantaloons, blue tunics and striped robes – and 'did their stuff quite well'. Not so the 2,000 Americans, chiefly from the 34th Division's 135th Infantry – victors of Hill 609 – who 'looked drab, uniforms rather sloppy'.[4]

Patton agreed. 'In spite of their magnificent [physical] appearance,' he wrote in his diary, 'our men do not put up a good show in reviews. I think that we still lack pride in being soldiers, and we must develop it.'[5]

The general consensus was that the 12,000 'British' troops – including Maoris and Sikhs – were the most impressive marchers, and got the best reception. Among them was young Second Lieutenant Peter Moore who had so narrowly avoided capture at Thala in his first action. He was one of six officers and 200 men chosen to represent the 2/5th Leicesters. The night before, he and his men had been allowed into Tunis to see the town 'which so many men had striven so long to capture'. His chief memory, as he wandered down the broad Avenue Gambetta, the route the procession would take, was of 'long queues of British and Allied troops, which practically met each other, and on both sides of the street, patiently awaiting their turn in the local brothels'.

For the parade itself, 'the watching crowd was vast and enthusiastic,' he wrote. 'As our detachment came opposite the saluting base and turned Eyes Right we saw on the platform the commanders who had been controlling our destinies during the last months . . . My first impression was of how disappointingly small they all looked.'[6]

Also part of the British contingent was Lance Sergeant John Kenneally of the 1st Irish Guards who had fought so heroically at the Bou two weeks earlier, but who would not learn of his Victoria Cross award for another couple of months:

> We spent hours cleaning and polishing, plus, as usual, we had extra drill to smarten us up ... The march past was a bit of a shambles. There were American units, the French Foreign Legion and Moroccan Goums, whose style of marching was bizarre to say the least. The whole thing was topped off by the French bands pounding away at about 140 beats [a minute] – they were too enthusiastic even for the light infantry who were used to that sort of thing; and for us, used to 90 beats, it was all rather frustrating.[7]

The watching crowds cheered regardless, particularly upon the arrival of the British guard of honour provided by the Grenadiers who, wrote Allfrey, looked as 'if they had never left London, and did their stuff in absolute silence really beautifully'. With the temperature nudging 92 degrees in the shade, a number of Guardsmen suffering from dysentery collapsed in the heat. But the onlookers did not notice because the regimental sergeant major 'used all his cunning to remove each sick man in turn without any spectator becoming aware of it'. The Guardsmen, as a result, shared with the flamboyant Moroccan Goums the loudest cheer of the day.[8]

For Lieutenant General Kenneth Anderson, who had been in Tunisia from start to finish, it was a highly moving occasion. 'Never have I seen,' he wrote, 'the equal of those men marching twelve deep in solid phalanx for more than two hours; magnificent in physique, bronzed and clear-eyed, conquerors they were and conquerors they looked as they swung by to the music of the massed pipes and drums, British and American regimental bands and the "musique" of the Foreign Legion playing its famous slow march "Le Boudin".'[9]

At the end of the procession came the tanks, armoured cars and artillery pieces, the latter burnished by their gunners until they shone like glass. It was, thought Charles Allfrey, 'a really good effort'.

When it was over, Juin hosted a sumptuous lunch for all the senior officers in the French Resident General's mansion. 'The *only* subject (almost embarrassingly so) of conversation,' noted Macmillan in his diary, 'among *all* the French and Americans was the British parade. I must say they were all very generous. Giraud said that when he had seen the Eighth Army at Sfax, he thought they must be unique. Now he had seen the First Army he realised they were as good.'[10]

The grumpy Patton described the meal as 'a very formal and uneatable affair', but at least there were 'no toasts'. Afterwards, while he and Bradley left to get back to their stations 'before dark', Ike and the other senior commanders were taken to meet the new Bey of Tunis, the uncle of the previous incumbent who had been ousted by the Allies as too pro-Axis.[11] In a 'colourful ceremony complete with gold throne, eunuchs, and native Tunisian troops', wrote Butcher, the Bey awarded decorations to Ike, Giraud, Cunningham, Alexander, Tedder and Anderson.[12]

Ike offered Macmillan a ride in his plane back to Algiers. As they passed Bizerte, they saw below them the first convoy to attempt the Mediterranean passage since 1941. It had left Gibraltar a few days before and would complete its journey to Alexandria without loss. Turning to Ike, Macmillan said: 'There, General, are the fruits of your victory.'

'Ours, you mean, ours,' said Ike, tears in his eyes. 'That we have all won together.'[13]

For the Western Allies, the scale of the Tunisian victory was unprecedented. At a cost of just over 70,000 casualties – including 10,000 fatalities – they had captured and killed more than a quarter of a million Axis troops, many of them veterans from crack formations.[14] The victory 'clearly signified to friend and foe alike', wrote Ike, 'that the Allies were at last upon the march'. He added:

The Germans, who had during the previous winter suffered also the great defeat of Stalingrad and had been forced to abandon their other offensives on the Russian front in favour of a desperate defence, were compelled after Tunisia to think only of the protection of their conquests rather than of their enlargement. Within the African theater one of the greatest products of the victory was the progress achieved in the welding of Allied unity and the establishment of a command team that was already showing the effects of a growing confidence and trust among all its members.[15]

That same team would direct the successive invasions of Sicily, mainland Italy and northern France – Operation Overlord, the long-awaited cross-Channel invasion of France – in July and September 1943, and June 1944, respectively, and the advance into Germany in 1945.

Many senior American commanders would insist after the war that it had been a mistake to postpone Operation Overlord until 1944, and that it prolonged the war for at least another year. Lieutenant General Kenneth Anderson, for one, did not agree:

> The Allies could not have adventured Overlord in 1943 without grave risk of failure, or, at best, prolonged and bloody stalemate. At the time we lacked any artificial harbours (Mulberries), efficient amphibious tanks or specialised armoured assault vehicles. 'Pluto' (the under-Channel petrol lines) could not have been ready; and even had the assault craft, air power, troops and materials of all kinds which were by then tied up in Italy been available in England I am convinced that our state of preparation would have been dangerously insufficient.

The Germans, moreover, would have been able 'to concentrate in immensely greater strength with no Italian campaign to divide their forces, with Italy still fighting, and with ample depth still available in which to hold off the Russians by rearguard tactics'.

For the Allies, noted Anderson, the victory in Africa had 'many direct and satisfying advantages'. By his tally, they had accounted for 'more than 320,000 Germans and Italians, killed, wounded and prisoners, and captured an immense quantity of equipment'. The enemy had also suffered a 'great lowering of morale', particularly the Italians.

The Allies, on the other hand, and in particular the raw American troops, had 'forged a splendid instrument, battle-hardened and supremely confident, to reinforce the Eighth Army, hitherto our only formation actively engaged against the Germans'. But the greatest profit of all, he believed (as did Ike), was the 'creation of a real spirit of Allied unity, which permeated all ranks'. It would prove to be 'the greatest of all war-winning factors' and the foundation was 'well and truly laid in Tunisia' by Ike and the soldiers of all three nations: British, American and French.[16]

Anderson hoped he would be given the opportunity to command the First Army in other theatres, but there were too many doubts over his leadership – voiced by people like Ike, Alex and Monty – for Brooke to ignore. The First Army was broken up and Anderson, after a stint preparing the Second Army for D-Day, was effectively sidelined for the rest of the war.[17]

Where Alex and Anderson could agree, however, was in the value of Allied cooperation. 'It was not inevitable by any means,' Alex insisted, 'that British and American troops would show, in the first battle they had fought together since 1918, such a whole-hearted spirit of comradeship, nor that the British and French, between whom the past three years had thrown many shadows, should recapture once more the same degree of trust and mutual respect which had animated the old alliance.' The credit should go, said Alex, to the soldiers of all three nations and in a 'very large degree to General Eisenhower who by word and example inspired these efforts'.

The campaign also marked, for Alex, the moment when the three services – army, navy and air force – set aside historic rivalries in favour of a cooperation that had become, by the close of the African campaign, 'close and automatic'. He credited Admiral Cunningham and the Air

Marshals Tedder and Coningham for this. Together they had won a victory that, in the final reckoning, was as good as annihilation. 'Never before had a great army been so totally destroyed,' wrote Alex. 'A quarter of a million men laid down their arms in unconditional surrender; six hundred and sixty-three escaped. Immense stocks of arms, ammunition and supplies of all natures were the booty of the victors. Our own casualties in the final battle were less than two thousand men.'[18]

To Harold Macmillan, a future prime minister, the victory was a high-water mark for British arms. 'At no time, perhaps, in the whole of the Second World War,' he wrote, 'did the prestige and power of Britain stand so high.'[19]

Early on 26 May, Winston Churchill set off from Washington DC to North Africa – via Newfoundland and Gibraltar, the first time this transatlantic crossing of 2,700 miles had been attempted – in a giant Boeing Clipper flying-boat, accompanied by Generals Marshall and Brooke. They completed the last leg from the Rock to Algiers in Churchill's new plane, a converted Lancaster bomber known as a 'York' – which was, Brooke noted, 'very comfortable, with special cabin for PM, drawing room, berths for 4 besides PM and lavatory' – and were met at Maison Blanche airfield at 4.30 p.m. on the 28th by, among others, Ike, Alex and Cunningham.

Churchill had come to Algiers to try to settle any differences between Giraud and de Gaulle. But his main aim was to capitalise on the fall of Tunisia by getting Ike to agree 'to invade Italy should Sicily be taken'. To that end, he insisted on accompanying Ike back from the airport, while Marshall was driven by Cunningham.[20] His lobbying continued during an impromptu conference at Ike's villa that afternoon, and at a late-night meeting on the 30th. 'We need to exploit our advantage in the Mediterranean,' he told Ike, 'to knock Italy out of the war while we have the chance.'

Ike pointed out that any exploitation would be 'somewhat limited' by the need to return seven divisions to the UK from 1 November so that they were available for Operation Overlord. He would, however, be able to determine early in the campaign for Sicily the attitude and defensive strength of the Italians on the mainland. 'If Sicily proves to be relatively easy,' said Ike, 'this would justify an immediate follow-up of a bridgehead on the toe of Italy across the Messina Strait. If the Italians fight stubbornly in Sicily, as they did when they were in good defensive positions in Tunisia, then we will be confronted with a long campaign, fighting for every hill-top. This will tie down our forces. It is simply too early to make a firm commitment now. But, like you, I don't want to lose any opportunity for exploitation that presents itself.'[21]

This was good enough for Churchill who, before leaving North Africa, paid a visit to the battlefields of northern Tunisia. There he inspected a knocked-out Tiger tank and was given a tour of the strong German defences at Hamman Lif by Major General Keightley whose tanks had made the breakthrough. He also gave an impromptu speech of 'praise and admiration' to a packed audience of First Army men in the Roman theatre at Carthage, built to house 5,000 spectators in the second century AD. 'Not even Scipio Africanus,'* noted a delighted General Anderson, 'addressing his victorious Legions could have received a more tumultuous welcome.'

Churchill soon forgot the contents of his speech, and even confused the location with the nearby Roman amphitheatre. 'Yes,' he told his dinner companions a day later, 'I was speaking where the cries of Christian virgins rent the air whilst roaring lions devoured them, and yet I am no lion and am certainly not a virgin!'[22]

Many times, in his long career as a soldier, war correspondent and politician, Churchill had witnessed the grim aftermath of battle. For

---

* In a nod to the great Roman general Scipio 'Africanus' who had conquered Carthage, Ike's former West Point classmates sent a congratulatory cable to 'Ikus Africanus'. (Butcher, *Three Years with Eisenhower*, p. 262)

those new to war, like American combat nurse Avis D. Schorer from Des Moines, Iowa, who arrived in Tunisia with the 56th Evacuation Hospital in late May 1943, the evidence of the recent 'bitter fighting' was a shock. 'Shell holes and bomb craters ripped the surface of the road,' she wrote. 'Wrecked tanks, burned planes, and abandoned vehicles were everywhere. Crude crosses marked the graves of Americans, British, and German soldiers. Bombs had recently levelled every hamlet.' Passing a large desert hill with a crude wooden sign that read 'Hill 609', she fought back tears. Her oldest childhood friend – a medic with the 34th Division of the Iowa National Guard – had been killed there.[23]

The Allied invasion of Sicily – Operation Husky – on 10 July was, for Italy, the beginning of the end. The huge amphibious operation involved more than 3,000 warships, supply vessels and landing craft converging on a 100-mile stretch of the southern coast with 160,000 troops, 14,000 vehicles, 600 tanks and 1,800 guns. Defending the island were 250,000 Axis troops, but the bulk were Italians who were poorly equipped and low on morale.

Landing largely unopposed, the two Allied armies – Monty's British Eighth and Patton's US Seventh – advanced inexorably to the north of the island on two coastal axes. With instances of Italians throwing away their weapons and fleeing, Kesselring reported that Sicily 'could not be held with German forces alone'. This prompted Hitler to leave Rastenburg and fly to Feltre, in northern Italy, for a summit meeting with Mussolini on 19 July. There, Hitler – pale and stooped – subjected the 'tired and unwell' Duce to a two-hour monologue. Devoid of substantive proposals, Hitler's words amounted to 'no more than a battery of propaganda, aimed at bolstering the Duce's faltering morale and preventing him from agreeing a separate peace'.

It made little difference. Six days later, Mussolini was arrested on the orders of King Vittorio Emanuele III who had, he admitted later, decided to end the Duce's regime in January 1943, but was waiting for the right moment. With Sicily about to fall, and Rome under air attack for the first time, that moment had come. He told the Duce that, since the war appeared lost and army morale was collapsing, he was replacing him as head of government with Marshal Pietro Badoglio, the former armed forces chief of staff. Badoglio had been holding secret talks with Ambrosio who, after the Klessheim conference, knew that Mussolini would never separate himself from Hitler and needed to be removed.

Hitler was at the Wolf's Lair when he heard the news of Mussolini's sudden removal. He was 'horrified' by 'the swift and bloodless end to fascist domination of Italy', and did not believe for a minute Badoglio's insistence that Italy would fight on. 'If only I could catch this filthy pig!' he roared.[24]

For just such an emergency, Hitler had plans in place to take control of northern Italy (Operation Alaric). Now he wanted to go further: occupy Rome and arrest the King, Badoglio and members of the new government. But Rommel, who had been summoned to Rastenburg to discuss the crisis, urged caution. 'It is important not to drive the Italians into the arms of the Allies,' he told Hitler, 'but instead be ready to act if they do try to make peace.'

Hitler went along with this, ordering Rommel to set up his HQ in Munich and take control of the northern passes into Italy. Over the next fortnight, eight German divisions were funnelled surreptitiously into northern Italy. They were in a position to act when news reached Hitler on 9 September that, five days after the Allied invasion of the toe of Italy (Operation Baytown), the Italians had capitulated after secret negotiations with the Allies. Rommel at once authorised Operation Axis, and within ten days his men had disarmed and interned 182 Italian generals, 13,000 officers and 402,600 soldiers, of whom 183,300 were transported to Germany.[25]

The situation was trickier in the southern half of Italy where Kesselring commanded Army Group South, particularly around Rome where the Italians had five divisions to Germany's two. Unable to coerce them by force, Kesselring's chief of staff, General der Kavallerie Siegfried Westphal, came up with the clever ruse of inviting them to surrender. Incredibly, they accepted the offer and, having handed over their arms, were allowed to return home.

Only the bulk of the navy and air force escaped to join the Allies. Within a few days, Italy had been occupied by its former Axis partner and Mussolini freed from his temporary prison in a ski hotel at Gran Sasso in the Appenines, thanks to a daring raid by German glider troops under the leadership of SS-Hauptsturmführer Otto Skorzeny. Two days later, the Duce arrived at the Wolf's Lair a 'broken man'.[26]

He wanted to retire but Hitler had other plans. For the next 600 days Mussolini would head the puppet Salo Republic in northern Italy as Hitler's catspaw until, on 27 April 1945, he and his mistress Clara Petacchi were captured by partisans as they tried to flee to Switzerland, and executed the following day. Their mangled and semi-naked bodies were later displayed, hanging upside down, in a Milan square.[27]

Mussolini's dream of carving out a new Roman empire in the Mediterranean and North Africa had turned into a nightmare in the featureless deserts, semi-arid highlands and rugged mountains of Tunisia. That seismic defeat – which had cost the German elements of Army Group Afrika up to 155,000 men[28] – put a severe strain on the Axis partnership that could only have been resolved if Hitler had been willing and able to conclude a separate peace with Stalin. That was not an option he ever seriously considered, nor was Stalin likely – particularly after the failure of Operation Citadel, the German attempt to pinch out the huge salient in the Russian line at Kursk in July 1943 – to have entertained a truce.

In the wake of 'Tunisgrad', therefore, it was only a matter of time before Italy dropped out of the war. The defeat had dealt the Axis alliance a mortal blow and would emerge – along with Guadalcanal in the Pacific and Stalingrad on the Eastern Front – as the third great turning point of the Second World War. As Churchill put it in *The Hinge of Fate*, the fourth and largest volume of his classic history of the conflict:

> Further successes lay right before us, and the Fall, or rather Liberation, of Italy was near ... Soon the German nation was to be alone in Europe, surrounded by an infuriated world in arms. The leaders of Japan were already conscious that their onslaught had passed its zenith. Together soon Great Britain and the United States would have the mastery of the oceans and the air. The hinge had turned.[29]

Acknowledgements

The genesis of this book was a late-night brandy with fellow historian James ('Jim') Holland in the bar of the RAF Club on Piccadilly. 'Why don't you,' he said, 'write about the Tunisia campaign? It's got everything: the first time the Western Allies fight side by side, a colourful cast of brilliant generals, including Ike, Monty, Alex, Patton, Bradley and Rommel, and proper jeopardy in that it was far from a foregone conclusion. It's also never been properly recognised as one of the key turning points of the Second World War; and I've got lots of sources – books, interviews and first-hand material – that you can use.'

It was typical of Jim's generosity: suggesting a brilliant idea that he might have kept to himself. But I still needed a title that summed up the campaign's significance and, while re-reading Rick Atkinson's 2004 history *An Army at Dawn*, I spotted the chapter heading 'Tunisgrad'. Bingo! I had it. A single word to describe a campaign so catastrophic the German public compared it to that other great disaster of early 1943 (and, as it turned out, huge hinge moment in the war), the destruction of Paulus's Sixth Army at Stalingrad.

Many other people helped with the research and writing of this book. I would particularly like to thank Mike Beckett, Darren Little, Jeremy Solel, Mat Lambert, Burton E. Etchison, Sarah Kirksey and

Darcy Walker Williams. And, once again, I owe a huge debt of gratitude to Iona McLaren who went through the manuscript with a fine-tooth comb, suggesting cuts, rewrites and big picture perspective that have hugely improved the book.

The research for this project was completed in multiple archives and thanks are due to the staffs of the Dwight D. Eisenhower Presidential Library and Archive in Abilene, Kansas; the Library of Congress in Washington DC; the Royal Navy Submarine Museum in Portsmouth; the Liddell Hart Centre for Military Archives, the National Archives, the Imperial War Museum, and the National Army Museum in London.

I'd like also to thank my dedicatee, Richard Foreman, who has been a close friend, advisor and collaborator for more than 20 years; my literary agent Caroline Michel; my publisher Arabella Pike and her excellent team at William Collins, notably Katherine Patrick, Sam Harding, Iain Hunt, Julian Humphries and Matt Clacher; and, last but not least, my wife Lou and daughters Nell, Tamar and Tashie who've put up with my long physical and mental absences from home life with remarkable stoicism.

References

PROLOGUE

1 Ian Kershaw, *Hitler*, 2 vols (London: Allen Lane, 2000), II, pp. 538–9; The Führerzonderzug: Hitler's Special Train, https://www.hitler-archive.com/articles.php?a=7 [accessed 5 June 2023]

2 Nicolaus von Below, *At Hitler's Side: The Memoirs of Hitler's Luftwaffe Adjutant 1937–1945* (Mainz: v. Hase & Koehler Verlag; repr. 2004), p. 157.

3 Walter Warlimont, *Inside Hitler's Headquarters 1939–45* (London: Weidenfeld & Nicolson, 1964), pp. 267–8.

4 Warlimont, *Inside Hitler's Headquarters*, p. 270.

5 Von Below, *At Hitler's Side*, p. 157.

6 Warlimont, *Inside Hitler's Headquarters*, pp. 267–8.

7 Kershaw, *Hitler*, II, p. 538.

8 *The Rommel Papers*, ed. B. H. Liddell Hart (London: Collins, 1953; repr. 1987), pp. 325–7.

9 *The Rommel Papers*, p. 326; Warlimont, *Inside Hitler's Headquarters*, pp. 268–9.

10 Von Below, *At Hitler's Side*, p. 156.

11 Kershaw, *Hitler: Nemesis, 1936–1945*, pp. 541–2; Julian Jackson, *France on Trial: The Case of Marshal Pétain* (London: Allen Lane, 2023), p. 231.

12 Von Below, *At Hitler's Side*, pp. 157–8

13 Kershaw, *Hitler: Nemesis, 1936–1945*, p. 543.

14 Warlimont, *Inside Hitler's Headquarters*, pp. 273–4.

15 Alexander Lüdeke, *Der Zweite Weltkrieg: Ursachen, Ausbruch, Verlauf, Folgen* (Berlin, 2007), p. 105.

1 'THE MOST DISMAL SETTING'

1 Dwight D. Eisenhower, *Crusade in Europe* (New York: Doubleday, 1948; repr. 1997), pp. 95–6.
2 Rick Atkinson, *An Army at Dawn: The War in North Africa, 1942–1943* (London: Little, Brown, 2003; repr. 2004), p. 5.
3 The National Archives, Kew (TNA), CAB 80/11, Chiefs of Staff Paper No. 168, 27 May 1940.
4 *Hansard* (Parliamentary Proceedings), House of Commons Debates, Volumes 360–2, 4 June 1940.
5 Max Hastings, *Finest Years: Churchill as Warlord, 1940–45* (London: HarperPress, 2009), p. 45.
6 Winston S. Churchill, *The Second World War*, 6 vols (London: Cassell, 1949–53), II, *Their Finest Hour*, pp. 22–4.
7 Jean Edward Smith, *FDR* (New York: Random House, 2007; repr. 2008), pp. 448–9.
8 Churchill, *The Second World War*, II, pp. 116–17, 186–91.
9 Kershaw, *Hitler*, II, p. 299.
10 https://lehrmaninstitute.org/history/index.html [accessed 14 June 2023]
11 Churchill, *The Second World War*, II, pp. 202–11.
12 Hastings, *Finest Years*, p. 69.
13 Jean Lacouture, *De Gaulle: The Rebel 1890–1944* (1984; repr. 1991), pp. 248–9.
14 Kershaw, *Hitler*, II, pp. 302–10.
15 Von Below, *At Hitler's Side*, p. 73.
16 TNA, WO 218/170, War Diary of No. 8 Commando (B Battalion, Layforce), January 1941; Churchill, *The Second World War*, III, *The Grand Alliance*, p. 56.
17 Saul David, *Military Blunders: The How and Why of Military Failure* (London: Robinson, 1997), pp. 186–96.
18 David, *Military Blunders*, pp. 333–48.
19 David Fraser, *Knight's Cross: A Life of Field Marshal Erwin Rommel* (London: HarperCollins, 1993; repr. 1994), pp. 219–40.
20 B. H. Liddell Hart, *The Other Side of the Hill* (London: Cassell, 1951), p. 250n.

2 'WE HAD WON AFTER ALL!'

1 Kershaw, *Hitler*, II, pp. 355–93.
2 Von Below, *At Hitler's Side*, p. 103.
3 *War Diaries 1939–1945: Field Marshal Lord Alanbrooke*, ed. Alex Danchev and Daniel Todman (London: Weidenfeld, 2001), p. 166.

4 Iain MacGregor, *The Lighthouse of Stalingrad* (London: Constable, 2022), pp. 36–9.
5 Atkinson, *An Army at Dawn*, p. 8.
6 Churchill, *The Second World War*, II, p. 539.
7 Brendan Simms and Charlie Laderman, *Hitler's American Gamble: Pearl Harbor and the German March to Global War* (London: Allen Lane, 2021), p. 336.
8 Richard Overy, *Why the Allies Won* (London: Jonathan Cape, 1995; repr. 2006), p. 304.
9 Overy, *Why the Allies Won*, p. 234.
10 Atkinson, *An Army at Dawn*, pp. 8–9.
11 Albert C. Wedemeyer, *Wedemeyer Reports!* (New York: Devin-Adair, 1958), pp. 15–21, 63–76; Jonathan W. Jordan, *American Warlords: How Roosevelt's High Command Led America to Victory in World War II* (New York: NAL Caliber, 2015), p. 97.
12 Overy, *Why the Allies Won*, pp. 234–5.
13 Overy, *Why the Allies Won*, p. 305.
14 Andrew Roberts, *Masters and Commanders: How Roosevelt, Churchill, Marshall and Alanbrooke Won the War in the West* (London: Allen Lane, 2008), pp. 69–70.
15 Hastings, *Finest Years*, p. 239.
16 Roberts, *Masters and Commanders*, pp. 129–30; Stephen E. Ambrose, *Eisenhower: Soldier and President* (New York: Simon & Schuster, 1990; repr. 2003), p. 68; 'Operations in Western Europe' [Marshall] Memorandum, April 1942, quoted in Churchill, *The Second World War*, IV, *The Hinge of Fate*, pp. 281–2.
17 Robert E. Sherwood, *The White House Papers of Harry L. Hopkins*, 2 vols (London: Eyre & Spottiswoode, 1949), II, p. 528.
18 Atkinson, *An Army at Dawn*, pp. 13–14.
19 Churchill, *The Second World War*, IV, p. 390.
20 Churchill, *The Second World War*, IV, pp. 342–4.
21 Churchill, *The Second World War*, IV, pp. 391–2.
22 Ian W. Toll, *The Conquering Tide: War in the Pacific Islands 1942–1944* (New York: W. W. Norton, 2015; repr. 2016), p. 10.
23 Atkinson, *An Army at Dawn*, p. 14.
24 Sherwood, *The White House Papers of Harry L. Hopkins*, II, pp. 605–6.
25 Sherwood, *The White House Papers of Harry L. Hopkins*, II, pp. 610–11.
26 Alanbrooke, *War Diaries 1939–1945*, p. 283.
27 Sherwood, *The White House Papers of Harry L. Hopkins*, II, p. 611.
28 Alanbrooke, *War Diaries 1939–1945*, p. 285.
29 Sherwood, *The White House Papers of Harry L. Hopkins*, II, p. 611.

30 George F. Howe, *Northwest Africa: Seizing the Initiative in the West* (Washington DC: US Army Center of Military History, 1993), p. 14.

31 Douglas Porch, *Defeat and Division: France at War, 1939–1942* (Cambridge: CUP, 2022), pp. 499–500.

32 Churchill, *The Second World War*, IV, pp. 429–35; Hastings, *Finest Years*, pp. 324–5.

3 IKE

1 Eisenhower, *Crusade in Europe*, p. 71; Stephen E. Ambrose, *The Supreme Commander: The War Years of Dwight D. Eisenhower* (New York: Doubleday, 1970), p. 80.

2 Eisenhower, *Crusade in Europe*, pp. 70–2.

3 Ambrose, *The Supreme Commander*, pp. 15–61, 318–19.

4 Kay Summersby Morgan, *Past Forgetting: My Love Affair with Dwight D. Eisenhower* (New York: Golden Apple, 1984), pp. 24–5, 85.

5 Ambrose, *The Supreme Commander*, pp. 320–1.

6 Abilene, Kansas, Dwight D. Eisenhower Presidential Library and Archive (DDE), Papers of Harry C. Butcher, Box 1, Factual Family Data on Lieutenant General Eisenhower (by Lieut. Comdr Harry C. Butcher), 16 July 1942.

7 Eisenhower, *Crusade in Europe*, p. 76.

8 Eisenhower to Marshall, 17 August 1942, in Joseph P. Hobbs, *Dear General: Eisenhower's Wartime Letters to Marshall* (Baltimore: Johns Hopkins University Press, 1971; repr. 1999), pp. 36–7.

9 Washington DC, Library of Congress (LoC), Manuscript Division, Papers of Paul M. Robinett, Box 6, 'Armored Commander: A Personal Story', p. 46.

10 Martin Blumenson, *The Patton Papers: 1940–1945* (Boston: Houghton Mifflin, 1974), Diary, 28 September 1942, p. 87.

11 Eisenhower, *Crusade in Europe*, p. 76.

12 Summersby Morgan, *Past Forgetting*, p. 78.

13 Eisenhower to Marshall, 17 August 1942, in Hobbs, *Dear General*, p. 37.

14 Howe, *Northwest Africa*, pp. 15–17.

15 Eisenhower, *Crusade in Europe*, pp. 77–80; Alanbrooke, *War Diaries 1939–1945*, 29 August 1942, p. 315.

16 Eisenhower, *Crusade in Europe*, pp. 80–1.

17 Harry C. Butcher, *Three Years with Eisenhower: The Personal Diary of Captain Harry C. Butcher, USNR* (London: Heinemann, 1946), 28 September 1942, p. 103.

18 LoC, Manuscript Division, Papers of George S. Patton, Box 27, Patton to Scott, 22 September 1942.

19 Eisenhower, *Crusade in Europe*, p. 82; Carlo d'Este, *A Genius for War: A Life of General George S. Patton* (London: HarperCollins, 1995; repr. 1996), p. 421.

20 Blumenson, *The Patton Papers: 1940–1945*, p. 87; Butcher, *Three Years with Eisenhower*, 9 October 1942, p. 111.

21 Eisenhower, *Crusade in Europe*, p. 83.

22 Eisenhower, *Crusade in Europe*, pp. 81–3.

23 Butcher, *Three Years with Eisenhower*, 9 October 1942, p. 115.

24 Eisenhower, *Crusade in Europe*, p. 85; Summersby Morgan, *Past Forgetting*, pp. 46, 80.

25 Summersby Morgan, *Past Forgetting*, pp. 48–59, 80–1.

26 Summersby Morgan, *Past Forgetting*, pp. 88–90; Butcher, *Three Years with Eisenhower*, pp. 136–7; Eisenhower, *Crusade in Europe*, pp. 94, 97.

4 'WELCOME TO NORTH AFRICA'

1 G. B. Courtney, *SBS in World War Two* (London: Robert Hale, 1983; repr. 2017), pp. 58–9; Portsmouth, Royal Navy Submarine Museum (RNSM), A19991/379, Richard Livingstone, 'Mark Clark's Secret Landing', p. 1116; Mark Clark, *Calculated Risk: His Personal Story of the War in North Africa and Italy* (London: George Harrap, 1951), pp. 83–4.

2 Eisenhower, *Crusade in Europe*, pp. 86–7.

3 Clark, *Calculated Risk*, pp. 73–5; Butcher, *Three Years with Eisenhower*, p. 123.

4 Clark, *Calculated Risk*, pp. 83–94; Courtney, *SBS*, pp. 59–62; Livingstone, 'Mark Clark's Secret Landing', pp. 1115–1119; Butcher, *Three Years with Eisenhower*, pp. 129–31.

5 Eisenhower, *Crusade in Europe*, pp. 99–101; Clark, *Calculated Risk*, pp. 99–102.

5 'SUICIDAL AND ABSOLUTELY UNSOUND'

1 Butcher, *Three Years with Eisenhower*, 7 November 1942, p. 144; Eisenhower, *Crusade in Europe*, p. 90.

2 Eisenhower, *Crusade in Europe*, p. 98.

3 Butcher, *Three Years with Eisenhower*, p. 143.

4 Eisenhower, *Crusade in Europe*, pp. 98–9; Howe, *Northwest Africa*, pp. 187–8.

5 Butcher, *Three Years with Eisenhower*, pp. 147–8; Clark, *Calculated Risk*, pp. 104–5; Eisenhower, *Crusade in Europe*, p. 103; Atkinson, *An Army at Dawn*, pp. 106–7.

6 TNA, DEFE 2/531, Report on Operation Reservist by Lieut. E. J. A. Lunn, SBS, 30 November 1942; Howe, *Northwest Africa*, pp. 47–8.

7 Atkinson, *An Army at Dawn*, pp. 70–1.

8 Private Papers (PP), Harry Holden-White, 'Goodbye to Old Hat', unpublished wartime memoir, Part II, Chapter 2; Howe, *Northwest Africa*, p. 189.

9 Report on Operation Reservist by Captain H. Holden-White; John Parker, *SBS: The Inside Story of the Special Boat Service* (London: Headline, 1997; repr. 2004), pp. 82–3.

10 Atkinson, *An Army at Dawn*, Chapter Two: Landing.

11 Holden-White, 'Goodbye to Old Hat', Part II, Chapter 5.

12 Report on Operation Reservist by Captain H. Holden-White.

13 Atkinson, *An Army at Dawn*, Chapter Two: Landing.

14 Ashcroft, *Special Forces Heroes*, pp. 79–80.

15 Report on Operation Reservist by Lieut. E. J. A. Lunn; TNA, DEFE 2/531, Report on Operation Reservist by Lieut. J. C. C. Pagnam.

16 Atkinson, *An Army at Dawn*, Chapter Two: Landing.

17 Viscount Cunningham, *A Sailor's Odyssey* (London: Hutchinson, 1951), p. 489.

6 'I'VE CAPTURED *MY* OBJECTIVE!'

1 William O. Darby, *We Led the Way: Darby's Rangers* (New York: Presidio Press, 1980), pp. 1–2, 6–7.

2 TNA, CAB 120/414, Churchill's memorandum to Ismay, 5 June 1940.

3 Robert W. Black, *Rangers in World War II* (New York: Presidio Press, 1992), pp. 4, 10–11.

4 Darby, *We Led the Way*, p. 26.

5 Dominic J. Caracillo (ed.), *1,271 Days a Soldier: The Diaries and Letters of Colonel H. E. Gardiner as an Armor Officer in World War II* (Dahlonega, GA: University of North Georgia Press, 2021), pp. 47–8.

6 Darby, *We Led the Way*, pp. 25–7.

7 Black, *Rangers in World War II*, pp. 10–15; Darby, *We Led the Way*, pp. 25–6.

8 Black, *Rangers in World War II*, pp. 22–3; Darby, *We Led the Way*, pp. 29–39.

9 Darby, *We Led the Way*, p. 48.

10 Darby, *We Led the Way*, pp. 10–14.

11 Black, *Rangers in World War II*, pp. 54–6; Darby, *We Led the Way*, pp. 17–18.

12 Saul David, *SBS: Silent Warriors* (London: William Collins, 2021), p. 159.

13 Black, *Rangers in World War II*, pp. 56–7; Darby, *We Led the Way*, pp. 18–23.

7 LITTLE NAPOLEON

1 Atkinson, *An Army at Dawn*, p. 222.

2 Robinett, 'Armored Commander', pp. 1–60; Heinz Guderian, *Panzer Leader* (London: Penguin, 1952: repr. 2000), p. 21.

3 Howe, *Northwest Africa*, pp. 195–9, 211–12; Robinett, 'Armored Commander', pp. 80–114.

4 Robinett, 'Armored Commander', pp. 114–17.

5 Howe, *Northwest Africa*, pp. 213–14.

8 'OLD BLOOD AND GUTS'

1 Howe, *Northwest Africa*, pp. 40–2.

2 D'Este, *A Genius for War*, p. 433.

3 Blumenson, *The Patton Papers*, pp. 97–8, 102.

4 D'Este, *A Genius for War*, pp. 256–90.

5 D'Este, *A Genius for War*, pp. 375–408.

6 D'Este, *A Genius for War*, pp. 1–2.

7 Summersby Morgan, *Past Forgetting*, p. 162.

8 Blumenson, *The Patton Papers*, p. 103.

9 Atkinson, *An Army at Dawn*, pp. 106–7.

10 Howe, *Northwest Africa*, pp. 121–7.

11 Howe, *Northwest Africa*, pp. 92–5.

12 Howe, *Northwest Africa*, pp. 133–4; Blumenson, *The Patton Papers*, p. 105.

13 Blumenson, *The Patton Papers*, p. 105.

14 D'Este, *A Genius for War*, pp. 434–5.

15 Blumenson, *The Patton Papers*, p. 106.

9 'FRANCE AND HER HONOUR ARE AT STAKE'

1 John D'Arcy-Dawson, *Tunisian Battle* (London: Macdonald, 1943), p. 17.

2 Zeynik Celik, *Urban Forms and Colonial Confrontations: Algiers Under French Rule* (University of California Press, 1997), p. 5.

3 Tag Barnes MM, *Commando Diary: 1942–1946* (Tonbridge Wells: Spellmount, 1991), pp. 16–17.

4 Howe, *Northwest Africa*, pp. 249–50; Atkinson, *An Army at Dawn*, pp. 94–5.

5 Jackson, *France on Trial*, p. 248.

6 Howe, *Northwest Africa*, pp. 249–50; Atkinson, *An Army at Dawn*, pp. 94–5.

7 Churchill, *The Second World War*, IV, pp. 548–50.

8 Atkinson, *An Army at Dawn*, p. 96.

9 Churchill, *The Second World War*, IV, pp. 550–1.

10 Atkinson, *An Army at Dawn*, pp. 95–6.

11 Barnes, *Commando Diary*, pp. 13–18.

12 Howe, *Northwest Africa*, p. 246.

13 Barnes, *Commando Diary*, pp. 18–20.

14 Howe, *Northwest Africa*, p. 248.

15 Barnes, *Commando Diary*, pp. 18–20; Howe, *Northwest Africa*, p. 248.

10 'MONEY FOR OLD ROPE'

1 Howe, *Northwest Africa*, pp. 234–6; David, *SBS*, p. 160.

2 PP, M. J. Beckett Papers, Diary of F. P. Bowen, No. 6 Commando, 7/8 November 1942.

3 Howe, *Northwest Africa*, pp. 236–7.

4 Howe, *Northwest Africa*, pp. 238–9.

5 Howe, *Northwest Africa*, pp. 241–5; Atkinson, *An Army at Dawn*, p. 97; Theresa M. Deane and Joseph E. Schaps, *500 Days of Front Line Combat: The WWII Memoir of Ralph B. Schapps* (New York: iUniverse, 2003), p. 46.

6 Howe, *Northwest Africa*, pp. 244–8.

7 David, *SBS*, pp. 157–8, 160–1.

8 Howe, *Northwest Africa*, pp. 251–2.

9 Eisenhower, *Crusade in Europe*, pp. 103–5.

10 Churchill, *The Second World War*, IV, p. 556.

11 Eisenhower, *Crusade in Europe*, pp. 104–5.

12 Clark, *Calculated Risk*, p. 106.

13 Eisenhower, *Crusade in Europe*, p. 104.

14 Clark, *Calculated Risk*, pp. 107–8.

15 Eisenhower, *Crusade in Europe*, p. 107; Churchill, *The Second World War*, IV, p. 558.

16 Jackson, *France on Trial*, p. 228.

17 Eisenhower, *Crusade in Europe*, p. 107; Clark, *Calculated Risk*, pp. 109–20.

18 Clark, *Calculated Risk*, p. 110.

19 Jackson, *France on Trial*, pp. 228, 231.

11 'THEY HAD BETTER HURRY UP'

1   Atkinson, *An Army at Dawn*, p. 163.
2   Howe, *Northwest Africa*, p. 255.
3   Albert Kesselring, *The Memoirs of Field Marshal Kesselring* (London: William Kimber, 1953; repr. 1988), pp. 140–2.
4   Howe, *Northwest Africa*, p. 255; Atkinson, *An Army at Dawn*, p. 164.
5   Kesselring, *Memoirs*, p. 142.
6   Eisenhower, *Crusade in Europe*, p. 111.
7   DDE, Dwight D. Eisenhower Papers, Box 6, General G. Barré to Eisenhower, 20 May 1949.
8   Atkinson, *An Army at Dawn*, p. 164.
9   Howe, *Northwest Africa*, pp. 255–7.
10 Kesselring, *Memoirs*, p. 142.
11 Atkinson, *An Army at Dawn*, p. 165; Howe, *Northwest Africa*, p. 258.
12 LoC, Robinett Papers, Box 4, Interview with General Walter Nehring, Karlsruhe, Germany, 4 September 1949.
13 Howe, *Northwest Africa*, pp. 258–9; Atkinson, *An Army at Dawn*, p. 165.
14 Robinett Papers, Box 4, Interview with General Walter Nehring.
15 TNA, CAB 106/708, Lieut. General Kenneth Anderson, 'The Allied Campaign in North Africa, 1942–43', p. 22.
16 London, Liddell Hart Centre for Military Archives (LHCMA), Papers of Field Marshal Alanbrooke, 6/2/53, Correspondence with Lieutenant General Sir Kenneth Anderson, Eisenhower to Brooke, 3 July 1943.
17 https://www.unithistories.com/officers/Army_officers_A06.html [accessed 25 August 2023]; Alanbrooke, *War Diaries 1939–1945*, p. 295.
18 Anderson, 'The Allied Campaign in North Africa', pp. 22–3; Atkinson, *An Army at Dawn*, pp. 173, 177; Howe, *Northwest Africa*, p. 277.
19 Diary of F. P. Bowen, 12 November 1942.
20 Lieutenant Colonel T. B. H. Otway, *Airborne Forces of the Second World War, 1939–45* (London: HMSO, 1951; repr. 2021), pp. 61–2.
21 Otway, *Airborne Forces*, p. 75; John Parker, *The Paras: The Inside Story of Britain's Toughest Regiment* (London: Metro, 2010), p. 44.
22 Diary of F. P. Bowen, 13/14 November 1942.
23 Diary of F. P. Bowen, 22 November 1942.

12 THE RACE FOR TUNIS

1   Papers of Field Marshal Alanbrooke, Correspondence with Lieutenant General Sir Kenneth Anderson 1942–1943, Anderson to Brooke, 16 November 1942.

2 Anderson, 'The Allied Campaign in North Africa', p. 24.

3 Howe, *Northwest Africa*, p. 279.

4 Anderson, 'The Allied Campaign in North Africa', p. 27.

5 Eisenhower, *Dear General, Ike to Marshall*, 30 November 1942, p. 93.

6 James Hill, in Max Arthur, *Men of the Red Beret: Airborne Forces 1940 to Today* (London: Century Hutchinson, 1990; repr. 1992), p. 39; Otway, *Airborne Forces*, p. 75.

7 Reg Curtis, *Churchill's Volunteer: A Parachute Corporal's Story* (London: Avon Books, 1994), pp. 95–6.

8 James Hill, in Arthur, *Men of the Red Beret*, p. 41.

9 Report of 'S' Coy Column activities 17/18 Nov. 42 by Major P. Cleasby-Thompson, in https://www.paradata.org.uk/media/146 [accessed 7 April 2022]

10 James Hill, in Arthur, *Men of the Red Beret*, p. 42.

11 TNA, WO 175/293, War Diary of the 1st Derbyshire Yeomanry, October–December 1942; London, National Army Museum (NAM), 1999-03-178-1, Lieut. M. Vincent Moore, 2 Troop, B Squadron, 1st Derbyshire Yeomanry, 'Memoir of the Tunisian Campaign, 1942–1943', pp. 9–10.

12 Moore, 'Memoir of the Tunisian Campaign', pp. 11–17.

13 TNA, WO 175/293, War Diary of the 1st Derbyshire Yeomanry, October–December 1942.

14 D'Arcy-Dawson, *Tunisian Battle*, p. 31.

15 Gilberto Villahermosa, *Hitler's Paratrooper: The Life and Battles of Rudolf Witzig* (Barnsley: Frontline Books, 2010; repr. 2014), pp. 132–3.

16 Anderson, 'The Allied Campaign in North Africa', p. 28.

13 'A HERCULEAN TASK'

1 Eisenhower, *Crusade in Europe*, pp. 118–19; Butcher, *Three Years with Eisenhower*, pp. 170–4.

2 Eisenhower, *Crusade in Europe*, pp. 120–1; Butcher, *Three Years with Eisenhower*, pp. 174–9.

3 Howe, *Northwest Africa*, pp. 280–1.

4 Villahermosa, *Hitler's Paratrooper*, pp. 134–6.

5 Anderson, 'The Allied Campaign in North Africa', p. 38; TNA, WO 218/32, War Diary of No. 1 Commando, December 1942; LHCMA, Allfrey Papers, 3/5, Operation 'Bizerte' Narrative (No. 1 Commando), 1–5 December 1942.

6 Howe, *Northwest Africa*, pp. 299–300; Anderson, 'The Allied Campaign in North Africa', p. 28; Robinett, 'Armored Commander', pp. 154–5.

7 D'Arcy-Dawson, *Tunisian Battle*, p. 33; Howe, *Northwest Africa*, p. 302.

8 Moore, 'Memoir of the Tunisian Campaign', p. 19.

9 Kesselring, *Memoirs*, p. 143.

10 Howe, *Northwest Africa*, pp. 300–1.

11 Robinett, 'Armored Commander', pp. 156–8.

12 Howe, *Northwest Africa*, p. 303.

14 'CUT TO PIECES'

1 Robinett, 'Armored Commander', pp. 147–8, 153, 163–5.

2 Anderson, 'The Allied Campaign in North Africa', p. 28; Howe, *Northwest Africa*, p. 305.

3 Robinett, 'Armored Commander', pp. 165–6.

4 Anderson, 'The Allied Campaign in North Africa', p. 29; Howe, *Northwest Africa*, pp. 305–6.

5 Anderson, 'The Allied Campaign in North Africa', p. 29.

6 Werner Baumbach, *Broken Swastika: The Defeat of the Luftwaffe* (London: Robert Hale, 1960; repr. 1974), pp. 135–6.

7 LoC, Robinett Papers, Box 4, 10th Panzer Division Combat Report of the Tebourba Engagement, 1–4 December 1942.

8 Howe, *Northwest Africa*, p. 306.

9 Gardiner, *1,271 Days a Soldier*, pp. 82–5; Howe, *Northwest Africa*, p. 308.

10 Howe, *Northwest Africa*, p. 309; John Frost, *A Drop Too Many: The Memoirs of World War II's most daring Parachute Commander* (London: Cassell & Co., 1980; repr. 1988), pp. 74–6; Lieut. Colonel J. D. Frost's report of the Depienne/Oudna operation, in Robert Peatling, *Without Tradition: 2 Para 1941–1945* (Barnsley: Pen & Sword, 1994; repr. 2004), p. 59.

11 Anderson, 'The Allied Campaign in North Africa', p. 29.

12 Frost, *A Drop Too Many*, pp. 74–7; Frost's report of the Depienne/ Oudna operation.

13 Frost, *A Drop Too Many*, pp. 78–80; Frost's report of the Depienne/ Oudna operation, pp. 61–2.

14 Frost, *A Drop Too Many*, pp. 80–95; Frost's report of the Depienne/ Oudna operation, pp. 66–9.

15 'Dennis Rendell recollects his disastrous Oudna experience', in Peatling, *Without Tradition*, pp. 79–80.

16 Frost, *A Drop Too Many*, pp. 96–103; Frost's report of the Depienne/ Oudna operation, pp. 69–71; Anderson, 'The Allied Campaign in North Africa', p. 29.

15 'A NASTY SETBACK'

1 Robinett, 'Armored Commander', p. 175.
2 Howe, *Northwest Africa*, p. 312.
3 Howe, *Northwest Africa*, pp. 314–15; Atkinson, *An Army at Dawn*, p. 221.
4 Robinett, 'Armored Commander', pp. 177–83.
5 Robinett, 'Armored Commander', pp. 177–83.
6 Gardiner, *1,271 Days a Soldier*, pp. 52, 55, 57, 77, 81–92.
7 Robinett, 'Armored Commander', pp. 181–2, 185.
8 https://vcgca.org/our-people/profile/1710/Herbert-Wallace-Le-PATOUREL [accessed 3 May 2024]
9 Howe, *Northwest Africa*, pp. 318–20; Atkinson, *An Army at Dawn*, pp. 223–5.
10 Papers of Field Marshal Alanbrooke, Correspondence with Lieutenant General Sir Kenneth Anderson 1942–1943, Anderson to Eisenhower, [No day] December 1942.
11 Eisenhower, *Dear General*, Ike to Marshall, 30 November 1942, pp. 92–4.
12 Howe, *Northwest Africa*, p. 320.
13 Butcher, *Three Years with Eisenhower*, p. 181.
14 Andrew Boyd, *British Naval Intelligence Through the Twentieth Century* (Barnsley: Seaforth, 2020), pp. 510–11.

16 'MY WORD STILL COUNTS FOR SOMETHING'

1 Liddell Hart (ed.), *The Rommel Papers*, p. 371.
2 Kesselring, *Memoirs*, p. 143; Warlimont, *Inside Hitler's Headquarters*, p. 308.
3 LoC, Robinett Papers, Box 4, Record of an interview with General Walther Nehring, 4 September 1949.
4 Fraser, *Knight's Cross*, pp. 8–10, 76–7, 150–1.
5 Fraser, *Knight's Cross*, pp. 207, 338.
6 Kesselring, *Memoirs*, p. 143.
7 John Gooch, *Mussolini's War: Fascist Italy from Triumph to Collapse, 1935–1943* (London: Allen Lane, 2020), p. 333.
8 Von Luck, *Panzer Commander*, pp. 128–30.
9 Gooch, *Mussolini's War*, pp. 333–4.

10 Liddell Hart (ed.), *The Rommel Papers*, pp. 363–5; Gooch, *Mussolini's War*, pp. 334–5.
11 Kershaw, *Hitler*, II, pp. 543–4.
12 Kershaw, *Hitler*, II, pp. 395–6.
13 Liddell Hart (ed.), *The Rommel Papers*, pp. 365–6.
14 Warlimont, *Inside Hitler's Headquarters*, pp. 307–8.
15 Warlimont, *Inside Hitler's Headquarters*, pp. 273–4, 282–3.
16 Liddell Hart (ed.), *The Rommel Papers*, pp. 366–7.
17 Gooch, *Mussolini's War*, p. 335.
18 Liddell Hart (ed.), *The Rommel Papers*, pp. 367–9, 372–3.
19 Fraser, *Knight's Cross*, p. 395; Liddell Hart (ed.), *The Rommel Papers*, p. 372.
20 Warlimont, *Inside Hitler's Headquarters*, pp. 296–8.

17 'IT WAS ALL SO UTTERLY POINTLESS'

1 Blumenson, *The Patton Papers*, pp. 124–5, 135, 137.
2 Butcher, *Three Years with Eisenhower*, p. 188.
3 Blumenson, *The Patton Papers*, p. 137.
4 D'Este, *A Genius for War*, p. 446; Robinett, 'Armored Commander', p. 199.
5 Atkinson, *An Army at Dawn*, pp. 227–8.
6 Robinett, 'Armored Commander', pp. 208–9.
7 Atkinson, *An Army at Dawn*, p. 228.
8 Robinett, 'Armored Commander', pp. 211–12.
9 Atkinson, *An Army at Dawn*, p. 230.
10 Eisenhower, *Crusade in Europe*, p. 123.
11 Howe, *Northwest Africa*, pp. 329–30; Robinett, 'Armored Commander', pp. 221–33.
12 Papers of Field Marshal Alanbrooke, Correspondence with Lieutenant General Sir Kenneth Anderson 1942–1943, Anderson to Brooke, 14 December 1942.
13 Anderson, 'The Allied Campaign in North Africa', p. 41.
14 Robinett, 'Armored Commander', pp. 234, 241–2.
15 D'Este, *A Genius for War*, pp. 446–7; Blumenson, *The Patton Papers*, pp. 137–8; Robinett, 'Armored Commander', pp. 244–5.
16 Robinett, 'Armored Commander', pp. 237–8.
17 D'Este, *A Genius for War*, pp. 445–6; Blumenson, *The Patton Papers*, p. 138.
18 Blumenson, *The Patton Papers*, pp. 138–9.

19 Papers of Field Marshal Alanbrooke, Anderson to Brooke, 14 December 1942.
20 Butcher, *Three Years with Eisenhower*, p. 191.
21 Papers of Field Marshal Alanbrooke, Anderson to Brooke, 14 December 1942.

18 'SIT STILL IN THE MIDDLE, GODDAMMIT, OR WE'LL ALL DROWN!'

1 Summersby Morgan, *Past Forgetting*, pp. 95–7; 'The Strathallan Story – The ship that died in secret', https://thestrathallan.com/wp/?page_id=2549&doing_wp_cron=1699291389.7324469089508056640625 [accessed 6 November 2023]
2 https://uboat.net/types/viic.htm; https://uboat.net/boats/u562.htm; https://uboat.net/men/commanders/404.html; 'The Strathallan Story', https://thestrathallan.com/wp/?page_id=2549&doing_wp_cron=1699291389.7324469089508056640625 [all accessed 8 November 2023]
3 Summersby Morgan, *Past Forgetting*, pp. 98–102; 'The Strathallan Story', https://thestrathallan.com/wp/?page_id=2557&doing_wp_cron=1699456369.2113258838653564453125 [accessed 8 November 2023]
4 https://thestrathallan.com/wp/?page_id=2537 [accessed 10 November 2023]
5 John Ellis, *The World War Two Databook* (London, 2003), p. 254.
6 Butcher, *Three Years with Eisenhower*, pp. 194–6; DDE, Papers of Harry C. Butcher, Box 1: Correspondence File 1942, Butcher to his wife Ruth, 29 December 1942; Eisenhower, *Crusade in Europe*, pp. 123–5; Papers of Field Marshal Alanbrooke, Anderson to Brooke, 25 December 1942.
7 Philip Jordan, *Tunis Diary* (London: Collins, 1943), p. 173.
8 Eisenhower, *Crusade in Europe*, pp. 124–6.
9 Butcher, *Three Years with Eisenhower*, p. 196.
10 Clark, *Calculated Risk*, pp. 129–30.
11 Summersby Morgan, *Past Forgetting*, pp. 108–11.

19 LONGSTOP HILL

1 Howe, *Northwest Africa*, p. 339; Atkinson, *An Army at Dawn*, p. 241.
2 D. C. Quilter (ed.), *No Dishonourable Name* (London: William Clowes and Sons, 1947), p. 40; https://www.britain-at-war.org.uk/ww2/Derrick_Jackson/html/training.htm [accessed 10 November 2023]

3 https://www.britain-at-war.org.uk/ww2/Derrick_Jackson/html/training.
   htm [accessed 10 November 2023]

4 Howe, *Northwest Africa*, p. 339; https://www.tracesofwar.com/
   persons/29958/Lang-Rudolf.htm [accessed 13 November 2023]

5 Hill, 'The Coldstream at Longstop: December 1942', in Quilter (ed.),
   No Dishonourable Name, p. 42; Howe, *Northwest Africa*, p. 339.

6 https://www.britain-at-war.org.uk/ww2/Derrick_Jackson/html/training.
   htm [accessed 13 November 2023]; Hill, 'The Coldstream at Longstop:
   December 1942', p. 43; Howe, *Northwest Africa*, p. 341.

7 Howe, *Northwest Africa*, pp. 341–2; Hill, 'The Coldstream at Longstop:
   December 1942', p. 44.

8 https://www.britain-at-war.org.uk/ww2/Derrick_Jackson/html/training.
   htm [accessed 14 November 2023]

9 Howe, *Northwest Africa*, pp. 342–3; Hill, 'The Coldstream at Longstop:
   December 1942', p. 44.

10 Hill, 'The Coldstream at Longstop: December 1942', p. 44.

11 https://www.britain-at-war.org.uk/ww2/Derrick_Jackson/html/training.
   htm [accessed 14 November 2023]

12 Howe, *Northwest Africa*, pp. 342–3; Hill, 'The Coldstream at Longstop:
   December 1942', pp. 44–6.

13 Howe, *Northwest Africa*, p. 343; Quilter (ed.), *No Dishonourable Name*,
   pp. 46–9; https://www.britain-at-war.org.uk/ww2/Derrick_Jackson/
   html/training.htm [accessed 14 November 2023]; Franklyn O. Johnson,
   *One More Hill: The Big Red One Blasts Hitler's Panzers from North Africa
   to Normandy* (New York: Bantam, 1983; repr. 1987), pp. 28–9.

14 Howe, *Northwest Africa*, p. 343.

15 Anderson, 'The Allied Campaign in North Africa, 1942–43', p. 33.

16 PP, James Holland Papers, Interview by Holland with Nigel Nicolson,
   15 September 2003.

17 PP, Nigel Nicolson Papers, Nicolson to his mother Vita Sackville-West,
   30 January 1943.

20 'IT IS KILLING THAT ANIMATES THEM'

1 Eisenhower, *Crusade in Europe*, p. 135; Butcher, *Three Years with
   Eisenhower*, pp. 196–7.

2 Churchill, *The Second World War*, IV, pp. 593–600; Atkinson, *An Army
   at Dawn*, pp. 266–7.

3 Anderson, 'The Allied Campaign in North Africa', p. 36.

4 David Nichols (ed.), *Ernie's War: The Best of Ernie Pyle's World War II
   Dispatches* (New York: Random House, Inc., 1986), pp. 3–15, 57–77.

5 https://www.americanairmuseum.com/archive/person/jack-m-ilfrey; https://p38assn.org/jack-ilfrey/ [both accessed 20 November 2023]

6 Nichols (ed.), *Ernie's War*, pp. 76–8.

7 Liddell Hart (ed.), *The Rommel Papers*, pp. 375–7.

8 Richard Overy, *Blood and Ruins: The Great Imperial War 1931–1945* (London: Allen Lane, 2021), p. 236.

9 Gooch, *Mussolini's War*, pp. 336–8; Kershaw, *Hitler*, II, p. 546.

10 Warlimont, *Inside Hitler's Headquarters*, p. 308.

11 Liddell Hart (ed.), *The Rommel Papers*, pp. 381–5; Gooch, *Mussolini's War*, p. 338.

21 DESERT RAIDERS

1 Vladimir Peniakoff, *Popski's Private Army* (London: Jonathan Cape, 1950; repr. 2002), p. 229.

2 IWM, Montgomery Ancillary Collection, Documents 1863, Brigadier Sir Edgar Williams' review of *Private Army* by Vladimir Peniakoff ('Popski'), 1950.

3 Peniakoff, *Popski's Private Army*, pp. xxiii–xxiv, 19–62.

4 Williams, review of *Private Army* by Vladimir Peniakoff ('Popski'), 1950.

5 Peniakoff, *Popski's Private Army*, pp. 62–108.

6 Williams, review of *Private Army* by Vladimir Peniakoff ('Popski'), 1950.

7 Peniakoff, *Popski's Private Army*, pp. 228–39.

8 Ben Macintyre, *SAS: Rogue Heroes* (London: Viking, 2016; repr. 2017), pp. 7–11.

9 Gavin Mortimer, *David Stirling: The Phoney Major* (London: Constable, 2022), pp. 24–9, 56–62, 85–93.

10 Macintyre, *SAS*, pp. 167–8, 174; Michael Asher, *The Regiment: The Real Story of the SAS* (London: Viking, 2007), pp. 176–9, 192.

11 Mortimer, *David Stirling*, pp. 206, 216; Macintyre, *SAS*, pp. 178–80.

12 Macintyre, *SAS*, pp. 180–3, 186–8; Asher, *The Regiment*, pp. 189–91; Mortimer, *David Stirling*, pp. 217–19, 229–33.

13 Liddell Hart (ed.), *The Rommel Papers*, p. 393.

22 THE CASABLANCA CONFERENCE

1 Hastings, *Finest Years*, pp. 352–3; Alanbrooke, *War Diaries 1939–1945*, p. 358.

2 Atkinson, *Army at Dawn*, p. 269.

3 Churchill, *The Second World War*, IV, pp. 604–5.

4 Hastings, *Finest Years*, pp. 352–3.

5 Roberts, *Masters and Commanders*, p. 348.

6 Alanbrooke, *War Diaries 1939–1945*, p. 348.

7 Roberts, *Masters and Commanders*, p. 303.

8 Roberts, *Masters and Commanders*, pp. 304–9.

9 Hastings, *Finest Years*, p. 353.

10 Alanbrooke, *War Diaries 1939–1945*, pp. 358–9.

11 John Miller Jr, *Cartwheel: The Reduction of Rabaul* (Washington DC: Office of the Chief of Military History, 1959), pp. 1–8.

12 Alanbrooke, *War Diaries 1939–1945*, p. 359.

13 Churchill, *The Second World War*, IV, p. 605.

14 Sherwood, *The White House Papers of Harry L. Hopkins*, II, pp. 666–71; Churchill, *The Second World War*, IV, p. 605.

15 Alanbrooke, *War Diaries 1939–1945*, p. 359.

16 Alanbrooke, *War Diaries 1939–1945*, p. 359.

17 Butcher, *Three Years with Eisenhower*, pp. 203–4; Eisenhower, *Crusade in Europe*, pp. 135–6.

18 Butcher, *Three Years with Eisenhower*, pp. 208–10.

19 Eisenhower, *Crusade in Europe*, pp. 136–8.

20 Roberts, *Masters and Commanders*, pp. 324–5.

21 Sherwood, *The White House Papers of Harry L. Hopkins*, II, pp. 671–2; Miller Jr, *Cartwheel*, pp. 1–8.

22 Roberts, *Masters and Commanders*, pp. 337–9.

23 Blumenson, *The Patton Papers*, p. 155.

24 Alanbrooke, *War Diaries 1939–1945*, pp. 360–1.

25 Churchill, *The Second World War*, IV, pp. 613, 616.

23 VICTORY OR DESTRUCTION

1 Liddell Hart (ed.), *The Rommel Papers*, pp. 388–90.

2 Von Below, *At Hitler's Side*, pp. 160–1.

3 Kershaw, *Hitler*, II, p. 547.

4 Von Below, *At Hitler's Side*, pp. 161–3.

5 Kershaw, *Hitler*, II, pp. 548–50.

6 MacGregor, *The Lighthouse of Stalingrad*, p. 272; David, *Military Blunders*, p. 207.

7 MacGregor, *The Lighthouse of Stalingrad*, pp. 275, 277–8; Kershaw, *Hitler*, II, pp. 550–1; Warlimont, *Inside Hitler's Headquarters*, pp. 300–2.

8 Kershaw, *Hitler*, II, p. 577; Von Below, *At Hitler's Side*, p. 161.

9 Butcher, *Three Years with Eisenhower*, pp. 210–11; Eisenhower, *Crusade in Europe*, pp. 139–40.

10 Anderson, 'The Allied Campaign in North Africa', p. 39.

11 Anderson, 'The Allied Campaign in North Africa', pp. 42–3; Howe, *Northwest Africa*, pp. 376–8; LHCMA, Papers of Lieut. General Sir Charles Allfrey, GB0099, Diary: 18–20 January 1943.

12 James R. Webb Papers, Box 1, 'First Waltz with Rommel', p. 1.

13 Robinett, 'Armored Commander', pp. 294–8; Anderson, 'The Allied Campaign in North Africa, 1942–43', p. 43; Howe, *Northwest Africa*, pp. 376–82.

14 LHCMA, Allfrey Papers, Diary: 21 January 1943.

15 Howe, *Northwest Africa*, p. 382.

16 Anderson, 'The Allied Campaign in North Africa', pp. 43–4; Howe, *Northwest Africa*, pp. 383–5.

17 Anderson, 'The Allied Campaign in North Africa', p. 44.

24 'SAVE YOURSELVES! SAVE YOURSELVES!'

1 Ambrose, *The Supreme Commander*, pp. 160–1.

2 Jordan, *Tunis Diary*, p. 197.

3 Eisenhower, *Crusade in Europe*, pp. 138–9.

4 Ambrose, *The Supreme Commander*, p. 164.

5 Butcher, *Three Years with Eisenhower*, pp. 212–14; Summersby Morgan, *Past Forgetting*, pp. 117–20.

6 Kesselring, *Memoirs*, p. 148.

7 Von Luck, *Panzer Commander*, p. 35.

8 Liddell Hart (ed.), *The Rommel Papers*, pp. 391–2.

9 Gooch, *Mussolini's War*, pp. 339, 352–3.

10 Liddell Hart (ed.), *The Rommel Papers*, p. 393.

11 Gooch, *Mussolini's War*, pp. 339–40.

12 Kesselring, *Memoirs*, p. 150.

13 Fifth Panzer Army War Diary, 24 January 1943, in history.army.mil/books/staff-rides/kasserine/vol-i-part_1.pdf [accessed 5 December 2023]; Liddell Hart (ed.), *The Rommel Papers*, p. 397.

14 Howe, *Northwest Africa*, pp. 391–2.

15 Howe, *Northwest Africa*, pp. 392–8; Atkinson, *An Army at Dawn*, 315–17; 1st Armored Division Report of Operations, 27 January–3 February 1943, in history.army.mil/books/staff-rides/kasserine/vol-i-part_1.pdf [accessed 5 December 2023]; Butcher, *Three Years with Eisenhower*, p. 217.

25 MONTY

1 Churchill, *The Second World War*, IV, p. 645; Danchev and Todman (eds), *War Diaries 1939–1945*, p. 379.

2 Churchill, *The Second World War*, IV, pp. 645–6.

3 PP, A. A. Blackwell Archive, Blackwell Album, p. 45.

4 Alanbrooke, *War Diaries 1939–1945*, p. 379.

5 Churchill, *The Second World War*, IV, p. 645; IWM, Montgomery Ancillary Collections 18, File 1, Montgomery's Letters to General Sir Frank Simpson, October 1942–September 1945, Monty to Brigadier F. E. W. Simpson, 6 February 1943; Stephen Brooks (ed.) *Montgomery and the Eighth Army: A Selection from the Diaries, Correspondence and other Papers of Field Marshal The Viscount Montgomery of Alamein, August 1942 to December 1943* (London: The Bodley Head, 1991), Monty to Brooke, 15 February 1943, pp. 135–6.

6 Ambrose, *The Supreme Commander*, p. 44.

7 Alun Chalfont, *Montgomery of Alamein* (London: 1976), p. 29.

8 *The Memoirs of Field Marshal Montgomery* (London: 1958), p. 35.

9 William Sheehan, *British Voices from the Irish War of Independence* (London: Collins, 2005), pp. 151–2.

10 Nigel Hamilton, *Monty: The Making of a General* (London: Hamish Hamilton, 1981), p. 214.

11 Alan Moorehead, *The Desert War: The North Africa Campaign, 1940–1943* (London: Hamish Hamilton, 1965), pp. 196–7, 199.

12 Dorman-Smith to John Connell (biographer of Wavell), 2 December 1958, in James Colvin, *Eighth Army Versus Rommel: Tactics, Training and Operations in North Africa 1940–1942* (Warwick: Helion & Co., 2020), p. 238.

13 PP, Holland Papers, F. C. Pogue's interview with Air Marshal Sir Arthur Coningham, 14 February 1947.

14 Monty to Simpson, 19 November 1943.

15 Rob Lyman and General the Lord Dannatt, *Victory to Defeat: The British Army 1918–40* (London: Osprey, 2023), pp. 312–13.

16 Field Marshal Lord Carver, 'Monty – Forty Years On', A Public Lecture in the Department of War Studies, King's College London, 8 March 1984.

17 Moorehead, *The Desert War*, p. 199.

18 Alanbrooke, *War Diaries 1939–1945*, p. 417.

19 Summersby Morgan, *Past Forgetting*, p. 130.

20 Eisenhower, *Crusade in Europe*, p. 211.

21 Moorehead, *The Desert War*, p. 199; Alanbrooke, *War Diaries 1939–1945*, p. 378.

22 Churchill, *The Second World War*, IV, p. 645.

23 Alanbrooke, *War Diaries 1939–1945*, p. 379.

24 Monty to Brigadier F. E. W. Simpson, 6 February 1943.

25 Churchill to Attlee, 5 February 1943, in Churchill, *The Second World War*, IV, p. 647.
26 Summersby Morgan, *Past Forgetting*, p. 123.
27 Churchill, *The Second World War*, IV, pp. 647–8.
28 Butcher, *Three Years with Eisenhower*, pp. 220–2; Churchill, *The Second World War*, IV, p. 648.
29 Ambrose, *The Supreme Commander*, pp. 165–7.

26 'LET'S GIVE ROMMEL
THIS ONE LAST CHANCE OF GLORY'

1 Liddell Hart (ed.), *The Rommel Papers*, pp. 394, 397.
2 Howe, *Northwest Africa*, pp. 405–6; Kesselring, *Memoirs*, p. 151; Order for Operation 'Frühlingwind', Fifth Panzer Army HQ, 8 February 1943, in https://history.army.mil/books/staff-rides/kasserine/vol-i-part_1.pdf [accessed 3 January 2024]
3 Liddell Hart (ed.), *The Rommel Papers*, p. 397; Ward Rutherford, *Baptism of Fire* (New York: Ballantine Books, 1970), p. 66; David, *Military Blunders*, p. 351.
4 Peter Hoffmann, *Stauffenberg: A Family History, 1905–1944* (Cambridge: CUP, 1995; repr. 2008), pp. 1–14, 51, 68–9.
5 Jürgen Schmädeke and Peter Steinbach, *Der Widerstand gegen den Nationalsozialismus. Die deutsche Gesellschaft und der Widerstand gegen Hitler* (Munich: Piper, 1986), p. 550.
6 Hoffmann, *Stauffenberg*, pp. 79–89, 114–16, 128–9, 132–3, 140, 151, 158–64; Sönke Neitzel (ed.), *Tapping Hitler's Generals: Transcripts of Secret Conversations, 1942–45* (Barnsley: Frontline, 2007), pp. 283–5.
7 Neitzel, *Tapping Hitler's Generals*, p. 305.
8 Ronny Kabus, *Jews of the Lutherstadt Wittenberg in the Third Reich* (Norderstedt, 2012), p. 85.
9 Neitzel, *Tapping Hitler's Generals*, p. 299.
10 Darby, *We Led the Way*, pp. 55–60; Black, *Rangers in World War II*, pp. 63–6.

27 'I'VE GOT A HUNCH THIS IS THE DANCE'

1 Ambrose, *The Supreme Commander*, pp. 168–9.
2 Summersby Morgan, *Past Forgetting*, pp. 124–6.
3 James R. Webb Papers, Box 1, 'First Waltz with Rommel', p. 1.
4 Ambrose, *The Supreme Commander*, p. 168.
5 James R. Webb Papers, 'First Waltz with Rommel', pp. 1–7.

6 Eisenhower, *Crusade in Europe*, pp. 141–2.

7 Butcher, *Three Years with Eisenhower*, p. 217.

8 Eisenhower, *Crusade in Europe*, p. 142.

9 Robinett, 'Armored Commander', p. 355.

10 Howe, *Northwest Africa*, pp. 410–11; Atkinson, *An Army at Dawn*, p. 325.

11 Robinett, 'Armored Commander', pp. 367–9.

12 Report by the Commander of the 168th Infantry, 7–17 February 1943, in https://history.army.mil/books/staff-rides/kasserine/vol-i-part_1.pdf [accessed 3 January 2024]

13 Summersby Morgan, *Past Forgetting*, pp. 126–7.

14 Eisenhower, *Crusade in Europe*, pp. 142–3; Robinett, 'Armored Commander', p. 369.

28 SIDI BOU ZID

1 DDE, World War II Participants and Contemporaries: Papers, Box 71, WWII Memoirs of Wade Walter Nyquist, p. 4.

2 WWII Memoirs of Wade Walter Nyquist, pp. 2–4.

3 Report of the Commander, 168th Regiment, 7–17 February 1943, in https://history.army.mil/books/staff-rides/kasserine/vol-i-part_1.pdf [accessed 3 January 2024]

4 'Life at the Front' by Ernie Pyle, 19 February 1943, in Nichols (ed.), *Ernie's War*, p. 81.

5 Report of the Commander, 168th Regiment, 7–17 February 1943, in https://history.army.mil/books/staff-rides/kasserine/vol-i-part_1.pdf [accessed 3 January 2024]

6 WWII Memoirs of Wade Walter Nyquist, p. 4.

7 Howe, *Northwest Africa*, pp. 410–12; Martin Blumenson, 'Kasserine Pass, 30 January–22 February 1943', Chapter 8 of *America's First Battles, 1776–1965*, in https://history.army.mil/books/staff-rides/kasserine/vol-i-part_1. pdf [accessed 3 January 2024]; Lessouda Force, 1st Armored Regiment, 13–17 February 1943 in https://history.army.mil/books/staff-rides/kasserine/vol-i-part_1.pdf [accessed 3 January 2024]

8 DDE, WWII Participants and Contemporaries, Box 120, Diary of Raymond Saidel.

9 Howe, *Northwest Africa*, pp. 411–12; Blumenson, 'Kasserine Pass, 30 January–22 February 1943'; Atkinson, *An Army at Dawn*, pp. 340–2.

10 Hudel and Robinett, 'The Tank Battle at Sidi Bou Zid', in https://history.army.mil/books/staff-rides/kasserine/vol-i-part_1.pdf [accessed 3 January 2024]; Lessouda Force, 1st Armored Regiment, 13–17 February 1943; Atkinson, *An Army at Dawn*, pp. 440–1.

11 Report of the Commander, 168th Regiment, 7–17 February 1943; Howe, *Northwest Africa*, p. 414.

12 Liddell Hart (ed.), *The Rommel Papers*, p. 398.

13 Ward Rutherford, *Kasserine: Baptism of Fire* (New York: Ballantine, 1970), p. 75.

14 Atkinson, *An Army at Dawn*, p. 346.

15 James R. Webb Papers, 'First Waltz with Rommel', pp. 14–15.

16 Eisenhower, *Crusade in Europe*, pp. 142–3.

17 Atkinson, *An Army at Dawn*, p. 346.

18 Summersby Morgan, *Past Forgetting*, p. 127.

29 'WE ARE GOING TO KICK HELL OUT OF HIM TODAY'

1 Nichols (ed.), *Ernie's War*, pp. 88–92.

2 Atkinson, *An Army at Dawn*, p. 349.

3 Nichols (ed.), *Ernie's War*, pp. 92–3.

4 Robinett, 'Armored Commander', pp. 370–1.

5 Nichols (ed.), *Ernie's War*, pp. 93–4.

6 Howe, *Northwest Africa*, pp. 419–21.

7 Nichols (ed.), *Ernie's War*, pp. 95–7.

8 Howe, *Northwest Africa*, pp. 421–2.

9 Howe, *Northwest Africa*, p. 423.

10 Robinett, 'Armored Commander', p. 372.

11 Anderson, 'The Allied Campaign in North Africa', pp. 50–1.

12 Report of the activities of the 2nd Battalion, 168th Infantry, 3–19 February 1943, in https://history.army.mil/books/staff-rides/kasserine/vol-i-part_1.pdf [accessed 3 January 2024]; Atkinson, *An Army at Dawn*, p. 354.

13 Report of the Commander, 168th Regiment, 7–17 February 1943; Report of Activities of 3rd Battalion, 168th Infantry, 7–20 February 1943, in https://history.army.mil/books/staff-rides/kasserine/vol-i-part_1.pdf [accessed 3 January 2024].

14 WWII Memoirs of Wade Walter Nyquist, p. 4.

15 Report of the Commander, 168th Regiment, 7–17 February 1943; Howe, *Northwest Africa*, p. 424.

16 WWII Memoirs of Wade Walter Nyquist, pp. 4–7.

17 https://valor.militarytimes.com/hero/6221 [accessed 18 January 2024]

18 *The Patton Papers*, p. 177.

19 Report of Activities of 3rd Battalion, 168th Infantry, 7–20 February 1943; Atkinson, *An Army at Dawn*, pp. 356–7.

REFERENCES

30 KASSERINE PASS

1 Liddell Hart (ed.), *The Rommel Papers*, p. 399.
2 Howe, *Northwest Africa*, p. 416.
3 Kesselring, *Memoirs*, p. 151.
4 Liddell Hart (ed.), *The Rommel Papers*, pp. 399–400.
5 Fraser, *Knight's Cross*, p. 405; *The Rommel Papers*, p. 400.
6 Fraser, *Knight's Cross*, p. 405; Howe, *Northwest Africa*, p. 425.
7 Liddell Hart (ed.), *The Rommel Papers*, p. 400; Darby, *We Led the Way*, p. 61.
8 Fraser, *Knight's Cross*, pp. 405–6; Liddell Hart (ed.), *The Rommel Papers*, pp. 400–2, 411.
9 Fraser, *Knight's Cross*, p. 406; Howe, *Northwest Africa*, pp. 444–5.
10 James R. Webb Papers, 'First Waltz with Rommel', p. 19.
11 David, *Military Blunders*, pp. 359–60; Atkinson, *An Army at Dawn*, pp. 369–70; Howe, *Northwest Africa*, p. 447.
12 Von Luck, *Panzer Commander*, p. 142; Butcher, *Three Years with Eisenhower*, p. 231.
13 David, *Military Blunders*, pp. 361–2.
14 Johnson, *One More Hill*, pp. 38–3.
15 Liddell Hart (ed.), *The Rommel Papers*, p. 403.
16 Hoffmann, *Stauffenberg*, pp. 170–1; Liddell Hart (ed.), *The Rommel Papers*, pp. 403–4.
17 David, *Military Blunders*, pp. 362–3; Liddell Hart (ed.), *The Rommel Papers*, pp. 404–5.
18 David, *Military Blunders*, p. 363; Liddell Hart (ed.), *The Rommel Papers*, pp. 405–6; Hoffmann, *Stauffenberg*, p. 171.
19 Peter Moore, *No Need to Worry: Memoirs of an Army Conscript 1941 to 1946* (Windsor: Winkfield, 2002), pp. 42–8.

31 'THE ENEMY HAS BROKEN THROUGH'

1 Robinett, 'Armored Commander', pp. 405–6.
2 Robinett, 'Armored Commander', p. 395.
3 Gardiner, *1,271 Days a Soldier*, pp. 136–7.
4 Robinett, 'Armored Commander', pp. 388–402.
5 Rutherford, *Kasserine*, pp. 122–3; Robinett, 'Armored Commander', pp. 403–10.
6 Liddell Hart (ed.), *The Rommel Papers*, p. 406.
7 Robinett, 'Armored Commander', p. 410.
8 Gardiner, *1,271 Days a Soldier*, p. 138.

9 Robinett, 'Armored Commander', p. 411.
10 Liddell Hart (ed.), *The Rommel Papers*, pp. 406–7.
11 Robinett, 'Armored Commander', p. 411.
12 Robinett, 'Armored Commander', pp. 416–17; Gardiner, *1,271 Days a Soldier*, p. 136.
13 Liddell Hart (ed.), *The Rommel Papers*, p. 407.
14 Kesselring, *Memoirs*, pp. 151–2.
15 Liddell Hart (ed.), *The Rommel Papers*, pp. 407–9.

32 ALEX

1 Hobbs (ed.), *Dear General*, pp. 103–4.
2 Ambrose, *The Supreme Commander*, p. 172.
3 Butcher, *Three Years with Eisenhower*, pp. 228–9.
4 Ambrose, *The Supreme Commander*, p. 172–4.
5 Eisenhower, *Crusade in Europe*, p. 146.
6 Hobbs (ed.), *Dear General*, p. 103.
7 Butcher, *Three Years with Eisenhower*, pp. 228–9.
8 Hobbs (ed.), *Dear General*, p. 103.
9 Eisenhower, *Crusade in Europe*, pp. 147–8.
10 Butcher, *Three Years with Eisenhower*, pp. 229–30.
11 Monty to Brigadier F. E. W. Simpson, 5 March 1943.
12 Brooks (ed.), *Montgomery and the Eighth Army*, pp. 156–7.
13 Brooks (ed.), *Montgomery and the Eighth Army*, p. 158; TNA, CAB 106/612, 'The African Campaign from El Alamein to Tunis', by Field Marshal Viscount Alexander of Tunis, II, p. 11.
14 Alanbrooke, *War Diaries 1939–1945*, pp. xxxix, 293; Saul David, *Mutiny at Salerno: An Injustice Exposed* (London: Brassey's, 1995), pp. 6–7; Holland, *Together We Stand*, pp. 251–5.
15 Alanbrooke, *War Diaries 1939–1945*, p. xxxix.
16 Alanbrooke, *War Diaries 1939–1945*, pp. 384–5.
17 Alexander, 'The African Campaign from El Alamein to Tunis', II, p. 12.

33 OPERATION *OSCHENKOPF*

1 Howe, *Northwest Africa*, pp. 501–2.
2 Liddell Hart (ed.), *The Rommel Papers*, pp. 407–9.
3 Howe, *Northwest Africa*, pp. 503–5; Villahermosa, *Hitler's Paratrooper*, pp. 153–4; Peter Hart, *Footsloggers: An Infantry Battatlion at War 1939–45* (London: Profile, 2023), pp. 79–81; Allfrey Papers, Diary: 1–2 March 1943.

4 PP, James Holland Papers, Transcript of Holland interview with Frank Read, 2004, https://www.griffonmerlin.com/wwii–interview/frank–read/ [accessed 7 February 2024]

5 PP, James Holland Papers, Corporal George Vaughan, 'Some Recollections of Sidi Nsir', p. 3.

6 Transcript of Holland interview with Frank Read, 2004.

7 Vaughan, 'Some Recollections of Sidi Nsir', pp. 3–7.

8 David Scott Daniell, *The Royal Hampshire Regiment: Volume 3, 1918–1954* (1955), pp. 106–7; Allfrey Papers, Diary: 26–27 February 1943; 'The Glorious 155th Battery Fought to the End', *The War Illustrated*, 7/158 (9 July 1943), p. 77.

9 Holland, *Together We Stand*, pp. 588–9.

10 Alexander, 'The African Campaign from El Alamein to Tunis', II, p. 13.

11 Frost, *A Drop Too Many*, p. 121.

12 Otway, *Airborne Forces*, p. 85.

13 Alexander, 'The African Campaign from El Alamein to Tunis', II, p. 13; Anderson, 'The Allied Campaign in North Africa', p. 58.

14 Liddell Hart (ed.), *The Rommel Papers*, p. 410.

15 Ambrose, *The Supreme Commander*, p. 175.

16 Eisenhower to Marshall, 3 March 1943, in Hobbs (ed.), *Dear General*, pp. 104–5.

17 DDE, James R. Webb Papers, Box 1, Draft article for the *Chicago Daily Tribune*, p. 7.

18 Ambrose, *The Supreme Commander*, p. 175.

19 Eisenhower, *Crusade in Europe*, p. 150.

20 *The Patton Papers*, p. 178.

21 Butcher, *Three Years with Eisenhower*, p. 235.

22 *The Patton Papers*, pp. 177–8.

23 Butcher, *Three Years with Eisenhower*, p. 235; *The Patton Papers*, pp. 180, 182.

24 *The Patton Papers*, pp. 180–1.

25 James R. Webb Papers, Draft article for the *Chicago Daily Tribune*, p. 7; *The Patton Papers*, p. 181.

34 MEDENINE

1 Liddell Hart (ed.), *The Rommel Papers*, pp. 410–15.

2 Hoffmann, *Stauffenberg*, p. 173.

3 Montgomery's diary notes on the Battle of Medenine, 3–6 March 1943, in Brooks (ed.), *Montgomery and the Eighth Army*, p. 167.

4 Monty to Brigadier F. E. W. Simpson, 5 March 1943, in Brooks (ed.), *Montgomery and the Eighth Army*, pp. 160–2.

5 Major General David Belchem, *All in the Day's March* (London: Collins, 1978), pp. 131–46.

6 Liddell Hart (ed.), *The Rommel Papers*, p. 415.

7 Hoffmann, *Stauffenberg*, pp. 173–4.

8 Belchem, *All in the Day's March*, pp. 146–8.

9 Hoffmann, *Stauffenberg*, p. 174.

10 Liddell Hart (ed.), *The Rommel Papers*, p. 415.

11 Hoffmann, *Stauffenberg*, pp. 174–5.

12 Liddell Hart (ed.), *The Rommel Papers*, p. 415.

13 Monty to Alex, 1145hrs, 7 March 1943, in Brooks (ed.), *Montgomery and the Eighth Army*, p. 166.

14 Liddell Hart (ed.), *The Rommel Papers*, pp. 416–18.

15 Von Luck, *Panzer Commander*, p. 144.

16 Liddell Hart (ed.), *The Rommel Papers*, pp. 418–19.

17 *The Goebbels Diaries*, p. 211.

18 Warlimont, *Inside Hitler's Headquarters*, p. 312.

19 Kershaw, *Hitler*, II, p. 581.

20 Liddell Hart (ed.), *The Rommel Papers*, p. 419.

21 *The Goebbels Diaries*, p. 226.

22 Liddell Hart (ed.), *The Rommel Papers*, p. 420.

35 'WE BEAT THE LIVING HELL OUT OF THEM'

1 D'Este, *A Genius for War*, p. 471.

2 Alexander, 'The African Campaign from El Alamein to Tunis', II, pp. 18–19.

3 *The Patton Papers*, pp. 185–90.

4 D'Este, *A Genius for War*, pp. 463–6.

5 D'Este, *A Genius for War*, p. 466; *The Patton Papers*, p. 188.

6 D'Arcy-Dawson, *Tunisian Battle*, p. 177.

7 Johnson, *One More Hill*, p. 48.

8 *The Patton Papers*, pp. 191–3.

9 D'Arcy-Dawson, *Tunisian Battle*, p. 178.

10 *The Patton Papers*, p. 192.

11 *The Patton Papers*, pp. 194–6.

12 Alexander, 'The African Campaign from El Alamein to Tunis', II, pp. 20–1; *The Patton Papers*, pp. 194–6; Howe, *Northwest Africa*, pp. 554–6.

13 Howe, *Northwest Africa*, pp. 557–60.

14 D'Arcy-Dawson, *Tunisian Battle*, p. 181.

15 D'Arcy-Dawson, *Tunisian Battle*, p. 181.

REFERENCES

16 D'Arcy-Dawson, *Tunisian Battle*, p. 182.

17 *The Patton Papers*, p. 199.

18 Alex to Monty, 29 March 1943, in Brooks (ed.), *Montgomery and the Eighth Army*, pp. 187–8.

19 Alexander, 'The African Campaign from El Alamein to Tunis', II, p. 21.

36 MONTY'S LEFT HOOK

1 NAM, 1998-08-24-1, Lionel Baker, 'A Newcomer's Life in the Eighth Army', p. 46.

2 Monty to Harding, 20 March 1943, in Brooks (ed.), *Montgomery and the Eighth Army*, pp. 177–8.

3 Captain Nigel Nicolson and Patrick Forbes, *The Grenadier Guards in the War of 1939–1945* (Aldershot: Gale & Polden Ltd, 1949), II, *The Mediterranean Campaigns*, pp. 296–309.

4 Alexander, 'The African Campaign from El Alamein to Tunis', II, p. 20.

5 PP, A. A. Blackwell Archive, Extract of Letter from Captain Alan Blackwell to his Parents, 2 April 1943.

6 Alexander, 'The African Campaign from El Alamein to Tunis', II, p. 20.

7 PP, A. A. Blackwell Archive, Diary of Captain Alan Blackwell, 23 March 1943.

8 Monty to Alex, 23 March 1943, in Brooks (ed.), *Montgomery and the Eighth Army*, p. 180.

9 Alexander, 'The African Campaign from El Alamein to Tunis', II, p. 20.

10 Monty to Alex, 23 March 1943, in Brooks (ed.), *Montgomery and the Eighth Army*, p. 180.

11 Alexander, 'The African Campaign from El Alamein to Tunis', II, p. 20.

12 Holland, *Together We Stand*, pp. 615–16.

13 Alexander, 'The African Campaign from El Alamein to Tunis', II, p. 21.

14 'Conclusion to Montgomery's diary notes on the Battle of Mareth, 20–28 March 1943', in Brooks (ed.), *Montgomery and the Eighth Army*, p. 186.

15 Alexander, 'The African Campaign from El Alamein to Tunis', II, p. 22; 'Conclusion to Montgomery's diary notes on the Battle of Mareth, 20–28 March 1943', pp. 185–7; https://teara.govt.nz/en/biographies/5n9/ngarimu-te-moananui-a-kiwa [accessed 15 May 2024]

16 'Conclusion to Montgomery's diary notes on the Battle of Mareth, 20–28 March 1943', pp. 185–7.

17 Carver, 'Monty – Forty Years On'.

18 Alexander, 'The African Campaign from El Alamein to Tunis', II, pp. 19–21; Alex to Monty, 29 March 1943, in Brooks (ed.), *Montgomery and the Eighth Army*, pp. 187–8.

19 Monty to General Sir Alan Brooke, 17 March 1943, in Brooks (ed.), *Montgomery and the Eighth Army*, p. 175.

20 Alex to Monty, 29 March 1943, in Brooks (ed.), *Montgomery and the Eighth Army*, p. 189.

37 'THE FÜHRER IS NOT READY TO THINK OF RETREAT'

1 Alexander, 'The African Campaign from El Alamein to Tunis', II, pp. 22–23.

2 LHCMA, Papers of Lieutenant General Charles W. Allfrey, Box 3/1, Diary, 24 March 1943.

3 https://www.paradata.org.uk/article/poetry-richard-dicky-spender [accessed 16 May 2024]

4 Frost, *A Drop Too Many*, pp. 156–65; Otway, *Airborne Forces*, pp. 86–7; Curtis, *Churchill's Volunteer*, p. 128.

5 LHCMA, Papers of Lieutenant General Charles W. Allfrey, Box 3/1, Diary, 28 March 1943.

6 Alexander, 'The African Campaign from El Alamein to Tunis', II, p. 23.

7 Jordan, *Tunis Diary*, pp. 221–2.

8 Von Luck, *Panzer Commander*, pp. 144–52.

9 Von Below, *At Hitler's Side*, pp. 167–8.

38 WADI AKARIT

1 Monty to Brigadier F. E. W. Simpson, 5 April 1943.

2 Eisenhower, *Crusade in Europe*, p. 151.

3 Ike to Marshall, in Holland, *Together We Stand*, p. 651.

4 Lieutenant General Sir Brian Horrocks, *A Full Life* (London: Collins, 1960), pp. 158–9.

5 Monty to Brigadier F. E. W. Simpson, 5 April 1943.

6 Ike to Marshall, 29 March 1943, in Hobbs (ed.), *Dear General*, p. 107.

7 Montgomery's diary notes on 'The Battle of the Gabes Gap, 5–7 April 1943', in Brooks (ed.), *Montgomery and the Eighth Army*, p. 197.

8 Francis Tuker, *Approach to Battle: A Commentary – Eighth Army, November 1941 to May 1943* (London: Cassell, 1963), pp. 318–20.

9 Montgomery's diary notes on 'The Battle of the Gabes Gap, 5–7 April 1943', p. 197.

10 Alexander, 'The African Campaign from El Alamein to Tunis', II, pp. 23–4.

11 Baker, 'A Newcomer's Life in the Eighth Army', pp. 94–122.

12 Alexander, 'The African Campaign from El Alamein to Tunis', II, p. 25.

13 Captain Ian C. Cameron, *History of the Argyll & Sutherland Highlanders 7th Battalion: From El Alamein to Germany* (London: Thomas Nelson & Sons, 1946), pp. 87–96.

14 Belchem, *All in the Day's March*, p. 154.

15 Alexander, 'The African Campaign from El Alamein to Tunis', II, p. 25.

16 Tuker, *Approach to Battle*, pp. 322–7; *The London Gazette*, 15 June 1943.

17 Alexander, 'The African Campaign from El Alamein to Tunis', II, p. 25.

18 Montgomery's diary notes on 'The Battle of the Gabes Gap, 5–7 April 1943'.

19 PP, A. A. Blackwell Archive, Major Andrew Edgar to Marjorie Blackwell, 10 April 1943; Mr Grey to Mr Blackwell, 24 April 1943.

20 PP, A. A. Blackwell Archive, Major Andrew Edgar to Mr Blackwell, 12 May 1943.

21 PP, A. A. Blackwell Archive, Private Leslie Binns to Marjorie Blackwell, 20 April 1943.

22 Montgomery's diary notes on 'The Battle of the Gabes Gap, 5–7 April 1943'.

23 Alexander, 'The African Campaign from El Alamein to Tunis', II, p. 25.

24 Hoffmann, *Stauffenberg*, pp. 178–87.

25 Belchem, *All in the Day's March*, pp. 157–8.

26 *The Patton Papers*, pp. 212–13.

27 Atkinson, *An Army at Dawn*, p. 465; Patton to his wife Beatrice, 8 April 1943, in *The Patton Papers*, p. 214.

39 MISSION IMPOSSIBLE

1 Douglas E. Delaney, *Corps Commanders: Five British and Canadian Generals at War, 1939–1945* (Vancouver: UBC Press, 2011), pp. 125–8.

2 Schaps, *500 Days of Front Line Combat*, pp. 63–4.

3 Alexander, 'The African Campaign from El Alamein to Tunis', II, p. 26.
4 Butcher, *Three Years with Eisenhower*, p. 242.
5 D'Arcy-Dawson, *Tunisian Battle*, pp. 199–200.
6 Moore, 'Memoir of the Tunisian Campaign', pp. 141–2.
7 Ike to Marshall, 16 April 1943, in Hobbs (ed.), *Dear General*, p. 108.
8 Eisenhower, *Crusade in Europe*, p. 151.
9 *The Patton Papers*, p. 218.
10 Ike to Marshall, 16 April 1943, in Hobbs (ed.), *Dear General*, pp. 108–9; Butcher, *Three Years with Eisenhower*, p. 245.
11 Robinett, 'Armored Commander', p. 476.
12 *The Patton Papers*, pp. 211, 219.
13 Butcher, *Three Years with Eisenhower*, p. 245; *The Patton Papers*, p. 220.
14 Gooch, *Mussolini's War*, p. 364.
15 Warlimont, *Inside Hitler's Headquarters*, p. 315; Gooch, *Mussolini's War*, pp. 364–5.
16 Kershaw, *Hitler*, II, p. 581; Von Below, *At Hitler's Side*, p. 169.
17 *The Goebbels Diaries*, p. 250.
18 Warlimont, *Inside Hitler's Headquarters*, pp. 312–13.
19 Gooch, *Mussolini's War*, pp. 365–6.
20 Churchill, *The Second World War*, IV, p. 690.
21 Alexander, 'The African Campaign from El Alamein to Tunis', II, pp. 26–7; Churchill, *The Second World War*, IV, p. 690.
22 Alexander, 'The African Campaign from El Alamein to Tunis', II, pp. 26–7.
23 Monty to Alex, 10 April 1941, in Brooks (ed.), *Montgomery and the Eighth Army*, pp. 201–2.
24 Alexander, 'The African Campaign from El Alamein to Tunis', II, pp. 27–8.
25 Alexander, 'The African Campaign from El Alamein to Tunis', II, pp. 28–9.

40 'THEY WERE BUNCHED LIKE A HERD OF CATTLE'

1 Monty to Brooke, 15 April 1943, in Brooks (ed.), *Montgomery and the Eighth Army*, pp. 208–9.
2 Monty to Brooke, 12 April 1943, in Brooks (ed.), *Montgomery and the Eighth Army*, p. 207; Alanbrooke, *War Diaries 1939–1945*, p. 418.
3 Jordan, *Tunis Diary*, pp. 233–4.
4 Alexander, 'The African Campaign from El Alamein to Tunis', II, pp. 29–30.

5 Paul Moon, *Victoria Cross at Takrouna: The Haane Manahi Story* (Wellington, 2010), pp. 100, 123; https://nzetc.victoria.ac.nz/tm/ scholarly/tei–WH2Maor–c11.html [accessed 1 June 2024]

6 Alexander, 'The African Campaign from El Alamein to Tunis', II, pp. 29–30.

7 Monty to Alexander, 21 April 1943, in Brooks (ed.), *Montgomery and the Eighth Army*, p. 215.

8 https://www.ibiblio.org/hyperwar/USA/USA-MTO-NWA/USA-MTO-NWA-31.html [accessed 13 March 2024]

9 Alexander, 'The African Campaign from El Alamein to Tunis', II, p. 30.

10 Monty to Brooke, 30 April 1943, in Brooks (ed.), *Montgomery and the Eighth Army*, p. 221.

11 Alexander, 'The African Campaign from El Alamein to Tunis', II, p. 30.

12 Sönke Nietzel and Harald Welzer, *Soldaten: On Fighting, Killing and Dying* (London: Simon & Schuster, 2011; repr., 2012), p. 295.

13 https://www.ibiblio.org/hyperwar/USA/USA-MTO-NWA/USA-MTO-NWA-31.html [accessed 13 March 2024]; Alexander, 'The African Campaign from El Alamein to Tunis', II, pp. 30–1; Jordan, *Tunis Diary*, p. 236.

14 Jordan, *Tunis Diary*, p. 237.

15 TNA, WO 98/8/785, Major John Anderson's Victoria Cross citation.

16 Richard Doherty, *The North Irish Horse: A Hundred Years of Service* (Spellmount, 2002), pp. 105–6.

17 https://www.ibiblio.org/hyperwar/USA/USA-MTO-NWA/USA-MTO-NWA-31.html [accessed 13 March 2024]; Jordan, *Tunis Diary*, p. 237.

18 John Kenneally VC, *The Honour and the Shame* (London: Kenwood, 1991; repr. 2008), pp. 72–5.

19 Kenneally, *The Honour and the Shame*, pp. 1–60.

20 Kenneally, *The Honour and the Shame*, pp. 127; https://vcgca.org/our-people/profile/1721/john-patrick [accessed 19 March 2024]

21 Alexander, 'The African Campaign from El Alamein to Tunis', II, pp. 32–3; Alex to Churchill, 30 April 1943, in Churchill, *The Second World War*, IV, p. 691.

22 Jordan, *Tunis Diary*, p. 248.

23 Eisenhower, *Crusade in Europe*, p. 155.

24 Butcher, *Three Years with Eisenhower*, pp. 247–9.

25 Cunningham to Pound, 28 April 1943 and Cunningham's Report on Operation Retribution, 13 November 1943, in Michael Simpson (ed.),

The Cunningham Papers, II, The Triumph of Allied Sea Power 1942–1946 (London: Routledge, 2020), pp. 75, 99.

26 Butcher, Three Years with Eisenhower, p. 250.

41 OPERATION STRIKE

1 D'Arcy-Dawson, Tunisian Battle, p. 232.

2 Alexander, 'The African Campaign from El Alamein to Tunis', II, p. 33.

3 Horrocks, A Full Life, pp. 168–9.

4 CMA, Allfrey Papers, Diary: 29/30 April 1943; Montgomery's notes for a talk with CIGS in June 1943, in Brooks (ed.), Montgomery and the Eighth Army, p. 231.

5 Horrocks, A Full Life, p. 169.

6 Tuker, Approach to Battle, pp. 354–64.

7 D'Arcy-Dawson, Tunisian Battle, pp. 229–32; Alexander, 'The African Campaign from El Alamein to Tunis', II, p. 33.

8 Horrocks, A Full Life, p. 170.

9 Robinett, 'Armored Commander', pp. 501–7.

10 PP, Nicolson Papers, Captain Nigel Nicolson to his parents, 13 May 1943.

11 Jordan, Tunis Diary, p. 252.

12 Horrocks, A Full Life, p. 171.

13 Howe, Northwest Africa, pp. 649–50; D'Arcy-Dawson, Tunisian Battle, p. 233.

14 Allfrey Papers, Diary, 6/7 May 1943; Howe, Northwest Africa, pp. 649–50.

15 Horrocks, A Full Life, p. 171.

16 Moorehead, The Desert War, pp. 237–8.

17 Moorehead, The Desert War, pp. 237–8.

18 D'Arcy-Dawson, Tunisian Battle, pp. 236–7.

19 Alexander, 'The African Campaign from El Alamein to Tunis', II, p. 37.

20 Horrocks, A Full Life, pp. 171–2.

21 Jordan, Tunis Diary, p. 253.

22 Orion C. Shockley, Random Chance: One Infantry Soldier's Story (Victoria, BC: Trafford Publishing, 2007), pp. 9–41.

23 Howe, Northwest Africa, p. 653.

24 Shockley, Random Chance, p. 42.

25 Alexander, 'The African Campaign from El Alamein to Tunis', II, p. 37.

42 'WE ARE MASTERS OF THE NORTH AFRICAN SHORES'

1 *The Goebbels Diaries*, 7 May 1943, pp. 274–5.
2 Gooch, *Mussolini's War*, p. 367.
3 Quoted in Kershaw, *Hitler*, II, p. 584.
4 *The Goebbels Diaries*, 8 May 1943, pp. 277–81.
5 Butcher, *Three Years with Eisenhower*, pp. 252–3; Alexander, 'The African Campaign from El Alamein to Tunis', II, p. 37.
6 Alex to Churchill, 8 May 1943, in Churchill, *The Second World War*, IV, p. 693.
7 Howe, *Northwest Africa*, p. 662.
8 Robinett Papers, Box 4, Master Sergeant T. Riggs to his parents, undated.
9 Pyle, *Ernie's War*, pp. 121–4.
10 Johnson, *One More Hill*, pp. 69–70.
11 Nicolson Papers, Captain Nigel Nicolson to his parents, 13 May 1943.
12 Vincent, 'Memoir of the Tunisian Campaign', pp. 162–8; D'Arcy-Dawson, *Tunisian Battle*, p. 244.
13 Alexander, 'The African Campaign from El Alamein to Tunis', II, p. 38; Anderson, 'The Allied Campaign in North Africa', p. 76.
14 Tuker, *Approach to Battle*, pp. 374–5.
15 Allfrey Papers, Diary: 12 May 1943; Tuker, *Approach to Battle*, pp. 375–9.
16 D'Arcy-Dawson, *Tunisian Battle*, p. 246.
17 Anderson, 'The Allied Campaign in North Africa', pp. 76, 78; Alexander, 'The African Campaign from El Alamein to Tunis', II, p. 38; Butcher, *Three Years with Eisenhower*, p. 259; Eisenhower, *Crusade in Europe*, p. 157; Ike to Marshall, 13 May 1943, in Hobbs (ed.), *Dear General*, p. 112.
18 Nicolson Papers, Captain Nigel Nicolson to his parents, 13 May 1943.
19 Freyberg to the prime minister of New Zealand, 27 May 1943, in https://nzetc.victoria.ac.nz/tm/scholarly/tei-WH2-2Doc-c9-20.html [accessed 12 April 2024]
20 Churchill, *The Second World War*, IV, p. 698.

43 'WE HAVE STRUCK A BLOW EQUAL TO STALINGRAD'

1 Churchill, *The Second World War*, IV, pp. 698–701.
2 Roberts, *Masters and Commanders*, p. 369.
3 Churchill, *The Second World War*, IV, p. 714; https://trove.nla.gov.au/newspaper/article/56282956 [accessed 16 April 2024]

4 Gooch, *Mussolini's War*, p. 368; Kershaw, *Hitler*, II, p. 585.

5 Von Below, *At Hitler's Side*, p. 171.

6 Kershaw, *Hitler*, II, pp. 578–80.

7 *The Goebbels Diaries*, 12–14 May 1943, pp. 296–9; Nietzl and Weltzer, *Soldaten*, pp. 246, 257.

8 Warlimont, *Inside Hitler's Headquarters*, pp. 313–17.

9 Gooch, *Mussolini's War*, p. 368; Kershaw, *Hitler*, II, p. 585.

EPILOGUE

1 Atkinson, *An Army at Dawn*, pp. 530–1; Harold Macmillan, *The Blast of War* (London: Macmillan, 1967), p. 322.

2 *The Patton Papers*, p. 253.

3 Butcher, *Three Years with Eisenhower*, pp. 263–4.

4 Allfrey Papers, Diary: 20 May 1943.

5 *The Patton Papers*, p. 253.

6 Moore, *No Need to Worry*, p. 78.

7 Kenneally, *The Honour and the Shame*, pp. 119–20.

8 Nicolson and Forbes, *The Grenadier Guards in the War of 1939–1945*, II, p. 345; Allfrey Papers, Diary: 20 May 1943.

9 Anderson, 'The Allied Campaign in North Africa, 1942–43', p. 80.

10 Allfrey Papers, Diary: 20 May 1943; Macmillan, *The Blast of War*, p. 324.

11 *The Patton Papers*, p. 253.

12 Butcher, *Three Years with Eisenhower*, p. 264.

13 Macmillan, *The Blast of War*, p. 325.

14 Howe, *Northwest Europe*, p. 675.

15 Eisenhower, *Crusade in Europe*, pp. 157–8.

16 Anderson, 'The Allied Campaign in North Africa', p. 80.

17 Papers of Field Marshal Alanbrooke, Ike to Brooke, 3 July 1943.

18 Alexander, 'The African Campaign from El Alamein to Tunis', II, pp. 39–40.

19 Macmillan, *The Blast of War*, p. 321.

20 Churchill, *The Second World War*, IV, pp. 726–30; Alanbrooke, *War Diaries 1939–1945*, p. 413.

21 Butcher, *Three Years with Eisenhower*, pp. 266–9.

22 Alanbrooke, *War Diaries 1939–1945*, pp. 415–16; Anderson, 'The Allied Campaign in North Africa', p. 80.

23 Avis D. Schorer, *A Half Acre of Hell: A Combat Nurse in WWII* (Lakeville, MN: Galde Press, 2000), p. 76.

24 Kershaw, *Hitler*, II, pp. 593–5; Gooch, *Mussolini's War*, pp. 384–9.

25 Liddell Hart (ed.), *The Rommel Papers*, pp. 431–40; Fraser, *Knight's Cross*, pp. 441–6.
26 Von Below, *At Hitler's Side*, p. 179.
27 Gooch, *Mussolini's War*, p. 410.
28 Howe, *Northwest Africa*, p. 676.
29 Churchill, *The Second World War*, IV, p. 743.

Bibliography

Primary Sources, Unpublished

Dwight D. Eisenhower Presidential Library and Archive (DDE), Abilene, Kansas
Papers of Harry C. Butcher
Papers of Dwight D. Eisenhower
Papers of James R. Webb
Papers of World War II Participants and Contemporaries

Imperial War Museum Archives (IWM), London
Montgomery Ancillary Collection

Library of Congress (LoC), Washington DC
Papers of George S. Patton
Papers of Paul M. Robinett

Liddell Hart Centre for Military Archives (LHCMA), London
Papers of Field Marshal Alanbrooke
Papers of Lieut. General Sir Charles Allfrey

Private Papers (PP)
M. J. Beckett Papers
A. A. Blackwell Archive
Harry Holden-White Papers
James Holland Papers
Nigel Nicolson Papers

Royal Navy Submarine Museum (RNSM), Portsmouth
Richard Livingstone, 'Mark Clark's Secret Landing'

The National Archives (TNA), Kew, London
CAB 80/11, Chiefs of Staff Paper No. 168, 27 May 1940
CAB 106/612, Field Marshal Viscount Alexander of Tunis, 'The African
   Campaign from El Alamein to Tunis'
CAB 106/708, Lieut. General Kenneth Anderson, 'The Allied Campaign in
   North Africa, 1942–43'
DEFE 2/531, Reports on Operation Reservist
HW 1/1169, Signals Intelligence passed to the Prime Minister, 26
   November 1942
WO 98/8/785, Major John Anderson's Victoria Cross citation
WO 175/293, War Diary of the 1st Derbyshire Yeomanry, October–
   December 1942
WO 218/32, War Diary of No. 1 Commando, December 1942
WO 218/170, War Diary of No. 8 Commando (B Battalion, Layforce),
   January 1941

The National Army Museum (NAM), London
1998-08-24-1, Lionel Baker, 'A Newcomer's Life in the Eighth Army'
1999-03-178-1, Lieut. M. Vincent Moore, 'Memoir of the Tunisian
   Campaign, 1942–1943'

Primary Sources, Published

Published Documents, Diaries, Letters and Memoirs
Alanbrooke, Field Marshal Lord, *War Diaries: 1939–1945*, eds Alex Danchev
   and Daniel Todman (London: Weidenfeld, 2001)
Barnes, Tag, *Commando Diary: 1942–1946* (Tunbridge Wells: Spellmount,
   1991)
Baumbach, Werner, *Broken Swastika: The Defeat of the Luftwaffe* (London:
   Robert Hale, 1960; repr. 1974)
Belchem, Major General David, *All in the Day's March* (London: Collins,
   1978)
Below, Nicolaus von, *At Hitler's Side: The Memoirs of Hitler's Luftwaffe
   Adjutant 1937–1945* (Mainz: v. Hase & Koehler Verlag; repr. 2004)
Blumenson, Martin, *The Patton Papers: 1940–1945* (Boston: Houghton
   Mifflin, 1974)

Brooks, Stephen (ed.), *Montgomery and the Eighth Army: A Selection from the Diaries, Correspondence and other Papers of Field Marshal The Viscount Montgomery of Alamein, August 1942 to December 1943* (London: Bodley Head, 1991)

Butcher, Harry C., *Three Years with Eisenhower: The Personal Diary of Captain Harry C. Butcher, USNR* (London: Heinemann, 1946)

Caracillo, Dominic J. (ed.), *1,271 Days a Soldier: The Diaries and Letters of Colonel H. E. Gardiner as an Armor Officer in World War II* (Dahlonega, GA: University of North Georgia Press, 2021)

Churchill, Winston, *The Second World War*, 6 vols (London: Cassell & Co., 1944–54)

Clark, Mark, *Calculated Risk: His Personal Story of the War in North Africa and Italy* (London: George Harrap, 1951)

Courtney, G. B., *SBS in World War Two* (London: Robert Hale, 1983; repr. 2017)

Cunningham, Viscount, *A Sailor's Odyssey* (London: Hutchinson, 1951)

Curtis, Reg, *Churchill's Volunteer: A Parachute Corporal's Story* (London: Avon Books, 1994)

Darby, William O., *We Led the Way: Darby's Rangers* (New York: Presidio Press, 1980)

D'Arcy-Dawson, John, *Tunisian Battle* (London: Macdonald, 1943)

Deane, Theresa M., and Joseph E. Schaps, *500 Days of Front Line Combat: The WWII Memoir of Ralph B. Schaps* (New York: iUniverse, 2003)

De Gaulle, Charles, *War Memoirs*, 3 vols (London: Simon and Schuster, 1959)

Eisenhower, Dwight D., *Crusade in Europe* (New York: Doubleday, 1948; repr. 1997)

Frost, John, *A Drop Too Many: The Memoirs of World War II's most daring Parachute Commander* (London: Cassell & Co., 1980; repr. 1988)

Goebbels, Joseph, *The Goebbels Diaries: 1942–1943* (New York: Doubleday, 1948)

Guderian, Heinz, *Panzer Leader* (London: Penguin, 1952: repr. 2000)

Hobbs, Joseph P. (ed.), *Dear General: Eisenhower's Wartime Letters to Marshall* (Baltimore: Johns Hopkins University Press, 1971)

Horrocks, Lieutenant General Sir Brian, *A Full Life* (London: Collins, 1960)

Johnson, Franklyn O., *One More Hill: The Big Red One Blasts Hitler's Panzers from North Africa to Normandy* (New York: Bantam, 1983; repr. 1987)

Jordan, Philip, *Tunis Diary* (London: Collins, 1943)

Kenneally, John, VC, *The Honour and the Shame* (London: Kenwood, 1991; repr. 2008)

Luck, Hans von, *Panzer Commander: The Memoirs of Colonel Hans von Luck* (New York: 1989; repr. 1991)

Macmillan, Harold, *The Blast of War* (London: Macmillan, 1967)

The Memoirs of Field Marshal Kesselring (London: William Kimber, 1953; repr. 1988)

The Memoirs of Field Marshal Montgomery (London: 1958)

Moore, Peter, *No Need to Worry: Memoirs of an Army Conscript 1941 to 1946* (Windsor: Winkfield, 2002)

Nichols, David (ed.), *Ernie's War: The Best of Ernie Pyle's World War II Dispatches* (New York: Random House, Inc., 1986)

Peniakoff, Vladimir, *Popski's Private Army* (London: Jonathan Cape, 1950; repr. 2002)

The Rommel Papers, ed. B. H. Liddell Hart (London: Collins, 1953; repr. 1987)

Schorer, Avis D., *A Half Acre of Hell: A Combat Nurse in WWII* (Lakeville, MN: Galde Press, 2000)

Shockley, Orion C., *Random Chance: One Infantry Soldier's Story* (Victoria, BC: Trafford Publishing, 2007)

Simpson, Michael (ed.), *The Cunningham Papers*, II, *The Triumph of Allied Sea Power 1942–1946* (London: Routledge, 2020)

Summersby Morgan, Kay, *Past Forgetting: My Love Affair with Dwight D. Eisenhower* (New York: Golden Apple, 1984)

Tuker, Francis, *Approach to Battle: A Commentary – Eighth Army, November 1941 to May 1943* (London: Cassell, 1963)

Warlimont, Walter, *Inside Hitler's Headquarters 1939–45* (London: Weidenfeld & Nicolson, 1964)

Wedemeyer, Albert C., *Wedemeyer Reports!* (New York: Devin-Adair, 1958)

Newspapers and Journals
Daily Telegraph
London Gazette
War Illustrated

Secondary Sources

Books and Articles

Ambrose, Stephen E., *Eisenhower: Soldier and President* (New York: Simon and Schuster, 1990; repr. 2003)

——, *The Supreme Commander: The War Years of Dwight D. Eisenhower* (New York: Doubleday, 1970)

BIBLIOGRAPHY

Arthur, Max, *Men of the Red Beret: Airborne Forces 1940 to Today* (London: Century Hutchinson, 1990; repr. 1992)

Asher, Michael, *The Regiment: The Real Story of the SAS* (London: Viking, 2007)

Atkinson, Rick, *An Army at Dawn: The War in North Africa, 1942–1943* (London: Little, Brown, 2003; repr. 2004)

Black, Robert W., *Rangers in World War II* (New York: Presidio Press, 1992)

Boyd, Andrew, *British Naval Intelligence Through the Twentieth Century* (Barnsley: Seaforth, 2020)

Cameron, Captain Ian C., *History of the Argyll & Sutherland Highlanders 7th Battalion: From El Alamein to Germany* (London: Thomas Nelson & Sons, 1946)

Celik, Zeynik, *Urban Forms and Colonial Confrontations: Algiers Under French Rule* (University of California Press, 1997)

Chalfont, Alan, *Montgomery of Alamein* (London: 1976)

Colvin, James, *Eighth Army Versus Rommel: Tactics, Training and Operations in North Africa 1940–1942* (Warwick: Helion & Co., 2020)

David, Saul, *Military Blunders: The How and Why of Military Failure* (London: Robinson, 1997)

——, *Mutiny at Salerno: An Injustice Exposed* (London: Brassey's, 1995)

——, *SBS: Silent Warriors* (London: William Collins, 2021)

Delaney, Douglas E., *Corps Commanders: Five British and Canadian Generals at War, 1939–1945* (Vancouver: UBC Press, 2011)

D'Este, Carlo, *A Genius for War: A Life of General George S. Patton* (London: HarperCollins, 1995; repr. 1996)

Doherty, Richard, *The North Irish Horse: A Hundred Years of Service* (Spellmount, 2002)

Edward Smith, Jean, *FDR* (New York: Random House, 2007; repr. 2008)

Ellis, John, *The World War Two Databook* (London, 2003)

Fraser, David, *Knight's Cross: A Life of Field Marshal Erwin Rommel* (London: HarperCollins, 1993; repr. 1994)

Gooch, John, *Mussolini's War: Fascist Italy from Triumph to Collapse, 1935–1943* (London: Allen Lane, 2020)

Hansard (Parliamentary Proceedings), House of Commons Debates

Hart, Peter, *Footsloggers: An Infantry Battalion at War 1939–45* (London: Profile, 2023)

Hastings, Max, *Finest Years: Churchill as Warlord 1940–1945* (London: HarperPress, 2009; repr. 2010)

Hoffmann, Peter, *Stauffenberg: A Family History, 1905–1944* (Cambridge: CUP, 1995; repr. 2008)

Holland, James, *Together We Stand: North Africa, 1942–1943 – Turning the War in the West* (London: HarperCollins, 2005)

Howe, George F., *Northwest Africa: Seizing the Initiative in the West* (Washington DC: US Army Center of Military History, 1993)

Jackson, Julian, *France on Trial: The Case of Marshal Pétain* (London: Allen Lane, 2023)

Jordan, Jonathan W., *American Warlords: How Roosevelt's High Command Led America to Victory in World War II* (New York: NAL Caliber, 2015)

Kabus, Ronny, *Jews of the Lutherstadt Wittenberg in the Third Reich* (Norderstedt, 2012)

Kershaw, Ian, *Hitler*, 2 vols (London: Allen Lane, 1998–2000)

Lacouture, Jean, *De Gaulle: The Rebel 1890–1944* (1984; repr. 1991)

Liddell Hart, B. H., *The Other Side of the Hill* (London: Cassell, 1951)

Lüdeke, Alexander, *Der Zweite Weltkrieg: Ursachen, Ausbruch, Verlauf, Folgen* (Berlin, 2007)

Lyman, Rob, and General the Lord Dannatt, *Victory to Defeat: The British Army 1918–40* (London: Osprey, 2023)

MacGregor, Iain, *The Lighthouse of Stalingrad* (London: Constable, 2022)

Macintyre, Ben, *SAS: Rogue Heroes* (London: Viking, 2016; repr. 2017)

Miller Jr, John, *Cartwheel: The Reduction of Rabaul* (Washington DC: Office of the Chief of Military History, 1959)

Moon, Paul, *Victoria Cross at Takrouna: The Haane Manahi Story* (Wellington, 2010)

Moorehead, Alan, *The Desert War: The North Africa Campaign, 1940–1943* (London: Hamish Hamilton, 1965)

Mortimer, Gavin, *David Stirling: The Phoney Major* (London: Constable, 2022)

Neitzel, Sönke, and Harald Welzer, *Soldaten: On Fighting, Killing and Dying* (London: Simon and Schuster, 2011; repr., 2012)

Neitzel, Sönke (ed.), *Tapping Hitler's Generals: Transcripts of Secret Conversations, 1942–45* (Barnsley: Frontline, 2007)

Nicolson, Captain Nigel, and Patrick Forbes, *The Grenadier Guards in the War of 1939–1945: Volume 2 – The Mediterranean Campaigns* (Aldershot: Gale & Polden Ltd, 1949)

Otway, Lieutenant Colonel T. B. H., *Airborne Forces of the Second World War, 1939–45* (London: HMSO, 1951; repr. 2021)

Overy, Richard, *Blood and Ruins: The Great Imperial War 1931–1945* (London: Allen Lane, 2021)

——, *Why the Allies Won* (London: Jonathan Cape, 1995; repr. 2006)

Parker, John, *The Paras: The Inside Story of Britain's Toughest Regiment* (London: Metro, 2010)

——, *SBS: The Inside Story of the Special Boat Service* (London: Headline, 1997; repr. 2004)

Peatling, Robert, *Without Tradition: 2 Para 1941–1945* (Barnsley: Pen & Sword, 1994; repr. 2004)

Porch, Douglas, *Defeat and Division: France at War, 1939–1942* (Cambridge: CUP, 2022)

Quilter, D. C. (ed.), *No Dishonourable Name* (London: William Clowes and Sons, 1947)

Roberts, Andrew, *Masters and Commanders: How Roosevelt, Churchill, Marshall and Alanbrooke Won the War in the West* (London: Allen Lane, 2008)

Rutherford, Ward, *Baptism of Fire* (New York: Ballantine Books, 1970)

Schmädeke, Jürgen, and Peter Steinbach, *Der Widerstand gegen den Nationalsozialismus. Die deutsche Gesellschaft und der Widerstand gegen Hitler* (Munich: Piper, 1986)

Scott Daniell, David, *The Royal Hampshire Regiment: Volume 3, 1918–1954* (1955)

Sheehan, William, *British Voices from the Irish War of Independence* (London: Collins, 2005)

Sherwood, Robert E., *The White House Papers of Harry L. Hopkins*, 2 vols (London: Eyre & Spottiswoode, 1949)

Simms, Brendan, and Charlie Laderman, *Hitler's American Gamble: Pearl Harbor and the German March to Global War* (London: Allen Lane, 2021)

Stiastny, Terry, *Believable Lies: The Misfits Who Fought Churchill's Secret Propaganda War* (London: W. H. Allen, 2025)

Toll, Ian W., *The Conquering Tide: War in the Pacific Islands 1942–1944* (New York: W. W. Norton & Co., 2015; repr. 2016)

Villahermosa, Gilberto, *Hitler's Paratrooper: The Life and Battles of Rudolf Witzig* (Barnsley: Frontline Books, 2010; repr. 2014)

Public Lectures

Field Marshal Lord Carver, 'Monty – Forty Years On', A Public Lecture in the Department of War Studies, King's College London, 8 March 1984

Websites

https://britain-at-war.org.uk/ww2/Derrick_Jackson/html/training.htm [accessed 10 November 2023]

https://history.army.mil/books/staff-rides/kasserine/vol-i-part_1.pdf [accessed 5 December 2023]

https://hitler-archive.com/articles.php?a=7 [accessed 5 June 2023]

https://www.ibiblio.org/hyperwar/USA/USA-MTO-NWA/USA-MTO-NWA-31.html [accessed 13 March 2024]

https://www.lehrmaninstitute.org/history/index.html [accessed 14 June 2023] https://www.nzetc.victoria.ac.nz/tm/scholarly/tei–WH2Maor–c11.html [accessed 1 June 2024]

https://nzetc.victoria.ac.nz/tm/scholarly/tei-WH2-2Doc-c9-20.html [accessed 12 April 2024]

https://www.paradata.org.uk/article/poetry-richard-dicky-spender [accessed 16 May 2024]

https://www.paradata.org.uk/media/146 [accessed 7 April 2022]

https://www.teara.govt.nz/en/biographies/5n9/ngarimu-te-moananui-a-kiwa [accessed 15 May 2024]

https://www.thestrathallan.com/wp/?page_id=2549&doing_wp_cron=1699291389.73244690 89508056640625 [accessed 6 November 2023]

https://www.thestrathallan.com/wp/?page_id=2537 [accessed 10 November 2023]

https://www.tracesofwar.com/persons/29958/Lang-Rudolf.htm [accessed 13 November 2023]

https://trove.nla.gov.au/newspaper/article/56282956 [accessed 16 April 2024]

https://www.unithistories.com/officers/Army_officers_A06.html [accessed 25 August 2023]

https://www.valor.militarytimes.com/hero/6221 [accessed 18 January 2024]

https://www.vcgca.org/our-people/profile/1710/Herbert-Wallace-Le-PATOUREL [accessed 3 May 2024]

Illustrations

Images from public domain unless specified.

American troops heading for Oran, Algeria, 8 November 1942.
British troops landing near Algiers, 8 November 1942.
Allied troops enter Oran, Algeria, 10 November 1942.
Generalfeldmarschall Albert Kesselring with Generalfeldmarschall Erwin
    Rommel, 1942.
Rommel, Ugo Cavallero and Maresciallo Ettore Bastico, Libya, 1942.
Lieutenant General Charles Allfrey, northern Tunisia, 5 December 1942.
Major General George S. Patton Jr, northern Tunisia, December 1942.
Men of the German 5th Parachute Regiment, Tunisia.
Franklin D. Roosevelt, Winston S. Churchill and chiefs of staff, January
    1943. Lieutenant General Henry H. 'Hap' Arnold, Admiral Ernest J. King,
    General George C. Marshall, Admiral Sir Dudley Pound, General Sir Alan
    Brooke, Air Chief Marshal Sir Charles Portal.
FDR inspecting Patton's troops in Morocco, January 1943.
General Sir Harold Alexander with General Dwight D. 'Ike' Eisenhower.
PFC Philip L. Mahoney and T/5 R. R. Pollard.
A knocked-out German Panzer III, 24 February 1943.
American GIs of the 2/16th Infantry, 26 February 1943.
British troops search a German prisoner, February 1943.
A British 17-pdr anti-tank gun in action, Medenine front, Tunisia, 11 March 1943.
Lieutenant General Patton with Eisenhower, mid-March 1943.
Patton observing enemy positions in March 1943.
A wounded soldier from the Durham Light Infantry and German prisoner,
    22 March 1943.

Monty congratulating troops, 2 April 1943.

Wadi Akarit. *(Courtesy of the A. A. Blackwell Archive)*

Captain Alan Blackwell. *(Courtesy of the A. A. Blackwell Archive)*

Blackwell's temporary grave at Wadi Akarit. *(Courtesy of the A. A. Blackwell Archive)*

Sergeants Brown and Randall (1st US Armored Division), 7 April 1943.

Oberstleutnant Claus Graf von Stauffenberg.

Lieutenant General Kenneth Anderson with Major General Omar N. Bradley.

Sherman tanks advance past a knocked-out German 88mm anti-tank gun, 23 April 1943.

A Douglas Boston light bomber of the RAF's No. 114 Squadron, 23 April 1943.

Stretcher bearers of the East Surrey Regiment, 23 April 1943.

Generaloberst Hans-Jürgen von Arnim.

A German Mark VI 'Tiger' tank.

German troops surrender to the crew of a British tank near Frendj, 6 May 1943.

British troops enter Tunis, 7 May 1943.

German prisoners being processed by American troops, 8 May 1943.

Giovanni Messe surrenders to Major General Bernard Freyberg, 13 May 1943.

Generaloberst von Arnim, 12 May 1943.

Spahi light cavalrymen, 20 May 1943.

Winston Churchill at Carthage in Tunisia with Lieutenant General Anderson, 1 June 1943.

Reichsmarschall Hermann Goering, Count Ciano, Adolf Hitler and Benito Mussolini.

The dead bodies of Mussolini, his mistress Claretta Petacci and three fellow fascists, Piazzale Loreto, Milan, 29 April 1945.

Index

Page numbers in **bold** refer to maps.